THE
PUSHCART PRIZE, IV:
BEST OF THE
SMALL PRESSES

1979–80 Edition

THE PUSHCART PRIZE, IV:

An annual small press reader. Founding Editors Anaïs Nin (1903–1977), Buckminster Fuller, Charles Newman, Daniel Halpern, Gordon Lish, Harry Smith, H.L. Van Brunt, Hugh Fox, Ishmael Reed, Joyce Carol Oates, Len Fulton, Leonard Randolph, Leslie Fiedler, Nona Balakian, Paul Bowles, Paul Engle, Ralph Ellison, Reynolds Price, Rhoda Schwartz, Richard Morris, Ted Wilentz, Tom Montag, William Phillips. Assembled with the assistance of over 100 staff and Special Contributing Editors for this edition, and with the cooperation of the many outstanding small presses whose names follow . . .

BEST OF THE SMALL PRESSES

BEST OF THE SMALL PRESSES

EDITED BY BILL HENDERSON

published by THE PUSHCART PRESS
1979–80 Edition

THE PUSHCART PRIZE, IV: 🔥 🔥 🔥

Library of Congress Card Number: 76–58675
ISBN: 0–916366–06–5
ISSN: 0149–7863

First printing, April, 1979

Manufactured in The United States of America
by RAY FREIMAN and COMPANY, Stamford, Connecticut

Also from
THE PUSHCART PRESS

THE PUBLISH-IT-YOURSELF HANDBOOK:
Literary Tradition and How-To
(eighth printing)

THE PUSHCART PRIZE: BEST OF THE SMALL PRESSES
(1976–77 edition)

THE PUSHCART PRIZE, II: BEST OF THE SMALL PRESSES
(1977–78 edition)

THE PUSHCART PRIZE, III: BEST OF THE SMALL PRESSES
(1978–79 edition)

THE LITTLE MAGAZINE IN AMERICA: A MODERN DOCUMENTARY
HISTORY

THE ART OF LITERARY PUBLISHING

ACKNOWLEDGEMENTS

The following works are reprinted by permission of the publishers:

"The Stonecutter's Horses" © 1978 *The Malahat Review* and Robert Bringhurst
"Snow Owl" © 1978 *Antaeus*
"The Stone Crab: A Love Poem" © 1978 *The Hudson Review*
"The Man Whose Blood Tilted The Earth" © 1978 *Red Cedar Review*
"Dream" © 1978 *Boxspring*
"I Show The Daffodils to the Retarded Kids" © 1978 *Southern Poetry Review*
"Running Away From Home" © 1978 *Kayak*
"Quinnapoxet" © 1978 *Antaeus*
"The Spanish Image of Death" © 1978 Red Hill Press
"For Papa (and Marcus Garvey)" © 1978 *Obsidian*
"Forgive Us . . ." © 1978 *Poetry Northwest* and George Venn
"Living With Animals" © 1978 *Greensboro Review* and the University of North Carolina at Greensboro
"Anonymous Courtesan In a Jade Shroud" © 1978 *Field*
"Grandmother (1895–1928)" © 1978 *American Poetry Review*
"Lot's Wife" © 1978 *Jam To-Day*
"Pig 311" © 1978 *Cedar Rock*
"The Ritual of Memories" © 1978 Graywolf Press and Tess Gallagher
"Things That Happen Where There Aren't Any People" © 1978 *Western Humanities Review*
"Some Carry Around This" © 1978 *Firelands Arts Review*
"Winter Sleep" © 1978 Bits Press and Mary Oliver
"To Ed Sissman" © 1978 *The Ontario Review*
"Meeting Mescalito At Oak Hill Cemetery" © 1978 Penca Books
"Plowing With Elephants" © 1978 *Indiana Writes* and Lon Otto
"Letters from A Father" © 1978 *Poetry Now* and Mona Van Duyn
"Made Connections" © 1978 *Massachusetts Review Inc.*
"Wildflower" © 1978 *Antaeus* and Stanley Plumly
"Lawrence At Taos" © 1978 *Field*
"Elegy" © 1978 *Poetry* and The Modern Poetry Association
"In Another Country" © 1978 City Lights Books
"Ice" © 1978 *Chicago Review*
"The Ownership of the Night" © 1978 *Field*
"from Laughing with One Eye" © 1978 *Poetry*
"Proteus" © 1978 *The Georgia Review*
"Night Flight to Stockholm" © 1978 *The Paris Review*
"The Biography Man" © 1978 *Iowa Review*
"Johnny Appleseed" © 1978 *Apalachee Quarterly*
"Sitting Up, Standing, Taking Steps" © 1978 Tuumba Press
"A Jean-Marie Cookbook" © 1978 *Sun&Moon* and Jeff Weinstein
"The Daisy Dolls" © 1978 *The Partisan Review*
"Lechery" © 1978 *Persea: An International Review*
"Home" © 1978 *Iowa Review*
"My Work in California" © 1978 *The Missouri Review*
"Ghosts Like Them" © 1978 *The Hudson Review*
"These Women" © 1978 *Gallimaufry* and Christine Schutt
"Early Winter" © 1978 *Massachusetts Review Inc.*
"Another Margot Chapter" © 1978 *Quarterly West*
"Rich" © 1978 *Intro*
"Sweetness, A Thinking Machine" © 1978 Douglas Messerli and Howard N. Fox
"Jeffery, Believe Me" © 1978 *TriQuarterly*
"from Kiss of the Spider Woman" © 1978 *Fiction*
"The Hat in the Swamp" © 1978 *Milk Quarterly*
"American Poetry: Looking for a Center" © 1978 *Black American Literature Forum*
"A Woman in Love With a Bottle" © 1978 Red Clay Books
"A Vision Expressed by a Series of False Statements" © 1978 *Some*
"Civilization and Isolation" © 1978 *North American Review*. Originally commissioned by Athabasca University for its Merrill Wolfe memorial lecture series.
"The Nerves of a Midwife: Contemporary American Women's Poetry" © 1978 *Parnassus: Poetry in Review* and Poetry in Review Foundation
"The Politics of Anti-Realism" © 1978 *Salmagundi*
"Contemporary Poetry and the Metaphors for the Poem" © 1978 *Georgia Review*
"A Renewal of the Word" © 1978 *The Kenyon Review*
"The Trial of Rozhdestvov" © 1978 Amnesty International
"Literature and Ecology: An Experiment in Ecocriticism" © 1978 *Iowa Review*

This book is for
Joyce Carol Oates
and
Raymond J. Smith

♨ ♨ ♨

INTRODUCTION:

About Pushcart Prize IV

LAST YEAR, the Kirkus Reviews commented on *Pushcart Prize III:* "in a publishing scene fast backing off from quality and lapping up the flashy and no-account, Pushcart's annual anthology of the previous year's best work from the small presses can no longer be complacently accepted as a showcase of 'alternative' literary endeavor; we have to see it, responsibly, as mainstream."

This confirmed what Pushcart has hinted at and sometimes hollered about since the Pushcart Prize series began—these days the mainstream of our literary culture is the small presses. As the variety of selections in *Pushcart Prize IV* indicates, it is a diverse mainstream, constantly infused by new work from authors with a vision of what is honest and important. Whenever burdened by bills or mailbags, Pushcart turns to these authors for a tonic of joy. It is this same sense of joy and purpose that maintains thousands of unrecognized and unpaid small press editors and writers.

With few exceptions, *Pushcart Prize IV* remains dedicated to these as yet uncelebrated authors and editors. So far in the series, 271 writers have been introduced from 170 small presses. We welcome here for the first time: *Apalachee Quarterly*, Bits Press, *Black American Literature Forum*, *Boxspring*, *Cedar Rock*, City Lights Books, *Firelands Arts Review*, Graywolf Press, *Greensboro Review*, *Indiana Writes*, *Intro*, *Jam To-Day*, *Kenyon Review*, *Malahat Review*, *Milk Quarterly*, *Missouri Review*, *Obsidian*, Penca Books, *Poetry Northwest*, Prescott Street Press, *Quarterly West*, *Red Cedar Review*, Red Clay Books, *Southern Poetry Review*, *Some*,

Sun&Moon, Tuumba Press and *Western Humanities Review*. As usual most of the presses in *IV* are new to the series.

It would be impossible to summarize *Prize IV's* 61 selections from 53 presses, but as a sample of the diversity picked from 4,000 nominations with the help of over 100 volunteer Pushcart editors, the following are mentioned.

In fiction: eighteen stories including the indescribable and unforgettable—Felisberto Hernández's "The Daisy Dolls" (*Partisan Review*); the sexually culinary—Jeff Weinstein's "A Jean-Marie Cookbook" (*Sun&Moon*); the outrageous—Dallas Weibe's "Night Flight to Stockholm" (*Paris Review*); the fantastic—Judith Hoover's first published tale "Proteus" (*Georgia Review*); the experimental —Ron Silliman's "Sitting Up, Standing, Taking Steps" (Tuumba Press) and other works that provide their own adjectives among them Shirley Ann Taggart's first published story from *The Hudson Review* and two efforts by Jayne Anne Phillips, who along with Tess Gallagher and Ishmael Reed appeared in a previous Prize collection.

In non-fiction: ten essays including the profound—Gerald Graff's "The Politics of Anti-Realism" (*Salmagundi*); the personal—Barbara Lovell's "A Woman In Love With A Bottle" (Red Clay Books); the sociological—Vine Deloria's "Civilization and Isolation" (*North American Review*); the sort-of pedagogical—John Love's "A Vision Expressed by A Series of False Statements" (*Some*); the experimental—William Rueckert's "Literature and Ecology: An Experiment in Ecocriticism" (*Iowa Review*), and many more.

As in previous collections, most of the selections in *IV* are poetry because most of small press publishing is devoted to poetry. Even a summary of more than 30 poems would be difficult but Pushcart would like to mention James Laughlin's "In Another Country"—the first appearance here for the poet (also known as the founder and publisher of New Directions) and for the press, City Lights Books, another literary legend. In choosing the annual Lamport Foundation "outstanding poet" we were stymied by the multitude of quality and decided on two poems to share the $100 award: "from Laughing With One Eye" by Gjertrud Schnackenberg Smyth (*Poetry*) and "Ice" by Ai (*Chicago Review*). The Lamport Award in fiction goes to Jayne Anne Phillips for "Home" (*Iowa Review*) and Barbara Myerhoff for "A Renewal of the Word" (*Kenyon Review*).

In *Pushcart Prize IV* the honors do not end where the reprints stop. The previous year was rich in talent, and since we can offer only a representation of that talent, the editors call the reader's attention to the "Outstanding Writers" section at the end of this volume. We urge you to read these authors in the original publications.

Finally a few messages of thanks from Pushcart: to Avon Books for a spirited promotion of the trade paperback edition of these Prize volumes in the year following our clothbound edition. And thanks of course to Pushcart's editors and Special Contributing Editors for *Prize IV* who made nominations and assisted in the final selection, and our thanks to you, the reader, who by reading this far may be tempted to continue on and discover the joy and caring of small press editors and authors.

Bill Henderson
THE PUSHCART PRESS

As we go to press, Pushcart is pleased to announce a new prize within the *Prize*: the $100 Hallie and Whit Burnett Award for a first-published short story goes to Shirley Ann Taggart for "Ghosts Like Them" (*Hudson Review*).

THE

PEOPLE WHO HELPED

FOUNDING EDITORS—*Anaïs Nin (1903–1977), Buckminster Fuller, Charles Newman, Daniel Halpern, Gordon Lish, Harry Smith, Hugh Fox, Ishmael Reed, Joyce Carol Oates, Len Fulton, Leonard Randolph, Leslie Fiedler, Nona Balakian, Paul Bowles, Paul Engle, Ralph Ellison, Reynolds Price, Rhoda Schwartz, Richard Morris, Ted Wilentz, Tom Montag, William Phillips. Poetry editor: H.L. Van Brunt.*

EDITORS—*Elliott Anderson, John Ashbery, Robert Boyers, Harold Brodkey, Hayden Carruth, Raymond Carver, Malcolm Cowley, Paula Deitz, Mort Elevitch, Raymond Federman, Carolyn Forché, Tess Gallagher, David Godine, John Irving, June Jordan, Karen Kennerly, Jerzy Kosinski, Richard Kostelanetz, Maxine Kumin, Mary MacArthur, Frederick Morgan, Cynthia Ozick, George Plimpton, Eugene Redmond, Teo Savory, Grace Schulman, Harvey Shapiro, Ron Sukenick, Anne Tyler, David Wilk, Bill Zavatsky*

SPECIAL CONTRIBUTING EDITORS FOR THIS EDITION —*Walter Abish, Sheila Ascher, Robert Bly, Bobbie Bristol, Michael Dennis Browne, Wesley Brown, Naomi Clark, Kathleen Collins, Norman Dubie, Larry Eigner, Loris Essary, Stuart Friebert, John Gardner, Louis Gallo, James Galvin, George Garrett, Lorrie Goldensohn, E.V. Griffith, Michael Gross, Barbara Grossman, C.W. Gusewelle, Robert Hass, Don Hendrie, Jr., Dick Higgins, Christopher Howell, Richard Howard, J.R. Humphreys, Laura Jensen, Mary Kinzie, Arthur and Kit Knight, Seymour Lawrence, Stanley*

Lindberg, Dan Masterson, McKeel McBride, Stephen Minot, Howard Moss, George Payerle, Michael Peich, Mary Peterson, Ben Pesta, Robert Phillips, Rochelle Ratner, Lynne Sharon Schwartz, Beth T. Shannon, Lynne Spaulding, Maura Stanton, Felix Stefanile, Margueritte Young, Yvonne, Suzanne Zavrian, Max Zimmer

HONORARY EDITORS (These people helped out for previous editions)—*Hallie Burnett, Stephen Dixon, Siv Cedering Fox, H.E. Francis, John Gill, Allen Ginsberg, Judy Hogan, Hilarie Johnston, Erica Jong, David Kranes, Allan Kornblum, Michael Lally, Phillip Lopate, Robie Macauley, Clarence Major, Theresa Maylone, Colleen McElroy, Bob Miles, Lisel Mueller, Carol Muske, Joel Oppenheimer, Noel Peattie, William Saroyan, Hugh Seidman, Ntozake Shange, Louise Simons, Mark Strand, Janey Tannenbaum, Carll Tucker, Mark Vinz, Marnie Walsh, Noel Young.*

DESIGN AND PRODUCTION—*Ray Freiman*

EUROPEAN EDITORS—*Kirby and Liz Williams, Genie D. Chipps*

AUSTRALIAN EDITORS—*Tom and Wendy Whitton*

JACKET DESIGN—*Barbara Lish*

POETRY EDITORS FOR THIS EDITION—*Naomi Lazard, Herb Leibowitz*

ASSOCIATE EDITORS—*Jon Galassi, DeWitt Henry*

EDITOR AND PUBLISHER—*Bill Henderson*

PRESSES FEATURED IN THE FIRST FOUR *PUSHCART PRIZE* EDITIONS

Agni Review
Ahsahta Press
Ailanthus Press
Alcheringa/Ethnopoetics
Alice James Books
American Literature
American Pen
American Poetry Review
Amnesty International
Anaesthesia Review
Antaeus
Apalachee Quarterly
Aphra
Assembling
Aspen Leaves
Barlenmir House
Bilingual Review
Bits Press
Black American Literature Forum
Black Rooster
Black Sparrow

Blue Cloud Quarterly
Blue Wind Press
Boxspring
California Quarterly
Capra Press
Cedar Rock
Center
Chariton Review
Chicago Review
Chouteau Review
Cimarron Review
City Lights Books
Clown War
CoEvolution Quarterly
Cold Mountain Press
Columbia: A Magazine of Poetry and Prose
Confluence Press
Confrontation
Cosmic Information Agency
Cross Currents
Curbstone Press
Dacotah Territory
Decatur House
December
Dryad Press
Duck Down Press
East River Anthology
Fiction
Fiction Collective
Fiction International
Field
Firelands Arts Review
Five Trees Press
Gallimaufry
Georgia Review
Ghost Dance
Goddard Journal
The Godine Press
Graham House Press
Graywolf Press

Greensboro Review
Greenfield Review
Hard Pressed
Hills
Holmgangers Press
Hudson Review
Icarus
Indiana Writes
Intermedia
Intro
Invisible City
Iowa Review
The Kanchenjunga Press
Kansas Quarterly
Kayak
Kenyon Review
Latitudes Press
Liberation
The Little Magazine
Living Hand Press
Living Poets Press
Lowlands Review
Lucille
Lynx House Press
Manroot
Magic Circle Press
Malahat Review
Massachusetts Review
Milk Quarterly
Montana Gothic
Missouri Review
Mulch Press
Nada Press
New America
New Letters
North American Review
North Atlantic Books
Northwest Review
Obsidian
Ohio Review

Ontario Review
Open Places
Oyez Press
Painted Bride Quarterly
Paris Review
Parnassus: Poetry In Review
Partisan Review
Penca Books
Penumbra Press
Pentagram
Persea: An International Review
Pequod
Pitcairn Press
Ploughshares
Poetry
Poetry Northwest
Poetry Now
Prairie Schooner
Prescott Street Press
Promise of Learnings
Quarry West
Quarterly West
Raincrow Press
Red Cedar Review
Red Clay Books
Red Earth Press
Release Press
Russian *Samizdat*
Salmagundi
San Marcos Press
Seamark Press
Second Coming Press
The Seventies Press
Shenandoah
A Shout In The Street
Sibyl-Child Press
Small Moon
The Smith
Southern Poetry Review
Some

Southern Review
Spectrum
St. Andrews Press
Story Quarterly
Sun&Moon
Sun Press
Sunstone
Telephone Books
Texas Slough
Transatlantic Review
Three Rivers Press
Thorp Springs Press
Toothpaste Press
TriQuarterly
Truck Press
Tuumba Press
Undine
Unicorn Press
Unspeakable Visions of the Individual
Vagabond
Virginia Quarterly
Western Humanities Review
Westigan Review
Willmore City
Word-Smith
Xanadu
Yardbird Reader
Y'Bird

CONTENTS

Contents

THE
PUSHCART PRIZE, IV:
BEST OF THE
SMALL PRESSES

1979–80 Edition

HOME

fiction by JAYNE ANNE PHILLIPS

from THE IOWA REVIEW

nominated by THE IOWA REVIEW, *DeWitt Henry and Seymour Lawrence*

I'M AFRAID Walter Cronkite has had it, says Mom. Roger Mudd always does the news now. How would you like to have a name like that? Walter used to do the conventions and a football game now and then. I mean he would sort of appear, on the sidelines. Didn't he? But you never see him anymore. Lord. Something is going on.

Mom, I say. Maybe he's just resting. He must have made a lot of money by now. Maybe he's tired of talking about elections and mine disasters and the collapse of the franc. Maybe he's in love with a young girl.

He's not the type, says my mother. You can tell *that* much. No, she says, I'm afraid it's cancer.

My mother has her suspicions. She ponders. I have been home
with her for two months. I ran out of money and I wasn't in love, so I
have come home to my mother. She is an educational administrator.
All winter long after work she watches television and knits afghans.

Come home, she said. Save money.

I can't possibly do it, I said. Jesus, I'm twenty-three years old.

Don't be silly, she said. And don't use profanity.

She arranged a job for me in the school system. All day I tutor
children in remedial reading. Sometimes I am so discouraged that I
lie on the couch all evening and watch television with her. The shows
are all alike. Their laugh tracks are conspicuously similar; I think I
recognize a repetition of certain professional laughters. This laughter marks off the half hours.

Finally I make a rule: I won't watch television at night. I will watch
only the news, which ends at 7:30. Then I will go to my room and do
God knows what. But I feel sad that she sits there alone, knitting by
the lamp. She seldom looks up.

Why don't you ever read anything? I ask.

I do, she says. I read books in my field. I read all day at work,
writing those damn proposals. When I come home I want to relax.

Then let's go to the movies.

I don't want to go to the movies. Why should I pay money to be
upset or frightened?

But feeling something can teach you. Don't you want to learn
anything?

I'm learning all the time, she says.

She keeps knitting. She folds yarn the color of cream, the color of
snow. She works it with her long blue needles, piercing, returning,
winding. Yarn cascades from her hands in long panels. A pattern
appears and disappears. She stops and counts; so many stitches
across, so many down. Yes, she is on the right track.

Occasionally I offer to buy my mother a subscription to something
mildly informative: *Ms, Rolling Stone, Scientific American.*

I don't want to read that stuff, she says. Just save your money. Did
you hear Cronkite last night? Everyone's going to need all they can
get.

Often I need to look at my mother's old photographs. I see her
sitting in knee-high grass with a white gardenia in her hair. I see her
dressed up as the groom in a mock wedding at a sorority party, her

black hair pulled back tight. I see her formally posed in her cadet nurse's uniform. The photographer has painted her lashes too lushly, too long; but her deep red mouth is correct.

The war ended too soon. She didn't finish her training. She came home to nurse only her mother and to meet my father at a dance. She married him in two weeks. It took twenty years to divorce him.

When we traveled to a neighboring town to buy my high school clothes, my mother and I would pass a certain road that turned off the highway and wound to a place I never saw.

There it is, my mother would say. The road to Wonder Bar. That's where I met my Waterloo. I walked in and he said, 'There she is. I'm going to marry that girl.' Ha. He sure saw me coming.

Well, I asked, why did you marry him?

He was older, she said. He had a job and a car. And mother was so sick.

My mother doesn't forget her mother.

Never one bedsore, she says. I turned her every fifteen minutes. I kept her skin soft and kept her clean, even to the end.

I imagine my mother at twenty-three; her black hair, her dark eyes, her olive skin and that red lipstick. She is growing lines of tension in her mouth. Her teeth press into her lower lip as she lifts the woman in the bed. The woman weighs no more than a child. She has a smell. My mother fights it continually; bathing her, changing her sheets, carrying her to the bathroom so the smell can be contained and flushed away. My mother will try to protect them both. At night she sleeps in the room on a cot. She struggles awake feeling something press down on her and suck her breath: the smell. When my grandmother can no longer move, my mother fights it alone.

I did all I could, she sighs. And I was glad to do it. I'm glad I don't have to feel guilty.

No one has to feel guilty, I tell her.

And why not? says my mother. There's nothing wrong with guilt. If you are guilty, you should feel guilty.

My mother has often told me that I will be sorry when she is gone.

I think. And read alone at night in my room. I read those books I never read, the old classics, and detective stories. I can get them in the library here. There is only one bookstore; it sells mostly newspapers and *True Confessions* oracles. At Kroger's by the checkout counter I buy a few paperbacks, best sellers, but they are usually bad.

The television drones on downstairs.

I wonder about Walter Cronkite.

When was the last time I saw him? It's true his face was pouchy, his hair thinning. Perhaps he is only cutting it shorter. But he had that look about the eyes. . . .

He was there when they stepped on the moon. He forgot he was on the air and he shouted, 'There . . . there . . . now . . . . We have contact!' Contact. For those who tuned in late, for the periodic watchers, he repeated: 'One small step. . . .'

I was in high school and he was there with the body count. But he said it in such a way that you knew he wanted the war to end. He looked directly at you and said the numbers quietly. Shame, yes, but sorrowful patience, as if all things had passed before his eyes. And he understood that here at home, as well as in starving India, we would pass our next lives as meager cows.

My mother gets *Reader's Digest*. I come home from work, have a cup of coffee, and read it. I keep it beside my bed. I read it when I am too tired to read anything else. I read about Joe's kidney and Humor in Uniform. Always, there are human interest stories in which someone survives an ordeal of primal terror. Tonight it is Grizzly! Two teenagers camping in the mountains are attacked by a bear. Sharon is dragged over a mile, unconscious. She is a good student loved by her parents, an honest girl loved by her boyfriend. Perhaps she is not a virgin; but in her heart, she is virginal. And she lies now in the furred arms of a beast. The grizzly drags her quietly, quietly. He will care for her all the days of his life. . . . Sharon, his rose.

But alas. Already, rescuers have organized. Mercifully her boyfriend is not among them. He is sleeping en route to the nearest hospital; his broken legs have excused him. In a few days, Sharon will bring him his food on a tray. She is spared. She is not demure. He gazes on her face, untouched but for a long thin scar near her mouth. He thinks of the monster and wonders at its delicate mark. Sharon says she remembers nothing of the bear. She only knows the tent was ripped open, that its heavy canvas fell across her face.

I turn out my light when I know my mother is sleeping. By then my eyes hurt and the streets of the town are deserted.

My father comes to me in a dream. He kneels beside me, touches my mouth. He turns my face gently toward him.

Let me see, he says. Let me see it.

He is looking for a scar, a sign. He wears only a towel around his waist. He presses himself against my thigh, pretending solicitude. But I know what he is doing; I turn my head in repulsion and stiffen. He smells of a sour musk and his forearms are black with hair. I think, it's been years since he's had an erection. . . .

Finally he stands. Cover yourself, I tell him.

I can't, he says. I'm hard.

On Saturdays I go to the Veterans of Foreign Wars rummage sales. They are held in the drafty basement of a church, rows of collapsible tables piled with objects. Sometimes I think I recognize the possessions of old friends: a class ring, yearbooks, football sweaters with our high school insignia. Would this one have fit Jason?

He used to spread it on the seat of the car on winter nights when we parked by country churches and graveyards. There seemed to be no ground, just water, a rolling, turning, building to a dull pain between my legs.

What's wrong? What is it?

Jason, I can't. . . . This pain. . . .

It's only because you're afraid. If you'd let me go ahead. . . .

I'm not afraid of you, I'd do anything for you. But Jason, why does it hurt like this?

We would try. But I couldn't. We made love with our hands. Our bodies were white. Out the window of the car, snow rose up in mounds across the fields. Afterward, he looked at me peacefully, sadly.

I held him and whispered, soon, soon. . . . we'll go away to school.

His sweater. He wore it that night we drove back from the football awards banquet. Jason made All State but he hated football.

I hate it, he said. So what? he said. That I'm out there puking in the heat? Screaming 'kill' at a sandbag?

I held his award in my lap, a gold man frozen in mid-leap. Don't play in college, I said. Refuse the money.

He was driving very slowly.

I can't see, he said. I can't see the edges of the road. . . . Tell me if I start to fall off.

Jason, what do you mean?

He insisted I roll down the window and watch the edge. The banks of the road were gradual, sloping off in brush and trees on either side. White lines at the edge glowed in dips and turns.

We're going to crash, he said.

No, Jason. You've driven this road before. We won't crash.

We're crashing, I know it, he said. Tell me, tell me I'm OK. . . .

Here on the rummage sale table, there are three football sweaters. I see they are all too small to have belonged to Jason. So I buy an old soundtrack, "The Sound of Music." Air, Austrian mountains. And an old robe to wear in the mornings. It upsets my mother to see me naked; she looks at me so curiously, as though she didn't recognize my body.

I pay for my purchases at the cash register. Behind the desk I glimpse stacks of *Reader's Digests*. The Ladies' Auxiliary turns them inside out, stiffens and shellacs them. They make wastebaskets out of them.

I give my mother the record. She is pleased. She hugs me.

Oh, she says, I used to love the musicals. They made me happy. Then she stops and looks at me.

Didn't you do this? she says. Didn't you do this in high school?

Do what?

Your class, she says. You did "The Sound of Music."

Yes, I guess we did.

What a joke. I was the beautiful countess meant to marry Captain Von Trapp before innocent Maria stole his heart. Jason was a threatening Nazi colonel with a bit part. He should have sung the lead but sports practices interfered with rehearsals. Tall, blond, aged in make-up under the lights, he encouraged sympathy for the bad guys and overshadowed the star. He appeared just often enough to make the play ridiculous.

My mother sits in the blue chair my father used for years.

Come quick, she says. Look. . . .

She points to the television. Flickerings of Senate chambers, men in conservative suits. A commentator drones on about tax rebates.

There, says my mother. Hubert Humphrey. Look at him .

It's true. Humphrey is different, changed from his former toady self to a desiccated old man, not unlike the discarded shell of a locust. Now he rasps into the microphone about the people of these great states.

Old Hubert's had it, says my mother. He's a death mask.

That's what he gets for sucking blood for thirty years.

No, she says. No, he's got it too. Look at him! Cancer. Oh.

For God's sake, will you think of something else for once?

I don't know what you mean, she says. She goes on knitting.

All Hubert needs, I tell her, is a good roll in the hay.

You think that's what everyone needs.

Everyone does need it.

They do not. People aren't dogs. I seem to manage perfectly well without it, don't I?

No, I wouldn't say that you do.

Well, I do. I know your mumbo-jumbo about sexuality. Sex is for those who are married, and I wouldn't marry again if it was the Lord himself.

Now she is silent. I know what's coming.

Your attitude will make you miserable, she says. One man after another. I just want you to be happy.

I do my best.

That's right, she says, be sarcastic.

I refuse to answer. I think about my growing bank account. Graduate school, maybe in California. Hawaii. Somewhere beautiful and warm. I will wear few clothes and my skin will feel the air.

What about Jason, says my mother. I was thinking of him the other day.

Our telepathy always frightens me. Telepathy and beyond. Before her hysterectomy, our periods often came on the same day.

If he hadn't had that nervous breakdown, she says softly, do you suppose. . . .

No, I don't suppose.

I wasn't surprised that it happened. When his brother was killed, that was hard. But Jason was so self-centered. He thought everyone was out to get him. You were lucky to be rid of him. Still, poor thing. . . .

Silence. Then she refers in low tones to the few months Jason and I lived together before he was hospitalized.

You shouldn't have done what you did when you went off to college. He lost respect for you.

It wasn't respect for me he lost—He lost his fucking mind, if you remember—

I realize I'm shouting. And shaking. What is happening to me? My mother stares.

We'll not discuss it, she says.

She gets up. I hear her in the bathroom. Water running into the tub. Hydrotherapy. I close my eyes and listen. Soon, this weekend. I'll get a ride to the university a few hours away and look up an old lover. I'm lucky. They always want to sleep with me. For old time's sake.

I turn down the sound of the television and watch its silent pictures. Jason's brother was a musician; he taught Jason to play the pedal steel. A sergeant in uniform delivered the message two weeks before the state playoff games. Jason appeared at my mother's kitchen door with the telegram. He looked at me, opened his mouth, backed off wordless in the dark. I pretend I hear his pedal steel; its sweet country whine might make me cry. And I recognize this silent movie. . . . I've seen it four times. Gregory Peck and his submarine crew escape fallout in Australia, but not for long. The cloud is coming. And so they run rampant in auto races and love affairs. But in the end, they close the hatch and put out to sea. They want to go home to die.

Sweetheart? My mother calls from the bathroom. Could you bring me a towel?

Her voice is quavering slightly. She is sorry. But I never know which part of it she is sorry about. I get a towel from the linen closet and open the door of the steamy bathroom. My mother stands in the tub, dripping, shivering a little. She is so small and thin; she is smaller than I. She has two long scars on her belly, operations of the womb, and one breast is misshapen, sunken, indented near the nipple.

I put the towel around her shoulders and my eyes smart. She looks at her breast.

Not too pretty is it, she says. He took out too much when he removed that lump.

Mom, it doesn't look so bad.

I dry her back, her beautiful back which is firm and unblemished. Beautiful, her skin. Again, I feel the pain in my eyes.

But you should have sued the bastard, I tell her. He didn't give a shit about your body.

We have an awkward moment with the towel when I realize I can't touch her any longer. The towel slips down and she catches it as one ends dips into the water.

Sweetheart, she says. I know your beliefs are different from mine. But have patience with me. You'll just be here a few more months. And I'll always stand behind you. We'll get along.

She has clutched the towel to her chest. She is so fragile, standing there, naked, with her small shoulders. Suddenly I am horribly frightened.

Sure, I say, I know we will.

I let myself out of the room.

Sunday my mother goes to church alone. Daniel calls me from D.C. He's been living with a lover in Oregon. Now he is back east; she will join him in a few weeks. He is happy, he says. I tell him I'm glad he's found someone who appreciates him.

Come on now, he says. You weren't that bad.

I love Daniel, his white and feminine hands, his thick chestnut hair, his intelligence. And he loves me, though I don't know why. The last few weeks we were together I lay beside him like a piece of wood. I couldn't bear his touch; the moisture his penis left on my hips as he rolled against me. I was cold, cold. I huddled in blankets away from him.

I'm sorry, I said. Daniel, I'm sorry please . . . what's wrong with me? Tell me you love me anyway. . . .

Yes, he said. Of course I do. I always will. I do.

Daniel says he has no car, but he will come by bus. Is there a place for him to stay?

Oh yes, I say. There's a guest room. Bring some Trojans. I'm a hermit with no use for birth control. Daniel, you don't know what it's like here.

I don't care what it's like. I want to see you.

Yes, I say. Daniel, hurry.

When he arrives the next weekend, we sit around the table with my mother and discuss medicine. Daniel was a medic in Vietnam. He smiles at my mother. She is charmed though she has reservations; I see them in her face. But she enjoys having someone else in the house, a presence: a male. Daniel's laughter is low and modulated. He talks softly, smoothly: a dignified radio announcer, an accomplished anchor man.

But when I lived with him, he threw dishes against the wall. And jerked in his sleep, mumbling. And ran out of the house with his hands across his eyes.

After we first made love, he smiled and pulled gently away from me. He put on his shirt and went to the bathroom. I followed and stepped into the shower with him. He faced me, composed, friendly, and frozen. He stood as though guarding something behind him.

Daniel, turn around. I'll soap you back.

I already did.

Then move, I'll stand in the water with you.

He stepped carefully around me.

Daniel, what's wrong? Why won't you turn around?

Why should I?

I'd never seen him with his shirt off. He'd never gone swimming with us, only wading, alone, disappearing down Point Reyes Beach. He wore longsleeved shirts all summer in the California heat.

Daniel, I said, you've been my best friend for months. We could have talked about it.

He stepped backwards, awkwardly, out of the tub and put his shirt on.

I was loading them on copters, he told me. The last one was dead anyway; he was already dead. But I went after him, dragged him in the wind of the blades. Shrapnel and napalm caught my arms, my back. Until I fell, I thought it was the other man's blood in my hands.

They removed most of the shrapnel, did skin grafts for the burns. In three years since, Daniel made love five times; always in the dark. In San Francisco he must take off his shirt for a doctor; tumors have grown in his scars. They bleed through his shirt, round rust-colored spots.

Face-to-face in bed, I tell him I can feel the scars with my fingers. They are small knots on his skin. Not large, not ugly. But he can't let me, he can't let anyone, look: he says he feels wild, like raging, and then he vomits. But maybe, after they removed the tumors. . . . Each time they operate, they reduce the scars.

We spend hours at the Veterans's Hospital waiting for appointments. Finally they schedule the operation. I watch the black-ringed wall clock, the amputees gliding by in chairs that tick on the linoleum floor. Daniel's doctors run out of local anesthetic during the procedure and curse about lack of supplies; they bandage him with gauze and layers of Band-Aids. But it is all right. I buy some real bandages. Every night I cleanse his back with a sponge and change them.

In my mother's house, Daniel seems different. He has shaved his beard and his face is too young for him. I can grip his hands.

I show him the house, the antiques, the photographs on the walls. I tell him none of the objects move; they are all cemented in place. Now the bedrooms, my room.

This is it, I say. This is where I kept my Villager sweaters when I was seventeen, and my dried corsages. My cups from the Tastee Freez labeled with dates and boys' names.

The room is large, blue. Baseboards and wood trim are painted a spotless white. Ruffled curtains, ruffled bedspread. The bed itself is so high one must climb into it. Daniel looks at the walls, their perfect blue and white.

It's a piece of candy, he says.

Yes, I say, hugging him, wanting him.

What about your mother?

She's gone to meet friends for dinner. I don't think she believes what she says, she's only being my mother. It's all right.

We take off our clothes and press close together. But something is wrong. We keep trying. Daniel stays soft in my hands. His mouth is nervous; he seems to gasp at my lips.

He says his lover's name. He says they aren't seeing other people.

But I'm not other people. And I want you to be happy with her.

I know. She knew . . . I'd want to see you.

Then what?

This room, he says. This house. I can't breathe in here.

I tell him we have tomorrow. He'll relax. And it is so good just to see him, a person from my life.

So we only hold each other, rocking.

Later, Daniel asks about my father.

I don't see him, I say. He told me to choose.

Choose what?

Between them.

My father. When he lived in this house, he stayed in the dark with his cigarette. He sat in his blue chair with the lights and television off, smoking. He made little money; he said he was self-employed. He was sick. He grew dizzy when he looked up suddenly. He slept in the basement. All night he sat reading in the bathroom. I'd hear him

walking up and down the dark steps at night. I lay in the dark and
listened. I believed he would strangle my mother, then walk upstairs
and strangle me. I believed we were guilty; we had done something
terrible to him.

Daniel wants me to talk.

How could she live with him, I ask. She came home from work and
got supper. He ate it, got up and left to sit in his chair. He watched
the news. We were always sitting there, looking at his dirty plates.
And I wouldn't help her. She should wash them, not me. She should
make the money we lived on. I didn't want her house and his ghost
with its cigarette burning in the dark like a sore. I didn't want to be
guilty. So she did it. She did it all herself. She sent me to college; she
paid for my safe escape.

Daniel and I go to the Rainbow, a bar and grill on Main Street. We
hold hands, play country songs on the juke box, drink a lot of salted
beer. We talk to the barmaid and kiss in the overstuffed booth.
Twinkle lights blink on and off above us. I wore my burgundy stretch
pants in here when I was twelve. A senior pinched me, then moved
his hand slowly across my thigh, mystified, as though erasing the
pain.

What about tonight? Daniel asks. Would your mother go out with
us? A movie, a bar? He sees me in her, he likes her. He wants to
know her.

Then we will have to watch television.

We pop popcorn and watch the late movies. My mother stays up
with us, mixing whiskey sours and laughing. She gets a high color in
her cheeks and the light in her eyes glimmers up; she is slipping,
slipping back and she is beautiful, oh, in her ankle socks, her red
mouth and her armour of young girl's common sense. She has a
beautiful laughter. She and Daniel end by mock armwrestling; he
pretends defeat and goes upstairs to bed.

My mother hears his door close. He's nice, she says. You've known
some nice people, haven't you?

I want to make her back down.

Yes, he's nice, I say. And don't you think he respects me? Don't
you think he truly cares for me, even though we've slept together?

He seems to, I don't know. But if you give them that, it costs them
nothing to be friends with you.

Why should it cost? The only cost is what you give, and you can tell if someone is giving it back.

How? How can you tell? By going to bed with every man you take a fancy to?

I wish I took a fancy oftener, I tell her. I wish I wanted more, I can be good to a man, but I'm afraid . . . I can't be physical, not really. . . .

You shouldn't.

I should. I want to, for myself as well. I don't think . . . I've ever had an orgasm.

What? she says. Never? Haven't you felt a sort of building up, and then a dropping off . . . a conclusion? Like something's over?

No, I don't think so.

You probably have, she assures me. It's not necessarily an explosion. You were just thinking too hard, you think too much.

But she pauses.

Maybe I don't remember right, she says. It's been years, fifteen years, and in the last years of the marriage I would have died if your father had touched me. But before, I know I felt something. That's partly why I haven't . . . since . . . what if I started wanting it again? Then it would be hell.

But you have to try to get what you want. . . .

No, she says. Not if what you want would ruin everything. And now, anyway. Who would want me.

I stand at Daniel's door. The fear is back; it has followed me upstairs from the dead dark bottom of the house. My hands are shaking. I'm whispering . . . Daniel, don't leave me here.

I go to my room to wait. I must wait all night, or something will come in my sleep. I feel its hands on me now, dragging, pulling. I watch the lit face of the clock: three, four, five. At seven I go to Daniel. He sleeps with his pillow in his arms. The high bed creaks as I get in. Please now, yes . . . he is hard. He always woke with erections . . . inside me he feels good, real, and I tell him no, stop, wait . . . I hold the rubber, stretch its rim away from skin so it smooths on without hurting and fills with him . . . now again, here, yes but quiet, be quiet . . . oh Daniel . . . the bed is making noise . . . yes, no, but be careful, she . . . We move and turn and I forget about the sounds. We push against each other hard, he is almost there and I am almost with him and just when it is over I think I hear my mother in the room directly under us. . . . But I am half dreaming. I move to get out of bed and Daniel holds me. No, he says. Stay. . . .

We sleep and wake to hear the front door slam.

Daniel looks at me.

There's nothing to be done, I say. She's gone to church.

He looks at the clock. I'm going to miss that bus, he says. We put our clothes on fast and Daniel moves to dispose of the rubber . . . how? The toilet, no, the wastebasket. . . . He drops it in, bends over, retrieves it. Finally he wraps it in a Kleenex and puts it in his pocket. Jesus, he swears. He looks at me and grins. When I start laughing, my eyes are wet.

I take Daniel to the bus station and watch him out of sight. I come back and strip the bed, bundle the sheets in my arms. This pressure in my chest . . . I have to clutch the sheets tight, tighter. . . .

A door clicks shut. I go downstairs to my mother. She refuses to speak or let me near her. She stands by the sink and holds her small square purse with both hands. The fear comes. I hug myself, press my hands against my arms to stop shaking. My mother runs hot water, soap, takes dishes from the drainer. She immerses them, pushes them down, rubbing with a rag in a circular motion.

Those dishes are clean, I tell her. I washed them last night.

She keeps washing, rubbing. Hot water clouds her glasses, the window in front of us, our faces. We all disappear in steam. I watch the dishes bob and sink. My mother begins to sob. I move close to her and hold her. She smells as she used to smell when I was a child and slept with her.

I heard you, I heard it, she says. Here, in my own house. Please . . . how much can you expect me to take? I don't know what to do about anything. . . .

She looks into the water, keeps looking. And we stand here just like this.

From LAUGHING WITH ONE EYE

by GJERTRUD SCHNACKENBERG SMYTH

from POETRY

nominated by Norman Dubie, Don Hendrie Jr., and John Irving

Walter Charles Schnackenberg
Professor of History (1917–1973)

NIGHTFISHING

The kitchen's old-fashioned planter's clock portrays
A smiling moon as it dips down below
Two hemispheres, stars numberless as days,
And peas, tomatoes, onions, as they grow
Under that happy sky; but, though the sands
Of time put on this vegetable disguise,
The clock covers its face with long, thin hands.
Another smiling moon begins to rise.

We drift in the small rowboat an hour before
Morning begins, the lake weeds grown so long
They touch the surface, tangling in an oar.
You've brought coffee, cigars, and me along.
You sit still as a monument in a hall,
Watching for trout. A bat slices the air
Near us, I shriek, you look at me, that's all,
One long sobering look, a smile everywhere

43

But on your mouth. The mighty hills shriek back.
You turn back to the lake, chuckle, and clamp
Your teeth on your cigar. We watch the black
Water together. Our tennis shoes are damp.
Something moves on your thoughtful face, recedes.
Here, for the first time ever, I see how,
Just as a fish lurks deep in water weeds,
A thought of death will lurk deep down, will show
One eye, then quietly disappear in you.
Its time to go. Above the hills I see
The faint moon slowly dipping out of view,
Sea of Tranquility, Sea of Serenity,
Ocean of Storms . . . You start to row, the boat
Skimming the lake where light begins to spread.
You stop the oars, mid-air. We twirl and float.

I'm in the kitchen. You are three days dead.
A smiling moon rises on fertile ground,
White stars and vegetables. The sky is blue.
Clock hands sweep by it all, they twirl around,
Pushing me, oarless, from the shore of you.

INTERMEZZO

Steinway in German script above the keys,
Letters like dragons curling stiff gold tails,
Gold letters, ivory keys, the black wood cracked
By years of sunlight, into dragon scales.
Your music breathed its fire into the room.
We'd hear jazz sprouting thistles of desire,
Or jazz like the cat's cry from beneath
The passing tire, when you played the piano
Afternoons; or "Au Clair de la Lune."
Scarlatti's passages fluttered like pages.
Sometimes you turned to Brahms, a depth, more true,
You studied him to find out how he turned
Your life into a memory for you.

*   *   *

In Number 6 of Opus 118,
Such brief directions, Andante, sotto voce:
The opening notes like single water drops
Each with an oceanic undertow
That pulled you deeper even as you surfaced
Hundreds of miles from where the first note drew
You in, and made your life a memory,
Something that happened long ago to you.

And through that Intermezzo you could see
As through a two-way mirror until it seemed
You looked back at your life as at a room,
And saw those images that would compose
Your fraction of eternity, the hallway
In its absolute repose, the half-lit room,
The drapes at evening holding the scent of heat,
The marble long-lost under the piano,
A planet secretive, cloud-wrapped and blue,
Silent and gorgeous by your foot, making
A god lost in reflection, a god of you.

WALKING HOME

Walking home from school one afternoon,
Slightly abstracted, what were you thinking of?
Turks in Vienna? Luther on Christian love?
Or were you with Van Gogh beneath the moon
With candles in his hatband, painting stars
Like singed hairs spinning in a candle flame?
Or giant maps where men take, lose, reclaim
Whole continents with pins? Or burning cars
And watchtowers and army-censored news
In Chile, in the Philippines, in Greece,
Colonels running the universities,
Assassinations, executions, coups—

You walked, and overhead some pipsqueak bird
Flew by and dropped a lot of something that
Splattered, right on the good professor, splat.

Now, on the ancient Rhine, so Herod heard,
The old Germanic chieftains always read
Such droppings as good luck: opening the door,
You bowed to improve my view of what you wore,
So luckily, there on the center of your head.

Man is not a god, that's what you said
After your heart gave out, to comfort me
Who came to comfort you but sobbed to see
Your heartbeat blipping on a TV overhead.

You knew the world was in a mess, and so,
By God, were you; and yet I never knew
A man who loved the world as much as you,
And that love was the last thing to let go.

"THERE ARE NO DEAD"

Outside a phoebe whistles for its mate,
The rhododendron rubs its leaves against
Your office window: so the Spring we sensed
You wouldn't live to see comes somewhat late.
Here, lying on the desk, your reading glasses,
And random bits of crimped tobacco leaves,
Your jacket dangling its empty sleeves—
These look as if you've just left for your classes.
The chess game is suspended on its board
In your mind's pattern, your wastebasket
Contains some crumpled papers, your filing cabinet
Heavy with years of writing working toward
A metaphysics of impersonal praise
Here students came and went, here years would draw
Intensities of lines until we saw
Your face beneath an etching of your face.
How many students really cared to solve
History's riddles?—in hundreds on the shelves,
Where men trying to think about themselves
Must come to grips with grief that won't resolve,
Blackness of headlines in the daily news,

And buildings blown away from flights of stairs
All over Europe, tanks in empty squares,
The flaming baby-carriages of Jews.

Behind its glass, a print hangs on the wall,
A detail from the Bayeux Tapestry.
As ignorant women gabbed incessantly,
Their red, sore hands stitched crudely to recall
Forests of ships, the star with streaming hair,
God at Westminster blessing the devout,
They jabbed their thousand needles in and out,
Sometimes too busy talking to repair
The small mistakes; now the centuries of grease
And smoke that stained it, and the blind white moth
And grinning worm that spiralled through the cloth,
Say death alone makes life a masterpiece.

The William of Normandy remounts his horse
A fourth time, four times desperate to drive
Off rumors of his death. His sword is drawn,
He swivels and lifts his visor up and roars,
Look at me well! For I am still alive!
Your glasses, lying on the desk, look on.

A RENEWAL OF THE WORD

by BARBARA MYERHOFF

from THE KENYON REVIEW

nominated by THE KENYON REVIEW

(editor's note—this essay was adapted from a series of interviews recorded by Barbara Myerhoff for a forthcoming book.)

> Stories are a renewal of the word, made alive by being spoken, passed from one to another, released from considerations of correctness and law. Rabbi Nachman of Bratzlav ordered that all written records of his teachings be destroyed. His words must be passed from mouth to mouth, learned by and in heart. "My words have no clothes," he said. "When one speaks to one's fellows, there arises a simple light and a returning light."

Every morning I wake up in pain. I wiggle my toes. Good. They still obey. I open my eyes. Good. I can see. Everything hurts but I get dressed. I walk down to the ocean. Good. It's still there. Now my day can start. About tomorrow I never know. After all, I'm 89. I can't live forever.

Death and the ocean are protagonists in Basha's life. They provide points of orientation, comforting in their certitude. One visible, the other invisible, neither hostile nor friendly, they accompany her as she walks down the boardwalk to the Aliyah Senior Citizens' Center.
  Basha dresses simply but with care. The purchase of each item of

clothing is a major decision. It must last, should be modest and appropriate to her age, but gay and up-to-date. And, of course, it can't be too costly. Basha is not quite five feet tall, like most of the men and women in the community of old people who live at the beach. She is a sturdy boat of a woman—wide, strong of frame, and heavily corseted. She navigates her great monobosom before her, supported by broad hips and thin, severely bowed legs, their shape the heritage of her malnourished childhood. Like most of the people who belong to the Aliyah Center, her early life in Eastern Europe was characterized by relentless poverty.

Basha dresses for the cold, even though she is now living in Southern California, wearing a babushka under a red sun hat, a sweater under her heavy coat. She moves down the boardwalk steadily, paying attention to the placement of her feet. A fall is common and dangerous for the elderly. A fractured hip can mean permanent disability, loss of autonomy, and removal from the community to a convalescent or old age home. Basha seats herself on a bench in front of the Center and waits for friends. Her feet are spread apart, well-planted, as if growing up from the cement. Even sitting quite still, there is an air of determination about her. She will withstand attacks by anti-Semites, Cossacks, Nazis, historical enemies whom she conquers by outliving. She defies time and weather (though it is not cold here). So she might have sat a century ago, before a small pyramid of potatoes or herring in the marketplace of the Polish town where she was born. Patient, resolute, she is a survivor.

Not all the Center women are steady boats like Basha. Some, like Faegl, are leaves, so delicate, dry, and vulnerable that it seems at any moment they might be whisked away by a strong gust. And one day, a sudden wind did knock Faegl to the ground. Others, like Gita, are birds, small and sharp-tongued. Quick, witty, vain, flirtatious, they are very fond of singing and dancing. They once were and will always be pretty girls. This is one of their survival strategies. Boats, leaves, or birds, at first their faces look alike. Individual features are blurred by dentures, heavy bifocals, and webs of wrinkles.

* * *

I sat outside the Center and thought about how strange it was to be back in the neighborhood where sixteen years before I had lived and for a time had been a social worker with elderly citizens on public relief. Then the area was known as "Oshini Beach." The word "shini" still made me cringe. As a child I had been taunted with it. Like many second-generation Americans, I wasn't sure what being a Jew meant. When I was a child, our family had avoided the words "Jew" and "Yid." We were confused and embarrassed about our background. In public we lowered our voices when referring to "our people" or "one of us." My grandparents had emigrated from an Eastern European *shtetl* as young people. Like so many of the Center folk, they too wanted their children to be Americans above all and were ashamed of being "greenhorns." They spoke to my parents in Yiddish and were answered in English. None of the children or grandchildren in the family received any religous education, yet they carried a strong if ambivalent identity as Jews. This identity took the form of fierce pride and defensiveness during the Holocaust but even then did not result in any of us developing a clear conception of how to live in terms of our ethnic membership.

I had made no conscious decision to explore my roots or clarify the meaning of my origins. I was one of several anthropologists at the University of Southern California engaged in an examination of Ethnicity and Aging. At first I planned to study elderly Chicanos, since I had previously done fieldwork in Mexico. But in the early 1970s in urban America, ethnic groups were not welcoming curious outsiders, and people I approached kept asking me, "Why work with us? Why don't you study your own kind?" This was a new idea to me. I had not been trained for such a project. Anthropologists conventionally investigate exotic, remote, preliterate societies. But such groups are increasingly unavailable and often inhospitable. As a result, more and more anthropologists are finding themselves working at home these days. Inevitably, this creates problems with objectivity and identification, and I anticipated that I too would have my share if I studied the Center folk. But perhaps there would be advantages.

There was no way that I could have anticipated the great impact of the study of my life, nor its duration. I intended to spend a year with them. In fact, I was with them continuously for two years (1973–74, 1975–76) and periodically for two more. In the beginning, I spent a great deal of time agonizing about how to label what I was doing— was it anthropology or a personal quest? I never fully resolved the question. I used many conventional anthropological methods and asked many typical questions, but when I had finished, I found that my descriptions did not resemble most anthropological writings. Still, the results of the study would certainly have been different had I not been an anthropologist by training.

Most of the 300 elderly members of the Aliyah Center were born and spent much of their childhood in one of the small, predominantly Jewish, Yiddish-speaking villages known as *shtetls*, located within the Pale of Settlement of Czarist Russia—an area to which almost half the world's Jewish population was confined in the nineteenth century. Desperately poor, regularly terrorized by outbreaks of anti-Semitism initiated by government officials and surrounding peasants, *shtetl* life was precarious. Yet a rich, highly developed culture flourished in these provincial, self-sufficient, semirural settlements, based on a shared sacred religious history, common customs and beliefs, and two languages—Hebrew for prayer and Yiddish for daily life. The folk culture, *Yiddishkeit*, reached its flowering there and, though it continues in various places in the world today, by comparison these are dim and fading expressions of it.

When times worsened, it often seemed that Eastern European *shtetl* life intensified proportionately. Internal ties deepened, and the people drew sustenance and courage from each other, their religion, and their community. For many, life became unbearable under the reactionary regime of Czar Alexander II. The pogroms of 1881-82, accompanied by severe economic and legal restrictions, drove out the more desperate and daring of the Jews. Soon they were leaving the *shtetls* and the cities in droves. The exodus of Jews from Eastern Europe swelled rapidly until, by the turn of the century, hundreds of thousands were emigrating, the majority to seek freedom and opportunity in the New World.

The scene surrounding the Center rarely penetrates the invisible, pulsing membrane of the community. The old people are too absorbed in their own talk to attend to the setting. Surfers, sunbathers, children, dogs, bicyclists, winos, hippies, voyeurs, photographers, panhandlers, artists, junkies, roller skaters, peddlers, and police are omnipresent. Every social class, age, race, and sexual preference is represented. Jesus freaks, Hare Krishna parades, sidewalk preachers jostle steel bands and itinerant musicians. As colorful and flamboyant as the scene is by day, it is as dangerous by night. Muggings, theft, rape, harassment, and occasional murders make it a perilous neighborhood for the old people after dark.

* * *

Among the Center people, life was highly ritualized, and their penchant for ceremony and symbol was aided by Judaism's particular richness in these domains. Drawing on their cultural background, Center people were able to elevate mundane affairs, bringing to each moment a heightened consciousness that rendered suffering and scarcity explicable and thus bearable. Being so rooted in their Judaism helped the old people in their struggles and celebrations. They were sufficiently comfortable with it to improvise upon it and adapt it freely as needed, for small requirements and large.

Basha exemplified this in her dinner preparations. She ate alone in her tiny room. Over an electric hotplate, she cooked her chicken foot stew (chicken feet were free at the supermarket). Before eating, she spread a white linen handkerchief over the oilcloth covering the table:

This my mother taught me to do. No matter how poor, we would eat off clean white linen, and say the prayers before touching anything to the mouth. And so I do it still. Whenever I sit down, I eat with God, my mother, and all the Jews who are doing these same things even if I can't see them.

Such a meal is a feast, superior to fine fare hastily eaten without ceremony, attention, or significance. I wondered if Basha's daughter knew how to dine so splendidly. Because of such things, I came to see the Center elderly as in possession of the Philosopher's Stone— that universally sought, ever-elusive treasure, harboring the secret which would teach us how to transmute base metals into pure gold. The Stone, like the Blue Bird's feather of happiness, is said to be overlooked precisely because it is so close to us, hidden in the dust at our feet.

My grandmother was very similar to these women and she looked like Basha. Sofie Mann, born in the Ukraine, had raised me. What Sofie knew, so did some of the Center people. Perhaps her story-telling was part of *shtetl* kitchen life. One winter day, I cried because I could not see outside and thought that meant no stories could be told. Sofie laughed and warmed a penny in her palm and then, pressing it against the frosted pane, make a small, round peephole. This framing suddenly transformed the view; the street, now focused and contained, became a magic scene. The houses on the hill rose and twirled about, animated by our gaze, dancing on chicken legs like the home of Baba Yaga, the Russian witch.

The best stories came on the days when I had a cold and was allowed to stay home from school. Then Sofie and I were alone all day, in the big, cold house on Taylor Road (coal was too expensive to heat a whole house just for two). Then she would tuck me into the big bed in the front room where at night three grownups slept. From the closet floor she would bring stacks of old magazines, and from the drawer one of Grandpa's huge hankies. The chicken soup was put on in the kitchen below. She lugged her huge sewing machine into the room. The stories pulsed out steadily, accompanied by the "*pocketa pocketa*" of the pedal, her feet riding up and down on invisible currents throughout the afternoon. Outside the snow settled evenly and in time the soup delivered up its primal odors. The world was ample, timeless and complete.

Many years later, Sofie and I shared a room again. Now it was my room, time and fortune having divested her of home and husband. She was a perpetual visitor in her grown children's households. I liked having her sleep next to me, though my mother thought an adolescent girl should have a room to herself. Sofie, toothless, shorn of braids, status, property, and independence, tossed and grunted on her bed like a beached porpoise. Sometimes she would awaken and we would begin whispering in the darkness, gathering in all our past, telling the stories again, forestalling everything that waited outside the room. When her eyes and legs were gone, in extreme old age, the stories were with her still, lasting as long as she needed them.

* * *

Shmuel Goldman was one of the most educated and interesting people in the community. I was looking for someone to study Yiddish with and Shmuel seemed ideal, if he would agree. We attempted a few Yiddish lessons together, but he was too impatient with my ignorance for me to continue. Still, we both enjoyed our time together. Shmuel loved recalling his childhood, and eventually I decided I would like to record his life history at length. He was doubtful at first but finally agreed; for the next two months we met at least once a week for formal, prearranged recording sessions, nearly all of which were taped. These were long and often taxing for both of us. In between, we met casually in and around the Center and Shmuel provided a running commentary on the people and events there. Shmuel was a philosopher, and an outsider, though he had lived in the neighborhood for thirty-two years. His psychology and principles made him intolerant of formal organizations and ideologically he was at odds with nearly everyone in the Center. But he was too sensible, too learned, and too deeply rooted in their common traditions to be ignored by them. He and the Center people could not leave each other alone, but neither could they find peace together.

"I have a friend. A woman I know already many years. One day she is mad at me. From nowhere it comes. I have insulted her, she tells me. How? I don't know. Why don't I know? Because I don't *know* her. She surprised me. That's good. That is how it should be. You cannot tell someone, 'I know you.' People jump around. They are like a ball. Rubbery, they bounce. A ball cannot be long in one place. Rubbery, it must jump.

"So what do you do to keep a person from jumping? The same as with a ball. You take a pin and stick it in, make a little hole. It goes flat. When you tell someone, 'I know you,' you put a little pin in.

"So what should you do? Leave them be. Don't try to make them stand still for your convenience. You don't ever know them. Let people surprise you. This likewise you could do concerning yourself. All this, I didn't read in any book. It is my own invention."

Invented, I was afraid, specifically to warn me. Shmuel delivered this speech as we trotted down the boardwalk on the way to his house, our arms linked tightly, less for closeness than to regulate our gait. He set a fierce pace. He didn't believe in strolling. I didn't mind. It gave me courage to walk with him in this way, regardless of his reasons.

Shmuel had agreed to let me record his life history. But clearly he was full of doubts about revealing himself to me and about my ability to understand him. I shared his fears but was prepared to put doubts aside and try. The differences between us seemed less formidable as I contemplated our long shadows running before us in the clear afternoon light. Many people believe that taking their picture captures their soul, and taking a life story is even more threatening. Inevitably, in trying to know him, I would be putting pins in him. Our shadows were exactly the same size—small, compact, heads enlarged by wiry curls. Despite the forty years that set us apart, despite our differences in sex, history, knowledge, belief, and experience, we resembled each other. Same big noses, dark eyes, sharp vaulted cheekbones. It could be seen that we were of the same racial stock. Shmuel had a way of reckoning all differences between us in his favor, mocking but without cruelty, yet in a way that always made me feel somewhat apologetic. I was grateful for all our similarities and read them as signs of hope in the validity of my attempt to comprehend him. It didn't help that I was a professor with a Ph D, for both of us were aware that his self-directed education was much broader than mine, not to mention his greater experience.

I had explained to him what anthropology was, how it was a way of attempting to penetrate someone else's world from within, to enter another person's culture imaginatively and experience it as he did. I talked to him about the methods of participant-observation, where by sharing a segment of his life—and Center life—I would try to know it first-hand to some degree, while at the same time preserving my separateness and a measure of objectivity. I explained what a "key informant" was and said that I had selected him to be a teacher about his culture, if he would agree.

"So you want me to be your 'native.' No, that's flattering but not good." he said. "I'm not typical. Get some of the others at the Center. I'm not like them. I don't join clubs. I'm not a Zionist. I don't believe in God. Find someone else."

Eventually I convinced him that I was drawn to him for his learning and philosophical approach, not for his typicality. He had thought more about his experiences than most, had struggled to make sense of them. He yielded to this argument. I added that this work had personal meaning for me as well. I had not had the opportunity to learn about the world of my grandparents directly. I wanted to hear a firsthand account of *Yiddishkeit* and the *shtetl*. My grandparents had not taught me this, and now they were dead.

"Your grandparents did not speak Jewish to you, or to their children?"[1]

"It was the usual story, Shmuel. They talked Yiddish to their children and the children answered in English. What there was to learn they ran away from as fast as they could, to become American."

"So now that you are big enough to choose for yourself, go talk to them."

"To late, Shmuel. They're all dead. I can only get it in this roundabout fashion. When I hear Yiddish and Hebrew, often I don't know what the words mean, but I know that they are part of me all the same."

"What you ask, we will try. But it needs patience and time. How much I have of that, I don't know. Now I begin by telling you to see something you would not notice without me at your side." He pulled me closer and I stuck my ear close to his mouth to catch his quiet words.

"Look at those women sitting there on the benches. Strong little grandmothers." I had noticed them. As usual on a sunny day, each bench held a brace of old women. Motionless, they emitted great determination. Their mere existence, then as now, was a political-social attitude. Their continuing survival mocked their historical enemies, and time itself.

"Look if you will at something important about these women," Shmuel whispered. "Each one is wearing a coat. What's so special about a coat? you could ask. These are poor women here. But still everyone has a coat. A coat is not an ordinary garment. It was our people who brought coats to this world. Before the little Jewish tailors came to America, what poor person could have a coat?"

I never knew if Shmuel's attitude toward his work came from his socialist beliefs, from some Judaic elements, or were entirely of his own making. Creativity and seriousness belonged to work. It was both religion and play. When he worked, his imagination was freed.

"The mind must be alive when you sew, if you are in a good shop or a bad. I have been in both, and all those in between. The outside conditions do not apply. You must bring it up from the inside, looking always for a way to express yourself.

"Do you know what this means for me? When I am in a shop, I am

[1]Shmuel preferred the term "Jewish" to "Yiddish" in referring to his native language, in order to emphasize its status as a bona fide language and not, as some supposed, a mere dialect.

told to make a whole coat for a dollar. It must be done. You can't tell the boss he is crazy. You can't quit. In my shop, the other men would say, '*Nu*,[2] I can do it.' They put down the little screw on the machine to make bigger stitches. But such a coat doesn't last the winter. This coat goes to a poor woman, her only garment for warmth. You wouldn't know this but it gives out in the Bible that a pawnbroker cannot keep a poor man's caftan or cloak for deposit or for pawn overnight, because a Jew can't profit from someone else's need. 'You shall not sleep in his pledge. When the sun goes down you restore to him his pledge, that he may sleep in his own cloak.' This comes from Deuteronomy, which no doubt you have not read. No, it is not the way of a Jew to make his work like there was no human being to suffer when it's done badly. A coat is not a piece of cloth only. The tailor is connected to the one who wears it and he should not forget it."

Shmuel's garments had lasted. He had always made clothes for his friends and his wife, Rebekah, saving shop remnants of his finest material for her. Rebekah still wore the long velvet skirts and frilly blouses he had made. She cut a fine figure in his garments.

We arrived at Shmuel's house, a single-story duplex a few doors from the boardwalk. "Do you want some tea? You are tired?" He knew I was and it pleased him that he was not. "Well, come in then, Rebekah will be glad to see you. By now she will be home from all her meetings."

We went into the large, rather bare living room, furnished with the landlord's cast-offs. Two golden naugahyde couches were pushed against the wall, and in between them stood a brave little table bearing heaps of magazines and papers—*Jewish Currents, Yiddishe Kultur Verband, Morgan Freiheit, The Nation, The People's World.* In one corner was a child's school desk and a kitchen chair, the drawers crammed with scraps of paper—Shmuel's poetry and essays in Yiddish, Hebrew, Polish, Russian, French, and English. Rickety bookcases held dictionaries, novels in all those languages, plus used college textbooks on political science, history, art, psychology, sociology, economics, and philosophy. In the center of the room, a huge, bare-breasted ceramic woman in yellow harem pants held aloft a tiny fluted lampshade.

I fiddled with electric sockets and my tape recorder while Rebekah put up water for tea. Shmuel waited quietly, wearing his quizzi-

[2]All right; so.

cal monkey look. He didn't look eighty. Time had sharpened his
facial planes, paring off all nonessential flesh. The lips were a thin,
neutral line, the eyes deep and close together, unclouded by
cataracts or glaucoma. His smile was restrained and rare. Only his
hair and ears and cheekbones were exuberant. His teeth were
jagged and stained but they were his own. I liked them and realized
how depressing I found the false white sameness of the others'
dentures. The cables of his neck wired his great, gaunt head onto a
springy, tidy frame.

Rebekah came to the couch and sat down next to Shmuel. She too
had her own teeth and, like him, lacked the equipment that makes
so many among the elderly look alike at first glance—the heavy
glasses, hearing aids, dentures. Rebekah was also small, energetic,
and erect. Even their hands were the same size, the backs blotched
with brown spots; but the fingers were uncrimped by arthritis.
Rebekah was seventy-four.

Both were healthy, apart from Shmuel's heart condition, for which
he frequently took nitroglycerine pills. "My doctor tells me not to
have emotions," he said. "I should damp down everything. Is this a
philosophy? To live longer by not being so much alive? Now, in
honor of your tape machine, I take one of his pills.

"So, you are here in our modest home. You see we are not poor.
We do not have too much money, not too little either. When this is
so, you pay attention. Spend carefully, eat carefully, you think about
what you wear, what you eat, chew slowly with pleasure. So you end
up paying attention to being alive. This is not such a bad thing. I
don't envy the rich. When we were young, in my little town—*that*
was poor. That was hunger. But because we didn't know anything
else we didn't think of ourselves as poor. Everyone lived the same in
the town. One was hungry, all were hungry. Not so hard as here
where you see there are very rich and very poor."

Shmuel held up a batch of papers covered with Yiddish. He had
prepared for today's session by writing out some of his recollections
from childhood. He put on his reading glasses and signalled that he
was ready to begin.

"Oh, how often in our dreams, like a bird, we fly back to the place
of our birth, to that little Polish town on the Vistula which would be
to you a small speck on the map, maybe even too insignificant for a
map. A few thousand people huddled together, hidden in the hills,

but with a view in sight of the beautiful river. In this place, the population was nearly equal Poles and Jews. All were poor. There were the poor and the poorer still.

"If you walked through the Jewish quarter, you would see small houses, higgledy-piggledy, leaning all over each other. Some had straw roofs; if shingles, some broken. No cobbles on the streets, and you might not even want to call them streets, so narrow and deep rutted from wagons. Everywhere, children, cats, geese, chickens, sometimes a goat, altogether making very strong smells and noises. Always, the children were dirty and barefoot, always the dogs were skinny and mean, not Jewish dogs. They came over from Gentile quarters looking for garbage and cats. You would go along this way until you crossed the wooden bridge into the main platz. Here were the women on market day, sitting in the open, or in little wooden stalls if they were well-off. Around the platz, a few Jewish stores, a stable, the pump with a roof and a bench.

"Most important you would see here two buildings, facing each other on opposite sides of the platz, without smiling. There was on one side the Catholic church, enormous, two big towers of bells, and across from it, the synagogue, small but dignified, topped by pagoda-like roofs covered with sheet metal. Under the sun, it was shining like silver, like a sparkle in God's eye. Otherwise it was all wood. The church stands there sternly, the synagogue's historical enemy—those two looked at each other all the day. The church was built with splendor inside and out. Its glittering beauty displayed itself when the great portals opened. The Jewish children were afraid even to look inside."

Shmuel warmed to his subject and broke off reading. "You see, that church was the biggest thing we ever saw. From everywhere in the town you could see the towers. You could never forget about it. It was such a beautiful building, but when the great bells tolled it meant trouble for us Jews. When we heard that, we children would run home as fast as we could, back into the Jewish streets. On Sundays and Easter, those were the worst times. The processions came out from the church. The peasants were drinking all the day and night, staggering down the road behind those pictures of the Saints they carry. Then, if they came across a Jewish child or woman, it could be murder. The hatred would pour out.

"You see, matters were never simple there. The pogroms were all around us. Then the soldiers on horseback would tear through the town and leave dead Jews behind. One time, we heard the big bell ring out and there was no reason for it. We were so scared we hid in the synagogue. That was probably the worst place to go, but we were small boys. All night we stayed huddling together there and heard terrible noises outside, horses, screams, shouts. We were afraid to light the lamps or stove. In the morning some men came to get us. Someone, it must have been a Pole, had warned the Jews with the bells that the soldiers were coming through. Everyone got away very quickly, hiding in the foret and in neighbors' homes. Who knows what would have happened without the warning? As it is, the soldiers tore up the Jewish streets, broke windows, threw the furniture out. We came out into the sparkling sunshine and the streets were white like in winter. Everywhere were feathers from where those Cossacks cut up our featherbeds. Dead animals also on our streets. From all this you can imagine our emotions when we walked past the great doors of the church. We would hardly throw a glance inside, even though the beauty would draw us like moths.

"Now, by comparison the synagogue you might not think was a beautiful place. It would be misleading to say it had any architecture. But do you think I noticed that? This synagogue was my first introduction to Judaism. The first time I went there I was with my beloved father who, up to the present moment, I feel is with me, so that when I think of the synagogue, I can still feel his hand in mine as he introduced me to the world it held.

"I will tell you a little bit what it looks like. You walked up ten broad steps to the door. Why ten? I don't know, but probably it had some meaning. Then to enter, you walked down again, ten steps more. Why? The reason I think is symbolical. Because from the depths of your heart, you seek God, and you should feel that brings you up. But right away, you realize you are in the presence of God. Your body vibrates with how high He is, and how you are very small. Of this you are reminded by the steps down. This is how I thought of it.

"But like most things symbolical, there is also a practical side. You see, the Poles had a law that the church must be the highest building in the town. So the Jews, to make their building high, built it up from the inside, very quietly. You could not see from the outside what was happening. This was typical of the way the Jews lived with the Poles at that time. Everything done inside so as not to attract notice. Oppression made us very cunning. In this here case, the floor of the synagogue was lowered. They dug down into the ground, so from the inside only it was a very tall building.

"Inside the synagogue, no saints, no gold. There is no big beauty. It is an empty room. Benches, a *bima*,[3] the ark, not very bright. Now here is another thing. In the top, by the ceiling, there were murals. Animals, Hebrew characters, flowers, birds of all kinds, and signs of the zodiac. There was also an elephant. Who had ever seen an elephant in Poland? Actually, he looked more like a deer with tusks. I raised my small head and looked up at that elephant until I thought my neck would crack. Some painter, some obsure fellow who never saw an elephant, he was the one who brought me all of a sudden to a thing I had never known before. You see, it was not a Jewish custom to decorate our homes. No pictures in our books. No carvings on the furniture. You know Jews forbid making religious pictures, and everything in those days was for religion. Why the synagogue was decorated at all, this I cannot answer. But in our little town, the only beauty which we could look at was the murals in the synagogue and the ones in the church which you were too frightened to have a good look at.

"Now, if you have enough tape, I will give you the best part. I will describe my favorite picture in that mural. Okay. This one was covered with musicians and angels playing horns and flutes. In the middle was a picture of Abraham in his devotion to God. He took his only son and got ready to sacrifice him for the sake of God, until the Angel took ahold of his knife and saved Isaac.

"It seems strange, but there have always been people who are ready to make sacrifices on an altar without reservation. So the Bible in this story is showing us that people have always been ready to sacrifice the younger generation. We still send the innocent out to be slaughtered.

"Now you see, these pictures formed me. I never forgot that. There is no such thing as a small place. Some people would call that little town a small *shtetl*, or say it was a small synagogue. But people are formed by their passions, in the same ways, no matter how small or big is the place they live. They become who they are, with all the troubles, all the passions, with all the things which are bound to come up and face them, from these childhood pictures. That picture of Abraham is such for me. So that to this day, when I see children

[3]Stand to hold the Torah during readings.

being sent out for slaughter, with those bugles playing and drums beating, while the angels are flapping their wings so you shouldn't hear the cries of the children being killed and shouldn't smell the blood, it stinks in my nostrils. But that is mankind. You cannot cut it out."

"Tell me, Shmuel," I asked, "didn't it confuse you, to love Judaism as you did, but see it condoning the sacrifice of an innocent victim for God's wishes?"

"Do you think that Judaism saves us from being men? Even as a boy, I saw Abraham's fault and knew it was his responsibility, not God's, to decide what was right.

"Like I said, sometimes things happen that make you realize how helpless you are. Not only were we children. We were Jews, and the outside would come up against us. This was like being a child twice over, you felt very small, very weak. To give you an example, sometimes the Polish nation would step into our hidden little world in the synagogue. This was when the Governor, appointed by the Czar, would visit our little town once a year on the Czar's birthday. When we knew he was coming, we cleaned everything, the best way we could. The women would come in and scrape all the candle wax and ashes off the benches and floors, oil the wood, make the books line up on the shelves. All the children would wear their best clothes, borrow shoes if they had to.

"The leadership of the synagogue was so afraid, not to displease the Governor. Everything was done to impress him. A rug was put down, from somewhere we got it. And a big chair put in the middle where the *bima* should be sitting. We, the boys, the Cantor, the Rabbi, would stand up there, straight and stiff, full of palpitations to receive him, as he entered the door, dressed in a beautiful jacket, grey, with red lapels of gold trim, with a huge cross hanging from his neck.

"As he entered we turned and faced him. He never smiled. We never smiled. He had little glasses that glittered. Very straight and big. He was much bigger than any of us, maybe six feet tall.

"The Rabbi would make him a receptional speech. This Rabbi was very short and bent over, a frail old man, near-sighted and scared to death. He held that paper right up to his nose, trembling all over from the ordeal. He delivered it in Russian, careful with all the words, to make it to the satisfaction of the Government. It filled my heart with pity to see that kind, old man so frightened, like a small, unloved boy.

"After the speech, we children began to sing the Russian hymn, a hymn on the dull side. But we sang with gusto. This hymn was also a delicate business, because it was introduced after Poland was partitioned by Russia. And we were Jews—not accustomed to placing any man superior to any other, except God himself. But this was the way we were required to pay homage. I will never forget this hymn. All mixed up with it was the fear if we make a mistake, something terrible will happen. I can hear still our beautiful clear voices, and see that tall man's fine uniform, with the synagogue so sparkling clean, and always I come back to the old Rabbi's terror. I get it all back together with the hymn."

Shmuel abruptly pushed back from the table. He tore his glasses off his nose and pulled himself up to his full five feet, two inches. Voice trembling, but sweet and grand, he gave forth the Russian hymn. I applauded when he finished and shouted bravo. For a few moments his tears and laughter spilled out freely. I had never seen him so unguarded. Neither of us heard Rebekah come in. Shmuel quickly reached for another pill.

"What am I hearing? Is it possible? Why do you sing that terrible song, Shmuel?" Rebekah asked sharply. "Those things only meant unhappiness for us. You shouldn't let him talk about those times," she reprimanded me. "It makes me shudder."

"Rebekah, Rebekah, it was there," Shmuel protested. "You won't make it any different if you say it wasn't there. The hymn, the Czar, the fear, the beauty, it was all there. It must be kept all together. To take out one part and lose the rest, to try to keep the good parts is to make every day the Sabbath. So far, the Messiah has not come. When every day is beautiful, we will be in Paradise."

"Shmuel has no understanding in some things." Rebekah turned to me. "He thinks because he has these ideas about things the world is changed. He will try to tell you living with the Poles was not so bad. He maybe hasn't told you what happened to him? Did he show you his scar? He met a boy, a *shagetz*,[4] and it was winter time, after Christmas. Shmuel wore a heavy sweater and scarf. This boy took out a knife and stabbed him in the neck."

[4]Non-Jewish boy.

"No, he hasn't told me. What happened, Shmuel?"

"I must have been about eleven years old. I was coming home from another village. I didn't see anyone. It was just growing dark and I was hurrying and took a shortcut through the woods. All of a sudden, something was on me with a knife, from the back. I felt a terrible pain in my neck and fell to the ground. He left me for dead. But it's not so easy to kill me. You know, they say that Jews are a stiff-necked people. He picked the wrong place to stab me. You could say my scarf saved me, or you could say maybe it was the characteristic of our people." Shmuel made his monkey face, eyebrows jumping up, mouth pulling down, eyes pushing out like raisins in a cookie.

"Well, this happened. It is true. I carry the scar to remind me till now. I never saw this fellow's face, but I knew who it was from the voice, one of our neighbors. Not a bad boy, but an ignorant peasant. But this is not characteristic. I cannot depict this here like it was a regular part of life in our little town."

"Did you see him again?"

"Of course, every day."

"Did you talk about it ever? Why do you think he did it?"

"No, we never spoke about it. After that, he was a little afraid of me. I think he thought I was some kind of a ghost. For why he did it, I can't say. He was a bully, and a small Jewish boy was like a fly to him. But it must be remembered that there were Jewish bullies also. Who knows what they would do if they wouldn't be caught and punished? Without the law to govern them, do they find it in their hearts always to behave? Because they were the Chosen People? Not even the Messiah would expect that. Without consequences, do you think men ever find it in their hearts to do what is right? If that was so, why would we need the Torah?"

"Why are you undoing your tape machine? Are you getting ready to go? I just got back." Rebekah was very disappointed. She had wanted to make a tape recording of a poem she had translated. I was already late for dinner but I knew if I left now, Rebekah would be annoyed with me for weeks.

Shmuel sensed my conflict and intervened. "Leave her alone, Rebekah," he said. "She'll come another day. She's a busy lady, and I'm a hungry man. Come, I'll walk you to your car. This is a dangerous neighborhood and my neck is stiffer than yours." He winked, gathered up my packages, and held open the door.

When we met again, Shmuel wanted to continue discussing his early life and how it had shaped him. This time he spoke spontaneously, no longer feeling it necessary to write out what he planned to tell me.

"Perhaps the deepest impressions of life are where the roots are set," he began, "but at the time we were not aware of it. Later it comes up to you, what that was. I was a happy boy, but did I know it? I was too busy. My middle name is Simcha, that means joy, and it seems that that name influenced me greatly. Until the present day, I would rather see life in a way that is full of color, also full of shade, because without the shade we don't have the color. On this Rebekah and I do not have the same views. She keeps track of the shade too much. But my view is more from Jewish wisdom. God is not all good, not all bad, like everything. This matches also common sense.

"My roots, you could not separate from what I was reading, from the very beginning of my life till now, that always made a big impression on me. Naturally, because of where I grew up, the only reading was religious until I was nearly grown.

"You can imagine that it didn't take me long to learn to read. Soon I was introduced to the Torah, the big history of our people. I was absolutely enchanted by it, even though it was really premature for me, since then I was only five years old when I began on it. I was brought by it to that Ancient People—very thrilling, different nations, tragedies, greatness, drama. It all came forward and took me into it, thousands of years among the Jewish people. I liked it immensely. The text itself gripped me and held me. I felt the greatness of it. Not till later did I understand what that was. Still, from the start, I was taken with its . . . how to say it, with the great unity and endurance of our people.

"Like all the small boys in our town, I started *cheder*[5] when I was only three years old. When I think about it, we had there a very strange way to learn. It was so noisy in that room you couldn't hear yourself think. For one thing, we were many small boys. The teacher had to do many things with us to keep our attention— games, riddles, jokes, tricks—because we couldn't sit still too long. So we made all the letters into different stories and songs. A *hey* was a man with a broken leg, so we would limp around the room. The *beys* was an open mouth, ready to take in learning. Some had morals like *giml-daled*, to be kind to the poor. We would say the *giml* looks at

[5]Religious primary school for Jewish boys.

the *daled* to remember we should look after the poor. But the *daled* turns away his face, so no one should see his shame at taking charity. The older boys would also use the pages in the books for guessing games, for gambling. So everyone used sacred books not only for wisdom but for enjoyment. We didn't stop learning when we left school, not like in this country. No, it went all through our time.

"We *cheder* boys were always together whenever we weren't helping our parents. We were raised on four cultures. We knew Jewish at home. We knew Polish, naturally. After the Czar took over, we had to learn Russian. And there was Hebrew, of course. Hebrew was our spiritual culture. The March of the Kings held us in that tongue. The people were so real for us—the melancholy King Saul, the brilliant, poetic Solomon, the angry, poetic suffering of Jeremiah; he was my favorite. We could always find heroes for us in there. We played our games in Jewish but from Hebrew came the ideas. Whenever we were free from school, we would play out certain games. We always fell back to the Bible itself and played it out.

"When you play like that you have to have a deep understanding of the characters, their psychology. It's not only like reading about something. These people in the Bible grew enlarged for us, how they behaved, what they did when we gave them situations and troubles to handle, that was our game. Until the present day, I can feel the greatness of those stories working in me, giving color, giving itself into my own way of thinking. Sometimes I'm really astonished to which extent it reached out into me, and this was completely without any other studies. So I would have to say it was the simple beauty of the Bible itself that became part of my makeup. Even now, when I come across certain words, certain phrases that I know, I can branch out on them and relate to other things I learned since. Many people went to school and studied many things, but it seems their attention was not riveted to what stories they came across as mine was.

"Going out from school, we would look for the right place to play. Where the earth was soft, somewhere outside the little town, and where we wouldn't bump into any Poles. Youngsters need such food for their imaginations. For example, we would talk about Jacob, what went wrong with him? We would compare him to our own fathers. You see, children, when you let them be like this, together, warm with those beautiful stories, the lessons of them ring out, very strong, very sweet. Those Bible stories taught us how to live.

"Now we also played the character of Isaac. He had troubles because he had no child for so long. With no children, what happens? There are standing in each and every corner of a room, people praying to a different God. Why? Because they have no common blood. As soon as a child is born, they are united by it. They have then one understanding and one God. You read such things as a child yourself, and you have no understanding. But gradually it comes out, when you take these parts into yourself. There's a deep thought that comes, but you can't yet put it into words. So later, you are grown and you find, from somewhere, you have ideas about how to raise children. It is these Patriarchs who have taught you that. So the Jewish ways get into you, from the earliest times, and you are raising children in a special way. It happens to be the Jewish way. I don't mean it is the best way, but it happens to be our way. That's all. It is planted in our gardens. Does that mean that other gardens should be destroyed?

"Now I will tell you about culture. Culture is that garden. This is not a thing of nations. It is not about Goethe and *Yeshivas*.[6] It is children playing. Culture is the simple grass through which the wind blows sweetly and each grass blade bends softly to the caress of the wind. It is like a mother who would pick up her child and kiss it, with her tenderness that she gave birth to it. We don't see this anymore. In the present time we see nations. They are not natural outgrowings. Their roots are too harsh. They grew up too fast. They have not got that natural sweetness."

"It sounds like most of your memories about your childhood in the little town are sweet," I said.

"It was a sweetness in the middle of fear and oppression. That is how the Jew lived and how the Jewish language was born. In the long journey from one nation to another, from one country to another, here and there, the Jew picked up a language. From the Arabs, the Germans, the Poles, the Russians. The Jews were like a flock of sheep. They would go into a place and against every tree they would leave some wool and pick up some moss. The Jew exactly. But it was in Germany that they were pushed to the point that they had to have a language all their own. Here they got their voice. Hebrew

[6]Schools of advanced Jewish studies.

was all right to speak to God, but when you had to speak man to man, to your own wife with love, or to your naughty child, when you had to curse your mule, Hebrew was no good for you. Too mighty. So little by little the Jew assembled his language.

"Now there are some people, even scholars and teachers, who you will hear say, Jewish is not a real language. For them, it was inferior. It came out of exile, or the language of exile, for the marketplace. It was for women to talk to children. Not good for big subjects. For these you need Hebrew or Russian or Polish or English. This is nonsense. Jewish we call the *mamaloschen*. That means more than mother tongue. It is the *mother's* tongue because this was the language the mother talked, sweet or bitter. It was your own. It is a language of the heart. This the Jewish writers knew, and they used it with love.

"It had another aspect. It was not only that Jews from everywhere could talk with this language. Also, it had words in it that could be used differently for the inside sweet world and the hard world outside. Now this *mamaloschen* kept apart the Jewish and Polish worlds. My father, for example, used to say, 'I took the shortcut, past the church, *lehavdl*,[7] to get to synagogue sooner.' That 'lehavdl' kept the church from being in the same breath with the synagogue. For cursing and blessing of all kinds, the Jewish language was the best. And it was a language that very few Poles understood. For us it was itself *lehavdl*, keeping us apart from the ones who hated us.

"So Jewish gave us unity. We passed by, we rubbed off, we gathered what we needed here and there. In the *shtetl* Hebrew was not the link, except for a few scholars. Whenever you went to the Judenstrasse in a new town, Jewish you spoke. Even in the schools, Jewish is standing by, patiently waiting to assist Hebrew. Always we travelled along in these two tracks, side by side. Hebrew and Jewish. Then another thing. In Hebrew you couldn't sing songs except for those Psalms which is not a song by itself. You couldn't amuse yourself in Hebrew. We could sing the deep, lyrical songs in Jewish. Lullabies, love songs. A boy likes a girl. He couldn't go up to her and say, 'I like you.' This would not be permitted. So how could he approach her and catch her attention? He would make up a song, and sing it as if to himself, naturally in Jewish, but so she could hear

[7]Hebrew: "to separate."

it. This is the sweet grass from which the language grew. Young boys singing songs. The language was our republic.

"Rebekah says I tell you too much about the sweetness in my little town. I have no hatred. Why should I? But she is right. It has to be said that terrible things happened there, like anywhere. Not only things the Poles did to the Jews. We make our own tragedies also, without their help. You see, much there was that was beautiful. But not only this. Many tragedies also in that town.

"When I was very young a beautiful, educated young man hung himself on the eve of the Sabbath in the synagogue. This was a desecration and a disgrace for the whole town, because he was driven to it. He got himself caught up in the rivalry between the Hasids and the Rabbis and he made an end to it in this way. What could have been worse? For me, something happened that was worse. Now this story tells a bad part about me in it, but I am telling you truthfully because that is part of it. We children would escape from the grownups on Saturday afternoons. Then my father and mother went to bed for a nap and we never knew what to do with ourselves. We would go any little place we could find outside of the town. We took off our shoes, our clothes, we came to play in that beautiful little lake.

"This is a very sad story. We were a few youngsters and we went over to the shallow part of the lake. Then some Polish youngsters came along and we hid. There were more of them than us, and it was Saturday so we did not want to fight. The boys of the village on Saturdays learned catechisms. I don't know what they learned there, but it was always better for the Jews to stay out of their way after those lessons.

"One of the boys stayed behind to swim after the others went away. He plunged into the water and began to shout. I was afraid but I went to the water anyway. But I was too young. I couldn't reach him. And then I saw coming a Polish man on the road. He was under the impression that it was a Jewish youngster there in the water. He looked at the boy, then walked on into the town. He didn't want to save a Jewish boy. We ran back to the town to tell someone, I remember I rushed so fast into town, I put my shirt on the wrong side.

"All the Jewish parents who didn't see their children there were afraid when that man told them the news. All those people rushed to the lake. By then someone had pulled the boy out. That was how people behaved. We knew the Polish man had passed him by, but we were afraid to tell on him. My teacher called us together when he heard about it. He took the boys out of school to the lake and said, 'Come be a witness as to how not to behave.' You see, people still make sacrifices of each other even though we no longer do it on altars.

"All right. Now here comes the bad part I am telling about me. I tried to save the boy myself, that's true. I could not manage it. But when I saw the man, that big Polish peasant on the road, why didn't I catch him to come down to the boy? I ran up to the road and there I stopped, frozen into speechlessness. We looked at each other a second, and then I ran away. In that silence, I helped kill a boy, out of my fear. This happened many years before that other one came at me with a knife. If the peasant later told anybody this happened, I doubt, because he was my accomplice. Did the knife come at me many years later in punishment, this I cannot doubt. Sooner or later, our actions come back to us with justice. This is my incurable wound with me all my life since then. I was like Jeremiah who also bore a terrible disgrace from his youth. Like Jeremiah I also was instructed by it. From this moment on, I cannot condemn my fellow man. Fear, *that* I condemn as our enemy, and this is not only for the Poles."

"Shmuel, did you ever tell anyone about it?"

"No, not my beloved father, not Rebekah, even. All these years I carried it alone."

"You know we have it recorded here on the tape."

"You think I'm so old I can't see the machine is turning?"

"Do you want me to erase it?"

"No, it belongs to the record, maybe the most important thing of all. Without knowing this, you don't know me. I told you this work would stick me with a pin, who knows how many sticks, before we finish."

"You don't have to tell me things that are so painful if you don't want to. Only you can decide what is necessary to include."

"Is this serious work we do here, or only a *bobbemeise*?[8] If you take my time, you take my life; at least you could make it right. Does it matter so much what you think of me, a tailor? No, what counts is

[8] A little story or folk tale.

what you learn from me. So much you don't know, I can hardly dent your ignorance.

"All of this makes no sense to me. Here you sit, all afternoon, listening to the life of an obscure tailor. Better I should make you a coat to express myself. I could do more with a needle and thread than with words. No one will get anything from this work."

"Let me give you an example, Shmuel. That story you told me about your attitude when you sew, about how it should feel to do the work, with attention, care and imagination. I think that has universal value."

"Bah! You are exaggerating again. Be careful."

"Okay, maybe I sometimes exaggerate, but I'm not. It's my opinion that your description of the attitude you bring to your work will have meaning for many people. It's a valuable lesson for anyone. No matter what one's task, it can be done as you describe, so that finally peeling potatoes, any routine job, instead of being monotonous, becomes full of possibilities. I really believe your life is infinitely richer than so many people's, for many reasons. This is just one example of what people can learn from you."

"There you go. 'Infinitely,' such a big word. Too big for what you mean."

"Okay, you don't like 'infinite.' I like it. It's the way I talk. I'm sorry if it annoys you."

"Will you put this in the record also, or will you wipe it out when I scold you?"

"I suppose I'll have to leave it in, won't I? To be fair to both of us. So we'll both be deflated, Shmuel."

"Maybe I'm too hard on you. You can't help your great ignorance. But you should watch out for exaggeration. When you exaggerate, it puts you outside of something. You are not treating it with care. I tell you this because of what I have just given over into your hands. If I'm hard on you, it's because I make this sacrifice of letting you deflate me. A teacher holds nothing back from his students. You should accept all this with the right approach. Now, we take our tea. Soon Rebekah will be home. If she catches me with this heavy heart she will be angry at both of us."

At another one of our taping sessions, Shmuel had forgotten a word he wanted and became very upset. I offered substitutes and finally suggested that we go on without it and return to the subject later. That upset him even more. In part, his agitation was due to his fear that this was a sign of senility. But when he discussed it later, it became clear that more was involved.

"You understand that one word is not like another," he said. "Just a particular one is needed to do the trick, none other. So when just the word I want hides from me, when before it has always come along very politely when I called it, this is a special torture designed for old Jews. Do you know what a word is to the Jew? Words don't just give a name. No, they change things around. This is why we pray, make blessings, make hexes, charms, all those things. When you have the right word, you have power over something. This is why a Jew never pronounces the Tetragrammaton. The Kabbalists believed if you said God's name you would die. This is because it could give you power even over God. When Jacob wrestled with the Angel, what do you think he asked him? He asked his name, because if he knew that, Jacob would be his servant. Everything about a word is important to a Jew, every letter. Rabbi Ishmael told one of the scribes of the Torah, 'My son, be careful in your work, for if you mix up even one letter you destroy the whole world.' "

It was not surprising that among Eastern European Jews the power of words was expressed in the practice of giving nicknames to anything or anyone—people, towns, animals, families. They summarized and fixed a single trait, feature of history or accident, character, or appearance for a lifetime. Nicknames lasted like legal names. Sholom Aleichem said they were "like a suit . . . made to order: measured, cut, hand-sewn and pressed—now wear it well!"

Words, among Jews and *shtetl* people, were no mere neutral labels; indeed, were so powerful that one might speak of word-magic. Words could affect what they named, and names contained something of the identity of that which they signified. As Shmuel said, words were alive and they had consequences in the world. In the Center, then, when people called each other names—derisive or laudatory—it had great seriousness. *Goniff, chazer, mishugene, reb, amoretz, yente, apikoros, schnorrer, filosofe, grauber, yekl, kunelemme*—these were permanent summary interpretations of the named one's very essence. Calling names was a significant form of social control among the Center people, and the consequences of name-calling went beyond merely stigmatizing. When one casts a spell or makes a curse, the words themselves are efficacious. There is only a slight shade of difference among spells, curses, prayers, and insulting names in a group that believes in word-magic.

Shmuel lapsed into silence. Outside the window a moth tapped lightly on the glass. The kitchen was dark and still. I could no longer see Shmuel's face. At last he began again slowly.

"What do we learn from all this? This little town I loved so much, with all its faults, I have to say we belonged there in such a way that we could never belong in America. Why? Because it was ours. Simple. Not so good or bad. But altogether Jewish. Now this is strange that I say we belonged there. Look how we lived. Hidden in a foreign land that we loved and hated. Even the beautiful river, the forests, none of these are ours. What did we have but fear and hunger and more hunger. So small, cramped, mostly very dirty. A life made up entirely from the imagination. We say our prayers for rains to come, not for us here in Poland, but for the Holy Land. We pass our lives to study the services of the Temple. What Temple? Long ago finished. It doesn't exist anymore. Where do our priests make the offerings? Only in our minds. We feel the seasons of Jerusalem more than the cold of Poland. Outside we are ragged, poor, nothing to look at, no possibilities for change. But every little child there is rubbing elbows with the glorious Kings and Priests of the Holy Land. The Prophets are in our daydreams, so we cannot forget their fight for freedom and justice. In this we find our home. We march and mingle in the teeming streets of Jerusalem and our visions rise. Ideas clash inside us like warriors. A spark of life comes into us.

"Would you say this is insanity? Your Dr Freud, would he call us schizophrenics? It could be. If we lived more in Poland and not so much in the Holy Land, would all these people be buried now in pits along the river? Do you think if we had had less to console us it would have made a different finish? These things I ask myself. Around and around it goes inside my head, making even the stories stop. When this happens, I lose myself. I think it may be dangerous for me to tell you these things. You should pay attention to the weather in America." Shmuel's voice had grown soft and dark. He shifted his body heavily in his chair and let out a sigh that was almost a groan. I couldn't see his face. "Go home now, child. I have nothing more for you today."

I stayed away from Shmuel for nearly two weeks after this session, saying that I wasn't feeling well. I wanted to give him time to mend and regain his composure. I felt he was angry at me for witnessing his grief, and I didn't know how to limit his growing inclination to probe his wounds. It was necessary to him, more than me, that he not hold back, and it had become clear that he, not I, would regulate and direct the flow of talk. I was afraid to stay away too long lest he think my feelings for him were altered by his revelations. It was quite a surprise when he accosted me cheerily on the boardwalk, scolding me gaily for wasting so much time.

"I have prepared some writings for you. Come to my house and I will read to you some happy things about my life. Also I have some poems you would like to make in your record."

It was a lovely day. Shmuel had set out flowers and arranged his poetry in piles on the desk.

"My thoughts always at Passover turn back to these things," he said. "In spring it was the finish of those terrible winters. People seem to become more tender at this time, the tight cords of the heart let go. I would walk out into the woods and see that river like a shining ribbon across the green fields, the wildflowers so small you had to lie down on the ground to see them, the smells of the wheat fields, mushrooms and berries calling to you when you walk through the woods, whether you want it to or not, taking you up in happiness. In springtime I think always of my beloved brother who had the misfortune to be a gifted artist. He left our town the Passover before I was twelve. He couldn't help himself. He loved beauty and saw it everywhere. Whether it was the beauty of the Jews or Gentiles made no difference. You see, this was a hardship for a Jewish boy to have this gift, finding a desire for art when the love of images is forbidden to him. Those who have a gift for music or words are not so afflicted. But those who are born to see and make pictures have another story. Such a one was this brother. In time he left for Paris, his mouth bare of French, his pockets not overstuffed with money, but his drawings spoke for him and he enrolled in the School of Fine Arts. In all his life he never tired of creating beauty. All that was around him became enriched, including myself."

"You lived with him in Paris for awhile, didn't you?" I asked.

"I went there and saw what he was doing," he replied. "I wanted to go to work to help support such a talent, but he was not one to nibble on his future greatness, letting others do for him. We lived together there, so poor we had one pair of good trousers between us. Whoever had the need that day, that one would take the trousers and the other stay home in bed. For him those were the happiest days. I have in my mind a picture of him sitting with the sun on his forehead, singing rich Polish songs with his hands flying up and back like swift white birds over the work he made.

"It was this brother who in his own way brought me a new awareness of our Jewish culture, even though he was himself less taken with it than any of us."

"How did that happen?"

"This brother of mine, and the other one, also older than me, were both revolutionaries. They had to smuggle in books from the bigger towns and cities. And this literature they had to hide from everybody, the officials, the Rabbis, their families. No one was supposed to read secular books, let alone revolutionary books. You could be arrested for that. But they had ways! They would smuggle pamphlets in their shoes, cut out pages from the religious books and put others inside. They could pretend to be chanting from the prayer books, but inside they had these other books they were reading. I knew something funny was going on. Then one day, my oldest brother leaves behind such a book. Was it by accident? I don't know. Anyhow, I fall upon it like a great treasure. Already it emerges to me as a new life. In Jewish, it was Karl Marx. From then on, I did not play Bible, the Talmud began to fade out for me until much later, when I was old enough to know the value of it. I went on from that to Dickens, Cervantes, and the great Russian literature.

"It was this," Shmuel said, "that brought me to understand some things about our Jewish language and literature, how it is different from others. Our writings bring us out of the morbid parts of life by laughter. The Jew has a joyful life regardless of the oppression he walks through, because he is a good swimmer. He always comes back to the surface. He tries to reach the other side, with his humor and irony. Great humor is based on pain and grief. And in this, the Jew proved to be the expert. To me, finding this other literature was a way to finding how Jewish life is written about.

"But all that is behind." He sighed heavily. "My brothers, my parents, all are gone. From fourteen children, only my sister and me are left. Of that big family, why are we only here? I often ask this. Are we the best ones? Why are we the lucky ones? I can't find an answer. It causes me great sorrow to think that we were allowed to live only because we were adventurous. Why should this be rewarded? It's not a necessary thing to be rewarded for, taking chances. Does this make a better man? I ask you, what kind of God could explain this?

"Now here I have some poems about my family, my beloved father and brother. These men when I write about them, it is a love story. We think of matters of the heart as something only between the sexes. But no, there are many kinds of love. That is what these poems tell you. I will show you the poem I wrote about my brother:

> This one, Menachem,
> A bright, gay man
> Whose eyes could find
> The beauty in a stone.
> Like many of them, gone.
> Swept away and buried
> In raging storms of hate.
> Where are his dancing eyes?
> Where are his gentle bones?
> Where is his glowing hair?
> A little heap of rubbish
> Somewhere.

"And your parents, Shmuel, what happened to them after your brother left?"

"From then on it was the beginning of all of us going out of that little town. After that brother left home, my mother was restless. The hand of enticement was on us, and already everyone is beginning to talk of America, America. Everyone grew nervous. Things were breaking up. *Yeshiva* boys were reading Karl Marx. Jewish boys carving images, young people beyond the reach of parents and Rabbis, going away from those poor, dear silent ones left behind. When they left they knew very well in their deepest convictions that they would never come back.

"Now my mother begins to nag my father to go out also, to follow the children. He doesn't want to leave. One Sabbath, she left the house and gave out all kinds of sweet cakes she had prepared to the children in the street. "What is this you're doing?' my father asks her.

"I'm getting myself a new set of grandchildren since I'll never see the others.'

"Now at this time my father is full with work but barely makes a living. 'I have first to finish my work,' he tells her. At this time there was a Rabbi passing through. She dressed up and went out to him, palpitating, in her Sabbath clothes. 'Rabbi, what do you say? Should we move from this little town?'"

"'Yes, go,' he tells her.

"'Will it go better with us?' She gives him then some money.

"'Yes, when you change you place, you change your luck,' he tells her.

"With this she comes back to my father. The cheeks of my mother were always red, but on this occasion, even more so. Looking very beautiful, in her fine dress, she says to my father, 'Now things are settled. We must move. The Rabbi said so.' How could he resist this?

"But this was a great tragedy for my father. He liked that little place immensely.

"The day comes to go. A summer day, beautiful. My father goes down to the cemetery and I with him. I couldn't stand to go too close to him. I loved him but the pain that was coming out from him kept me away. Like flames, going out in waves. First he walked up and down. Finally, he gave the Rabbi there some money to say prayers and keep up the graves. Then he walked over to the grave of his father. He cried, tears coming down and down his face. His hair was black and grey. Old as he was, there was a youthfulness about him, very remarkable. At this time, I saw that youthfulness go out from him forever, like the departure of a spirit. I could not take this sight in, and hid my eyes. Still, when I looked up, he stood there like a small boy crying. He walked over to the others' graves, his mother, his sisters and brothers, then back again to his father. He started up a conversation there, telling his father why he was leaving, asking him for forgiveness and a blessing. All the while his tears are running through his beard until his shirt front is altogether drenched.

"You understand, it had never occurred to him that he would leave that place. His father lived there and his father before him, and so all the way back. My father had the custom of going often to his father's grave. Not just to keep it up, but to talk to him. When he had a trouble he couldn't solve, a fight with his brothers, or when there was a *simcha*. It was frequent among Jews to go to the graves in this way and invite the dead person to come to weddings and celebrations. So to leave all this behind meant something of the highest seriousness to him.

"Finally he had cried his heart full and he remembered me. He smiled and took up my small hand and kissed it. Both of us walked out of there without talking. I remember all our wealth was packed in two huge bundles placed on two skinny horses tied up outside. That's how we walked out of the little town, behind the skinny horses. A girl I knew was standing there when we passed her by. She said to me, 'Is this all? Is this your worldly fortune, all you gathered up in all the time you were living here? I said, 'No. There's another big bundle coming along with us, but you can't see it.' So we walked along the road out from there forever."

Shmuel leaned back heavily and rested briefly.

"In all this talking we do, I am finding myself carried back and back to my town. Out of my vision have come these pictures, these stories, colored and lively as if they are still there. I would sit down and write about it myself but I wouldn't want to make an end of it. An end, you see, it has its own, without me finishing it off a second time. Besides this, I talk about it for 120 years, it wouldn't be finished. How can I hope to tell you about what life used to be? So much we have talked, so much there is still left out. If I made the full story I would have to tell you how it was in Poland going back to my father's father, how they all lived.

"All this I give you was broken up, torn out, and thrown into the ovens. What words are there to lament this sufficiently? Even if Jeremiah himself would come back and cry out, 'Let my eyes run down with tears night and day, and let them not cease. For my dearly beloved people is smitten with a great wound. With a very grievous blow.' Even this would not be strong enough. When Jeremiah ran through the streets of Jerusalem, his eyes running like fountains, still it would not be enough crying. No lamentation could be strong enough to depict this tragedy. It was not only what befell the Jews. The ones who did it, they were no better off than the Jews. They lost their humanity; we lost only our people and our way of life. Although Hitler committed suicide, it was actually mankind who committed suicide, and this can never be undone.

"I cannot say goodbye to all that. As long as my eyes are still open, I'll see those beloved people, the young, the old, the crazy ones, the fools, the wise, and the good ones. I'll see the little crooked streets, the hills and animals, the Vistula like a silver snake winding in its beauty, and then I fall into a dream. It's a dream you can feel, but you cannot touch it. You see it still, you feel it, you become a part of it.

Spring with its promises passes out, then very peacefully winter
enters, gradually becoming stronger until it is a fury all around you.
Then the elderly men bend over in the streets and the children run
with smoke coming out of their mouths, their poor feet blistering in
the cold through the skimpy shoes. Maybe from wisdom, maybe
from cold, the old men walk slower, bent over with age until their
beards fall over their hands held for warmth against the breast. The
walk has a heavier tread. The black caftans shine with frost. All this is
natural. It has no moral, no consequence.

"In that little town there were no walls. But we were curled up
together inside it, like small cubs, keeping each other warm, growing from within, never showing the outside what is happening, until
our backs make up a strong wall. It is not the worst thing that can
happen for a man to grow old and die. But here is the hard part.
When my mind goes back there now, there are no roads going in or
out. No way back remains because nothing is there, no continuation.
Then life itself, what is its worth to us? Why have we bothered to
live? All this is at an end. For myself, growing old would be altogether a different thing if that little town was there still. All is
ended. So in my life, I carry with me everything—all those people,
all those places, I carry them around until my shoulders bend. I can
see the old Rabbi, the workers pulling their wagons, the man carrying his baby tied to his back, walking up from the Vistula, no money,
no house, nothing to feed his child. His greatest dream is to have a
horse of his own, and in this he will never succeed. So I carry him. If
he didn't have a horse, he should have at least the chance to be
remaining in the place he lived. Even with all that poverty and
suffering, it would be enough if the place remained; even old men
like me, ending their days, would find it enough. But when I come
back from these stories and remember the way they lived is gone
forever, wiped out like you would erase a line of writing, then it
means another thing altogether for me to accept leaving this life. If
my life goes now, it means nothing. But if my life goes, with my
memories, and all that is lost, that is something else to bear.

"We talked a lot here about God. Do I believe in God, you asked
me? What does any of this have to do with God? This I cannot say.
Some people are afraid to be alone and face life without God.
Hemingway killed himself because he was searching for something
and couldn't find it. The wise man searches, but not to find. He
searches because even though there is nothing to find, it is necessary

to search. About God, I would say I am an agnostic. If there is a God, he is playing marbles with us.

"On this note about God, we finish now," he said. "You have all I can give you. Take it and do something with it. What it is I don't know. You have to take it in your own way. How you will do this with all your ignorance, I cannot think, but maybe something comes together and makes sense for you.

"We'll see. Now, *maidele*.[9] go home with all this package of stories. I'm tired."

Shmuel had never used an affectionate term to me before. I was deeply moved by it, but remembering his discomfort with my "exaggeration," I refrained from telling him how much all this meant to me. I wanted to hug him more than anything, but managed to hold off and only shook his hand. For the only time since I had been visiting his house, he did not walk me to the door, but remained sitting quietly as I let myself out.

Three days later Rebekah called me to tell me that Shmuel had died peacefully in his sleep two nights before.

[9] Little girl.

ICE

by AI

from THE CHICAGO REVIEW

nominated by George Payerle and Carolyn Forché

breaks up in obelisks on the river,
as I stand beside your grave.
I tip my head back.
Above me, the same sky you loved,
that shawl of cotton wool,
frozen around the shoulders of Minnesota.
I'm cold and so far from Texas
and my father, who gave me to you.
I was twelve, a Choctaw, a burden.
A woman, my father said, raising my skirt.
Then he showed you the roll of green gingham,
stained red, that I'd tried to crush to powder
with my small hands. I close my eyes,

and it is March, 1866 again.
I'm fourteen, wearing a white smock.
I straddle the rocking horse you made for me
and stroke the black mane cut from my own hair.
Sunrise hugs you from behind,
as you walk through the open door.
You lay the velvet beside me
and I give you the ebony box
that holds the baby's skull.
You set it on your work table,
comb your pale blond hair with one hand,
then nail it shut.
The new baby starts crying. I cover my ears,
watching as you lift him from the cradle

and lay him on the pony skin rug.
I untie the red scarf, knotted at my throat,
climb off the horse and bend over you,
as you kneel beside the boy.
I slip the scarf around your neck,
and pull it tightly, remembering how I strangled the other baby
and laid her on your stomach while you were asleep.
You break my hold and pull me to the floor.
I put my hand inside my pocket,
while you walk around me slowly taking off your clothes.
I scratch you, bite your lips, your face,
then you cry out,
and I open and close my hands
around a row of bear teeth.

I open my eyes.
I wanted you then, and now
and I never let you know.
I kiss the headstone.
Tonight, wake me like always.
Talk and I'll listen,
while you lie on the pallet
resting your arms behind your head,
telling me about the wild rice in the marshes
and the empty .45 you call *Grace of God* that keeps you alive,
as we slide forward, without bitterness, decade by decade,
becoming transparent. Everlasting.

IN ANOTHER COUNTRY

by JAMES LAUGHLIN

from IN ANOTHER COUNTRY (City Lights Books)

nominated by Hayden Carruth

tesoro

she would say with that succulent
accent on the middle o as if she
were holding something as precious
as the golden testicle of a god.

Credere!

OBBEDIRE! COMBATTERE! I guess
it was the same then everywhere all over Italy in big
white letters painted up on

walls and especially on railroad
retaining walls at the
grade crossings and to make
a good record and show how

things were in ordine they
would let down the crossing
bars ten minutes before the
trains came so people were

backed up on both sides in

crowds shouting across to
each other all a big joke
and that's how we met where

we first saw each other I
was on the up side walking
back to town from swimming
& she was on the other with

her bicycle heading to the
cove wearing her tight white
sweather with nothing under
it & her grey checked skirt

& sandals era come Beatrice
al ponte quando si videro la
prima volta there by that
bridge in Florence where he

first saw her (later one day
she brought her schoolbook
of Dante so I could see the
famous painting) com' allora

al ponte only neither of us
was shy first we were looking then we were smiling and
when the train had finally

passed and we met in the middle I just took hold of her bicycle and walked beside her
but you have swum already I

can see your hair's all wet
why do you want to go again?
why do you think? I said ma
brutta I'm ugly sono brutta

and at the cove she changed
behind a big rock into her
suit it was white and tight
too ti piace? she asked you

like it? the water was very
clear that day and the rocks
were warm there was a German
boy came nosing around but

she wasn't nice to him and
he went away after we swam
we sat on the rocks sunning
& talking I only knew a few

words of Italian then but we
found another language that
did well enough I'd draw a
picture of the word I wanted

with my finger on her thigh
or she on mine the sky was
clear the air was soft with
just a little breeze I was

18 she was 15 and her name
was Leontina going back to
town she had me ride her on
the handlebars and put her

arms around my neck to keep
from falling off she didn't
want an icecream mamma m'as-
petta alla casa my mother's

waiting for me so I'd better
go just leave me here ma se

tu vuoi 'sta sera dopo la
passeggiata al angolo near

the newsstand quando sono
le nove yes I said yes I'll
be there alle nove after the
churchbells sound at nine.

Giacomino!

she called vieni qua splashing her
arms in the clear green water vieni
subito and so I followed her swimming around a point of rock to the

next cove vieni qua non hai paura
and she slipped like an eel beneath
the surface down through the sunken
entrace to a hidden grotto where

the light was soft and green on fine-
grained sand é bello no? here we can
be together by oursleves nobody else
has ever been here with me it's my se-

cret place here kiss me here I found
it when I was a little girl now touch
me here é strano questa luce com' un
aitro mondo so strange this light am

I all green? it's like another world
does that feel good? don't be afraid
siamo incantati we're enchanted in
another world O Giacomino Giacomino

sai tu amore come lui è bello? come' è
carino sai quanto tu mi dai piacere?

sai come lei ti vuol' bene? lie still
non andare via just lie still lie still.

Genovese

non sono I'm Roman it comes from
my father look at my nose it went
straight down from her forehead
like coins you see from Etruria.

Tornerai?

she wept will you come back
for me I wanted to slip away
but she found out the time
of the train and was there

in the compartment wearing
her Sunday dress & the Mil-
anese scarf I had given her
tornerai amore mio will you

come back and bring me to
America crying and pressing
my hands against her breasts
my face wet with her tears

& her kisses till the train
stopped at Genova and they
made her get off because I
couldn't buy her a ticket.

𝕭 𝕭 𝕭

THE DAISY DOLLS

fiction by FELISBERTO HERNÁNDEZ

from THE PARTISAN REVIEW

nominated by THE PARTISAN REVIEW, *Sheila Ascher and Max Zimmer*

Nᴇxᴛ ᴛᴏ ᴀ ɢᴀʀᴅᴇɴ ᴡᴀs ᴀ ꜰᴀᴄᴛᴏʀʏ and the noise of the machines came through the plants and trees. And deep in the garden was a dark weathered house. The owner of the "black house" was a tall man. At dusk his slow steps came up the street into the garden, where the crunching sound they made on the gravel could be heard over the noise of the machines. One autumn evening, as he opened the front door, squinting in the strong light of the hall, he saw his wife standing halfway up the staircase; and noticing how the steps spread into the middle of the courtyard, it seemed to him she was wearing a great big marble dress, gathered up in the same hand that held onto the balustrade. She realized he was tired, that he was on his way up to the bedroom, and waited for him with a smile. They kissed, and she said:

"Today the boys finished setting up the scenes . . ."

"I know, but don't tell me anything."

She saw him up to the bedroom door, tweaked his nose and left him to himself. He was going to try to sleep a bit before dinner: the dark room would separate the day's worries from the pleasures he expected of the night. He listened fondly, as he had since childhood, to the muffled sound of the machines, and fell asleep. In his dream he saw a lamp shining on a table. Around the table stood several men. One of them wore tails and was saying: "We have to turn the blood around so it'll go out the veins and back the arteries, instead of out the arteries and back the veins." They all clapped and cheered; and then the man who wore tails jumped on a horse in the yard and galloped off, through the cheers, on clattering hooves that drew sparks from the flagstones. Remembering the dream when he woke up, the man of the black house recognized it as an echo of something he'd heard that same day—that the traffic, all over the country, was changing from the left to the right hand—and smiled to himself. Then he put on his tails, once more remembered the man in the dream and went down into the dining room. He approached his wife and, running his open hands through her hair, said:

"I always forget to bring a lens to have a good look at the plants in the green of your eyes. But I know you get your skin color rubbing olives in it."

She tweaked his nose again, then poked his cheek, till her finger bent like a spiderleg, and answered:

"And I always forget to bring scissors to trim your eyebrows."

She sat at the table and seeing him leave the room asked:

"Did you forget something?"

"Who knows."

He came right back and she decided he hadn't had time to use the phone.

"Won't you tell me where you went?"

"No."

"And I won't tell you what the men did today."

He'd already started to answer:

"No, my dear olive, don't tell me anything until after dinner."

And he poured himself a glass of French wine.

But his wife's words had been like tiny pebbles dropped into the pond of his reveries; and he couldn't give up the thought of what he expected to see that night. He collected dolls that were a bit taller than real women. He'd had three glass cases built in a large room. In the biggest one were all the dolls waiting to be chosen to compose scenes in the other cases. The arrangements were in the hands of several people: first of all, the caption writers (who had to express the meaning of each scene in a few words). Other artists handled settings, costuming, music, etc. Tonight was the second show. He'd watch while a pianist, seated with his back to him, across the room, played programmed works. Suddenly the owner of the black house remembered he mustn't think of all this during dinner. So he took a pair of opera glasses out of his pocket and tried to focus them on his wife's face.

"I'd like to know if the shadows under your eyes are also plants."

She realized he'd been to his desk to fetch the opera glasses and decided to make a joke of it. He saw a glass dome, which turned out to be a bottle. So he put down the opera glasses and poured himself some more French wine. She watched the burbling drops fall into his glass, splattering black tears on the crystal walls as they ran to meet the wine on its way up. At that moment Alex—a White Russian with a pointed beard—came in bowing at her and served her a plate of ham and beans. She used to say she'd never heard of a servant with a beard; and he used to say it was the only condition Alex had set for accepting the job. Now her eyes shifted from the glass of wine to the tip of the man's sleeve, where a tuft of hair grew, crawling all the way down his hand to his fingers. As he waited on the master of the house, Alex said:

"Walter—" (the pianist) "is here."

After dinner Alex removed the glasses on a tray. They rang against each other, as if happy to meet again. The master, who had fallen into a sleepy silence, was pleasantly stirred at the sound and called out after him:

"Tell Walter to go to the piano. He mustn't talk to me as I come into the room. Is the piano far from the glass cases?"

"Yes, Sir, on the other side of the room."

"Good. Then tell Walter to sit with his back to me, to start on the first piece of the program and keep repeating it without stopping until I flash the light at him."

His wife was smiling at him. He went up to kiss her and for a moment rested his flushed face on her cheek. Then he headed for the little parlor off the big showroom. There he started to smoke and drink his coffee, waiting for the right mood to come over him before he went in to see the dolls. At first he listened vaguely for the noise of the machines and the sounds of the piano, which reached him in low murmurs, as if he were underwater. At moments he started, imagining some of the sounds were hinting at something meant for him alone, as if he were being singled out among several people snoring in a room. But when he tried to concentrate on them, they scattered like frightened mice. He sat there puzzled for a minute, then decided to ignore them. But suddenly he realized he wasn't in his chair anymore: he'd gotten up without noticing it. He remembered having just opened the door, and now he felt his steps taking him toward the first glass case. He switched on the light in the case and through the green curtain he saw a doll stretched out on a bed. He opened the curtain and mounted the podium. It was actually a small rolling platform on rubber casters, with a railing. From there, seated in an armchair at a little table, he had a better view of the scene. The doll was dressed as a bride and her open eyes stared at the ceiling. It was impossible to tell whether she was dead or dreaming. Her arms were spread in an attitude of what could be either despair or blissful abandon. Before opening the drawer of the little table to read the caption, he wanted to imagine something. Maybe she was a bride waiting for the groom, who would never arrive, having jilted her just before the wedding. Or maybe she was a widow remembering her wedding day; or just a girl dressed up to feel like a bride. He opened the drawer and read: "A moment before marrying the man she doesn't love, she locks herself up, in the dress she was to wear to her wedding with the man she loved, who is gone forever, and poisons herself. She dies with her eyes open and no one has come yet to shut them." Then the owner of the black house thought: "She was really a lovely bride." And after a moment he was happy to realize he had survived her. Then he opened a glass door and entered the scene to have a closer look. But at the same time, through the noise of the machines and the music, he thought he heard a door slam. He left the case and, caught in the door to the little parlor, he saw a piece of his wife's dress. As he tiptoed over to the door, he thought she must have been spying on him, probably as another joke. He snatched the door open and her body fell on him. He caught it in his arms; but it seemed very light; and he immediately recognized Daisy, the doll who resembled her. Meantime his wife, who was crouching behind an armchair, straightened up and said:

"I also wanted to give you a surprise. I just had time to get her into my dress."

She went on talking, but he didn't listen. Although he was pale, he thanked her for the surprise. He didn't want to discourage her, because he enjoyed the jokes she made up with Daisy. But this time he'd felt uncomfortable. So he handed Daisy back to her, saying he didn't want too long an intermission. Then he returned to the other room, closing the door behind him, and walked toward Walter. But he stopped halfway and opened another door that gave on his study, where he shut himself in, took a notebook from a drawer and proceeded to make a note of the joke his wife had just played on him with Daisy, and the date. First he read the previous note, which said: "July 21. Today, Mary"—his wife's name was Daisy Mary; but she liked to be called Mary; so when he had a doll made to look like her, they decided to use the rusty name Daisy for the doll—"was leaning out the balcony over the garden. I wanted to surprise her, putting my hands over her eyes. But on my way to the balcony I saw it was Daisy. Mary had seen me go to the balcony; she was right behind me, laughing." Although he was the only one to read the notebook, he signed each note with his name, "Horace," in large letters and heavy ink. An earlier note said: "July 18. Today I opened the wardrobe to get my suit and found Daisy hanging there. She was wearing my tails, which looked ridiculously large on her."

Having made a note of the latest surprise, he was back in the showroom, heading for the second glass case. He flashed a light at Walter for him to go on to the next piece on the program and started to roll up the podium. In the pause Walter made before taking up the new piece, he felt the machines pounding harder; and as the podium moved, the casters seemed to rumble like distant thunder.

The second case showed a doll seated at the head of a table. She held herself upright, her hands on either side of her plate, between the two long rows of silverware. Her posture and the way her hands rested on the silverware made her look as if she were at a keyboard. Horace looked at Walter, saw him bent over the piano, his tails dangling over the edge of the stool, and thought of him as a bird beating black wings. Then he stared at the doll and, as on other occasions, seemed to sense that she was moving. The movements didn't always begin right away; nor did he expect them when the doll was dead or lying down; but this time they started too soon, possibly because of her uncomfortable position. She was trying too hard to look up; nodding slightly, with effort; so that the moment he left her face to gaze at her hands, her head dropped noticeably. He in turn quickly raised his eyes to her face again; but she was already back in her original position. He then began to imagine her story. Her dress and surrounding objects suggested great luxury; but the furniture was coarse and the walls were of stone. On the far wall there was a small window, and behind her a low half-open door, like a false smile. She might be in a dungeon in a castle. The piano made stormy noises and every now and then lightning flashed in the window. Then he remembered that a minute ago the rolling casters had reminded him of distant thunder, and he felt uneasy. Also, before entering the room, he'd been hearing those insinuating sounds. But, returning to the doll's story: maybe she was praying God, at that very moment, to free her. Finally, he opened the drawer and read: "Second scene. This woman is expecting a child soon. She is now living in a light-house by the sea. She has withdrawn from the world, which has blamed her for loving a sailor. She keeps thinking: I want my child to listen only to himself and the sea.'" He thought: "This doll has found her true story." Then he got up, opened the glass door and slowly went over her things. He felt he was defiling something as solemn as death. He turned to the doll, trying to find a point where their eyes could meet; and after a moment he bent over the unhappy girl, and as he kissed her on the forehead it gave him the same cool, pleasant sensation as Mary's face. He'd hardly taken his lips off her forehead when he saw her move. He was paralyzed. She started to slip to one side, losing her balance, till she fell off the edge of the chair, dragging a spoon and a fork with her. The piano was still making sea noises; and there were still the flashes in the windows and the rumbling machines. He didn't want to pick her up, and hurried out of the case and the room, through the little parlor, into the courtyard. There he saw Alex and said:

"Tell Walter that's enough for today. And have the boys come in tomorrow to fix up the doll in the second case."

At that moment Mary appeared:

"What's the matter?"

"Nothing: a doll fell—the one in the lighthouse . . ."

"How did it happen? Is she hurt?"

"I must have touched the table when I went in to look around . . ."

"Ah! So you're getting upset!"

"No, I'm very happy with the scenes. But where's Daisy? She certainly looked pretty in your dress!"

"You'd better go to sleep, darling," answered Mary.

But instead they sat on a sofa, where he put his arms around her and asked her to rest her cheek on his for a moment, in silence. As their heads touched, his lit up with memories of the two fallen dolls: Daisy and the girl in the lighthouse. He knew what this meant: the death of Mary. And, afraid his thoughts would pass into her head, he started to kiss her ears.

When he was alone again in the darkness of the bedroom, he concentrated on the noise of the machines and thought of the warning signs he'd been receiving. He was like a garbled wire that kept intercepting hints and calls meant for others. But this time all the signals had been aimed at him. Under the noise of the machines and the sound of the piano he'd detected those other hidden noises, scattering like mice. Then there'd been Daisy falling into his arms when he opened the closet door, as if to say: "Hold me, for Mary is dying." And it was Mary herself who had prepared the warning, as innocently as if she were showing him a disease she wasn't yet aware of. Then, later, there'd been the dead doll in the first case; and, before reaching the second case, the unexpected rumble of the podium, like distant thunder, announcing the sea and the woman in the lighthouse. Then the woman slipping out from under him: like Mary, who would no longer bear a child. And finally Walter, like a dark bird, beating his wings as he pecked away at his black box.

II

Mary wasn't ill and there was no reason to think she was going to die. But for some time now he'd been afraid of losing her and dreading the prospect of life without her. So one day he'd thought of having a doll built to resemble her. At first the idea seemed to have failed. He felt only dislike for Daisy, as for a poor substitute. She was made of kidskin, scented and colored like Mary. Yet when Mary asked him to kiss her, he tasted leather and had the feeling he was about to kiss a shoe. But in time he'd begun to notice a strange relationship developing between the two women. One morning he saw Mary singing while she dressed Daisy: she was like a girl playing with a doll. Another time, when he got home in the evening, he found Mary and Daisy seated at a table with a book open in front of them. He had the feeling Mary was teaching a sister to read, and said:

"It must be such a relief to talk to someone who can keep a secret!"

"What do you mean?" said Mary, springing up in anger and leaving the room.

But Daisy went on staring at the book, like a friend maintaining a tactful silence. And that same night, after dinner, to keep him away from her, as they shared their usual sofa, Mary put the doll between them. He glanced at Daisy's face and disliked it again: it was cold and haughty, as if to punish him for slighting her. A bit later, he went into the showroom. At first he strolled back and forth along the glass cases. Then, after a while, he opened the big piano top, removed the stool, replaced it with a chair—so he could lean back—and started to walk his fingers over the cool expanse of black and white keys. He had trouble combining the sounds, like a drunk trying to unscramble his words. But meantime he was remembering many of the things he knew about the dolls. Slowly he'd been getting to know them, almost without realizing it. Until recently, he'd kept the store that had been making his fortune. Alone, after closing hour every day, he liked to wander through the shadowy rooms, looking at the dolls in the show windows. He went over their dresses, with an occasional almost casual glance at their faces. He observed the show windows from an angle, like a director watching his actors in a play. Then he started finding expressions similar to those of his salesgirls in the doll's faces. Some inspired the same distrust in him; others, the certainty that they were against him. There was one with a snub nose that seemed to say: "Who cares?" Another, which appealed to him, had an enigmatic face: just as she looked good in either a summer or a winter dress, she could also be thinking almost anything, and accepting or rejecting him, according to her mood. In any case, the dolls had their secrets. Although the window decorator knew how to display each of them to her best advantage, at the last moment she always added a touch of her own. It was then that he started to think the dolls were full of portents. Day and night they received countless greedy looks; and those looks formed nests and bred warnings. Sometimes they settled on the dolls' faces like clouds on a landscape, shadowing and blurring their expressions; or lingered and tainted their innocence. Then the dolls were like creatures in a trance, on unknown missions, lending themselves to evil designs. On the night of his quarrel with Mary, he reached the conclusion that Daisy was one of those changeable dolls who could receive warnings and transmit messages. Since she lived in the house, Mary had been showing increasing signs of jealousy. Even before, whenever he flirted with a salesgirl, he'd felt her reproach in Daisy's knowing look. That was back in the days when she kept pestering him to give up the store. But now her fits of jealousy at the sight of any other woman had reached the point where they couldn't even spend an evening out together anymore.

On the morning after the quarrel he made up with both of them. His dark thoughts bloomed at night and faded in the daytime. As usual, they went for a walk in the garden. He and Mary carried Daisy between them—in a long skirt, to cover her lifeless legs—as if propping up a sick relative. (The neighbors had cooked up a story about how they'd let a sister of Mary's die, to inherit her money, whereupon, to do penance, they'd taken in a doll who resembled her, as a constant reminder of their crime.)

After a period of happiness, during which Mary prepared surprises for him with Daisy and he hastened to enter them in his notebook, came the night of the second show, with its announcement of Mary's death.

He then hit on the idea of buying his wife a number of strong dresses—to remember her by later on—and made her try them on Daisy. She was delighted and he also pretended to be, when—at a hint from him—she decided to have some of their closest friends to dinner one night. It was storming out, but the guests all sat down gayly to eat; and he, thinking of all the memories the evening was going to leave with him, tried to be the life of the party. First he twirled his knife and fork—like a cowboy with a pair of guns—and aimed them at a girl next to him. She, going along with the joke, raised her arms, and he tickled her plucked armpits with the knife. It was too much for Mary, who burst out:

"Horace, you're being a brat!"

He apologized all around, and soon everyone was having fun again. But when he was serving his French wine, over dessert, she saw a big black stain—the wine he was pouring outside the glass— growing on the tablecloth; and trying to rise, clutching at her throat, she fainted. They carried her into her bedroom; and when she recovered she said she hadn't been feeling well for days. He sent at once for the doctor, who said it was nothing serious but she had to watch her nerves. She got up and saw off her guests as if nothing had happened. But alone with him later on, she said:

"I can't stand this life any more. You were playing with that girl right under my nose."

"But, Mary . . ."

"And I don't just mean the wine you spilled gaping at her. What about in the yard afterwards, when she said: 'Horace, stop it'?"

"But, darling, all she said was: 'A boring topic.'"

They made up in bed and she fell asleep with her cheek next to his. But, after a while, he turned away to think about her illness. And the next morning, when he touched her arm, it was cold. He lay still, gazing at the ceiling for several grueling minutes before he managed to shout: "Alex!" At that moment the door opened and Mary came in; and he realized it was Daisy he'd touched and that Mary had put her there next to him, while he slept.

After much reflection, he decided to send for his friend Frank, the doll manufacturer, and ask him to find a way to give Daisy some human warmth.

Frank said:

"I'm afraid it's not so easy, old boy. The warmth would last about as long as a hot water bottle."

"All right—fine. Do what you want, just don't tell me. I'd also like her to be softer, nice to touch, not so stiff . . ."

"I don't know about that either. Think of the dent you'd make every time you laid a finger on her."

"Well, anyway, she could be more flexible. And, as for the dent, I don't think that would be such a drawback."

The day Frank took Daisy away, Horace and Mary were sad.

"God knows what they'll do to her," Mary kept saying.

"Now then, darling, one mustn't lose one's sense of reality. After all, she was just a doll."

"Was! You sound as if she were dead. And you're a fine one to talk about sense of reality!"

"I was just trying to comfort you . . ."

"And you think that's the way to do it! She was more mine than yours. I dressed her and told her things I've never told anyone, do you realize that? And she united us more than you can imagine."

He was heading for his study; and she went on, raising her voice:

"Think of all the surprises we prepared for you. Wasn't that enough, without asking for 'human warmth'?"

By then he'd reached the study and slammed the door behind him. The way she'd pronounced "human warmth" not only made him feel ridiculous but soured all the pleasures he was looking forward to when Daisy returned. He decided to go for a walk.

When he got back, Mary was out; and when she returned, they spent a while hiding the fact that they were unexpectedly glad to see each other.

That night he didn't go over his dolls. The next morning he was busy. After lunch he and Mary strolled in the garden. They both felt Daisy's absence was temporary and shouldn't be made too much of. He even thought it was easier and more natural to put his arm around Mary. They both felt light and gay, and went out again. But later, at dinnertime, when he went up to the bedroom for her, he was surprised to find her there alone. He'd forgotten for a moment that Daisy was gone, and now her absence made him strangely uneasy. Mary might well be a woman without a doll again; but he could no longer separate the two in his mind, and the fact that the house didn't seem to notice she was missing was like a kind of madness. Also, the way Mary wandered back and forth in the room, apparently not thinking of Daisy, reminded him of a madman drifting around naked, in a daze, forgetting to dress. They went down to dinner. And there, sipping his French wine, he stared at her in silence, till finally he thought he caught a hint of Daisy in her. Then he began to understand what the two women meant to each other. Whenever he thought of Mary, he remembered her fussing over Daisy, arranging her clothes, sitting her up straight so she wouldn't sag and planning to surprise him with her. If Mary didn't play the piano—as, for instance, Frank's girl friend—it was because she expressed herself in her own original way through Daisy. To strip her of Daisy would be like stripping an artist of his art. Daisy wasn't just part of her personality but her most charming side; so that he wondered how he could ever have loved her before Daisy came. Perhaps in those days she'd found other means or ways to express that part of herself. But a while back, when he'd gone up to the bedroom for her and found her alone, she'd seemed strangely insignificant. "Besides," he went on to himself, still sipping his French wine, "Daisy was

was an unknown obstacle," which probably explained why he kept on tripping over her on his way to Mary.

After dinner he kissed Mary's cool cheek and went in to look at his glass cases. One of them showed a Carnival scene. Two masked dolls, a blonde and a brunette, in Spanish costumes, leaned over a marble balustrade. To the left was a staircase with masks, hoods, paper streamers, and other objects scattered on the steps with artful neglect. The scene was dimly lit; and suddenly, watching the brunette, he thought he recognized Daisy. He wondered whether Mary had sent for her as a surprise. Before going into the matter, he opened the glass door. On his way up the staircase, he stepped on a mask, which he picked up and threw over the balustrade. The gesture gave the objects around him an unpleasantly physical sensation, and he was disappointed. He moved to the podium, irritated at the way the noise of the machines seemed to clash with the sounds of the piano. But after a few minutes he turned to the dolls again and decided they were probably two women who loved the same man. Then he opened the drawer and read the caption: "The blonde has a boy friend. He discovered, not long ago, that he preferred her friend, the brunette, and declared his love. She was also secretly in love with him, but tried to talk him out of it. He persisted, and on this Carnival night has just told the blonde about her rival. Now the two girls meet for the first time, knowing the truth. They haven't yet spoken as they stand there in a long silence, wearing their disguises." At last he'd guessed one of the captions, he thought; but then wondered whether the coincidence wasn't a portent or warning of something that was already going on between him and the two dolls, and whether he wasn't in love with Daisy. The question— which drew him back into the glass case for a better look—led to others: What was it about Daisy that could have made him fall in love with her? Did the dolls perhaps give him something more than a purely artistic pleasure? Was Daisy really just an eventual substitute for his wife? And for how long would she be happy to play second fiddle to her? It was absolutely necessary for him to reconsider their roles. He didn't want to take these worries up to the bedroom with him; so he called Alex, had him dismiss Walter, then sent him for a bottle of French wine, and sat with it for a while, listening to the noise of the machines. Then he walked up and down the room, smoking. Each time he came to the glass case he drank some wine, and then set out again, thinking: "If there are spirits that haunt empty houses, why wouldn't they also haunt empty dolls?" He thought of those haunted castles, full of spooked objects and furnishings joined in a heavy sleep, under thick wraps, where only ghosts and spirits roam, among whistling bats and marshy sighs. . . . At that moment he was struck by the noise of the machines and he dropped his glass. His hair stood on end, as it dawned on him that if spirits had voices, they were probably the stray sounds of the world, speaking through them, and so maybe the spirit that lived in Daisy spoke the language of the machines. Trying to shake off these thoughts, he felt chills running up his spine. He dropped into an armchair and went on thinking: no wonder such strange things had happened on a recent moonlit night. They were out in the garden, all three of them, and suddenly he started chasing his wife. She ran, laughing, to hide behind Daisy—which, as he realized, wasn't the same as hiding behind a tree—and when he tried to kiss her over Daisy's shoulder, he felt a strong pinprick. Almost at once, he heard the machines throbbing, no doubt to warn him against kissing Mary through Daisy. Mary didn't know how she could have left a pin in the doll's dress. And he could have hit himself for being foolish enough to think Daisy was a reflection of Mary, when in fact they reflected each other. . . . Now, coming back to the noise of the machines, he remembered what he'd been suspecting all along; that it had a life of its own, like the sounds of the piano, though they belonged to different families. The noise of the machines was of a noble family, which was perhaps why Daisy had chosen it to express her true love. On that thought he phoned Frank to ask after Daisy. Frank said she was nearly ready, that the girls in the workshop had found a way to . . . Whereupon Horace interrupted him, saying he didn't want to know the details. And, hanging up, he felt a hidden pleasure at the thought of all those workshop girls putting something of themselves into the doll.

The next day, at the lunch table, he found Mary waiting for him with an arm around Daisy's waist. After kissing his wife, he took the doll in his arms, and for a moment her soft warm body gave him the pleasure he'd been hoping for; though when he pressed his lips to hers, she seemed feverish. But he soon got accustomed to this new sensation and began to enjoy himself.

That night, at dinner, he wondered: "Why must the transmigration of souls take place only between people and animals? Aren't there cases of people on their deathbed who've handed their souls over to some beloved object? Besides, it's not just by chance that a spirit comes to dwell in a doll who looks like a beautiful woman. Why not suppose it might have guided the hands of those who built the doll? When someone has a purpose in mind, doesn't he use all the means at his disposal, especially an unexpected helping hand?" Then he thought of Daisy and wondered whose spirit was living in her.

Mary had been in a bad mood since early evening. She'd scolded Daisy while she dressed her because she wouldn't stay still. Now that she was full of water, Daisy was a lot heavier than before, and kept tipping forward. Horace thought of the relations between his wife and the doll, and of the strange shades of enmity he'd noticed between women who were such close friends that they couldn't get along without each other. At the same time, he remembered the same thing often happened between mother and daughter. . . . A minute later, he raised his eyes from his plate and said:

"Tell me something, Mary. What was your mother like?"

She jumped at the question: "Why? Do you want to trace my defects to her?"

"Of course not, darling! I wouldn't think of it!"

He spoke in a soothing voice. So then she said:

"Well, I'll tell you. She was my complete opposite. Calm as a clear day. She could spend hours just sitting in a chair, staring into space."

"Perfect," he said to himself. Though, on the other hand, after pouring himself a glass of wine, he thought: "I can't very well use Daisy to have an affair with the spirit of my mother-in-law."

"And what were her ideas on love?"

"Do you find mine inadequate?"

"Mary, please!"

"She had none, lucky for her. Which was why she was able to marry my father to please my grandparents. He had money. And she made him a fine wife."

Horace relieved, thought: "Thank God for that. One thing less to worry about."

Though it was spring, the night turned cold. Mary refilled Daisy, dressed her in a silk nightie and took her to bed with them, like a hot water bottle. As sleep came on him, Horace felt himself sinking into a warm pool, where all their legs tangled, like the roots of trees planted so close together there was no way to tell them apart.

III

Horace and Mary were planning a birthday party for Daisy. She was going to be two years old. Horace wanted to present her on a tricycle. He told Mary he'd seen one at a Transportation Day exhibit and was sure he could get it. He didn't tell her the reason for using this particular device was that he remembered seeing a groom elope with his bride on a tricycle in a film years ago. The rehearsals were a success. At first he had trouble getting the tricycle going; but as soon as the big front wheel turned it grew wings.

The party opened with a buffet dinner. Soon the sounds from human throats and necks of bottles mixed in a loud murmur. When it was time to present Daisy, Horace rang a school bell in the courtyard and the guests all went out, holding their glasses. They saw him coming down a long carpeted hallway, struggling with the tricycle, which at first was almost invisible. Of Daisy, who rode behind him, only her flowing white dress showed. He seemed to be floating on a cloud. Daisy's feet were on the axle that joined the small back wheels, her arms thrust forward hugging him, with her hands in his trouser pockets. The tricycle came to a stop in the center of the yard, and in the midst of cheers and applause, Horace reached over and stroked her hair. Then he started pedaling hard again, and as the tricycle headed back up the carpeted hallway, gathering speed, everyone watched in breathless silence, as if it were about to take flight. The performance was such a success that he repeated it; and the laughter and applause were beginning again when suddenly, just as he reached the yard, he lost a back wheel. There were cries of alarm, but when he showed he wasn't hurt, there was more laughter and applause. He'd fallen on his back, on top of Daisy, and was kicking his legs in the air like an insect. The guests laughed till they cried. Frank gasped and spluttered:

"Boy, you looked like one of those wind-up toys that goes on walking upside down!"

Then they all went back into the dining room. The men working on the props in the glass cases had surrounded Horace and were asking him to lend them Daisy and the tricycle for a scene. He refused; but he was so happy he invited everybody into the show-room for a glass of French wine.

"If you could tell us what you feel watching the scenes," said one of the boys, "I think we could all learn something."

He started to rock back and forth on his heels, staring at his friends' shoes. Finally he made up his mind and said:

"It's very difficult to put into words, but I'll try. If you promise meantime to ask no more questions and accept anything I care to say."

"Promised!" said one who was a bit hard of hearing, cupping a hand to his ear.

Still, he took his time, clasping and unclasping his hands; and then, to quiet them crossed his arms and began:

"When I look at a scene . . ." Here he stopped, and then took up the speech again, with a digression: "(It's very important to see the dolls through a glass, because that gives them a certain dreamlike quality, like memories. Before, when I could stand mirrors—now I can't any more, but it would take too long to explain why—I liked to see the rooms reflected in them.) So . . . When I look at a scene, it's like catching a woman in the act of remembering an important moment of her life. A bit—if you'll forgive the expression—as if I were opening a crack in her head. Stealing her memory, like a bit of underwear. Then I can use it to guess and invent all sorts of things, even to break into her most intimate thoughts. Sometimes I have the feeling the woman is dead; and then it's like picking a corpse, waiting for something to stir in it . . ." Here again he stopped, not daring to tell them of the strange stirrings he'd seen.

The boys were also silent, till one of them thought of emptying his glass of wine at a swallow and the others imitated him. Then another said:

"Tell us something more about yourself: your personal tastes, for instance."

"Ah, as for that," said Horace, "I don't think it'll be of any help to you in making up your scenes. For instance, I like to walk on a wooden floor sprinkled with sugar. That little crunching noise . . ."

Just then Mary came in to ask them all out into the garden. It was a dark night and the guests were supposed to form couples and carry torches. Mary took Horace's arm and showed the way. At the door that led into the garden, each guest picked a small torch from a table and lit it at a flaming bowl on another table. The glow attracted the neighbors, who gathered at the low hedge, their faces like shiny fruit with watchful eyes among the trees, glinting with distrust. Suddenly Mary crossed a flower bed, flicked a switch, and Daisy appeared, all lit up in the top branches of a high tree. It was one of Mary's surprises and was met with claps and cheers. Daisy was holding a white fan spread on her breast. A light behind the fan turned it into a bright colored web. Horace kissed Mary and thanked her for the surprise. Then, as the guests scattered, he saw Daisy staring out toward the street he took on his way home every day. He was leading Mary along the hedge when one of the neighbors shouted at others coming up the street: "Hurry! The dead woman's appeared in a tree!" They made it back to the house, where everyone was toasting Daisy. Mary had the twins—her maids, who were sisters—get her down from the tree and change her water for bed.

About an hour had gone by since their return from the garden, when Mary started looking around for Horace and found him back in the showroom with the boys. She was pale and everyone realized something serious had happened. She had the boys excuse Horace and led him up to the bedroom. There he found Daisy with a knife stuck in her chest. The wound was leaking hot water down her dress, which was soaked, and dripping on the floor. She was in her usual chair, with big open eyes. But when they touched her arm, they felt it getting cold.

Horace was holding Mary, who had burst into tears saying:

"Who could have dared to come up here and do such a thing?"

After a while she calmed down and sat in a chair to think over what was to be done. Then she said:

"I'm going to call the police."

"You're out of your mind," he said, "We can't do that to our guests, just because one of them . . . And what are you going to tell the police? That someone stuck a knife in a doll and she's leaking? The best is to say nothing. One has to know how to lose with dignity. We'll send her in for repairs and forget about it."

"I can't," said Mary. "I'm going to call a private detective. Don't let anyone touch her: the fingerprints must be on the knife."

He tried to reason with her, reminding her the guests were waiting downstairs. They agreed to lock the doll in, as she was. But the moment Mary left the room, he took out his handkerchief, soaked it in cleaning fluid, and wiped off the handle of the knife.

IV

Horace finally managed to convince Mary to say nothing about the wounded doll. The day Frank came for her, he brought Louise, his girlfriend. She and Mary went into the dining-room, where their voices sounded like a lot of chattering birds being let out of their cages to mix in the air. They were used to talking and listening at the same time.

Meantime Horace and Frank shut themselves in the study. They spoke one at a time, in undertones, as if taking turns at drinking out of a jug.

Horace said: "I was the one who stuck the knife in her, so I'd have an excuse to send her in to you."

And they stood there, bowing their heads in silence.

Mary was curious to know what they were discussing and, deserting Louise for a minute, came to listen at the door. She thought she recognized her husband's voice; but it sounded hoarse and blurred. (At that moment, still mumbling into his chin, Horace was saying: "It may be crazy, but I've heard of sculptors falling in love with their statues.") In a while, Mary came back to listen again, but could only make out the word "possible," pronounced first by her husband, then by Frank. (Actually, Horace had just said: "It must be possible," and Frank had answered: "If it's possible, I'll do it").

One afternoon, a few days later, Mary realized Horace was acting strange. He'd be watching her fondly and then suddenly turn away, looking worried. As he crossed the courtyard at one point, she called him, went out to meet him and putting her arms around his neck said:

"Horace, you can't fool me. I know what's on your mind."

"What?" he said, gaping wildly.

"It's Daisy."

He turned pale.

"What gave you such an idea?"

He was surprised she didn't laugh at his odd tone.

"Oh, come on, darling . . . After all, she's like a daughter to us by now," Mary went on.

He let his eyes linger on her face, and with them his thoughts; going over each of her features, as if reviewing every detail of a spot he'd visited daily through many long happy years. Then he broke away and went and sat in the little parlor, to think about what had just happened. At first, suspecting his wife had found him out, he'd felt certain she'd forgive him. But then, seeing her smile, he'd realized it was madness to suppose she could imagine, let alone forgive, such a sin. Her face was like a peaceful landscape, with a bit of golden evening glow on one of her cheeks, the other shaded by the small hump of her nose. He'd thought of all the good left in the innocence of the world and the habit of love, and the tenderness with which he always came back to her face after his adventures with the dolls. But in time, when she discovered, not only the true nature of his affection for Daisy, but the length and depth of his deceit, her face would collapse. She'd never be able to understand the sudden evil in the world and in the habit of love, or feel anything but horror at the sight of him.

So he'd stood there in the yard, gazing at a spot of sun on his coat sleeve. As he'd shifted, the spot had moved, like a taint, to her dress. Then, heading for the little parlor, he'd felt his insides lump and sag, like dead weights. Now he sat on a little stool, thinking he was unworthy of being received into the lap of a family armchair, and felt as uncomfortable as if he'd sat on a child. He hardly recognized himself and shuddered at the thought of being made of such base metal. But, to his surprise, a bit later, in bed with the covers pulled up to his nose, he went straight to sleep.

Mary was on the phone to Frank, saying:

"You'd better hurry with Daisy. Horace is worrying himself sick."

Frank said:

"I have to tell you, Mary: it's a bad wound, right in the middle of the circulatory system. We can't rush it. But I'll do what I can."

In a while, Horace woke up under his pile of covers, blinking down a kind of slope, and saw a picture of his parents on the far wall. He felt they'd cheated him: he was like a trunk full of dirty rags instead of riches; and they were like two thieves who'd fled before he grew up and exposed the fraud. But then he was ashamed of these monstrous thoughts.

At dinner, he tried to be on his best behavior.

Mary said: "I called Frank about hurrying Daisy."

If only she'd known the madness and betrayal she was contributing to by hastening his pleasure! he thought, blindly casting about, right and left, like a frightened horse.

"Looking for something?" asked Mary.

"No, here it is," he said, reaching for the mustard.

She decided if he hadn't seen it standing there right in front of him he must not be well.

Afterwards he got up and slowly bent over her, till his lips grazed her cheek. The kiss seemed to have dropped by parachute, on a plain not yet touched by grief.

That night, in the first glass case, there was a doll seated on a lawn, surrounded by huge sponges, which she seemed to think were flowers. He didn't feel like guessing her fate so he opened the drawer with the captions and read: "This woman is sick in the head; no one knows why she loves sponges." "As if I didn't pay them to find out," he thought; then, bitterly: "They must be to wipe away her guilt."

The next morning he woke up rolled into a ball and couldn't help remembering who he was now. He imagined himself signing a bad check, under a false name. His body was sad, as it had been once before, when a doctor told him he had thin blood and a small heart. But that other time he'd gotten over the sadness. Now he stretched his legs and thought: "Formerly, when I was young, my skin was a lot thicker: I didn't care so much about hurting others. Am I getting weak with age? Or is it a late flowering of shame and guilt?" He got up feeling much relieved; but he knew the dark clouds were still around somewhere, not far away, and that they'd be back with night.

V

A few days later, wanting to distract Horace, Mary took him for a walk. Along the way, she kept wondering whether he was missing Daisy or the real daughter they'd never have any more.

The afternoon Daisy got back, he didn't seem particularly glad to see her, and again Mary thought she wasn't the reason for his sadness. But, a moment before dinner, she caught him lingering over her fondly, and felt relieved.

After that, for several nights, as he kissed his wife before going in to see the dolls, he searched her face with sharp eyes, as if to make sure there was nothing strange hidden there. He hadn't yet been alone with Daisy.

And then came a memorable afternoon when, in spite of the mild weather, Mary filled Daisy with hot water, packed him into bed with her for his nap, and went out.

That evening he kept scanning her face as if watching for an enemy. She noticed his quick, nervous gestures, his stilted walk. He was waiting for the sign that he'd been found out.

Finally, one morning, it happened.

Once, some time ago, when Mary had been complaining of Alex's beard, Horace had said: "Better than those twin maids of yours that you can't tell apart!"

She'd answered: "Why, do you have anything special to say to either one of them? Have you gotten them mixed up in some way?"

"Yes, I was calling you once, and who do you think came in? The one that just happens to carry your name."

After which the twins had been ordered to stay out of sight when he was home. But seeing one vanish through a door once at his approach, he'd chased her, thinking she was a stranger, and run into his wife. Since then Mary had them come in only a few hours in the morning and never took her eye off them.

The day he was found out, Mary had caught the twins raising Daisy's nightie when it wasn't time to dress her or change her water. As they left the bedroom, she went in. In a little while the twins saw her rush across the courtyard into the kitchen, and back again, with the big chopping knife. They were frightened and tried to follow her; but she slammed the door on them. When they peeped through the keyhole her back blocked their view; so they moved to another door. She had Daisy spread on a table, as for an operation, and was stabbing her all over, flailing away as the water splashed in her face. Two small spurts rose from one of Daisy's shoulders, mixing in the air, like the water from the fountain in the garden; and there was a gush from her belly, stirring under her torn nightgown. One of the twins had knelt on a cushion, with a hand over one eye, the other eye stuck to the keyhole. When the draft that came through the hole made her eye run, she changed places with her sister. Mary was also crying as she finally dropped the knife on Daisy and fell into an armchair, burying her face in her hands. The twins lost interest in the scene and returned to the kitchen. But soon she called them back up to help her pack. She'd decided to handle the situation with the wounded dignity of a fallen queen. Determined to punish Horace, she instructed the twins to say she would not receive him, in case he showed up before she was ready. She started making arrangements for a long trip, and gave the twins some of her dresses. Finally, she drove off, leaving the twins wailing in the garden. But, back in the house with their new dresses, they cheered up. They drew open the curtains that covered the mirrors—to spare Horace the shock of seeing himself in them—and held the dresses up to their bodies for effect. One of them saw Daisy's mangled form in a mirror and said: "What a beast!" She meant Horace, who had just appeared in a door, wondering how to ask them to explain the dresses and the bare mirrors. But, suddenly catching sight of Daisy sprawled on the table in her ripped nightie, he changed course. The twins tried to sneak out of the room; but he stopped them: "Where's my wife?"

The one who had said "What a beast!" stared him full in the face and answered:

"She's on a long trip. She gaved us these dresses."

He dismissed them and stood there thinking: "The worst is over." Then he glanced at Daisy again. The chopping knife still lay across her belly. He wasn't too unhappy, and for a moment even imagined having her repaired. But then he pictured her all stitched up and remembered a rag horse he'd had as a child, with a tear in it. His mother had wanted to patch it up; but he'd lost his taste for it and thrown it out.

As for Mary, he was convinced she would return. He kept telling himself: "I have to take things calmly." And in fact, he felt bolder than he had for years. Looking back over the morning's events, he already saw himself betraying Daisy. A few days ago Frank had shown him another doll: a ravishing blonde with a shady past. Frank had been spreading word of a manufacturer in a northern country who made these dolls. He'd imported the designs, and the first samples had been a great success. Soon an elderly shy man had visited him, with big pouchy eyes gleaming under heavy lids, to ask for details. Frank had shown him photographs of the dolls, saying: "Their generic name is Daisy; but then each owner gives them whatever pet name he wants. These are the samples that came with the designs." He'd displayed only three photographs, and the man had picked one, almost at random, and asked the price, cash in hand. Frank had quoted a stiff sum and the buyer had blinked a couple of times; but then he'd signed the order, with a pen shaped like a submarine. Horace had seen the finished blonde and asked Frank to hold her for him; and Frank, who had others on the way, had agreed. At first Horace had thought of setting her up in an apartment; but now he decided to bring her home and keep her in the glass case where he kept the dolls waiting to be assigned their roles. As soon as the servants retired, he'd bring her up to the bedroom; and before they rose in the morning, he'd put her back in the glass case. Meantime, he hoped Mary wouldn't turn up in the middle of the night. Since Frank had put the doll at his disposal, he'd felt himself riding a lucky streak he hadn't known since youth. His having missed Mary's departure was a good sign; so was his youthful sense of being in control. If it was that easy to give up one doll for another, it was no use wasting tears on a corpse. Mary was sure to be back, now that he no longer cared about her; so he'd leave the corpse to her.

Suddenly Horace started to edge along the wall like a thief. Sidling up to a wardrobe, he drew the curtain across the mirror. He repeated the gesture at the other wardrobe. He'd had the curtains hung years ago. Mary was always careful to shield him from the mirrors: she dressed behind closed doors and made sure the curtains were back in place before leaving the room. Now he was annoyed to think the twins had not only been wearing her clothes but had left the mirrors uncovered. It wasn't that he didn't like to see things in mirrors; but his sallow face reminded him of some wax dolls he'd seen in a museum one afternoon. A shopkeeper had been murdered that day, like many of the figures represented in the dolls, and the splotches of blood on the wax were as repulsive to him as if he'd actually caught the murderer at work with his knife. The only uncovered mirror in the room was the one on the dresser. It was a low mirror where he could bend for a quick glimpse at the knot of his tie, as he went by every day. Since he combed and shaved by touch, it had never seen his face; so that now, feeling safe, he passed it as usual, but with the same unpleasant feeling he would have had at the sight of his face, as suddenly it pictured his hand against his dark suit. He realized then his hands were also the color of wax. At the same time, he remembered some loose arms he'd seen in Frank's office that morning. They were pleasantly colored and shaped like those of the blond doll; and, like a child asking a carpenter for scraps, he'd told Frank: "I could use some of those arms and legs, if you have any left over."

Frank couldn't imagine what for; so he'd explained: "I'd like the boys to make up some scenes with loose arms and legs. For instance, an arm hanging from a mirror, a leg sticking out from under a bed and so on."

Frank, bent over his work, had watched him askance.

At lunch that day, Horace drank his wine as calmly as if Mary were out spending the day with relatives. He kept thinking of his good luck. He got up feeling elated, sat at the piano for a while, letting his fingers roam, and finally went up for his nap. On his way past the dresser, he thought: "One of these days I'll get over my fear and face the mirrors." He was already looking forward to the surprises he'd find in their jumbled images. Then, with another glance at Daisy, who would have to wait until Mary got back, he went to bed. As he stretched out under the covers, he touched a strange object with the tip of his foot and jumped up. For a moment he stood there, then pulled back the covers. It was a note from Mary that said: "Horace: here's your mistress. I've also stabbed her. But I can admit it—not like a certain hypocrite I know who just wanted to send her in to have filthy things done to her. You've sickened my life and I'll thank you not to look for me. Mary."

He went back to bed, but couldn't sleep and got up again. He avoided her things on the dresser as he avoided her face when they were quarreling. Then he went to the movies. There he shook hands with an old enemy, without realizing it. He kept thinking of Mary.

When he got back, there was still a bit of sun filtering into the bedroom. As he went by one of the covered mirrors, he saw his face in it, through the wispy curtain, catching the sun, which made it look bright as a ghost. With a shudder, he closed the windows and lay down. If his luck was coming back, after all these years, it wouldn't be for long; nor would it come alone, but wrapped in strange circumstances, as the ones he'd been coping with because of Daisy, who still lay there, a few feet away. At least her body wouldn't rot, he thought, wondering at how little it had to do with the spirit that had once inhabited it. And so, mightn't that spirit have deliberately provoked Mary's wrath, so there would be a corpse between them. Horace and Mary? He couldn't sleep, watching the ghostly shapes of the room, which seemed to echo the noise of the machines. He got up, went to the table and drank some wine. As the evening wore on he became more and more aware of Mary's absence. He missed their kiss after dinner. Alone with his coffee in the little parlor, he decided he ought to avoid the house while she was gone; and when he went out for a walk a bit later, he looked for a student hotel he remembered seeing in the neighborhood. A palm grew in the doorway and a row of glinting mirrors led all the way up the stairs; so he walked on. The sight of so many mirrors in a single day was a dangerous sign. But then he remembered what he'd told Frank early that morning about wanting to see an arm hanging from a mirror. He also remembered the blonde doll, and his new boldness, and turned back. He brushed past the palm and tried to climb the stairs without looking at himself in the mirrors. It was a long time since he'd seen so many at once and the confusion of images made his head spin. He even thought there might be someone hidden among the reflections. The lady who ran the place met him upstairs and showed him the free rooms, which all had great big mirrors. He chose the best and said he'd be back in an hour. At home, he packed a small suitcase; and on his way back to the hotel he remembered it had once been a brothel: which explained the mirrors. There were three in his room, which looked its best in the largest one, by the bed. So that was the one he watched, wondering for how many long years it had been reflecting the same vaguely Chinese sceneries. The gaudy red wallpaper was faded by now, but, according to the mirror, still showed traces of what looked like yellowish bridges with cherry trees sunk in the bottom of a lake. He got into bed and put out the light, but went on seeing things in the glow that came in from the street. He had the feeling he'd been taken into the bosom of a poor family, where all things were friends and had aged together. But the windows were still young and looked out; they were twins, like Mary's maids, and dressed alike, in clinging lace curtains and velvet drapes gathered at the edges. It all gave him a strangely borrowed sense of wellbeing, as if he were in someone else's body. The loud silence made his ears hum and he realized he was missing the noise of the machines and that he was glad he'd left it behind in the black house. If only he had Mary at his side now, he'd be completely happy. As soon as she came back he'd have her spend a night with him in the hotel. But then he dozed off thinking of the blonde doll, and dreamed of a white arm floating around in a sort of dark haze. A sound of steps in a neighboring room woke him up. He got out of bed, on bare feet, and paced the rug, but saw a white spot following him, and recognized his face, reflected in the mirror over the fireplace. He wondered why someone didn't invent a mirror that showed objects but not people; though of course that was absurd; not to mention the fact that a man without an image in the mirror would have to be dead. He lay down again, just as someone turned on a light across the street. The light fell on the mirror by the bed; and he thought of his childhood, and other mirrors he'd known, and fell asleep.

VI

Horace now slept in the hotel; and the same pattern of events repeated itself every night: windows went on across the street and the light fell on his mirrors; or he woke up and found the windows asleep.

One night he heard cries and saw flames in his mirror. At first he watched them as if they were flickers on a screen; but then he realized if they showed in the mirror they must be somewhere, and springing up he saw them dancing in one of the rooms across the street, like tiny devils in a puppet show. He jumped out of bed, threw on his robe and put his face to a window. The flashes in the glass made the window seem as frightened as he was. There was a crowd down below—he was up on the second floor—and the firemen were coming. Just then, he saw Mary leaning out another window of the hotel. She'd already noticed him and was staring at him in surprise. He waved, shut the window and went up the hall to knock on what he thought was her door. She came right out saying:

"You're wasting your time following me."

And she slammed the door in his face.

He stayed there quietly, till he heard her sobbing inside. Then he said:

"I wasn't following you. But since we've met, why don't we go home?"

"You go on if you want," she said.

He thought he sensed doubt in her voice; and the next day he moved back happily into the black house. There he basked in luxury, wandering like a sleepwalker among his riches. The familiar objects all seemed full of peaceful memories, the high ceilings braced against death, if it struck from above.

But when he went into the showroom after dinner that evening, the piano reminded him of a big coffin, the resonant silence of a wake. He raised the top of the piano and, suddenly terrified, let it fall with a bang. For a moment he stood there with his arms up, as if someone were pointing a gun at him, but then rushed out into the courtyard shouting: "Who put Daisy in the piano?"

As his shouts echoed, he went on seeing her hair tangled in the strings, her face flattened by the weight of the lid. One of the twins answered his call, speechless. Finally Alex appeared and said: "The lady was in this afternoon. She came to get some clothes."

"These surprises of hers are going to be the death of me," Horace shouted, losing control. But suddenly he pulled himself together: "Take Daisy to your room and have Frank come for her early tomorrow morning. Wait—" he shouted again. "Come here." And as the twins left—lowering his voice to a whisper: "Tell Frank to bring the other doll when he comes for her."

That night he slept in another hotel. He got a room with a single mirror. The yellow wallpaper had red flowers and green leaves woven in a pattern that suggested a trellis. The bedspread was also yellow and irritated him: he had the feeling he was sleeping outdoors.

The next morning he went home and had some large mirrors brought into the showroom to multiply the scenes in the glass cases. The day passed with no word from Frank. That evening, as he came into the showroom with the wine, Alex dropped the bottle . . .

"So, what's all the fuss about?" said Horace.

He was wearing a black silk mask and yellow gloves.

"I thought you were a thief," said Alex, as Horace's laugh blew billows in the mask.

"I can't breathe or drink with this thing on. But before I remove it I want you to take down the mirrors and lean them on chairs—like this," said Horace, taking one down and showing him.

"They'd be safer if you turned the glass to the wall," objected Alex.

"No, because I still want them to reflect things."

"You could lean their backs on the wall then."

"No, because then they'd be at the wrong angle and show my face."

When Alex had done as he was told, Horace removed his mask and began to sip his wine, pacing up and down a carpet in the middle of the room. The way the mirrors tipped forward, toward him, leaning on the chairs that separated them from him, made him think of them as bowing servants watching him from under raised brows. They also reflected the floor crookedly through the legs of the chairs. After a couple of drinks, he was bothered by this effect and decided to go to bed.

The next morning—he'd slept at home that night—the chauffeur came, on Mary's behalf, to ask for money. He gave it to him without asking where she was, but assumed it meant she wouldn't be back soon. So, when the blonde doll arrived, he had her taken straight up to the bedroom. At dinnertime, he had the twins dress her in an evening gown and lead her to the table. He ate with her sitting across from him; and afterwards, in front of one of the twins, asked Alex: "What do you think of this one?"

"A beauty, sir—very much like a spy I met during the war."

"A lovely thought, Alex."

The next day he told the twins:

"From now on you're to call her Miss Eulalie."

At dinnertime, he asked the twins (who no longer hid from him): "Can you tell me who's in the dining room?"

"Miss Eulalie," both the twins said at once.

But out of earshot, making fun of Alex, they said:

"It's time to give the spy her hot water . . ."

VII

Mary was waiting for him in the student hotel, hoping he'd return there. She went out only long enough for her room to be made. She carried her head high around the neighborhood, but walked in a cloud, thinking: "I'm a woman who has lost her man to a doll. But if he could see me now he'd be drawn to me." Back in her room, she opened a book of poems, bound in blue oilcloth, and started to read out loud, in an absent voice, waiting again. When he didn't show up, she tried to see into the poems, as if someone had just left a door open by chance for her to peep in. Then, for a moment, it seemed to her the wallpaper, the folding screen, even the bright taps of the washbowl also understood the poems, swept up in their lofty rhythms and noble images. Often, in the middle of the night, she switched on her lamp and chose a poem as if she were choosing a dream. Out walking again the next day, she imagined her steps were poetry. And one morning she decided: "I'd like Horace to think of me walking alone among trees, with a book in my hand."

She packed again, sent for her chauffeur and had him drive her out to a place belonging to a cousin of her mother's: it was a tree-lined suburb. The cousin was an old spinster who lived in an ancient house. When her huge bulk came heaving through the dim rooms, making the floor creak, a parrot squawked: "Hello, milksops." Mary poured her heart out to her without a sniffle. The fat cousin was horrified, then indignant, and finally in tears. But Mary calmly dispatched the chauffeur to get money from Horace. In case Horace asked after her, he was to say, as if on his own, that she was walking among the trees with a book in her hand. If he wanted to know where she was, he should tell him. Finally, he was to report back at the same time the next day. Then she went and sat under a tree with her book, and the poems started to float and spread through the garden as if filling in the shapes of trees and clouds.

At lunch the fat cousin brooded; but then she asked: "What are you going to do with the pig?"

"Wait for him and forgive him."

"Not at all like you, my dear. This man has turned your head and you're still dancing to his tune like one of his dolls."

Mary lowered her eyes in blissful silence. But later that afternoon, the cleaning woman came in with the previous day's evening paper, and Mary noticed a headline that said: "Frank's Daisy Dolls." She couldn't help reading the leaflet announcing "a fancy display on the top floor of our smartest department store. We understand some of the dolls wearing the latest fashions will be Daisies. And that Frank, the famous doll manufacturer, will at the same time be joining the firm that runs the store. More evidence of the alarming rate at which this new version of original sin—to which we have already referred in previous editions—is spreading among us. Here is a sample of a flier left at one of our main clubs: Are you ugly? Don't worry. Shy? Forget it. No more quarrels, back talk, gossipy relatives. A Daisy Doll for all, offering her silent love."

Mary was shaking all over:

"The nerve—to think he can use the name of our. . . !"

Still grasping for words, she raised flashing eyes, aimed them in fury, and shouted:

"Look at this!"

The fat cousin, seated nearby, blinked and rummaged in her sewing basket, looking for her glasses. Mary said:

"Listen to this." And she read out the leaflet. "I'm not just going to divorce him, but kick up the biggest row this country has ever seen."

"Now you're talking sense!" shouted the fat cousin, taking her hands—which were raw from scrubbing pans—back out of the basket. And, at the first chance she had, while Mary strode frantically up and down, tripping over innocent plants and flowerpots, she hid the book of poems from her.

The next day the chauffeur came in wondering how to evade Mary's questions about Horace; but she only asked him for the money and then sent him back to the black house to fetch Mary, the twin. Mary—the twin—arrived in the afternoon and told her all about the spy and how they all had to call her Miss Eulalie. At first Mary—Horace's wife—was terrified, and asked faintly:

"Does she look like me?"

"No, Madam—she's blonde and dresses differently."

Mary—Horace's wife—jumped up, but then dropped back into her armchair, crying at the top of her voice. The fat cousin appeared and the twin repeated the story. The fat cousin's heaving breast shook as she burst into loud moans; and the parrot joined the racket screeching: "Hello, milksops."

VIII

Walter was back from a holiday and Horace was having his nightly showings again. The first night, he'd taken Eulalie into the showroom with him, sat her next to him on the podium and kept his arms around her while he watched the other dolls. The boys had made up scenes with more "personalities" than usual. There were five in the first glass case, representing the board of directors of a society for the protection of unwed mothers. One of them had just been elected President of the board: another, her beaten rival, was moping over her defeat. He liked the rival and left Eulalie for a moment to go plant a kiss on her cool forehead. When he got back to the podium he thought he heard the noise of the machines filtering through gaps in the music and recalled Eulalie's resemblance to a spy. In any case, his eyes feasted greedily on the various dolls that night. But the next day he woke up exhausted and toward evening he had dark thoughts of death. He dreaded not knowing when he would die, or what part of his body would go first. It was harder for him every day to be alone. The dolls were no company, but seemed to say: "Don't count on us—we're just dolls." Sometimes he whistled, but soon felt the thread of sound thinning out till he lost track of it. Other times, he talked to himself aloud, stupidly commenting on what he was doing: "Now I'm going to the study for the inkwell." Or he described his actions as if he were watching someone else: "The poor idiot—there he is, opening a drawer; uncovering the inkwell. For all the good it does him." Finally, frightened, he went out.

The next day he received a box from Frank. He had it pried open: it was full of loose arms and legs. He remembered his request and hoped the box didn't include any loose heads. Then he had it carried in to the glass case where he kept the dolls waiting to be assigned their roles. He called the boys on the phone to explain how he wanted the arms and legs to take part in the scenes. But the first trial was a disaster and angered him. The moment he drew the curtain, he saw a doll dressed in mourning, seated at the foot of what looked like some church steps. She was staring straight ahead, with an incredible number of legs—at least ten or twelve—sticking out from under her skirt. On each step above her was an arm with the hand turned up. "Clumsy fools—couldn't think of anything better than to use all the arms and legs at once," he thought; and without trying to figure out the meaning of the scene, he opened the drawer with the captions and read: "This is a poor widow who spends her time wandering around looking for something to eat. The hands are like traps snapping up alms." "What silly nonsense," he kept thinking. He went up to bed in a bad mood; and on the point of falling asleep, he saw the widow walking with all her legs, like a spider.

After this failure Horace felt very disappointed in the boys, the dolls and even Eulalie. But, a few days later, Frank took him out for a drive. Suddenly, going up the highway, Frank said:

"See that little two-storey house by the river? That's where that old guy lives—the shy little man who has your blonde's sister: your—uh—sister-in-law . . ." He slapped Horace on the leg and they both laughed. "He comes only at night. Afraid his mother will find out."

The next morning, toward noon, Horace returned alone, to walk down the dirt road that led to the house by the river. He came to a closed gate, next to which there was another even smaller house probably belonging to the forester. He clapped and an unshaven man in a torn hat came out chewing.

"Looking for someone?"

"I've been told the owner of that house over there has a doll . . ."

The man—now leaning back on a tree—broke in to say:

"The owner is out."

Horace drew several bills from his wallet; and the man, eyeing the money, began to chew more slowly. Horace stood there thoughtfully rippling the bills, as if they were playing cards. The man swallowed and watched. When he seemed to have had enough time to imagine everything he could do with the money, Horace said:

"I might just want to have a look at that doll."

"The boss comes at seven."

"Is the house open?"

"No, but I have a key. In case anyone finds out," said the man, reaching for *the loot*, "I don't know anything." He pocketed the money, taking out a big key: "Give it a couple of turns . . . The doll is upstairs . . . And make sure you leave everything *jest* as you find it."

Horace strode down the road, once again full of youthful excitement. The small front door was as dirty as an old hag and the key seemed to squirm in the lock. He went into a dingy room with fishing poles leaning against the walls. He picked his way through the filth and on up a recently varnished staircase. The bedroom was comfortable; but there was no doll. He looked everywhere, even under the bed; and at last he found her in a wardrobe. At first it was like running into one of Mary's surprises. The doll was in a black evening gown dotted with tiny stones like drops of glass. If she'd been in one of his show cases he would have thought of her as a widow sprinkled with tears. Suddenly he heard a blast, like a gunshot. He ran to look over the top of the stairs and saw a fishing pole lying on the floor below, in a small cloud of dust. Then he decided to wrap the doll in a blanket and carry her down to the river. She was light and cold; and while he looked for a hidden spot under the trees he caught a scent that didn't seem to come from the forest, and traced it to her. He found a soft spot on the grass, spread out the blanket, holding her over his shoulder, and laid her down as gently as if she'd fainted in his arms. In spite of the seclusion, he wasn't at ease. A frog jumped and landed nearby; and as it sat there panting, he wondered which way it was going to jump next. In a moment, he drove it off with a stone. But still, to his disappointment, he couldn't concentrate properly on the doll. He didn't dare look her in the face, for fear of her lifeless scorn. Instead he heard a strange murmur mixed with the sound of water; and turning toward the river, he saw a boy in a boat, rowing up with horrible grimaces. He had a big bloated head and tiny hands and seemed to move only his mouth, which was like a piece of raw flesh, hideously twisted into its strange sound. Horace grabbed the doll and ran for the house.

Later, on his way home, he thought of moving to some other country and never looking at another doll. When he arrived, he went straight up to the bedroom to throw out Eulalie; but he found Mary sprawled face down on the bed, crying. He went up and stroked her hair, but realized the doll was on the bed with them and called in one of the twins, with orders to remove her and have Frank come and take her away. He stretched out next to Mary and they both lay there in silence waiting for night to fall. And then, taking her hand and searching painfully for words, as if struggling with a foreign language, he told her of his disappointment in the dolls and the emptiness he'd felt in his life without her.

IX

Mary thought Horace's disappointment in the dolls was final, and for a while they both acted as if happier times were back. The first few days, neither of them mentioned Daisy; but then they began to fall into unexpected silences, and each of them knew whom the other was thinking about. One morning, strolling in the garden, Mary stopped in front of the tree where she'd put Daisy to surprise Horace. There, remembering the story the neighbors had made up and the fact that she'd actually killed Daisy, she burst into tears. When Horace came out to ask her what was wrong, she met him with an angry glare. He realized she'd lost much of her appeal, standing there alone with folded arms, without Daisy. Then, one evening, he was sitting in the little parlor, blaming himself for Daisy's absence, brooding over his guilt, when suddenly he noticed a black cat in the room. He got up, annoyed, intending to scold Alex for letting it in, when Mary appeared saying she had brought it. She was in such a gay mood, hugging him, as she told him about it, that he didn't want to upset her; but he hated it for the stealthy way it had crept up on him in his guilt. And soon it, too, came between them, as she got into the habit of taking it up to bed with her, making it lie on the covers. He waited for her to fall asleep, then started an earthquake under the covers till he got rid of it. One night she woke up in the middle of the earthquake:

"Was it you shaking the bed?"

"I don't know."

She grumbled and defended the cat. Till one night, after dinner, he went into the show room to play the piano. For some days now he'd done without the scenes in the glass cases and, against his habit, left the dolls in the dark, alone except for the noise of the machines. He lit a lamp by the piano, and there was the cat, a dark shape on the lid, watching him with bright eyes. Startled, he chased it off, then went after it, as it jumped and ran into the little parlor. There, clawing to get out, it ripped a curtain off the closed door that led into the yard. Mary was watching from the dining room. She rushed in with strong words, ending with:

"You made me kill Daisy and now I suppose you want me to kill the cat."

He put on his hat and went out for a walk. He was thinking she had no right to treat him that way any more since they'd made up. At one point, he remembered, she'd not only forgiven him his madness but actually said she loved him for it. In any case, seeing her lose her appeal without Daisy was already punishment enough. The cat cheapened her, instead of adding to her charm. Seeing her tears, on his way out, he thought: "So, it's her cat and her guilt." But at the same time he had the uneasy feeling that her guilt was nothing compared to his, and that if she couldn't quite live up to his expectations it was because of the weight she was carrying for him. And so it would always be, even on his deathbed. He imagined her still at his side, on his unpredictable but probably cowardly last days or minutes, sharing his dread. Perhaps—he couldn't think which was worse—he wouldn't even realize she was there.

At the corner he stopped to gather his wits so he could cross without being run over by a car. For a long time he wandered with his thoughts, down dark streets, till suddenly he woke up in a park and went and sat on a bench. There he thought about his life, staring into the trees. Then he followed their long shadows, to a lake, where he stopped to wonder vaguely about his soul, which was like a heavy silence on the dark water: a silence with a memory of its own, in which he seemed to recognize the noise of the machines. Perhaps the noise was the wreckage of a lost boat, full of dolls, sunk in the night. Starting suddenly, he saw a young couple come out from under the trees. As they approached, he remembered kissing Mary for the first time in a fig tree, nearly falling off, after picking the first figs. The couple moved past, a short distance away, crossed a narrow street and went into a small house. He noticed several other small houses, some with rent signs; and, though he made up again with Mary when he got home, later that night, when he was alone for a moment in the showroom, he thought of renting one of the small houses with a Daisy Doll.

The next day at breakfast he was struck by the fact that the cat had green bows in its ears. Mary explained people took their newborn kittens to the druggist to have their ears pierced with one of those machines used for punching holes in file paper. He liked the idea and thought it a good sign. From the street, he phoned Frank to ask him how he could distinguish the Daisy Dolls from the others on show at the fancy department store downtown. Frank said at the moment there was only one available, near the cash register, wearing a single earring. The coincidence, he decided, was providential: she was meant for him. And he began to relish the thought of returning to his vice as to a voluptuous fate. He could have taken a tram; but he didn't want to break the mood; so he walked, thinking about how he was going to pick out his doll. Now he was also caught up among other people, pleasantly lost—it was just before Carnival—in the holiday crowd. The store was farther away than he had calculated. He began to feel tired, and anxious to meet the doll. A child aimed a horn at him and blasted it in his face. He started to have horrible misgivings and wondered whether he shouldn't leave the visit for the afternoon. But when he reached the store and saw other dolls dressed up in the show windows he decided to go in. The Daisy Doll was wearing a wine-colored Renaissance dress. A tiny mask added to her proud bearing and he felt like humbling her; but a salesgirl he knew came up with a twisted smile, and that drove him off.

A few days later he'd installed the doll in one of the small houses near the park. Two nights a week, at nine o'clock, Frank sent a secretary over with a cleaning woman. At ten, they filled the doll with hot water and left. He'd asked them to leave her mask on. He was delighted with her and called her Hermione. Once when they were both sitting in front of a picture, he saw her eyes—thoughtful eyes, shining through the mask—reflected in the glass. From then on, they sat in the same place, cheek to cheek. Whenever he thought the eyes in the glass—it was a picture of a waterfall—took on an expression of humbled pride, he kissed her passionately. Sometimes he crossed the park with her—he seemed to be walking a ghost—and they sat on a bench near a fountain. But suddenly he realized her water was getting cold and hurried her back into the house.

Not long after that there was a big fashion show in the fancy department store. A huge glass case filled the whole of the top floor: it was in the middle of the room, leaving just enough space on all four sides for people to circulate. Because people came not only for the fashions but also to pick out the Daisy Dolls, the show was a great success. The showcase was divided into two sections by a mirror that reached all the way to the ceiling. In the section facing the entrance, the scene—arranged and interpreted by Horace's boys— represented an old folk tale, "The Woman of the Lake." A young woman lived in the depths of a forest, near a lake. Every morning she left her tent and went down to the lake to comb her hair. She had a mirror which some said she held behind her, facing the water, in order to see the back of her head. One morning after a late party, some high society ladies decided to pay the lonely woman a visit. They were to arrive at dawn, ask her why she lived alone and offer their help. When they reached her, the woman of the lake was combing her hair. She saw their elegant dresses through her hair and curtsied humbly at their approach. But at their first question she straightened up and set out along the edge of the lake. The ladies, thinking she was going to show them some secret, followed her. But the lonely woman only went round and round the lake, followed by the ladies, without saying or showing them anything. So the ladies left in disgust, calling her "the mad woman of the lake." And since then, in that part of the country, a person lost in silent thought is said to be "going round the lake."

In the showcase, the woman of the lake appeared seated at a dressing table on the edge of the water. She wore a flimsy white robe embroidered with yellow leaves. On the dressing table were a number of vials of perfume and other objects. It was the moment in the story when the ladies arrived in their party dresses. All sorts of faces peered in at them, along the glass case, looking them up and down, and not only for their dresses. Glinting eyes jumped suspiciously, from a skirt to a neckline, from one doll to the next, distrusting even the virtuous ones, like the woman of the lake. Other wary eyes glanced off the dresses as if afraid to come into contact with the dolls' skins. A young girl bowed her head in Cinderella-like wonder at the worldly splendors she imagined went with the beautiful dresses. A man frowned and lowered his eyes before his wife, hiding his urge to own a Daisy Doll. The dolls, in general, didn't seem to care whether they were being dressed or undressed. They were like haughty tarts oblivious to everything but their "poses."

The other section of the showcase was divided into two parts: a beach and a forest. The dolls on the beach wore bathing suits. Horace had stopped to watch two in a "talking" pose: one with a series of concentric circles, like a target (the circles were red), drawn on her belly, the other with fish painted on her shoulderblades. With his small head (another doll head) bobbing among the spectators, he moved on, to the forest. The dolls there were natives and almost naked. Instead of hair, some grew plants with tiny leaves on their dark heads, vines that trailed down their backs; they had flowers or stripes on their dark skins, like cannibals. Others were painted all over with bright human eyes. He took an immediate liking to a negress, who looked normal, except for a couple of little black faces with button lips painted on her breasts. He went on touring the show until he ran into Frank and asked him:

"Which of the dolls in the forest are Daisies?"

"Why, in that section they're all Daisies."

"I want you to send me the negress—out to the house by the park."

"It'll take at least a week, old boy . . ."

But, in fact, twenty days went by before he had her in the house. She was in bed, waiting for him, with the covers drawn up to her chin.

Now he didn't find her so interesting any more; and when he pulled back the covers she let out a wild cackle in his face. It was Mary, laughing at him, in bitter spite, explaining how she'd learned of his new deceit. It turned out his cleaning woman also worked for "Milksops." He listened absently, as if distracted. She noticed his strange calm and stopped for a moment. But then, hiding her amazement, she went on:

"So now what do you have to say for yourself?"

He went on staring blankly, as a man sunk into a stupor, after an exhaustion of years. Then he started to turn on his heels, with a little shuffle. Mary said: "Wait," and got up to wash off the black paint in the bathroom. She was frightened and had started to cry and sneeze at the same time. When she got back, he was gone. But she found him at home, locked in a guest room, refusing to talk to anyone.

X

Mary kept asking Horace to forgive her for her last surprise. But he stuck to his wooden silence. Most of the time he was shuttered in the guest room, almost motionless, it seemed (except for the empty bottles of French wine that kept turning up). Sometimes he went out for a while in the evening. When he got back, he ate a bite and then collapsed on the bed again, with open eyes. Mary often went in to look at him, late at night, and found him stiff as a doll, always with the same glassy stare. One night she was startled to see the cat curled up next to him. She decided to call the doctor, who started to give him injections. He was terrified, but seemed to take more of an interest in life. So she called in the boys to set up a new show for him.

That night they had dinner in the big dining room. He asked for the mustard and kept sampling the wine. Afterwards, he drank his coffee in the little parlor; and soon he went into the showroom. The first scene had no caption: among softly lit plants, in a big rippling pool, he made out a number of loose arms and legs. He saw the sole of a foot stick out through some branches, like a face, followed by the leg, like a roving beast. As it touched the glass wall it stopped and contracted. Then came another leg, followed by a hand and arm that slowly wound around it as they met, like bored animals in a cage. He stood there for a while, absently watching the different combinations of limbs, till there was a meeting of toes and fingers. But suddenly the leg involved began to straighten out in the commonplace gesture of standing on its foot. He was disappointed and flashed his light at Walter, as he moved the podium on to the next scene. There he saw a doll on a bed, wearing a queen's crown. Curled up next to her was Mary's cat. This distressed him and made him angry at the boys for letting it in. At the foot of the bed were three nuns, kneeling on prayer stools. The caption said: "The queen died giving alms. She had no time to confess, but the whole country is praying for her." When he looked again, the cat was gone. But he had the uneasy feeling it would turn up again at any moment. He decided to enter the scene—watchfully, in case of any unpleasant surprises. Bending to peer into the face of the queen, he leaned a hand on the foot of the bed. At that moment, he felt another—one of the nuns'—hands on his. He must not have heard Mary's voice pleading with him, because the minute he felt the other hand he straightened up, stiff as death and started to open his mouth and move his jaws like a bird trying to flap its wings and caw. Mary took his arm; but he brushed her off in terror and began turning himself around with a little shuffle as he had the day she laughed in his face, pretending to be his negro mistress. She was frightened again and let out a scream. He tripped over a nun and knocked her down. Then, heading back out of the scene, he missed the small door and walked into the glass wall. There he stood beating on the glass with his hands, which were like birds knocking against a closed window. Mary didn't dare take his arm again; she ran to call Alex, who was nowhere to be found.

Finally, thinking she was a nun, he came in asking what she wanted. She said, crying, that Horace was mad. They went into the show-room, but couldn't find him. They were still looking for him when they heard his steps in the gravel of the garden. When they caught him, beyond the flowerbeds, he was going toward the noise of the machines.

translated from the Spanish by Luis Harss

SNOW OWL

by DAVE SMITH

from ANTAEUS

nominated by Howard Moss

In snow veined with his blood and the white bruise
of a broken wing, the hiss in the mouth
salutes my hand and will have still
its pink plug of flesh.
Big as I am he would nail me
if only the legs lasted, those numbs
never made for this crawling, for the wings,
all night, beat nowhere. He is himself. *Here,*

here, I say, on my knees edging toward him,
my own mastery the deceit of words.
His eye cocks, the hinged horn
of beak-bone cracks and rasps,
comes cold again, and shrill,
again, the shragged edge of wind
speaking the language of his world,

his kind, giving a blunt answer to all pain.
My words fall on his white attention
like a rain he can't escape.
At each angle his bad wing
sends a screen of snow
between us, a blind conceit,
until I leave him, beaten,
who I never leave in this life . . .

and go home, blood-specks and snow's feathering
for new clothes. In the spit of weather

I go without tracks, lips drawn
back for the least gusts
of harsh breath, and know
the moon that leads me is
an eye closed long ago
to the world's dark, large secrets.

LOT'S WIFE

by KRISTINE BATEY

from JAM TO-DAY

nominated by JAM TO-DAY

While Lot, the conscience of a nation,
struggles with the Lord,
she struggles with the housework.
The City of Sin is where
she raises the children.
Ba'al or Adonai—
Whoever is God—
the bread must still be made
and the doorstill swept.
The Lord may kill the children tomorrow,
but today they must be bathed and fed.
Well and good to condemn your neighbors' religion;
but weren't they there
when the baby was born,
and when the well collapsed?
While her husband communes with God
she tucks the children into bed.
In the morning, when he tells her of the judgment,
she puts down the lamp she is cleaning
and calmly begins to pack.
In between bundling up the children
and deciding what will go,
she runs for a moment
to say goodbye to the herd,
gently patting each soft head
with tears in her eyes for the animals that will not understand.
She smiles blindly to the woman
who held her hand at childbed.

It is easy for eyes that have always turned to heaven
not to look back;
those that have been—by necessity—drawn to earth
cannot forget that life is lived from day to day.
Good, to a God, and good in human terms
are two different things.
On the breast of the hill, she chooses to be human,
and turns, in farewell—
and never regrets
the sacrifice.

THE STONE CRAB: A LOVE POEM

by ROBERT PHILLIPS

from THE HUDSON REVIEW

nominated by THE HUDSON REVIEW, *Nona Balakian and Joyce Carol Oates*

("Joe's serves approximately 1,000 pounds of crab claws each
day"—Florida Gold Coast Leisure Guide)

Delicacy of warm Florida waters,
his body is undesirable. One giant claw
is his claim to fame, and we claim it,

more than once. Meat sweeter than lobster,
less dear than his life, when grown that claw
is lifted, broken off at the joint.

Multilated, the crustacean is thrown back
into the waters, back upon his own resources.
One of nature's rarities, he replaces

an entire appendage as you or I
grow a nail. (No one asks how
he survives that crabby sea with just one

claw; two-fisted menaces real as night
-mares, ten-tentacled nights cold
as fright.) In time he grows another—

meaty, magnificent as the first. And,
one astonished day, *Snap!* it too
is twigged off, the cripple dropped

back into treachery. Unlike a twig,
it sprouts again. How many losses
can he endure? . . . Well,

his shell is hard, the sea is wide.
Something vital broken off, he doesn't
nurse the wound: develops something new.

NIGHT FLIGHT TO STOCKHOLM

fiction by DALLAS WIEBE

from THE PARIS REVIEW

nominated by THE PARIS REVIEW *and DeWitt Henry*

I OWE ALL THIS TO GABRIEL RATCHET. It was he who arranged for the round-trip ticket, two seats side by side, on Scandinavian Airlines, got me my reservation in the King Gustaf Holiday Inn, deodorized my basket, put in the new sheets, put on my new, formal black sack with the white ribbon drawstring around the top and bathed my suppurating stumps for the journey. He even carried one end of my wicker laundry basket when I went aboard. In the darkness, I heard him instructing the stewardesses as to how to clean me, how to feed and water me and when to turn me. I heard money changing hands. I heard his stomachy laugh and the ladies' bovine grunts. I think I heard a stewardess pat his little bald head. Then came my first lift-off. The great surge of the old Boeing 747 sliding my butt and stumps against one end of the basket and then the floating and my ears popping. Into glorious, golden dreams in my black chute. Into non-stop gliding through images of published books, careful emendations, green surgical gowns, and the rustle of paper money, the clink of prizes and the odor of immortality. It was Gabriel Ratchet who gave me this slow drifting in the darkness 50,000 feet over Iceland, the North Atlantic, Ireland, England, the North Sea and Norway as we, as I hear from the pilot, descend into our landing pattern for Stockholm and me about to meet the king of Sweden and, I assume, his wife and all the little royalties. I wonder what they'll sound like; I wonder how they'll smell.

I owe all this to Gabriel because he is an expert in contracts. He's made contracts for musicians, painters, sculptors, quarterbacks, pole vaulters, jugglers, born-again Christians and presidents. He's negotiated the careers of farmers, professors, poets, priests, baseball pitchers, terrorists and airline pilots. For the past thirty years he's had his hand in more success than you can shake a scalpel at because of his immense number of contacts. He says he brought it with him from the womb. I can believe it.

Gabriel—his clients call him Gabe or Gabby—was born on the western slope of Muckish Mountain in Donegal in 1935, exact day unknown he says, when his mother saw some white horses hung with silver bells. He came to Chicago, IL., he says, when the potato crop failed around Bloody Foreland in 1951. I don't remember any potato famines in Ireland since the nineteenth century, but I'm always willing to lend him an ear and listen to his stories. He came to Chicago, he says, because he is a creature of our own flesh and blood and likes a city where every man has his price. He says his contracting business didn't go well at first. In fact, he was on his last leg when he met Isobel Gowdie in October, 1956, in the Chicago Art Institute while he and she were standing and staring at some water lilies by Monet. According to his account, Gabriel sighed and said, "Hell, Peg Powler can paint better than that." Isobel, having an eye to the main chance, immediately answered, "Richard Tarlton has one foot in the grave. Can you give him a hand?" Gabe's life as a public servant and a successful entrepreneur began with that moment because he negotiated a contract whereby for a shake and a cut Ambroise Paré became the first wealthy one-armed undertaker in Hellwaine, ME.

I first met Gabe in the lobby of the Palmer House in December of 1977 when I was there for an MLA convention. He was loitering around the packed lobby, looking, I later found out, for failures with whom he could do some business. He was sidling about, handing out, quietly and covertly, little business cards, red letters on green, that gave his name, Gabriel "Ballybofey" Ratchet, his office, 1313 Spoorne Ave., Chicago, his telephone number, 393-6996, his office hours, "At Your Convenience," his profession, "Contractor," and his motto, "Don't limp in obscurity; get a leg up on this world." He gave me his last card and said he'd never seen so many potential clients. He said he'd had his eye on me for some time and I was cut to the quick. We chatted, there in that mob, for a while and I asked him about himself. He told me that he was short because of that potato famine in his youth. His nose and ears were gnarled because his mother had been frightened by Peg O'Nell when she, his dear mother, was nursing him and her left teat had immediately dried up while in his mouth. His teeth were rotted out and his head was bald because his wife of two years, Joan Tyrrie of Creke Abbey, MT., had tried to poison him with bat slobber. He managed, he said, to overcome the poison by eating stuffed grasshoppers, roasted ants and mice roasted whole and threw her into the Chicago River. He said she'd been bad from the start and he was surprised his marriage in the year of 1955 lasted the two years that it did. Gabe said that her stepmother had given her a bottle of flat beer and some sour bread for a dowry and that after their marriage in Calkett Hall all she wanted to do was to be friendly with the goats and comb their beards. He said there was saltpeter in her heaven and gold in her hell and that her angels were sufficiently embodied to be impeded by their armor and damaged by gunpowder. I told him my problems and he said that I was too old to fool around any longer, that I would have to fight tooth and nail to make it. I said I'd call him if I needed his service.

I needed his help a lot sooner than I thought then because my paper which I presented at that MLA convention was laughed at. When I began my opening remarks I heard tittering. When I asked for silence, they guffawed. When I introduced my paper— "Metaphorical Thinking as the Cause of the Collapse of British and American Literature" by Professor Meyric Casaubon, Department of English, University of Tylwyth Teg, Wales, OR.—they hooted and snarled and shot out their lips. They waggled their beards and gnashed their teeth on their pipe stems. Even my old friend, Bock Urisk, who claimed he could hear grass growing, could run so fast when he was young that he had to keep one leg over his shoulder to stay in sight, could break stones on his thighs they were so hard and could spin a windmill by blowing through one nostril, waved his open palms past his ears and held his nose. I got the message when Richard Tynney of Gorleston, DE., the chairman of the panel, and Sir John Shepe of Wanstrowe, IA., the moderator, got up, dropped their pants and showed me their bare asses. I was mooned for metaphors and that was the end, I thought. I walked off the stage, my green suit striking among the black turtle necks, my thick black hair bobbing over the seated howlers, my hooked nose, my protuberant chin and my green eyes lifted high in disdain, even though I was without socks and my huge belly bounced and rumbled. I walked out of the room, my white Converse All-Stars squeaking on the waxed floors, my white tie and my blue shirt spotted with my sweat. I decided then to go back to what I'd always been doing anyway, writing fiction. I took out the green card with the red letters.

It was a Thursday when I lifted the phone and called him. I said, "Gabe, I'm going to be sixty-six tomorrow, Friday, January 13, 1978, and I've been writing fiction all my life and no one's ever published a word of it and I'd give my left pinkie to get into *The Paris Review*." And I did because Gabriel was interested at once and told me that he'd get in touch with me the next day because he thought he might find a buyer. He did. The next day Gabe came around and said he had a friend, Tom Reid, whose ancestor was killed at the battle of Pinkie in 1547 and who needed to get his self-respect back. According to Gabriel, Tom had agreed to see to it that my story, "Livid With Age," would be published in *The Paris Review* for my left pinkie. And he did. He told me to type my story, doublespaced, on clean white paper. Not to use eraseable paper. He said I should make my setting exact in place and time, not to moralize at the end of my story and to get rid of the false intensifiers like "literally," "really," "utterly," "just," "veritable," "absolutely," "very" and "basically." Create emphasis by syntax, he said. He also told me to clean the sweat stains off. I did all that and when my story came out, I went to Dr. Dodypol and had the finger removed surgically and under anesthesia. His head nurse, Kate Crackernuts, wrapped the finger in cotton bandages and in red tissue paper with a yellow ribbon around it and I walked out a published author and weighing three ounces less than when I walked in. And made money on it too, because the operation cost fifty dollars and I was paid sixty for my story.

A month after the appearance of "Livid With Age," I sent another story out. "Liam Sexob Lives in Loveland," to *TriQuarterly*. It seemed like it came back the same day, although of course it didn't, and I knew that I needed Gabriel Ratchet again and his influence. I found him sitting in the Trywtyn Tratyn Pub, drinking Habitrot and flirting with Jenny Greenteeth. "Look, Gabe," I said, "I need help. I'd give my left testicle to get my story in *TriQuarterly*." Gabe didn't even look at me when he said, "Make it two and I think I can get you a deal." I allowed as how I'd probably go along with it and he said he'd talk to Marmaduke Langdale, who needed them for his Whitsun Rejoicings. Gabe did and I did. Dr. Nepier from Lydford in Bercks and his head nurse, Sarah Skelbourn, removed them on a cold Friday in December of 1978. Sarah wrapped them in white bandages, green tissue paper and red ribbons. I took them to Gabriel, who was satisfied with the merchandise and told me that Marmaduke Langdale said I should change the title of the story to "Silence on the Rive Gauche," change the name of the main character Liam Sexob to Burd Isobel, eliminate the doublings, get rid of the colloquial style, erase the tear stains from the margins of pages 4, 14 and 22, and stop using exclamation points, dashes, underlinings for emphasis and the series of periods that indicate ellipses. I did all that. Retyped the story on good, twenty pound linen bond and sent it off to *TriQuarterly*. They accepted it within a week and I was on my way to my second story in print.

When "Silence on the Rive Gauche" came out, I asked Gabriel Ratchet to be my permanent agent. He agreed and in July of 1979 Dr. Louis Marie Sinistrati and his colleague, Isidore Liseaux, removed my left hand which I figured I didn't need anyway because I can only type with my right hand and right arm, wrapped it in blue and red striped gift paper, tied it with black ribbon, and sent it to Mr. Greatorex, the Irish Stroker, who wrote back from the Island of Hy Brasil, MD., that I should stop using participial phrases, get the inactive detail out of my descriptions, stop using literary language with its euphemisms and circumlocutions and not to use exclamations such as "needless to say," "to my amazement" and "I don't have to tell you." He also suggested that I not send in pages with blood stains on them. I did everything he said and *Esquire* accepted my story, "Moles' Brains and the Right to Life."

Even though I was still anemic from my last publication, I decided in January of 1980 to bid for the *New Yorker*. Gabe sent out the message and Durant Hotham wrote from Yatton Keynel, ME., that he would do it for a pair of ears if I would promise to stop using abnormal word order, get rid of the *faux-naif* narrator, eliminate all cliches from my narrative, would isolate point of view in one character or one narrator and would clean my snot off the manuscript. I did what he said and sent in the manuscript of "Muckelawee." Durant wrote back his thanks for the contract and told me to visit Peg Powler at 1369 Kelpie Street and she would have some directions for me. I went. She had directions and told me to go to Dr. Arviragus at the Abbey Lubbers Clinic. I went. When I walked out of the Clinic, I had my ears in a red and gold bag tied at the top with green ribbon. The stumps on the sides of my head tingled in the cold air as I walked out into a new reputation as one of the finest short story writers in America.

When I suggested a book of short stories to Gabriel, he shivered. He suggested that I rest for a while and get myself together before I made any more deals. I told him he'd made a lot of money off my publications and that he would make a lot more. Just to do his work as my agent and let me worry about the parts. He did admit that he had an offer. That he needed a left arm, even if there was no hand attached to it. A Dr. William Drage of Hitchin, AR., needed it to fit out Margaret Barrance so that she could attend a ball because not having a left arm there was nothing for her to lay across the shoulder of her male partner while she danced. Gabriel told me that I would have to go to Hitchin for the transplant. I agreed and I did in March of 1981. But before he removed the left arm, he told me that the deal was contingent on my editing my manuscript carefully, to carefully control the secondary patterns, to make the deuteragonist more important in all the stories, to research materials for the stories, to make the stories more weird, more strange, more uncomfortable for the reader. Clean the ear wax off my pages. I promised I'd do all he told me to do and he took my arm and sewed it onto Margaret, who six months later danced in her first ball at the age of thirty-three, wearing a blue and gold dress with a red sash around her waist, while Doubleday published my collection of short stories, *The Cry of Horse and Hattock* (September, 1981).

Because my recovery times were lengthening, I decided that a novel should be my next reduction and when I mentioned it to Gabriel Ratchet he fell on the floor and chortled. I told him to get his little carcass off the floor and get to work. He did. He got bids for my nose, my feet, my legs, my eyes, my penis and my kidneys. I bid one left foot. The law firm of Morgue, Arsile and Maglore handled the negotiations and in February of 1982 Ratchet finalized the contract with Miss Ruth Tongue of Somerset, KS., by which I agreed to furnish her with one left foot in return for the publication of my novel, *Flibberty Gibbet*, by Knopf. My part of the contract was that I had to stop misusing "transpire," "problematical," "livid," "momentarily," "presently" and "loin." My sentences were to be made more simple. I was to use more active verbs with agents doing actions. I was to get out the melodrama. I also agreed not to use any anthropomorphizing metaphors, not to personify anything not human, to make only direct descriptions of characters, objects and actions and not to leak urine on my manuscript. Gabriel also negotiated an interesting addendum to the contract and that was that if the book could be made to win a national prize then my part of the bargain was the left foot and the whole left leg. Wouldn't you know; Ms. Tongue got the whole leg when *Flibberty Gibbet*, clad in a dust jacket of red, black and orange, won the National Book Award for 1982. They carried me up to the podium in a rocking chair and I shook hands for the last time when I accepted the award.

Ratchet's account books, which he read to me before I left O'Hare, read as follows after that:

April 4, 1983: Right foot. To Tommy Rawhead of Asmoday, ND. Complicate the emotional and psychological dimensions of the action. Careful selection of names. Vary sentence rhythms. Tonal variation. Shit off pages. Novel: *Brachiano's Ghost*. Macmillan. Black and grey cover. Red chapter headings. Plus right leg: Pulitzer Prize. Done.

July 16, 1984: Right hand. To Elaby Gathen of Hackpen, MI. Correct spelling of "existence," "separate" and "pursue." No redundancy in nouns and verbs and their modifiers. Play games with readers. No slobbering on pages. Book of short stories: *The Blue Hag of Winter*. Random House. Gold on black cover. Red title page. Right arm also: O'Henry Award, St. Lawrence Award for Fiction and Chair at Columbia. Done.

February 10, 1985: Two eyes. To Billy Blind of Systern, DE. No use of "etc.," the suffix "-wise," correct use of "as." No rhetorical questions in narrative. No openings with dialogue. No flashbacks.

Include all senses in descriptions. No pus on pages. Two volume novel: *Sammael*. Little, Brown. Red, green and blue cover. Nobel Prize. Done.

As I float over the shadowed northern world, I think now that we all go off into darknesses, bit by bit, piece by piece, part by part. We all disintegrate into our words, our sentences, our paragraphs, our narratives. We scatter our lives into photographs, letters, certificates, books, prizes, lies. We ride out the light until the records break one by one. We sit out the days until the sun gets dimmer and dimmer. We lie about in the gathering shadows until North America, South America, Australia, Antarctica, Asia, Africa and Europe lie about on the dark waters of our globe. It is crack time in the world of flesh. It is shatter time in the world of limbs. It is splatter time in the world of bones. It is the last splinter of the word. I have tasted the double-deal. I have smelled the slight-of-hand. I have heard the cryptic whisper. I have felt the cold riddle. Because no one stands apart from his stone. No one laughs apart from his crust. No one breathes apart from his shriveling. No one speaks apart from his silence. To lie down in a wicker basket is not to lie apart. To be turned on soft, pus-soaked sheets is not to be turned alone. To be fed through tubes is not to eat alone. To drink and choke is to spit up for all. To float through the night is the journey we all take sooner or later until the bright and shining morning star breaks and there is no more.

I can feel the huge plane starting to descend. My seventy-four year old ears are popping. The stewardess who smells like a dead dog has already rolled me over so that I won't aspirate if I vomit. She's strapped me tightly in place on my two seats. I can feel the safety belts across my rump and ribs. I feel the descent into darkness and I know that I have not given up anything that I could not do without. I know that you can live with less than you came in with. I know that wholeness is not everything and that if you will give an eye for a prize you'll be a sure winner. I can feel my long, white hair sliding and shaking over my stumpy ears as the plane bucks and banks for the landing. I can imagine the attendants in black knickers with the little black bows by the knees who will carry me onto the clapping stage. I can imagine the old black king squinting through his thick glasses down into the wicker basket with the two handles and the white Cannon sheets. As my snot begins to leak out over my upper lip, I can hear myself asking him to clean the ear wax out of my shallow ears so that I can hear him clearly when he extols the virtues of long-suffering, when he prattles about how some people overcome severe handicaps and go on to greatness, when he maunders about the indomitable will of the human spirit, while the old black queen gurgles and snickers down at the heady, winning lump. And I hope it's a prince, princess or princeling who will hold the microphone down into the basket so that while pus oozes from my eye sockets I can whisper my acceptance speech. I hope I can control my saliva. I hope I don't shed tears. I wonder if there will be flowers to add their smells to the noises, the tastes and the temperatures. I wonder if anyone will manage to get a sip of Champagne to me. That thumping, bumping and bouncing must be the runway.

LITERATURE AND ECOLOGY: AN EXPERIMENT IN ECOCRITICISM

by WILLIAM RUECKERT

from THE IOWA REVIEW

nominated by Louis Gallo

"It is the business of those who direct the activities that will shape tomorrow's world to think beyond today's well being and provide for tomorrow."
—Raymond Dasmann
Planet in Peril

"Any living thing that hopes to live on earth must fit into the ecosphere or perish."
—Barry Commoner
The Closing Circle

". . . the function of poetry. . . . is to nourish the spirit of man by giving him the cosmos to suckle. We have only to lower our standard of dominating nature and to raise our standard of participating in it in order to make the reconciliation take place. When man becomes proud to be not just the site where ideas and feelings are produced, but also the crossroad where they divide and mingle, he will be ready to be saved. Hope therefore lies in a poetry

through which the world so invades the spirit of man that
he becomes almost speechless, and later reinvents language."

—Francis Ponge
The Voice of Things

1/Shifting our locus of motivation

Where have we been in literary criticism in my time? Well. like
Count Mippipopolus in *The Sun Also Rises*, we seem to have been
everywhere, seen and done everything. Here are just some of the
positions and battles which many of us have been into and through:
formalism, neoformalism, and contextualism; biographical, historical, and textual criticism; mythic, archetypal, and psychological
criticism; structuralism and phenomenology; spatial, ontological,
and—well, and so forth, and so forth. Individually and collectively,
we have been through so many great and original minds, that one
wonders what could possibly be left for experimental criticism to
experiment with just now.

Furthermore, there are so many resourceful and energetic minds
working out from even the merest suggestion of a new position, that
the permutations of even the most complex new theory or methodology are exhausted very quickly these days. If you do not get in on
the very beginning of a new theory, it is all over with before you can
even think it through, apply it, write it up, and send it out for
publication. The incredible storehouse of existing theories and
methods, coupled with the rapid aging (almost preaging, it seems) of
new critical theories and methods, has made for a somewhat curious
critical environment. For those who are happy with it, a fabulously
resourceful, seemingly limitless, pluralism is available: there is
something for everybody and almost anything can be done with it.
But for those whose need and bent is to go where others have not yet
been, no matter how remote that territory may be, there are some
problems: the compulsion toward newness acts like a forcing house
to produce theories which are evermore elegant, more baroque,
more scholastic, even, sometimes, somewhat hysterical—or/and,
my wife insists, testesical.

I don't mean to ridicule this motive; in fact, I have recently
defended it rather energetically.[1] I'm really reminding myself of

how things can go in endeavors such as this one, so that I can, if possible, avoid the freakism and exploitation latent in the experimental motive. Pluralism, a necessary and valuable position, which is not really a position at all, has certain obvious limitations because one always tries to keep up with what's new but must still work always with what has already been done and is already known. So what is to be done if one wants to do something that is worth doing, that is significant; if one is suffering from the pricks of historical conscience and consciousness; wanting to be "original," to add something new, but wanting to avoid the straining and posturing that often goes with this motive, and above all, wanting to avoid the Detroit syndrome, in which the new model is confused with the better or the intrinsically valuable. Whatever experimental criticism is about, the senseless creation of new models just to displace or replace old ones, or to beat out a competitor in the intellectual marketplace should not be the result. To confuse the life of the mind with the insane economy of the American automobile industry would be the worst thing we could do.

The more I have thought about the problem, the more it has seemed to me that for those of us who still wish to move forward out of critical pluralism, there must be a shift in our locus of motivation from newness, or theoretical elegance, or even coherence, to a principle of relevance. I am aware that there are certain obvious hazards inherent in any attempt to generate a critical position out of a concept of relevance, but that is what experiments are for. The most obvious and disastrous hazard is that of rigid doctrinal relevance—the old party-line syndrome. I have tried to avoid that. Specifically, I am going to experiment with the application of ecology and ecological concepts to the study of literature, because ecology (as a science, as a discipline, as the basis for a human vision) has the greatest relevance to the present and future of the world we all live in of anything that I have studied in recent years. Experimenting a bit with the title of this paper, I could say that I am going to try to discover something about the ecology of literature, or try to develop an ecological poetics by applying ecological concepts to the reading, teaching, and writing about literature. To borrow a splendid phrase from Kenneth Burke, one of our great experimental critics, I am going to experiment with the conceptual and practical possibilities of an apparent perspective by incongruity. Forward then. Perhaps that old pair of antagonists, science and poetry, can be persuaded to lie down together and be generative after all.

2/Literature and the biosphere

What follows can be understood as a contribution to human ecology, specifically, literary ecology, though I use (and transform) a considerable number of concepts from pure, biological ecology.

The problem now, as most ecologists agree, is to find ways of keeping the human community from destroying the natural community, and with it the human community. This is what ecologists like to call the self-destructive or suicidal motive that is inherent in our prevailing and paradoxical attitude toward nature. The conceptual and practical problem is to find the grounds upon which the two communities—the human, the natural—can coexist, cooperate, and flourish in the biosphere. All of the most serious and thoughtful ecologists (such as Aldo Leopold, Ian McHarg, Barry Commoner, and Garret Hardin) have tried to develop ecological visions which can be translated into social, economic, political, and individual programs of action. Ecology has been called, accurately, a subversive science because all these ecological visions are radical ones and attempt to subvert the continued-growth-economy which dominates all emerging and most developed industrial states. A steady or sustainable state economy, with an entirely new concept of growth, is central to all ecological visions. All this may seem rather remote from creating, reading, teaching, and writing about literature; but in fact, it is not. I invoke here (to be spelled out in detail later) the first Law of Ecology: "Everything is connected to everything else." This is Commoner's phrasing, but the law is common to all ecologists and all ecological visions. This need to see even the smallest, most remote part in relation to a very large whole is the central intellectual action required by ecology and of an ecological vision. It is not mind-bending or mind-blowing or mind-boggling; it is mind-expanding. As absurd as this may sound, the paper is about literature and the biosphere. This is no more absurd, of course, than the idea that man does not have the right to do anything he wants with nature. The idea that nature should also be protected by human laws, that trees (dolphins and whales, hawks and whooping cranes) should have lawyers to articulate and defend their rights is one of the most marvelous and characteristic parts of the ecological vision.

3/Energy pathways which sustain life

I'm going to begin with some ecological concepts taken from a great variety of sources more or less randomly arranged and somewhat poetically commented upon.

A poem is stored energy, a formal turbulence, a living thing, a swirl in the flow.

Poems are part of the energy pathways which sustain life.

Poems are a verbal equivalent of fossil fuel (stored energy), but they are a renewable source of energy, coming, as they do, from those ever generative twin matrices, language and imagination.

Some poems—say *King Lear*, *Moby Dick*, *Song of Myself*—seem to be, in themselves, ever-living, inexhaustible sources of stored energy, whose relevance does not derive solely from their meaning, but from their capacity to remain active in any language and to go on with the work of energy transfer, to continue to function as an energy pathway that sustains life and the human community. Unlike fossil fuels, they cannot be used up. The more one thinks about this, the more one realizes that here one encounters a great mystery; here is a radical differential between the ways in which the human world and the natural world sustain life and communities.

Reading, teaching, and critical discourse all release the energy and power stored in poetry so that it may flow through the human community; all energy in nature comes, ultimately, from the sun, and life in the biosphere depends upon a continuous flow of sunlight. In nature, this solar "energy is used once by a given organism or population, some of it is stored and the rest is converted into heat, and is soon lost" from a given ecosystem. The "one-way flow of energy" is a universal phenomenon of nature, where, according to the laws of thermodynamics, energy is never created or destroyed: it is only transformed, degraded, or dispersed, flowing always from a concentrated form into a dispersed (entropic) form. One of the basic formulations of ecology is that there is a one way flow of energy through a system but that materials circulate or are recycled and can be used over and over. Now, without oversimplifying these enormously complex matters, it would seem that once one moves out of the purely biological community and into the human community, where language and symbol-systems are present, things are not quite the same with regard to energy. The matter is so complex one hesitates to take it on, but one must begin, even hypothetically, somewhere, and try to avoid victimage or neutralization by simple-minded analogical thinking. In literature, all energy comes from the creative imagination. It does not come from language, because language is only one (among many) vehicles for the storing of creative energy. A painting and a symphony are also stored energy. And clearly, this stored energy is not just used once, converted, and lost from the human community. It is perhaps true that the life of the human community depends upon the continuous flow of creative energy (in all its forms) from the creative imagination and intelligence, and that this flow could be considered the sun upon which life in the human community depends; but it is not true that energy stored in a poem—*Song of Myself*—is used once, converted, and then lost from the ecosystem. It is used over and over again as a renewable resource by the same individual. Unlike nature, which has a single ultimate source of energy, the human community would seem to have many suns, resources, renewable and otherwise, to out-sun the sun itself. Literature in general and individual works in particular are one among many human suns. We need to discover ways of using this renewable energy-source to keep that other ultimate energy-source (upon which all life in the natural biosphere, and human communities, including human life, depends) flowing into the biosphere. We need to make some connections between literature and the sun, between teaching literature and the health of the biosphere.

Energy flows from the poet's language centers and creative imagination into the poem and thence, from the poem (which converts and stores this energy) into the reader. Reading is clearly an energy transfer as the energy stored in the poem is released and flows back into the language centers and creative imaginations of the readers. Various human hungers, including word hunger, are satisfied by this energy flow along this particular energy pathway. The concept of a poem as stored energy (as active, alive, and generative, rather than as inert, as a kind of corpse upon which one performs an autopsy, or an an art object one takes possession of, or as an antagonist—a knot of meanings—one must overcome) frees one from a variety of critical tyrannies, most notably, perhaps that of pure hermeneutics, the transformation of this stored creative energy directly into a set of coherent meanings. What a poem is saying is probably always less important than what it is doing and how—in the deep sense—it coheres. Properly understood, poems can be studied as models for energy flow, community building, and ecosystems. The first Law of Ecology—that everything is connected to everything else—applies to poems as well as to nature. The concept of the interactive field was operative in nature, ecology, and poetry long before it ever appeared in criticism.

Reading, teaching, and critical discourse are enactments of the poem which release the stored energy so that it can flow into the reader—sometimes with such intensity that one is conscious of an actual inflow; or, if it is in the classroom, one becomes conscious of the extent to which this one source of stored energy is flowing around through a community, and of how "feedback," negative or positive, is working.

Kenneth Burke was right—as usual—to argue that drama should be our model or paradigm for literature because a drama, enacted upon the stage, before a live audience, releases its energy into the human community assembled in the theater and raises all the energy levels. Burke did not want us to treat novels and poems as plays; he wanted us to become aware of what they were doing as creative verbal actions in the human community. He was one of our first critical ecologists.

Coming together in the classroom, in the lecture hall, in the seminar room (anywhere, really) to discuss or read or study literature, is to gather energy centers around a matrix of stored poetic/verbal energy. In some ways, this is the true interactive field because the energy flow is not just a two-way flow from poem to person as it would be in reading; the flow is along many energy pathways from poem to person, from person to person. The process is triangulated, quadrangulated, multiangulated) and there is, ideally, a raising of the energy levels which makes it possible for the highest motives of literature to accomplish themselves. These motives are not pleasure and truth, but creativity and community.

4/Poems as green plants

Ian McHarg—one of the most profound thinkers I have read who has tried to design a new model of reality based upon ecology—says that "perhaps the greatest conceptual contribution of the ecological view is the perception of the world and evolution as a creative process." He defines creation as the raising of matter from lower to higher order. In nature, he says, this occurs when some of the sun's energy is entrapped on its path to entropy. This process of entrapment and creation, he calls—somewhat cacophonously—negentropy, since it negates the negative process of entropy and allows energy to be saved from random dispersal and put to creative ends. Green plants, for example, are among the most creative organisms on earth. They are nature's poets. There is no end to the ways in which this concept can be applied to the human community, but let me stay close to the topic at hand. Poems are green plants among us; if poets are suns, then poems are green plants among us for they clearly arrest energy on its path to entropy and in so doing, not only raise matter from lower to higher order, but help to create a self-perpetuating and evolving system. That is, they help to create creativity and community, and when their energy is released and flows out into others, to again raise matter from lower to higher order (to use one of the most common descriptions of what culture is). One of the reasons why teaching and the classroom are so important (for literature, anyway) is that they intensify and continue this process by providing the environment in which the stored energy of poetry can be released to carry on its work of creation and community. The greatest teachers (the best ecologists of the classroom) are those who can generate and release the greatest amount of collective creative energy; they are the ones who understand that the classroom is a community, a true interactive field. Though few of us—maybe none of us—understand precisely how this idea can be used to the ends of biospheric health, its exploration would be one of the central problems which an ecological poetics would have to address.

5/The remorseless inevitableness of things

As a classic textbook by E. Odum on the subject tells us, ecology is always concerned with "levels beyond that of the individual organism. It is concerned with populations, communities, ecosystems, and the biosphere." By its very nature it is concerned with complex interactions and with the largest sets of interrelationships. We must remember Commoner's first Law of Ecology: "Everything is connected to everything else." The biosphere (or ecosphere) is the home that life has built for itself on the planet's outer surface. In that ecosphere there is a reciprocal interdependence of one life process upon another, and there is a mutual interconnected development of all of the earth's life systems. If we continue to teach, write, and write about poetry without acknowledging and trying to act upon the fact that—to cite a single example—all the oceans of our home are slowly being contaminated by all the pollutants disposed of in modern communities—even what we try to send up in smoke— then we will soon lose the environment in which we write and teach. All the creative processes of the biosphere, including the human ones, may well come to an end if we cannot find a way to determine the limits of human destruction and intrusion which the biosphere can tolerate, and learn how to creatively manage the biosphere. McHarg and others say that this is our unique creative role, but that as yet we have neither the vision nor the knowledge to carry it out, and that we do not have much more time to acquire both. This somewhat hysterical proposition is why I tried to write this paper and why, true to the experimental motive intrinsic to me as a human being, I have taken on the question of how reading, teaching, and writing about literature might function creatively in the biosphere, to the ends of biospheric purgation, redemption from human intrusions, and health.

As a reader and teacher and critic of literature, I have asked the largest, most important and relevant question about literature that I know how to ask. It is interesting, to me anyway, that eight years ago, trying to define my position, I was asking questions about the visionary fifth dimension and about how man is *released from the necessities of nature into this realm of pure being by means of literature*. Four years ago, attempting to do the same thing. I was writing about history as a symbol and about being boxed in the void, convinced that there were no viable concepts of or possibilities for the future, and about literary criticism as a necessary, endlessly dialectical process which helps to keep culture healthy and viable throughout history.[2] Nothing about nature and the biosphere in all this. Now here I am back on earth (from my heady space trips, from the rigors and pleasures of dialectic, from the histrionic metaphor of being boxed in the void) trying to learn something about what the ecologists variously call the laws of nature, the "body of inescapable natural laws," the "impotence principles" which are beyond our ability to alter or escape, the remorseless inevitableness of things, the laws of nature which are "decrees of fate." I have been trying to learn something by contemplating (from my vantage point in literature) one of ecology's basic maxims: "We are not free to violate the laws of nature." The view we get of humans in the biosphere from the ecologists these days is a tragic one, as pure and classic as the Greek or Shakespearean views: in partial knowledge or often in total ignorance (the basic postulate of ecology and tragedy is that humans precipitate tragic consequences by acting either in ignorance of or without properly understanding the true consequences of their actions), we are violating the laws of nature, and the retribution from the biosphere will be more terrible than any inflicted on humans by the gods. In ecology, man's tragic flaw is his anthropocentric (as opposed to biocentric) vision, and his compulsion to conquer, humanize, domesticate, violate, and exploit every natural thing. The ecological nightmare (as one gets it in Brunner's *The Sheep Look Up*) is of a monstrously overpopulated, almost completely polluted, all but totally humanized planet. These nightmares are all/if then projections; *if* everything continues as is, *then* this will happen. A common form of this nightmare is Garrett Hardin's ironic population projection: if we continue our present 2% growth rate indefinitely, then in only 615 years there will be standing room only on all the land areas of the world.

To simply absorb this tragic ecological view of our present and possible futures (if nothing occurs to alter our anthropocentric vision) into the doomsday syndrome is a comforting but specious intellectual, critical, and historical response; it dissipates action into the platitudes of purely archetypal and intellectual connections. Better to bring Shakespearean and Greek tragedy to bear upon our own biosphere's tragedy as a program for action than this—anyday. I will not attempt to deal here with the responses to the tragic/ doomsday ecological view generated by a commitment to the economic growth spiral or the national interest. Others have done it better than I ever could. Let me say here that the evidence is so overwhelming and terrifying that I can no longer even imagine (using any vision) the possibility of ignoring Ian McHarg's mandate in his sobering and brilliant book, *Design With Nature:*

Each individual has a responsibility for the entire biosphere and is required to engage in creative and cooperative activities.

As readers, teachers, and critics of literature, we are used to asking ourselves questions—often very complex and sophisticated ones—

about the nature of literature, critical discourse, language, curriculum, liberal arts, literature and society, literature and history; but McHarg has proposed new concepts of creativity and community so radical that it is even hard to comprehend them. As readers, teachers and critics of literature, how do we become responsible planet stewards? How do we ask questions about literature and the biosphere? What do we even ask? These are overwhelming questions. They fill one with a sense of futility and absurdity and provoke one's self-irony at the first faint soundings of the still largely ignorant, preaching, pontificating voice. How does one engage in responsible creative and cooperative biospheric action as a reader, teacher (especially this), and critic of literature? I think that we have to begin answering this question and that we should do what we have always done: turn to the poets. And then to the ecologists. We must formulate an ecological poetics. We must promote an ecological vision. At best, I can only begin here. Following McHarg and rephrasing a fine old adage, we can say that "where there is no ecological vision, the people will perish." And this ecological vision must penetrate the economic, political, social, and technological visions of our time, and radicalize them. The problem is not national, but global, planetary. It will not stop here. As Arthur Boughey points out, "There is no population, community, or ecosystem left on earth completely independent of the effects of human cultural behavior. Now [this human] influence has begun to spread beyond the globe to the rest of our planetary system and even to the universe itself."

6/The central paradox: powerless visions

One has to begin somewhere. Since literature is our business, let us begin with the poets or creators in this field and see if we can move toward a generative poetics by connecting poetry to ecology. As should be clear by now, I am not just interested in transferring ecological concepts to the study of literature, but in attempting to see literature inside the context of an ecological vision in ways which restrict neither and do not lead merely to proselytizing based upon a few simple generalizations and perceptions which have been common to American literature (at least) since Cooper, and are central to the whole transcendental vision as one gets it in Emerson, Thoreau,

Whitman, and Melville. As Barry Commoner points out, "The complex web in which all life is enmeshed, and man's place in it, are clearly—and beautifully—described in the poems of Walt Whitman," in Melville's *Moby Dick* and everywhere in Emerson and Thoreau. "Unfortunately," he says, with a kind of unintentional, but terrible understatement for literary people, "This literary heritage has not been enough to save us from ecological disaster." And here we are, back again before we even start, to the paradoxes which confront us as readers, teachers, and critics of literature—and perhaps as just plain citizens: the separation of vision and action; the futility of vision and knowledge without power.

7/The harshest, cruelest realities of our profession

Bringing literature and ecology together is a lesson in the harshest, cruelest realities which permeate our profession: we live by the word, and by the power of the word, but are increasingly powerless to act upon the word. Real power in our time is political, economic, and technological; real knowledge is increasingly scientific. Are we not here at the center of it all? We can race our verbal motors, spin our dialectical wheels, build more and more sophisticated systems, recycle dazzling ideas through the elite of the profession. We can keep going by charging ourselves back up in the classroom. In the end, we wonder what it all comes down to. Reading Commoner's (or almost any other serious ecologist's) statements, knowing they come from a formidable scientific knowledge, from direct involvement with the problems and issue from a deeply committed human being, can we help but wonder what we are doing teaching students to love poetry, to take literature seriously, to write good papers about literature:

Because the global ecosystem is a connected whole, in which nothing can be gained or lost and which is not subject to overall improvement, anything extracted from it by human effort must be replaced. Payment of this price cannot be avoided; it can only be delayed. The present environmental crisis is a warning that we have delayed nearly too long.

> . . . we are in an environmental crisis because the means
> by which we use the ecosphere to produce wealth are
> destructive of the ecosystem itself. The present system of
> production is self-destructive. The present course of
> human civilization is suicidal. In our unwitting march
> toward ecological suicide we have run out of options.
> Human beings have broken out of the circle of life, driven
> not by biological need, but by social organization which
> they have devised to conquer nature . . .

All my literary training tells me that this is not merely rhetoric, and
that no amount of rhetoric or manipulation of the language to political, economic, technological, or other ends, will make it go away. It
is a substantive, biosphere-wide reality we must confront and attempt to do something about.

8/The generosity of the poets

I will use what I know best and begin with the poets. If we begin
with the poets (who have never had any doubts about the seriousness and relevance of what they are doing), they teach us that
literature is an enormous, ever increasing, wonderfully diverse
storehouse of creative and cooperative energy which can never be
used up. It is like the gene-pool, like the best ecosystems. Literature
is a true cornucopia, thanks to the continuous generosity of the
poets, who generate this energy out of themselves, requiring, and
usually receiving, very little in return over and above the feedback
from the creative act itself.

This is probably nowhere more evident than in a book such as
Gary Snyder's *Turtle Island*; or, to take quite a different kind of text,
in Adrienne Rich's *Diving Into the Wreck*. What the poets do is
"Hold it close" and then "give it all away." What Snyder holds close
and gives away in *Turtle Island* is a complete ecological vision which
has worked down into every detail of his personal life and is the
result of many years of intellectual and personal wandering. Every
poem is an action which comes from a finely developed and refined
ecological conscience and consciousness. The book enacts a whole
program of ecological action; it is offered (like *Walden*) as a guide
book. It has in it one of the most useful and complete concepts of
renewable, creative human energy which can be put to creative and

cooperative biospheric ends that I know of. Its relevance for this paper is probably so obvious that I should not pursue it any longer.

The Generosity of Adrienne Rich's Diving into the Wreck. Things are very different in this book of poems, and not immediately applicable to the topic of this paper. But this book is the epitome—for me—of the ways in which poets are generous with themselves and can be used as models for creative, cooperative action. Without exception, the poems in this book are about the ecology of the female self, and they impinge upon the concerns of this paper in their treatment of men as destroyers (here of women rather than of the biosphere, but for remarkably similar reasons). As Margaret Atwood's profound ecological novel, *Surfacing*, makes clear, there is a demonstrable relationship between the ways in which men treat and destroy women and the ways in which men treat and destroy nature. Many of the poems—and in particular a poem such as "The Phenomenology of Anger"—are about how one woman changed and brought this destruction and suppression to an end, and about what changes must occur to bring the whole process to an end. A mind familiar with ecology cannot avoid the many profound and disturbing connections to be made here between women and western history, nature and western history.

The Deconstructive Wisdom of W. S. Merwin's: Lice. One of the most continuously shattering experiences of my intellectual life has been the reading, teaching, and thenceforth re-reading and re-teaching of this book of poems. This is one of the most profound books of poems written in our time and one of the great ecological texts of any time. Whatever has been argued from factual, scientific, historical, and intellectual evidence in the ecology books that I read is confirmed (and more) by the imaginative evidence of this book of poems. Merwin's generosity consists in the extraordinary efforts he made to deconstruct the cumulative wisdom of western culture and then imaginatively project himself into an almost unbearable future. Again, as with Adrienne Rich, these poems are about the deep inner changes which must occur if we are to keep from destroying the world and survive as human beings. I know of no other book of poems so aware of the biosphere and what humans have done to destroy it as this one. Reading this book of poems requires one to unmake and remake one's mind. It is the most painfully constructive book of poems I think I have ever read. What these poems affirm over and over is that if a new ecological vision is to emerge, the old destructive western one must be deconstructed and abandoned. This is exactly what Rich's poems say about men and women.

The Energy of Love in Walt Whitman's Song of Myself. This energy flows out of Whitman into the world (all the things of the world) and back into Whitman from the things of the world in one of the most marvelous ontological interchanges one can find anywhere in poetry. This ontological interchange between Whitman and the biosphere is the energy pathway that sustains life in Whitman and, so far as he is concerned, in the biosphere. There is a complete ecological vision in this poem, just as there is in Whitman's conception of a poetry cycle which resembles the water cycle within the biosphere. Whitman says that poems come out of the poets, go up into the atmosphere to create a kind of poetic atmosphere, come down upon us in the form of poetic rain, nourish us and make us creative and then are recycled. Without this poetic atmosphere and cultural cycle, he says, we would die as human beings. A lovely concept, and true for some of us, but it has not yet resolved the disjunction (as Commoner points out) between vision and action, knowledge and power.

The Biocentric Vision of Faulkner's Absalom, Absalom! Can we not study this great fiction, and its central character, Thomas Sutpen, in relation to one of the most fundamental of all ecological principles: "That nature is an interacting process, a seamless web, that it [nature] is responsive to laws, that it constitutes a value system with intrinsic opportunities and constraints upon human use." There is an ecological lesson for all of us in the ferocious destructiveness of human and natural things brought about by Thomas Sutpen.

Looking upon the World, Listening and Learning with Henry David Thoreau. Does he not tell us that this planet, and the creatures who inhabit it, including men and women, were, have been, are now, and are in the process of becoming? A beautiful and true concept of the biosphere. His model of reality was so new, so radical even in the mid-nineteenth century, that we have still not been able to absorb and act upon it more than a hundred years later.

Entropy and Negentropy in Theodore Roethke's "Greenhouse," "Lost Son," and "North American Sequence." Was there ever a greater ecological, evolutionary poet of the self than Roethke, one who really believed that ontology recapitulates phylogeny, one so close to his evolutionary predecessors that he experiences an interchange of being with them and never demeans them with personification and seldom with metaphor. Kenneth Burke's brilliant phrase—vegetal radicalism—still takes us to the ecological centers of Roethke, self-absorbed, self-obsessed as he was.

But enough of this. The poets have always been generous. I mean only to suggest a few ecological readings of texts I know well. Teaching and criticism are the central issues here, so let me move on toward some conclusions.

9/Teaching and critical discourse as forms of symbiosis

"Creativeness is a universal prerequisite which man shares with all creatures." The central, modern idea of the poet, of literature, and of literary criticism is based upon the postulate that humans are capable of genuine creation and that literature is one of the enactments of this creative principle. Taking literature to ecology by way of McHarg's statement joins two principles of creativity so that humans are acting in concert with the rest of the biosphere, but not necessarily to the ends of biospheric health. That has always been the problem. Some of our most amazing creative achievements— say in chemistry and physics—have been our most destructive. Culture—one of our great achievements wherever we have gone—has often fed like a great predator and parasite upon nature and never entered into a reciprocating energy-transfer, into a recycling relationship with the biosphere. In fact, one of the most common antinomies in the human mind is between culture/ civilization, and nature/wilderness. As Kenneth Burke pointed out some time ago, man's tendency is to become rotten with perfection. As Burke ironically formulated it, man's entelechy is technology. Perceiving and teaching (even writing about) human creativity in this larger ecological context could be done in all literature courses and especially in all creative writing courses. It could only have a salutary effect. It would make the poet and the green plants brothers and sisters; it would charge creative writing and literature with ecological purpose.

Symbiosis, according to McHarg, is the "cooperative arrangement that permits increase in the levels of order": it is this cooperative arrangement that permits the use of energy in raising the levels of matter. McHarg says that symbiosis makes negentropy possible; he identifies negentropy as the creative principle and process at work in the biosphere which keeps everything moving in the evolutionary direction which has characterized the development of all life in the biosphere. Where humans are involved and where literature provides the energy source within the symbiotic arrangement. McHarg says that a very complex process occurs in which energy is transmuted into information and thence into meaning by means of a process he calls apperception. As McHarg demonstrated in his book, both the process of apperception and the meaning which results from it can be used to creative, cooperative ends in our management of the biosphere. The central endeavor, then, of any ecological poetics would have to be a working model for the processes of transformation which occur as one moves from the stored creative energy of the poem, to its release by reading, teaching, or writing, to its transmutation into meaning and finally, to its application, in an ecological value system, to what McHarg variously calls "fitness and fitting," and to "health"—which he defines as "creative fitting" and by which he means to suggest our creation of a fit environment. This work could transform culture and help bring our destruction of the biosphere to an end.

Now there is no question that literature can do all this, but there are a lot of questions as to whether it does in fact do it, how, and how effectively. All these concerns might well be central for teachers and critics of literature these days. We tend to over-refine our conceptual frameworks so that they can only be used by a corps of elitist experts and gradually lose their practical *relevance* as they increase their theoretical *elegance*. I am reminded here of the stridently practical questions Burke asked all through the thirtys and early forties and of the scorn with which they were so often greeted by literary critics and historians of his time. But none of these questions is antithetical to literature and there is a certain splendid resonance which comes from thinking of poets and green plants being engaged in the same creative, life-sustaining activities, and of teachers and literary critics as creative mediators between literature and the biosphere whose tasks include the encouragement of, the discovery, training, and development of creative biospheric apperceptions, attitudes, and actions. To charge the classroom with ecological purpose one has only to begin to think of it in symbiotic terms as a cooperative arrangement which makes it possible to release the stream of energy which flows out of the poet and into the poem, out of the poem and into the readers, out of the readers and into the classroom, and then back into the readers and out of the classroom with them, and finally back into the other larger community in a never ending circuit of life.

10/But . . .

I stop here, short of action, halfway between literature and ecology, the energy pathways obscured, the circuits of life broken between words and actions, vision and action, the verbal domain and the non-verbal domain, between literature and the biosphere—because I can't go any further. The desire to join literature to ecology originates out of and is sustained by a Merwin-like condition and question: how can we apply the energy, the creativity, the knowledge, the vision we know to be in literature to the human-made problems ecology tells us are destroying the biosphere which is our home? How can we translate literature into purgative-redemptive biospheric action; how can we resolve the fundamental paradox of this profession and get out of our heads? How can we turn words into something other than more words (poems, rhetoric, lectures, talks, position papers—the very substance of an MLA meeting: millions and millions of words; endlessly recirculating among those of us in the profession); how can we do something more than recycle WORDS?

Let experimental criticism address itself to this dilemma.

How can we move from the community of literature to the larger biospheric community which ecology tells us (correctly, I think) we belong to even as we are destroying it?

Free us from figures of speech.

NOTES

I have not documented all of the quotations from, paraphrases of, and references to ecological works because there are so many of them and I wanted the paper to be read right through. The paper is literally a kind of patchwork of ecological material. I have identified my major sources and resources in the bibliography. The only things I felt should be identified were my own works because the references to them would be obscure and quite incomprehensible otherwise.

1. In "Literary Criticism and History: The Endless Dialectic," *New Literary History*, VI (1974–75), 491–512.
2. Respectively, in:
   a) "Kenneth Burke and Structuralism," *Shenandoah*, XXI (Autumn, 1969), 19–28.
   b) "Literary Criticism and History."
   c) "History as Symbol: Boxed in the Void," above.

BIBLIOGRAPHY

I have drawn upon the following books in a great variety of ways. I list them here to acknowledge some of the ecological resources I have used.

Marston Bates, *The Forest and the Sea: A Look at the Economy of Nature and the Ecology of Man*, Mentor, 1906.
Gregory Bateson, *Steps to an Ecology of Mind*. Ballantine, 1972.
Arthur S. Boughey, *Man and the Environment: an Introduction to Human Ecology and Evolution*. Second Edition, MacMillan, 1975.
Barry Commoner, *The Closing Circle: Nature, Man, and Technology*. Bantam Books, 1972.
The Crisis of Survival. Scott Foresman and Company, 1970.
Raymond Dasmann, *Planet in Peril: Man and the Biosphere Today*. New York: World Publishing, 1972.
Garrett Hardin, *Exploring New Ethics for Survival: The Voyage of the Spaceship Beagle*. New York: Viking Press, 1972.
The House We Live In: an Environmental Reader. New York: MacMillan, 1971.
Edward J. Kormandy, *Concepts of Ecology*. Concepts of Modern Biology Series, Prentice-Hall, 1969.
Aldo Leopold, *Sand County Almanac*. Ballantine, 1966 (original publication).
Ian McHarg, *Design with Nature*. Doubleday/Natural History Press, 1971, (original date, 1969).
Helen and Scott Nearing, *Living the Good Life: How to Live Sanely and Simply in a Troubled World*. New York, Schocken Books, 1970.
Eugene Odum, *Ecology*, Modern Biology Series, Holt, Rinehart, Winston, 1963.
G. J. C. Smity, H. J. Steck, G. Surette, *Our Ecological Crisis: Its Biological, Economic, and Political Dimensions*. New York: MacMillan, 1974.
Gary Snyder, *Turtle Island*. New York: New Direction, 1974.
The Subversive Science: Essays Toward an Ecology of Man. Ed., Shepard and McKinley. Boston: Houghton Mifflin, 1969.
Who Speaks for Earth. Papers from the 1972 Stockholm conference. New York: Norton, 1973.

GHOSTS LIKE THEM

fiction by SHIRLEY ANN TAGGART

from THE HUDSON REVIEW

nominated by THE HUDSON REVIEW

I. AUNT AMANDA JANE

DEAR AMANDA JANE, SHE WRITES. But she is too ashamed and guilty to continue. Ashamed of her contempt and fear of Amanda Jane, of the name Amanda Jane itself, the way it makes her think of black women in white kitchens, of Aunt Jemima. Although, she herself had loved Aunt Jemima once; as a little girl. A little girl dreaming on her aunt's front porch. Dreamed Aunt Jemima into the kitchen to bake special cakes for Angela Powers. But Aunt Jemima always turned in those dreams and viciously locked the oven door, so that she, Angela, would have to watch all the cakes turn black and burn to ashes. But when she woke up crying, Aunt Amanda Jane, sitting on that porch with her, would take Angela into her big arms and tell her sternly that bad dreams was God's reminder to sinners to make their peace with the Lord, and you was never too young to make your peace, to drive off the devil.

So how can she write Miss Amanda Jane Powers, Natchez, Mississippi, without feeling her soul burning and going to hell, without seeing her Aunt Amanda Jane with her straw hat and the Bible she couldn't read, rocking on an old weathered rocking chair on her front porch. Her Aunt Amanda Jane with her old black eyes fumbling in their yellow sockets, grabbing at Angela's face, her thin body, saying, "Amen, girl, Amen. I been there and back. Yes, Lawd, I been there and back." An old heavy black woman who is neither particularly impatient nor particularly peaceful with all her flesh, just a little tired of it, a little bored with it. "But it jes a house, Angela Ann, jes a house, honey, and the Lawd seen fit to give me a big one and if He seen fit to do it, then I seen fit to keep it."

Yesterday from Philadelphia, Pennsylvania, Angela Powers said, "How is she?" Her mother in Mississippi said, "She's an old woman, Angela." Her mother sighed into the telephone not in sympathy or resignation, but just as a habit. "But you don't think she'll die, do you Mama?" And she imagined her mother shaking her head, sad and intense and tired herself, before she said, "Honey, that old woman's been dead a long time now, her body just ain't believed it yet."

Ten years ago, she, Angela Powers, had sat on that old rotting front porch with her. A skinny nineteen-year-old girl from a poor Mississippi family of eleven children, all younger than her, yet home from college in those summers not to teach the children, but the aunt (who even then was well into her eighties, well into dying). A promising young woman on a full scholarship to a northern university, mysteriously compelled home into that fiercely hot summer sun in Natchez, to teach her aunt that the Lord didn't give her a fat body, a tired body; that, she, herself, made her body fat, made it tired.

Going off every day to her aunt's porch until her mother had said, "Lawd, child, what do you want with that old woman?"

And she would shrug her awkwardly tall and thin body and say, "I don't know, Mama."

But she had refused dates to sit on that porch with her, refused offers to drive into town with the tall predatory young men and sometimes older men, that hovered around her aunt's front gate, its broken-down condition, its peeling paint.

"I ain't never read me no books," was all her aunt had said, "and girl I ain't about to now." And then she sang, "Ain't about to leave you, Lawd. Ain't about to."

But Angela, always patient and polite, would continue sitting there reading out loud; sitting with her hair pulled painfully and neatly straight back from her high-cheekboned face, her continually washed and creamed face. Whose aunt had even said she could smell the mothballs and cleaning liquids still on Angela's sweaters and skirts. An old aunt whose voice would come on with a sudden power like a radio left on high, violently plugged in, and would sink into Angela's ears, anchor in her heart. "You stink, chile. You stink like a new bicycle and you gonna rust, chile. I knows, chile. I knows."

So sometimes she had hated her, her Aunt Amanda Jane; rocking there on that front porch that looked out over nothing now but broken rhubarb stems and ghosts of cotton plants. Hated that old woman singing and rocking there; picking at her decayed teeth between songs, and tapping on her chair a different beat from whatever songs she sang; as if there was such a multitude of songs, such an urgency to sing them, that they had had to appear in pairs, multiples. And how that had confused Angela, tangled up her words, until her aunt, alert to sounds, their patterns in space, had said, "Don't mumble, girl."

Yes, and hated her aunt's laziness too, her preaching from a rocking chair she never left to know one way or another what she was preaching about. Angela's mother had told her that Amanda Jane had been a flirt, a tease, but that men sensed that stubborn density of her soul, its competence and independence too; the Amanada Jane Powers who could go out in a heavy storm, her hair all done up for a date and a new dress just sewed; could go out and direct all her brothers and sisters to getting the animals inside and who brought in the last pig herself. So she had plenty of proposals, although one sweetheart was killed, but she said she wasn't about to marry him anyway, so who knows. But she never did get married, never did anything past 25, when her father died and left her in the house; had brothers and cousins and then nephews and then great-nephews to look after her. Took right to the porch, sewing in the beginning, and talking about opening a sewing place, selling her quilts and dresses, but then after awhile, just rocking and remembering. So, of course, Angela couldn't help pitying her, pitying the way her life slipped into the wood she rocked in; but pitying her from far away exactly like she thought some white northerner with a brand new color TV might, turning into a documentary on the south, taking time to sigh and shake their heads before turning the channel. But then she would feel ashamed. Because, really, she loved her aunt.

But couldn't write to her. Even said she didn't have time to visit her the last time she was home. Said she didn't have time to see an old woman rock and sing and not even know you're there; an old woman who might even die right there, right in front of Angela herself. Although her mother had laughed that same mournful trying to be joyful sound of her aunt's songs, and said, "No, honey, you ain't about to see that." But when her mother had turned back to washing down the kitchen floor, she had said, "Then you wouldn't have to worry about death no more, child. You'd have to worry about the ressurection."

No, wasn't going over to see her aunt six months ago when she was home, until her mother had leaned her own deep, dark face into Angela's and said, "You my daughter, girl, my flesh and blood; but girl, you as cold as the north you live in." So it was fear that got her over those three-hundred yards to her aunt's porch; guilty and ashamed in that hot stagnant Mississippi air.

Was it fear of her aunt dying, she had thought, or fear of an aunt who at ninety-five, wouldn't die?

Yet she loved her.

And was afraid of her. Of the way she sang, so loud and uncontrolled. Afraid of the wrinkles in her aunt's face, the wrinkles even in her faded white socks pulled down below her heavy black ankles. And Angela would become a little dizzy at this loss of moisture and life in her aunt's skin, even mirrored in her aunt's clothes, as if the woman herself had already left them, routinely and unsentimentally abandoned them, moved inward. Her Aunt Amanda Jane turning inward upon herself like a dead star in space.

In the last summer before she graduated from college, she had gone over to see her aunt and her aunt had said, "A woman's got to be saved, chile. She was His second thought and He wasn't yet done with her when the world got started. So she needed a man, honey."

But she hadn't needed those men in Mississippi, men who hung around on a broken gate, smelling of chewing tobacco and a boisterous camaraderie. "Good afternoon, Mizz Angela. Ain't it a good afternoon, Mizz Angela. Now ain't it just a real fine afternoon?" Dragging out the word fine with their wide mocking toothy grins.

Her aunt said, "If a woman not saved by love and childruns, her soul jes dries up and dies, chile. Dries up and dies. Oh Lawdy, you can hear it crack. Yes, Lawd. Happened to women I knows. Women, I knows, chile."

So in the late summer afternoons of 1967 Angela dreamed she saw images in the haze of her aunt's front porch. Of her savior who would be the strongest, blackest man she had ever seen. One day washing dishes with her sisters she thought she saw him coming through the field in the back. But up close, she recognized him as a preacher and saw him put his arms around their mother who had run out the back door drying her hands on her dress. Angela stood stiff and still when her mother came back inside. "Was it . . . ?" And she was surprised at her panic, her fear, and her coldness. "Why honey, no," her mother had said startled, guessing her question. "It was Grandma Powers who went with the Lord." And she wondered how she could have forgotten her Grandmother Powers deathly sick in her bed and still reciting her tales of Mississippi that Angela's brother Latent, at 16, convinced of his pending importance and superiority, had generously vowed to write and publish. So that later, the preacher had said she had died slightly frantic, angry at the Lord for taking her too soon, right in the middle of that final story. The end lost forever in ordinary Mississippi dirt and rock.

But her brother, Latent, believed in ghosts, in his grandmother reappearing, in the ending being revealed to him. He believed in ghosts, more than in her, his sister, who he admitted was exceptionally bright, but whom he was convinced would get lost, become anonymous and harmless in marriage and fertility, like so many other sisters, all the sisters he had ever known. Impotent with their big bellies and their big breasts, he had said. But it was all right. Acceptable for women. Only men needed to commit suicide.

In the late summer evenings her savior committed murder and theft. In the movies downtown. Breaking up rocks on a chain gang with Sidney Poitier. Or maybe even Sidney Poitier himself. A man so strong she imagined she could smell his sweat, like hot burnt rubber, all the way through the paper movie screen in the concrete church basement on Farm Street. Heard his cry through the giggling and whistles, when he finally broke the rock, when he said in that fierce amplified whisper, his black face blazing with sweat, "God, I can't stay here. These men are dead. And I'm still alive." And when he was sentenced to die she dreamed that she was the woman he saw in that movie, the woman who turned his soul to love and repentence; and mystically, magically this saved her. She was saved.

II. ENRIQUE JONES

In real life she was also finally saved. His name was Enrique Jones, a tall, exotic looking black man who wore hand embroidered Swedish shirts and vests sent to him by a sister in Scandinavia, so that he almost looked like a shepherd, lost in the wrong land, the wrong contour of the earth, in the mountainless, flat, sea-level city of Philadelphia. Enrique Jones, her savior. His mother was Spanish and his father was black and the combination of strange bloods never quite jelled, so that Enrique never quite understood Spanish and never quite identified with blacks, with any of their rallies, their tears, their rage. He only understood rage in a purer, more impersonal sense and when he broke Angela's nose with his fist, he had cried. Gently and lovingly he tried to persuade her that it wasn't personal, that it wasn't even because he hated his job, hated collecting people's trash, because, he joked, even those rich, smart-assed politicians had to do that, all that wealth and power and they still had to take people's trash every day! And they couldn't even punch out at 4:00 either. Enslaved forever with other people's trash! And he would laugh heavily, heartily, at this irony until he had had too much beer or until his friends left or until he felt sick. And then he might hit her again, punch her in the stomach. But it wasn't personal, he would tell her; he loved her, god how he loved her. And then he would watch television, watch people in new clothes wander into ski lodges and unwrap fancy bottles of booze in front of a fireplace, and over their heads, wooden rafters, that someone could have rubbed their skin, their goddamn soul out polishing. And through those big glass windows was new snow; all white and clean like those faces, all those contented, uncluttered white faces smiling at him. And on another channel, doctors staring seriously, thoughtfully at patients; prescribing perfect treatments, exercises, love. White male doctors. Over 40. Fatherly and respected. And then suddenly they were younger. And then women. And now black. But all with the same smiles, all pointing fearlessly, confidently, to the remedy, the cure. But he could never quite focus on the cure, never quite concentrate on those prescriptions because he would be trying to remember when it started. When he first saw them. Those doctors. And it gives him a headache, a pounding and throbbing in his head trying to remember all those puffy, broken-up streets in his old neighborhood; his youth in those potholes, those bars, so cloudy and noisy with the same people, the same dudes, the same friendly slaps, the same angry punches. But the TV was always going, he remembers that, remembers the exact day they got color TV's downtown, has a good memory; but there were never black doctors, never, he would have noticed. And he can't imagine who snuck out, Jesus Christ, who would even think of sneaking out and masquerading as a doctor?

So he broke her nose, and her glass Christmas tree ornaments, and their daughter's wrist. When she left, he said it was personal, it was personal now. Very personal. He said, "Woman, I'll kill you if you leave." He said, "You hear? You hear that woman?" And his rage had finally taken shape, crystallized. But when she was out the door he ran after her, yelled from the sidewalk to her, "Get your fucking little ass out of here, woman. And don't you come running back. Don't you ever come running back."

And she could feel him behind her, watching her, trying to hypnotize her with his eyes, trying to pull her back to him. So she didn't turn around once. Not once. And then what? And then nothing.

III. ANGELA POWERS JONES

She just walked straight ahead and didn't look back. Walked into this apartment with Mandy, her nine-year-old daughter, and signed the lease, signed him out of her life, and she didn't cry once. Since then she hasn't seen him, doesn't want to, but hasn't bothered with a divorce the way the people in this neighborhood don't always bother with marriage, with written laws; the powerful inertia of all those words and papers that drive educated men to horror movies and roller coasters, to get going again, to get their blood moving again.

But she still lives in Philadelphia, a city with historic landmarks, the Liberty Bell. The cracks in the bell for when freedom starts to break apart, break down into slavery again. But when she married Enrique and had a child, there were things she had to do, meals she had to cook, love she had to give to a man who was her husband. And she didn't cry when he hit her, hardly moved at all. He said she was so good, even her body was so good, not crazy and out of control like his body; and then he would start to cry and she would comfort him. Other times he caressed her and said, "How do you live with me? How are you so brave?"

Didn't whimper or scream like her sisters did, five sisters still in that shack at home on that burned-out farmland in Mississippi with a hundred kids and animals and lovers running over them, keeping their faces down so close to the dried-up useless soil that they wouldn't leave because it wouldn't feel right, because that was their home. But with no way out for them anyway; no scholarships and no beauty. Their mother had said Angela was the only one about to get anywhere. And if she didn't get anywhere, her mother had said, no one she knew in the whole world would.

But once when he slapped her, slapped her hard, and then looked right into her face, into how hard she tried not to change that face, not to remember that slap, he had gotten angry and said, "Je-sus woman. Are you human?" But she was always in love with him. She doesn't remember a time when she wasn't in love with him, just a time when she had to go away and not look back. Like going away to college had been. And now she dreams of walking in tunnels. Of doors being slammed shut. And this bothers her. Because wasn't leaving home, going to college, leaving a husband who beat her, weren't these good decisions? Wise decisions? Wouldn't psychiatrists agree with this, applaud her; so many people couldn't do that well. Couldn't just walk out of a life like that. Like she did.

But she still lives in the same kind of neighborhood, a neighborhood that is a little worn-out and neglected. A neighborhood starting to shrivel, crack, like old photographs kept too long, kept in too much light; as if the light from the city was too powerful for neighborhoods so close and unprotected. A neighborhood that could burn and turn to ashes, like something in a childhood nightmare that she can almost taste, that makes her uneasy.

So she sits on guard at her window on the fourth floor. Looking out for whole days while Mandy's in school. At the holes in the streets. The broken bottles and old tires in yards, wherever there are yards.

At the collasped buildings. The condemned buildings. At the collapsing wooden fence around a vacant lot across the street with "Jarcy and Jimmy '77" in big awkward red letters, and in a corner on that same fence, in piercing angular black print: "You die, man."

In the afternoons she watches the adolescent boys stand around and pass out plastic bags of drugs and put them in their jackets. Watches them push each other against the fence and laugh, imitating violence, but not violent yet, not ready in the daylight to try and blast the souls out of their own or each other's bodies yet; but excited, desperate to get out, to take off, to get away finally from so many people so close screaming into each other's hearts, or on hot nights, all vegetating in crowds outside on their steps like colonies of seals. She thinks that's what it looks like from up here, from her window.

And in the mornings she watches the prostitutes come home in their flashy clothes and heavy make-up. And the old men and old women asleep or drunk on someone's front steps. The most harmless people in this neighborhood and yet these are the ones that panic her, like dead fish washed up on beaches always do, as if there was some disaster just out of the corners of her eyes that could suddenly move in and destroy her. But she knows these old people are not dead, not even very dramatic, just lonely and tired. But she would like to take their pulses, listen to their hearts; shake their old bony shoulders right out of their skins just to make sure they are still there.

But most of the time she watches the strangers, well-dressed strangers not from this neighborhood, who walk quickly from block to block, absorbed and entranced by their destinations, seeing nothing.

Her destination today was the supermarket, the welfare office. But she tells herself it's all right, the welfare, the food stamps, won't always be like this, things will change, get better, after all she has a college degree, a diploma, something magic, the first in her family. So she has to remember that. "But in history?" An employment counsellor had said, astonished, but a very familiar, routine astonishment. He had said, "Well, you know you can't do anything with that." And then he asked her what machines she could operate, was she familiar with any of the machines on this list?

But one of the employment counsellors was friendly, sympathetic. She was a little older than Angela, a white woman, pretty, but a woman who wore a little more make-up, a little more force in her smile than Angela. She studied her a minute and then said, "Your boyfriend made a bad husband and you got a couple kids, right? And you don't know what to do. Oh, honey, I know." She took her hand. "I know. And look at this, you graduated from college. But honey, I got a kid in here today with a master's degree in something you couldn't even pronounce, and I don't want to discourage you, but she was useless, good lord, didn't know anything you need to know to live, to keep alive."

And good grades. Angela always had good grades, and good grades must mean something. She was convinced of it. She must be able to do something. Her mother said she could come home, that's what she could do. She said Latent was working in a plant in Birmingham part-time, "but he still thinking about his ghosts, still waiting for Grandma's ghost to finish that book of his. Amanda Jane has a touch of the flu, been in bed all week, nothing serious, but wants to hear from you. Keeps asking if there's a letter from Angela Ann. Keep the Lord in your heart and come home. Love, Mama."

She tears up the letter. She didn't believe in ghosts, she didn't even believe in her fear of ghosts, only Aunt Amanda Jane believed in that. She would tell Angela's stiff little body, "Now don' you worry bout them ghosts Latent tell you bout, he ain't gonna conjure up no ghosts. Even if he could, oh, Lawdy, help us, they never hurt you honey, cause ghosts is the soul. Theys not the body that does, theys the soul that is. Ghosts like them, they might wanna scream up the grass in the winna, and oh, Lawdy, they in pain, yes, Lawd; but ghosts like them, chile, they jes can't do nuthin. They jes can't."

She throws the pieces of the letter into a wastebasket in her living room.

Her living room is a greenish-brown, with a little blue. A couple of worn blue tweed chairs and the wallpaper is light green with brown dancing women who have cried the whole way down one wall, the wall that faces the street, the rain and the snow. She asked the landlord about the leaks, said he was letting his own apartment depreciate, it wasn't her wallpaper after all. He had smiled, the kind of smile babies smile by accident, with a burp. He had said, "Yes." Just yes. So she let them cry, all those women who lost their limbs, their faces. Good, she thought that they should be mutilated by nature and not by men. But how did it happen? How did her husband break her nose? And how could she know when even

Sidney Poitier on a chain gang, a convicted murderer, gave her such a gentle, loving look? Her mother agreed with Enrique's gentle soul; she had said, "You treat this man good, honey." Of course Angela had known Enrique had gotten into fights, knifed someone once. A long time ago. But his life with her would be different. Saved by their love. Protected. Yes, she admitted she was tired and needed protecting. But wasn't that her privilege, after all, as a woman? No, those were someone else's words. She, Angela Powers Jones, advocated equality. And in their marriage they both had had an equal chance to escape, to die gracefully.

Dear Amanda Jane, she writes from an old round kitchen table with a formica top. Writing Dear Amanda eternally, she believes, into her one hundredth year of life. One hundred sheets of her daughter's tablet paper crumpled up and stuffed under the exposed pipes of her kitchen sink, although later she would dig them out and count them and find that, really, there were only 15. Dear Amanda Jane, she writes, but a friend of hers from college, whom she hasn't seen since college, comes over and interrupts her with her good clothes, her good job, her advanced degrees; she takes her hand and says, "Oh, Angela." Her friend's face is disappointed, compassionate, going out of control. But Angela's face, her perfect smile, her perfect bone structure and perfect teeth are convincing, persuasive. She says, "It's not so bad, really. It's just the wallpaper. It's such an awful color." Later, her friend, brave in her expensive dress, her neatly sculptured afro, her solid gold hoop earrings, asks, "But a man like that, Angela? A man who would physically abuse you?"

Angela shrugs. She looks out the window at the buildings. Buildings like her building. Old and dirty with small cement yards. And she thinks that some place else in Philadelphia things must be growing, coming alive. She thinks of trees and grass and flowers, and she feels suddenly deserted, angry.

Her friend makes an effort to sit neatly in one of Angela's sagging chairs, not to get stuffing on her dress. She says, "Angela Powers. Our social conscience. That Angela Powers shrugs?" She makes another effort to laugh, to joke about this. Then enthusiastically she says, "Angela, remember that paper you read in sociology? About our people struggling to get up north where the cold air will revive them, but with the cotton still caught under their fingernails. Remember? And about their new life in the north, how ironically it wasn't new at all, but the same. The same rats and the same weariness to be white, so that they felt cheated, as if they had been purposefully distracted at that moment when things were going to change. Remember that? God, Angela, we couldn't believe it was you . . . you were always so quiet. And remember our professor, Miss Dover, a white conservative woman, a little sickly, and how we swore she turned even whiter, embalmed right there at her own familiar worn desk she had written a poem about. Do you remember that? A poem about a *desk!* But anyway, your paper and Miss Dover, god, I've remembered that all these years!" Angela says nothing and after a minute her friend leans out of her chair and reaches over and touches Angela's hand again. She says, "If you ever want to talk about it. . . ." Angela doesn't move, she thinks only how hot it is. As hot as Mississippi. And it's only April. Only spring and still expected to be pleasant, comfortable.

She gets up and opens the window, feeling a little dizzy, a little tired. But in her mind she sees that her sociology professor does turn a little whiter, paler, behind that solid mahogany desk. A little shocked on such a routinely drowsy late May afternoon. And Angela feels that this, this must be something.

Her friend says, "Angela . . . ?" She says other things also, but Angela is only aware of the beat of that other black woman's voice, aware of the beat of the tires, the horns outside, a faster, more demanding beat that continually assaults and wears down the streets and eardrums of her neighborhood. And she wonders what the beat is like in Africa in 1978, the Africa she sees on the news, and whether the beat of a thousand guns and bodies being pounded into the ground will destroy their forests; their jungles. But secretly, she wonders how really this has anything to do with her.

Her friend says, "Angela, can I help you? Is there any way I can help?"

"You help them," a skinny, angry young college woman of the 1960's says in her mind, "You help them set up programs. You give them food. And yet they deceive you, they cheat you and your government. They take your money and watch your televisions, your dreams. Because their dreams aren't so visible, so concrete. Surely you know that. And your dreams are too expensive, too impossible for them. And they know this, they smell this like they smelled those sweet suffocating lilacs, that wet cotton and oily sweat that permanently opened, widened their nostrils."

Words rehearsed over and over in a life she can hardly remember so it is a surprise they are still there, still in perfect order. She looks out the window and the bricks in the building across the street make her feel dizzy and confused, the way she felt dizzy for two months before her freshman year in college, alarming her parents. What was she just thinking about? Suddenly she can't remember. But who was that vicious accusing college girl with all those white faces staring at her, and four black ones too, all staring blankly at her. And who was this woman now who stared out her window all day, rocking on a rocking chair. No, that at least, wasn't true, she didn't have a rocking chair. And she did do something, she did take care of her daughter, of course, and she does have a college degree. . . .

Her friend comes over to her, concerned with her silence, her appearance of nausea and sickness, concerned also with the dust that makes her cough, blown in from somewhere she can't see. But she manages to ask Angela if she is all right. Is she all right? Angela, her mind blank now, not dizzy anymore, assures her she is fine, fine in her strong thin, handsome black body, she is just tired. Saw her lover last night, not a violent man either, not very violent at all. And her daughter will be home from school soon. And the dishes have to be washed, and the roaches chased off the counters; her daughter is very fussy, squeamish; not good at all in the role of a poor minority child. Her friend says, "God, Angela, look at me. You can do better, girl. Girl, you can do so much better." Angela says of course, she plans on it. She smiles and says, "Don't worry about me, Rennie." She stares at her hands, so long and thin and graceful. "I think I'll become a doctor. Enrique hated doctors. Was scornful of them. Scornful of healing itself." She says, but today she is just so tired. Her friend nods, and they walk together to the door. Her friend hugs and kisses her good-bye. She says, "But you still look good Angela. Fantastic. Remember that. You still have a chance."

When her friend leaves, she falls asleep and dreams she is in a jungle in Africa and a tribal chief whom she knows is a murderer, insists she is his wife. She is attracted to him and thinks maybe this is true, but she somehow feels she is married to someone else, although she can't remember him, can't picture him at all. And then she thinks of her Aunt Amanda Jane and she can't remember if she is dead or alive, but surely if she were dead, surely she would remember the funeral? So she comes to the conclusion in the dream that she must have amnesia. And in her amnesia married the tribal chief. A handsome man who treats her gently. So why should she strain to remember a life she's already forgotten? And she can't think of a reason why. And yet she feels uncomfortable. And is glad to wake up.

Since it is 1:00 in the afternoon she fixes herself a light lunch. Some lettuce and tuna fish. She thinks about her dream and laughs because the tribal chief looked like Sidney Poitier, although she is a little ashamed to have dreamed herself so easily married to a murderer.

Sitting in a light cotton dress at her kitchen table, having finished eating now, and absent-mindedly peeling the formica off the top of the table. White and black formica, although the white has yellowed a little. Has given up writing to an old inert woman furiously trying to rock away her life on a porch in Mississippi that won't quite collapse and give up like that fence across the street; and not even Angela. Angela's elevation and rise into the mystical white forests of the north could save her. And of course Angela's marriage didn't work out, couldn't save anyone.

She cuts her thumb peeling the formica, but stubbornly she keeps peeling it, breaking it off in her fingers. And yes, it's true, she is ashamed of her aunt, an old ignorant woman who won't move and won't listen and won't die. Yes, so ashamed of her aunt, that she can't even write to her when she is sick in bed, a ninety-five-year-old woman of her own blood sick in bed, waiting to hear from her and she can't even tolerate her name, Amanda Jane, and yet she named her own daughter Amanda. Ashamed of her shame.

At 2:00 she gets up and goes over to the window and looks out, vaguely daydreaming, vaguely watching for her daughter to come home from school. She has been waiting, watching at this window for such a long time, so many months, and nothing has happened. A "dangerous, high risk" neighborhood where, after all, there is no danger, no risk. A disappointment. Disappointing that the women on this wall cry, suffer, for only bad weather, too much spring rain. So she is surprised when there is an accident outside in front of her building, and her heart is pounding. A man hit by a car! A black man in a gold suit, hit and thrown to the sidewalk. Two men run away, quickly, deftly, and other people gather, press against each other, greedy for a better view. Kids run over and circle the area, kicking aimlessly at the garbage and then pushing and jostling each other to see the man.

Angela watches this from her window. She watches the people

move slowly closer to that man lying on the ground not quite twisted out of shape, out of their reach. And she thinks of insects. Insects around a light. Swarms. Swarming. But the movement, the whispers, are choked off suddenly by sirens, police cars, an ambulance. And then someone yells. A thick, heavy voice, heavy with rage, pain, yelling, "He's dead so get the fuck out of here."

But they come anyway, the police, the ambulance. Two men bring out a stretcher. They cover the man on the ground with a white sheet. And Angela dreams of ghosts rising from the sidewalk, of white socks on black legs. And she wonders where this dream comes from and where it goes from here, wonders if she is going crazy finally, when there has never been any sign of it, no hint at all. They put the stretcher in the ambulance. They close the doors and drive away. She is shaking. Violently cold on such a warm spring day. Ashamed. Guilty. Almost sick. But she can't quite cry. She can't quite cry with the hundred other women in this apartment. A hundred brown women crying. And one who isn't. But after all she didn't even know him. "I didn't even know him," she says to no one of them in particular.

🔥 🔥 🔥

ELEGY

by DAVID ST. JOHN

from POETRY

nominated by Stuart Friebert and Grace Schulman

> *If there is any dwelling place*
> *for the spirits of the just;*
> *if, as the wise believe, noble souls*
> *do not perish with the body,*
> *rest thou in peace . . .*

Tacitus

Who keeps the owl's breath? Whose eyes desire?
Why do the stars rhyme? Where does
The flush cargo sail? Why does the daybook close?

So sleep and do not sleep.

The opaque stroke lost across the mirror,
The clamp turned.
The polished nails begin the curl into your palms.
The opal hammock of rain falls out of its cloud.

I name you, *Gloat-of-*
The-stalks, drowse-my-embers, old-lily-bum.
No matter how well a man sucks praise in the end
He sucks earth. Go ahead, step
Out into that promised, rasp gratitude of night.

Seeds and nerves. *Seeds*

And nerves. I'll be waiting for you, in some

Obscure and clarifying light;
I will say, Look there is a ghost ice on the land.

If the page of marble bleeds in the yellow grass,
If the moon-charts glow useless and cold,
If the grains of the lamp outlast you, as they must—
As the tide of black gloss, the marls, and nectar rise

I will understand.

Here are my gifts: *smudges of bud,*
A blame of lime. Everything you remember crowds
Away. Stubble memory,
The wallpaper peeling its leaves. Fog. Fog
In the attic; this pod of black milk. Anymore,

Only a road like August approaches.

Sometimes the drawers of the earth close;
Sometimes our stories keep on and on. So listen—

Leave no address. Fold your clothes into a little
Island. Kiss the hinges goodbye. Sand the fire. Bitch
About *time.* Hymn away this reliquary fever.

How the sun stands crossing itself in the cut glass.

How the jonquils and bare orchards fill each morning
In mist. The branches in the distance stiffen,
Again. The city of stars pales.
In my fires the cinders rise like black angels;
The trunks of the olives twist once toward the world.

Once. I will walk out into the day.

THE RITUAL OF MEMORIES

by TESS GALLAGHER

from UNDER STARS (Graywolf Press)

nominated by GRAYWOLF PRESS, *Grace Schulman, Raymond Carver and Laura Jensen*

When your widow had left the graveside
and you were most alone
I went to you in that future
you can't remember yet. I brought
a basin of clear water where no tear
had fallen, water gathered like grapes
a drop at a time
from the leaves of the willow. I brought
oils, I brought a clean white gown.

"Come out," I said, and you came up
like a man pulling himself out of a river,
a river with so many names
there was no word left for it but "earth."

"Now," I said, "I'm ready. These eyes
that have not left your face
since the day we met, wash these eyes.
Remember, it was a country road
above the sea and I was passing
from the house of a friend. Look
into these eyes where we met."

I saw your mind go back through the years
searching for that day and finding it,
you washed my eyes
with the pure water
so that I vanished from that road
and you passed a lifetime
and I was not there.

So you washed every part of me
where any look or touch
had passed between us. "Remember,"
I said, when you came to the feet,
"it was the night before you would ask
the girl of your village to marry. I
was the strange one. I was the one
with the gypsy look.
Remember how you stroked these feet."

When the lips and the hands
had been treated likewise and the pit
of the throat where one thoughtless kiss
had fallen, you rubbed in the sweet oil
and I glistened like a new-made thing, not
merely human, but of the world gone past
being human.

"The hair," I said. "You've forgotten
the hair. Don't you know it remembers.
Don't you know it keeps everything. Listen,
there is your voice and in it the liar's charm
that caught me."

You listened. You heard your voice
and a look of such sadness
passed over your dead face that I wanted
to touch you. Who could have known
I would be so held? Not you
in your boyish cunning; not me
in my traveler's clothes.

It's finished.
Put the gown on my shoulders.
It's no life in the shadow of another's joys.
Let me go freely now.
One life I have lived for you. This one
is mine.

𝄐 𝄐 𝄐

PLOWING WITH ELEPHANTS

by LON OTTO

from INDIANA WRITES

nominated by INDIANA WRITES

"It is stated that in Ceylon, elephants are employed in
Plowing rice-fields and in preparing new ground for the cultivation
of coffee, pepper, &c. One of these animals, well-trained, it is said,
will do the work of twenty oxen; consequently more labor is
performed in a given time, and the period is hastened for putting in
the crops. The price of an elephant in Ceylon varies from $50 to
$75. Could not the elephants exhibited in the caravans in this
country be more profitably employed in plowing our prairies of the
west?"
The American Agriculturist
August 1847

It is stated that one farmer on the Nebraska prairie
took for gospel eastern words to the west,
saw succession of wild flowers in unbroken country
asked more than oxen like mice—asked elephants;
so the barn-big harness was made, the plow forged: plowing
waited only the profitless, gay caravan.

A day like a bell marked the coming of the caravan
in a jungle of dust to the last town on the prairie.
The farmer bargained from sun down to stars, plowing
deep into debt, and with five years saved from the stingy west,
won, behind canvas, a senile bull elephant,
long lost in dreams of a raining, forest country.

For one short season the madness drew to the country
spectators from Council Bluffs and Omaha in caravans
to witness, at dawn, the harnessing of an elephant,
the burning man and his boy bringing to the prairie,
to the black edge of the waving west,
the enormous, ramshackle parody of plowing.

One season loud with the monstrous plowing
and an iron harsh winter crushed shut the country,
ending the mad plan to cultivate the west
The dragging out of the carcass to caravans
of wolves, horses jangling wild eyed to a sink on the prairie,
gored grave-long nightmares with the tusks of an elephant.

The sullen boy suffered ridicule for years for the elephant;
seized manhood early, wore out debts by right plowing;
neither forgave nor understood, but set a chair on the prairie
for the stone deaf, oblivious contriver of a country
filled with the rumbling of sail-eared caravans,
unsettling thunder in the mind of the west.

The old man rocked to his end staring west,
hands once more glorious on the plow traces of an elephant.
Mastodon and mammoth pushed south in shaggy caravans,
pushed down from the arctic for a man who died plowing,
impossibly deep, the cold guts of a country,
not drawing its life from his bones on the prairie.

It is said that the west was won by plowing
an elephant into the bison's country.
It is said that a caravan sometimes haunts the prairie.

MEETING MESCALITO AT OAK HILL CEMETERY

by LORNA DEE CERVANTES

from CANTO AL PUEBLO (Penca Books)

nominated by Naomi Clark and Robert Hass

Sixteen years old and crooked
with drug, time warped blissfully
as I sat alone on Oak Hill.

The cemetery stones were neither erect
nor stonelike, but looked soft and harmless,
thousands of them rippling in the meadows
like overgrown daisies.

I picked apricots from the trees below
where the great peacocks roosted and nagged
loose the feathers from their tails.
A lizard introduced himself. I knelt to him
with my hands on the earth, lifted him
and held him in my palm, reflecting how
Mescalito was a true god.

Coming home that evening, I realized
nothing had changed. I covered mama on the sofa

with a quilt I sewed myself, locked my bedroom
door against the stepfather and gathered
the feathers I'd found that morning, each
green eye in a heaven of blue, a fistfull
of understanding,

and late that night I tasted
the last of the sweet fruit, sucked the rich pit
and thought nothing of death.

A JEAN-MARIE COOKBOOK

fiction by JEFF WEINSTEIN

from SUN & MOON

nominated by SUN & MOON

I STOLE TWO COOKBOOKS and read them when I knew I should be doing other things. I wanted to make a casserole of thinly-sliced potatoes, the non-waxy and non-baking kind, although the dish would be baked in cream. I found out from reading that what I wanted to do was no good unless I rubbed a clove of garlic around the inside of the pot, not that I'm adding the garlic itself, but that the cream seems to imbibe the flavor and hold it until you are ready. It was these fine points I wanted to know, the right and the wrong way to slice, the effective use of spices, why an earthenware dish 'worked' (the way yeast 'works') while a glass one didn't: the secrets

of cooking. Some people argue that something should be done a
certain way so it will taste a certain way, but how do they know that
when they taste a dish they are all tasting the same thing? Experience makes a difference. For example, once I threw up when I ate a
noodles and cheese casserole, so I won't eat one again, no matter
how good. Experience even tells me how to feel about cooking
something like a fried egg sandwich. I make them in bacon fat now,
but for a long time I thought only big households with dirty tin cans
filled with drippings, or a great constant cook like my friend Kit,
could save bacon fat and properly cook with it. For years I would
throw the good clear fat down the drain, and I still don't know how or
why I changed. It's like baking; I can't bake now, although I read
baking recipes and work them through in my head, but only if I see
that they apply to someone else, to someone *who can bake*. The
most difficult transition I know is to move from one sort of state like
that to another, from a person who doesn't bake to one who does. I
would like to find out how it is done.

*

It seems that Jean-Marie took on the cloak of 'gay' life in San
Diego. He was a graduate student of art, interested in frescoes and
teaching French on the side. Then, a year after he whispered he was
going to remain celibate, mouthing the word as if he wasn't sure of its
pronunciation, he started to skip classes. And one night he walked
into the local gay bar, the one where people danced, called the Sea
Cruise. At first he walked into the bar with women he knew from
school and danced, commandeering them around the floor. Then he
came with his old friend Mary, a head taller than he was, and they
jerked around, absolutely matched. All this progressed over
months; I would see Jean-Marie and Mary every time I was there,
which probably means they were at the bar more often than I was. I
can be sure they were always there together. I never ate dinner with
them but I assume they would try to 'taste' things the same way.
Considering their need to think of themselves as alike, the idea of
them kissing is interesting. They would want to think they were
feeling the same thing, mutual tongues, mutual saliva. Their pleasure would not be mutual, and they would have to avoid thinking
about that. Can you like kissing yourself? Can you like kissing

someone you falsely imagine to be like yourself? It seems like deception to me, and I wonder why they do it.

*

Good cooking knives are indispensible to good cooking, which I learned by reading. I am told that carbon steel is better than stainless steel, that it wears away and gets more flexible with use, but such knives have to be dried after they are washed, their tips protected by corks, and you are supposed to yell at anyone who uses your knives for opening jars or other obviously damaging things. I don't mean to be facetious here, but apparently knives are important. I stole a set of Sabatier (lion?) knives that I thought were the best, stainless steel, but later I found out about the carbon versus stainless and got a sinking feeling in my stomach, though I also knew I would cherish them less and use them more.

*

Then Jean-Marie discovered men, or males rather, and started dancing with them, kissing them, and going out with them. The first was a sixteen year old boy whose personality was all Jean-Marie's idea, and every time they met his time was spent looking for it, the way Puritans scanned nature to find signs of God. He and Jean-Marie probably did not sleep together, or if they did share a bed sometimes they probably didn't have sex. When this ended, by the boy leaving for San Francisco, Jean-Marie used disappointment as the excuse to pick up guys at the Sea Cruise, first the ones who liked to be mooned at, the quiet regulars, then the drugged-out ones, and then the ones made of stainless steel. He made the transition from gown to town by moving away from school to a dark house in the city, full of wood and plants and no light to read by. He slowly withdrew from the University and backed into San Diego, dropping old associations and living with a different opinion of himself. He sold his car so he could ride the municipal buses, and considered getting food stamps and general relief.

*

Here is a recipe I invented, a variation on scrambled eggs:
  2 eggs at room temperature
  cream, or half-and-half, sour cream, yogurt, though cream is best
  freshly ground black pepper
  a little salt
  butter (not margarine) unsalted butter is best
You take the eggs, beat them well but not frothy, then add a good
lump (I call it a dollop) of cream or whatever, and *stir* it in. Grind in
some pepper, add a little salt. Heat a good frying pan very slowly
(this is important) and melt in it a dollop of butter. When the butter
starts to 'talk' add the egg mixture. Cook it slowly until it starts to
curdle; this takes time, as it should, in the gentle heat. In the
meanwhile get your toast ready and some tea. You can't rush this.
Move the eggs around with a wooden spoon or fork; metal is not
good. When they look done, creamy and solid, turn them into a
warm plate. You may want to throw on some fresh chopped herbs,
watercress, cilantro, parsley, but plain is wonderful. I don't know
why these are a 'variation' on scrambled eggs, but they do taste like
no others. They even come out different every time, although some
people can't tell the difference, and a few people I know won't even
touch them.

*

   When I met Jean-Marie on the bus he told me he got a poem
published, and I suspected it was about love:
  His beating heart
  My moist lips, etc.
It *was* about love, in rondelle form, for he hadn't left school as much
as he thought. The next night I had a friend over for dinner. I heard
he was a gourmet so I was nervous to impress him, although I'm not
usually like that. Unfortunately I got home late and had to rush
around to get everything ready, muttering to myself, but all at once I
changed my mind about the matter and decided I was doing something which should be a pleasure, so I stopped worrying about it.
Everything went well, basically because John wasn't much of a
gourmet. We had: sherry, iced mushrooms with lemon juice and no
salt, gratin dauphinois—a simple (hah!) casserole of thinly sliced
washed dried new potatoes so thin that two pieces make the thickness of a penny, baked in a covered earthenware bowl rubbed with

garlic, salted, peppered, and filled with cream. The cover is taken off towards the end of the baking so a brown crust forms. Eaten right away, and it was heaven. We were talking about Cretan art. It's important that the bowl be earthenware, that it be rubbed with garlic, and that the cream and potatoes come to within ¾ of an inch of the top of the uncovered casserole. We went up to the roof to grill the steaks and talked about the view and how odd it was to be in California. These steaks are called biftecks a la mode du pays de vaux, grilled and seasoned fillet steaks on a bed of chopped hard-boiled eggs, fines herbes (I had only dried herbs but I reconstituted them if you know what I mean), lemon juice, and salt and pepper. I also added some chopped watercress. Then you heat it all. It was in this French glass dish I bought when I was so bored I could have killed myself. I stole the fillets. We drank wine and talked of sex. Then we had a salad of deveined spinach. He was really impressed; and I was surprised, both that he was so easily moved and that it all turned out so nicely. *I* was impressed too.

John brought a dessert, which was a home-baked apple pie, really a tart, and it was not as good as all that, but I was happy he brought it. It tasted much better the second day. We made out on the sofa then, but all of a sudden I got an urge to break away and go dancing, and John readily agreed. At the bar he fell 'in love' with this beautiful Spaniard name Paco, who was drunk. They danced a lot together, badly, but John finally had to take me home. I wondered if he went back to meet Paco, but I thought not. John said he would see me when he got back from his trip to the East Coast. I had a dream that night in which I felt completely perverted and inhuman, and I think the meal had something to do with it.

*

Jean-Marie, after his year out in San Diego, wrote a long letter about promiscuity to the San Diego Union, which of course didn't get printed, although a month after he sent it in they lifted a small part of it and passed it off as opinion about a case where a lot of men got arrested in the bathroom of the San Diego May Company, 'for indiscriminate reasons' the paper said.

Dear Sirs: I am a gay male in San Diego and I want to talk about sex, or the problem of promiscuity so many of us face. Most of us, gay or not gay, are looking for someone to love, for a day, a year, or forever, and admittedly this is hard to do. But we have to try. However I don't understand why the only way many of the gay guys in San Diego try is by tricking. For those of you who don't know what tricking means, it's meeting someone, at a gay bar, in the park or on the street, going home and having sexual contact. Sometimes you don't even talk, because it would ruin everything. But when you do start conversations, they all go like this: what's your name (and you give your first name only), where are you from, what do you do, did you see . . . . . (a movie), etc., completely anonymous conversations, which is sad. Why do we do this? I don't really understand why, or why people hang around bathrooms, or even worse. It could be lust, but lust is just a screen for loneliness. Why doesn't the city of San Diego (or all cities) provide a place for people, gay and non-gay, to talk, dance, like a coffeehouse? This has worked elsewhere. But I do think that we as people should honestly question what they are doing. Sometimes I get so sick of what I am doing, going to bars every night, drinking when I don't want to drink, flirting when I don't want to flirt, staying out until two in the A.M. sweating and waiting for the right person, or at that point any person, that I don't know what to do. I could go back to the University, but I know the University is worse. I wonder if I was roped into this. There are some people I meet at the gay bars that I really think should be put away because of the way they act, and treat others. But other times I don't think that at all, and I just feel sorry for them. I wish I understood my appetites better, and I wish the city would do something about it.

*

I have never made a real dessert before, one that requires more than chopping up some fruits and adding whatever liqueurs I have around, so I thought I'd try something out of a cookbook, something called a chocolate bombe. I stuck to that one partly because I liked the name and partly because I like chocolate and also because I had some Mexican vanilla extract which would go well in it. 'Chocolate Bombe' I realized later would make a good title for a screenplay, but it would have to be about food, and very few things are. Food is shown in some movies, like the gourmet concoctions in Hitchcock's *Frenzy* or the banquet in *The Scarlet Empress* or in any number of bakery scenes with pastry on one side of the window and little faces, of boys usually, on the other. But nothing masterful or mature, and I don't think it's because food is silly or insignificant, but because it's hard to visualize people at a meal where food stands for their relationships or essences in some way, like the beef dish in *To The Lighthouse*. How can I say I was 'in the mood' to make something with cream, to watch something gel, to fill the beautiful mold sitting in the cupboard.

After I made the bombe, enough for ten people, there was so much left over that I left the key to my apartment outside the door and asked the couple in the next apartment to go into the freezer and help themselves, which they did, but other people helped themselves to my typewriter and television.

Chocolate Bombe (about ten servings)

Soak 1½ teaspoons of gelatin in one cup of cold water. Stir and bring to the boiling point 1 cup of milk, 1½ cups of sugar, and two tablespoons of unsweetened cocoa. Dissolve the gelatin in the hot mixture. Cool. Add one teaspoon of vanilla extract. Chill until about to set. Whip 2 cups of cream until thickened but not stiff. Fold it lightly into the gelatin mixture. Still-freeze in a lightly-greased mold, and unmold ½ hour before serving.

It tasted rich, although there were too many ice crystals in it. The best part was sampling the gelatin mixture before the cream was added, because it was so sweet and cold, just gelling, redolent of chocolate and Mexican vanilla. By the way, it doesn't come out tasting like pudding or jello; it's full of weight, like home-churned ice cream. It wasn't perfect, but because it came out at all I imagined it was better than it was.

Sometimes I eat because I'm lonely or disappointed. In fact, as I drive away from the bar at night, I tell myself (or the others in the car) it was 'amusing' or 'boring' or 'kinda fun', but almost always at the same point in the turn to the main stretch home I feel a hollow feeling, which, when I recognize it, says I'm hungry, and I look forward to something to eat. It's almost absolutely predictable: the masking talk, the turn, and then the hunger, and often I overeat before I go to bed. The few times I've gone home with someone from the bar I've been hungry in the same way, so I assume these sexual episodes aren't really happy ones. Sometimes I've been nauseous, but that's a different feeling for different reasons. I've gone home with only one person who offered me a full breakfast in the morning or who lived as if he cooked himself full meals. That was in New York

City, with a very nice guy who just wanted to fuck me and get me to sniff amyl. He did get up early, and seemed to be making a lot of money, although the only thing I can remember about how he spent it was a really hideous gilt and glass table in his living room, and the fact that he bought towels at Bloomingdale's the afternoon before, spending more than a hundred dollars. The towels were hanging in the bathroom without even having been washed. We took a taxi home to his place, I remember now, I wasn't hungry and only slightly sick to my stomach. I ate underripe bananas with a guy I was 'in love' with, but he was angry because I couldn't fuck him. And once, in Denver, the only thing I found in the refrigerator of this guy who picked me up, fucked me, and fell asleep at eight in the evening was one of those mealy chocolate flavored wafers you use to gain weight if you eat them with things or lose weight if you eat them alone. There was literally nothing else in there. I forgot about David. David made me a poached egg which tasted slightly of the vinegar in the water, on whole wheat toast, and fresh juice, and tea. I had many more of those breakfasts, even though we didn't have sex, but I loved to sleep with David, and still would if we hadn't had that fight about a story I wrote concerning him.

*

Jean-Marie became more and more bitter about his life, although he didn't realize to what extent he was excluding himself from his old friends, and especially from women. The world looks cruel when you concentrate only upon the males you know or want to know, and women become generalized and ignored, somehow peripheral. Jean-Marie got sick of this but he didn't know why, and none of his new friends could tell him. Certainly he was less stiff after a year in the Sea Cruise, and sloughed around the dance floor as if he had done it before, but . . .

But, he said, I'm special. I am a feminine man, and that's good, even better than being a woman. He would peer into mirrors, for mirrors were all over the walls of the rooms he haunted, and play with disconnecting 'Jean-Marie' from the little boy he grew up with. His head would twist and arch, one shoulder would rise, his nostrils flared as he imagined what could be possible. He never looked further down than his neck, and avoided parts of himself like his nose or the jut of his ears. Certainly he was bitter because he couldn't store this mirror-feeling, when his blood rushed and he could do anything. It wasn't vanity, this play in front of mirrors, nothing was being judged or compared, except perhaps the old with the new.

Oh ugh hmm. Do you really think so? Really I couldn't how could I? It wouldn't work . . . do you think so? Hmmm well. In far Peru there lived a llama he had no papa he had no mama he had no wife he had no chillun he had no use for penicillin . . . Jesus . . . yes of course I can come when do you want me . . . the brie please . . . fine I'll leave anytime of course but will they understand my English yes I know how important it is . . . God you're cute and you've gained weight hummph why do I get so much pleasure out of this . . . it's true isn't it.

*

I have made some errors in cooking, but these aren't nearly as important as errors in menu, or rather in the meal. I just heard of someone who swallowed a handful of aspirin, which made her sick. People are constantly eating to make themselves sick, to poison themselves, poison others, to forget, or to die. Someone once said stupidity takes corporeal form. I seem to have an aptitude for planning a happy meal, the combination of people, appetites, and what I called the 'attitude' of the food: the amounts, the way a hot dish is followed by a cool one, the interplay or colors, the sequence of dishes and their values. I do this best when I am alone because people eating at my house sometimes make me nervous, and although I plan the food, I can never plan the run of old friendships at a dinner table. There's a whole history of ruining meals; in certain places, if you wanted to get even with a family you ground up the bones of their bird or some other possession into the food you served to them—it's a way of breaking up hospitality. One example of this was a stew which consisted of the guests' children. People no longer realize the potential power in the act of sharing food, but they do suffer from the consequences whether or not they're aware of it. The menu of the most awful meal I ate:

mulligatawny soup and saltines
three bean salad

'oven-fried' chicken, I had the drumstick
mashed potatoes
green beans with butter
white bread and butter
ice cream and sugar wafers

There was something wrong with the soup but I didn't know what; it tasted bitter, not from any single ingredient but from the expression on the face of the person who stirred it. Really. It was bitter exactly the way a person is, in its 'sweat'. After the soup I said something nasty to a guest who was invited just to meet me, and everyone was embarrassed and tried to cover up. Mel belched out loud and George got annoyed but didn't say anything; he merely stabbed at his chicken and pushed it away. Judy spilled her milk on my pants, accidentally I'm sure, so I had to get up and change. When I got back George wasn't speaking to Nancy, and Mel was winking and nodding with no subtlety at all across the table. It could be that there were too many of us in the room, but we all had the same bad taste in our mouths.

I once had breakfast (brunch) in a gay bar, waiting an hour for a plate of bacon, two vulcanized eggs, and the pre-hashed potatoes that get scraped around a hot surface for a few minutes until their fetid water evaporates and they take on some color. Someone I didn't know was rubbing my knee and my only friend there kept drinking those morning drinks that make you anticipate evening, while the air smelled of the night before. How could I eat? I did eat, ravenously, but managed only by insisting to myself that except for my appetite I wasn't at all like the others around me. How long would that last? One more meal there could do the trick, so I swore I'd never eat at that bar again. I went home alone and looked at myself in the mirror to see if I had changed, for the grease from the potatoes was already beginning to appear on my forehead.

My God no. If you put a flower in a vacuum all its essence leaves. The fog might just be getting tired and collapsing into puddles . . . grease . . . damp . . . those little flakes of skin sticking in patches, nothing to show for all that reading, nothing to wear that fits, too big or too small and who can keep up with all that sewing even when I sew it unravels around my stitches. I'll throw it all out.

*

Two Mirror Snacks

1) bacon fat or a mixture of butter and oil, not too much, a few
   small potatoes, boiled in their skins (leftovers are best) one
   or two peeled and crushed cloves of garlic the pulp, fresh or
   canned, of one tomato plenty of basil
   optional: cut pitted black olives, about 6
              a few sliced mushrooms
              a few celery leaves

Heat the fat or oil and butter in a small frying pan until very hot, put
in the potatoes and mix them around, breaking them into chunks but
not mashed. Add the garlic and some coarse salt if you have it,
stirring constantly until they take on some color. Add the rest of the
ingredients in any order you like (I add the olives last). Don't stir
towards the end, so the bottom burns a little. Turn out onto a plate,
add salt and freshly ground black pepper to your taste, and eat with
white wine or beer. Be sure to scrape all the burnt particles and
grease out with a spoon and eat them.

2) (you need a blender for this one)an egg
   a few big spoonfuls of plain yogurt
   enough wheat germ to cover it, but not more than a Tbsp.
   a good ripe banana, broken into pieces
   one cup of any mixture of:milk, half & half, fruit juice
   ½ tsp. of real vanilla extract (try Mexican vanilla)
   some sweetner, honey, sugar, ice cream, just a bit
   optional: a few spoons of protein powder
              a spoon of soy lecithin
              a tsp. of polyunsaturated flavorless oil

Add to the blender in the order mentioned, but don't fill to more
than ⅔ capacity. Most protein powder tastes awful, so add only as
much as you think you need. Non-instant dried milk is a good
substitute. Blend at low speed for a few seconds, uncover, make sure
the wheat germ isn't sticking in clumps to the yogurt, and scrape the
now agglutinated protein powder off the sides of the blender and
repulverize, all with a rubber spatula. Smell it, taste it, add more of
what you think it needs. Cover and blend at medium speed for half a
minute. Have right away or refrigerate, but it will settle. Sometimes

I add an envelope of chocolate flavored instant breakfast or some powdered chocolate because the chocolate and orange juice (if that's your juice) taste great together. Fruit jam is also good. Obviously this recipe can take a lot of things, but remember your purpose.

Note that each mirror snack is a different response to feeling bad.

*

In his response to the bar, or in his response to the person he was afraid of becoming, Jean-Marie resorted to interests connected neither to school nor to the bar life he was now trying to avoid. He taught himself to knit, but when he found himself mooning over pictures of models in scarves and sweaters, he realized he didn't want to. Then he thought he'd learn to cook, revolted by the cold stupid meals he fixed for himself and by his unquestioning dependence on others for anything hot. One evening he had dinner with some of his University friends, baked ham and guacamole salad, for old times' sake. After dinner Jean-Marie asked them to try and describe the worst meal each of them could remember. He was stunned by his boldness—he never started things—but he was comfortable after the food and sat back to listen.

As they talked, Jean-Marie thought this was the most interesting conversation he'd heard since he left the University. He hated school, hated the lab scientists and art professors and the pretty jock behind the locker room cage who demeaned every woman as soon as she walked away. Yet even though the gay people at the Sea Cruise were gentle, they were more miserable with their lives than any group of people he knew. It was 'they' now, but tomorrow it could be 'we'. What could he do? Could he straddle the two and possibly be happy? He was beginning to guess that happiness isn't the issue here, and survival is more crucial. 'In what way' he thought 'is survival related to being happy?'

*

The most difficult dishes in any cookbook are the 'everyday' recipes, luncheon, bruncheon, egg, family dishes, cooking for survival when you have more important things to do or don't have much money. Let's assume you don't have a family to feed but haven't much time and want to be happy with what you are eating. Here is a list of staples for 'everyday' meals:

milk
eggs, bought fresh a few at a time if possible
onions
oil or bacon drippings (bacon)
a little butter, unsalted
tomatoes, fresh and canned
garlic
cheap greens, vegetables in season
some cheese
bread, or flour to bake it
fresh boiling potatoes
chicken, all parts of it
lemons, possibly oranges
salt, black pepper
beer or wine

Staples are defined here not as what you need, but as what holds things together. I know this list assumes there is an 'everyday'. Some people, I know, have to cadge their next meal, for a place to prepare it, for a place to eat. These are people you should ask in for a meal, if possible.

I asked Jean-Marie to dinner. We agreed, although I don't re-member why, to have a cooking contest. The rules were to prepare a menu. We would each cook our own menu and then each other's, which would take four nights. We decided on a judge who needed the meals but who also understands more about food than anyone we knew without being disgusting.

Jean-Marie's menu, using the staple list, one good piece of flesh or fowl, some extra money, and one day's work:

consomme, iced, with chervil
carrotes marinees
boned leg of lamb, mustard coating (gigot a la moutarde)
boiled new potatoes with parsley butter

sliced iced tomatoes with basil and olive oil
orange pieces flambe
cafe espresso
the meal is served with a good French red wine'

My menu, with the same 'limitations':

cream of potato and watercress soup
stuffed mushrooms
cucumbers and lemon juice
roast duck with tangerine stuffing, lemon glaze
parsley garnish
garlic mashed potatoes
spinach and cilantro salad, lemon juice dressing
strawberry lemon ices
the meal is served with cold Grey Riesling (California)

See appendix for comments on the selections. These are expensive
meals, requiring not only food but many utensils and a lot of heat
and cold (energy).

Jean-Marie and I met our judge, J., at my house the first evening,
where I cooked my menu. J. said very little as we ate, although at
one point he asked me for my recipe for stuffed mushrooms and their
history:

Edythe's Stuffed Mushrooms

'My mother invented these one night when she ran out of clams to
stuff. My father was rather demanding about the food their party
guests (or rather his party guests) were served, and although my
mother prided herself on her stuffed clams, it was still sort of
slave-work for her. This is not to say that my father didn't like to
cook—he did—but he would not clean up after his filth, to use my
mother's words. She liked these mushrooms, which were moist and
tasty, and I took her recipe and adjusted it to my tastes:

large open mushrooms, the bigger the better, 3 per person
at least one bunch of parsley
juice of one lemon
6 or so cloves of garlic, peeled

one or two cans of minced clams, drained
seasoned bread crumbs, Italian style
basil, fresh or dried
coarse salt
freshly ground black pepper
olive oil
plenty of freshly grated parmesan and/or romano cheese

The reason the quantities are vague is because I never measured them; the frying pan, a good heavy one, should determine the amount of everything. It almost always works out, and any leftover stuffing is delicious, although it should be refrigerated so you don't get food poisoning. The tricky part of this dish is making sure the mushrooms don't dry out, and all the soaking is for this purpose. Carefully twist the stems out of the mushrooms, so you are left with the intact cap and gills. Reserve the stems. With a spoon scrape the gills and all excess stuff out of the caps, so you are left with little bowls. As you finish this process, eating any mushrooms you may have broken, place the caps in a large bowl of cool water into which you've squirted the lemon juice. The mushrooms will soak in this; the acid prevents them from turning too brown. Mince the parsley flowerettes. Mince the garlic. Now, take each mushroom stem, chop off and discard the woody half, the part which stuck in the ground, and dice the remaining halves. Grate your cheese. Heat the frying pan slowly, then add at least ¼ inch of olive oil. This may seem like a lot, but it's necessary. When the oil gets fragrant, add the garlic. Before the garlic browns, add the clams and saute. Add the minced mushrooms, stirring constantly, the parsley, and keep cooking. Make sure nothing burns. Add salt, pepper, and enough bread-crumbs to soak up the excess clam and mushroom liquid. The basil should have been crushed and thrown in some time before; do add quite a bit. The stuffing should now be loose and moist but not liquid, and very hot. Remove from heat, and add most of your grated cheese, reserving some. Stir it all, and put it aside. If you think the mushrooms have soaked long enough, take each one out, shake out the water, and with a spoon put the stuffing in. Do this with a light hand and keep the stuffing as particulate as possible. Stuff all the mushrooms. Now, if you must, you can leave them sit for a while (do not refrigerate), but it is best to immediately put them into a lightly greased broiling dish, having preheated your oven or broiler sometime before, arrange touching in some kind of pattern, salt the tops, sprinkle with grated cheese and maybe a little olive oil, and run them under a hot broiler or in a very hot oven until both the stuffing is completely heated and the tops of the caps are not too tough and brown; it is an exact point. By that time the water in the mushrooms should have just steamed them, so they are perfectly cooked, neither raw and brittle nor rubbery and slick. If you want to be fancy, place the mushrooms, before you broil them, on a bed of carefully washed and deveined leaves of spinach, and broil them together. Some of the mushroom juice will run out onto the perfectly cooked spinach, which can be used to sop it all up.'

On the first evening Jean-Marie paled a bit when he tasted my mushrooms, perhaps because he didn't know how easy they were to make. On the second night Jean-Marie cooked, and we both knew our food was good, so this time we talked nicely and forgot the pretense of competition.

'But I know Louis the 15th had a head shaped like a pear.'

I should note that I did not tell our judge who cooked what. J. ate well, asking us to save portions of everything, so by the fourth night there should be two versions each of two different meals, three in miniature. Of course we were sickened at the prospect of so much rich food, but the concept of a cooking contest was still strange enough to be interesting. On the fourth night we talked about writing cookbooks and tasted a little bit of everything. Jean-Marie managed to make the mushrooms but could not even fake the ices, and my version of his marinated carrots was pale and sticky.

I say this in retrospect because at some point in our meal I couldn't tell what food was mine, or where it came from. Jean-Marie looked contemplative and sick. Our judge was so quiet we didn't see him most of the time. The courses were served by ghosts. Critical faculties must have faded, and we thought only of parody and death.

The grotesque prudishness and archness with which garlic is treated in this country has led to the superstition that rubbing the bowl with it before putting the salad in gives it sufficient flavor. It rather depends whether you are going to eat the bowl or the salad.

Jean-Marie left, J. left, I was left sitting alone not knowing when they had gone. There was a note:

I cannot tell the difference among your dishes because each bite was a universe. Why do you insist so much on difference and comparison? I was so happy to be eating, and it was all good food, that my joy overran any pose of judgment. When you cook something, and put it aside, how do you know who cooked it? Who were you that day? Who could have doctored the food, soured it, stolen it away and left a note of gibberish in its place? Certainly you can write a cookbook, but could it possibly predict a meal? It's an odd mirror to stare into, with no certainty in it. There was a point when I almost swallowed a bone, and some sherbet dribbled down my chin and stained the tablecloth. Did you notice? Would you have cooked that meal, or any meal, if I hadn't been there to eat it? Will your tablecloth wash out? (No matter, I blotted up the spill.) I do think you expect too much, but I would be pleased if you arranged your life so you could continue to cook. However I don't see that a cookbook could be anything but a reflection of imagined life, which is not a bad thing. I'd be happy to visit you again.

APPENDIX

Jean-Marie comments on his menu:
My menu is mainly French, relying on the good fresh vegetables of Southern California. The cold soup whets your appetite, the marinated carrots, which is a French country specialty, excites your now raging hunger and prepares your palate for the mustard flavor of the lamb. After all that cold stuff, the lamb and hot simple potatoes are a happy change. The red wine supports and is not pushed over by the strong flavors of the main dish. People should be talking at this point, as soon as the initial gobbling has stopped. The iced tomatoes provide color, if the conversation doesn't, and the basil is yet another welcome flavor. After a pause (which I never think is long enough) the oranges cool your mouths, 'degrease them' so to speak, and the espresso should be strong and black.

Comments on the other menu:
These are things I like. If the duck doesn't smoke up the whole house it can be quite a surprise, because people don't expect duck the way they expect chicken or lamb. The spinach and cilantro salad is also a surprise (especially if you don't wash the spinach enough) but seri-

ously people see the blue-green leaves of the spinach and think it's lettuce but the light is funny, and then the cilantro, a lighter yellow-green, flashes like little bits of afterglow or whatever that visual phenomenon is called. And when they eat it, it's the same thing, because all the bland cuddy spinach juice is punctuated by the herb, utterly unexpected. Ices cool everyone after the duck. The menu works; I don't have to explain exactly why, do I? By the way, Jean-Marie shouldn't repeat the mustard of the carrots in his lamb.

THE POLITICS OF
ANTI-REALISM

by GERALD GRAFF

from SALMAGUNDI

nominated by SALMAGUNDI, *Elliott Anderson and Cynthia Ozick*

*(editor's note; Gerald Graff's article was the central argument in a symposium con-
ducted in Salmagundi #42. It was answered by essays from several of the writers he
discusses. In his introduction to Graff's piece,* Salmagundi *editor Robert Boyers
says—*

*"Though I couldn't go all the way with Graff on every detail—and he knows
better than to court perfect agreement—I was convinced that no previous item I'd
read had so persuasively criticised the cultural radicalism of our time. Nor had any
other essay so well exposed the dangerous myths that equate cultural radicalism
with effective political action. Graff had gone after some of our best writers and
thinkers, largely refusing to applaud the important work they'd done. But he'd set
himself another, more difficult task, which was nothing less than a profile of the intellectual milieu we inhabit. Others would have to apportion credit and blame and set
the record straight on Leslie Fiedler, Roland Barthes, Richard Poirier, Herbert Marcuse and the others. For Graff's purposes they were important because they'd
helped to create a revolution in the way we think about art and politics, and because
they'd contributed to the general confusion we share. Graff's essay makes us feel
there may be a way of dealing effectively with this confusion, and that too is an
achievement in a period so suspicious of positive suggestions as ours has been. . . .")*

WITH THE WANING of the political radicalism of the sixties,
"cultural radicalism" has grown proportionately in influence. The
radical legacy of the New Left and the counter culture seems increasingly to lie in the sphere of culture rather than of politics.
"Cultural radicalism" and "cultural revolution" are vague terms, of
course. They denote no particular school of thought but rather a
certain style of thinking, a pattern of typical oppositions and iden-
tifications whose rationale is usually left unformulated. This style of
thinking can be found today in structuralists and post-structuralists,
phenomenologists, post-Freudians and Jungians, existential and
Hegelian Marxists, and innumerable other manifestations of the

vanguard spirit in art, criticism, and social thought. More broadly
still, the patterns of radical cultural thought have become part of the
folk mythology of intellectuals as a group—and of those whose
outlook is shaped by intellectuals. The names and the movements
may change, but the structures of thought persist. Anybody today
who endeavors to think "advanced" thoughts about culture and
society is likely to think them through at least some of the patterns I
try to describe in this essay.

Central to the outlook of cultural radicalism is a romantic theory of
history which sees the progressive evolution of objective rationality
as a fall from the organic unity of prereflective stages of being. One
style of romanticism sought to overcome this fall, or escape its
consequences, by an imaginative return to the preindustrial past—
to antiquity, the Middle Ages, primitive or folk culture. Another
style of romanticism aimed not to reverse the course of progress but
to carry forward and fulfill its promise of human liberation. This
"romanticism of the left" sought to overcome the fall into reason by
using the imagination not retrospectively but prophetically, to
further the recovery of organic unity through a revolution exemplified by the sensibility of art. This radical romanticism at once
overturned the utopian assumptions of the Enlightenment and re-
stated them in a new form, the avant-garde quest for a progressive
expansion of the frontiers of consciousness.

Radical Parallelisms

The assumption cultural radicalism inherits from this left wing
romanticism is that a parallelism exists between psychological, epistemological, esthetic, and political categories of experience. Repression in psychology, rationalism in epistemology, representa-
tionalism and the elitism of high culture in esthetics are parallel
expressions of bourgeois social domination. A statement by Joyce
Carol Oates, in an essay entitled "New Heaven and Earth," illustrates the neatness of alignment sometimes attained by this parallelism:

> We have come to the end of, we are satiated with, the "objective,"
> valueless philosophies that have always worked to preserve a status
> quo, however archaic. We are tired of the old dichotomies: Sane/
> Insane, Normal/Sick, Black/White, Man/Nature, Victor/Vanquished,

and—above all this Cartesian dualism I/It. . . . They are no longer useful or pragmatic. They are no longer *true*.[1]

Political domination (Victor/Vanquished) is the correlative both of the epistemological separation of the knower from his object (I/It) and the psychological or medical differentiation of sanity from insanity. The central assumption here is that objective thought is the psychological and epistemological counterpart of political tyranny. There are several senses in which this is held; objective thought requires us to repress our emotions, to take a "valueless" stance in the interests of operational efficiency. This "reification" destroys the unity between ourselves and what we perceive and turns the "other" into an alien thing, ripe for domination and manipulations. In a parallel fashion, Western civilization turns both nature and human beings into manipulable things through technological mastery on the one hand and colonialism and exploitation on the other. Finally, by taking for granted the existence of a stable world "out there," objective thought presupposes a reality that is essentially unchangeable. By adjusting to the "reality principle," we reconcile ourselves to the established concensus as if it were an eternal law of nature. Thus Roland Barthes can assert that "the disease of thinking in essences . . . is at the bottom of every bourgeois mythology of man."[2]

Far from representing the culmination of man's struggle against ignorance and superstition, then, objective thought emerges as at best a precondition of the expanded material basis on which a non-aggressive society must depend, as a stage in the evolution of consciousness toward a reunified sensibility. It follows that the cultural revolution must be conceived as a revolt against the reality principle in the name of the pleasure principle, as the overcoming of repressive reason by imagination—or by a new "reason" based on Eros, fantasy, non-aggressive desire. The struggle, as Herbert Marcuse defines it, is "between the logic of domination and the will to gratification," both asserting their claims "for defining the reality principle. The traditional ontology is contested: against the conception of being in terms of Logos rises the conception of being in a-logical terms: will and joy. This countertrend struggles to formulate its own Logos: the logic of gratification."[3] By undermining the

[1]Joyce Carol Oates, "New Heaven and Earth," *Saturday Review of the Arts*, Vol. LV, 45 (November, 1972), p. 53.
[2]Roland Barthes, *Mythologies*, trans. A. Lavers (New York: Hill and Wang, 1972), p. 75.

epistemological and instinctual bases of domination, the cultural
revolution prepares the way for the political transformation of society, though the precise nature of this transformation may as yet be
only vaguely forseeable. At present, it may only be possible to say, as
Richard Poirier says, that any political solutions "will require a
radical change in the historical, philosophical, and psychological
assumptions that are the foundation of any political or economic
system. Some kind of cultural revolution is therefore the necessary
prelude even to our capacity to think intelligently about political
revolution."[4]

Art plays a key role in the social vision of the cultural revolution,
but not as propaganda art or as socialist realism. For though in
content these methods may be radical, in their *forms*, and the modes
of perception embodied in their forms, they are conventional and
reactionary. Overthrowing the established form of society means
overthrowing realism, or going "beyond realism." Art, defined as an
autonomous expression of the imagination, not passively receiving
its laws from nature but freely dictating them to nature, is seen as the
epitome of liberated sensibility. The romantic opposition between
discursive and creative meaning, between language used as a practical *sign* and language used as a constitutive *symbol*, corresponds to
the distinction between tyranny and liberation. The imagination's
independence from reality exemplifies the human spirit's break with
political oppression and psychic repression, with all preestablished
ideas of reality. As Frank Kermode writes, ecoding Barthes, "the
whole movement towards 'secretarial' realism" represents "an
anachronistic myth of common understanding and shared universes
of meaning."[5] By refusing to hold a mirror up to nature and by
exploding the very idea of stable "nature," art undermines the
psychological and epistemological bases of the ruling order. The
revolt against realism and representation is closely tied to the revolt
against a unitary psychology of the self. As Leo Bersani argues in *A
Future for Astyanax*, "the literary myth of a rigidly ordered self," a
myth perpetuated by realism, "contributes to a pervasive cultural

---

[3]Herbert Marcuse, *Eros and Civilization: A Philosophical Inquiry into Freud* (New York:
Vintage Books, 1962), p. 113.
[4]Richard Poirier, *The Performing Self: Compositions and Decompositions in the Languages of
Contemporary Life* (New York: Oxford University Press, 1970), p. 144.
[5]Frank Kermode, "Novels: Recognition and Deception," *Critical Inquiry*, Vol I, 1 (Sept.,
1974), p. 112.

ideology of the self which serves the established social order."[6]

Radical art ruptures not only the forced unification of the self but also the linguistic "contracts" which impose uniform assumptions, reassuring us that reality is known in advance. Alain Robbe-Grillet says that "academic criticism in the West, as in the Communist countries, employs the word 'realism' as if reality were already entirely constituted (whether for good and all or not) when the writer comes on the scene. Thus it supposes that the latter's role is limited to 'explaining' and to 'expressing' the reality of his period."[7] In a similar vein, Roland Barthes disparages the conventions of narrative fiction as "formal pacts made between the writer and society for the justification of the former and the serenity of the latter."[8] "Classical language," says Barthes, "is a bringer of euphoria because it is immediately social,"[9] implying a world known and agreed upon in advance—packaged, as it were, for the convenience of the consumer. Narrative realism is "the currency in use in a society apprised by the very form of words of the meaning of what it consumes."[10] Preestablished codes imply a myth of preestablished reality and order, and "the content of the word 'Order' always indicates repression."[11]

The move beyond the "correspondence" theory of language entails a rejection of the mimetic view of criticism along with the mimetic view of literature. Just as literature must explode the bourgeois myth of a real world independent of human perception and fantasy, so criticism must divest itself of the academic myths of "the work itself," the "intention" of the author, and the "text" as a reified object. The theory that literature radically "defamiliarizes" our perception of reality spawns the corollary, that criticism ought to defamiliarize our perception of literature. Just as the literary work destroys our complacent agreement about the nature of reality, criticism "deconstructs" the static, canonical interpretations by which conventional scholarship entraps the work and domesticates its potentially explosive energies. These moves beyond realism and beyond objective interpretation are paralleled in turn by a third

[6]Leo Bersani, *A Future for Astyanax: Character and Desire in Literature* (New York: Little, Brown, 1976), p. 56.
[7]Alain Robbe-Grillet, *For a New Novel* (New York: Grove Press, 1965), p. 160.
[8]Barthes, *Writing Degree Zero*, trans. A. Lavers (New York: Hill and Wang, 1953), p. 32.
[9] *Ibid.*, p. 49.
[10] *Ibid.*, p. 32.
[11]*Ibid.*, p. 26.

impulse, which seeks to go beyond elitist hierarchies of high and low culture. The old-fashioned writer's conformity to a preestablished reality or the old-fashioned critic's conformity to an objective text or to a body of critical principles and criteria are emblems of the mass man's conformity to the propaganda and manipulation of organized technological society. These equations may not coexist in all radical theories, but they form a logical unity. I propose to examine them in turn.

Beyond Realism

One of the most systematic attempts at an anti-realistic theory of radical esthetics has been made by Herbert Marcuse, whom I shall treat at some length here. Unlike Barthes, Marcuse resists the equation of "classical language" and classical form with bourgeois political domination; he attacks Herbert Read and other avant-garde irrationalists for assuming that "classicism is the intellectual counterpart of political tyranny." Bourgeois art, including bourgeois realism, according to Marcuse, "transcends all particular class content." Through its expression of specifically bourgeois concerns, this art achieves a "universal meaning" that may be liberating for all classes.[12] Agreeing with Trotsky's strictures against an exclusively proletarian culture, Marcuse holds that the cultural revolution should not repudiate bourgeois culture, but should try to "recapture and transform" its "critical, negating, transcending qualities."[13] Marcuse's own esthetic theory attempts to use the concepts of Kant, Schiller, and Freud while overcoming their bourgeois limitations. Marcuse's respect for classical art distinguishes his position from that of Barthes. But Marcuse defends classical art only by describing it in romantic terms. Hence, he, like Barthes, opposes art to classical rationality and anything resembling mimesis. As thoroughly as any romantic theorist, Marcuse identifies art with the pleasure principle and denies its dependence on the reality principle. Following Kant and Schiller, Marcuse defines art as a "non-conceptual truth of the senses."[14] Though art may *use* concepts as part of its raw material, it

[12]Marcuse, *Counterrevolution and Revolt* (Boston: Beacon Press, 1972), pp. 89–90.
[13]*Ibid.*, p. 93.
[14]Marcuse, *Eros and Civilization*, p. 169. "The norms which govern the aesthetic order are *not* 'intellectual concepts'" (*Counterrevolution and Revolt*, p. 95).

is not obliged to reflect conceptual or theoretical truth. Marcuse thus rejects Lukács' praise of bourgeois critical realism for depicting "the basic laws which represent capitalist society." This requirement, he says "offends the very nature of art. For the basic structure and dynamic of society can never find sensuous, esthetic expression: they are, in Marxian theory, the essence behind the appearance, which can only be attained through scientific analysis, and formulated only in terms of such an analysis. The open form cannot close the gap between the scientific truth and its esthetic appearance."[15]

Such a passage suggests how ambivalent Marcuse can be with respect to classical rationality, how he hovers on the edge of romantic irrationalism without ever quite taking the plunge. On the one hand, he calls for a new "conception of being in a-logical terms: will and joy," a "logic of gratification."[16] On the other hand, he does not reject Marxist "scientific analysis." We shall return to this problem later. For the moment, the important point is that though Marcuse does not wholly deny the possibility or desirability of an objectivist or realistic epistemology, he distinguishes this epistemology from that of art, contrasting art with science in the customary romantic fashion. For the creative imagination, he says, summarizing Kant, "the experience in which the object is thus 'given' is totally different from the every-day as well as scientific experience; all links between the object and the world of theoretical and practical reason are severed, or rather suspended."[17] Presumably, these oppositions between the esthetic and the theoretical and practical realms are "transcended" by the work of art itself, or by the revolutionary realization of artistic vision in the society of the future. But art remains for Marcuse a non-conceptual mode of experience. It does not reflect reality.

A similar, though more equivocal rejection of realism characterizes much of the current revival of Marxist criticism. Siding with Brecht over Lukács, the New Marxism often leans toward the kind of analogical reasoning—long common in bourgeois avant-garde circles—which regards "open" forms as progressive, "closed" ones as reactionary. Thus Terry Eagleton, in *Criticism and Ideology*, opposes "Lukács' nostalgic organicism, his traditionalist preference for closed, symmetrical totalities," to "open, multiple forms which

[15]Marcuse, *Counterrevolution and Revolt*, p. 125.
[16]Marcuse, *Eros and Civilization*, p. 113.
[17]*Ibid.*, p. 162.

bear in their torsions the very imprint of the contradictions they lay
bare."[18] But how can open, multiple forms "lay bare" contradictions
when they are, so often, themselves expressions of a viewpoint
distorted by alienation? Where does literature get the perspective
that permits it to present distortion *as* distortion, to make itself a
criticism of contradictions rather than a symptom of them?

In another book, *Marxism and Literary Criticism*, Eagleton
hedges on these questions. He says that art can "yield us a kind of
truth," but this truth is "not, to be sure, a scientific or theoretical
truth." Rather, it is "the truth of how men experience their conditions of life and how they protest against them." In other words,
"though art is not in itself a scientific mode of truth, it can, nevertheless, communicate the *experience* of such a scientific (i.e., revolutionary) understanding of society. This is the experience which
revolutionary art can yield us." This sounds like a left-wing version of
Susanne Langer's theory that art yields a "virtual experience" of
understanding without the content of understanding, or like T. S.
Eliot's view that poetry does not solicit beliefs but shows us "what it
feels like" to have beliefs. The separation between the conceptual
and the experiential, so familiar in bourgeois esthetic theory, is not
overcome. Or is it? Eagleton does suggest that art somehow gives a
critical perspective toward ideology:

> Science gives us conceptual knowledge of a situation; art gives us the
> experience of that situation, which is equivalent to ideology. But by
> doing this, it allows us to "see" the nature of that ideology, and thus
> begins to move us towards that full understanding of ideology which
> is scientific knowledge.[19]

It is not clear how a work of art can let us "see" the nature of an
ideology (and why the quotation marks?) without communicating a
conceptual apprehension of the ideology. Either the audience perceives the ideology *as* an ideology, in which case it conceptualizes it,
or it does not see the ideology at all. The same equivocations over
realism can be found in other current Hegelian and existential
Marxists, but I cannot dwell on these theories here. One can appre-
ciate the determination of the neo-Marxists to avoid the crudities of

[18]Terry Eagleton, *Criticism and Ideology: a Study in Marxist Literary Theory* (London: NLB,
1977), p. 161.
[19]Eagleton, *Marxism and Literary Criticism* (Berkeley: University of California Press, 1976),
p. 74, p. 83, n. 16.

vulgar Stalinist realism with its dismissal of modernist experiment forms. But in their sympathy with the anti-realistic premises of modernism, the neo-Marxists may have abandoned the critical standpoint which makes Marxism a corrective to conventional modernist literary positions. Marcuse avoids these contradictions by unequivocally denying the realistic and theoretical nature of art. But Marcuse, too, as we shall see, has problems when he attempts to account for the subversive power of art.

How *does* Marcuse account for this subversive power? Marcuse says this power resides not in the content of art but in its form. It is art's freedom from conceptual reality, in fact, its ability to create out of the autonomy of the imagination that "other nature" which, as Kant theorized, supplies a "completeness of which there is no example in nature," that makes art a criticism of the existing order. By freely dreaming new possibilities of desire that have never been embodied in the actual world, art gives us a measure of the unsatisfactory reality around us. In this sense, all art for Marcuse is formalistic art—even realism. For though the world of a work of art may, as he says, be "derived from the existing one," it transforms this raw material according the esthetic laws of art and the psychological laws of the mind.[20] In other words, though art may employ realistic conventions, it cannot serve a realistic ontology. "The norms governing the order of art are not those governing reality but rather the norms of its negation,"[21] a negation implicit in the form and style of art as such. Marcuse connects Kant's idea of the imagination and Schiller's idea of art as "play" with the Freudian concepts of the pleasure principle, Eros, and "the return of the repressed."[22]

Art then, regardless of its specific content, evokes "the power of the negative." Its very structure is made up of "the words, the images, the music of another reality, of another order repelled by the existing one and yet alive in memory and anticipation. . . ."[23] This means that even the artist who sets out to justify the established political order actually ends up subverting it. Marcuse thus arrives at a different sort of justification for explicitly "reactionary" art than that of traditional Marxist criticism, which also seeks to locate a "progressive" content unintended by the creator of the work. Marx,

[20]Marcuse, *Counterrevolution and Revolt*, p. 92.
[21]*Ibid.*, p. 95.
[22]Marcuse, *Eros and Civilization*, p. 130.
[23]Marcuse, *Counterrevolution and Revolt*, p. 92.

Engels, and Lukács praised the novels of Balzac for giving a picture of social reality unwittingly at odds with the author's intended legitimist message. For Marcuse, such writings are revolutionary not because they imitate the real world but because they negate it. Form is not transparent representation but transformation of reality, and for this reason subversive.

On the other hand, Marcuse holds that the purely esthetic nature of artistic negation limits the political effectiveness of art: "the critical function of art is self-defeating. The very commitment of art to form vitiates the negation of unfreedom in art." The element of "semblance" in art "necessarily subjects the represented reality to esthetic standards and thus deprives it of its terror."[24] This fact explains for Marcuse why societies have often been able to domesticate radical art and render its rebellion harmless. Marcuse's esthetic writings are studded with warnings against overestimating the power of art by itself to precipitate a revolution. Nevertheless, despite these cautions, Marcuse does not cease affirming that art embodies the very spirit of human liberation. And in *Essay on Liberation*, a kind of manifesto of the late sixties, Marcuse judged that the "disorderly, uncivil, farcical, artistic desublimation of culture constitutes an essential element of radical politics: of the subverting forces in transition."[25]

In the esthetic of the cultural left, one of the chief means by which art presumably exercises a subversive political effect is by shattering familiar modes of perception. This esthetic of "defamiliarization," as it has been called,[26] has its roots in the romantic idea that art strips away the veil of customary perception and permits us to see the world in a new light. At first sight, this doctrine appears antiformalistic, and indeed it became one of the guiding assumptions of literary realism in the nineteenth century, in those realists who saw themselves as unmasking the false appearances of society. But formalism may itself appear as an esthetic of defamiliarization, an esthetic that seeks to explode the familiarities of realism. Formalism defamiliarizes experience not in order to reveal some truth behind

[24]Marcuse, *Eros and Civilization*, p. 131.

[25]Marcuse, *Essay on Liberation* (Boston: Beacon Press, 1969), p. 48.

[26]See Robert Scholes' discussion of this concept in Russian formalist criticism in *Structuralism and Literature: an Introduction* (New Haven: Yale University Press, 1974), pp. 83–85, pp. 173–76; also Jonathan Culler, *Structuralist Poetics: Structuralism, Linguistics, and the Study of Literature* (Ithaca: Cornell University Press, 1975), p. 134.

the veil, but rather in order to dislodge us from our expectation of ever encountering truth. It is this use that Marcuse makes of the concept of esthetic defamiliarization, enabling him to reconcile his Kantian formalism with a kind of surrealism.

Marcuse writes of "surrealistic forms of protest and refusal" as the needed solvent of "repressive reason" in one-dimensional society.[27] He celebrates the verbal disruptions of experimental literature, which break the oppressive rule of the established language and images over the mind of man. He stresses that art dissolves the film of familiarity and cliché which, in advanced society, intercedes between reality and our perceptions:

> Non-objective, abstract painting and sculpture, stream-of-consciousness and formalist literature, twelve-tone composition, blues and jazz: these are not merely new modes of perception reorienting and intensifying the old ones, they rather dissolve the very structure of perception in order to make room—for what? The new object of art is not yet "given," but the familiar object has become impossible, false. From illusion, imitation, harmony to reality—but the reality is not yet "given"; it is not the one which is the object of "realism." Reality has to be discovered and projected. The senses must learn not to see things anymore in the medium of that law and order which has formed them; the bad functionalism which organizes our sensibility must be smashed.[28]

Art in this way brings into being a "new sensorium." In the universe of art, Marcuse says, everything "is 'new,' different—breaking the familiar context of perception and understanding, of sense certainty and reason in which men and nature are enclosed.[29]

This concept of radical perceptual disruption informs the esthetics of "self-conscious" fiction, science fiction, and other departures from realism. David Ketterer, for example, writes of the "radical disorientation" produced in the reader by science fiction conventions, and Darko Suvin calls this effect one of "cognitive estrangement." According to Ketterer, the new epistemology of science fiction tends to "destroy old assumptions and suggest a new, and often more visionary reality."[30] A similar view is advanced by Robert Scholes. Science

[27] Marcuse, *Essay on Liberation*, p. 30.
[28] *Ibid.*, pp. 38–9.
[29] Marcuse, *Counterrevolution and Revolt*, p. 98.
[30] Quoted by James Stupple, "Fiction Against the Future," *The American Scholar*, Vol. 46, 2 (Spring, 1977), p. 219.

fiction, Scholes says, "can regenerate a criticism of present life . . . through the construction of models of the future." Science fiction can serve this "model-making" critical function, according to Scholes, precisely because it is not burdened by the reactionary constraints of realistic probability but is "freed," as Scholes says, "of the problem of correspondence or noncorrespondence with some present actuality or some previously experienced past."[31] Similarly, for critics writing in this vein, literary reflexivity is radical: by calling into question the referential adequacy of the categories of understanding, it shakes us loose from our susceptibility to ideology.

Structuralism has served the purposes of radical esthetic theory by demonstrating that language is an affair of conventions, cultural creations that do not necessarily rest on truths of nature. Structuralism shows that signification is not a closed system, regulated by eternal meanings, but a process infinitely open to interpretation. In Barthes' use of structuralism, the departures of modern poetry from the "naturalized" cultural norms of prose have an exemplary value, shattering the illusion of a natural link between conventions, and the ideologies underlying them, and nature. Barthes contrasts realistic prose, that presupposes a closed, completed universe, with "the terror of an expression without laws" evoked by modern poetry, where "the word is no longer guided *in advance* by the general intention of a socialized discourse."[32] "Each poetic word is thus an unexpected object, a Pandora's box from which fly out all the potentialities of language"—a discourse "terrible and inhuman."[33] The modern poet in this way exposes the worthlessness of bourgeois "currency," for underlying it is only the fiction of an eternal order of reality.

Both Barthes and Marcuse are aware of the paradoxical and equivocal nature of this mode of artistic negation. Marcuse cites Barthes' *Writing Degree Zero* in *One-Dimensional Man* as an example of the kind of vanguard theory which is forced, by "the total mobilization of all media for the defense of the established reality," to call for a "break with communication" itself.[34] Marcuse recognizes

---

[31] Robert Scholes, "The Fictional Criticism of the Future," *TriQuarterly*, No. 34 (Fall, 1975), p. 242.
[32] Barthes, *Writing Degree Zero*, p. 48.
[33] *Ibid.*, p. 26.
[34] Marcuse, *One-Dimensional Man: Studies in the Ideology of Advanced Industrial Society* (Boston: Beacon Press, 1964), p. 68.

that such anti-art may be politically innocuous, along with the art that expresses "a fashionably desublimated, verbal release of sexuality."[35] He condemns the irrationalism and mysticism of Norman O. Brown, Charles Reich, and the counter culture. He argues that the "revolution in perception" is vitiated when, through drugs or other stimulants, "its narcotic character brings temporary release not only from the reason and rationality of the established system but also from that other rationality which is to change the established system."[36] In the early seventies in particular, Marcuse seemed to retract some of the sympathy he had previously expressed for the irrationalistic ruptures of vanguard art. In *Counterrevolution and Revolt* (1972), Marcuse attacks Artaudian Theater of Cruelty, Living Theater, and rock culture as symptoms rather than criticisms of a sick society: "to the degree to which it makes itself part of real life," he says, this art "loses the transcendence which opposes art to the established order. . . ."[37] The criticism is well taken. What is not clear, however, is why Marcuse's own endorsement of formalism and surrealism, indeed Marcuse's definition of all art, should be immune to it. The shattering of the reality principle Marcuse calls for, the overcoming of the subject-object distinction, the emergence of a "new sensorium"—these things would seem to entail the very merging of art and life which Marcuse here deplores.

Radical esthetics without realism has been expounded by several American critics in a form that at first appears to be anti-political. In *The Confusion of Realms*, Richard Gilman attacks all artistic theory and practice which takes literature to be "an employment of language for ends beyond itself."[38] Invoking recent self-reflexive experimental fiction (Barthelme, Gass, Updike) and the criticism of Susan Sontag, Gilman argues that literary works are self-sufficient, self-justifying universes within themselves, not second-order representations of some already existing reality. Literature is properly an "increment," not a "complement," Gilman says;[39] it need not communicate "experience of any kind except an esthetic one,"[40] and

---

[35] Marcuse, *Counterrevolution and Revolt*, p. 118, n.
[36] Marcuse, *Essay on Liberation*, p. 37.
[37] Marcuse, *Counterrevolution and Revolt*, p. 101.
[38] Richard Gilman, *The Confusion of Realms* (New York: Random House, 1969), p. 49.
[39] *Ibid.*, p. 264. p. 48.
[40] *Ibid* p. 48.

it has "no reason for being other than to test and exemplify new forms
of consciousness, which, moreover, have had to be invented precisely because actuality is incapable of generating them."[41] Elsewhere, Gilman applauds "the secularization of art," which is to say,
"its chastening and the removal from it of the 'values' that ought to be
obtained elsewhere, i.e., the moral, social, and philosophical values
which literature and art were once expected to communicate."[42]
Richard Poirier, advancing an esthetic of "the performing self,"
agrees with these sentiments. He endorses Gilman's attack on those
who "confuse realms" by subordinating art to political ends and
holds that "literature has only one responsibility—to be compelled
and compelling about its own inventions."[43] In A World Elsewhere,
Poirier argues that American literature, in its classic embodiments,
can be seen as a series of attempts to create fictive worlds of pure
"style" against the alien laws of politics, morality, and social behavior. These works create "an imaginative environment that excludes
the standards of that 'real' one to which most critics subscribe."[44] A
similarly anti-political formalism appears in the theories of Susan
Sontag, Leo Bersani, and many others. These critics suggest that the
psychic experimentalism of modern art is incompatible with the
collective goals of humanitarian social reform, whether liberal or
socialist. For them the cultural revolution speaks for antinomian
energies which cannot be domesticated within the organized forms
of politics and cannot be tailored to fit the requirements of any
imaginable society, however ideal.

   In its very disengagement from society and politics, however, this
formalism reveals its political animus. The ostensibly chastened
renunciation of humanistic pretentions for literature serves the
aggressive aim of subverting the bourgeois mentality. Gilman's assertion that literature ought not be "an employment of language for
ends beyond itself" contradicts his assertion that literature's purpose is to "test and exemplify new forms of consciousness," for the
new forms of consciousness are obviously designed to subvert the
old ones. Like Marcuse, Gilman proposes formalism as a weapon—

[41] Ibid., p. 72.
[42] Gilman, "The Idea of the Avant-Garde," Partisan Review, Vol. XXXIX (Summer, 1972), p.
395.
[43] Poirier, The Performing Self. p. 31.
[44] Poirier, A World Elsewhere: the Place of Style in American Literature (New York: Oxford
University Press, 1966), p. 7.

the epistemological solvent of the bourgeois reality principle and the "old Mediterranean values" which "are making some of us sick with a sense of lacerating irony."[45] The glorification of literature as a "world elsewhere," in the very process of divorcing literature from politics, betrays political resentment. It bespeaks a perception that, as Poirier puts it, "there is nothing within the real world, or in the systems which dominate it, that can possibly satisfy" our aspirations.[46] The same impulse that turns formalism against society turns it against radical politics, seen as a mere extension of the over-organized, over-rationalized social order.

Beyond Objective Criticism

As I have noted in a previous essay,[47] some recent commentators have seen the strangulation of art by criticism as a kind of literary counterpart of imperialism or industrial pollution. Thus Susan Sontag: "Like the fumes of the automobile and of heavy industry which befoul the urban atmosphere, the effusion of interpretations of art today poisons our sensibilities." Interpretation, she adds, is "the revenge of the intellect upon art."[48] It follows that art must get its own back by defining itself as the revenge of sensibility against the intellect, which is to say, against a culture whose political repressiveness is presumably exemplified in its overintellectuality. In this spirit, Leslie Fiedler calls for a postmodern criticism that abandons hollow pretentions to correctness and asserts itself unabashedly as creative writing, a criticism "poetic in form as well as in substance."[49] As if in response to Fiedler's call, a number of theories have arisen, including Ihab Hassan's "paracriticism" (which makes "mixed use of discomfirmation and discontinuity, of space, silence, self-query, and surprise"), Roland Barthes' evocation of the text as "a body of bliss consisting solely of erotic relations," Stanley Fish's

---

[45] Gilman, *The Confusion of Realms*, p. 19.
[46] Poirier, *A World Elsewhere*, p. 5. I discuss Gilman and Poirier at greater length in "Aestheticism and Cultural Politics," *Social Research*, Vol. XL (Summer, 1973), pp. 311–343.
[47] See "What Was New Criticism? Literary Interpretation and Scientific Objectivity," *Salmagundi*, No. 27 (Fall, 1974), pp. 72—93.
[48] Susan Sontag. *Against Interpretation* (New York: Delta Books, 1967), p. 7.
[49] Leslie Fiedler, "Cross the Border, Close the Gap," *Playboy*, Vol. 16 (December, 1969), p. 230.

"affective stylistics," and Harold Bloom and J. Hillis Miller's arguments for the necessity of "misreading."[50] These theories argue not only that the reader must create the text—a proposition defensible enough if understood in the right way—but that he must (or should) create it without reference to any control outside the fictions imposed by his subjectivity or by the open-ended possibilities of language. That the reader is thereby "liberated" in some way is taken to be beyond argument, even though not all these theories conceive the liberation in political terms.

But in some instances, the attack on objective interpretation has been given a Marxian twist, with the suggestion that the very concept of textual determinacy is an extension of the system of private property. Again, the reasoning is highly analogical. Objectivity is a kind of police force suppressing the creative flow of interpretation. Or objective interpretation treats the text as a kind of "currency," bound by linguistic "contracts" to the existing class system. By freeing the text from the author's intended meaning and treating it as "multivalent," "plural," and open to the uninhibited and loving "play" of interpretation, the critic, it is implied, trangresses the bourgeois system of ownership:

> A multivalent text [Barthes argues] can carry out its basic duplicity only if it subverts the opposition between the true and the false, if it fails to attribute quotations (even when seeking to discredit them) to explicit authorities, if it flouts all respect for origin, paternity, propriety, if it destroys the voice which could give the text its ("organic") unity, in short, if it coldly and fraudulently abolishes quotation marks which must, as we say, in all *honesty*, enclose a quotation and juridically distribute the ownership of the sentences to their respective proprietors, like subdivisions of a field. For multivalence (contradicted by irony) is a transgression of ownership.[51]

Barthes' disengagement in *S/Z* of Balzac's "Sarrasine," then, from its author's apparent intention is aimed at bourgeois "propriety" (paralleled by bourgeois "paternity"), not merely the external propriety of

---

[50] Ihab Hassan, "Joyce, Beckett, and the Postmodern imagination," *TriQuarterly*, No. 34 (Fall 1975), p. 181; Barthes, *The Pleasure of the Text*, trans. R. Miller (New York: Hill and Wang, 1975), p. 16; Stanley Fish, "Interpreting the *Variorum*," *Critical Inquiry*, Vol. II, 3 (Spring, 1976), pp. 463–85; Harold Bloom, *A Map of Misreading* (New York: Oxford University Press, 1975); J. Hillis Miller, "Deconstructing the Deconstructers," *Diacritics* (Summer, 1975), p. 30.

[51] Barthes, *S/Z*, trans. R. Miller (New York: Hill and Wang, 1974), pp. 44–45.

social and literary decorum but the structures of possession and control this decorum rationalizes. At the very least, this kind of reading presumably undermines the ideology of professional literary study.

Critics who wish to liberate the reader from the determinacy of the text often write as if the only alternative were a kind of critical Final Solution that shuts off all disagreement out of a neurotic fear of uncertainty. Thus Barthes dismisses the problem of interpretive truth with the assertion that "the language each critic chooses does not come down to him from Heaven."[52] He thereby implies that if you are looking for truth in your interpretations, you are probably longing for some kind of theocratic authority to relieve you of the anxiety of choice. Start believing in the existence of an objective world or text, and the next thing you know you will be calling out the ideological police—demanding censorship and suppressing disagreement. At the very least, you convict yourself of existential cowardice. This reduction of the issue to a simple polarity of tyranny vs. freedom, bad faith vs. authenticity, is seen in an often-quoted statement by Derrida:

> There are thus two interpretations of interpretation, of structure, of sign, of freeplay. The one seeks to decipher, dreams of deciphering, a truth or an origin which is free from freeplay or from the order of the sign, and lives like an exile the necessity of interpretation. The other, which is no longer turned toward the origin, affirms freeplay and tries to pass beyond man and humanism, the name of man being the name of that being who, throughout the history of metaphysics or of ontotheology—in other words, through the history of all of his history—has dreamed of full presence, the reassuring foundation, the origin and the end of the game.[53]

Quoting this passage, Frank Kermode characterizes the contrast between types of interpretation as a contrast between "the old, Puritan, strict, limited, theocratic, radiating certainty about emblems and types," and "the new, which depends on the activity of

[52] Barthes, "What is Criticism?", *Critical Essays*, trans. R. Howard (Evanston: Northwestern University Press, 1972), p. 260.
[53] Jacques Derrida, "Structure, Sign, and Play in the Discourse of the Human Sciences," *The Structuralist Controversy: The Languages of Criticism and the Sciences of Man*, ed., E. Donato and R. Macksey (Baltimore: Johns Hopkins University Press, 1972), p. 264.

the individual creative mind, on the light of imagination."[54] The
choice having been reduced to one between defensive Puritanism
and open-minded creativity, not much remains to argue about.

Beyond High Culture

Like literary realism and objective criticism, the distinction between high and low culture is attacked as a sympton of elitist
ideology. Not only is a preference for high over mass culture presumably "elitist," but this label is sometimes applied to virtually any
critical reservations about mass culture. Leslie Fiedler, for example,
equates high culture with the "finicky canons of the genteel tradition."[55] Against this genteel tradition Fiedler poses an insurgent,
anti-hierarchical, irreverent popular culture, and a postmodern art
and criticism impatient with the old boundaries and determined to
"cross the border, close the gap." "The final intrusion of pop into the
citadels of high art," Fiedler says, presents "the exhilarating new
possibility of making judgments about the goodness and badness of
art quite separated from distinctions between high and low, with
their concealed class bias."[56]

Richard Wasson expresses a similar exhilaration. The merging of
high and mss culture in the sixties, Wasson believes, signalled the
end of the dichotomy of action and contemplation that has kept the
intellectual in a position of sterile isolation. The sixties, he writes,
"give us a series of metaphors of culture which we might categorize
as incarnational: culture leaves its sacred cloister and goes into the
world to participate in the joys and sorrows of the human community
and to work for its redemption."[57] One of Wasson's examples of this
"incarnational" overcoming of distinctions is Northrop Frye's system
of archetypes, which permits us to "demystify the discipline of
English studies" by showing that the same mythic and generic
structures pervade high and low forms alike. "That is why the
standard criticism of Frye—that one can fine archetypes
everywhere— is so absurd; it's precisely because they are omnipresent that the literary critic can speak to the problems of civilization, can use his special competence to participate in the efforts of

[54] Kermode, "Novels: Recognition and Deception," p. 119.
[55] Fiedler, "Cross the Border, Close the Gap," p. 230.
[56] *Ibid.*, p. 256.
[57] Richard Wasson, "From Priest to Prometheus: Culture and Criticism in the Post-Modern
Period," *Journal of Modern Literature*, Vol. III, 5 (July, 1974), p. 1201.

mankind to shape the world."[58] And again: "for Frye the job of the man of culture is not to defend highbrow culture but to demystify forms of communication by revealing their connections."[59] In Marcuse and Frye, Wasson concludes, "imaginative culture" transcends traditional distinctions; it "furthers the cause of Eros, of freedom, of liberation; it is not a spiritual discipline, an inner check, a hostile force opposed to the mass and popular arts, but a vehicle of liberation."[60]

The logic of this argument leads Wasson to congratulate Frye for declining to "consider advertising as 'bad' or 'false' or a mass media to be opposed by highbrow taste." He refers specifically to a statement by Frye that "to protect ourselves in a world such as ours" we have to look at advertising ironically, so that instead of rejecting it we "choose what we want out of what's offered to us and let the rest go." Here, Wasson comments, "advertising is appropriated into the total form of literature, into the world of archetypes. We react to advertising in the context of our understanding of verbal statements, of the visions of the world that literature gives, and in that context we accept or reject the vision. Literature, literary criticism, and literary education play then a decisive role in shaping the civilization we have and the civilization we want."[61]

This argument is elusive: if, as Frye suggests, advertising is something from which we need to protect ourselves by means of irony, then where does this irony come from if not from some external perspective superior to advertising? Is not irony a bit condescending, a bit "elitist"? Wasson evidently recognizes the need to maintain a critical view of mass culture, yet the need to avoid the elitism of "highbrow taste" encourages the elimination of critical distance. What do we do when mass culture fails to correspond, precisely, to "the civilization we want"? And how do we know "what we want" unless we examine our desires critically and objectively? Critical principles seem to be required somewhere here, yet such principles seem incompatible with culture defined as an expression of the joys of Eros and of "incarnational unity of being." If detachment and dualism are equated with elitism, then the very resistance of intel-

[58] *Ibid.*, p. 1195.
[59] *Ibid.*, p. 1197.
[60] *Ibid.*, p. 1201.
[61] *Ibid.*, p. 1197.

lectuals to society comes to be suspect. In the name of radical egalitarianism, criticism has to be liquidated.

Radical Contradictions

Here we can begin to see how the typical equations and oppositions of radical esthetics open it to difficulties. By equating imagination, Eros, and the pleasure principle with liberation and conceptual rationality with repression and elitism, radical esthetics accedes to the kind of technological dissociation of sensibility that it aims to oppose. Though this esthetics protests against positivistic and philistine reductions of art to the status of mere fantasy and myth, it reinstates these reductions in its own definition of art as an explosion of the unrationalized aspects of the psyche. Radical esthetics may claim to "reconcile" art and reason, but the reconciliation is prevented by the repudiation of mimetic theories of art and by the antinomy of theoretical and imaginative truth. Presupposing the degraded view of reason that identifies it with functional rationality, radical esthetics embarks on a self-defeating effort to make creative imagination, Eros, the senses do the work that only the reasoning intellect can do. This effort implants a familiar contradiction into radical culture; in exposing objective reason as an ideology, radicalism leaves itself no means of legitimizing its own critique of injustice and exploitation. If objectivity is a myth, then the rationale of tyranny is undermined, but so is the rationale of principled resistance to tyranny. Radical esthetics equates liberation with the transcendence of the subject-object distinction, as embodied in art and in the new sensibility. But such transcendence blurs the distinction between reality and myth and undermines the possibility of criticism.

The chronic ambiguity of its epistemology makes formalism an equivocal basis for an esthetic of radical intransigence. Formalism vacillates between opposing itself to reality and to the languages of practical discourse and appropriating them. Though formalism likes to oppose art to life, it also frequently confuses art with life, turning "life" itself into a set of literary fictions. When formalists like Gilman and Poirier suggest that "reality" is a myth of the imagination they perpetrate the "confusion of realms" they attack. If one strategy of formalism is to turn its back on politics and history and withdraw into the "world elsewhere" of art, another is to take revenge on politics and history by annexing them into the structures of art, turning them into manifestations of the imagination and the ego.

Thus Poirier, for example, asserts that "all expressed forms of life, reality and history" are "fictions": "Where is the Civil War and how do we know it? Where is the President and how does anyone know him? Is he a history book, an epic poem, or a cartoon by David Levine?"[62] Art reacts against the general invasion of life by theatricality and unreality by universalizing it, abolishing reality itself. In the process, art loses its critical perspective.

Radical esthetics confuses the acceptance of a common reality with capitulation to political tyranny. It is this confusion that causes Barthes, for example, to denounce the esthetics of representation and realism, for such an esthetics, deriving from "classical" (or in Derrida's term, "logocentric") assumptions about language, presupposes a common reality as the ground of language. As Jonathan Culler summarizes Bathes' argument (with apparent agreement), representational writing "depends heavily on readers' ability to naturalize it and to recognize the common world which serves as point of reference; and consequently changes in the social situation, which make it clear that the world is not one, undermine this *écriture*."[63] It is a historical fact that the loss of a sense of a common world, shared by the various classes and nations, was a principal cause of the decline of mimesis as a literary mode. But it does not follow that we can accept the absence of a common world as a literal philosophical truth, nor certainly as a shibboleth of radicalism. To reject the existence of a common world as a bourgeois myth is simply to invalidate political discourse, which depends on the possibility of giving a uniform reference to terms such as "exploitation," "justice," "equality," "oppressor," and "oppressed."[64] These terms, of course, may be perverted in systematic ways by the conventional languages of a particular ruling class, but our ability to identify the perversion as a perversion depends on our ability to refer to a common world. By mistaking shared reality and shared language with a stifling conformity, Barthes ends up attacking no particular society but the process of socialization. He is led to promote an antinomian defini-

---

[62] Poirier, *Performing Self*, p. 29.

[63] Culler, *Structuralist Poetics*, p. 135.

[64] Culler acknowledges the necessity of a "common world" when he says that "the possibility of critical argument depends on shared notions of the acceptable and the unacceptable, a common ground which is nothing other than the procedures of reading" (*Ibid.*, 124). Culler notes that Barthes occasionally concedes this too (*Ibid.*, pp. 190–91).

tion of freedom as the refusal of community—a bourgeois definition of freedom if there ever was one.[65]

A radical esthetic based on formalism and defamiliarization encounters other kinds of problems. By breaking with the common language, such an esthetic deepens the division between art and society and perpetuates the spiral of artistic alienation and impotence. The more violently the arts overturn objective consciousness, the representational view of art, and the common language, the more surely do they guarantee their marginality and harmlessness—a condition which in its turn inspires renewed artistic attempts to overturn objective consciousness, representation, and common language. Aiming at intransigence, art ends up collaborating with its enemies, science, utilitarianism, and commerce, to ensure its unimportance. Redefining its alienation from society as a model of liberation, art boasts of its "secularization" as if it were a consciously chosen position rather than a consequence of antagonistic conditions. The strategic refusal of obedience to social demands on art permits the artist to ignore the fact that society has stopped making them.

The formalist strategy (and I include here those aggressive formalisms that do not retreat from life but absorb it through the projection of myth) is really a renunciation and an adaptation. It exploits the incidental virtues of the homelessness, impotence, and marginality which capitalism thrusts on the artistic intellectual. The esthetic affirmation of the spirit of "play," of the uninhibited exploration of the frontiers of consciousness, ignores the severely restricted boundaries within which this play and this exploration must take place. The play and the exploration presuppose the artist's dispossession of an interpretation that would permit him to master social experience. The formalist vocabulary assumes the alienation of the artist from society, but with the understanding that alienation and estrangement do not need to call themselves by these names. Separation from society and the loss of the perspective by which this

---

[65] See Culler's critique of the *Tel Quel* group (*Ibid.*, pp. 241–54). Eagleton writes well against those who see criticism as "the repressive father who cuts short the erotic sport of sense between text and reader, binding with the briars of its metasystem the joyfully pluralist intercourse of meanings between them. A libertarianism of text and reader, in short, typical of the *Tel Quel* group, which like all libertarianism fatally inverts itself into a mirror-image of bourgeois social relations" (*Criticisms and Ideology: a Study in Marxist Literary Theory* [London: NLB, 1977], pp. 42–3).

separation might be understood cease to be merely the unfortunate condition of art under a certain form of society, and become part of the very definition of art.

But the self-induced separatism of art represents only one side of a contradictory state of affairs. As the arts have wilfully separated from society they have, in certain new and paradoxical ways, become reunited with it. The estrangement of art from society has coincided with the estrangement of society, or of great segments of society, from itself. As the middle class has become disillusioned with science, commerce, affluence, and consumption and sceptical toward traditional bourgeois certainties, the separatism of the arts has actually drawn art and society into closer relation. Advanced art is, after all, not socially marginal; or rather, its very marginality makes it central in a society where displacement from the center (or no relation to the center, the sense that there is no center) has become the common fate.[66] If art, like the family and the church, has become what Christopher Lasch calls a "haven in a heartless world,"[67] a refuge of "humanness" that serves as a sort of vacation from the menacing world of work and competition, this fact only establishes its common ground with the community. If formalist esthetics is a way of living with alienation, this fact is more and more a source of social reconciliation than of social separation. In its ability to redescribe displacement from centrality as a revolutionary form of freedom and potency, advanced culture furnishes a model by which social powerlessness can be experienced as gratification. In this sense, those (largely on the left) who think that intellectuals like themselves have no power and those (largely on the right) who think

[66] As early as 1878, in *Anti-Dühring*, Engels saw the evolution of corporate capitalism rendering the capitalist himself superfluous:

> If the crises revealed the incapacity of the bourgeoisie any longer to control the modern productive forces, the conversion of the great organizations for production and communication into joint-stock companies and state property shows that for this purpose the bourgeoisie can be dispensed with. All the social functions of the capitalists are now carried out by salaried employees. The capitalist has no longer any social activity save the pocketing of revenues, the clipping of coupons, and gambling on the Stock Exchange, where the different capitalists fleece each other of their capital. Just as at first the capitalist mode of production displaced the workers, so now it displaces the capitalists, relegating them, just as it did the workers, to the superfluous population, even if in the first instance not to the industrial reserve army. (Frederick Engels, *Anti Dühring*, trans. E Burns [New York: International Publishers, 1972], p. 304).

[67] Christopher Lasch, "The Family as a Haven in a Heartless World" *Salmagundi*, 35 (Fall, 1976), pp. 42–55.

such intellectuals have too much are both right. In the cultural world today, powerlessness (and the command of its intellectual paradigms) confers power.

The terms in which it defines revolution and liberation make radical esthetics congenial to many elements of consumer society, for liberation from traditional constraints is an essential condition of the expansion of consumption. Consumer society, in its destruction of continuity through the exploitation of fashion, ephemeral novelty, and planned obsolescence, effects a "systematic derangement of the senses" that makes the disruptions and defamiliarizations of vanguard culture look puny by comparison. The superannuation of the past, the fluidity of personal relations, the malleability of the physical environment before technology and the spiritual environment before the myth-making of advertising, journalism, entertainment, and political propaganda combine not only to erode our assurance of reality but our ability to recognize this erosion and see it as harmful. Alienation from work, from the possibility of community, from belief in the possible intelligibility of reality have increasingly become the shared ground of middle class life. As this has occurred, adversary epistemologies that challenge the "logocentric" correspondence of language and mind with things lose their oppositional force. In demanding that words be liberated from the significations, fixed in advance, of socialized discourse, Barthes and other radical critics forget the extent to which advertising and mass culture have already accomplished this end. Their exposure of the inherently ideological nature of thought finds an echo in the popular cynicism that says that all judgments are "matters of opinion," and "who is to say" what is real and what is not?

Not only does consumer society generate feelings of social uselessness, it also helps shape the diagnoses of these feelings and the proposed remedies. Hence the emergence of new industries for the profitable dissemination of advanced theories of alienation and liberation. The politics of the self, which reduces history to the psychodrama of the autonomous imagination contending against a repressive superego, spreads from the esoteric discussions of intellectuals into everyday social and even commercial life. But again, commerce, advertising, and popular entertainment surpass the power of the most visionary art in offering a prospective escape from the limitations of ordinary human existence by way of a life of infinitely multiplying personalities, "life styles," and "environments." Through commodities symbolic of the open and liberated life, personal autonomy is consumed as a compensation for the superfluousness of the consumer. Recapitulating the fate of romantic art, the individual achieves autonomy at the very moment his contribution ceases to matter. Just as the autonomous artistic imagination is placed beyond criticism, the modern self is consoled for its dispossession of history, community and reality by having its "needs" placed beyond criticism. The "triumph of the therapeutic" closes the gap between sophisticated and lay cultures: no great distance separates the literary critic who looks to art for "a body of bliss consisting solely of erotic relations" from the encounter-group participant seeking to "get in touch with his body."

The "adversary culture," with its stylish powerlessness redefined as a form of erotic potency, thus becomes indistinguishable from the "adversary." Though advanced art is not necessarily popular or commercially successful, neither unpopularity nor commercial failure can any longer be plausibly attributed to the public's intolerance of innovation. The antinomian disparagement of "bourgeois values" is celebrated by the agencies of publicity, exploited by the manipulators of cultural fashion, and emulated in personal conduct—an additional reason why the ante of provocation and radical experiment must continually be raised if the arts are to justify their vanguard credentials. Perhaps only by refusing to assume material existence at all can art succeed in disappointing—though even this proposition is rendered dubious by the recent enthusiasm extended to Conceptual Art. The point seems to have been reached at which artistic intransigence is indistinguishable from celebration of the dynamisms of mass society. It is impossible to say whether the artistic "vanguard" is actually leading society or struggling to keep up with it.

In short, cultural radicalism ignores the disappearance of the paternalistic repressions it seeks to dissolve. Though "conservatives" may here and there protest the triumph of godlessness and immorality, no conservatism opposes the necessary expansion of consumer markets. Whereas power once required the appearance of sanction by the spiritual ideas of high culture, power today finds it possible to do without such sanctions, to exploit a culture of radical pluralism and ideological dissonance. Far from representing tradition and "elitism," the contemporary corporation is hostile to the fixity of traditional standards, which stand in the way of progress.

Hence the tolerance shown by corporate society to the kind of culture that crosses all the borders and closes all the gaps. Attacks on the vestiges of high cultural standards and realistic sensibility only further the transformation of culture into an appendage of the fashion industries, the subjection of all art and ideas to the law of planned obsolescence. The blurring of cultural levels celebrated by Fiedler and Wasson as an overcoming of "concealed class bias" only bespeaks the irrelevance of traditional discriminations of taste to the goals of managers and publicists. Insofar as radicalism makes the extirpation of high cultural snobbery the central objective, it encourages the illusion that mass culture is the democratic expression of the people, as if mass culture were not owned and operated by private interests.

The situation in the university departments of literature and the humanities echoes that of the social macrocosm. Just as the esthetics of radical defamiliarization blends with the dynamics of consumer society, attacks on the traditional modes of criticism and interpretation coincide with the spirit of academic professionalism. The departments of the humanities some time ago became the principal patron and expounder of esthetic innovation. There is no visible reason why they should not encourage radical innovation in criticism. The antithesis of "academic" and "avant-garde" is as obsolete as the antithesis of "bourgeois" and "bohemian." Just as a post-scarcity economy may depend on the liquidation of traditional social restraints, academic professionalism may even *require* radical critical innovation as a continuation of its expansion. Where quantitative "production" of scholarship and criticism is a chief measure of professional achievement, narrow canons of proof, evidence, and logical consistency impose a drag on progress. The new wave of paracritical improvisation in criticism and the transformation of interpretation into prose poetry may be arriving just in time now that conventional modes of qualifying for professional advancement seem to be wearing thin.

Repressive Desublimation

But the cultural radicals have not ignored these social changes. For some of them, the new accommodation of established society to vanguard art and ideas is merely the conclusive evidence that the revolution has already arrived. For those less sanguine about the present situation, this accommodation threatens the success of the

cultural revolution—but by no means discredits its essential outlook. For Marcuse, the new popularity of vanguard cultural attitudes
is a manifestation of "repressive desublimation"—the dominant
society's repression of culturally revolutionary ideas by assimilating
them in harmless forms. Marcuse observes acutely that high
bourgeois culture, with its idealism, its love of beauty, renunciation,
and sublimation, "has ceased to be the dominant culture." Therefore, a new question arises:

> if today we are witnessing a disintegration of bourgeois culture which
> is the work of the internal dynamic of contemporary capitalism and
> the adjustment of culture to the requirements of contemporary
> capitalism, is not the cultural revolution, then, inasmuch as it aims at
> the destruction of bourgeois culture, falling in line with the capitalist
> adjustment and redefinition of culture? Is it not thus defeating its own
> purpose, namely, to prepare the soil for a qualitatively different, a
> radically anticapitalist culture? Is there not a dangerous divergence,
> if not contradiction, between the political goals of the rebellion and its
> cultural theory and praxis? And must not the rebellion change its
> cultural "strategy" in order to resolve this contradiction?[68]

In the fifty pages following this passage in *Counterrevolution and
Revolt*, I find no statement which addresses these extremely perti-
nent questions. Marcuse concedes that the revolutionary program
has been all too easy to vulgarize and divert into frivolity and
self-deception, but this fact is not permitted to call into question the
program itself. Marcuse is content to reaffirm his faith that "the
cultural revolution remains a radically progressive force."[69]

In other words, Marcuse declines to draw the logical conclusion to
which his own social theory leads him: that the new sensibility in art
and culture does not so much negate "one-dimensional society" as
mirror it. And does not Marcuse's formalist esthetic mirror the
self-validating autonomy which Marcuse and other social critics have
discovered in the technological, bureaucratic, and economic processes of advanced society? In *One-Dimensional Man*, Marcuse says
the language of one-dimensional society "controls by reducing the
linguistic forms and symbols of reflection, abstraction, develop-

---

[68] Marcuse, *Counterrevolution and Revolt*, p. 85. See also Barthes' remarks about the political
innocuousness of avant-garde theatre: "Whose Theater? Whose *Avant-Garde?*", *Critical
Essays*, pp. 67–70.
[69] Marcuse, *Counterrevolution and Revolt*, p. 103.

ment, contradiction; by substituting images for concepts. It denies
or absorbs the transcendent vocabulary."[70] But the substituting of
images for concepts is according to Marcuse's Kantian esthetic the
essence of art, which aims at "the non-conceptual truth of the
senses." Defined as sensuous "experience" severed from conceptual
correspondence with reality, art has no more basis than the techno-
cratic language of one-dimensional society for transcending existing
reality. It becomes an aspect of what it rebels against.

Here is the main difficulty with the subversive claims made
widely for the disorienting and "model-making" powers of art,
whether these claims are advanced specifically for certain anti-
realistic genres or for art in general. It does not follow that a work
that serves to "destroy old assumptions and suggest a new, more
visionary reality" necessarily induces its audience to see the world
more critically. The radical disorientation of perception and the
cognitive estrangement brought about by self-reflexive fiction may
result in a dulling of the audience's sense of reality or in a shell-
shocked relativism suspicious not only of ideology but of truth. The
"models for the future" seen by critics in science fiction may stimu-
late escapist fantasies rather than critical thinking, all the more
probably if these models are inserted into an already uncritical,
fad-worshipping mass culture. In other words, there is no way of
determining the critical character of a literary work unless we know
its disposition toward reality. If esthetic disruption and projection
are not regulated by a rational respect for reality—that is, by a
controlling realism—their critical value cannot be taken for granted.
Radical esthetics, determined to liberate fantasy from "the problem
of correspondence or noncorrespondence with some present actuality or some previously experienced past," has no way of making good
its claims for the critical power of fantasy. James Stupple points to
this problem with science fiction itself: "rather than encouraging
analysis," Stupple writes, the use of disorienting conventions in this
genre "actually impedes it, putting an end to critical thought."[71]
Whether fantasy makes us more critical or merely more solipsistic
and self-indulgent depends finally on its accountability to what is
outside itself. But it is just such accountability that radical esthetics
confuses with acquiescence.

That a great deal of putatively radical art has become an aspect of

[70] Marcuse, *One-Dimensional Man*, p. 103.
[71] Stupple, "Fiction Against the Future," p. 219.

the confusion it rebels against is, as we have already seen, the very criticism Marcuse himself levels at the irrationalistic impulse in contemporary art and in the counter culture. In merging art with life, Marcuse observes, the new sensibility often "loses the transcendence which opposes art to the established order."[72] But this same criticism logically applies to Marcuse's own conception of art. Since he puts art under no obligation to reflect conceptual reality, Marcuse has no way of explaining why art should "transcend" established reality in a critical rather than a solipsistic or escapist fashion. His theory deprives itself of the critical principle needed to distinguish between substantial and trivial forms of artistic imagination. Marcuse sees art as "another reality, another order repelled by the existing one." But how can a work of art be "repelled" by existing reality unless it has the power to understand what that reality is? Art must be granted the power to conceptualize the existing reality, to see it *as* distorted, before it can effectively negate it.

Marcuse and other cultural radicals do not follow the logic of their position to its natural conclusions. If they were to do so they would have to abandon their belief in the parallelism of cultural and political revolution. They would have to acknowledge that the esthetic of defamiliarization and projection, of formalist assault on the reality principle, falls in line with "the capitalist adjustment and redefinition of culture." This, in turn, would call into question the larger assumption that the liberation of Eros and the pleasure principle from repression is a necessary counterpart of the revolt against oppression. And then one might ask, must we have a new cultural sensibility, a "new sensorium," a reorientation of perception, an "a-logical" celebration of being, a release of "will and joy" and Eros, a flight beyond humanism and the logocentric idea of man, if we seek to bring about greater justice and truthfulness? Or has the goal of relieving boredom replaced justice and truth as the purpose of politics? But to think these thoughts is to question the very foundation of cultural leftism. That the cultural revolution is regrettably vulnerable to "cooptation"—this can be conceded. But that the cultural revolution itself is fundamentally misconceived—this is unthinkable.

---

[72] Marcuse, *Counterrevolution and Revolt*, p. 101.

WINTER SLEEP

by MARY OLIVER

from THE NIGHT TRAVELER (Bits Press)

nominated by BITS PRESS

If I could I would
Go down to winter with the drowsy she-bear,
Crawl with her under the hillside
And lie with her, cradled. Like two souls
In a patchwork bed—
Two old sisters familiar to each other
As cups in a cupboard—
We would burrow into the yellow leaves
To shut out the sounds of the winter wind.

Deep in that place, among the roots
Of sumac, oak, and wintergreen,
We would remember the freedoms of summer,
And we would begin to breathe together—
Hesitant as singers in the wings—
A shy music,
Oh! a very soft song.

While pines cracked in the snow above,
And seeds froze in the ground, and rivers carried
A dark roof in their many blue arms,
We would sleep and dream.
We would wake and tell
How we longed for the spring.
Smiles on our faces, limbs around each other,
We would turn and turn
Until we heard our lips in unison sighing

The family name.

6 6 6

WILDFLOWER

by STANLEY PLUMLY

from ANTAEUS

nominated by Grace Schulman, Stanley Lindberg, Joyce Carol Oates and Carolyn Forché

Some—the ones with fish names—grow so north
they last a month, six weeks at most.
Some others, named for the fields they look like,
last longer, smaller.

And these, in particular, whether trout- or corn-lilly,
onion or bellwort, just cut
this morning and standing open in tapwater in the kitchen
will close with the sun.

It is June, wildflowers on the table.
They are fresh an hour ago, like sliced lemons,
with the whole day ahead of them.
They could be common mayflower lillies-of-the-valley,

day-lilies, or the clustering Canada, large, gold,
long-stemmed as pasture roses, belled out over the vase—
or maybe solomon's-seal, the petals
ranged in small toy pairs

or starry, tipped at the head like weeds.
They could be anonymous as weeds.
They are, in fact, the several names of the same thing,
lilies of the fields, butter-and-eggs,

toadflax almost, the way the whites and yellow juxtapose,
and have "the look of flowers that are looked at."

rooted as they are in water, glass, and air.
I remember the summer I picked everything

flower and wildflower, singled them out in jars
with a name attached. And when they had dried as stubborn
as paper I put them on pages and named them again.
They were all lilies, even the hyacinth,

even the great pale flower in the hand of the dead.
I picked it, kept it in the book for years
before I knew who she was,
her face lily-white, kissed and dry and cold.

LETTERS FROM A FATHER

by MONA VAN DUYN

from POETRY NOW and PLOUGHSHARES

nominated by POETRY NOW, PLOUGHSHARES *and Maxine Kumin*

1.
Ulcerated tooth keeps me awake, there is
such pain, would have to go to the hospital to have
it pulled or would bleed to death from the blood thinners,
but can't leave Mother, she falls and forgets her salve
and her tranquilizers, her ankles swell so and her bowels
are so bad, she almost had a stoppage and sometimes
what she passes is green as grass. There are big holes
in my thigh where my leg brace buckles the size of dimes.
My head pounds from the high pressure. It is awful
not to be able to get out and I fell in the bathroom
and the girl could hardly get me up at all.
Sure thought my back was broken, it will be next time.
Prostate is bad and heart has given out,
feel bloated after supper. Have made my peace
because am just plain done for and have no doubt
that the Lord will come any day with my release.
You say you enjoy your feeder, I don't see why
you want to spend good money on grain for birds
and you say you have a hundred sparrows, I'd buy
poison and get rid of their diseases and turds.

2.
We enjoyed your visit, it was nice of you to bring
the feeder but a terrible waste of your money
for that big bag of feed since we won't be living
more than a few weeks longer. We can see

them good from where we sit, big ones and little ones
but you know when I farmed I used to like to hunt
and we had many a good meal from pigeons
and quail and pheasant but these birds won't
be good for nothing and are dirty to have so near
the house. Mother likes the redbirds though.
My bad knee is so sore and I can't hardly hear
and Mother says she is hoarse from yelling but I know
it's too late for a hearing aid. I belch up all the time
and have a sour mouth and of course with my heart
it's no use to go to a doctor. Mother is the same.
Has a scab she thinks is going to turn to a wart.

3.
The birds are eating and fighting, Ha! Ha! All shapes
and colors and sizes coming out of our woods
but we don't know what they are. Your Mother hopes
you can send us a kind of book that tells about birds.
There is one the folks called snowbirds, they eat on the ground,
we had the girl sprinkle extra there, but say,
they eat something awful. I sent the girl to town
to buy some more feed, she had to go anyway.

4.
Almost called you on the telephone
but it costs so much to call thought better write.
Say, the funniest thing is happening, one
day we had so many birds and they fight
and get excited at their feed you know
and it's really something to watch and two or three
flew right at us and crashed into our window
and bang, poor little things knocked themselves silly.
They come to after while on the ground and flew away.
And they been doing that. We felt awful
and didn't know what to do but the other day
a lady from our Church drove out to call
and a little bird knocked itself out while she sat
and she brought it in her hands right into the house,
it looked like dead. It had a kind of hat
of feathers sticking up on its head, kind of rose

or pinky color, don't know what kind it was,
and I petted it and it come to life right there
in her hands and she took it out and it flew. She says
they think the window is the sky on a fair
day, she feeds birds too but hasn't got
so many. She says to hang strips of aluminum foil
in the windows so we'll do that. She raved about
our birds. P. S. The book just come in the mail.

5.
Say, that book is sure good, I study
in it every day and enjoy our birds.
Some of them I can't identify
for sure, I guess they're females, the Latin words
I just skip over. Bet you'd never guess
the sparrows I've got here, House Sparrows you wrote,
but I have Fox Sparrows, Song Sparrows, Vesper Sparrows,
Pine Woods and Tree and Chipping and White Throat
and White Crowned Sparrows. I have six Cardinals,
three pairs, they come at early morning and night,
the males at the feeder and on the ground the females.
Juncos, maybe 25, they fight
for the ground, that's what they called snowbirds. I miss
the Bluebirds since the weather warmed. Their breast
is the color of a good ripe muskmelon. Tufted Titmouse
is sort of blue with a little tiny crest.
And I have Flicker and Red-Bellied and Red-
Headed Woodpeckers, you would die laughing
to see Red-Bellied, he hangs on with his head
flat on the board, his tail braced up under, wing
out. And Dickcissel and Ruby Crowned Ringlet
and Nuthatch stands on his head and Veery on top
the color of a bird dog and Hermit Thrush with spot
on breast, Blue Jay so funny, he will hop
right on the backs of the other birds to get the grain.
We bought some sunflower seeds just for him.
And Purple Finch I bet you never seen,
color of a watermelon, sits on the rim
of the feeder with his streaky wife, and the squirrels,
you know, they are cute too, they sit tall

and eat with their little hands, they eat bucketfuls.
I pulled my own tooth, it didn't bleed at all.

6.
It's sure a surprise how well Mother is doing,
she forgets her laxative but bowels move fine.
Now that windows are open she says our birds sing
all day. The girl took a Book of Knowledge on loan
from the library and I am reading up
on the habits of birds, did you know some males have three
wives, some migrate some don't. I am going to keep
feeding all spring, maybe summer, you can see
they expect it. Will need thistle seed for Goldfinch and Pine
Siskin next winter. Some folks are going to come see us
from Church, some bird watchers, pretty soon.
They have birds in town but nothing to equal this.

So the world woos its children back for an evening kiss.

EARLY WINTER

fiction by MAX SCHOTT

from THE MASSACHUSETTS REVIEW

nominated by THE MASSACHUSETTS REVIEW

THE MEADOW or, as they called it, the swamp, was a ranch in itself, some sixty miles off the pavement and a long hundred from town. And the swamp or meadow, big as it was (it would summer a thousand cows and grow the hay to winter them too) big as it was, was just a pock on the desert, the junipered high desert with its big river cuts and occasional badlands of broken black rock that you could hardly lead a horse through and which they called devils'-gardens; the meadow was nothing but a pock in the desert that ran changingly on and filled the big meeting corners of three states.

On the steep at the edge of the meadow was a set of corrals and a barn, a gas motored power-plant and a good house. For more or less

239

than six months of the year the road was passable, though it would go anytime it rained, even in the summer. And there was a telephone which worked a surprising amount of the time as long as it wasn't storming. If you were riding the desert you would run into that thin bare wire that staggered from tree to tree to pole as randomly as if it belonged there, and I mean really run into it if you weren't watching, because often it was low enough to unhorse you.

Fall was more than with them. Spring calves, big now, had sucked the fat off their mothers with the milk. The good was gone out of the feed. It was come-home time. Little groups of range cattle were finding their ways into the come-home lanes or just wandering down the fence lines, walking along with their heads down, spoiled to preferring a winter of hay, captivity, mud and tractor-broke snow, to the risky pickings of wintering out. Coming down randomly, just like the Indians in that part of the country used to, where they would bunch-up in the lowlands, fifty together in those close and stinking communal houses with the chiefs sitting closest to the air-holes, and argue over how many months of winter were left. Ben watched the cattle as he drove along, he couldn't help it.

Behind him swayed his pot-bellied mare, his saddle was cinched to the racks. Beside him on the seat and floor of the truck-cab was a whole pile of stuff: bridles, brushes, halters and lass-ropes, medicines for doctoring cattle, a raincoat, chaps, rubber boots made to fit a stirrup, matches, a furred cap and so on.

At home he had dried up the one cow and turned the nursecalves on the other, and he had fixed a place where the two skim-milk pigs—one he was fattening for his brother and the other for himself—where they could get in out of the weather. The irrigation water was shut out of the ditches clear back at the county locks. His fields were frozen. There was enough old growth standing to hold his cattle for a month (after that he would have to pitch hay). In other words, there wasn't much to do outdoors but to keep an eye out. Marian had no hard outdoor chores to do, and they wouldn't be owing to Clyde for anything except to keep a watch after Ben's cattle, to look in on Marian and drink her coffee.

At home: that farmland, fenced and cross-fenced, square as a house—as the house it owned, and flat as a table, with its touchy domestic grasses and shedding poplars. Bare branches, shed-out now; a wintry place it was, home, already it was looking wintry, and when it was wintry it was dead and sad. The desert though was various, rolling and live. It escaped the seasons and penetrated the horizons, jumped its own gorges and flew on. He supposed that's why even those sudden gorges and sheer cliffs were only called cuts and breaks. Because the desert belittled its own monuments. No landmark really broke or season really killed it. Juniper, wildplum and sage—they shed no leaves; paw a foot of snow off a clump of bunchgrass and you'll find it just as green as summer would have.

Ten miles in he passed a big weathered house together with a big roughly leveled field. Twenty years ago a dry-farmer had failed there. Now it was Sterling's, and the house was fenced off with a good, bright four-wire fence, to keep Sterling's cattle from worrying the place down, as a cow is likely to run a nail in her foot, or even to wander inside and get in a tight she can't get out of. It's odd though, Ben thought, to see a house fenced like that, four bright wires all around, with no break, no gate.

He passed Goose Lake, round as a dollar, seeming not to reflect the clear blue sky but to glitter opaquely with a kind of tin-foil energy of its own. In its center a wooden float, broken, down on which the P-38s used to practice diving, fifteen years before. That was how the float got lopped off, too, he'd heard. There was one that, as if to prove its excellent aim, never pulled up. Imagine that, Goose Lake's only wave. But looking at the lake he couldn't imagine it. It could only enter splashless, as in a dream.

Beyond it, a real landmark: the cylindrical mountain, Horse Cock, the same from every side, with its peculiarly convex mesa and swollen underlip, like a flashlight on end or a cake that swelled over and out of the pan it was baked in, a muffin—but more like its namesake, the tumescent penis of a stallion, than any of those. And some in-between in the Forest Service had changed the name to Horse Mountain when it came time to make a map.

He widened the road a little on the curves, as if he was trying to outrun his own dust, but there wasn't any. The old mare stood behind his shoulder, spraddle-legged, tilting wide outside with the brown eye of experience, a little frightened, gauging through the slats. She stumbled and he saw her eye. Well, he slowed himself down. If he could get it through his head that he was being paid by the day now rather than the mile, and that there was no reason to hurry. So used he had become to hauling cattle for so much a mile. Certainly he didn't mean to overwork himself or his truck or his mare for Sterling. Sterling, who always set before a man more than he could possibly get done, hoping that way to surprise him into turning an extra lick or two over his hours and wages.

Forty miles in, he crossed water, a young creek in the center of a broad and shallow wash; a slab had been laid over the crossing, so that the only part of this desert that was paved was the thirty feet that was under water. Above that on the far side, a herder's camp, a box of a trailer with a pin hitch that would push a car more directions than the car would ever pull it, if you dared it on the highway. Parked now, under a tree, and in front of it a big dust-encrusted woman. Well, any woman was a rarity in a sheep camp. Still, she could have bathed. Probably she was so used to dry camps that she didn't know what to make of a watered one.

Near her, a hobbled and saddled horse. It was not long after noon. He figured that a band of sheep was probably over some rise with a dog or two and that the sheepherder would be asleep in the trailer or under a tree behind it. He thought these things idly, for no reason. No, the herder would be inside, this day, which had too much sting to it even at noon to let a man sleep away from a blanket or fire, though you couldn't really call it cold.

The woman looked at him with no show of interest, sitting dumb and expressionless though he could tell by the deadness of the tiretracks in the road that he was the first to pass here in at least a day or two and more likely a week.

He thought, well you might have to be out here a quite a while before you would want her, but when you did she would certainly be there. No matter who was chasing who she would never outrun you, or even wander very far from camp, let alone leave on you. . . .

The road fell down over a steep, as off a ridge, but he'd been traveling flat for a hundred miles; the road fell down the bank, dropping some hundred feet in a quarter of a mile, and the meadow was there, as round as anything five miles across that isn't pure water can be. The house was flung out in a pocket at the foot of the hill and below it a maze of privy and pump-house and calf-sheds and the housing of the generator and a sorry tangle of little fences for keeping in, and separated, a milkcow or two and the house-calves: or had—it was all empty now, and below that a good barn and some pole corrals big and solid enough that you could work a thousand cattle at a time through them or a few hundred horses, but it was all empty now, not even a saddlehorse around, though farther out the meadow was dotted, and anywhere you looked on the desert you could see a cow or two among the junipers.

The place was empty now because Sterling's man had died and it was hard to get another one. They would stay a few days or a week and leave. Rare the single man who would stay long way out here, but Sterling had come up with one, who had stayed a long time, even if he was having trouble coming up with another.

Ben had ridden out mornings after cattle with Sterling's man, a half-deaf old fellow not much more than five feet tall. All alone he had stayed out here for years, apparently having nothing better to do until he died, which he'd finally gone ahead and done last winter, though he'd gone to town to do that. Shorty was his name and Ben had ridden with him, the one as unused to speaking as the other was to shouting, so that little was said. Except once when he told Ben to go down in the mosquitoes and move a sixteen foot canvas dam, Ben had managed to yell "If you want it done, do it yourself. I take all my orders from the man who makes out the checks."

The one person that would talk to Shorty, and had talked to him, was Sterling. They would stand shouting at one another, Shorty telling Sterling where there was a sick cow, which waters were wet and which dry and where there was too many cattle and not enough feed, or the other way round, or where a man might borrow a chain harrow, and then Sterling would tell Shorty what to do about it. On and on they would go, standing eyeball to bellybutton and shouting, the two giants, Ben called them, the big giant and the little giant.

In the house, on a yellow wall above a narrow iron bedstead a list had been nailed. Ben looked at it. Imagine Shorty going to sleep every night under—living under—a list of chores. He wouldn't have forgot what he was there for, that was certain. To ride with Shorty had been the next thing to being alone, and in fact at those times Ben if he'd had his rathers would rather have been alone, had wished he was alone. Now he wished him life, just for the company.

Ben rattled around the place. What was he doing here, anyway? A question not of sense, he knew what he was doing here.

Part of the trouble was that the place was too big, he thought. House, outbuildings, barn, the roar of the big gas-engined generator that he'd just fired up, roaring now like a tremendous dose of silence, like all the silence of the empty corners of three states buzzing, like a fly in your ear. Even Shorty had no more than camped here all those years. It was a place for a family, hired-man, hay crew, a few teams of horses. Yet you couldn't get a family to stay here either. The kids couldn't get to school, for one thing. And what woman nowdays would stand being snowed, frozen and mudded in from more or less Thanksgiving until more or less the first of May?

Ben went back out of the house and hayed the mare and wired the gate shut so she'd be there in the morning. It was colder here than at home, and the long ride hadn't done her any good, so that her long hair which had already "come-in winter" was standing on end like the fur of a dead rabbit. He looked at the clouds blowing up over Oregon and opened the barn door for the mare so that she could get in out of the weather if she liked.

There had been a family here, before Shorty, which was why the place was what it was, the house and all; two brothers, one with a wife. And they were the kind to tough it out and like it, thrive on it, though they never owned it. Sterling owned it then, too. And it was typical of Sterling's luck, his good luck, that the woman never could conceive, so that they were here for twelve years. Until at last they managed to adopt a child, and when it grew, had to move somewhere near a school bus.

Well they were long gone now, he thought, the only sign of them being an extravagant wood-stove, the kind with a confusing lot of vents and dampers and heat-shifting levers and two warming ovens above the fire-box and two regular ovens below it and a trashburner, and weighing so much that it had sunk on one side through the kitchen floor. Now mice and even chipmunks went back and forth through the hole.

Ben shook a spider out of the coffeepot, banged a few sticks of wood together and built a fire in a corner of the stove, knocked the cobwebs off the broom and swept the kitchen, ran some of the rust out of the water pipes and filled the coffeepot and sat down and stared at the wall, putting him in mind of other walls he'd stared at. Outside it got dark. What was he doing here?

Money, yes, and that was reason enough to come. But the answer really had nothing to do with the question. What in the world was he doing here? He had spent enough nights alone in his life and even one more was too many. Besides that, it was somehow silly, with her sitting there alone and lonely and he here. And her worse off, when he thought of it, because she would be the victim of Sterling's wife or Clyde's wife or someone's, who would insist on sitting with her, which she wouldn't want but would accept.

All the walls he had stared at: walls of line-camps and construction camps and road building camps and trail cutting camps and logging and mining camps, not to mention the shacks and cabins and hotels and rooms in people's houses and yards. Brick, stone, tin, canvas, cardboard even. Worst the thin walls of hotels, stained at the level of the bed from the spittle and semen of men more single than he had ever been, penetrated by the coughing and pure terrors of men out of wine and coming down, men more married—at least more hopelessly married—to the bottle then he ever was. And when he sat straight up in bed out of sleep in the middle of the night to the tune of that! Yes, and at that time of night in those places alone your skin gets pretty thin and your self respect along with it.

He hardly marked when it started to snow.

He remembered one Labor Day's drunk, the end of a great drunk, of almost a whole summer's drunk really. Because hadn't he been either drunk or on his way to getting sober (he never made it), from June to September! That was the summer when his ranch, the ranch he'd saved up five thousand dollars to lease and stock, when his ranch was going belly-up. But that isn't quite the way he was thinking of it now. He was simply picturing the end of a great drunk, himself up on a great black rock at a Labor Day celebration, driving steel with a ten pound hammer, drunk, and he smiled a little as he thought of it. He stared at one spot on the wall and he saw that one picture. It remained at the center, but other incidents circled and fed it.

Himself on the rock wearing a plaster cast, and he thought for an instant of the day in the spring of the year when he took a flyer off a spilling wagonload of meadowhay. Flung he was, and crushed his ankle when he lit. He remembered making the doctor set it with him awake. "How much pain can you stand?" the man asked. "What I have to." Because he didn't want to be unconscious and them messing with him. Especially strangers, especially doctors. He would no more have let them put him to sleep than he would have fallen asleep in a barber chair with a razor on his neck. Of course he knew there was no rhyme or reason to it, that they would go on and do what they would do anyway, and that finally, awake or asleep, he would have to just go on and let them.

He remembered raking a lot of hay with a one horse buckrake, his plaster leg propped straight out in front of him on a forked stick. The hay, he even remembered, had gone shelly from laying around too long in the sun while he tried to borrow a baler, so that most of the grain spilled back onto the ground, and the next tenant would have a good crop of volunteer oats at the expense of Ben's hay. And he remembered playing housewife to the hay-crew, so that when they were getting up at four he was getting up at two-thirty to build them breakfast. Right down to the butane stove and the kerosene lantern and the radio turned to KXLA which would bring in western music all the way from Los Angeles until about daylight, when it began to fade. . . . And in the evenings he would imagine them, the others, down at the river, their bodies drawn along by the current, the water pulling at the fine, burning chaff, while he chafed under his plaster and tossed grapes to the dog from the back steps.

After the hay was in he began to drink. There was nothing else to do. Every Sunday they would catch another laying hen and eat her. Sometimes he could dance like a sound-legged man. One day the barn burned; the shingles glided flaming all over the hillside like runaway kites and they went chasing them and he prayed for it all to burn, every tree of it.

Then one night he woke to the insistent yapping of the dog and when he got to the barnyard heard the frantic squawking of a hen and finally found her with a cow standing on her leg, the cow too placid or uncaring or dumb to move, and he thought that was how it should be, not a weasel in the hen house but a cow standing on a chicken, on his ranch.

The black rock on an iron-ribbed wagon. On Labor Day the whiskey had flowed. Someone had managed to have the rock loaded onto the wagon and towed it downtown with a tractor. Jamestown— that had been a town to fit him then; the man he was then it fit wonderfully well, the Mother Lode dead a hundred years almost but the town still a good Saturday night town. Fourteen bars and a grocery store and a hotel, and the people loose and at loose ends, tied and not very tightly to those old slow-diers, the mills and the dwindling woods and mined-out mines and sheeped-out hills . . . Someone—a one-eyed trader drunker than he was—had been fool enough to hold the drill for him while he swung at it with the hammer (hit it, too), his plaster cast propped some way he couldn't remember. Drunken fools. And right now sitting in this kitchen with his coffee boiling over probably the first time he'd ever thought of it since and not been ashamed of the spectacle.

He got ready to go to bed. You had to go out to the generator to turn it on, but to cut the power you had only to flick a switch in the kitchen: just like uptown, except that the light and sound going at once was a shock. So that then, for a time, all he could hear standing in the dark was the roar backward in time.

He turned to the window and watched it snow, and then the roar went away, and he began to hear—sounding like sleep might sound—the soft loud hush of snowing.

The next morning when he went out Ben couldn't say he was surprised: he'd had a good notion through the night of how heavily it was snowing. Yet as he stood on the porch pulling on his gloves he couldn't help being astonished by the landscape. The meadow and the desert—all snow.

On the top edge of the open barn door, on every top fence rail and balanced on the top of each post were the most symmetrical, delicate peaks of unbroken snow. Even the four-pronged barbs on the wire were fluffy, or looked like big crystals.

The cows and calves were already trompling and making the trackless meadow imperfect. Irregular patches of snow, melting and steaming, rode on their backs. Ben buckled up his rubber boots and stepped off into it.

When he went to hay his mare he stopped and leaned on the fork and hooked an elbow over her warm hip and said a few admiring words about her not being about to get her old back wet—which he might never have done hadn't they been stuck out here all alone together. A magpie walked out of the barn before him and fluttered onto a rail.

Ben went out too. The magpie walked the fence, kicking off snow, too close to him, walking and cawing and kicking off snow. Cawing, two-toned, puffed up and gaudy. They were vile enough anytime, but every winter especially they grew impertinent. This one was rushing the season to boot. So that he went to the trouble to work a rock out from under the snow and flung it.

It missed the bird and hit the fence, scattering snow, and made a thwack that gave a start to every cow for a hundred yards. Even the mare jumped and snorted. All sorts of exaggerated spookiness spread on across the white meadow; tails and hackles stood straight up on end as if the dry air were really electric. But the bird only hopped a little further from him and kept on with its nasty cawing.

His job of work had changed. He could see that the weather was now going to do the most part of his cow-gathering for him. Twos and threes of them with their big calves trailing along behind, were winding down off the slopes, dark among the whitened junipers everywhere. The weather had given him a new job too, and one he cared for less. The feed on the meadow—feed that usually would have carried the cattle another month, until it had a good ordinary right to snow—all that was inundated now. So he had to feed hay. He could see the stacks, the big stacks of loose summer-cut hay dotting the big meadow, each with a fence around it to keep the cattle off. And he'd seen a sled, parked dry and cobwebby in the shed. And he knew where the harness hung. So now what he had to do was to wrangle a team and go to pitching hay. A job he cared a lot less for than riding after cattle, though he didn't care so much for that anymore either. Well, it didn't pay to give it much thought. Besides, he did like having to give himself up to the weather. He began wondering where he might find a team.

Where might he find a team? He knew that Sterling had a few workhorses turned loose down here somewhere, or did have, and Ben tried to estimate which way across the unfenced desert they might have wandered.

While the mare ate, he went back to the house and softened some coffee with canned milk and poured some water into the top of a flour sack and squeezed together some dough and rolled it out and cut off some biscuits with a waterglass and baked them. The kitchen was warmed to the corners with the fire he'd built when he got up and his coffee'd done a good deal of boiling while he was out, even though he'd left it on the corner of the stove.

When he was done he threw a saddle on her and rode out, a few strips of jerky in his pocket, remembering that when he was a young man he'd always packed himself a good lunch and was wanting at it by ten o'clock, while now he would ride out with an ounce or two of jerky and as often as not would find it still in his pocket when he rode in at night.

He had no real notion of where the horses were, and all sign was covered. Idly he began looking for them in his mind's eye, picturing them in this place and that, some of the places being so far away that he hated to think of them really being there. Until giving in to some chance mixture of indecision and intuition, he took off northeast and came on them three hours' straight ride later—noon it was. "I must be living right," he said when he saw them, half-a-dozen bigfooted workhorses, who threw up their big craggy heads at the sight of him and started a trail back toward the ranch, glad enough not to have to paw snow for a meal, he supposed, only needing someone to start them, to jog their memories a little, to remind them there was such a thing as captivity and a haypile. In the spring of the year it would have been another story: they would have been trying to break back over the top of him every chance they saw, trying to stay in the country, out among the wild ones and the new grass, but not now.

He let them go. They broke trail for him, heading straight for the ranch. It was a shining day, but a short one, and cold. He pounded his gloved hands on the saddlehorn until he knocked a little sting into them. When his feet began to lose feeling he got off the mare and walked. He was afoot, coming along a ridge, when he saw the horses below him trotting right along and then suddenly split from their direction, taking a hard break too, right up a drifted gully, bounding through deep snow. And that surprised him, until he looked down again and saw what they'd seen or got wind of: a big bull, stretched out dead with the turkey vultures on it and around it. Their hard eyes snapped at him. They already had it half undressed. "Well there's one old baloney bull who will never make Chicago now," he said. Then he looked around and saw a good windfall and decided to thaw out.

He knocked a little snow off the deadfall: he shook it and peeked in among the branches. It was a regular good nest of twigs and sticks, besides the well-weathered branches of the tree that began it. If he'd had any sense at all he would have pulled out some of the sticks, dug a hole in the snow and built a small fire. Instead he peeled a handful of tinder, set it inside and just set the whole thing afire.

It flamed up big, as how could he help but know it would? Too hot to stand near, and his feet were what was cold. He had to squat off at some distance. He watched the vultures. They hated and gauged him too, snatching their heads away from their work, cocking their heads toward him with their black snapping eyes working on him. With strings of flesh in their mouths—they never stopping stringing flesh.

His fire flamed up bigger and hotter; after all, it was a whole tree. His face stung and glowed with fresh heat and embarrassment. He decided he must have been a little out of his mind when he lit it.

Then he became preoccupied with a whole series of trifling occurrences, that he felt like he was taking notice of for the first time, though they must have actually entered his imagination with great purity and force just minutes before:

the surprised head of the first work horse, when he'd rode up on them, tossed up—ears pressed forward, pop-eyed, nostrils as wide and still as tea-cups, pure attention against the blank white land.

:the reins, wrapped around his glove, tensing and slacking as he leads the mare along the ridge, him trying to stalk, bent-kneed, from one big new hoofprint to the next.

:when he ungloves, the veined pallor of his hands; the kindness or gentleness visible in the very shape of those worked and weathered hands of his.

:the squeak of his boots, his rubber boots, against the fine dry snow, electric and lonely sound in the dry air until he hears the timbred voice, reminding him of a musical instrument, say "Well there's one old baloney bull who will never make Chicago now."

While he was recontemplating these things a coyote slipped up to the carcass. She was already working it, when Ben finally took notice. Life was doing her no favors, you could just glance at her and see that. Her swaying string of hairy teats were the biggest part of her. He guessed she had a litter of big summer pups hid somewhere, and probably fat, who kept the meat sucked off her old bones. "You could do with a weaning too, couldn't you sister," he said, thinking of the cows and their big spring calves.

His fire wasn't blossoming like it had been. He got closer and closer to it, until he was heated up all the way through. For the first time in several hours he could feel his ulcer churn. He imagined it as a coal, a good live coal heating him outward. He imagined himself as a candidate for spontaneous combustion, like a load of green hay, boiling secret and airless at the center, until it goes off. That amused him, even the words amused him—spontaneous combustion. He watched the birds and went on hating them with an excellent, hot little hatred, so pure and concentrated that he could have almost located and extracted it too, like an object, like a coal.

When he got on his mare he left his right hand ungloved and took down his summertime lass rope, which in this weather had gone stiff as a board, and as he rode down off the ridge he built a little creaky loop. He would have loved nothing so much as to have lucked it on one of those vultures just one time, just to change the look in those eyes one time. But they flapped on out of reach as coolly as they did everything else, not even bothering to fly. The bitch coyote though was apparently ravening. By the time she looked up and saw him coming, he was already closer than he should have been. She panicked and leapt out in a squeeze between the mare and the bull, right past him. And the loop which he threw just for the hell of it, to see if he could, because he'd never roped a coyote and because it was ready in his hand—the loop whipped up around her neck and he sucked the slack out of it in one motion and snatched her right around out of the air.

She flung herself back against it, shutting off her own air and striking and snapping mostly at nothing, because the rope was at best a blur and most of the time above her and out of her sight altogether.

He had to laugh at himself. He'd only wanted to catch her, not to be tied to her. Now he remembered what he already knew, that some things are easier to get into than out of. He wanted his rope back. Anyway he figured he had more use for it than she did. There was no use in her running herself more ragged than she already was, trying to get away from it, or getting herself tied for all time to a bush.

She was surely gaunt. He'd roped lots of soggy little calves not half as tall as she was, and not many of them could he have held with the rope just in his bare hand, like he could easily her. All long hair. Even throwing the fit that she was, she felt to him like a jackrabbit on the line, which was a sorry way to start a winter, that thin.

She wouldn't hang back and choke herself long, he knew, before she'd be making a desperate run at him and his mare, and maybe really get him in a jackpot. So he tied the rope to the saddlehorn and tied the mare's head to the rope so that she, if she lost her nerve, couldn't turn tail and run off. Then he started pretty gingerly down the line, stopping to pull his glove on, cursing himself all the way for his foolishness, and wondered why a man his age would still play pranks.

As he came on she hauled back harder and wilder, her head flapping and popping, tongue out, until when he is about six feet from her she jumps toward him as she was bound to, trying to get at him or by him, he couldn't tell. But he had the rope in his hand and stepped aside and snatched the slack from her and popped her sideways, so that she flew to the end of it again like a cork on a string. And while she still suffered from that he managed to get to her and run the arch of his foot right down the rope and hard onto her throat and head, though not without getting his boot slashed. Then he had her pinned, her head right under his foot, squashed down into the snow, one eye bugging out of its socket not at him or anything. The rest of her flopped two or three times like a beached fish, and that's all. She quit. He saw that her teats had been actually sucked raw, and suddenly he imagined a pup trying to sneak up and suck her in the dark, and in his mind she roars with pain and rage, and her teeth flash.

He wondered if he was giving her too much. He didn't want to kill her, and he didn't want to get his hand bit, especially when he saw that she'd gone through both of his boots, the rubber and the leather, clear to his sock. When at last he lifted his foot off of her, she didn't move. He pulled her toward the mare, stuck his gloved hand between the rope and her furred neck, and pulled off the loop.

Ben thought he should see whose bull it was. He couldn't find a brand showing, so he looped the hind legs and took a turn or two around the saddle horn and rolled him. It was Sterling's all right. And he'd like to be able to tell him what the bull died of, like a good cowboy should. You couldn't tell anything with this new snow. You couldn't tell whether he's laid here a long time and just wasted away slowly, down sick, or if he'd just laid down here and died, or if he'd suffered and tore up the ground in his pain, or what. So he tried to do some pathology—looked at the tongue, the eyes, the feet, the liver—couldn't tell a thing. It looked like a good active bull. His hooves were slick and hard as a new black axe, like he'd done a lot of traveling over the desert rocks. Altogether as healthy and sweet a dead bull as Ben had seen around—he'd tell Sterling that.

The sun was already gone from the hollow; it was getting late in the day. Ben climbed back up the hill to his fire. Now he was glad he'd built it so big—it was still coaling. He stuffed a chunk of saddle blanket down his split boot. Then he cut off a couple of leather saddle-strings, dug some holes in his boot leathers and produced a kind of make-do lace.

When he left her she was still lying there. But she was breathing, he could see her breathing. He wondered—if she staggered up after a while, would she go right back to her meal? He guessed she would.

It was night before he was halfway home. But it seemed light as day, with the moon lighting up the snow for miles around. And the workhorses marked a trail straight for the barnyard.

It was a fine night. When he rode into the barnyard himself, he felt good, even if he was tired and his feet were cold. He knew there were feet there but they didn't have enough feeling in them to seem to belong to anyone. Yet they carried him all right when he got down. Of the six workhorses he only needed two, and he thought this as good a time as any to kick the other four out on the meadow. Three of them he managed to let out a gate. But the fourth one stuck with the two he wanted. So he thought he would just throw a rope on him and lead him out.

The big gentle horse, surprised by the rope in the night, raised up against the moon, striking. Then happened what sometimes does in the moonlight, a weird confusion of distances, and they were right at one another, when it seemed they had been a rope's length separate. Ben threw his arms up in front of his face and his right arm was instantly slapped back down along his side. Then the horse led off quietly and he turned him loose and threw them all some hay.

He kept thinking about it. He tried to make himself know that death had maybe just brushed him by. That he just missed inches of being struck on the skull by a gentle fifteen hundred pound horse pawing out at blank air. But he couldn't make it real. Sure, no death makes sense but some are a good deal more fitting than others, somehow, or to someone. And some were nonsense, nonsense, and he thought of Judy again—a girl with a fever and then a tiny sucked-out smell, like a room after a party; that one had never made the least bit of sense or dislodged from his mind in thirty years. So that to this day he could easier stand in a gale than a certain kind of airless room. Something he had not made sense of in all that time and believed now he never would or could, for there was none in it.

When he was thawed out again by the stove, he started thinking of Marian. Just suddenly, as if he just recalled who he was and that he had a wife up by town.

For some reason he remembered a night not too long after they were married and just after they'd come here and he'd started trying to farm again. He'd promised her for a couple of weeks or more to take her to Reno and she could pick out some furniture. But he was always busy with something and kept putting it off. Until this one night after they had gone to bed she started getting onto him over it, lying with her back to him and talking about how long he'd put her off and how many promises he'd broken and how if he hadn't intended to do it he shouldn't have ever said he would and on and on. He hadn't said anything in return and was feeling quite chilled by it, until he laid his hand up against her back and knew from the feel of it that what she was doing was all fakery, her tone, and her having her back turned to him talking, even if she did mean what she said. And when he ran the back of his hand on down her back and around between her legs, she had broke down completely, laughing, and swore at him because she did break down and laughed and swore again.

He drug his bed into the kitchen tonight and built the stove up one last time. He didn't feel very lonely. He was terribly tired. He dreamt of oranges. On the sideboard Marian had filled a bowl full of oranges. He opened a cupboard that should probably have had clothes or canned goods in it, and it was full of oranges too, all in a loose pile, tight-skinned oranges of all sizes, still striped green around their stems.

From the very beginning he suspected that this wasn't just an early snow but winter. The sky held bright and clear. There was no sign of thaw. At night it was cold enough that in the morning it took a good jab with a pointed shovel to even crack the trough-ice. From the meadow you could look up any time and see more cattle trickling down to the feedground from the surrounding hills.

Ben just about knew what would happen. As soon as Sterling decided too that this was the start of an early winter and not an early snow only, then he would send Wesley down in a sled to pick him up. With Wesley, Sterling would send some poor fellow or other, old or young, fated to spend the winter down here alone, forking hay and reading through the pile of old ranch romances and catalogs, poking wood into the stove and trying to find a radio station that would come in, anything to listen to besides the sound of the generator and snow falling. Ben and Wesley would see to getting the calves weaned and started on feed, eating grain and away from their mothers, and would show the new man what to do. Then they would go on in the sled back, with his mare tied on behind trying to trot with her feet in a runner track, like a rope-walker, or maybe pulling the sled herself.

He took the battery out of his Diamond-T. Here the truck was going to sit until spring came, or more likely summer. He cursed his luck for that: hauling was their grocery money all winter. But for just a minute or two, before he thought it out, he was almost glad. Sometimes he imagined he would rather starve in the house warm than to get out again and wrestle those truck chains among the icicles or spill cows up and down those slick ramps or wade around in the slogs of icy black holes that the farmyards got to be every winter.

But starving was a bad joke. He would need a little money, and he didn't know anyone dumb enough to hire him to sit by the fire, though that was the job he preferred. When he thought about it seriously he knew that more than likely he would end up leasing another truck, or maybe he could shame Sterling out of his for a while. He would keep hauling and so keep the trade he'd built up. But even if he didn't he could bet that whatever else he might find to do wouldn't be any warmer.

For a couple of days, every time he looked at his snowbound truck, these things ran around in his head past what they were worth. Well, this wasn't a place to make your mind operate. There was no one to talk to, and after a while even thinking seemed a waste of time. Within only a couple of days he'd begun talking to himself out loud and to the team and the mare and the cattle, which amounted to the same thing. If he hadn't gone through the same thing times before, he would have worried about himself.

To pitch hay to that many cattle took him five hours, cold dull ones, and that each day. In the afternoons he saddled his mare and rode back over the feedgrounds, doctoring sick calves when he saw them and studying the cows so that he could recognize the sick ones and doctor them later, when he had help.

There were lots of cattle on the meadow now, and in the afternoons they sometimes spread out considerably from where he'd fed them, so that they might be anywhere on the meadow, which was a big one. He rode the meadow slowly, probably not seeing all the cattle on any one day, but really looking at every cow he saw and thinking about her. This went on routinely for three or four days, which might as well have been years, and then he began having troubles, which afterward went from bad to worse.

There were bridges on the meadow and anytime you rode across it you had to cross one or two—little rough cedar bridges that spanned the canal. The canal wound around all over the meadow, so that you were surprised to finally figure out it was only one canal and that it must flow downhill from one place to another like any other. In the spring it helped to slowly dry the bog, the canal did, and in the summer you could maneuver the big canvas dams across it and shoot water back out across the grass.

The snow itself, except for being clumsy and inconvenient, wasn't bad to catch and doctor cattle in. The footing was all right. But the bridges were icy. In a roundabout way, that was where his troubles began. He'd come across a cow with a horn that had grown in half a circle and the point of it was starting back into her skull. If he drove her up to the barn he could trap her in a chute and saw it off. He had to make her cross one bridge. She wouldn't set foot on it so he roped her and started to drag her across. But the mare's feet got to spinning on the icy boards and he had to turn the cow loose with his rope to keep from going down. That was all right: he could catch her another time and he had plenty of ropes. He decided to take the mare back to the barn and sharpshoe her with calks before he did anything else.

This was on the fourth afternoon. It was clouding up again and so seemed colder, though it probably wasn't. He found the calked shoes hanging in the barn; they were just about her size, too. He got doubled up under her and went to work. Cold as it was, he poured off sweat for the biggest part of an hour. Before he was done he could look out through the cracks of the barn siding and see it snowing again. All the time—while he pulled the old shoes off and leveled her feet and nailed and clinched the calked shoes on—he talked to the mare: "Okay, mother, that's all right, let me see your other foot now . . . give it to me . . . here, stand up now, don't lay on me or I'll flog your old noggin for you . . . That's a good little dear—now see if you can keep yourself right side up next time you go ice-skating," and so on.

It was the first horse he'd shod himself for some years. Ordinarily he got Wesley or someone to do it for him. Yet he got doubled up under her and was able to get the new iron nailed on all right, pretty well, really, he thought, not badly done. But then when he straightened clear up from the last foot he felt rotten. And from that time on, from the moment he straightened up after shoeing the mare, he imagined his stomach took to him harder and more often than it ever had. Of course he knew as well as anyone that if that hadn't started it something else would have. But from that time on he began to wish he was somewhere else, and not down here alone.

Even before that, too, he had begun to indulge himself in not eating—with no one around to prod him or cook for him—though he should have known better. It snowed most of the night. In the morning he stood on the porch again and got ready to go feed. While he pulled on his gloves and the furred cap and wound the muffler slowly round his neck, he looked out at the meadow.

This time, when he stepped off the porch, he sank to his knees. He felt out his own previous tracks, then he only had to deal with last night's snow. Later on, when he got the team harnessed and went out on the meadow with the sled, he would try to drive over the old sled tracks too, so that the horses would have the best possible go at it. But that wouldn't be so easy. Beyond the barnyard was nothing to sight by but a few fence lines in the distance, the curving willow-lined canal and the lay of the big haystacks. He knew already how the team would keep sliding off the buried invisible bands of packed snow and feeling their way back on.

When he reached the barn he saw that the first magpie had been joined by another, exactly like itself. He guessed it snowed magpies here, one per storm. Now when he saw there were two he gave up furiously on magpies and spit on the ground.

The fork was in the sled. Ben harnessed the team and drove out across the meadow to the first haystack, where he stopped by the stackyard gate.

The gate was made of barbed wire and upright sticks; this kind of weather drew it up tight. He had built hundreds of them and opened thousands. What they called them back home he couldn't re-member, but down in most of California they called them Portagee gates and way out here they called them Indian gates. Sterling liked to say that it takes five minutes to build one and half an hour to open it.

Before he put his shoulder to the gate Ben brushed a little peak of snow off the vertical so it wouldn't be falling down his neck. When he pressed the upright hard with his shoulder the top wire popped, twang, like a banjo string. "Well you don't know your own strength yet, old son," he said out loud, bad-naturedly—sarcastically.

Cattle were all around him waiting. More were coming; they bucked clumsily in the deep snow, cold and feeling fine. He shut them out of the stackyard. Then he proceeded to load.

For every forkful of loose hay in the stack there is a kind of natural pry-point, the key he called it, and if you don't find it you are setting your back against the whole great tangled stack itself. Since he was, say, fifteen years old, he'd been feeling his way to it gently, and it felt good to find it even now. But even so, when he came away neatly with this first big forkful, and got his hip under it and pitched it on the sled—there was a sudden grabbing pain. It didn't hurt as much as it worried him, because he didn't think there was a way around it. And it was there again, each time, a point of strain at the inert start of the swing, just as the hay came free of the stack, just at the unavoidable dead beginning of the arc. There was no way around it. He felt as if his key had been found too.

After he loaded the sled he drove back to the stackyard gate and opened it and drove through it, hollering hungry cattle out of his way all the time, and got out again and closed it and got in again and started his team off across the new snow, trying to divine his old tracks. Then he got into the back of the sled and forked off hay as they went, clucking to the horses all the time, for they were tentative today and would have liked to stop at every step. He fanned the hay off across the field. The cows lined up over it. And then back to the stackyard. Three trips from this stackyard and three each from two others: nine loads of hay forked onto the sled and forked off, spread across the meadow; then he was done with it, early in the afternoon, and drove back to the barn and put up his horses and went back to the house and the fire.

Later in the afternoon he rode through the cattle. Most of them were lying down now, kept warm by their own full-bellied ruminations, chewing their cuds, lying along the fouled feedgrounds among a scattering of hay stems.

He noticed a heifer calf standing by her mother, who was down resting. The calf was standing a little too squarely on her legs, with her head thrust out, looking altogether a little sad. She was a big calf, an excellent deep-hearted full-flanked calf and glowing. She glowed even through her long hair: so she wasn't sick, at least not yet, but only hurting.

When he got around on the other side of her, Ben saw what was wrong. She was blinking a swollen eye. Underneath it, the thick curly white hair of her face was stained and twisted into wisps, stained yellow all below the weeping eye.

She wasn't the first calf he'd seen like that this week. The others he'd caught and doctored. Like the others she had probably rooted around in this meadowhay with her whole head, caught a seed of bronco grass on an eyelash and blinked it right onto the surface of the eye. From there it worked its way under the lid. Eventually the seed might get dissolved by the eye-fluids themselves, but by that time she would go blind in that eye and have an iris white as a pearl.

This was the biggest of the lot. He thought that if a man could raise a whole pasture full of calves like this one and peddle them each fall, then he could soon kiss the bank and their seven percent goodbye and be working on his own money and land—farting in silk like he'd said to the girl. So when the mother cow got up to her feet, he looked her over. She wasn't a big, high-priced breedy looking cow but just a common spindly-assed little cow, with a pretty head and what he liked to call a motherly eye. He tried, as he'd done for most of his life, to get one more clue about why one cow will raise a calf like that every year and another cow who looks like by the book she should, won't.

Anyway that was a dead dream. Snow would burn before he would make money. Besides that, he wasn't all that interested any more. He wondered why those old habits of thought wouldn't leave him alone, but seemed to flow on as long as blood would.

He had all the room in the world to catch her. He didn't try to catch her right away but let the mare chase her awhile, to take some of the sap out of her, because he didn't want to take her on fresh the way she was—as big as she was and full of wild grass and milk. So he let her run herself down, and then he roped her. When she hit the end of it she bawled, and when she bawled her mother bawled too and started trotting toward them, bawling anxiously.

The heifer did not battle, just lay back against the rope strangling. She had her legs spread and braced and wouldn't fall. He couldn't throw her. He had her front leg in his hands, shoving it against her, locked in joint and square, so that it made a good prypole. Ben strained with his old thin legs and back and belly against the pure sagging spraddle-legged inertia of her, but he couldn't tip her over. The mother cow came up behind him. She snuffled and snorted and he felt her breath blowing against him right through his hip pocket. He snorted back at her and she jumped away and in her excitement jumped against the rope which in turn slapped the old mare alongside the neck like a rubber band. When the mare jumped the calf was jerked into motion and he pulled the leg to him and then shoved it back at her hard and she went down.

With his knee on her shoulder and her forefoot doubled up in his hands he held her flat. After she quit thrashing he took the short rope from his belt, eased her hindlegs across the front one and tied her down. Her good eye looked up at him, bulging so that he could have flicked it off with his fingernail. He paddled more snow back to the mare and led her ahead so he could loosen the rope and take it off the heifer's neck before she choked entirely. All the time the old cow danced around moaning.

The cow didn't frighten him. He didn't know why. There wasn't a mean bone in her body but that was no good reason not to be afraid of her. Once out of sheer nervousness and in the same circumstance a black cow had bowled him over. And he really had no way of knowing that this one wouldn't. He rolled the heifer over so that her bad eye was up, and squatted down over her. The cow was all around him. She snorted and blew little beads of water on his elbow. Her hot, grassy breath, smelling truly like fermented grass, blew on the back of his neck and fanned both his cheeks. She was really beside herself. But she didn't bother him.

It was nothing but the feathery seed of a bronco grass, but it was something the way it hid itself, burrowing down into the corner of the socket. Because even when he peeled back the two lids as far as possible between his thumb and forefinger, all the hidden surface of the candy-striped eyewhite had seemed to be revealed, but nothing else. Until he spread the lids more forcibly at the very corner, the inside corner of the socket. Even then he could finally see just the tiny tail, a few filaments. These he caught between his nails—drew out the seed and flicked it away. She rolled her sweet, stupid brown eye around a time or two and then let it settle back to center where it could look out at him and mother and the world again.

Whatever it was started before he even got back on the mare. He figured he had borne up under so much pain in the last fifteen or so years that changes in it frightened him more than they actually hurt him. As if he was his own wife worrying. Anyway now he knew he wasn't going to have to ride anywhere more today but back to the barn.

He rode like he had a board stuffed down his shirtback, but in spite of that, listening and out of time, unable even to keep up with the easy familiar swaying motion of the mare walking.

When he got to the barn and unsaddled, instead of throwing his saddle up on the wooden rack like he always did, like anyone would, he found himself just shoving it through the tackroom door. He left it on the floor mashing its own skirts. When he looked at it he was surprised that he had done that.

He unbridled the mare, turned her loose and began walking one step at a time to the house. It wasn't hard: he seemed weightless. Yet he wasn't really sure he would make it: as if he was a wind-up toy that might peter out any time. When he opened the housedoor he noticed that he hadn't left the bridle in the barn: it was swinging from his forearm. He chucked it in the corner. Blood in his mouth ran up against the back of his gums and across against the underpinning of his tongue. He spit in the sizzling stove.

Wood enough was piled in the two crates by his chair to feed the stove for several hours. (More was on the porch.) Good. He didn't want to move. The last thing he wanted was to have to get up. He didn't want to lie down. He didn't even want to take his boots off right yet. He was weak as a cat. He liked what the woodfire did to his tingling limbs and face. He shed his coat and his muffler and cap onto the floor. There was no way he could go fork hay off that cold sled tomorrow morning, no way, and that was fine with him.

The next afternoon, when Wesley came, Ben was still sitting there. Through the kitchen window he saw the sled come over the rim and start down the sidehill.

A couple of minutes later he saw the horse's head reappear just outside the window, not fifty feet from him. He saw it—the head of the sorrel horse bowed into the bridle, pushing at it, face rubbed afoam by the bridle-leather, the tongue of the downsliding sled shoving the horse along and Wesley's hands set against it, hauling back on the reins, so that the horse was all bunched together in a ball, curled and glistening like a red shrimp. Wesley reminded him a little of popeye. His forearms were solid as logs. Above his heavy jaw the near cheek pooched out, disfigured by a plug of tobacco. He was wearing his mud-colored hat. Another bundled-up capped figure sat beside him on the sled, showing a good crop of gray whiskers. Ben saw it all, just as he knew he would see it—which was strange because how would he know what he would see?

He was half out of his head, Ben was. But he saw it all, whiskers and all. That other figure was the new chore man. It wasn't his wife. No, but the new man without a doubt. The new man whiskers and all. And what business had he looking for his wife? How could he think, why had he thought, that it might be his wife? And wouldn't he have been furious at her for coming way down here? Say, wouldn't he! He'd have read her a good one—or better yet, he wouldn't have spoken.

He imagined Wesley's perplexity and delighted in it. He imagined it to its finest details and delighted in all of them. He saw through Wesley's eyes. So certain he was of everything. Coming over the ridge Wesley first sees *the smoke coming out the stove-chimney. Fine*, Wesley thinks, *everything as it should be*. (If he'd had any doubts before that, it was because a few cows could be heard bawling hungrily even from the ridgetop. Maybe that would bother him, but he would hardly be aware of it himself, and then he would see the smoke and be relieved, and hardly know that either.)

Then as he dips down past the house (he can't see into the half-dark kitchen, though he tries)—as he dips past the house and goes on to the barn, he sees *them lined up at the fence, stretching out their necks, more and more of them bawling with excitement at the sight of a sled, though it hasn't hay in it.*

Now Wesley is puzzled. He is on the watch for signs now. A blind man couldn't miss some of them. When he gets up to the barn to unharness, *the hungry workhorses and the saddlemare like to paw the mangers down at the sight of him. The tackroom is open to the weather.* He steps inside to hang up the harness. *Ben's saddle is all in a crush on the floor.*

Ben saw all this paced out in time, so that he knew, or at least thought he knew, just the moment when Wesley hung the harness up and saw the saddle. Wesley tells the new man *to put up the horse and feed all the animals in the barn. Himself he hurries toward the house. Wesley hurries along in Ben's own tracks, almost running. The tracks satisfy him that Ben is in the house. What is that sort of lizard-trail ripple in the snow, alongside the boot-tracks?* (That had been made by the bridle reins that dragged all that way. Ben remembered that the ends of them had been snow-wet when he got to the house: but Wesley would never figure that out.)

Ben saw it all. Otherwise he hasn't a clear or even a sensible thought in his head. He is occupied by a perverse, mistaken glee. Mistaken, because he keeps imagining how surprised Wesley is going to be—Wesley who expects to find a man very sick, if not crippled, burnt or God knows what. Instead Wesley is going to find him, Ben, taking his ease, sitting with his boots on, his feet up on the stove, keeping warm and—well just sitting like any keeping warm man.

At the right instant Wesley did come in, fast, betraying himself, banging the door, just as Ben knew he would. But what Ben became aware of really when he looked at Wesley's face was his own appearance. All the heat he possessed had seemed to gather suddenly—or rather he suddenly became aware that it was so gathered—at two places: the high points of his cheeks and in his eyes. Otherwise he was cold and felt himself drained of color. His hair was matted on his scalp. A parade of cold sweat, large drops sticky as sap, lined the lowest furrow of his forehead. He was unshaven, he was tangled, he was pale, his teeth even were out. All that he read in Wesley's eyes—and for just a moment reawakened to the real world, but only for a moment and then was as quickly off again into something else.

Without saying hello or anything else he said: "What kind of man did Sterling find to sit down here and chuck hay to his cows all winter?"

Wesley simply looked at him.

"What?" Ben said.

"You look wrung out. What happened? You look like you've been sitting right there since the world began. What's wrong with you? Can you get around?"

With a belligerence Wesley had never noticed before in him or even imagined, Ben said: "Pull that sled up to the kitchen door and point it to town and we'll find out if I can get around," and then shifted as quickly and said, "No, my legs are all right in themselves only they won't hold up the rest of me, son. Just hand me my hat and we'll head back on up the country. How's the weather to home, anyway? Ain't this a bitch!"

"Sure," Wesley said.

The new man, who was a stranger, came in and pulled off his cap and gloves. He was a used-up looking man, as glum and purposeless looking as old Shorty before him. Ben glared at him as if he was all his enemies rolled into one.

"Look, do you know what's wrong with you?" Wesley asked Ben.

"Wrong? I feel pretty uneven. That's what's wrong. Anyone can tell that by looking at me. Can't they?" Ben kept looking at the new man. "Can't they? How about you? Do you like the way I look?"

The new man wore cast-off britches four sizes too big for him. He had more stubble than Ben had and from the looks of him it was more habitual. He just glowered back at Ben fearlessly.

"How about you?" Ben asked him. "You're not one to say, are you!

Careful who you try too far, partner! You'll get in over your head, and for you that's not far—deep, I mean, deep, deep." Then Ben turned to Wesley and said nastily: "Well, didn't Sterling find a man to chuck hay to his cows?"

"John Rhodes, this is Ben Webber," Wesley said.

"Yes!" said Ben loudly, punctuating his own name.

"What is he, drunk? or just tailing off of one?" asked John Rhodes.

"Now that's stupid of you to say," said Ben coolly. Of course it was true that when he was drinking he used to act a lot like he was acting now, and the remark actually seemed to pacify him.

"Well boys, there's a lot of cows to feed before dark," he said, "and I'm a little late getting my feet under me this morning." Saying this he stood up with his fingertips on the stove and sat back down again. "You boys feed them: I'll tend the soup."

"No morning, it's suppertime where I come from," said Rhodes, an evidently humorless man.

"Is that true?" said Ben. "If I'd known it was you coming I'd of shaved. For supper too. Maybe you could have phoned."

"You keep your loonies a long way from town," Rhodes said to Wesley.

Once Wesley decided to take Ben back it was the sooner the better. However he had Rhodes to worry about too. He might not take to spending his first evening at the swamp feeding eight hundred cattle alone by lantern light. Not that Wesley cared if he took to it or not, but he might sull up and want to go in the sled back, or who knows what. So Wesley went feeding.

When he did get the sled pulled up by the kitchen door it was way after dark. He told Rhodes he would be back in a day or two to wean calves.

The night was a clear one. A waning moon had risen. Ben, stretched out on his back, was swaddled in blankets and packed in meadowhay. The last thing Wesley did was load some rocks that he had heated and wrapped in burlap sacks. He stashed them all around Ben's legs and thighs. Like an admiring child, Ben watched Wesley load the stones. "Aren't those heavy?" he asked.

"It won't hurt the fat bitch to pull a few rocks," Wesley said, misunderstanding. That was when Ben noticed his own mare harnessed and hitched.

"If they're still warm when we hit the ridge over Goose Lake, they'll feel fine," Ben said.

"I don't imagine they'll make it quite that far," Wesley said, "but you're pretty well wrapped up out of the weather."

"I'll say I am." In fact never had he felt safer or warmer, more helpless or better cared for. At the same time, predictable and unpleasant thoughts contrasted his mood directly, if such a thing is possible. These thoughts seemed to surround him, not touching him but to float by persistently, at a distance.

Here he was, wrapped up so and flat on his back. If he hadn't the energy to mind it now, he at least knew he was going to mind it later. He was afraid they could do what they wanted to him now. Flat on his back to their ministrations, their overkind concern—doctors, neighbors, his brother. He could see it coming.

That, and he had been hired to do a job of work he couldn't get done. (Sterling had made a mistake.) He wished that he had made a mismove, had a stroke of bad luck or committed a piece of stupidity—got injured somehow, or taken sick for no reason. Those things could happen to anyone and everyone knew it. But no, his old motor appeared to have just strained and run down bit by bit. That's how they would treat it. That's the way he felt about it himself, nearly forgetting about his stomach now and the blood he spat. That's how they would treat it, though they would never say. Sterling would see it like that. So would Clyde, who had tried to old-woman him out of coming down here in the first place.

Before Sterling, who he was costing money, he would have to be apologetic and grateful. And if he refused to act that way, well it amounted to the same thing. He was costing Wesley his sleep. He had gone out of his mind. He had acted the fool before Wesley and a stranger too. Even now, when he spoke he was so naive-seeming and mellow that Wesley must wonder. These things he thought of for a while, but was soon lulled by the wide, indifferent night. He wished it to go on, the night—afraid of his own chair in his own front room, where they were going to poke and pull him. At the same time he really wanted nothing so much as to get home. . . .

In his sleep he began to ride inclined, gravitating toward the back of the sled. His legs instinctively stiffened, and that woke him. It was darker than it had been. Or so it seemed. He saw where the moon had set, leaving a little glow on the mountain. But the stars had grown pale: it couldn't be long till daylight. He had certainly been sleeping. He was warm. His feet braced themselves against the heel of the sled. The sled-runners whispered; the mare breathed heavily.

By that hard breathing and the incline of his body he recognized that they were climbing up the ridge over Goose Lake. In a couple of more hours they would be back to the pavement, where the snowplows ran and where Wesley had a truck parked.

Halfway up the ridge Wesley let the mare turn crossways to the slope and get her air. "How are you making it?" Ben asked.

"Not bad, but I've been warmer," Wesley said. "How about yourself?"

"Oh, just right," Ben said.

At the top Wesley let her stop and blow again. Ben raised up a little and looked around once. Now it was coming dawn; no true colors yet anywhere. The snow wasn't white anymore and the sky wasn't blue. Neither dark nor light. The last stars flickered weakly like bad low voltage connections. The lake looked fleshy as a new leaf and as little like water. As the sled once more broke into motion he fell back to sleep like a baby and didn't move until they rattled over the railroad tracks that ran parallel to the highway.

MY WORK IN CALIFORNIA

fiction by JAMES B. HALL

from THE MISSOURI REVIEW

nominated by George Garrett and DeWitt Henry

I. *The Younger Factory*

Of the one hundred passengers arriving from Seattle (Boeing) my job was only with thirty-four industrialists from Asia. Of this group a dozen were unexpectedly tall; a few wore dark, prescription glasses; only one man had two briefcases as carry-on. Not one delegate looked back at the aircraft or took a picture of the Oakland charter terminal.

My welcome sign at the baggage claim area read in Japanese and Hindi: Industry Tour Delegates Here. They manufactured something or were of engineering backgrounds; therefore they were urbane and kept my placard in view but did not cluster about. Most of them spoke Oriental languages, but to me they used English: "Our weather is identical of here weather." "We have eaten considerately while at flying," and so on.

At the luggage carousel one man from Korea claimed only a backpack and pair of blue skis. By way of explanation their chief delegate, a Mr. Hognisko, said our gentleman from Korea join this California Inspection at last minute: all very good.

Beyond the terminal entrance our bus was parked, its engine running.

For this I was relieved. In my work a great many things can go wrong.

Finally, our bus headed south towards San Leandro and the plant which was not far beyong Fremont.

By courtesy, Mr. Hognisko had boarded first and had claimed a seat immediately behind the driver. Now Mr. Hognisko leaned forward very intently; in a small notebook he recorded the RPM and fuel gauge readings. I made a mental note to arrange later for him actually to drive our bus—under supervision—inside the factory yard: a litttle thing like that for a delegate is very memorable.

As the bus went steadily through the last of the morning fog, I walked the aisle and answered their polite queries: Those salt flats at the edge of Upper Bay, were in production? The Alameda container-shipping facility, was it eighty-percent automated? Concerning Blacks in major California cities: how much Blacks?

The Korean's backpack was in the aisle beside him. Intensely, mostly with his arms, he was speaking to a man across the aisle; the man listened, did not change expression, but finally repeated the question to me in English:

"Gentleman with valuable pack here say he makes fashion-purses—very many. Also: how far is Disneyland?"

I replied that Disneyland was in the Los Angeles area, specifically at Anaheim, which was approximately four hundred miles south, about one hour flying time.

"Gentleman says Disneyland not so far away."

At first the factory appears on the horizon as several hundred aligned ventilators, exhaust stacks, and air-scrub towers; closer, the immense roofs rise slowly from the ground and fill the bus windows. Only then do they really see the factory walls.

I understand the reaction: they have flown a long way to see this absolutely state-of-the-art complex; in their own countries they may wish to build a replica. When at last in a moment of bus-window vision our factory becomes manifest, they fall silent, are a little reverent, a little stunned. I, myself, often view it at mid-morning in the California sunshine and still I have some slight feeling of awe.

Our bus stopped at the entrance gate: There will be a slight delay.

Actually, I believe these foreign-delegation delays have internal function. Not every unit of our Younger factory operates at any given time; therefore all tour routes are selectively programmed.

The question is a good one: as an experienced guide, have I seen the complete layout, all units in production? Or: have I ever been programmed twice on the identical tour-route? Possibly, but my sole interest is professional: the art of tour-satisfaction.

In about twenty minutes, as expected, a young woman in her three-wheeled golf car rides out across the vast parking lot to our bus. She hands me the route-skip chart. Often we work together.

Inside our bus, the young woman from Public Relations speaks to this delegation in English, German, and then in Turkish. First, an apology for this routine delay. Then her rundown of statistics: number of fenced areas, square-footages under roof, water gallonage daily; the architects and major contractors for the Beginning, Middle, and Final Coordinate modules.

Her speech is always impressive. No questions.

As our delgation enters rountinely through the East-Arch plaza, I sense the usual change of mood: casual talk ceases. Here the corridors are vaulted-steel, air-conditioned, and are virtually aseptic. The big surprise is the color-coding systems: all Receiving and Primary Incalculation areas are in tones of red; at tour's end, near the West Exit gates, the color coding ranges from indigo through violet.

Therefore, when one delegation looked down from the catwalk into their first full-production module, they saw that the nitrous tubing, conduits, and the work-persons' smocks were an identical shade of green. Because the high-speed machines are virtually silent, my voice was easily heard.

"Below, Gentlemen, our syntax looms. From left to right, inside translucent tubes, the Youngers are admitted, then loomed."

Each delegate at once became fascinated with a single aspect of the process: with the emission tubes or water-recovery sumps; with the sensor areas or the green, intricate thread-lines which glisten in the cool light. As though they were encased, merely passive objects, all Youngers are sorted, then pass at high speed through the looms. Here all syntax patterns were confirmed. No one person can ever register all the coordinated movements; in the end, all visitors merely stare.

"All loom thread is 90% nylon—linen is no longer used." And to Mr. Hognisko, "Syntax is a general term: in addition to speech, it also encompasses larger cultural patterns."

He made a note.

In the loom pits below, the machinery seemed to breathe, and for an instant to glow deeply inside the intricate thread barriers. A workperson, a woman in a green smock, emerged from the corridor between the extraordinary, winking shuttles, as though ejected or born from the loom itself; she glanced upward, gestured, then placed one hand lightly—testing for heat—on a rotor housing. The breathing looms slowed perceptively. The vault darkened as we moved on.

No further questions.

Our delegations lined up behind the glass barriers of a typical organic unit: here all Youngers receive their viral program injections; these modules are typical of one of the more advanced procedures.

All in a row, faces pressed to the glass barriers, the delegates watched intently. Smiling or asleep in their little sacs, the Youngers passing in the troughs seem almost a blur. When twins with Oriental features went past, the delegates gesticulated, were much pleased.

As we watched, the sensor banks read the fluid codes: abruptly, the twins were shunted off together, disappeared. Farther along we viewed the more refined sorting and incalculation: one strain was for sensitivity to metal objects (cars, gold coin, tempered steel—as in guns). This one is standard, takes very well. The more complex motives of power (money and banking) or indiscriminate knowledge (for teachers) is less predictable.

From my point of view, however, nothing *seems* to happen in the organic modules; they are low delegate interest. The crux forge and the sports verifier are more melodramatic. For Youngers, however, the entire process is without pain; doubtless it passes in a mild semi-biotic dream. As to overall effectiveness, not all types of irradiated tendencies are final; in California, a complete program-rejection at some later age is not common. Being exotic, our viral incalculation modules elicit few questions.

None? Very well: move along now to a typical production unit, V.T.

In V.T. all action is overt. Here all delegates have floor privilege. They may stand at a machine-of-choice. They move about freely. Only a repeated call for the lunch-snack disengages most foreign observers. I also like these sections quite a bit.

Of course, the unexpected noise is the first contrast. The hubbub is most life-like: here all the machine operators call out. They curse one another and their balky machines; they chew tobacco where they stand. In V.T. the work rules are posted in several languages, especially Spanish; the operators belong to a loose, ineffectual union. Here Management leaves well enough alone.

At once all delegates scattered. Now they stood beside the machines, avidly speaking with the operators, if only in sign language. At last here was something everyone understood.

Mr. Hognisko was immediately beside a Stealth Elaborator. The Younger is placed (in sac) on a rotating metal plate; the eccentrically-balanced flywheel lowers—delicately or too deeply—and roughs the sac with the wheel's random abrasives. All Youngers appear to be terribly shocked, are in momentary pain; inside the sac we see their little hands row the fluid. Oddly, however, certain Youngers laugh; others withdraw or become merely fetal. The fascination, of course, is with the *variety* for at the Violence Tannery no two Youngers ever react precisely in the same way. The reason for this is not known.

No matter: because of altercations and workmen shouting obscenities, there can be neither questions or answers. Naturally these conditions divert delegates from our more refined techniques: A & A (Animal Affiliaton, usually of the horse-prone variety); A & T (Alliance and Trauma-consequence, as in multiple divorce); A & C (Attenuated Cruelty, wide-spectrum). If asked directly, I say those more isolated sheds are reserved for some future visitation.

Because this particular delegation would not leave the machines, time did not permit them a view of the flower-decked, elaborately color-coded Reunion Ramps. Here all Youngers are delivered—emotionally, melodramatically—to parents, guardians, etc. With manufacturers, a little reconciliation doubtless goes a long way, for their interest is with distribution. In any event, after our luncheon-snack I answered questions:

—Yes: all water is re-cycled. Our California model conforms to Regional and Federal clean-air standards, or is being modified accordingly.

—No: Those Upper-Bay salt flats have no bearing on this choice
of site.

In some distant area of the plant, at a place I have never been, I
heard a reverberating, deep, explosion. All cafeteria lights went
dim—then again became bright.

The delegates looked at each other but did not change expression.

Through a third party who spoke some English, the man from
Korea asked about profit margins, and projected return on capital
investment.

These figures, I said, are not available at the present time.

Before lunch was over, I noted that Mr. Hognisko has disappeared.

When we went outside to our boarding ramp, I saw Mr. Hognisko
driving our bus (under supervision). He steered in large, swerving
figure-eights, all over the now totally deserted parking lot.

When the regular bus driver saw me waiting, he directed Mr.
Hognisko to park at our ramp.

As they boarded, each delegate said the tour had been most
interesting and educational.

Whereupon I returned with the delegation to a downtown San
Francisco hotel and checked them in for the night.

II. *The Snow Orchestration*

A Bedouin party had toured California sixteen days when I was
detailed to their "caravan" at a highway intersection just south of
Yosemite.

Majestically, their polished-aluminium motor coaches all in a row
floated around a curve, became larger; closer, in the mid-morning
sun, the silver coaches seemed still wet. They parked in echelons-
of-two beside the highway. Beneath the windshields, I saw
sprayed-on, national colors; all license plates were of diplomatic
issues. Their coaches carried twenty-eight persons, excluding drivers; the TV, radio, citizen's band antennae, and the rooftop air
conditioners implied money was no object. They were much more
than one hour late.

When no one got out, I walked from my car back to the first motor
coach. Above and from behind his windshield, a driver in white
coveralls waved casually. Their door did not open until I knocked
again.

The Sheik greeted me cordially. He was in native dress and spoke with a distinct Cambridge accent. We shook hands. Inside it was a series of elaborate, meaningless introductions in Arabic; I presumed the names and titles were also on my roster.

The large forward compartment of this coach was lined with satin pillows; a white canopy of cloth hung overhead. With waterpipes and provocative sex magazines scattered about, the effect was that of a lavish tent, temporarily at ease on a desert oasis. From each dais, however, I noted each Arab could see both the driver's back and the instrument panel of the coach.

Naturally, my concern was to discuss at once our exercise: its engineering, cultural function, project costs, and projected useful life—everything. Unfortunately, either it was now tea time or I was served ritualistically. Inwardly I fretted at this further delay but made conversation and watched them drop many lumps of sugar into their delicate teacups. Time passed. The canopy filled with blue, sweet, Arabic smoke.

Suddenly an older man who had remained withdrawn in shadows leaned forward. He spoke emotionally in Arabic. I understood not a word, but I felt accused—of something.

"This cousin," the Sheik said not calmly, "*believes* one of our drivers is a State Highway Patrolman. In disguise, of course."

I requested details.

"As we go, we hear only this driver: *his* citizen-band radio is *active*. On our monitor in this coach we hear his *every* word."

They nodded: it was a communal judgment.

"This Number-Three driver conveys—Oh, slyly in code—information."

Patiently, I explained: all caravan drivers assigned are Teamster-Union members. By custom these drivers, via CB, convey harmless greetings to other passing Teamster-Union drivers. They alert one another to speed traps, the presence of Highway Patrol cars, and so on.

"But we have diplomatic plates!"

Finally I resolved it by two promises: a possible substitute driver; secondly, immediate warning to Number Three. Meanwhile, with their permission, I would brief all drivers; on this final leg to the valley ahead their caravan would simply follow my official car. This was discussed at some length: agreed.

Therefore I walked back to the other coaches to alert the drivers and to counsel Number Three—who appeared to be Pakistani. The third and fourth coaches carried only women and children. On identical television consoles I saw the identical program, an episode from "Gunsmoke"—with Arabic soundtrack. The women in *perda* and their children watched the screens very intently.

Number-Five coach carried servants, supplies, one accountant-scribe, and a physician; inside it smelled rancid with coffee grounds, smoke, and household pets.

At the head of the convoy, from the middle of the highway, I waved one arm in a circle: start your engines.

Slowly I led the way upward along the treacherous, curved highway for another sixty-two miles. We were now so behind schedule that the two guards at the gateway arch of stone waved us immediately to the promontory. Not far from the guard rails at the cliff's edge, the motor coaches again parked in echelons-of-two. Again I walked back to their first coach and knocked several times to gain admission.

I said the news was good: although well past noon, the atmospheric conditions at the altitude were still satisfactory. Our observation parapets lay immediately ahead.

Most opportunely, the Sheik said, this pause coincides precisely with the customary hours for lunch. Naturally I would be their honored guest?

"Very well," I had to reply, for clearly my status was that of servant. "Possibly this pause is foreordained—for our better fellowship?"

Everyone who understood smiled; my remark was then translated. The older men nodded wisely, then repeated in Arabic what I thought was the word "foreordained."

Our meal was elaborate. The lamb and the goat had been slaughtered, then fast-frozen in their home country, flown to California, and only last night delivered by taxi to this caravan. I admired the planning; the Sheik replied that such was their custom while abroad. Eventually everyone took a waterpipe and began to smoke. More time passed.

Amost inadvertently, much later, I glanced at my wristwatch.

Everyone stood up as though I, myself, had engendered this by-now-ruinous delay. At once two men took citizen-band microphones from beneath their pillows and began to give orders. Then everyone was talking at once in Arabic.

When all members of the party gathered on the promontory,

there was a drawn-out uninformed discussion: was the snow exercise
suitable for male children (under puberty), women, or servants?
Eventually the physician, all young girls, and the eldest women
were returned to the caravan; for security, all drivers to remain *in*
their vehicles—and no CB transmissions.

So it was very late when finally I led their party to the viewing
ramparts. Once seated, the Bedouins wrapped themselves in their
robes and stared at the amphitheater headwalls of granite. Already I
saw shadows in the east crevasse.

Over an intercom which connects all observation sites, I gave the
set-speech: superb feat of modern technology superbly adapted to
the unusual California resources and terrain. The exercise exploits
three basic elements: light, wind-activation, and snow. Although
apparently preserved in its superb natural state, our amphitheater
below in fact is artfully lined with recessed ducting, elaborate banks
of discharge nozzles, and panels of sequestered lights. From geo-
thermal wells—Nature's bounty—high-density CO_2 rises, is compressed, and is then released sequentially. The gas escaping becomes "snow." All energy-transfer systems draw power from distant
hydroelectric sites. Hurriedly, I reviewed the volume of released
gasses, miles of buried tubing, square-footage estimates, the main
designers, primary contractors, and maintenance budgets, *per
capita*. Were there questions?

If the Bedouins registered my voice, they gave no sigh.

Oddly—I confess it—when an orchestration begins, I forget the
parties visiting. No two orchestrations are identical; I am always
surprised. In one way I am proud to be part of it, and at those
moments I wish everyone in the world could share this experience,
especially when the program is complete and in sunlight at noon—
which is the proper time.

As always, and especially with the Bedouin party, I had the usual
feeling of anticipation—something like terror—when the first flakes
of snow floated upward from the walls. Lights suddenly transformed
the vast granite amphitheater into alabaster. The first "winds" blew.
The panoramic wall began imperceptibly to writhe.

The snow builds, is caught in random drifts as though the wind
were a shaping hand: the first portraits emerge. As it is with the vast
faces carved in stone against the sky at Mount Rushmore, so now do
portraits of snow range across the light-breathing walls for our initial
contemplation. Because of the programmed wind, the hair on the

snow-sculptured heads seems to rise as though the massive heads had tossed back in pain from the azure light.

On this particular day the faces at once extended into full-length figures: two prehistoric Asiatics in postures of sacrifice, their ritualistic knife piercing again and again the maimed child of snow. Face averted, an Indian woman undulates in postures of sexual invitation below the priest who is riding a burro. Whereupon the amphitheater resolves into concentric rings, each ring smaller and lower until the lowest depths become an eye, an enfolded flower of blazing snow, more fluid, more gold than the sun at noon. From the top rings, driven by winds, the snow overflows then falls like giant slabs of wax dripping into the molten eye. Always I imagine music would contribute to their better understanding of our past, but there is no sound beneath the sky.

The full-length figures dissolve into violet light. Now there is a wall of forests, all trees falling. Oxen and a thousand horses rear or are solidly yoked, pulling first crude sledges across the headwall, and then pulling grotesque mills down, down through a crevasse into that deepest core. All growing things are now gone away, the walls turn incredibly green, are supine beneath the faceless wind. These things I know are prelude only and I wait.

The sun came to rest on the farthest rim of the mountain. That first suggestion of nightfall was like the giant, whistling shadow of a bird's wing scything above our parapets.

The snow orchestration became suddenly frenzied. The lights blinked, shuddered; the wind rose. Everywhere snow erupted, became untrammeled drifts, then rolled down, down, as a thousand small avalanches into the darkness.

The amphitheater became mauve, then red. The wind swirled, lifted the red snow in rising, cyclonic columns. At eye-level those columns tilted, and I saw into the calyx of a monstrous flower. Within, I saw neither face nor figure—only the snows: iridescent, without motion, a roil of fire wherein nothing burned.

The lights turned a violent orange. The snow column died into the fissures of the granite wall; the wind also went away. As though the world itself had ended, there was neither breath nor sound.

In that spectacular, truncated way—abruptly—the orchestration of snows for the Bedouins stopped. If viewed in sunlight at noon, they would have understood everything; they, themselves, had delayed. I made no apology. I did not explain.

Their robes blown by late-evening winds, the Bedouins straggled back in little groups to the darkening promontory and to their aligned coaches. Only the guardrails seemed unchanged.

As it turned out, however, I never did answer the usual questions. At once their physician and their accountant-scribe requested audience.

Very mysteriously, Number-Three driver had disappeared. He had transmitted no CB messages; no property was missing; no known enemies. With the Sheik, I inspected that coach; the driver had simply vanished.

At once the Sheik withdrew with his immediate family and counselors. I waited outside the closed vehicles for what seemed a very long time. Finally, everyone reappeared and I was told a decision:

Most assuredly this thing was unfortunate. On the other hand, could it be entirely astonishing: had not I, myself, agreed previously both to the reprimand and also to driver-replacement? Being a Pakistani—very possibly naturalized for convenience—the man was obviously incompetent. For this surely the Teamsters Union bears much blame. Concerning the driver's family: in any way, here or abroad, might they be contacted?

I said probably in some way they could be tracked down.

Excellent. But to the main point: an alternate driver.

I did not reply.

"Being the most qualified," the Sheik said, "by reason of my own extensive limousine holdings, *I* will drive this vehicle for the remainder of this day. I have closely observed all drivers—also the instrument panel. For me this will be educational. Agreed?"

I said the next stop was outside Fresno, where they were expected.

"Well done," the Sheik said very affably, for he was eager to drive.

One-by-one the engines started. Their noise reverberated upward in the chilled, rising wind from the mountains.

Going back down the highway, the Sheik followed my automobile much, much too closely. Continually he honked the airhorns. He drove recklessly—on the inside of all curves.

At that time—and to this day—it was pointless for me to report to anyone higher up that very plainly I saw bloodstains near the driver's seat when I inspected the vehicle. I suspect their physician. But as the Sheik had so rightly said, "We have diplomatic plates."

No matter: at the final intersection their caravan turned south. I honked once, and waved goodbye. In my report I intended to say that—in fact—the delegates noted many parallels between our snow orchestrations and their own rich, essentially Persian cultural heritage.

Exactly at the speed limit I drove north to my motel which was at the edge of Stockton.

III. *At the Coma Pavilions*

"My hobby geology," the surveyor from Penang told me. "Long time ago this place under water."

I said probably so.

On our drive south to the coast this group of scholars, a recuperating Swiss physician, educators, etc., had become better acquainted and were now a lively, well-motivated interest group. Our station wagons were to park here; older ladies—probably ex-schoolteachers—changed to hiking boots for this last-mile descent to the valley floor.

No recording equipment or cameras beyond this point, please.

Below, melodramatically, the valley divides; each parallel branch ends in white sand at the beach. Beyond, the sea was iridescent, rising, turquoise. For me this tour marked the season's end; already I was thinking of Palm Springs.

Energetically, our ex-schoolteachers started down the path; farther along, one voice, in German, began a marching song. Mainly to permit the Swiss physician a moment's rest beneath the rock overhang of a shelter carved years ago from solid rock by the first inhabitants, I called a halt and then reviewed our inspection guidelines:

Speech with inhabitants permitted *only* if resident-initiated. However: technically qualified observers—physicans, our pathologist, etc.—may touch or otherwise manipulate comatose subjects. Only gross anatomical evaluations are customary; use of a stethoscope is all right. "Why-type" queries are unsettling, hence counterproductive. In a word, ladies and gentlemen, we are professionally-oriented observers.

"Yes, yes," the group responded, mostly in English. "Is understood."

Questions?

—Certainly: All of them enjoy State, Federal, and Constitutional safeguards regardless of race, etc., Percentage of resident, native Californians is not available—estimates vary, yes.

—No: not an "exhibit" or a "theme park" impulse (e.g., Under Six Flags). If motivations appear incomprehensibly complex, consider the complexity of life today.

No others? I thank you.

Around the first, abrupt corner, against the sky and almost bridging the canyon walls, they saw their first Counseling Mobile. The light was very good.

To me, this one is largely amusing. To all educators and to our shockingly emaciated priest, *en route* to the Vatican, it was fascinating. At once, they climbed the ladders and from the high platforms leaned over the railings the better to observe.

I explained the site-logic: here coastal winds converge where the canyon narrows. The boom and cable arrangements suspended also converge—then regress—from the Resource Wheel—the large one, centered horizontally. The dissonant noises are their voices and also wind among their cables. In mid-air, the subjects forever pass; being electrically charged, however, they can never touch. By attraction then repulsion they move continually—what, one hundred fifty feet above these rocks?

Suddenly, exhibitionistically, one in a loincloth, its body dried totally by the winds, swooped down: arms outstretched, wide-eyed, the sun caught as fire on its enormous, steel-rimmed glasses. For a second it was suspended above our astonished heads, then with tackle screaming, it rose in a great rush of air, was gone.

"Dead," the Swiss physician said. "Long time." Our pathologist from Edinburgh, concurred.

Aloft on the highest platforms the educators tried to interpret the sound of the cables and the voices in the sibilant air. Again I called: Rejoin, please, your group immediately?

Because the sun was not yet too high we walked mostly in the shade of the canyon walls. Being of mature years, this group viewed with little interest the Excess Pavilions: a Consumer Cavern, the Cervix-Renewal and Depletion Station where desires of a purely sexual nature are changed monthly by surgical intervention. Surprisingly, the emaciated priest scarcely paused at an elaborate Meditation Pavilion dedicated to programmed Faith-Loss.

Their age-group considered, possibly I kept them overly long at the Matriarch Escarpment. I, myself, am oddly drawn to this ever-expanding sequence which is best viewed from elevated walkways along the opposite canyon wall. I explained:

Opposite: a typical encampment painted ochre and blue. Architecturally, the primitive forms hang on: seen in the platforms, square or shaped to the cliff face; seen in the shelters, rooflines peaked or typically convex; observed in the child-transfer poles (one per sibling) anchored like horizontal flagpoles, extending out from the platforms; also below—bars vertical or horizontal—their individual men-pens. Now: either supine or pacing continually in the prescribed patterns—two examples visible, extreme left—the woman controls all architectural improvements, equipage, monies. Moreover. . . .

"A-hoh!" the priest said, for he was coughing. Deeply absorbed, the Swiss physician said nothing, but his nurse spoke vehemently, "Disgusting, I think." The physician nodded, "Is so."

Along the cliffs, the women had finished eating and had fed the little children—gentle or with cruel dispatch. Actually, I find the children very pleasing to watch, for they frolic about the platforms, at times terrifyingly near the unguarded edge. Now, however, it was time for them to descend.

Note the psychological play. Having been fed, the children understand they are to be lowered, head-down, from the anchored flagpoles to the man-cage level of the structure. While being rigged by the ankles for their over-the-canyon suspension, the children whimper or kick. If a reactive type, the mother screams; if brutal, she often abuses the child.

Observe: at the instant of lowering, a child now smiles, laughs, calls to the man! See the Black babies bounce and whirl themselves and sing out?

At cage-level, the man reaches out. Variously he speaks, touches the girls' genitals, see? Swings them far out over the canyon—their play. Soon the man gives each suspended child its ritualistic mid-day bath. So: now along the escarpment, high and low, the children are raised back to the mother's platform. Now their little faces are very sober, or they simulate tears, or great glee—as the mother requires. There: all done for this day.

Being myself the son of parents long separated, a Pomona College graduate, and as a person who lives in celibacy—save the two winter months at Palm Springs—really, I am drawn to this escarpment. In fact, I forgot to ask for questions.

The surveyor from Penang spoke. "How make more babies?"

"At night," I replied. "Someway at night."

"Surely," the pathologist said, "there is a hole in the platforms. Possibly by a trapdoor access is gained—after dark or not."

"Hole somewhere," the surveyor replied. "But why he go up there anymore?"

A discussion ensued and eventually I led this group to the place where first we hear plainly the long, cloth-tearing sound of waves dying on the white sands.

Among thwarted beach pine and oak trees at the valley's mouth, in pits, or aloft on poles exposed to the heavy sledge of the sun, abruptly, we came upon crucifixion platforms.

The stench of kelp and ruined shellfish at first is shocking, but this group did not at all draw back from this littoral of self-imposed agonies. The pathologist and the surveyor and the German philologist (ret.) ran forward to see more. In a second all the others scattered wildly among the trees.

Abandoned, I watched them go. Officially, I appear interested in a great many things; unofficially, however, my enthusiasms cannot be totally legislated from higher up. In my work-year of ten months, I see no other place of such consummate, natural beauty; yet, inwardly, I find this quarter-mile of sand truly revolting. Farther along I hear even the ex-schoolteachers cry out among the oak trees at some macabre, almost-sought-for recognition. In this place I keep my personal participation to the level of description, and the tight little smile.

In general: our Crucifixion Beach presents three general categories: Situations-Financial (Credit Pits, Tax-Supplicators, and others); Conformist Poles (Stakes, also Bamboo); and finally, the Coma-Pavilions proper. Since no one in the party either wanted or needed to hear more, I went directly ahead to the place where they would re-assemble. As I walked rapidly ahead, certain members of our party called out.

Two school teachers, their walking boots deep in sand, asked about a woman, burned by the sun, her hair blowing, seated—or buried—navel-deep in her pit. Mechanically, steadily, the woman threw sand upward into the wind; the wind blew the sand back into the pit and into her eyes. "Either credit-possessive," I explained,

"Or a person forever sailing on packaged tours. It is the same. By going deeper she expects—some-time—to find water, from the sea."

The Swiss doctor was separated from his nurse. He was beside a platform about the height of a hospital bed, the platform larger than a circus ring, made up of old hatch covers, planks, and other flotsam from the sea. The bodies—perhaps one hundred—were hopelessly intertwined, comatose, save for the eyes which at random opened, stared for awhile at the sun, then closed. Stethoscope in place, the doctor was tracing the arterial blood supplies in the arms and the legs of the men and women. On his right hand the doctor wore a rubber, surgical glove. He glanced up from his very serious examination and said, "Nefer hemorrhoids in a homosexual—I have nefer seen it."

The professional educators and also the German philologist (ret.) called down from the very top of a conformist pole. Aloft those poles sway in the wind, first towards the valley of stone, then towards the sea. Their voices seemed to be calling, "Accounted for . . . allll accounted for. . . . " but I could not be certain.

Even the priest, who was said to be *en route* to the Vatican and who had heard so much during his life, was apparently overwhelmed. Withdrawn in shadows, I passed him beside the pilings of some vast towering platform. In sand, from below, he stared aloft at the underpinnings. The priest was extraordinarily pale beside the black, creosoted poles.

The surveyor from Penang was the first to join me as I waited at the exit path where pines and oak and sand almost touch the tides running.

Without wishing to be so, I was sitting eye-level before the final and certainly the largest single pavilion. Here incredibly old men and women sit on a platform, elaborately put together, iron-reinforced against any storm. In the wind, in the terrible sun, at night and in salt spray these persons beyond speech each hour thrust thorns, or splinters of wood, or even fractured abalone shells—any debris—beneath their own flesh, and into the shoulders and the backs of one another.

In the end, always, their infections are overwhelming and they lie down, more than a thousand, still working, still moving a little, then comatose, unable to register either the sea or clouds, the valley or the sun burning in the sky overhead. Forever, their large and their small wounds fester, suppurate, fester, and grow.

"Okay," the surveyor said after awhile. "They pay for something?"

I said probably so.

Only when the first shadows rose from the sea and fell all at once across the beach did this party leave the Pavilions and gather at the exit path. Going back, no one at all sang. This day and this season were now ending. For the first time since I began this kind of employment, I found it a little depressing: for the past hour I had waited, and had thought vividly of Palm Springs. The station wagons were still parked on the cliff above.

Only after we were on the freeway returning to the hotels and to the city from whence we had come did the surveyor from Penang whisper in my ear:

"German, one who start singing. He stay back there. On a pole."

I did not reply. The pathologist and the priest and the Swiss physician were already asleep, and besides these things happened more often than the surveyor knew: about two per party, on a yearly average.

The station wagon seemed to throw itself even faster through the dark, headed towards the high, lighted escarpment of the San Francisco skyline. I thought only about tomorrow—and of Palm Springs.

This year, again, no doubt I will meet someone interesting.

I always do.

THE OWNERSHIP OF THE NIGHT

by LARRY LEVIS

from FIELD

nominated by FIELD *and Carolyn Forché*

1.

After five years,
I'm in the kitchen of my parents' house
Again, hearing the aging refrigerator
Go on with its music,
And watching an insect die on the table
By turning in circles.
My face reflected in the window at night
Is paler, duller, even in summer.
And each year
I dislike sleeping a little more,
And all the hours spent
Inside something as black
As my own skull . . .
I watch
This fruit moth flutter.
Now it's stopped.

2.

Once,
Celebrating a good year for Muscatel,
My parents got away to Pismo Beach,
Shuttered and cold in the off season.

When I stare out at its surf at night,
It could be a girl in a black and white slip,
It could be nothing.
But I no longer believe this is where
America ends. I know
It continues as oil, or sorrow, or a tiny
Island with palm trees lining
The sun-baked, crumbling
Asphalt of its air strip.

A large snake sleeps in the middle of it,
And it is not necessary to think of war,
Or the isolation of any father
Alone on a raft in the Pacific
At night, or how deep the water can get
Beneath him . . .
Not when I can think of the look of distance
That must have spread
Over my parents' faces as they
Conceived me here,
And each fell back, alone,
As the waves glinted, and fell back.

3.

This evening my thoughts
Build one white bridge after another
Into the twilight, and now the tiny couple
In the distance,
In the picture I have of them there,
This woman pregnant after a war,
And this man who whistles with a dog at his heels,
And who thinks all this is his country,
Cross over them without
Looking back, without waving.
Already, in the orchards behind them,
The solitary hives are things;
They have the dignity of things,
A gray, precise look,
While the new wasps swarm sullenly out of them,

And the trees hold up cold blossoms,
And, in the distance, the sky
Does not mind the one bird in it,
Which by now is only a frail brush stroke
On a canvas in which everything is muted and
Real. The way laughter is real
When it ends, suddenly, between two strangers,
And you step quickly past them, into the night.

THE SPANISH IMAGE OF DEATH

by CÉSAR VALLEJO

from SPAIN LET THIS CUP PASS FROM ME (Red Hill Press)

nominated by RED HILL PRESS

THERE she goes! Call her! That's her rib cage!
That's death on her way through Irun,
with her accordion gait, her swear word,
the yard of cloth I've told you about,
the ounce of weight grown silent . . . when it was the others!

Call her! Hurry! She looks for me among the rifles,
as if she knew well where I could beat her,
which are my best tricks, my specious laws, my awful codes.
Call her! She walks just like a man, even among beasts,
she leans against that arm wrapped around our leg
as we sleep against the parapets,
she waits by the elastic door of sleep.
And now she's shouted! Shouted her basic, sensorial scream!
She must be screaming with shame,
seeing that she's fallen among plants,
seeing how far she's come from animals,
hearing us say: It's death!
After wounding our vital interests!

(Because that drop I told you about, comrade,
falls and develops its own liver; and gorges itself on
the neighbor's soul.)
Call her! We must follow her
to the foot of the enemy tanks,

death is a being one becomes by force,
whose beginning and end I carry graven
at the head of my hopes
though she may run that ordinary risk that you,
that you know,
pretending that she pretends to ignore me.

Call her! She has no being, this violent death,
she's just barely the most laconic happening;
her style, when attacking,
is closer to a simple tumult without orbit or canticles of joy,
it tends to its own daring bits
of timing, to imprecise pennies,
full of deaf carats, to despotic applause.
Call her! For in calling her with passion, with numbers
you help her drag her three knees
the way, at times,
those enigmatic, global fractures hurt us, puncture us,
the way, at times, I touch myself and cannot feel a thing.

Call her! Hurry! She's looking for me
with her cognac, her moral cheekbone,
her accordion gait, her swear word.
Call her! We can't lose the thread by which I bewail her.
From her stench upwards; oh dust of mine, comrade!
From her pus upwards; oh whip of mine, lieutenant!
From her magnet down; oh tomb of mine!

translated by -
Alvaro Cardona-Hine

FOR PAPA (AND MARCUS GARVEY)

by THADIOUS M. DAVIS

from OBSIDIAN

nominated by OBSIDIAN

Sundays of walls and attic fans
  Meant
The Claiborne car clacking over
  wide neutral grounds
   hiding from the sun under
    china ball trees
The Journey
  coasting over land to water
The Crescent
  urging city dwellers
   to the curve of the past

Those Sundays meant
Breathing each other's air
Looking back seeing where we had been.
Knowing we could not go back

        Papa
Staunch bright with seeing and saying
Proud marching Garveyite
Marshalled his Black Cross Nurses
  his African Legion with
"Up up you mighty race
You can accomplish what you will"
The Black Star Line must get to the river
  The bend is waiting

289

Sundays meant Papa's sermons of
    Dark Water and Dark Men
Oiled flesh loading cane sweet yam banana
    Displaced fruit of Zambeze soil
Strong men of broad souls
    from green river villages
    a milennium old
Deflected descendants of voyagers
    bound in earth clutter
      boxes and bails

Land locked men left to lower and lift
    sing
      LOADUMM LOADUMM
In time to remember the time
Dark men called generations to dark waters

Sundays bridged waters with lives
Papa preached
Dark water and dark men made Sundays
Year after year Sundays recall what Papa preached

🔥 🔥 🔥

A VISION EXPRESSED BY A SERIES OF FALSE STATEMENTS

by JOHN LOVE

from SOME

nominated by SOME

I HAD A DREAM that John Ashbery was reading the entire *Double Dream of Spring* to a cafetorium full of high school kids in Brooklyn. Paper Concordes swooped over kids who were drawing cartoons of Ashbery as a bionic aardvark, and wadded-up paper baseballs landed in the Afros of kids who were fast asleep on pillows of Geometry books. In the back row Jose was giving Clarissa an anatomy lesson. Ashbery could barely be heard over the hundreds of animated conversations about the Bermuda Triangle, zombies, and UFOs. Suddenly the scene changed: Ashbery was reading the Manhattan phone book at the Guggenheim Museum. A packed house of hushed admirers and graduate students perked to hear his every syllable.

I had a dream that Robert Bly was reading Kabir at Eleanor Roosevelt Junior High, 182nd and Amsterdam. "The musk is inside the deer," he said with a flourish of his poncho, "but he wanders around looking for grass." Suddenly loud guffaws rocked the room, an Adidas sneaker went sailing toward the podium, and the scene switched to the Donnell Library, where Bly was getting a standing ovation from David Ignatow and Harvey Shapiro.

I had a dream that Ezra Pound, before he came to rest in the Venetian Lagoon, was reading the *Pisan Cantos* to a lunchroom full of English teachers in New Rochelle. The teachers were yawning and passing notes to each other about car payments and salary increments, and kept checking their digital watches.

I had a dream that Pablo Neruda was reading "Nothing But Death" to the advanced bilingual class at I.S. 52 in the Bronx, home of the Savage Skulls. He got to the part about the caskets sailing up the river of the dead, the river of dark purple, when Hector turned to Maria (his main squeeze) and blurted loudly: "Man, that's *bor*-ing! He got all those crazy *pictures* in his head! This guy is *mental!*"

*

Roethke spoke of reading poetry to audiences as "the killer": the idea being that turning your mind inside-out in front of people can be terrifying. "We always try to hide the secret of our lives from the general stare." He must have had a premonition of the national Poets-in-the-Schools program . . . that poets someday would be reading their work and the work of others in front of people who didn't necessarily want to be there.

Menacing, involuntary audiences. People under 18 harboring the most primitive notions about poets and poetry. Skateboard champions who can't sit still. Sons of hardhats wearing RANGERS T-shirts and snide grins. Jaded TV addicts. Miniature Fonzies. Stoned-out Led Zeppelin disciples. Speedy young geniuses who invent solar-powered submarines during Social Studies. Expressionless neat kids who stay in a polite coma all day, who seem to be extras off the set of "Valley of the Chalk People." Young girls in tight white Levis with looks of impossible longing, as if they're suffering an exile from a miraculous disco. Gigglers and pranksters. Doodlers and Magic Marker wizards drawing spaceships, colliding galaxies, death rays, and Farrah Fawcett-Majors in heat. A room in a public school in America is a room of glares, sneers, snickers, and bored yawns. Is this the toughest room a poet will ever play?

Most poetry readings—in bars, cafes, and auditoriums—*aren't* a terror. They're relaxed gatherings of friends, usually people who have some direct or indirect connection with one of the seven ruling families of the Poetry Mafia. A quick mental scan of the audience proves this, revealing: several subscriptions to *Field, Kayak*, and the *American Poetry Review*, fifteen failed CAPS applicants; six CCLM members; an N.E.A. fellowship winner; two MacDowell colonizers; twelve small-press editors, including one who produces a literary magazine printed inside fortune cookies—people whose brains crackle with images of Columbia writing seminars, the Poetry Project, the Gotham Book Mart, and the use of elision in the work of W. S. Merwin.

In a world of entertainment, of Peter Lemongello packing them in at the Rainbow Grill, poetry audiences are a rare and subtle breed. They come to listen to language do its stuff. They don't come to see exploding strobes or guitars that vomit blood. They come to hear words. As Pound might have said in that faculty lunchroom: "literature is nutrition of the impulses." A poetry audience is a friendly group of the convinced and faithful, come to listen to one of their own kind.

That's why the "involuntary" audience really is terrifying. They didn' pay to see this show; they don't get all warm inside at the mention of "poetry." They sit with blank looks. It means facing a group that doesn't share your basic premise . . . something like a WASP walking into the 2nd Avenue Delicatessen and ordering a rare pork sandwich, a glass of milk, and a side of mayo.

I walked into a class of tenth graders in Pearl River, New York, and asked them to write their "image of a poet." They wrote, verbatim:

> . . . *a poet is an elderly sissy who tries to be famous and sophisticated by using syllables to sound smooth.*
> . . . *I think a poet is an egghead petunia who wears a sheet over his body and walks through the fields talking in rhymes.*
> . . . *I think a poet is a boring old guy with a wrinkled mug who stays inside all day in Greenwich Village on Welfare, with a sack of pencils*

and a bunch of scribbled-on papers all around his desk.

. . . A poet—I don't come upon many. I would be shocked if I saw one. It would have a beard, be messy and weak. And also old.

. . . A poet is someone old and strict with a harsh voice, a tall hat, a long black robe, carrying books in his hands and when he reads them it would sound funny because of the way he says them.

. . . A poet tries to get his feelings across with inspirations. First he figures them out, then he sells them to a company. He has long red hair and is lonely.

. . . A boring person who stays indoors and writes about experiences he has never experienced.

. . . A dull dreary person who is bald and you can't understand him, continually mumbling to himself in a kind of daze of thoughts.

. . . a carefree middle-aged person who reads a lot and is therefore quiet.

. . . About 62. Stuffy. Got time to look around. Owes money.

One girl wrote at the bottom of her paper: "Do you think you can profit from going around speaking poetry? Doesn't it take up and bore your whole life and girl relationships?"

At one point I asked the students to write a definition of an image in poetry. One kid wrote: "An image is a vision expressed by a series of false statements."

Suddenly you realize that the poems your friends will applaud in a bar won't necessarily work here. "The poet's job," Williams wrote, "is to body that sacred and secret presence into the world, but nobody will know what he's talking about."

Poets in the parks encounter the same thing: puzzled looks on the faces of lunchtime passersby, amused surprise . . . as if someone had slipped a page of Gertrude Stein into their copy of *Jonathan Livingston Seagull*.

But: does it matter if a bunch of fifteen-year-olds, or a bunch of officeworkers, can't understand poetry? Does that mean we should all re-write our poems, or write a separate set they can relate to? Or have different sets of poems specially written for different people? With all the people in the world, it could become ridiculous . . . poems for retired Japanese home-run kings, poems for orthodontists who grew up in Vermont, poems for Republican librarians, poems for imprisoned ventriloquists.

This is a big issue, bigger than the both of us. Why doesn't somebody write an intelligent essay in *Field* about this? The issue is:

is poetry, spoken poetry, a "popular" art? Should it try to touch a large audience of all kinds and sorts? Or does its very nature, as compressed imaginative language, mean that it's meant for the few? Should spoken poetry move toward the popular arts (music, theatre, movies, bullfighting, base-running) or toward the private arts (decoupage, bonsai, needlepoint, ships-in-bottles)? Should poetry try to seduce people away from TV bowling? Or should the audience be an elite, incestuous club: *The New York Review of Each Others' Books?*

Do you get smarter when you're dead? I don't know, but here are three dead poets who attack this issue with smarts:

Frank O'Hara, in "Personism: A Manifesto": *"But how can you really care if anybody gets it, or gets what it means, or if it improves them? Improves them for what? For death? Why hurry them along? Too many poets act like a middle-aged mother trying to get her kids to eat too much cooked meat, and potatoes with drippings (tears). I don't give a damn whether they eat or not . . . nobody should experience anything they don't need to, if they don't need poetry bully for them. I like the movies too. And after all, only Whitman, Crane, and Williams, of the American poets, are better than the movies."*

Ezra Pound (in a bad mood), in *Poetry*, June 1916: *"Therefore we read again for the one-thousand-one-hundred-and-eleventh time that poetry is made to entertain. As follows: 'The beginnings of English poetry . . . made by a rude warfaring people for the entertainment of men-at-arms! . . .*

(The works of Homer) were made for no man's entertainment, but because a man believing in silence found himself unable to withhold himself from speaking.

Such poems are not made for after-dinner speakers, nor was the eleventh book of the Odyssey. Still it flatters the mob to tell them that their importance is so great that the solace of lonely men, and the lordliest of the arts, was created for their amusement."

Ezra Pound (in a better mood), in *The Serious Artist*, 1913: *"You are a fool to read classics because you are told to and not because you like them. Also you are a fool not to have an open mind, not to be eager to enjoy something you might enjoy but don't know how to.*

Now art never asks anybody to do anything, or to think anything, or to be anything. It exists as the trees exist, you can admire, you can

*sit in the shade, you can pick bananas, you can cut firewood, you can
do as you damn well please."*

William Carlos Williams: *"I wanted to write a poem that you would
understand, because if you can't understand it, what good is it? But
you have to try real hard."*

Hector and Maria may never like Neruda, and who's to say that's a
tragedy? They can't get into it, no matter how powerful it is. They'd
rather go see Bruce Lee in *Hurt Me Deeply.* Yankee Stadium will
never fill to the upper decks with poetry lovers. Baudelaire compared the public to a dog: it hates the scent of a rare cologne, but
loves to chew garbage.

"Nobody should experience anything they don't need to." True,
but everybody should have an accurate idea about what's available to
experience.

Some people—kids especially—simply don't know what's happening with writing. They've got no idea what's in there. Never
touch the stuff.

Sometimes when I look out at a classroom of kids I have the
haunting feeling that out there somewhere is a replica of myself, who
in the famous long ago thought of poetry as an agony somewhere
between prune juice and poison ivy. I remember that time in the
September of seventh grade: there she was: Miss Haines, five-foot-
one, in a granny dress with a brown sparrow print, hair in a bun,
spectacles, about a hundred and forty-six years old, dragging us to
the dreary shores of Gitche Gumee and the Big Sea Water. Or on a
sing-songy Midnight Ride, leavened with some knee-slappers by
Ogden Nash. Nearly anything held more mystery for a twelve-
year-old: a Frisbee, a treehouse, *Lassie*, dreams, even Suzy Men-
denhall across the aisle. I was one of the dummies who didn't need to
experience *The Legend of Sam McGee.*

It's not pop evangelism that sends poets into the schools and parks
and onto the public stage, but simply an impulse to let people know
what's happening this side of *Hiawatha.* You don't want to bully
anybody, collar people on the streetcorners or barge into an uptown
bodega shouting early Lorca. You don't want to force-feed anybody;
you simply want to free those replicas of yourself from a horrifying
time-warp where elderly sissies in long black robes prance through

the fields mumbling rhymes. There are words they ought to know about that can give them a kick, that may actually incite them to continue to continue.

The "involuntary audience" can feed the poet some kicks, too. It's refreshing to know, as you look at faces, that *not one person* in the audience has ever read Charles Olson's *Projective Verse*, been to a meeting of the James Joyce Society, or submitted poems to *The New Yorker*. Their innocence of the literary who's-who, the style-schools and movements, makes them ideal listeners. You save the quirky inaccessible stuff for later. (Berryman on Stevens: "Mutter we must as best we can. He mutter spiffy.") You save the spiffy stuff for later, because an audience like this has got a healthy restlessness. They have a low threshold of boredom (Yeats: "The more vivid their nature, the greater their boredom.") They've got no time for subtle enjambments or literary in-jokes. They'd really rather be outside, but if they have to listen to poems they want it up front: a story, a song, a strong mood, a dream.

They're full of energy and they want a talky, energetic poetry. Body electric. They like visual language; kids in school (I don't know about people lunching in Bryant Park) can usually write images of their own that would make Yannis Ritsos run to sharpen his pencil.

They're sharp critics. They hate depressing poems of staring-out-the-window-at-the-rain, or lemme-tell-you-about-my-operation-and-generally-sad-life. They like poems about real experiences: a brush with death, gettin' burned by your girl, the dullness of the workaday, sex on the mountaintop, a deja-vu for lunch. They love humor, "that delight that death teaches" (Edson). They like poems about mysterious stuff: they're as interested in ESP and UFO's as Yeats was in magic, astral projections, and invisible folk who come out of the mountains at night. They want music in words, exactly the thumping pulse Roethke loved.

Poets should welcome such an audience. It throws responsibility on them, makes them clean up their act. "You've got to try real hard."

An incredibly generous government is giving poets the chance to meet this open audience: readings are being funded in libraries, restaurants, nursing homes, cafes, galleries, schools, parks, and museums. With so many poets on stage, it would seem that before long the primitive ideas about poetry would be erased, and we'd become a nation of poetry consumers: poetry in Bloomingdales, poetry at half-time at the Super Bowl, poetry books made into movies, Poetry Burgers, where would it stop?

That'll never happen, even though more poets than ever are trying hard to touch the untouchables. It won't happen because every poet, even the most tame, will defend to the death the right to create stuff that won't play to the balconies. Writing has to be invention, experiment, curiosity, and discovery—or else it's dead furniture. "Troubadour" comes from the word for "finder" etc. And experiment means you try everything once. This can include maddening incomprehensible imagery, wails belches swoons rallingcries and whispers of whatever feelings come knocking. "Cling to the inner calypso" (Knott). If you seek new places, those places are often confusing, stark, or overwhelming: "and when he reads them it sounds funny and you can't understand them."

I had this dream. I don't remember it too well, some guy standing in front of this huge cafetorium full of America: New Jersey in the pit, Ohio in the second row, then Texas out on the left, California way in back and Alaska doing the lights. He was talking, but talking special: pictures would come into the air, and hypnotizing music, and the people were actually listening. These were kids and workers. One of them, in Michigan in the twelfth row, turned to another and said Hey, this is better than the movies.

ゟ ゟ ゟ

JEFFERY, BELIEVE ME

fiction by JANE SMILEY

from TRIQUARTERLY

nominated by TRIQUARTERLY, *Jonathan Galassi, and Barbara Grossman*

MY FONDNESS FOR YOU I set aside. That you have always attracted me I set aside. That I had gone seven weeks (since Harley,
you will remember) without, even that I set aside. I swear to you,
Jeffery, my motives were altruistic to the last degree. Humanity was
what I was thinking of. Humanity and, specifically, the gene pool.

I might, as you would perhaps suggest, have consulted you.
Needless to say, I thought of it. But where? Over café mocha after
dinner, inserted somehow into both our speculative glances at the
waiter, do I lean across the table dripping necklaces into the dessert
and say, "Let's make a baby, Jeffery"? Do I risk having to retreat into
my chair and endure rejection while tonguing *mousse au chocolat* off

my gold chains? My mother once dipped her left breast into a wedding cake, and my father licked the half-moon of *crême beurre* from her peach satin, but that is precisely the point, Jeffery. We aren't on such familiar terms. I will clue you in, J., with no condescension but only respect for your separate but equal experience: one whispers "So-and-so, let's make a baby!" only in the most passionate or most boring of circumstances. One always means it, but never does it.

And, truthfully, by the time I was ready to consult you, I had made up my mind. You are a thoughtful man, even cautious. "But let's talk about it," you would have said. "Let's wait a bit." Perhaps then, "I think we'd better not." Mine is the necessary affectionate nature, and I have plenty of money. The internal logic, the organic growth of my plan could possibly have been distorted. I wanted it to be perfect. Persons are not created lightly. Who can tell the lifelong effect of a cacophonous conception?

I eventually decided against alcohol and in favor of marijuana. The point was not to incapacitate you, but to confuse you. I admit I was foraging about among a pastiche of high school and college experiences reconsidered. You were right to sense something odd in my insistence that dinner could not be put off an evening, though I know you work on Tuesdays. But when one has to deal with thirty hours, calculated rhythmically and astrologically, one is not interfered with by the trivialities of custom. You arrived punctually, considerate as always, three-piece suited as always, bringing, as always, a bottle of St.-Emilion, though I hadn't told you about the roast chicken. You were right to mistrust my mood. The tentatively seductive me you had not before seen, silk skirt and no underpants (mindful that we had once agreed on the aesthetic virtues of my buttocks), the knees never crossed, slipping unconsciously apart, the shirt unbuttoned between the breasts. All for my benefit, not yours. Indeed, you only subliminally noticed (we were discussing your mother, I believe, and you asked twice if somebody else were coming). How haltingly the conversation moved. I told you I was tired, unable to talk fluently, and you believed me. Actually, now that I had decided, had gone so far as to lay my snare in the brownies, I could not withhold my glance. I will never forget the pepper-and-salt trousers you wore, the way the material fanned away from each inseam and stretched smoothly around each thigh. Cuffs. Those pants had cuffs and you wore black socks with russet clocks and tan shoes.

Set aside your modesty and think carefully what sort of man you are. Review your life. Look in the mirror if need be. To begin with, forty long (a graceful size) and thick curly hair (indeed, ringlets). Look into your eyes, Jeffery. In all honesty, how much bluer could they be? And how much thinner and more arched your nose? And disfigurement. Where are the large pores? Is there the thread of a varicose vein? I know you have never worn glasses, had a pimple, used an Ace bandage. Even the soles of your feet are warm, not shockingly cold (take it from me) in the middle of the night.

I wanted to hear about your new pipe, that calabash you got in the city. But though you carefully explained, I still don't know what meerschaum is. I just know how you take out your pipe and put it back in, how the tip of your tongue flicks out to lick the mouthpiece, how you bite down on it and draw back your lips to keep talking, how unconscious and competent you are in lighting the match and watching the bowl and sucking in the air. And you take it out and put it back in, out of your mouth and in. Why had we never talked about cherries and briars and clays and corncobs before?

Our aperitif conversation augured well, I thought. After pipes, you will remember, we moved on to the marriage of Eileen and Dave, her third, his second. I, the experienced one, derogated the institution and marveled at their attachment to it. You replied, "And if you can't create your own life-style in the twentieth century, what consolation is there?" I chattered about angst and apocalypse in the usual fashion. How were you to know my visions of blue bootees with pompoms, velvety baby necks, and minuscule toes? Nothing, you seemed to have said—and, more important, no one—is illegitimate at the latter end of human history.

Dinner was intended to relax you. I don't like beef consommé, but I know you do, and you always want roast capon for the wine; Caesar's salad and fresh croutons, your favorite, and infant peas sautéed with baby onions *aux fines herbes*, mine; the usual bread; a fresh tangerine ice (home- and handmade, J., beaten every quarter hour all afternoon). The brownies perhaps were a bit obvious, great slabs of chocolate lathered with icing, walnut pieces scattered through like confetti, not a seed, not a stem, the dope ground into marijuana flour and disguised by a double dose of double dutch. And then you said, "I can't."

"Maybe over coffee," gnashing my teeth at my own vanity, my anxiety to impress you with my cooking, as if I had wanted marriage rather than motherhood. In my lap I held my hands because they wanted to touch you. You drank coffee. Did you notice the Jersey cream? I said, "Want a brownie?" I could tell by your smile that you wanted to please me. "In a while. Have a cup of coffee with me. I'll get it." And there was your round little butt passing sideways between my chair and the coffee table, nearly brushing my face. You would put a dollop of Kahlua in it, I seemed jumpy. Oh that I had bitten your left bun right then. "Thank you." Do you remember how demurely I said thank you, smoothing the silk in my lap?

But Jeffery, as adults we pretend that handsome is as handsome does. Really, you have done handsomely. Music, for example, is only your hobby, and yet you play three instruments. Everyone agrees you are a masterful raconteur, and yet a temperate man (that last, indeed, was the greatest obstacle to my plot). You have a graceful and generous mind. What was the last spiteful comment you made? There are none within my memory. Your minor virtues are countless: you leave proper tips, you hang up your clothes, you are not too proud to take buses. This is just living, you would say, and yet all those thank-you notes add up. Not wishing to embarrass you, I will drop the subject, adding only that we both know what a remarkable child you were and that you have been steadily successful.

When the coffee cup was heavy in my hands, you sat down on the table and looked at me. "I'm concerned for you," you said. I was flattered. When you leaned forward, you smelled like tobacco, wool, and skin. The bowls of your cobalt irises float well above the lower lids, and there is white in them like skeletons. I had never noticed that before. The pupils dilated. You do like me. It was time to take your face between my palms and gain your favors with one passionate, authoritative, skilled, yet vulnerable kiss. I said, "Harley is threatening to cut his throat again." I hadn't heard from Harley, but it's a threat he offers preferred women every few months.

"When did he call?"

"My mother is dying."

"Of what?"

"The police beat up my grandfather for passing out deaf-and-dumb cards."

"Both your grandfathers are dead."

"My sister anticipated a walk light, and a taxi ran over her feet."

"What did you do today?"

"I washed DDT off infant peas and baby onions. What do you think of babies, Jeffery?"

"They're very flavorful." This game we play when I want to tactfully inform you that I am strong enough for the urban nightmare. Your concern must have been assuaged; you removed to a chair beyond the table. We talked about the granular universe, as I remember.

"Please have a brownie?" My offer perhaps seemed tiresome. For me, I knew you would. I did, too. They tasted indescribably musty. I wanted to say, "It's only the marijuana." You were too polite to mention it. You must have felt hungry, because you had another. Then another. I wanted to ask, "And why do you prefer men, Jeffery?" but I merely said, "You smell good," and got up to clear the table. We had cleaned the chicken of every morsel of flesh. When I came back, you were asleep. Post nitrates, post Hitler, post strontium-90. I got a hand mirror out of my purse and held it before your nostrils. A healthy fog. Still, I was disappointed. You would indeed be staying the night, but in a near coma.

Woman, Jeffery. Joy, by Jean Patou, a dollar a dab. Fragrant, smooth, rosy. Draped in fragrant (lavender), smooth (silk spun by the very worms themselves), and abundant tissues of robin's egg and full-bodied burgundy. Woman standing in a draft in her tawny stockings regarding her erect nipples with her brown but really yellow eyes, her black hair shifted shinily forward in the light, her clean clean clean face, every pore purged. Let me tell you, J., that I, too, have falled asleep *in media seductione*. But good heaven, he was not only a freshman given to wearing an orange and black stocking cap to bed on football weekends; he had three splinted fingers and was there on a wrestling scholarship. I removed your shoes.

After finishing the dishes, dusting and wiping out the china cabinet, mopping the floors, washing the woodwork, replacing the light bulb in the front-hall closet and the one in the back pantry, Windexing the mirrors, sorting through all my makeup bottles and the medicine chest, and hemming up a new dress, I removed your jacket.

Frankly, Jeffery, the building of model ships for nautical museums and private collections is nothing so much as honorable. You fashion every mahogany plank and rosewood mast, you overcast raw edges of sails, you braid the lines and lanyards, you tie the microscopic knots. Remember the time I nosed around your mullion-windowed shop?

"Of course I'll tell you."

"Is it with long tweezers, the way they do radium?"

The masts and sails nestled together on the deck like bat wings. You slid the hull gently, tightly, through the neck and positioned it on the floor of the bottle. "Pull this string." I pulled. The masts stood up and the sails spread and the bottle filled with wind. Won't you believe the lifelong importance of this mystery to me?

I disrobed. I brushed my teeth twice and flossed them. I plucked two hairs between my eyebrows. I washed my face with glycerine-rosewater soap. I brushed my hair a hundred strokes and poured peroxide into my ears and navel. I applied cups of water to my eyeballs. I gargled. I blew my nose. I emptied my bladder. I cleaned under my fingernails. I buttoned my cotton pajamas crotch to chin, then zipped myself into a turtleneck bathrobe and sat down on the bed. The only, though enormous, bed.

As if I had intended to all along, I walked up to you in the living room, removed every stitch you had on, and threw it all down the air shaft in the hall. I was touched by the frayed waistband of your Munsingwears. When I came back you were shivering every so often, but still comatose. I turned up the heat and, for the time being, covered you with an antique quilt, rose of Sharon pattern, as one such as I, a woman, a cook, a believer in simple plants like yeast, might set the dough on to rise. I pulled on my mukluks, muffled my neck, and sat down with Roland Barthes.

But you (it) were (was) inescapable. Perfectly lubricated in your bendings and unbendings, eyes almost completely closed, with every manifestation of presence and yet gone, gone. I threw down the Barthes, yanked off the quilt and took a good look. My eye, of course, flew at once to your penis for evidence of your inner life. But I dragged my gaze away. There wasn't much of you to see, mostly skin not unlike my own. I fingered some of it. It pinched up elastically, resumed its shape, changed white to red to pink. I laid my cheek, my breast, my shoulder, my knee on various parts of you, to tune you in over unusual receivers. I smelled you. You smell like hollandaise for some reason. Experimentally, I applied lips and tongue to your penis. It grew to a firm, tasteful size, unblemished, stem and cap nicely differentiated. I let it wilt. I am not a necrophiliac. Like all of us raised by the scientific method, simply curious. I said, still robed, pajamaed, slippered, and muffled, picking Roland B. up off the carpet and smoothing wrinkled pages, "Jeffery! I'll put you to bed." The first voice in hours, all night. You answered promptly. "Watch your fingers."

"What?"

"Power drills are a dangerous business." Thus your inner life inexorably proceeded, not exclusive of these hands with which I stood you up, the sharp corner of the table around which I steered you, the toilet I placed you next to, but relegating all of our surroundings with no compromise. "Piss!" I ordered. "That's easier said than done," you said, already doing it, your eyes adamantly closed.

Man, unconscious, naked in my bathroom, warm skin in jeopardy of cold surfaces, porcelain and metallic. The fluorescent light whitening and fattening him, the muscles in his narrow bony feet (the little piggy that stayed home shorter than the one that went to market) tensing and relaxing as he loses and regains degrees of balance.

Your body. I guided it into the bedroom and set it up at the end of the bed. "Lie down, Jeffery," I said, poking the small of its back. It toppled onto the bed, face down. I covered it up, pink sheet, red thermal blanket, white quilt; under its cheek, a down pillow. I hung up my own clothes, climbed into bed with it, turned out the light. Black shades, navy curtains, it was dark. I did, as you can imagine, kiss it on the cheek, laid an amicable hand on its scapula. I thought again of Einstein. I fell asleep, and woke up disoriented, fucking. "Where am I?" I said. In response, you came. By way of explanation, I added, "It's very dark." You simply said, "Mary." Truly, that is my name, although the name of many. You used a very one-in-the-afternoon, fully conscious, what-shall-we-have-for-lunch sort of intonation. In the morning you were gone in a pair of my jeans and a sweat shirt.

It is January. I was glad to have kept your shoes. Since then, four weeks ago, where have you been? I do not accuse, I simply wish to know. That and where you intend to be, which will become increasingly important from now on.

SWEETNESS,
A THINKING MACHINE

by JOE ASHBY PORTER

from SUN & MOON

nominated by John Ashbery

I WAS IN A RESTAURANT trying to read Hawthorne, but distracted by the conversation of two blonde young women near me, when I was transported to a dimly lighted hotel room. From where I lay it seemed I could look out a window into the narrow street below. There before a brilliant plate glass window a tiny figure gesticulated wildly, dancing and shaking his fists above his head. "It is merely an illusion," said a person in the room with me. "The window is higher. Sit up and you will see." In fact, the street below was empty.

There was a time in my youth when things began to grow disconcertingly complex. I ignored them but at length I could do so no more. As I forlornly wandered the dwindling spaces between them I happened on a solution to my dilemma. It turned out that, pierced with my earnest gaze, they collapsed like balloons.

It seems I flee from a furious rider down a road like silver ribbon over the hills and valleys ahead—I can hear the gasping of the horse. Stars seem to burn on my forehead. I gesticulate wildly, feinting and dancing to avoid the scythe that comes out of billowing robes like lightning. I have been interested in the scattered jokes of our time. I suppose them to be decaying leaves fallen from a mighty tree which itself is perhaps not at all comic. I need a quiet out-of-the-way place, a simple cabin with a table and chair and a jug of clean water.

2

Once the devil appeared to me in the guise of an acquaintance, an agreeable young blonde man with a short curly beard. A tall thin black adolescent whom I had never seen before was with him. We were in a shower room which seemed to be at the apex of the known world, standing near one another and talking of women. The devil described his relations with a certain woman in such detail that the three of us quickly developed erections. The devil smiled, laying his hands over our shoulders in a brotherly fashion, and then he bent over me to perform fellatio. The young black bent to kiss my thighs.

Nothing of the sort had ever happened to me before. The ideas but not the feelings of guilt and remorse came and went. The apparent fact that I had passed a point of no return exhilarated me. I felt much affection and even some gratitude toward the devil and his friend. As I relinquished a fatigued and unclean naiveté for the sake of freedom and seeming innocence I breathed easier. I grasped the organs of the two men and leaned back, looking up at the deep black sky, itself like us in consummation.

3

Afterwards I spent several months with the devil—I did not see the young black again—in a beautiful old lodge at the same altitude as the shower room. It was a pleasant and relaxed period. The devil called it by a scientific name, explaining that it was a prelude to my re-entry into society. During the day I wandered in the gardens or sat in the sun on a balcony which hung over a sheer cliff affording a splendid view of the world below. The air was pure and invigorating.

Usually I took breakfast and lunch alone, but almost always I dined with the devil, and in the evenings we sat together in the library before a fire, while the wind howled outside. He did not make any further sexual advances toward me.

Our conversations, sometimes animated but more often quiet and meditative, ranged over a wide variety of subjects, returning most often to questions of a philosophical and psychological nature. Throughout, his main objective was to prepare me for the consequences of the incident in the shower room.

One such was that I had gained the ability to fly at great speed in perfect comfort. Accompanied by the devil, I soared and looped through many famous cities of the world. I saw much of the secret and private life of people, much that I would never have suspected before, as we paused in the air outside windows, or even made our way into rooms. We were never observed. Sometimes one of those we watched would stiffen, sensing our presence behind him, and then whirl—but we were away. I should add that for the actors of all the scenes I witnessed I felt only tenderness and love. I learned that the sole complete destruction is self-destruction: that those who seek to destroy destroy themselves always; and that harm is thus endlessly diminished.

The capacity of flight soon disappeared however, and the devil was primarily concerned with permanent changes I had undergone. Since I was by no means yet aware of these, he enumerated them in some detail. He said that I should no longer fear anything very much. The minds of others—their motives and their feelings— would for a long time be obscure to me and I should not presume to understand them. On the other hand I should trust people as never before. Men would enjoy my company and many women love me. I would no longer be intrigued by children. My life had ceased to be dramatic.

4

I am occasionally alone in a bright airy restaurant bounded on two sides by plate glass in late summer afternoon. A gentle rain falls from low clouds into the street outside. Across the street stand palms of various shapes, some tall and thin, others like pineapples. Beyond is a slow river, then low flat land, then white beach and then the warm shallow Atlantic Ocean on which this same rain is falling. In the street calm automobiles pause for the traffic signal and then pass in a sweetly ordered procession, their tires hissing and splashing on the warm wet pavement, their windshield wipers moving at various speeds. I sip my coffee and watch them. Some turn at the corner, signalling with small winking lights. Through the rain-dimpled windshields I can distinguish motionless figures in the shadowy interiors. Nothing could be sweeter than the peaceful movement of these cars through the rain. The stars on my forehead are quenched. And the littered jokes of our time? For the moment they are all washed away.

5

Some years ago I was among the fifteen or twenty weekend guests at the spacious New England seaside estate of a couple with whom I was but slightly acquainted. I was the youngest of the party, which consisted mostly of couples in their forties. It was late summer—I was already engrossed in plans for returning to my studies at college.

While the group was interesting and colorful, to my eyes at least our host so eclipsed the rest of us that I can scarcely recall anyone else. The vitality of my host's slightest word or movement commanded attention irresistibly. As the weekend progressed I noticed that he escorted by turns most of the women present into a stand of pine behind the house. I remember I saw one of the younger women enter a room, place her hand on her husband's shoulder, bend down and say she was going for a walk in the woods with the host.

My hostess had passed her physical prime yet she was one of the most attractive women I have ever met. Except for her large mild brown eyes her features were not striking. Her beauty derived rather from her soft clarity of attitude and manner.

On the last afternoon we played football on the lawn and then after an excellent dinner we danced and talked, and drank a great deal. We were somewhat melancholy because we had enjoyed one another's company in the peaceful house, and because we should almost certainly never again all be together. I sat alone for a time on the veranda looking out over the sea. The night air was gentle and luminous. I saw my host strolling off into the woods, alone. At length I entered the living room, which was lighted by a single kerosene lamp in the corner. A few of the guests sat at their ease here and there, and in the center of the room my hostess stood and sang. She paused to explain to me that the song was one she had performed in a musical comedy when she was at college. It was a maudlin torch-song which she delivered with few gestures. Her voice was low, unmelodious and sweet. We applauded quietly.

She accompanied me into the hallway and I expressed my thanks for the pleasant weekend. "For people like us," she said, "such times don't come without some thought and allowance. I think you understand." I knew nothing to say. Then somewhat timidly she suggested that we walk in the woods. Trembling, I told her I was very tired and needed sleep to be fresh for the next day's drive. "You know best," she said, smiling and laying her hand on my arm.

One evening soon after I came down from the devil's lodge to rejoin society I happened to see this woman again at a fashionable ball in a large city. In the vast smoky hall during one of the orchestra's intermissions we came toward one another through an opening in the crowd. She was lovelier than I had remembered her. She was dressed in black velvet after the fashion of Madame Gautreau in the portrait by Sargent. But her skin was golden-toned instead of white; she seemed submissive, inviting and undramatic; and the famous dress was sweetly old-fashioned.

She smiled up at me and I saw in her brown eyes much the same expression I had seen before. I led her from the hall, up increasingly narrow twisting flights of stairs to a small secluded bedroom where we made love and where afterwards I gave thanks for all the events I have related here.

TO ED SISSMAN

by JOHN UPDIKE

from THE ONTARIO REVIEW

nominated by THE ONTARIO REVIEW

I

I think a lot about you, Ed—
tell me why. Your sallow owl's face
with the gray wart where death had kissed it,
drifting sideways above your second gin
in Josèph's, at lunch, where with a what-the-hell
lurch you had commanded the waiter
to bring more poison, hangs in my mind
as a bloated star I wish to be brave on.

I loved your stuff, and the way
it came from nowhere, where poetry
must come from, having no credentials.
Your talk was bland, with a twist of whine,
of the obvious man affronted. You stooped
more and more, shouldering the dark for me.

II

When you left, the ceiling caved in.
The impossible shrunk to the plausible.
In that final room, where one last book
to be reviewed sat on your chest, you said,
like an incubus, transparent tubes
moved in and out of your veins
and nurses with volleyball breasts
mocked us with cheerleader health.

You were sicker than I, but I huddled in
my divorcing man's raincoat by your bed
like a drenched detective by the cozy fire
a genial suspect had laid in his manor,
unsuspecting he is scheduled Next Victim.
I mourned I could not solve the mystery.

III

You told me, lunching at Joseph's,
foreseeing death, that it would be
a comfort to believe. My faith,
a kind of rabbit frozen in the headlights,
scrambled for cover in the roadside brush
of gossip; your burning beams passed by.
"Receiving communications from beyond": thus
you once described the fit of writing well.

The hint hangs undeveloped, like
my mental note to send you Kierkegaard.
Forgive me, Ed; no preacher, I—
a lover of the dust, like you,
who took ten years of life on trial
and lent pentameter another voice.

THE MAN WHOSE BLOOD TILTED THE EARTH

by M.R. DOTY

from RED CEDAR REVIEW

nominated by RED CEDAR REVIEW

They made him dance
in a circle of peas
he didn't want to
but it was all they had
and he knew it
so he danced

When he was so tired
that he could no longer stand
on his red feet
he asked
will you help me

Not if you stop dancing
before midnight
they said nor if you
step on a pea

But my mother is sewing
the red coat for Elizabeth
he said and I must
be there to see her
try it on

Elizabeth is dead
they answered
dance on jig

But my mother is cooking
the gray goose from the fair
I must be there to help
carve it

The gray goose is waiting
to eat the peas stupid
dance

The boats came in
from the sea
the lights went out
in the stores
still he could not stop
they threw water
on him then ashes
then whiskey then wheat

He looked like a wide white
asphodel bobbing
in a circle of peas

You are our
cloud-late-in-the-year
they screamed
you will save us
from the winter storms
and the blight in the spring

I'm just a little dancer
he tried to say
who got left by
a one eyed medicine man
I can't tilt the earth for you

Tilt the earth for us
they panted as they
threw broken glass in his circle

At midnight they lifted his body
from the glass and the wheat
and as their last moon
fell into their last sea
one of them said
he had so much blood
in him surely it
will tilt the earth

LAWRENCE AT TAOS

by SHIRLEY KAUFMAN

from FIELD

nominated by FIELD

And . . . out of eternity a thread
separates itself on the blackness
*   a horizontal thread*
that fumes a little . . .

*   –"The Ship of Death"*

1

She said a white cloud
followed them up the hill
and hovered above the crazy androgynous
phoenix with its plump white breasts
like lids of sugar bowls.

Both of them noticed it
and told each other later.
So I didn't just make it up
she said. It looked like the soft
underside of an egret's wing.

When they had stood a long time
over his ashes the cloud
turned into smoke or steam
or shimmeriness, that was the word
she wanted, and was gone.

316

2

In Taos we eat sopapillia
with honey butter at La Cosina
and pay one dollar to see
the obscene paintings, banned in London,
by the author of *Lady Chatterley's Lover.*

They fly back into paradise
as he kept running through
the gates of the wrong gardens.
He went to Mexico and almost died.
Back to the ranch. But didn't stay.

When Frieda returned to Taos
with his ashes, she forgot them
on the train. They had to
flag the train down at the next stop
to get them back again.

3

Someone keeps looking in the window,
stealing Brett's paintings off the wall,
the drawings she made of him.
The sun's too bright. That's why
her eyes are covered with milk.

She has to be lifted, heavy
lumps of her, into the chair.
She turns up her hearing aid.
Ah Lawrence. Telling us how
she touched him to make him calm.

And she goes on about the cabin
and the horses dragging the wood in,
photographs of her quite

beautiful and slender next to a tree
or in a doorway, watching him.

4

A lizard runs over Frieda's tomb,
his green tail longer than the rest
of his body. There are fresh
pine boughs on the ground.
And a visitors' book

full of ecstatic letters
to the dead. Someone pasted
a poem in the little chapel
over two roses in a bottle.
So many women in love,

their souls like small eggs
spilling out of their shells.
From here the sky is stretched
so taut at the horizon
we can't see the thread.

CONTEMPORARY POETRY AND THE METAPHORS FOR THE POEM

by CHARLES MOLESWORTH

from THE GEORGIA REVIEW

nominated by THE GEORGIA REVIEW, *Robert Boyers, and Joyce Carol Oates*

IT WOULD BE POSSIBLE TO WRITE a lively and perceptive literary history by tracing the rise, development, and eventual fading of each epoch's central metaphor for the literary "work." One classic study, M. H. Abrams' well known *The Mirror and the Lamp*, explores these two polar images of art as incarnating either a mimetic or an expressive base for aesthetic objects. Another, implicit in Cleanth Brooks's title *The Well Wrought Urn*, is the sense of the poem as a construct built of tensions and opposing forces, somehow "fixed by the artist's use of paradox as the verbal means of resolving these tensions. For the Romantic era, Keats's poetry and letters are filled with phrases,

as suggestive as Donne's "well wrought urn," that could easily serve
such a metaphoric role. Recall, for example, how Keats speculated
that the events in a man's life were an allegory, and his poems could
be seen as the commentary on that allegory; surely much of the
Keats criticism in the last forty years has tried to come to terms with
this notion in discussing Keats as a literary-biographical subject.

The metaphors for the poem, then, can be various, overlapping,
and even centrifugal, catching up notions of psychology and the
poet's career as well. But now and again there are shifts in these
metaphors that mark undeniably important developments in literary history, though the larger the shift the more difficult it is to trace
the exact moment when a new metaphor wins dominance. We might
even speculate that after Rimbaud the central focus has fixed on
metaphors for the poet, rather than the poem; and voyager, madman, shaman, aesthete, and so on have suggested themselves as
unifying roles, both to locate the poet for his audience and often to
insist on his remoteness. Also implicit in the metaphor for either
poem or poet is an evaluation, sometimes polemical, of the place
poetry has in the epoch, since the metaphor might sharply dif-
ferentiate between what is available, or necessary, for a poem to do
and what a novel or play might achieve. Though it can't be relied
upon as an universal key, the prevailing metaphor for the poem
might help readers, directing them to the scope, the intent, and
even the texture of the poetic act.

Once the poetry editor for the *Saturday Review*, John Ciardi,
wrote a book that employed the assumptions and standards of the
"New Criticism." It was called *How Does A Poem Mean?* and it
advanced the notion that a poem was "a machine for making
choices." The formalism of the book's title was given perhaps a
too-clear thrust in this metaphor of a machine, picking and choosing
words as it went along, each choice more and more circumscribed,
but when well made, more and more forceful in its "integrity." This
aesthetic was a dominant one in the decade of the 1950's, and its
sense of the poem as a self-regarding, self-justifying statement was
instilled into many readers and would-be writers of poetry in American universities. Because of the role universities played in fostering
poetic talent, this aesthetic came to influence the writing of poetry in
a special way, as it carried with it a special authority and a built-in
defense. The poem became a kind of academic set-piece, an object
so hemmed round with ironic deprecation, so often reliant on allu-

sion to other poems, and so internally consistent—the poem had always to be well "brought off"—that it demanded explication before experience, analysis before assent. No transcendent values could be directly affirmed, since these might raise questions about the poet's "intentions"—thorny questions that had also been ruled out of bounds by another tenet of formalism, the intentional fallacy. This tenet held either an artist realized his intentions in the poem, and so we didn't need an independent account of them, or he hadn't, and in this case we had no way of establishing what those failed intentions were, except through another statement by the poet that could be as equally flawed as the poem. Therefore, all that was left was the poem itself—logically, an unassailable argument, but one that ignored how reading, being made up of anticipated meanings as well as realized ones, actually occurs. Only an assumption that poems were objects, removed totally from use or any dialectical shifts in meaning caused by history or cultural patterning, could subtend such an abiding faith in formalism.

Gradually this dominant sense of a poem as an autotelic, self-explaining statement, or "object," began to lose its force. In its place in the late fifties and early sixties came at least three other metaphoric images for the poem: 1) the poem as a force-field; 2) the poem as a "leaping" or associatively linked cluster of nondiscursive images; and 3) the poem as commentary on some unspoken myth—what Galway Kinnell has called a "palimpsest." The first of these was formulated with especial drive by Charles Olson, in his "Projective Verse," written in 1950, but not widely known till some years later. The second has as one of its chief proponents Robert Bly, who coined the term "leaping," but there are many poets who sympathize with its emphasis on nondiscursive elements without necessarily agreeing completely with Bly. The third metaphor, clearly the least well defined of the three, has no one major theoretician, but would include among its practitioners such poets as W. S. Merwin, Mark Strand, and various avant-garde poets like Clayton Eshelman, Robert Kelly, and others. But, perhaps most importantly, each of the three metaphors is at odds with any sense of the poem as a completed, self-enclosed artifact. Whatever their usefulness for readers, or for poets, and whatever larger cultural forces they might reflect and syncretize, these three metaphors helped put an end to the poem as a machine or "well-wrought urn." Though all the poems written out of these three new metaphoric senses might not differ radically from previous poems, clearly an aesthetic boundary had been redrawn.

1. Composition by Field

Charles Olson drew much of his metaphoric language in "Projective Verse" from his reading in the philosophy of Alfred North Whitehead and from the developments in theoretical physics near the turn of the century. Olson was never a systematic thinker, of course, and the extent to which he had actually mastered either Whitehead or force-field theory is not really relevant. What is relevant, however, is Olson's attempt to get outside the tradition of the Western lyric as it had developed since the Renaissance. "The lyrical interference of the ego"—this was how he termed what he considered the main stumbling block. Olson was after a poetics that cut short any subjective indulgence in emotive states for their own sake; he wanted to restore poetry to its mythic potency, that is, he wanted to use it to investigate and record those activities and cultural habits that men needed words to embody.

Throughout Olson's work, his poetry and his theory, there appear two aspects of the same drive: to present some transcribed evidence, and to cut against the grain of assumptions built up by any kind of social narcosis, since through such narcosis men had used language more as a shield than a sword. Olson's use of a persona in his Maximus poems has a completely different intent from that of most other contemporary poets; unlike Berryman, say, whose persona was a way to display and toy with his authorial ego at the same time, Olson used his character to achieve a larger base and thus give more resonance, historically and morally, to what he said. This use is in many ways profoundly conservative, and Olson's political vision is in many ways a pre-capitalist one, as if he adapted agrarian principles to the fishing village of Gloucester, Massachusetts. "It is hard to be a historian and a poet at the same time," he says at the end of the *Mayan Letters*, and he shows in those letters how he wanted to return poetry to its central, and centralizing, position in the culture. For this centering, poems had to be more than set-pieces; they had to reflect and register forces that were at the edges of formulability, and give shapely utterance to values that were pervasively dispersed through the cultural consciousness. This is why his poems often revert to incidents and even texts from foreign cultures, in order to gain a "perspective by incongruity," and why they often seem (and are) fragmentary, like random jottings or the quick and barely traceable path of a sub-atomic particle. The poem is like a force-field: on and through it occur seemingly random recognitions, but if the poet properly positions himself, in order to increase his attentiveness, he can use the poem to register indefinite but powerful forces that would otherwise pass unnoticed. The poem is neither mirror nor lamp, since the poet neither imitates or expresses; rather, the poem is a mental construct drawn up to record the underlying structure of phenomena.

Olson says in "Projective Verse" that the poet must follow the "track" that "the poem under hand declares for itself"; furthermore the poet must be "aware of some several forces just now beginning to be examined." In a sense Olson's poetics is passive, since its main concern is to superinduce in the poet a kind of altered consciousness. Once this pervasive awareness is fostered, the poet turns his focused awareness to the job of recording it. But he must be aware that this new consciousness cannot use the old language, especially the old *patterns* of the language. Instead, he must "step back here to this place of the elements and minims of language" and there "engage speech where it is least careless—and least logical." The sense here that the poet is engaged upon an attempt resembling the exploration of sub-atomic particles is deliberate, of course, and is Olson's way of dealing with that urge towards primitivism in all modernist thought, but it is also his way of depersonalizing the activity.

That peculiar sense of language as completely free ("least logical") and completely determined ("least careless") supplies Olson with the dialectic that runs throughout his poetry. He wants to posit a completely formed utterance—often a document or historical notation or first version of a tale—and have it be seen in context with the freely generated utterances that it gives rise to (we might almost say gives permission to). The "sweetness of meter and rime" Olson calls a "honey-head," that is, he sees prescriptive meters as the equivalents of social narcosis, taking over and gumming up the production, even the "emission," of syllables. Replace the meter with the syllable, he insists, shift the instruments to a new field. Or to put it differently, "Listening for the syllables must be so constant and so scrupulous . . . that the assurance of the ear is purchased at the highest . . . price." The poet must be able to register all the forces at work in his consciousness, even the proto-semantic.

Olson's theories are idiosyncratically presented, and—he resembles Emerson among others in this regard—through selective quotation, he can be made to say almost anything. But I think most critics (even Robert Bly is culpable in this regard) are wrong to present Olson as offering some innovative technical advice, some key like "breath-line" that can be taken over by all poets for whatever "message" they can adapt it to. Olson's work fundamentally challenged poetry as it was being written in 1950; it did more than simply extend Pound's theories (though his relation to Pound's theories is both obvious and reciprocal) because it took the scientistic metaphors strewn through Pound's criticism and used them seriously and consistently. But only if the poet abandons the lyric mode, at least as it is generally practiced, and turns toward narrative or something like a mythic, epical structure, will the "technique" of Olson be completely useful. Otherwise, what Olson had to say about the poem—his metaphor for the poetic act—is no more (and no less) than what Pound and Eliot had said, that the "emotional slither" of etiolated Victorianism had to be replaced with the concision, the affective exactitude of such diverse poets as Villon, Donne, and Baudelaire.

William Carlos Williams, for one, saw that Olson was after more than technique, and he reprinted a large portion of "Projective Verse" in his *Autobiography*. In doing so, Williams acknowledged that both he and Olson were engaged in a common task: to present "the reconstruction of the poem as one of the major occupations of the intelligence in our day." Williams understood Olson's sense of "field," and the chapter in which he reprints "Projective Verse" is to my mind the subtlest and in some senses the most complete of Williams' aesthetic formulations. Williams devotes the remainder of the chapter to an account of his friend, the painter Charles Sheeler, and the "adaptations" Sheeler has made of Shaker furniture, his Russian wife's past, and the environment of his Hudson River Valley farm. Sheeler's house, or rather the field of forces that he is conscious of, working in and through his house, becomes Williams' metaphor for the reconstruction of the poem. "To transfer values into a new context, to make a poem again" is how Williams puts it, restating his lifelong concern to "make it new" and invent aesthetic order at the same time. But, like Olson, Williams is concerned with a new sensory and evaluative interaction, not for the sake of newness, not simply to provide grist for some technical innovation, but because the old ways of expressing awareness, of showing the mind to itself, aren't effective. The mind occludes itself when it relies on a previously shaped language or on a language imported from some other location, some other "field." "Nothing can grow unless it taps into the soil," he says at the end of the chapter. But the organization of the poem proceeds both from and towards another organization:

> It is ourselves we organize in this way not against the past or for the future or even for survival but for the integrity of understanding to insure persistence, to give the mind its stay.

Integrity of understanding describes quite accurately what field theory tries to provide physicists, since such theories rely heavily on a statistical or phenomenological model which interweaves data from several sources into an integrated whole. For Williams and for Olson the evidence they were after was simply not obtainable, or at least not capable of being accurately registered, with the traditional "object" of verse. What Williams and Olson sought is what is always "at hand"—this is what makes them inventors—but what is at hand can often only be revealed by a discharge into our consciousness of some remote historical energy—and this is what makes them con-servers. Some of the poets who place themselves in the Williams-Olson "line" (poets such as Levertov, Creeley, and Snyder) are aware they don't have the same mythic concerns as the two older poets, but they also realize that the metaphor of the poem as a "field of forces" satisfies the modernist demands for accuracy of perception and complexity of apprehension. After the example of Olson, many contemporary poets proceeded with much more care to the record-ing instruments, knowing that the way they drew up the evidence was as important as the audience they addressed.

II. Associative Poetry

We see in Robert Bly's theories, though of course in different terms and with different emphases, many of the same polemical aims that animated Charles Olson. Bly wants the poem to record more than a pre-established emotional truth, some previously mediated value-statement that the poet offers to his audience to reassure them all is well. On the contrary, Bly, like Olson, wants most deeply the word behind the words, some statement that will be both a befuddlement and a challenge to our daily chatter. Also like Olson, Bly develops a way of proceeding towards this statement, a kind of moral discipline in the form of a poetics, but unlike Olson, Bly does not want to talk about "technique." This avoidance, one might almost call it a fear, of technical skill comes from Bly's belief that to plot an arrival, to plan an intuition, is inherently self-defeating. One must proceed differently if what is desired is what has been missing. All of Bly's theory revolves around this key sense: that something is missing, a knowledge, an awareness was once available to us, and a conspiracy of rationality and order keeps it from us. Evidence must be gathered, but if we trust the ordinary evidentiary schemes we are foredoomed to arrive at the same conclusions. Unlike Olson, Bly is willing to admit personal, subjective testimony as valid (in fact he insists on it), but at the same time such subjective speaking must not insist on ownership or self-regard. Bly's experience of two years of enforced solitude and silence in a snow-bound Minnesota cabin convinced him that only after such an experience did he truly know what he wanted to say. In other words, Bly's discipline must lead through the self, beyond the self. This is what produces in Bly's poetry that otherwise curious mix of pastoral quietism and moral harangue. The image—the truth leaped toward, beyond the connectiveness of rational discourse—will say it all, but it must be strictly attended to. Any attempt to transliterate the image, to use one's "technique" to make it presentable, will not only betray its accuracy, but will involve us in a disauthenticating ego-game.

Bly has edited an anthology of short poems,* statements that ask for no involved justification, cries of joy or insight that rest their case on the belief that what is missing is so large and has been hidden for so long that the most we can manage, the most we can bear, are quick glimpses. For Bly the poem as leap becomes a way back to a different order of understanding, for the missing truth has left its traces, its broken and frayed connections that can spark into conductivity once again. Bly challenges the lyric poem to resume one of its aboriginal functions, to rectify a mode of awareness that is pre-rational. In this sense, both Bly and Olson are indebted to books like Bruno Snell's *The Discovery of the Mind* or Eric Havelock's *Preface to Plato*, with their investigation of how mythological modes of thought precede rational ones, though it is through the poets' addition that this temporal priority can be equated with moral authority.

The Sea and the Honeycomb: A Book of Poems (Madison, Minnesota: Sixties Press, 1966).

Bly's metaphor for the poem, then, is deeply polemical, and he stresses just those elements in poetry that are absent from prose, fictional and nonfictional: articulation of parts, discursiveness of procedure, and a penchant to "see around" the problems and seek comprehensiveness rather than instanteity of expression. Bly's poetic gets much of its tension, however, from its seeing the poem simultaneously as image and as leap, as a mythically authoritative presence and a self-saving gesture. In fact, over the last decade or so (from the theoretical pieces in his magazine *The Sixties* to his contribution to the anthology *Naked Poetry*, called "Looking For Dragon Smoke," and on to the first number of *The Seventies*) we can sense a shift in Bly's concern from an image-centered poetry, where the danger was in producing a kind of endless series of sensory fragments, to a more energized *movement*, where the poem pointed a direction rather than simply presented a picture. It is almost as if Bly sensed that his body-centered mysticism needed another dimension, that to rely too exclusively on the images was to produce another version of a contemplative poetry which included all the dangers of egoism and "plots" that he had so energetically avoided. The "image" might be mistaken for an object, but the same danger could not apply to "leaping."

III. The Poem as Myth

Part of what shapes the theories of Bly and Olson is a feeling that the lyric poem ought to assume a larger role in the shaping of culture, that it was only when poets settled on poems as "set-pieces" that they abandoned what was a traditionally important function of poetic language, namely to contain and rectify the crucially operative values in any society. This sense also animates those poets who write a poetry heavily indebted to a study of myth and the modes of mythic consciousness. Since Yeats's *A Vision*, however, it has become increasingly difficult for any poet to enunciate a mythic "system" that might justify or elucidate individual lyric poems. Poets now knew that one crucial element in a *mythos* was its social purpose, that is, a myth operated with fullest potency only when it formed the belief system of many individuals, all of whom drew their value-terms from its reservoir of assumptions and exemplary acts. In the fifties, following in part the misleading example of Eliot's *Waste Land*, many poets began to use mythic material, often of a Greek or

Roman source, to serve as individualized psychological paradigms for the lyric poem. This practice still goes on, of course, and its main limitation is clear: it tends to melodramatize the poet's mundane concerns, and at the same time it may trivialize the myth. Also aware of this limitation, many contemporary poets use myth ironically, to suggest or measure the gap between an archaic but heroic culture and our more self-conscious, but commonplace, egocentricity. At two of its more brittle extremes, this use of myth can degenerate into a manipulation of motifs, a purely decorative use, or, on the other hand, it can simply retell the ancient story in modern terms, where the poet acts as a noninstitutionalized teacher, conveying cultural riches from the past. It would be extremely unusual to find, say, a Yale Younger poet or a National Book Award winner between 1950 and 1965, whose book did not include at least one poem named after a Greek or Roman deity, and whose structure didn't resemble these two extremes.

As the use of myth by poets became more self-conscious over the last two decades, the understanding of myth and its various social and cultural functions also developed in almost exponential ways. Mythography seemed to generate a kind of cultural warehouse of mythical motifs, and the revolution marked by Frazer's *Golden Bough* appeared commonplace. The *Golden Bough* was subject to at least two qualitatively different perspectives: it could demonstrate the economy of the mythic imagination, always using a limited number of basic structures, though capable of producing myriad variations, or it could foster a thorough-going cultural relativism. In either case, the poet's awareness might be compromised, since he was free to use mythic material without the need to vindicate it specifically in terms of his own experience. Myth threatened to assume the status of rhetoric in Renaissance poetics, that is, it answered several formal questions without raising troublesome notions of sincerity, all the while it allowed the poet to achieve a "public" (even "universal") resonance.

Some poets were aware of these shortcomings and took several measures to avoid them; others felt the difficulties, but stayed with a more or less traditional use of myth. Examples of the former would include many avant-garde poets, such as Armand Schwerner, whose *Tablets* is an extended work based on the notion that certain fragmentary codicies are being translated by him; and Michael McClure, whose tantras featured animal noises and proto-semantic sounds; and Ed Dorn, whose *Gunslinger* took over certain material formed around the American West, but used it to deal with philosophical questions in a half-comic vein. McClure also wrote plays that featured a mythologized version of such people as Billy the Kid and Jean Harlow, while Dorn's *North Atlantic Turbine* was a brilliant attempt to break open the myths of Anglo-American imperialism. In other words, there are several poets who use myth for personal or satiric or merely lyric ends, or a mix of these three purposes and more. For some of these poets, myth-making becomes intertwined with personal fantasy, and can arise out of a need to deal with social issues in a nonpropagandistic way; for example, Diane Wakoski's *George Washington Poems* are simultaneously a debunking of the public-school myths of our first president, an extended meditation on role-making and the masculine "mystique," and a surreal autobiography.

In these new uses of myth, contemporary poets often strove for a trans-personal scope by adapting a body of historical materials to their purposes, or, as in the case of Robert Duncan's *Passages* and *Structure of Rime*, a more or less traditional notion or structure which then allowed them maximum inclusiveness. Often the larger works that resulted from such procedures were purposely kept fragmentary, "in process," since myth has come to be seen as a dialectic, often involving a growth and development of stories or motifs through many versions, the "total" truth being a construct that spanned and included but also went beyond the single versions. In many such poetic "sequences" a kind of "projective verse" was employed, though in weaker cases this simply meant the breaking up of any typographical consistency in the poem. Part of this aesthetic developed, of course, from the example of such poets as Yeats and Stevens, and others such as Blake before them, who invited the reader to consider all the poet's separate lyrics as parts of a unified statement: Stevens, for example, had considered calling his collected poems *The Whole of Harmonium*. The poet's myth in this case becomes the transrational "vision" articulated by all his or her poems, not locatable in any specific poem or passage, but animating and pervasive throughout them all. But with many contemporary poets, unlike Stevens and Yeats, the "system" is something self-consciously chosen; it doesn't slowly arise out of several decades of poetic practice and it isn't later pieced together by critics and scholars.

Another way myth is used by contemporary poets can be seen at the level of diction. To strip one's words of most particularity and specific detail, and still to write a highly charged syntax so that instead of vague emotive drift one creates a portentous but abstract narrative tension, to use a certain group of nouns like door, stone, ring, or feather that vaguely resemble the key objects in a primitive ritual: all of this comes together (with a different "mix" for certain poets, to be sure) to form a poetic language with a definite "mythic" feel. Many of the poets who write in this mode are also translators, and working with the demands of that discipline they seem to have developed what we might call a "secondary" language, that is, a flat syntax and bland diction that resembles what is often used in translations. This language also must avoid slang, colloquial idioms, and any overly specific noun that would place or date the work. Clearly this language often produces parables, where archetypal actions and symbolic detail suggest a mythic consciousness at work. Here is an example, the first several lines of a poem by W. S. Merwin:

> Fear
> there is
> fear in fear the name the blue and green walls
> falling of and numbers fear the veins that
> when they were opened fear flowed from and
> these forms it took a ring a ring a ring
> a bit of grass green swan's down gliding on
> fear into fear and the hatred and something
> in everything and it is my death's
> disciple leg and fear no he would not
> have back those lives again and their fear as
> he feared he would say but he feared more he
> did not fear more he did fear more
> in everything it is there a long time
> as I was and it is within those
> blue and green walls . . .

Merwin's poems often use this language, and certain devices occur fairly frequently in his and others' poetry to create a sense of anonymity and at the same time to suggest a very strong ego at work in the language (this particular poem ends: "there is fear in everything and it is/ me and always was in everything it/ is me.") There is often a vague "other" in the poem, often a use of certain mythological topics, such as an aetiological or apocalyptic terminus for the action, and often a stylized repetition or ambiguity to suggest ritual structure. In a sense this particular example can be read as a stream-of-consciousness lyric about a child's first experience of fear, but the elaborate structure and riddling intertwining of phrases make for considerable complexity. (Often this complexity can mask a fairly banal content, as the last three lines of the poem might indicate.) Often we sense in Merwin's poetry a conflict between a need to use mythic material and the impulse to shape individual lyrics on a "self-bound" scale; this conflict some readers see as Merwin's main asset, while others find it produces poems that read like well-dressed truisms. In any case, his poems are more like hierophantic testaments than songs, as if he had created a litany in search of a redeeming mystery, hoping that after the half-gods of melody depart, the gods of rapture would arrive.

*   *   *

No one of these three metaphors for the poem now dominates contemporary poetry; in fact, their overlapping and mutual interaction often accounts for the strength of individual poets, and it certainly adds to the pluralism of styles available today. This pluralism of styles is both cause and effect of a mushrooming of theoretical speculation about poetry and how best to "achieve" it. I say "achieve" it, rather than write it, because what such metaphors often do is provide individual poets with a way to anchor their practice, to promote and justify a way of entering into their own poetry. As more and more isolation threatens the writer, as more and more the interview takes the place of the creative utterance, and as more and more the figure of the poet or the sense of the "poetic" outstrips the importance of individual poems, these metaphors may increase in importance. But while they are more than the trapping of artistic speculation, the metaphors might be called upon to do too much of the work of generating poetic meaning and excellence. Ours is an age when linguistic philosophy—words about words—seems at times to usurp the entire domain of philosophy. So far, poets have not settled for making only poems about poetry, but it is a temptation that needs stout resistance.

ANOTHER MARGOT CHAPTER

fiction by R.C. DAY

from QUARTERLY WEST

nominated by Raymond Carver

I LIKE DAYS WHEN THE CIRCLES CLOSE. Begin with breakfast, end with dinner, lend a little money, collect a debt, mail something out, find a nice something in the mailbox. I like waking up with Margot, and sleeping with her again at night. She's been gone several days now and I keep listening for the crunch of tires on gravel, her blue Ford returning, and herself contrite, languorous, needing the circle of my arms as I need the circle of hers. A lovely woman, Margot, whose needs sometimes take her away but always bring her back. She's a dancer, with long, strong legs and an incomparable body. Any day when she doesn't return has no bottom to it, and I fall and fall through the night, shivering, putting in the hard hours till daybreak.

Things haven't gone well for me lately; it seems I've been improvident. Strangers have been asking for me, and I've had to avoid the main streets and the Jambalaya, where I like to drink beer in the late afternoon. Going to the post office, I stay off the town square, for there I'm anyone's game; I slip along the storefronts instead, poised to fly inside or up an alley. They've tracked me to where I live. Yesterday, a woman came to my door collecting, she said, for Lungs, and I shook a few pennies into the can with the double cross on it. A collector though not for charity, that one; she wanted a look at my furniture. Those shrewd, appraising eyes, the tight nostrils sniffing out my assets, the hand iron-steady on the double-cross can: a heartless professional.

I can play really good days on the harpsichord—or could if I still owned one. The patterns of a good day make fine music. They group in clear configurations, open in the manner of a Bach fugue, and then return as the day draws on. For all the separation among the parts, they close at the end, all discord resolved. Margot understands this language, as of course a dancer would, and often we've ended a really good day in each other's arms, talking, happy after making love. "We're in the coda," I say, "the soft downsong." Though we're in the dark, I know her sleepy smile as she murmurs, "Oh, Jim, this one is fine."

But Margot isn't here, and that sound of tires on gravel might or might not be the blue Ford returning. A door slams with a loose clang, and then another. A do barks. There are strangers between the house and study. Someone says, "This is nice, Guthrie," and someone else calls out: "Dibs on the tree—I'll make a treehouse." The first voice again: "Look, they have chickens."

A broad face appears at my window, eyes bulging, low mongoloid forehead pressed against the glass. It's a boy of some sort, and it has a mother, who crowds up to the window and says, "Here's somebody, Guthrie—hello in there, we're looking at your house."

Watch out. It might be an exploration only, or might be the final assault. I set my face and go to the door. Besides the two at the window, there's a stocky, long-armed man with a hog-bristle haircut and big yellow teeth, who sticks out a hand and says, "Guthrie. This here's my missus. We didn't see no car in the drive, so we come on in."

I don't touch the hand. He's grinning at the study, the house, the redwood tree, the chicken coop. He grins at the missus and at his son, who, with the musculature and popcorn brain of a young Hercules, drives my ax into the chopping block and cleaves it with a single stroke. The missus is a rolling-fat woman done out in red stretch-pants and a blue, tent-like blouse. She says, "Do the chickens go with the place?"

It might be only an accident. They seem innocuous enough. I decide to give them an opening. "Yes, the chickens go with the place." But the place, I think, isn't going anywhere, for an owner has rights if his title is clear.

The trouble is, the title might not be all that clear. Perhaps I've too heavily encumbered the property, or they've found a small invalidating clause in the agreement. I'm in arrears, I'll confess. Debt grows like moss on my heart. Every shadow is a creditor, every stranger a repo-man.

"How much you asking?" Guthrie says.

From the other side of the house comes a kind of daughter, a lumpish girl about fifteen, with no neck, a tiny head, and stiff hair parted in the middle and sticking out on both sides like a birdhouse roof. She has in tow a couple of gray, silent spectres almost transparent with age. Their hands tremble, mouths work in wordless speech. They're too elaborate for stage dressing, too pathetically real.

"We druv past and saw the sign," Guthrie says. "How much?"

"It's a dead end. You can't drive past."

"The sign says For Sale."

He's so simple and obstinate that he's probably the Guthrie he says he is. But who can tell? Collectors pose as repairmen, meter readers, piano tuners, salesmen, tax assessors, Jehovah's Witnesses, building inspectors—anything to gain access to the house, where they suddenly turn rough and carry out the moveables. I lost my harpsichord to a seeming musician in a black suit, by his looks a retired mortician. He'd heard I had a harpsichord, he said, and wanted to come in and try a few passacaglias on it. Who would deny a fellow musician? I stepped back. Then two brutes leaped from the bushes and pushed in after him. While the old one held me off—he was stringy as a chimpanzee—the others hauled the instrument out to a truck, and that was the last I saw of it.

I grant this Guthrie full play. "Go in and look around." Unless he can carry out a stove or refrigerator, what harm can he do? The house has already been picked clean.

While they're inside thumping the walls and hallooing to each other, I go around front where, sure enough, there's a For Sale sign. I uproot it and throw it across the street behind some trees. It might be a practical joke, a hint from the neighborhood, or an Act of God. But it's probably the bank. You miss a little payment or two and they slap a For Sale sign on your house in the middle of the night. Like ingenious packrats they scurry, hustle, never rest—and they love night work. One night they took my car. A week later they made off with a good chrome dinette set, the color TV, and a leather couch, while Margot and I were asleep in the bedroom. We didn't hear them come or go. Not a sound. Spooky.

The Guthries come back single file, the two ancestors tottering at the rear. Guthrie says, "I can fix it up, I reckon. How much you want?"

"Two hundred thousand dollars."

He waits for me to laugh. But I give him a steady stare, and add: "Not including mineral rights."

He bites down on his teeth, makes fists. "Mama, Junior, git in the pick-up. Sue-Ann, bring gampa-n-gamma." He turns to me. "I'll have yore ass in court quick as an eyeflash."

I follow around and watch them climb into the rust-rotted truck, the two young ones in back with their rangy, ugly, reddish-brown dog, the four others stacked in the cab. Guthrie lets her roll, pops the clutch; the engine catches, roars, shakes the air. He turns around in my driveway and, through a cloud of oil-smoke, spits at my shoe. The dog gives a curl-lipped growl. They have the marks of authentic Guthries, and I'm sorry to have offended them, but what reception would I get at their house if I came snooping?

In the study I'm writing my autobiography. The study is really just a shed with a pot-bellied stove; I lined it with wallboard to keep the wind out, made a desk of plywood, and set up a lamp. It's my last line of defense. If the house goes, I can shrink my perimeter to the study and sleep on the old mattress by the stove. Since the electricity went off last week, I've been using a kerosense lamp for light. The water went too, so I dug a makeshift latrine below the chicken coop. It's inconvenient, but one lives according to his circumstances and does what he must do. At bottom there are more important things than convenience. Margot, for example, and my autobiography.

I send off a piece of myself every few days to a New York agent who handles that kind of thing. At least I think he handles that kind of thing; he mails me a postcard every time I send him something:

"Received, Chapter Six." Or twelve, or twenty. I assume he's doing what an agent should, passing them around to editors, mentioning them over lunch to book publishers, and generally getting my name known in the right places.

But of course I can't be sure. Perhaps he too has a pot-bellied stove and uses them to light fires with. I can't afford to think that way, and yet I can't help worrying, for some of those chapters are spun out of my soul's fiber, my very life. I'm thinking of one in particular, about chickens. I know more than anyone else in America about those loathsome, stupid, intractable birds; I have seven hens, cannibals all, eating their own eggs, pecking at each other's eyes, dropping excrement in the food dish. They're unbelievably filthy. They stink like the original cesspit. One day, no doubt, I'll be down to eating them. My stomach heaves at the thought.

The chapter I'm working on now is about my marriage to Margot. In it I'm playing the harpsichord, as I often did, while she's across the room writing a poem. The light falls wonderfully on a bowl of yellow jonquils in the window. I'm playing Margot, myself, the bright jonquils, and our arrangement in the space of the room. The themes impinge on each other, cavort, touch here, there open away in a mirror-image, mathematical sequence of notes—and turn on the F-sharp of the jonquils. In this chaper she writes a poem to me and places it on the carved music rack. As I read it, my fingers can't help modulating, slipping from the major to doleful minor. For the poem begins like this:

> You must know I have other lovers.
> How could you not know,
> Living with me in this tight room?
> How could you not sense,
> When your arm goes over me in the gray dawn,
> That something in me is not for you?
> Oh, I have roots going down and down,
> My belly is knotted cypress, and
> Tough wood twists in my arms.
> Don't you feel the rough bark
> As your fingers touch my thighs?

It's a true poem; Margot isn't exclusively mine. The minor is just right for that part of our relationship: she goes away. But she always returns, and the chapter will pivot on that *but* as the harpsichord composition pivots, anchors, on the yellow F-sharp. This is such a fine piece; its figures rise so lyrically into the pattern that, I think, I'll do the score for it, record it, and send chapter, score, and tape together to my agent as a kind of orchestration, a total work. Imagine his astonishment when he receives it, the eagerness with which he'll pick up the telephone and ask some powerful editor to lunch.

Right now, though, I set love aside. My inventory is down to a refrigerator, lamp, kitchen stove, electric sander, some of Margot's leotards and dresses, a few odd shirts and trousers of my own, and a handful of worthless trifles in the livingroom. I choose the sander as being portable and the most likely to bring a bid at the exchange. Strictly speaking the sander isn't mine; I borrowed it from my friend, Ray, a successful writer who no longer smooths anything but his prose. Ray has been in lots of tight corners; he'll understand. I need money. I'd like to have the water on again when Margot gets back, for she'll be fastidious about going in the hole behind the chicken coop.

But as I'm leaving I spot the real thing there in the street, glaring at my house. He's wearing a tan whipcord suit, the coat open over a tapered brown shirt and western-style string tie. A lean fellow with wire-rim glasses, truculent chin, and a murderer's eyes. He's slapping some papers on his leg. Everything about him says, "Experience in the field." He stands planted, waits for me and says, "Where's the sign I put up here last night?"

He isn't the sort you walk around and ignore. The papers in his hand might or might not mean anything; a professional always has a set of papers, official looking, more intimidating than a gun though he might have one of those, too. This one and several like him will be shown for what they are when I get to that harsher chapter in my Life. They're dogs, single-minded and vicious; your only hope is to face them down. If you shy away they'll tear you to pieces, and they might tear you up anyway, for plain fun.

"You're too late, the place is stripped," I say. "This sander is all I could find, except the shotgun. He's sitting with it over his knee, just waiting for someone to come through the door. I'm John Phillips—Amalgamated Credit."

"John Crot," he says unhappily. "Furniture gone? What about the stove and refrigerator—they're on my list."

"He's sitting on the stove, with the shotgun. I almost ran right into him. Scared the hell out of me. I grabbed this and cut out."

"I'll take the goddamn house with him in it,"Crot says.

I laugh in sympathy. "You'll need a big truck."

"Or lots of little ones," he says.

"Well, good luck. The shotgun's a 12-gauge Browning. It ought to be worth something, if you can get it away from him."

I leave the dog snarling there. At the corner I glance back; he's still in the street, staring at the house.

A good rule to follow is never stake all in a single game. In one game the sander is my ace, but the pot's small and I haven't much of a hand. The most it will bring is ten dollars—not enough to convince City Water to unlock my turn-on valve. But I'm in a bigger game as well; I not only owe but am owed. An acquaintance of mine, a photographer, did a picture book about the coastline here, and I wrote poems for the text. Wonder of wonders, he found a publisher who offered a 2,000-dollar advance, one-tenth of which is mine. Poems are hard to write. I wrote those, I'd guess, at the rate of ten cents an hour. But 200 dollars will save my life. I can have power and water restored, with a ten or two left to buy flowers and brandy for Margot.

I've stopped at Andy's every day since he was offered his advance; I was there yesterday and the check hadn't come. Today, on my way downtown, I find an envelope tacked to his apartment door an inside it no money, just a note: "I'm off to Dothan, Alabama, on a really big deal. Things are breaking at last. Don't worry about the money, I'll get it to you. It's a debt of honor. Thanks for everything." I turn the envelope over and shake it.

For a few moments I lose my head. I try the doors and windows. I hammer the front door with my fists, both fists, and am ready to heave a rock through the window—I'll blow the walls down, seize the TV, muscle out anything that will bring 200 dollars in the second-hand market—when the next-door tenant comes around the porch and says, "He moved out this morning. Bought a new Chevy pick-up, loaded everything in, and went to Oregon."

"Oregon?"

"That's what he said. But between you and me, I think he was heading for Idaho. He's got a girlfriend in Twin Falls."

"Then why did he say Oregon?" Coming from me, this is not an intelligent question; I already know why he said Oregon.

"Heavy-duty debts," says the tenant. "Some mean looking people have been coming around after him."

I drop the rock. He gives me a pitying smile, with a touch of glee in it. No money. For the title page of my Life, I'll use that pathetically humorous cartoon logogram, a dollar-sign with wings, flying away. But no humor for the Deadbeat Andy chapter: soul language, as thick and bitter-dark as bile.

At the exchange downtown my broker allows only five dollars on Ray's sander. He remembers that I persuaded his assistant, once, to give sixty dollars for a Montgomery Ward guitar which hadn't cost more than fifty new. Now he loves it when I come in. He gave me a dollar for a shiny G.E. toaster, and only two dollars for a leather briefcase worth thirty times that much. He toys with me, cackles, sneers. I'm his and he knows it; he's the only ready-money broker in town.

Still, five is better than nothing. With the crisp bill in my pocket I see that the day is sunny-bright. There are old folks, lovers, children, and dogs on the town square, delighting in the green lawn. I don't cross the square but skirt it as I've mentioned, on my way to the post office to see how I stand in that game.

The post office, like slow disease, eats me little by little. There'll be a Post Office chapter somewhere in my Life, with the postal authorities as fate-figures. Those impassive, ironical, blue-uniformed clerks know me intimately; they enjoy my apprehension as I come to my box, bend, shade my eyes, and peer through the little glass window. When I drop a chapter in the slot, they tear it open, read it aloud for their amusement; they throw it away or send it on as whim suits them. They're as merciless as sharks, cobras, killer-dogs, or bankers.

I enter in a sweat. At my box I stoop to the door and squint inside—to be sure the clerk hasn't set something in there to surprise me, say a jack-in-the-box, or a poniard on a spring to stab my groin.

Today there's a letter and a pink card telling me I have a package around at the counter. The letter is from Acme Collections, a form letter which says in bold print: THE PARTY IS OVER. Around the lettering there are cartoon sketches of sexy partygirls drinking champagne and partyboys smoking big cigars and throwing money around. At the bottom I read an ominous little handwritten note:

"I'll be calling on you, friend." It's signed Alex Troc, in a transparent anagrammatic disguise for Crot, the professional I met earlier. At least I've seen the man, so I know what kind of dog I'm dealing with.

The package, though, brings worry. It isn't my birthday or Christmas, and God knows I haven't ordered anything from L. L. Bean, Abercrombie's, or Brooks Brothers. Of course, it could be something good sent to me by mistake, or even a small gift from Margot; but the odds are against it. A trick, then? A postal refinement on some basic practical joke?

I creep to the counter, give the pink card. "Box 947." The clerk, middle-aged, with a lop-sided moustache, might or might not be the one assigned to my affairs. Stone-faced, he finds the package and turns it over a couple of times before handing it to me. It's heavily wrapped in brown paper, about six inches thick and longer than it is wide. Taped to the outside is a first-class letter come piggy-back all the way from New York.

Without thinking I tear the letter open, then catch myself and look quickly at the clerk. There's a flicker of amusement in his eyes, a slight, ironic thawing of his frozen face. He could almost permit himself to snicker.

Foul news! A spring-driven poniard and no mistake, this letter from Marvin X. Sylvester, now my ex-agent. "I am returning your manuscripts. You should find an agent who can submit your work with more enthusiasm. Good luck. Yours, etc., M.X.S."

A mountain climber, a thousand feet up the rock-face, hears his rope part with a twang. The drowning man barely misses the life-ring thrown to him. A window in a jet blows out and the nearest passenger is sucked through the hole. I'm those catastrophies, and more.

I use the five dollars to buy a stiff whiskey at the Jambalaya, and, at a table alone, I open the package. I read a page here, a paragraph there; it's like walking through the graveyard where I'm buried.

I knock back the whiskey and call for another. With my only contact cut off, I might as well be living on a rock in the Bering Sea: no boat, no radio, and food only for another week. The first snowstorm begins, flakes hiss in the dark sea-moil, and winter sets in for good.

"Has Margot been around?" I ask the bearded barman.

"Not today." He conforms to the barman's code of ethics. Had

Margot left five minutes before, he would've said the same. This bearded fellow, name of Morry, owns everyone's secrets and never breathes a word of them. I owe him for saving me a few times when pursuit was close. He, of course, owes me nothing.

I trudge outside, my autobiography as heavy as a headstone under my arm. Amid dogs, children, mooning lovers, and old folks I plod across the square. There's no language for how wretched I feel. "Shoot!" the sapper says, and all in one motion, a single sudden plunge, the graceful bridge drops in the river.

It takes a good while to get home with a soul turned to stone, my body cast iron. On my street Crot, or Troc, is nowhere in sight, which means that he's staked out in the bushes. Coming closer, though, I spot a strange car in the driveway, a newish Chrysler, and my heart leaps to Margot whom someone has delivered home. I fling the manuscripts in the study and hurry through the cold house. "Margot?" The walls echo, there's nothing in the place; motes dance slowly in the sunlight. Out on the deck I look around and call, "Hey!" But there seems to be no one outside, either.

Just then a coin lands ringing at my feet, rolls along the boards, disappears through a crack. I hear a laugh above me. Someone on the roof? No, there he is, perched high on a limb in the redwood tree between house and study. Another coin traces a silver arc, a quarter, which bounces over my shoe then off the deck. "Enough!" I yell up at him. "What the hell, Ray."

I'm amazed as he swings down from limb to limb. Built like a bear but agile as a mandrill, he descends in swoops, and at the bottom limb he scoots out over the deck on all fours. Casually balanced, he swings under the branch as it bends, and alights cool as anything beside me. "Can you spare some gin, brother?" he says.

"I suppose you want your sander." My voice is bitter with bad luck. "I'm sorry, but I had to lend it out."

"What sander?" Lord help us, he's forgotten. But why should he remember? He had a short story in last month's Esquire; a publisher is bringing out a collection of his fiction soon. He has an agent. Why should he clutter his mind with trifles?

"My sander is your sander," he says. "Keep it. I'm traveling light for awhile."

"Where are you going?"

"New York. There are some people I want to talk to, and I can't do it from the West Coast. Where's Margot? I thought I'd take you two out to dinner."

"She's away for awhile." That's all I need say, for Ray and I have known each other a long time. He was married once and split up after nightmare scenes. He's seen all there is in man-woman relationships; there's nothing to tell him about my situation that he wouldn't already know.

"No gin, Ray. Scotch?"

Hoping Crot hadn't beaten me to it, I go to the study and overturn a pile of chickenfeed sacks, kick aside a broken canvas chair, and lift some boards off a stack. There, in the pocket where I hid it, is the fifth of Cutty Sark I've been saving to treat flesh-wounds or see me through some final, arctic night. But I'd share my last with Ray.

"No ice," I tell him. "My automatic ice-maker went out last week."

He laughs. "A little water then."

"No water."

"Can it be that bad? No water? Let's have a look at the problem." He takes me to the Chrysler, opens the trunk, and finds a pair of bolt-cutters. "I wouldn't go anywhere without these," he says. "Where's your tie-in with the main?"

I lift the City Water trapdoor at the curb. With an easy double snip of the bolt-cutters, he drops the padlock from the valve. "Lo, there was water after all," he says, turning the little wheel.

He's bought the Chrysler, or rather made the down payment, with the advance on his book, and other winged dollar-signs have flocked to his shoulders. For now at least, he's pretty well off. He says nothing about my empty house, nor do I; we share such knowledge without speaking of it. We talk about old times, close calls, bizarre circumstances—tales, yarns, stories to be written. He thinks I should call my autobiography *Shards and Remnants*, but I favor *Cross Currents, Debris and Foul Effluvia*.

We work pretty far through the bottle. My lost-harpsichord episode makes him laugh till he's weeping, then he responds with three of his own. I tell him my Vanishing Agent story, the Poniard in the Post Box, and Deadbeat Andy, all soon to be chapters in my Life. As we talk, trouble doesn't disappear exactly; I know that Crot and his henchmen are waiting out there. I'm surrounded, I know that. But the worry withdraws a little, leaving me a kind of green-belt of happy space. Inside it, I have a very good time getting drunk with Ray.

Finally he asks, "Do you think Margot will be back soon?"

"Can't say for sure."

"Well, let's take leave for a spell and go for dinner. Is Garcia's still in business?"

The sun has set and it's chilly on the deck. Hungry as I am, I take time to give the hens a couple of scoops of laying mash, on the off chance they'll lay an egg or two. They're disgusting creatures, but there's nothing like a fresh egg for breakfast.

The Chrysler hums, glides, slides along, heater going, springs eating the street-bumps. A luxury car is a fine thing to have, even short-term, and if my luck should change I might put a down payment on one like Ray's, take Margot for some rides, maybe drive to San Francisco or Santa Fe. If the Life has any defect so far, it's one of stasis; I could use some traveling chapters.

At Garcia's, half-starved, I seriously overorder. I work through enchiladas, rellenos, burritos, and refried beans, then double back and take a tostada I've had my eye on. Ray, who's been eating regularly, can't quite believe I'm putting all that away. When I finally overequalize and can't chew a bite more, he says, "Jesus, you'll blow up." I haven't touched El Zapato, the shoe, an enormous flour tortilla packed with meaty wonders. I request a doggy-bag for El Zapato, though it's no dog I'll feed. All too well I know how hunger comes up with the sun.

At my place Ray sits still and leaves the engine running. He wants to make part of the distance tonight. "Look," he says, "I just sold a story to Playhouse for 1,000 dollars. Let me help you out a little, all right?" He stuffs something in my shirt pocket and I could cry for having such a friend.

"Ray, damn it, thanks. I'll pay you back. A debt of honor. Tell you what, you can have my Poniard in the Post Box. Take it, write it up—I'll leave it out of my Life."

He claps me on the shoulder and laughs. "No, that's yours. I wouldn't know how to tell it." As I step out, he says, "Hang in there, you skinny bastard."

Almost silent the Chrysler, a great ocean liner on fat rubber, eases away and leaves me watching its stunning taillights.

There'll be Ray chapter in my final work, no question about that.

When I light the lamp in the study, I find he's given me 250 dollars, a short, thick cigar-roll of bills. Incomparable friend, I'll redeem your sander, I swear I will, and I'll put fifty away to send when you're flat.

A few hours go by. Then footsteps on the gravel. Margot's back. No sound of tires, no blue Ford. "I lost it," she says, which means only that she no longer has it.

"I've missed you, Margot." Since there seems to be activity around the house, we hole up in the study. I build a fire in the stove. When its belly is cherry red, we undress and make love on the mattress. She's languorous and insistent by turns, an exceptional lover, and I'm exceptional too, having suffered those days without her. I ask no questions and want no explanations, but fold her in and am in turn enfolded. "Margot, Margot, Margot," I say, and she murmurs my name in triple response. The world has drawn in to the stovelit mattress. I whisper her a piece of a John Donne poem:

> Such wilt thou be to me, who must
>   Like the other foot, obliquely run;
> Thy firmness makes my circle just,
>   And makes me end where I begun.

"I should be reading that to you," she says. "I'm the one's been gone."

"Let's read to each other—both at once."

We read with body's language, give all our books with lyric grace. The stove darkens, cools to coals, and we lie holding and held.

What matter the stealthy light-beam playing about outside, the soft footfalls, the muffled curse, the creak of boards being pried? Listen. Isn't that a heavy truck rolling, engine off, down the graveled street? Crot and crew are repossessing it after all, shingles coming up, roofboards, rafters, the roofbeam—pulled loose and passed down to waiting hands. Seven sharp squawks and the hens are sacked. A soft ripping noise, the spang of wire: the tarpaper roof leaves the chicken coop.

"Hear that, Margot?"

"Yes, they must have the whole credit bureau out there."

"And the postal workers, on night duty."

"And artists' agents. Ooooh, it's frightening. Hold me."

We laugh into each other. In the dark I run my fingers along her splendid back, down over her superb, muscular buttocks, and along those dancer's thighs. I'm of half a mind to light the lamp, to look and touch at the same time. "I love you, Margot. I'm glad you're back."

"Do you remember," she says, "when you used to play the harpsichord while I danced? It was almost like I was the harpsichord, and you played me."

"And like you danced in my fingers," I say, reversing the cliche and straining it a little. "Margot, would you want us to have a harpsichord again?"

"We can't afford that," she says.

"We might . . ."

A wall topples with a resonating crump. Dogs bark. Flashlights dart this way and that in consternation. Someone says, "My God, he's under there." I hope it fell on Crot; but again no luck, for I recognize his raspy voice: "Ready, heave. All right, now drag him out. That's good, he'll live."

"Ray came by today," I say. "He gave me some money. Enough for a down payment."

"Where would we put it?"

"I'll push the desk over a little. Clean out the feed sacks and boards. There's always room for a harpsichord."

"It'll be nice to have music," she says.

Walls fall, floors come up, joists and stringers protest and are vanquished. By morning they'll be down to the gray foundation. The noise gets a little loud but not enough to intrude between us. As Margot falls asleep in my arms, I think of doing a chapter called The Purloined House, one called Dogs, and another Margot chapter, muscular, rhythmical, exquisitely counterpointed. I palm the dimpled small of her back, that lovely incurve. Still in the downsong, she stirs, murmurs, drifts deep again.

I drift a bit myself, thinking how much I love this fine woman. A pipe-wrench clatters on a fitting, nails shriek softly, dogs bark in the night.

SITTING UP, STANDING, TAKING STEPS

fiction by RON SILLIMAN

from TUUMBA PRESS

nominated by Dick Higgins and Tuumba Press

Hɪɢн ɢʀᴀʏ sᴋʏ. A large wood table with only a green bottle of "white" Rhine wine atop it (empty). An open umbrella upside down in one corner of the room. Ritz crackers topped with cream cheese and, beside them, crayolas. Gray plastic bottle of lemon ammonia on its side on the green tile in back of the toilet. My red-and-black checked CPO jacket atop a guitar in my rocking chair. Butter on the knife. Dobermans and Danes. The walkin and his cutout. A callus around the ring. Slice of toast on a saucer on a corner of the wood table. The low fast foreign car. The girl with green eyes. The venetian blind. One day of Crash City. Water table. The fatal florist in the forest. The thickness of my mother's ankles. Poise of the pen. Yellow

Buick. The numbers and kinds of irreducible acts. Cloud shadow on the still bay. Crips and walkies. Black sock. Extension and the nature of existence. The transfer point. Red orange. Solidity. Fog. The green felt-top table in the tavern light. The geometry of cues. His sister. The olive trees of Sacramento Street. Chipped cup. The submarine on the horizon in the sunset. State of null karma. Undefined descriptive predicate. Little lobes. Some handsome hands. Statue of a dog with a fish in its mouth. Something about cowboys in bus depots. The real heat. Great sloping grove of clover. The bell curve. Woman in a pink blouse. Amber, ochre. The action faction or the praxis axis. Chapstick. Cheesy smell of a dog stool. Hiss of traffic. Sunset debris. Jackalope. Pudding cups. Bruise on her thigh. Crab grass. Eggplant in the shape of a face or dolphin. Blue bench. Prairie apple. Albino with a beard. Hard edge. Pornographic motherhood. Chess people. World behavior. Knuckle archives. Sausage. Saucer. Long legged women on platform, short skirts, streaks of blonde in their hair, lipstick a deep, deep red. Itch of the coccyx or the cuticle wall. A net of concrete atop the planet, streets and roads and boulevards. Oily leather skin of the shopping bag lady. Experimental sheep. Mouldy towel. Hair in a shag, with large white earrings. As tho under a footbridge. A small man in a big brimmed hat. In a heliport by the sea wall in the fog. A new white pen to write with. The bus to the suburbs. A store full of reptiles. Rows of white headstones. Toll bridge. The eyes of the bus driver in the rearview mirror. A small mole on the female stranger's upper lip. An old Chinese woman with black slacks on under her dress. Helicopter, harbor, filmy morning light. A green suit, a white shirt and a loud tie or a gray suit, a blue shirt and a striped, quiet tie. Three kinds of prose. Color films of dead people. Burned out buses among backlot dillweed, Military Ocean Terminal. Deer fetus wine of China. Pigeons in the eaves of a Queen Anne's tower. All toes of identical length. Odor of stale soap, bus depot john. Abductor muscles. The bitterness of women. The problem of truth in fiction. Abandoned railroad cars on a siding by the rock quarry. Advanced life support unit. Geometry of the personal. Midget in a large felt hat. Fork lift. Abandoned industrial trackside cafeteria amid dillweed stalks. My droor thing. Corridor of condos. Post-nasal drip. Hot hamster. Sand in the notebook. A salt-water cave. Eroded ruins. The bend in the pelican's wing-spread. Algae in a tidepool. An old windowless house of concrete, its door rusted off, with nothing inside it but odor and an

open safe. Pepper on the eggs. Jaws. One of several small silver
bracelets. A thin layer of sand, a coarse film, in my nose and hair.
Under a willow beside the pile of raked leaves, the lawn mower in
the graveyard. Density or sleep. The Paradise Cafe. A small heap of
grey, broken bird wings. Puka shell necklace. The woman with the
shawl or the woman with the apple. The angle of the pile of un-
washed plates. Red goose shoes. A terrible dirigible incident. Natural gas pipeline. Lubricated prophylactic. Legend of the Pony Express. Midmorning. Dark stools. Rice paper wafer. Longer boat
under the bridge. The brown boot. Bananas. This way. A linguistic
emulsion. Feedback. Radial tires in the mud. The constant knocker.
The bridge of the nose. A location or condition of the mind. Prodder.
Curlews and herons in the lagoon at low tide, the red sky of night,
sailor's delight, moss on the willow, shoes off, pebbles between toes.
Frigate. Ceramic blue star. Briar patch. Friend or lover. The long
pier. A system, an argot. The window in the windsurfer's sail. Geese
of the lagoon. Long shadows. A field of woven grass. A superficial,
professional verbal exchange. Outdoor basketball courts as a form of
sculpture. Sharp shadows on the fennel that constitute a description
of dawn. Article-starved predicate. World of ski-boots. Root beer.
Big damp grey dog. Panda plant, ice plant, wandering Jew. Along
the coast, on cots, in coats. A warm new storm. Blue ink on a white
page between red lines. Words after words. Chard. The loose goose.
The late dawn of December. Duck soup. A cheeselike discharge in
her vagina. The fat cat's flat hat. Glass beads, tortoise shell ring.
Legendary bladder, legendary weak bladder. Stable, half-supple
string of terms and relations. Hang glider. Forgotten sentence.
Deep blue dome of sky above still grey plane of water. Between
movies, not cinema, not films, not here, between movies. Condo
door awning. A not-fat dalmation. Schizo. Things to know versus
things to do. Ochre school bus. The objects of thought, qualities and
relations. The chapter on things. Corn row hair style. Shower or
storm. Bozos, yoyos, turkeys, geeks. Slope-shouldered fuckoff.
Henry Africa's. Curlew, sandpiper, tern, gull, godwit. Swizzle stick.
Cuticle. Static electricity. Mauve. Towaway zone. Blue mailbox.
Cabin cruiser. Itchy balls. Half-eaten apple. Helen Frankenthaler's
newer works. The Jello word for the day. Spurs. A duck that looks
just like Groucho. Banana-flavored taffy. Mirror image. A fire in the
oil fields. Motown. Spewn shrapnel-like remnants of a helicopter.
Tripod. Cumshot. Certain, possible, impossible. During. Herons

about a boat hull at low tide. Pink crayon, blue crayon. Fat black dog. Bloody earlobe. Faucets. A field of clover over there. The towers of the bridge. The pillars. Odor of paper. Orange and green quilt. Hair in an Afro-blowout. Golden saxophone. Key of C. Tail of an afghan. Vapor trail in a light blue sky. Trace of a vapor trail. Memory and imagination. New page. A park on a hillside. A valley full of water, a bay. Green and round and in pain. Toy boat. Kite in the shape of a moth. Gray day. Slow trombones. Red lines. Gentle smell of dust. Duck pond by the freeway. Bo Diddley's hat. The damaged guitar. Expository sentence. More than this. Walnut desk in foodstamp office. Halfhour of videotape. Boulevards. Studebaker. Blue-grey eyes. Not nouns. A series of ankles. An investment. Phil Whalen's "platter of little feet." His shaved head, light colored eye-brows, thin lips, wide ears. The precise odor of pavement. The fog before dawn. The missing felt-tip pen. The ability. Kidney beans, pinto. Inherent danger in. Ninth. Lithographers, associates. Spurs, chaps, myth. The inflamed hangnail. As big as. Red goose shoes. Watermelon tattoo. Hoosier state. Bean factory. Wart upon nose. Ice tea. Colorless dawn sky. Sloop. Verb. One mean mastiff. Tugrope. Slide guitar. Man of no fortune. Worm time. Macro-. Oat Willie's cappucino. Towards words. Determiner. Faucet. Tattoo of a watermelon. Light blue summer morning sky. Swordfish. Seahorse. Recent problems in the general theory of karma. Revisionaries. His class origin versus his class stand. One rim job. Butch. A lad with an Afro blowout. A stinger. Number or doobie. Next to the last. Texaco, Arco, Exxon. Garden Street, Treat Street, Canty Lane, Highland Place. Tamal, Represa, Corona, Stormdrawer, Marion, Butner, Steilacoom, Sandstone, Redwing, Starke. Facials and manicures upstairs. Pronominal anaphor. The stragglers, the shudders, the White House horrors. Alcatrax shade and blind. The hustle, the bump. Crash City. Neck, bridge, nut, fret. Meat rack. An attitude towards the verbal. An old man in a straw hat in the shade with a Dr. Pepper. Yellow mustard dispenser. Hotter, more hot. A deposit of red pepper on a lettuce leaf. Horny high school students. The politically conscious meter maid. Charred hill. Dry leaf. Cecil the seasick sea serpent, Rags the tiger. Neighbor. Burnt eucalyptus. The first poem about Kefir. Capitol of North Dakota. Turmoil. The sexually-active dental technician's very good friend's larger but younger Spaniel. A stairway to heaven. Nancy and Sally and Suzy. Kevin and Kirk. Kevin and Patty. Patty and Andy. Patty and Frank or

Darrell. Tony and Roberta. Frank again and Nora and Eric. Richie and Joan and Carol. Aaron and a different Carol. Jesse and Sarah. Maxine or Ashleigh. Jeanne and Peter. Fame as a subject. Fame as an object. Mister tooth decay. Ferry terminal. Quarry. Hobo camp, the ranch. Population. Flouride. Peonson's bald head (pate). Cope or thieves or cops and thieves. The dry dock. Bison, bison. Blue Capri. Still more pronominal anaphors. Her red fuzzy muff. Ambivalence, an autobiography. Good buddy. Bachelors together. Hoop, rim, backboard. Fine white smoke of a grass fire just east of San Quentin on the first day of July. Forgotten things. The headmaster's daughter. Low in tar. Mucous. The red scooter. Almond mask. His sock. Each new first time. Description, an invention. Slice of life pie. Marigolds. White white jumpsuit. Echoes. Concentration camps by the name of bantustans. Clarinet. At first. The day before Barbara's birthday, two before Chuck's. Brown or red brick. Blue toothpaste. On stage. Ferry terminal. Four day week. Interpol or Cointelpro or Burns. Namibian difficulties. The recent unpleasantness between Japan and the U.S. List lover. Trailer park. Underpass. Tuesday, a.m. What, alarm, ceiling, clock, dull light, urine, toothpaste, blue shirt, jeans, water for coffee, bacon, eggs, soy toast, phoney earth shoes, bus, another bus, typewriter, telephone, co-workers, salad, iced tea, more co-workers, bus, ambulance on freeway, another bus, a beer, chicken, rice and squash, today's mail, feces, tv, glass of chablis, darkness. Rare delta fog. Plywood, fiberboard. Couch, divan, chesterfield, sofa. String of silver elephants on a chain about her neck. Her inevitably turned-up levi cuffs. The moderately successful wage slave. Morning in North Beach, Sunday in Chinatown. Locked bumpers, a problem in front of Rincon Annex, inside WPA murals of the working class, back from Ghana at forty. The tease. Sky blue wall of the racket club. Space cowboy. The cotton rings around the mountain, bum rhythm, the limp, the gimp. Googoo dada dada. P soup. For the entire family. 2 Disney smash hits. The All ★ Game. Two ponies in a brick red trailer behind a brown pickup with a bale of hay in the back. Bush jacket from China. Names of the cross streets. A restful orange. A restful orange bridge. The water, the haze, the sky, all blue, a line drawing. Or not blue but grey or gray. All the same. Industrial park. Heliport. Saliva. Canal at low tide. Pompidour sheriff's yacht by the curious name of Bijou, a year's wages. Shade over shade over shade. The curl of the ear. The tongue behind the teeth behind the lips, at the entrance of the throat. Remainder of a cigar. Calm blue eyes. Bells and chimes and wooden drums. Straw horse. Off-white piano. High hat. Blue couch. An old pair of Frye boots. Summer. The sun. High gray sky.

♭ ♭ ♭

MADE CONNECTIONS

by MICHAEL HARPER

from THE MASSACHUSETTS REVIEW

nominated by DeWitt Henry

> *the wages of dying is love*, GALWAY KINNELL

Rich with gifts on your return to Edinburgh
your voice quakes in sayable poems chiming
images of your ancestors, the kite in the eye
drawn off into highland village of first
offerings, the misspelt bookmarker for *Alex
Kinell, 1843*, given by his beloved; your grandfather's
snuffbox made from horn into an animal
full of snuff, the gift-bible of the pastor
to your father on his first trip to this city:
all these caretaken by a yawning ninety year old
aunt, your relatives rolling in the omphalos
dreams of castles, high manors of war in words.

We sit awhile in first-class bypassing derailment,
the sea suggesting your father's ship, crestfallen
with his leaving homelands for the Boer War;
I open the paper to a photo of a black man bleeding
at the feet of a South African policeman, his boots
caked in "riots"; one schoolboy locked in a room
littered with corpses, babies and old grannies
moaning on litters, chants his lessons in Afrikaaner
begging to get out; the train lumbers on thick with uniformed
cadets in fatigues on their way to maneuvers.

Locked in trenches of France and Belgium,
or jumping ship in West Virginia with a friend,

your father makes cabinets as his son makes
testimony in stone, images scribbled on a rocking
train, the image of kite being drawn off into the Hebrides,
or the village where a young girl gave the gift of passing
hours, her tongue forcing books to give up light
knowing he would come back to read to an old
woman, of war and travel, the comfort of a sleepy
child, in the moon-arms of her father, made in America.

ANONYMOUS COURTESAN IN A JADE SHROUD

by BRENDA HILLMAN

from FIELD

nominated by FIELD

In an unknown century of your country's life,
they staked your body out
and bound it with rocks the color of grass
and sewed the rocks with golden filaments,
They flattened your breasts, and in your bald head
made a hollow valley for the eyes.

I walk around you, wanting to see
inside—how the chandelier of sun
makes its way through,
what became of your fingernails, your hair.

Perhaps you were not beautiful, but had
a sickly look, nothing to recommend you
but a famous father or a gift for talk.

I wonder how you made it
to the afterlife; did your soul
seep out the narrow cracks?
Or was it better than anything you knew

just to lie flat on your back

like a garden, well cared-for, unchanging,
and so valuable—each frozen cell—
nothing could tempt you to let the rich man in.

🔥 🔥 🔥

A WOMAN IN LOVE WITH A BOTTLE

by BARBARA LOVELL

from LOVE STORIES BY NEW WOMEN (Red Clay Books)

nominated by RED CLAY BOOKS

Lady wants a story about that, about a woman in love with a bottle. O.K. Once upon a time there was a bottle named vodka-scotchcointreauretsinaB&B and cheap Gallo sherry. Woman's name was Barbara. Then you give a little description, a little background stuff, and crank up the plot—girl meets bottle, falls in love with bottle, overcomes a few obstacles to her passion with a bit of suffering; they of course get married, you put the sex parts in here somewhere. How it ends: they get a divorce, this being a modern story, BUT they live happily ever after which is unfashionable and won't sell worth a damn because we all crave that lonely existentialist anguish, right? You want to hear how it goes anyway?

Background stuff: broken home, acne, some confusion about sexual identity, immortal longings in her, artist and all. She cannot live with people, any one person long because screwing gets stale and predictable and so does what he or she says in the morning and when they get home from work at night. The ring around the bathtub isn't worth the trouble. There is also a lot of anger. That gets complex and subtle, part of the immediate plot. Develop as we go along.

Let's do it in the first person and start in the middle. With the sex. Scene: *Fucking the Vodka*.

I wake up feeling low down and good and excited. Secret. I am in East Orange, New Jersey, I am thirty-eight years old. The September sun is just pearling in. I stare at the wall, the usual first-light, leaf shadow filigree at four a.m. I want it not to dance so sharply from wind through the birch outside this second story window. I want nothing to move. My husband is sleeping; my child is sleeping across the hall; the whole campus is sleeping; there is no traffic.

The bed we sleep in, this man I'm married to and I, is a large wooden platform holding two single foam slab mattresses, constructed so as not to jostle one another as we toss in our nightmares. Clever and particularly satisfactory at this moment as I sit up carefully. Carefully. Because the usual morning evil gets going in the skull the minute the head is lifted from the pillow: the jackhammer, the waves tilting the seasick cochlea, the icepicks puncturing the retina to split a brain full of neurons with no defense. And carefully because it is important to move soundlessly, to make no sudden movement that will wake him. I must not wake anyone, only myself to keep this appointment at dawn. I am a thief in my own house; I move with stealth.

I do not flush the toilet. The stairwell is just outside the bathroom door. The third step down creaks, I have learned, if you step on the side near the bannister. I avoid it automatically.

Illicit love does, after a time, take on its sordid aspects. In the kitchen my breath comes short; I can't get across the room to the cabinet under the sink fast enough, and my hand reaching for the familiar beautiful blue-labeled clear gallon of vodka trembles. My eyes have stopped seeing the setting: grease scummed dishes in the sink, the wilting avocado plant in the window, the dog's water bowl slimy and stale. Sordid. I couldn't care less. I want what I've come for and I want it bad and I'm about to get it. Wanting. All the nerve ends tensely erect, begging, sweetly aching and stretching for contact. A spring coiled tight and coiling tighter every long second somewhere between belly and crotch.

I am skilled at illicit love. Even as I stand there shaking, really shaking with desire, the bottle on the counter now and my fingers tenderly unscrewing the lid, my eye makes instantaneous, careful note of just how far down the label the level is. Not halfway yet, just about at the top of the final "f" in Smirnoff. Sometimes when you're fucking you can't even take time to get undressed, it's too urgent. This is urgent, that spring may snap, and I don't fool with a glass. No foreplay, just the long, sweet release. Bad prose there, same modifier in less than 100 words. But the aching is sweet and the coming is sweeter—no other word for it, it is very, very sweet: that spring finally letting go, the starved nerves getting full and fed and satisfied, relaxing down now, pleasantly limp, sort of purring. In the belly that spreading lifeglow it had been tight for. And warm, so warm. Real good. Jackhammer, icepicks gone. Hand steady. You can walk a straight line and prove it down the linoleum squares. The inner ear feels fine, hums a little in delight. Every cell saying thank you.

I water that sad avocado, but I don't want to think about how it got so sad; I am too happy. I save some of the water in the measuring cup for the blue-labeled gallon, bring the level back up to the "f." Which creates certain problems I'll solve later. Foreshadowing here: hidden bottle bound to arrive on the scene. Right now this bottle and I guard our secret, no one will know.

Back up the stairs, the world still sleeping. I crawl into my side of the bed, into my customary fetal position, my back to this man to whom I have just been unfaithful, and sleep the sleep of a woman who has just been thoroughly and expertly loved.

That takes care of the middle up to the turning point, the—so to speak—climax. Where does the beginning begin, the necessary flashback: courtship, assignations, admissions, the deep sworn vows?

It's such an old story.

Twenty-three years ago. The only undergraduate in a faculty member's living room with six graduate students. Bessie Smith and Jelly Roll Morton on the player. Always, from the first, that funky, low down mood. Everyone drinking martinis, no, Gibsons—it was the smart, in-thing. Everybody except me because in those days drinking was against the honor code for undergraduates. In spite of the blues on the hi-fi and the Gibsons, everybody was feeling pretty miserable. We had gathered at the home of this faculty member, a kind of mentor, to console ourselves for a failure. We, who? Jill the dancer, Anne the painter, Louise the violinist, Helen the playwright, I the poet, and John the Renaissance man, a nineteen year old philosopher and aesthetician who knew all things. It was the first night of Christmas vacation which also happened to be the deadline for entries for the Spring fine arts festival. For weeks we had worked and talked with the total faith and enthusiasm of the young at the age when they believe that they and they alone have seen the light. We had invented, we thought, a New Art Form. It was to be all the arts in one, staged in a new, incredible, perfect harmony. And of course we had not gotten it together. And we had done a lot of talking and made a lot of promises to the whole school, including skeptical professors we were going to prove wrong. So. We could hardly face ourselves, how were we to face the world. Or go home and have a Merry Christmas.

After the second Gibson, Jill, who was six feet tall and all long bones and angles, rose in one motion from her crosslegged position on the parquet floor and began to dance her parody of our tragic plight—clutched brow, mortified slump, quick, static posture of agony, the dying fall. Helen began to giggle and recite *Four Saints, Three Acts: when this you see, remember me*, John and Louise tangled on the sofa, first in a mock fight and then settling down to necking, John still holding his Gibson in his left hand and exploring Louise's blouse front with his right. I watched Louise reach to loosen her ponytail and let her dark hair fall free, something I'd never seen before.

I sat well back in the corner, desolate, furious with them, openly weeping. As far as I was concerned it was the end of the world, life could not go on. Anne, to whom I was closest, Anne who had eyes straight out of Etruscan paintings and which, I thought, saw everything, watched me weep for a while and then said to Claire, our faculty hostess, "For god's sake, give Barbara a drink."

Claire brought me some tomato juice. "Legal." It was the best tomato juice I had ever tasted. The first swallow I felt better. Immediate relief to all that pain and grief and shame. I drank it straight down and felt wonderful. Claire brought me another. That warm glow, that satisfied well-being. The hell with the New Art

Form, this was something really worth my time. Got up and mimed our absurdity with Jill, I who had never danced, never used my body to express anything at all. And so fell in love, first kiss, with someone whose name I didn't even know. I was in love, I later learned, with Bloody Mary.

And sang it in the shower for months afterwards: "Bloody Mayree is th' gurl I lo-ove." I was really happy. And kept going back to Claire's every chance I got for more. I got a lot of chances. It was a fine year.

The analogy grows tedious: first blackout, loss of virginity, beginning cocktail hour a little earlier, taking care as I brought them in from the kitchen that the scotch on the rocks in my left hand was mine because it held the extra, secret, generous splash, gradually working it so we had three drinks before dinner instead of one, establishing the nightcap as legal-assignations, stolen moments, whatever. You get the drift, let's drop it.

Scenes from a Bigamy:

Every couple has a formula: let's play house tonight, see you later alligator, with a significant look. Ours was simply, let's try to get to bed early tonight. Goody, put off grading papers (though my cleverness had somehow allowed me to drink wine to get through that onerous task) and make gimlets, drink gimlets, lots of them, nobody counting; prolong "foreplay" for hours and get blissfully numb. Three or four nights a week. And more and more my suggestion. Afterwards one more to go to sleep on (pass out on), celebrate because it had all been so good, we were so skilled, so compatible, so inventive, so free. The lies.

Across the street from us on faculty row lived Cathy: blonde, Scandanavian, sculptress—metal welding—very good at her work. Not pretty but a good face, reminded me of Clavdia Chauchat in *The Magic Mountain*. Unhappily married like everyone else in the world. And funny. I, over cocktails one noon at the Metropolitan Museum, "Cathy, have you ever been abroad?" She, "Only for thirty-two years." Bright, smart, sensitive. We used to go into the city, gallery hopping and doing the museums. She knew the names and dates of every Kline and DeKooning in the Modern. We talked intensely about art and poetry. We talked wittily about bad marriages. She was a jazz freak, too. I liked her. My friendships with women have always been close, too close sometimes. When I was too drunk to drive to the liquor store Cathy would go for me. I liked her so much I gave her my husband. This generosity took care of my guilt and eventually allowed me a separate bedroom and a private bottle right there when I wanted it— which was most of the time. I could stay there for hours; I think it was along in here I switched to sherry for daytime love, for writing my inspired poetry. I, of course, couldn't loosen up to write without a drink. Could anybody? Don't all poets drink?

Quadrangle: him, Cathy, me, Gallo sherry. I liked Cathy so much I very nearly gave her my child. She had none of her own and adored children, especially my nine year old daughter who returned her adoration. Cathy taught her to play the piano, took her to work with her on sets at the college theatre, and would happily come over to my kitchen and fix lunch when Stacy came home from school if I were too drunk to pour the milk or find the pimento cheese. Up to a point, I was grateful.

That point: one fine afternoon in spring I come home from school. (Pattern then: pre-dawn rendezvous with the blue label which, supplemented with spiked orange juice at breakfast, enabled me to function with my classes, home for sherry lunch which got me through in pretty good shape until the early cocktail hour, a few clear hours in the afternoon holding on to the promise of that hour.) That afternoon I had an inspiration. I'd take Stacy to Turtleback Zoo, we'd have a fine time, just the two of us. They had a new acquisition, a small furry beasty, a hyrax, but *kin to an elephant*. Which knocked me out. Stacy and I both adored animals, any animals. This was a special thing I could give her.

When I walked in, my husband, Cathy, and Stacy were down on the green rug in the living room playing poker—a passion he and Cathy shared and Stacy had contracted. Stacy was bright, too; sometimes she won and was noisily triumphant. We all thought it was marvelous.

I, "Hi, gang. Stacy, finish that hand and get your jacket, I've got a big surprise."

Stacy had green eyes, the real thing, like her father. When she looked up at me that afternoon they were cloudy, hidden somehow. What was this? I'd never seen that before. Something in the bottom of my stomach grabbed the answer before it got to my head. She didn't want to go. Playing poker with them was more fun than going anywhere with me. There was embarrassment. Resentment. Even annoyance. I was suddenly an intruder. When this message got to my brain, I scrambled, bribed.

"The zoo, honey, we'll go to Turtleback. They've got something new and really amazing. And we'll get an icey."

She looked down at her cards, raised the ante. She didn't know what to say to me. My husband and Cathy were laughing at her bet. I didn't exist.

"*Stacy*, the *zoo!*" Something in my tone reached Cathy.

She, "It's all right, honey, you can go."

I could not believe it. Cathy was giving *my* child *permission* to go out on a spring afternoon with her own mother. Stacy still did not look up. She didn't want permission; she didn't want me.

So now I hated my good friend Cathy. Jealousy is a much more uncomfortable emotion than guilt. She could have my husband, but not my child. I needed a drink. And had one, a long one straight from the bottle an hour and a half before cocktail hour; and another one until something, pain I think, but not the rage, eased. Then upstairs to my room, slamming the door as hard as I could and heading straight for the bottom dresser drawer where the Gallo sherry resided under my sweaters. On the bed fully clothed. The nerves that had been listening for every sound from them, hoping for Stacy's steps coming up the stairs, gradually began not to give a damn, and I let the sherry seduce me into blankness. Just not think, turn off. Pass out.

I don't yet know what they said, how they got dinner, got to bed. The next morning Stacy brought me coffee in bed and hugged me. Neither of us said anything. I knew, in some way, it was only that she had been having fun. And then, too, I *had* been gone from her in one way or another a long time. But Cathy. Terror began to rise. I reached for the Gallo which tasted terrible. Cancelled classes and stayed in bed until time for Stacy to come home from school. For a couple of days I coped. We never did go to the zoo.

Repeat this scene any number of times. Except that when Cathy came over I went upstairs. And the coping got foggier. And the terror more intense.

I guess that's the climax. Or this: one morning that summer lying on the couch caught in the terror cycle. Staring into a cold fireplace, the winter ashes still not taken out. Stacy was just outside the door to the left of the fireplace on the screened porch teaching herself magic card tricks. I could see from the window across the room Cathy weeding the flower bed along her front walk. My husband was at the college teaching in summer session. I had a salty dog, very little grapefruit juice, propped on my chest. I was trying to break the terror cycle so that I could walk. I wasn't drunk. Just frozen. I wanted to go out to the backyard and cut the old-fashioned tea roses—one bush was actually orange—we had inherited from some flower loving faculty member at least twenty years back. I wanted to put them in a certain blue-grey salt glaze vase we'd gotten in Nashville, Tennessee, before Stacy was born. She loved flowers, I did too. We all did. This was the first year I hadn't helped her plant her own flower garden, her zinnias and nastursiums. I really *wanted* those roses on the teakwood table before lunch. But I couldn't move. The terror cycle is awful. It had grown familiar, become a daily battle. It's hard to describe. There's the ice in the belly. Then something rising up, constricting the throat, invading the brain, actually impairing eyesight. Rationality departs, you cannot think, the heart thuds, knees weaken. It's worse than that. It is, I suppose, a kind of reverse of that satisfying warm and soothing feeling of liquor going down the gullet to the belly, that hot *yes* that then spreads to the nerves, the head, and the consequent illusion of being unusually clear-headed, in control and at ease. It's a cycle because liquor helps immediately, thaws the ice and you can breathe. It must be like an adrenalin injection when you're choking with asthma, nitroglycerin for angina, morphine for the junkie—I don't know. It's a cycle because it doesn't last. The liquor wears off more and more quickly as the months pass, terror returns, even worse, requires more liquor. And so on. This morning I drained the salty dog and nothing happened. The ice was still right there. The gin bottle was on the rug beside me, I filled the glass, hands shaking so badly I splashed as much on the rug as into the glass, and drained it— nothing, no help, just out of my mind terrified. I threw the glass shattering into the fireplace and screamed, not from the brain, but from the ice in the belly and in a voice I couldn't recognize as mine, "Oh, god, I want to die!" I meant it.

Stacy came running in and there was *my* terror in *her* green eyes, "Mother, mother, don't curl your fingers like that. Mother please!"

I looked at the catatonic claws that were my hands still in the motion of throwing that glass. I looked at her terrified face. "Go get Cathy."

Denouement. More of the same cycle, but not the screaming. Stacy having nightmares, clearly uneasy when her father wasn't around. Psychiatrists, marriage counselors, even one comic, idiotic scene when my husband was in a committee meeting and Stacy was over at Cathy's, with the two over-rouged evangelical women from A.A. I thought they were cheap and contemptible. I still do.

I struggled to an understanding of my hang-ups from a broken-home childhood, my anger and resentment at being married to a man much brighter than I was and, more important, a better writer, my anger at myself for having given that man my mind, the humiliation when a colleague would ask what I thought about some fairly elementary literary matter and my complete loss: I have to go home and ask my husband what I think about Pound's contribution to Eliot's development as a poet. Anger at having given away the child I worshipped. Anger at having failed to do the writing I had always believed I had to do and wanted to do. A lot of anger. A lot of understanding. No good. Terror. And liquor the only help.

One week that summer my husband took Stacy to visit his parents. I was in no shape to go and didn't want to and even knew, dimly and reluctantly and heartbreakingly, Stacy's need to be away from me for a while. I, of course, promised him not to drink, that I'd get straightened out, etc., both of us knowing I was lying. The dog stayed with me.

For about an hour after the car pulled away from the curb, I felt a great calm. No fear. This is nice. I'll feed the dog. Dog bowl by kitchen cabinet containing blue-labeled vodka bottle, as you remember. So have a drink, a nice normal unterrified drink. Then do something pleasant, take a walk, pick the roses. Yeah.

Well, something new: the liquor triggered the terror. For three days I lived on valium from the first psychiatrist, thorazine from the second, and vodka. I forgot to feed the dog. Didn't eat myself, most of the time just plain forgetting to. When I remembered, I got nauseated. I remember noticing a white crinkled scum of mold on the surface of a pot of Scotch Barley soup on the stove, and vomiting in the kitchen sink.

I was afraid to sleep in my own bed. I slept in Stacy's which kept her own special sweet odor, trying, I think, to make some kind of hopeless contact with her. For some reason I read Graham Greene's

Complaisant Lover over and over, the print blurring, not remembering when I got to the end what I had read and so compulsively reading it over again. I must have read it twenty-five times.

Wandering the empty rooms, driving back roads, bottle in the passenger seat, getting lost and too scared to cry. For days I had been having convulsive stomach spasms and flushing of face and chest; it had happened from time to time before, and the doctors had never been able to explain it, but now it was constant. One night spasming on the couch, in the dark, staring at the spot where I knew the fireplace was, I had this sudden, kinesthetic, claustrophobic feeling: I cannot inhabit my own skin anymore, I've got to get out. How do you get out of your own skin? A drink to get to the telephone. "Cathy, can you come?" A drink while I waited. The last one.

The medical doctor, the specialist in alcoholism who'd been working with me, met us at the hospital. He was a big, fatherly, gentle, reassuring man. He put his arms around me, and I had the illusion, like that peaceful moment when my husband and child had driven away, that it was going to be o.k. My dignity was somewhat salvaged by the admitting diagnosis, acute gastritis. In the wheelchair, up the elevator, sitting limply on a chair by the door while nurses moved around doing something efficient. Cathy left. Dr. Berlan left. I needed a drink. Badly. My roommate was the typical fascinated-with-illness, tactless, fake commiserative type, "What's wrong with you, my dear?"

"I'm a goddamned alcoholic." Silence.

In bed, hooked up to the I.V., shot full of some kind of tranquilizer that's supposed to help. The silent, disapproving resident leaves. The nurses leave. The roomie goes to sleep. The panic returns in a rush, as bad as it's ever been. Worse. I jerk the I.V. needle from the vein, ring the bell. I've got to get out of here. I've got to get to Stacy. To the nurse when she comes, "This is a mistake, I have to get out of here." She takes one look, wheels around, and I hear them paging the resident. Another nurse comes in. We fight. I want out of that bed and she holds me down. I've *got* to get to Stacy. The woman in the next bed is praying for me. The resident comes in in a hurry. He is very angry and very rough. Informs me I could easily have died, have been very stupid, there are people really sick in this hospital, he will not tolerate such nonsense.

Something strange happens to time at this point. All at once I notice that there is an awful lot of blood on the sheets they are changing, that he is Philippino, that the needle has been reinserted, my arm strapped to a board, my feet tied to the foot of the bed, my cigarettes gone, the side rails up, and the roomie is moaning of pain and interrupted sleep while they jab a needle into my right buttock. I want a drink.

I must have slept. It is light. Dr. Berlan stands over me, a hand on my shoulder. He informs me gently that today will be the worst, that he'll give me shots for the withdrawal symptoms. He's right. The day is agony. The slightest movement on my part, the nurses', the roomie's scrapes, flays every raw nerve and they're all raw. I try now to think of some neat literary simile and fail. If the whole body and brain were a skinned knee and they poured on iodine, it wouldn't even come close. But the worst is the I.V. The eternity between each drop and I am hypnotized, have to watch, wait, beg that hanging drop to fall. Trying to force the level in the bottle to go down but can't perceive it, the way you can't perceive the hour hand on a clock move. I beg for shots, and the nurses get angry, and I'm beyond caring.

This goes on for three days. When my husband and Stacy come to get me, she brings me huge red and blue Mexican paper flowers. When Dr. Berlan dismisses me he explains about the metabolic process of the liver and antabuse, how I won't drink anymore now because I'm intelligent and understand that this will make me very, very ill, I'll feel absolutely lousy.

He's wrong. What woman in love ever was rational, when did intelligence ever win, over desire? He was right about the antabuse. You feel like hell. You think you're going to die.

Repeat the above scene, omitting the part about jerking the needle out, three times. Lovers are slow learners.

Then one day it's over. All over. The analogy applies. You just aren't in love anymore. It's gone flat, magic fled, the thrill is gone— all the sentimental pop songs are right. No will power involved at all. No strength of character. It's just all over, no magnetism there, nothing.

So that's the denouement. Of course I left my husband, left Stacy with him where she belongs. Some years have passed. She visits me and we have a good time. She's my best friend. I have a new dog. I go to drinking parties, me and my diet cola, and it's great fun. I'm in love again. With myself. With this pen on this page. With a poet I see from time to time, another writer better than I, but that's somehow irrelevant now. In love with my students. With this good life. I wake up feeling good, secret, excited. Who knows, this may be the day I write something good. I can't wait.

Lady wanted a story about a woman in love with a bottle. Wonder if this is it?

𝔥 𝔥 𝔥

PROTEUS

fiction by JUDITH HOOVER

from THE GEORGIA REVIEW

nominated by THE GEORGIA REVIEW *and John Gardner*

T HE CURTAIN FALLS, the house lights go up, and the performance is over. If the audience hesitates, if it takes just a few seconds for their attention to turn back to themselves, you have mastered them. If, in that hesitation, there is a jolting surprise and flash of unfocused anger, you have successfully deceived them, Stefan Mira: they will come back again and again but they will not forgive you.

Stefan takes the portrait of Madame Henriot and a self-portrait of Van Gogh with him to every new city, to every new hotel room; he believes he could not sleep if they were not constantly watching him, if, when he turned over in the strange bed and opened his eyes, he could not be assured of seeing them. He carries them himself, wrapped tightly in brown paper and bound with yellow string, and won't let the cabdrivers or the bellboys or the porters take them from him. On the train he buys two seats: one for himself, one for the paintings. The public applauds his eccentricities because he is a celebrity and a foreigner.

For the stage he uses the name "Proteus." He has awed his audiences by transforming his body into unthinkable shapes, by seeming to expand to the size of a giant and then squeezing into a child-sized coffin. He has changed his facial features to resemble any volunteer from the floor who will stand on the stage beside him, man, woman, or child, and has, at the end of each performance, appeared to melt like a warm wax doll into a puddle on the floor.

Now Stefan is sitting uncomfortably on a train leaving Pittsburgh. This is where his father had come, and looked, and then written his mother to tell her yes, there was work for him in America and yes, it was good work. This is where his mother had brought him and his sisters and the baby, crossing the Atlantic on the crowded deck of the *Kaiser Wilhelm*; the baby had died from exposure on the way. When they had arrived in Pittsburgh on the train from New York City and his mother saw the blackened buildings, streets, people, sky, and thinner, blackened husband she had refused to get off the train. His sisters had cried while Stefan and his silent father struggled with his mother, finally lifting her down the steps of the train onto the platform and holding her there until the train departed and she stopped fighting. She did not speak to her husband for the first two weeks of her life in America, did not look at him until he told her he would buy tickets for the train and boat home as soon as he made enough money. When he said this, sighing the soft Czech words and staring down at her brown shoes on the wooden floor, she took his hand and accepted America as prison and home. She died three years later, just after Stefan had finally persuaded her to let him teach her English.

The train follows the river outside of the city, into the farmland. Last night after the performance, when Stefan was reaching for his suit in the closet, he had uncovered the hiding place of a small boy. He had a thin, pointed face and black hair, and Stefan had not been surprised when the boy had asked in Czech for his autograph. He smiled and wrote "Proteus" on the wrinkled scrap of paper the boy offered him. It is not unusual for children to approach him with their notebooks, autograph books, or pieces of paper, but this was the first time any of them had gotten all the way into his dressing room without being seen by one of the guards. Stefan smiles again remembering the boy's shaking voice and frightened eyes; he hopes he did not disappoint the boy by showing himself capable of wearing a black suit and tie as easily as a stage costume. "You are the greatest magician in the world," the boy had said in Czech. "I am not a magician," Stefan answered in English, but the expression of the boy's face did not change; he did not understand the language.

Stefan had led the boy from his dressing room through the maze of two-dimensional props and rows of hanging costumes as far as the stage. From there he had pointed the way out. He never enters the stage after a performance; he never looks past the thick, dark curtain after a show. Once in the early part of his career he had gone back to talk to one of the directors who had summoned him, just after he had removed his makeup. In what had become instinct he had turned at center stage to face the audience—the silence—the darkness—the rows and rows and two balconies of empty seats—the loss of his audience—the recognition that people came to see him perform, or did not see him at all. . . . He had begun moving backwards, his hands reaching behind him until they touched the folds of the heavy, immobile curtain, then ran to his dressing room, paced from closet to mirror to closet and because he needed to do something and because he could think of nothing to do he had begun reapplying his makeup.

From his window he can see lines of wire fence surrounding farms of white barns and white farmhouses. He measures the speed of the train by how solid the blur of wire looks, the blur closest to the tracks. His father had promised his mother he would quit the mill and buy a farm as soon as he made enough money. Yes, yes, she had nodded, her long brown arms stretching wet clothes across a line: I will wait. She had always allowed her husband his dreams; he came home from the steel mill with his matchbook opportunities—excited, planning, promising—waving his blistered hands in the air as if conjuring dreams into existence. At least once a week he swore to quit his job after the next paycheck. They would have a farm, he would buy a store, he would become a salesman and wear a new gray suit, he and Stefan would start a newspaper for the Slavs who couldn't, or wouldn't, read the American papers, he and Stefan would build a shop and make and sell furniture, he and Stefan would join a construction company and in a year buy their own machinery and start their own company.

Young Stefan accepted each new dream as though the preceding ones had never been mentioned, had never been heard. He was willing to wonder at these untouchable lives without expectation of more than that wonder. He had learned to watch his mother's face for the degree of possibility of each scheme his father presented to her; when she sat back and nodded silently, her most common signal, he knew he could accept without hope, without disappointment.

The cows are lying down in the fields: it will rain soon. Even that is not magic, Stefan thinks. Hopefully the rain is coming from the west, behind the train; hopefully the train is the faster. He closes his eyes, attempts to be more comfortable in the seat but fails, looks up quickly at the brown-covered paintings across from him, then sleeps.

"You are the greatest magician in the world," a small boy is telling him, repeating it louder and louder. "You are, I know you are." But he is speaking English and Stefan cannot understand him, though he knows by the wonder on the boy's face what he must be saying. He thinks he must be the boy's father because they are in the yellow kitchen of the old house outside of Pittsburgh, or the kitchen of the older house in Moravia. He sees a woman in the corner whom he does not recognize but knows she is his wife; both wife and son have thin, pointed faces and black hair and Stefan realizes that they resemble him, and then that they are mocking him, putting their hands on their hips at the same moment he does, both copying his expression of annoyance at what the boy is saying. "I told you never to say that in this house," he reprimands the boy, and wife and son echo his Czech statement with an English one. Stefan turns to run out the door but finds he can only move very slowly, his feet almost too heavy to lift, and he panics at the way he must strain to pull them from the floor. He looks up quickly and sees his wife and son are in front of him again, sees that he has not been able to turn away from them, that he has been trying to run towards them and not out the door at all. The woman now is putting on some sort of mask; when she has fit it to her face Stefan sees that it is a mask of Madame Henriot, but there are holes for eyes and mouth and the woman's own are showing through, making Madame look malicious instead of beautiful. Stefan watches the boy raise his hand to his ear, sees him laughing at him now while his eyes are still large with wonder. He tries to look down or away or to close his eyes but he cannot and he tries to stop the terrible slow running but he has no control and he sees his son has a knife in his hand and is beginning to saw off his ear and Stefan tries to tell him to stop but cannot open his mouth and just as he reaches them just as he is about to touch them he sees that they are no longer there and he is holding his own bleeding ear in one hand and falls slowly down trying to tear the mask of Madame Henriot from his own face. But it only grows tighter, pressing into his skin; there is no hole for the mouth for him to breathe and he is choking, the mask burying itself into his face.

The jerk of the steel brakes wakes him. Looking out his window he sees a wooden platform without shelter and a man standing alone in the rain. The engine slows down just enough for the man to step aboard, the whistle screams, and the train moves on.

Stefan is wiping the sweat from his forehead with a white handkerchief when the conductor opens the door of his compartment and ushers the man in. He does not look at Stefan but hands the conductor his ticket and takes the seat next to the paintings. The brim of his wet hat hides his forehead and eyes; he leans back into the seat and appears to be trying to sleep.

The appearance of the man disturbs Stefan; a musty smell has begun to fill the compartment and the windows are becoming frosted with steam. Stefan can see no part of the man's body which is not covered by clothing, even his hands are curled in gray gloves. Puddles are forming around the black shoes and drops of water drip rhythmically from the wide brim of the hat onto his chest and lap. There seems to be enough water soaked into the man to flood the entire compartment, the train itself.

Closing his eyes, Stefan tries to sleep again. His dreams do not frighten him because he can never remember them, though he has had this same one, with variations, many times. But the presence of this new passenger with his warm smell of soaking clothes and skin makes Stefan uneasy, afraid to close his eyes before the man.

"You are the magician Proteus, aren't you?"

His voice is deep and rumbling, and he does not look up at Stefan. The water is still dripping from his hat.

"I . . . yes. But I have never been billed as a magician."

The new passenger seems undisturbed by the last remark, though

Stefan has found people are usually aroused to question or deny it. He still does not move, and is silent for a while. Opposite him Stefan shifts his position to stare out the window, after waiting expectantly for the man to ask or say more. The rush of the fields outside makes him dizzy, his eyes tired, and he must constantly wipe the window clear of steam.

There is a movement, and Stefan's eyes are jerked from the wet fields to watch the shoes of the new passenger scrape back beneath the wooden seat, the knees pull slowly back towards the folds of the jacket, the back unbend and extend from waist to chest, the shoulders spread, the neck uncurl, and chin stretch into the air. Now the movement is stopped, or held back; there are seconds of hesitation, Stefan holding his breath, when the new passenger finally releases a long sigh of whistling air and the movement flows down from chin to shoes to refold his body like a wave receding.

He lifts his head and slowly opens his eyes, eyes yellow and large, the whites a lighter, dirtier shade of yellow, as if bruised.

"I have seen many of your performances." He speaks slowly; Stefan is staring back at the eyes which stare into his, does not even notice the mouth moving, the nose or the shape of the face.

"I have had occasion to be in many cities at times when you were on the stage. Oh yes, I have been a member of, I would think, most of your audiences. A salesman: I'm a travelling salesman." Here the man pats the brown suitcase on the floor between his legs, but Stefan does not look down, will not look away; he is relaxed staring into the yellow eyes, and the man calmly returns the look.

"Watches: wristwatches, pocketwatches, watches on ornamental pins for ladies, watches with compasses on the back, any type and style of small timepiece you can imagine. I like to claim that my motto is *I sell Time*. Not such an inaccurate statement, I think. These watches do, to some degree, encapsulate Time, don't you think? Contain it? And, in a sense, they give a form to Time: a body, if you will. A man who owns such a thing might be able to persuade himself that he controls Time—winding or refusing to wind the mechanism as he chooses."

As he speaks, the man feels for his suitcase again, and raises it to his lap; he reaches into a pocket of his wrinkled jacket and brings out a single key. With his last statement he opens the suitcase and presents its contents to Stefan, who blinks his eyes and looks down.

There is a cacophony of syncopated, disharmonious ticking as the lid is raised and at least a hundred timepieces are visible to him. Gold and silver flash even in the dim sunlight coming in the window, gold and silver chain and ornament sparkle like the pirate booty of a treasure chest.

"Hm, yes: I sell Time," the man says proudly, watching the expression on Stefan's face change from amazement to interest to the look of a man captured and seduced by an enemy. He closes and locks the suitcase, then places it on the floor between his legs.

The steam whistle blows loudly and the brakes begin to scrape against the iron wheels; peering out the window to left then to right, the new passenger grabs the handle of his suitcase and opens the door of the compartment.

"Well, my stop here," he says, speaking rapidly, sharply now. "You're probably going on to the city: Philadelphia? New York? South to Washington? I'll be in each of those places before two weeks are over. We'll meet again, Mr. Proteus; no doubt of that, no doubt of that." The door slides shut and Stefan hears the squelching sound of the wet shoes hurry down the corridor. He clears a small space of the steamy window and waits for the man to step from the train to the platform, but when the machine moves forward again no one has jumped off. He watches for a long time after the platform is out of sight, then decides that the man must have left from the other side of the train. This stop was like the last one, where the new passenger had boarded: a single raised platform without shelter, a dirt road disappearing into the fields of corn or hay, no city or town visible from the tracks.

From nowhere into nowhere is no place of business for a travelling salesman, Stefan says to himself. The window is defogging by itself now; the warm, wet smell becomes less noticeable.

A parade? What makes me think of a parade?

The image in Stefan's memory becomes clearer and stronger as he stares at the steam-muted windows, and just as his hand touches the pane to wipe it clear the image snaps sharp and he remembers.

He remembers that he was standing in the kitchen in the old house, his mother was cooking, and because there was a great noise of bells, band music, laughing, and shouting he was wiping the steam from the kitchen windows to look outside. His mother scolded him for smearing the windows she'd have to wash—no, he'd have to wash them, he'd smeared them—before the guests came to supper.

"What would they think, our only friends in America?" his mother had asked him, biting down on the foreign word "America."

He remembers next that he was outside and that his father was with him, explaining what a parade was by saying "There's a circus at the far end of it, past the Post Office," and then explaining what a circus was by saying "where the parade stops."

And then he was at the circus past the Post Office, seeing so many things that had to be explained but weren't; his father dashed straight to a small purple tent with silver stars and moons sews onto it, and they went in: "to see the future," his father said. They entered the purple tent with only one candle on a round table in the center when it needed at least five streetlamps, he thought, in a row inside that tent, because that old woman sitting at that round table looked like someone he would want to be able to see clearly, someone whose every move he would want to be able to watch carefully.

He stood behind his father, who sat down at the table opposite the old woman, and over his father's shoulder watched her squinting at them both. His father reached out his hand and she grabbed it—Stefan jumped forward against the table to grab it back from her, but his father caught him and said that it was all right, that this was how she was going to tell him the future. Stefan ran out of the tent.

He turns his head from the window and looks at the two paintings covered in brown paper on the seat across from him. "I am not a magician," he says aloud.

What I do is not trickery, or deceit: it is pure physical ability. I have never performed a "stunt": what I do is the result of . . . not triumph over the limitations of the body, but the discovery that there are no limitations. I have expanded my body to the height of a man two feet taller than me, I have contracted my muscles until I am the size of a nine-year-old. And I do not yet know the limitations: how much taller or smaller I am capable of teaching myself to become.

Yes: teaching. The body must learn that it is not restricted, it is not imprisoned within the dimensions of tape measure or yardstick. How do I know that I cannot teach my body to become larger than this Pullman compartment? If I try and cannot, it is because I have failed, not because it is impossible.

There is no "gift of magic" in this: it is talent, it is skill. It is a triumph over space if they insist on billing it as a "triumph" over anything. . . . And time . . . it is a triumph over time as well. Because I have given it form.

A porter slides open the door of Stefan's compartment and announces that the dining car is now serving lunch.

A parade of passengers begins a clumsy, bumping march down the aisle toward the dining car. As it moves past Stefan's compartment individual faces peer in at him now sitting alone: a careless, automatic curiosity, thinks Stefan, watching them. Just as they will carelessly, automatically grow old: thoughtlessly resigned to process. None of them will ever wake up one morning, none of them, to find to their astonished discomfort that they have become much older than they believed they had. There will be no privilege of surprise allowed them.

I will not wait to be changed.

Moving along with that monotonous march of the passengers is a man who smiles and tips his still-dripping-wet hat to Stefan as he is pushed past the compartment. Stefan jumps up and shouts "Wait!" but the forward motion of the line of bodies has already carried the salesman far down the aisle. Sliding open the compartment door Stefan tries to step out and squeeze into the line, but is pushed back and aside by arms and voices yelling. He keeps his eye on the familiar hat floating fast to the front of the car and finally pushes himself out into the aisle; finding no room to get past anyone in front of him, he can only wait until the open space of the dining car allows him to search for the man there.

The dining car is crowded with passengers in gaudy holiday outfits or wrinkled travelling clothes, who shout in auctioneer voices for their lunches, who fight for a cup of muddy coffee. Stefan scans each face, but the salesman is not there; he retraces his steps down the aisle, emptied now, looking through the glass of each compartment, but the salesman is not in any of them. He returns to his own compartment, to his uncomfortable seat, and stares at the brown-covered paintings until, exhausted but resisting calm, he falls asleep.

The man carries his suitcase filled with Time across the sand to the edge of the ocean, and stands. It is dusk, the horizon is swallowing the sun, and the tide is pulling the sand from under his shoes, already and always heavy with warm saltwater. His jacket is wrinkled across his bent shoulders, the weight of the suitcase stretches the fingers of one gray glove, the brim of his hat curls limply over his forehead. Slipping with the sand, he sighs and lifts his head, and steps slowly into the water until the bottom of the suitcase in his hand is gliding heavily along the tops of the waves.

As he walks farther and farther into the water the waves swell and crash higher and higher onto the sand, as if there is barely enough space in the ocean to easily contain the weight of the tired god's body, and its age, or as if his return has stirred a boundless ecstasy.

QUINNAPOXET

by STANLEY KUNITZ

from ANTAEUS

nominated by Tess Gallagher

I was fishing in the abandoned reservoir
back in Quinnapoxet,
where the snapping turtles cruised
and the bullheads swayed
in their bower of tree-stumps,
sleek as eels and pigeon-fat.
One of them gashed my thumb
with a flick of his razor fin
when I yanked the barb
out of his gullet.
The sun hung its terrible coals
over Buteau's farm: I saw
the treetops seething.

They came suddenly into view
on the Indian road,
evenly stepping
past the apple orchard,
commingling with the dust
they raised, their cloud of being,
against the dripping light
looming larger and bolder.
She was wearing a mourning bonnet
and a wrap of shining taffeta.
"Why don't you write?" she cried
from the folds of her veil.
"We never hear from you."
I had nothing to say to her.

But for him who walked behind her
in his dark worsted suit,
with his face averted
as if to hide a scald,
deep in his other life,
I touched my forehead
with my swollen thumb
and splayed my fingers out—
in deaf-mute country
the sign for father.

THINGS THAT HAPPEN WHERE THERE AREN'T ANY PEOPLE

by WILLIAM STAFFORD

from WESTERN HUMANITIES REVIEW

nominated by WESTERN HUMANITIES REVIEW, *Grace Schulman and Laura Jensen*

It's cold on Lakeside Road
with no one traveling. At its turn
on the hill an old sign sags and
finally goes down. The traveler rain
walks back and forth over its victim
flat on the mud.

You don't have to have any people when
sunlight stands on the rocks or gloom
comes following the great dragged clouds
over a huddle of hills. Plenty of
things happen in deserted places, maybe
dust counting millions of its little worlds
or the slow arrival of deep dark.

And out there in the country a rock has been
waiting to be mentioned for thousands of years.
Every day its shadow leans, crouches,
then walks away eastward in one measured stride
exactly right for its way of being. To reach
for that rock we have the same reasons
that explorers always have for their journeys:
because it is far, because there aren't any people.

🔥 🔥 🔥

LECHERY

fiction by JAYNE ANNE PHILLIPS

from PERSEA: AN INTERNATIONAL REVIEW

nominated by PERSEA: AN INTERNATIONAL REVIEW, Wesley Brown, DeWitt Henry and Seymour Lawrence

THOUGH I HAVE NO MONEY I must give myself what I need. Yes I know which lovers to call when the police have caught me peddling pictures, the store detectives twisting my wrists pull stockings out of my sleeves. And the butchers pummel the small of my back to dislodge their wrapped hocks; white bone and marbled tendon exposed as the paper tears and they push me against the wall. They curse me, I call my lovers. I'm nearly fifteen, my lovers get older and older. I know which ones will look at me delightedly, pay my bail, take me home to warm whiskey and bed. I might stay with them all day; I might run as the doors of their big cars swing open. Even as I run I can hear them behind me, laughing.

I go down by the schools with my pictures. The little boys smoke cigarettes, they're girlish as faggots, they try to act tough. Their Camels are wrinkled from pockets, a little chewed. I imagine them wet and stained pinkish at the tips, pink from their pouty lips. The boys have tight little chests, I see hard nipples in their t-shirts. Lines of smooth stomach, little penis tucked into jockey briefs. Already they're growing shaggy hair and quirky curves around their smiles. But no acne, I get them before they get pimples, I get them those first few times the eyes flutter and get strange. I show them what I do. Five or six surround me, jingling coins, tapping toes in tennis shoes. I know they've got some grade-school basketball coach, some ex-jock with a beer gut and a hard-on under his sweat pants in the locker room; that kills me. They come closer. I'm watching the ridged toes of their shoes. Now I do it with my eyes, I look up and pick the one I want. I tell him to collect the money and meet me at lunch in a park across the street, in a culvert, in a soft ditch, in a car parked under a bridge or somewhere shaded. Maybe I show them a few pills. One picture; blowsy redhead with a young blond girl, the girl a kneeling eunuch on white knees. The redhead has good legs, her muscles stand out tensed and she comes standing up. I tell them about it. Did you ever come standing up. I ask them, they shift their eyes at each other. I know they've been in blankets in dark bedrooms, see who can beat off first. Slapping sounds and a dry urge. But they don't understand their soft little cocks all stiff when they wake up in daylight, how the bed can float around.

So at noon I wait for them. I don't smoke, it's filthy. I suck a smooth pebble and wait. I've brushed my teeth in a gas station. I press my lips with my teeth and suck them, make them soft. Press dots of oil to my neck, my hand. Ambergris or musk between my breasts, down in the shadowed place where hair starts in a line at my groin. Maybe I brush my hair. I let them see me do it, open a compact and tongue my lips real slow. They only see the soft tip of my tongue, I pretend it's not for them.

Usually just one of them comes, the one I chose, with a friend waiting out of sight where he can see us. If they came alone I can tell by looking at them. Sometimes they are high on something, I don't mind. Maybe I have them in an abandoned car down in a back lot, blankets on the seat or no back seat but an old mattress. Back windows covered up with paper sacks and speckled mud, sun through dirty windows or brown paper makes the light all patterns.

He is nervous. Right away he holds out the money. Or he is a little mean, he punches at me with his childish fist. A fine blond boy with a sweet neck and thin collar bones arched out like wings, or someone freckled whose ashen hair falls loose. A dark boy, thick lashes and cropped wooled hair, rose lips full and swelling a little in the darkened car. I give him a little whiskey, I rifle through the pictures and pretend to arrange them. I take a drink too, joke with him. This is my favorite time; he leans back against the seat with something like sleep in his eyes, I stroke his hard thighs, his chest, I comfort him.

I put the pictures beside us, some of them are smaller than post cards. We put our faces close to see them. A blond girl, a black girl, they like to see the girls. One bending back droops her white hair while the other arches over, holds her at the waist, puts her mouth to a breast so small only the nipple stands up. In the picture her mouth moves in and out, anyone can tell. A black hand nearly touching pale pubic hair, a forefinger almost tender curls just so, moves toward a slit barely visible just below the pelvic bone. I don't like pictures of shaven girls, it scares them to see so much. It makes them disappear.

I do things they've never seen, I could let them touch but no. I arrange their hands and feet, keep them here forever. Sometimes they tell me stories, they keep talking of baseball games and vicious battles with their friends. Lips pouty and soft, eyes a hard glass glitter. They lose the words and mumble like babies; I hold them just so, just tight, I sing the oldest songs. At times their smooth faces seem to grow smaller and smaller in my vision. I concentrate on their necks, their shoulders. Loosen their clothes and knead their scalps, pinching hard at the base of the head. Maybe that boy with dark hair and Spanish skin, his eyes flutter, I pull him across my legs and open his shirt. Push his pants down to just above his knees so his thin thighs and smooth cock are exposed; our breathing is wavy and thick, we make a sound like music. He can't move his legs but stiffens in my lap, palms of his hands turned up. In a moment he will roll his eyes and come. I'll gently force my coated fingers into his mouth. I'll take off my shirt and rub my slick palms around my breasts until the nipples stand up hard and frothy. I force his mouth to them. I move my hand to the tight secret place between his buttocks. Sometimes they get tears in their eyes.

In the foster homes they used to give me dolls and I played the church game. At first I waited till everyone left the house. Then it didn't matter who was around. I lined up all the dolls on the couch, I sat them one after the other. They were ugly, most of them had no clothes or backwards arms. They were dolls from the trash, the Salvation Army at Christmas, junk sale dolls. One of them was in a fire. The plastic hand was missing, melted into a bubbled fountain dribbling in nubs down the arm. I lined them up, I made them quiet. We faced the front of the room. I made us sit for hours unmoving, listening to nothing at all and watching someone preach.

Uncle Wumpy gave me a doll. They call him that. Like his pocked face had rabbits ears and soft grey flesh. His face is pitted with tiny scars, his skin is flushed. We won at the carnival; cowboy hats, a rubber six-gun, a stuffed leopard with green diamond eyes for Kitty. We were on our way out between booths and machines, sawdust sticky with old candy and beer, to pick Kitty up at work. We passed the duck-shoot. Wumpy was so drunk I had to help him with the gun and we drowned them all. Little yellow ducks with flipped up tail feathers and no eyeballs; they glided by hooked to a string. We hit them, knocked them back with a snap like something breaking. We hit twelve; the whole group popped up, started gliding by again as eyeless as before. So we kept shooting and shooting. . . . The barker came out from behind the counter with his fat long-ashed cigar. He held it pinched in two fingers like something dirty he respected. Then he sucked on it and took the gun away. The crowd behind us mumbled. He thrust the doll into my arms. She was nearly three feet tall, pearl earrings, patent heels. Long white dress and a veil fastened with a clear plastic bird. I took the bird, lit it with Wumpy's lighter. Its neck melted down to a curve that held its flat head molded to its wings. I liked to keep the bird where no one saw it. Finally I buried it in a hole, I took it to a place I knew I'd forget.

How I found Wumpy. I was twelve, I lived with Minnie. She made me work in the luncheonette, swab formica tables with a rag. Bend over to wipe the aluminum legs, clotted ketchup. By the grill her frozen french fries thawed out limp and fishy. She threw them in sooty fat; they fizzled and jumped and came out shining. Her old face squinched like a rat's, she was forty. Wore thick glasses and a red handkerchief on her head, liked the gospel shows turned up loud. One hand was twisted. She had the arthritis, the rheumatism, the corns, the bunions on her knotted toes as she walked to the shower at home. Hunched in her long robe she fixed her eyes on the bathroom door. Scuttled clinching herself at the waist and slammed the door.

After school I walked to the restaurant and helped her clear tables till seven. She cursed the miners under her breath. Slapped my butt if I was slow, moved her hard hand, its big twisted knuckles. Grabbed the curved of my ass and squeezed.

Wumpy came in every night for coffee, he cut brush for the State Road Commission. Watched Minnie and me. Kitty started coming in with him. Cellophane baggie full of white crosses, cheap speed. She'd order a pepsi, take a few pills, grind a few more to power on the tabletop. She winked, gave me hair ribbons, said she'd like to take me to the movies. Wumpy told Minnie I needed some clothes, he and Kitty would take me to Pittsburgh and buy me some dresses. They gave her thirty dollars.

In the motel I stood in the bathroom and vomited. Soapers floated in the bowl, clumps of white undissolved powder in a clear mucus. I puked so easy again and again, I almost laughed. Then they came in naked and took off my clothes. I couldn't stand up, they carried me to the bed. Wumpy got behind her and fucked her, she kept saying words but I couldn't keep my eyes open. She pulled me down. She said Honey Honey. In the bottom of something dark I rocked and rocked. His big arms put me there until he lifted me. Lifted me held my hips in the air and I felt her mouth on my legs, I felt bigger and bigger. The ceiling spun around like the lights at the Care Center spun in the dark halls when I woke up at night. Then a tight muscular flash, I curled up and hugged myself.

I stood by the window and fingered the flimsy curtains. I watched them sleeping, I didn't leave. I watched Wumpy's broad back rising and falling.

Wumpy would never do it to me, he gave me pictures to sell. I wanted to give him the money, he laughed at me. He had little stars in the flesh of his hands. He took me to bars. We took a man to some motel, Wumpy said he always had to watch. . . . stood by the bed while I choked and gagged a little, salt exploding in my throat.

The dream is here. It is here again and again. Natalie made the dream. I slept with her when I was eight, six months we slept together. She whimpered at night, she wet the bed. Both of us wards of the state, they got money for us. Cold in the bedroom, she wrapping her skinny arms around my chest. Asking can she look at me. But I fall asleep, I won't take off my clothes in bed with her. I fall asleep and the same dream comes.

Natalie is standing in the sand. Behind her ocean spills over, the waves have thick black edges. Natalie in her shredded slip, knobby knees, her pale blue eyes all watery. Natalie standing still as a dead thing spreads her legs and holds herself with her hand. Her fingers groping, her white face. She squeezes and pulls so hard she bleeds. She calls for help. She wants me. Faces all around us, big faces just teeth and lips to hold me down for Natalie. Natalie on top of me. Natalie pressing down. Her watery eyes say nothing. She sighs with pleasure and her hot urine boils all around us.

I remember like this: Natalie watches me all the time. They're gone all day, we stay alone with the silent baby. Once there's no food but a box of salt. Bright blue box, the silver spout pops out. The girl with the umbrella dimples and swings her pony tails, flashes her white skin. I can eat it Natalie. I can eat it all. She looks out the window at the snow. I know she's scared. I sit down on the floor at her feet. The box is round like a tom-tom, I tip it up. Salt comes in my mouth so fast, fills me up but I can't quit pouring it . . . I start to strangle but Natalie won't look, she screams and screams. She kicks at me with her bare blue feet, the box flies across the room throwing fans of salt. When it gets dark, salt gleams on the floor with a strange cool light. Natalie stays in her chair without moving and I get to sleep alone.

I got lavish cards at the Care Center, I think a jokester sent them. To Daughter from Mother At Christmas, scrolls of stand up gold and velvet pointsettias. I used to think about the janitors, those high-school boys with smirky eyes and beer breath, licking the envelopes. . . . somehow mailing them from Wichita or Tucson. The agency moved me from home to home. Holidays I spent at the Center, they did paper work to place me again. Every time there was a different pasty-faced boy with ragged nails, dragging a dun-colored mop. The cards came, they were never quite right. When I was ten. For Baby's First Christmas—a fold-out hobby horse, a mommy with blond hair and popped eyes. I was seven, the card said Debutante in raised silver script, showed a girl in mink and heels. After I started getting arrested the psychiatrist told them to hold my mail. They said I might go to an asylum.

Baby Girl Approximately 14 Months Abandoned December 1960. Diagnosed as Mute. But when I was three I made sounds like trucks and wasps, I screamed and sang. They think I'm crazy, this is what happens.

I like to lock the bathroom door late at night. Stand in front of the mirrors, hold a candle under my chin. Stare at my shadowed face and see the white shape of a skull. I lay down on the cold tile floor and do it to myself by the stalls. I do it. I lay on my stomach. Hold my breath, riding on the heels of my hands I'm blind; I feel the hush hush of water pipes through the floor. Ride up over a hump into the heat the jangling it holds me. When I opened my eyes and roll over, the ceiling is very high it is the color of bone, lamplight through the barred windows. I make myself good I do it. Lay on the cold floor, its tiny geometric blocks. My skin goes white as porcelain, I'm big as the old sinks and toilets, the empty white tubs. White glass, marble, rock, old pipes bubbling air. When those white streaks flash in my vision I run here. I watch her. I know she is me. She runs from stall to stall flushing toilets, she does it again and again. Slushing water louder and louder, then high-pitched wail of the tanks filling. Crash and wail. I crouch on the floor and listen. I don't let anyone in.

I think Natalie is dead, she said she would die when she was twelve. But only then. In August under trees we sat heaving rocks. She buried her feet in sand and said she was a stone. I could pinch her till my nails rimmed with red; if she didn't cry out I had to do what she said. She wanted to play house again: I'm a house I'm a giant house. Crawl through my legs Its the door. And she heaved herself onto my back, cupped my chin in her hands. Pulled my head back to see her face above me. She stroked my throat, pointed her pink tongue in my ear and hissed. Shhhh. Hissing. Shhhhhh. Purring breathing deep in her belly. She pretended her voice was a man. I love you You're mine Eat your food. And I licked her hand all over, up and down between her fingers.

Once the man came after us. We were in the shed behind the house. Natalie liked that room with the tools and jugs, rusted rakes, wood in splintered piles and the squeaking rats. She took off her clothes, draped them on random nails to make an armless girl. A man's big black boots swallowed her ankles. She white and hairless, jingling the metal clasps. Natalie laughing and laughing. We held the blunt nosed hammers, we threw them hard. Indented circles on the floor, piles of circles pressing down in the old wood like invisible coins. Natalie said we made money. More and more, on the wall, on the floor. Natalie at the windows crashing, glass in glittered piles on her shiny black rubber boots.

He opens the creaky door. What the hell are you doing. I hide by the work bench, back in the webs and spiders. The unbuckling, quick snaky swish of his belt against his pants. He catches her, throws her over the work bench. Natalie gets quiet, the big boots fall off her feet. Her feet almost have faces, dangling, alabaster, by my face; her thin white legs hanging. Slaps of the belt and drawn-out breathing. You little bitch. He takes a penny and throws it to shadows in the dust. She knows She always knows She finds it. Handfuls of clattering coins. Natalie walks in her goose-pimpled skin, makes a pile of copper pennies by his shoes. He pushes her down on her knees. Natalie is laughing just a little. I see his back, his wide hips, the green work pants. Touch it, he says, Natalie says she can't, her hands are poison.

I'm pure, driven snow. I clean the house, make soup from a can. Wumpy drinks a beer. Squeezes cans till they buckle and fold, throws them in a corner. I want to touch him, squeeze him hard; he closes his eyes to make sounds in his scratchy voice. If I take off my shirt he hits me. Kitty hugs me. My Baby. She wants me to do what she wants. Wumpy does what she says. More and more, she wants what I want. We move around on the checkerboard floor.

Kitty is on probation. We give her lots of coffee and get her walking. Every Saturday the parole officer wants her to talk. Maybe she scores, comes back with smack in an envelope. Darker and darker, snow feathers down to wrap us up. Kitty nods out on the window sill, curls up like a dormer mouse in her bulky red coat. She likes to lean out almost too far. Wumpy: I watch him through a lopsided hole in the bathroom door, he wants to be alone. Ties off, bulges a vein to hit. Hums and sighs. Pipes make watery yawns and wheezes, they come together in the tunneled walls. It's so quiet I hear the click of the neon sign before it changes and throws a splattered word across the floor. Rooms it says, blue Rooms. When I see someone move I'm afraid; If Natalie weren't dead she would find me.

ὰ ὰ ὰ

CIVILIZATION AND ISOLATION

by VINE DELORIA

from THE NORTH AMERICAN REVIEW

nominated by Carolyn Forché

"Men can be provincial in time, as well as in place," Alfred North Whitehead once remarked. When we apply this insight to the realm of human knowledge, quite frequently we refer to the non-western peoples and point out that they have failed to keep pace with the technical developments that other peoples, particularly western peoples, have made. Thus non-western societies are considered by many social scientists as remnants of stages of human evolutionary growth struggling to reach levels of sophistication that were achieved and surpassed by Europeans many centuries ago. Rarely is the question of provinciality applied directly to western European peoples, and on those occasions we find that provinciality is applied as a criterion to determine efficiency and sophistication within the worldview of that tradition.

Provinciality, however, is a characteristic of societies and individuals who fail to conduct periodic critiques of their beliefs and who assume, with some degree of smugness, that the knowledge they possess, because it has been their possession for so long, provides the basis for intelligent existence in a world of sudden and unexpected change. Western Europeans have been so much dazzled by their own technology that they have fallen into a provinciality in regard to human knowledge so narrow as to exclude major portions of human experience. Whitehead called this attitude the "fallacy of misplaced concreteness," and he meant by this the exclusionary approach to the physical world coupled with the belief that whatever approach one did use properly excluded things that have no value.

When Native Americans have been forced to confront this attitude on the part of non-Indian neighbors we have generally come off second best. A good many factors must be included in any analysis of our failure to confront and overcome the attitude of superiority which non-Indians have thrust upon us. The most important factor would probably be the efficiency of technology which non-Indians brought with them. Marvelous instruments and tools of iron and other metals blinded us and produced an uncritical assumption that whatever the white man was doing must be based upon some superior insight into the world of nature. We forgot, to our detriment, that the first Europeans we encountered thought they were going to sail over the edge of the world, that succeeding expeditions had fantasies about Fountains of Youth, Cities of Gold, and northwest passages to Cathay.

Native Americans did not realize that Europeans felt a dreadful necessity to classify us within a view of the world already made obsolete by discovery of our continent. While we could not participate in the heated theological discussions concerning our origins —whether we derived from Noah's Ark or were survivors of the Ten Lost Tribes of Israel—we perhaps could have been more insistent on making the non-Indians provide more and better arguments for their version of world history and human knowledge. Any group that frantically dug gold in the west in order to transplant it to the east and bury it cannot be quite right and their insights cannot form the highest achievement of our species.

The world is much more sophisticated today, and groups of widely varying backgrounds can communicate with each other even though they form the minority of particular societies. Thus the modern emergence of Indian peoples and the concentration by them on revival and revitalization of culture should include a persistent emphasis on the validity of their own histories, technologies, and social and political institutions. In some measure Indian groups have already begun this process of defending and justifying cultural insights tribes have preserved over the centuries of contact with Europeans. Unfortunately, much of this activity has been phrased in an anti-white format which does not produce a justification of the Indian tradition but merely points out the inadequacies of the non-Indians. We do not take time to adapt this approach to the problem. One glance at the western democracies and we discover that the political leaders, when they are not lusting in their hearts after forbidden fruit, are demonstrating that intelligent life probably does not exist on the planet or, in the alternative, are planning ways to extinguish whatever intelligent life might accidentally arise here.

Transcending this childish tactic of accusatory relationship with the non-Indian is not difficult but it involves creating or re-creating a confidence in the Indian traditions. Such a task initially involves a determination of the techniques which Indians used to accumulate, evaluate, and perpetuate their knowledge of the world and to translate this knowledge into western terms that can speak rationally and intelligently to those people within the western cultural milieu who are prepared to listen. That is a lot of "lates," but above all it is not *too* late. So I will attempt to outline the variances which I see between the western European traditions and the Indian traditions, primarily the North American peoples, with the hopes that the differences —and there are radical differences to be seen—will be illustrated so clearly as to enable us to embark on a new interpretation of human knowledge which is not provincial in either time or space.

If I were to choose the single attribute that characterizes the western approach to human knowledge, indeed to almost all human activities, I would unhesitantly choose "isolation." In scientific and philosophical terms we are perhaps speaking of William of Occam and his famous razor which has cut the throat of more than one effort to synthesize human knowledge. Briefly, we can rephrase this doctrine as the belief that by continual subdivision of any problem we can reach a certain and ultimate knowledge. For most of the last couple centuries the scientific concern with finding the tiniest element of the atom demonstrated the potency of this belief. It also, incidentally, illustrated the basic western belief in the primacy of matter over spirit. But isolation remains the dominating attitude which western peoples have adopted toward the world. We see this approach eloquently in our political institutions and the assumption that one human being is interchangeable with another and that the conglomerate of human decisions, counted statistically, produces the proper course of action for a nation to adopt. This belief reduces wisdom to public opinion polls and produces those nasty and distasteful compromises which substitute for intelligent activities in most of the western democracies.

We find additional confirmation of this belief in isolation in the various religious traditions that are characteristic of western peoples. Almost always, in the last analyses, we find the solitary individual in the hands of an angry, or at least disgruntled, god. Even those western peoples who have rejected the traditional religious denominations of their culture have not found another approach to the religious question but have simply adopted the Oriental version of solitude, listening to one hand clapping, and other symbolic gestures, and are now contentedly recycling their own energies endlessly. Even the atheists and humanists ground their justifications in the primacy of the individual rather than the maturity of the species.

One reason for the scientific and philosophical isolation of the elements of experience is the belief, deeply held although rarely practiced, that one cannot trust sense perceptions, human emotions, or the intuitional abilities of the human personality. This article of faith must certainly go as far back as the Greek philosophers and the prophetic movement in Israel, but was not a dominating factor in western existence until the relatively late period when Descartes, Leibnitz, and Newton demonstrated the efficiency of the mathematical descriptions of the physical world. Since that time western peoples have increasingly depended upon mathematics for their analyses and insights of nature. The approach has proven spectacular in the physical sciences, particularly physics, and the technology that has been produced as a by-product of physical theory has only served to entrench in western minds the belief that mathematics is the proper description of reality. So influential is this attitude that in the last century we have seen the development of social sciences which seem to suggest that statistical truth is equivalent to ultimate reality. The social sciences now insist that all human activities can be described as functions of complicated formulas. I have seen this attitude applied to elections in the United States, but I have generally rejected that approach and bet on the people who counted the votes rather than on those statistics which projected who would vote. Mayor Richard Daley of Chicago, now deceased, never failed me in this respect.

As mathematics has been more influential in representing the scientific quest, and as the scope of human knowledge has expanded, the old tendency toward isolation has produced a strange phenomenon in which human knowledge is divided into separate categories variously called disciplines, fields of study, or what have you. As sciences have given rise to subgrouping of knowledge and specialties have been developed, knowledge itself has suffered a fragmentation and the sole guarantee of the validity of knowledge has been in the similarity of techniques employed to accumulate and interpret data. Briefly, even this field of methodology has degenerated as the various disciplines have moved away from each other, so that the sole criterion of truth today seems to lie in the sincerity of the researcher and his or her relative status within the specific field of endeavor. Sincerity is no guarantee of anything except an emotional state and quite often not much of a characterization even of that.

Isolation, in the oriental context, seems to be the isolation of emotions and personality, but in the western context can only be understood if seen in the context of the physical universe conceived as a giant machine that operates according to certain immutable laws. Conceiving physical reality as if it were a machine not only squeezes emotions and intuitions out of the data but introduces into the data the belief that the unusual cannot occur. Casuality becomes the primary mode of interpreting data and eventually becomes the manner in which people describe a situation, so that even observations of events become incomplete and only the mechanical aspects of the happening are reported.

When this attitude emerges in the field of history its effect is to reduce the intensity of experience and homogenize human activities so that everything can be classified under the same categories of interpretation. History becomes at first a chronology and eventually a trivial commentary that has no criteria by which factors are described or understood. Most contemporary interpretations of world history are simply the imposition of uniformitarian principles on factual data that has been emptied of any human content. Ultimately, history becomes a collection of data of what we would like to believe about the world as dictated by the ideals we hold, rather than even an accurate chronology of what actually happened. We become helpless integers involved in a process over which we have no control and with respect to which we have little understanding.

Perhaps the final consequence of approaching the world with the intent to isolate and thereby achieve dominance over things is the belief that the way we see things is the proper manner of describing them. Thus we approach and reunite with the original contention that we are dealing with the fallacy of misplaced concreteness. But we have not engaged in a reasoning process as much as taken a tour around the intellectual and conceptual universe of the western European to illustrate the various modes that this basic error can take. A few illustrations may be in order, to demonstrate both the provinciality of the western attitude and the manner in which Indians and dissatisfied non-Indians can begin to move away from this mooring and expand the horizons of all concerned. The treatment of non-western peoples, particularly North American Indian peoples, provides a perfect setting in which we can examine the manner of escape.

The Europeans, arriving in North America, discovered a people that had no written language, laws, religions, or customs, yet governed themselves so well that the American constitutional fathers were encouraged by Benjamin Franklin to model themselves after the Iroquois League when they came to devise a constitution. Europeans, looking at Indian societies, decided that these people lived in savagery because they had no written rules and regulations to govern them. Here we find the intense desire to objectify, to render human activities to mechanical form, and to accord respect by discovering similarity and homogeneity. Finding a qualitative difference between Indians and themselves, the Europeans promptly characterized the North American peoples as a lawless breed devoid of the attributes of civilized society. A great many wrongs were done to Indians because non-Indians believed them to be without laws and therefore unable to make intelligent or just decisions regarding their lives.

All of these beliefs about Indians changed as social science became more influential in western society and more sophisticated in its observations. In 1926, with the publication of Malinowski's famous book, *Crime and Custom in Savage Society*, which demonstrated that customs could be as restrictive and socially integrating as written codes and laws, the perception of people made a radical shift and Indians were considered savages because they were so tightly bound by custom and lacked the freedom of western democratic peoples. How a whole race could shift in one century from most lawless to most law-bound remained a mystery to the Indians who came into contact with western intellectual history, but it should have been an indication to non-Indians that all was not well with the western way of perceiving human activities.

This example illustrates that much of what western peoples have understood as knowledge is simply a reorientation, within their own framework, of the thesis used to interpret phenomena, and is not a corresponding development in the phenomena itself. Even more, the example indicates that no final statement, and perhaps no reliable statement, can ever be made concerning knowledge of the world. There is always another viewpoint by which interpretations of data can be made and when this situation becomes entrenched in the academic worldview of a culture, inevitably the reality that it describes becomes a verbal or mental reality. When phenomena do not fulfill our expectations, they are disregarded, downgraded, or derided and the opportunity to come to grips with another facet of reality escapes us.

When we turn to the North American Indian worldview we discover an entirely different perspective on the world. Instead of isolating things, Indians encompassed them; togetherness, synthesis, and relatedness characterized their experiences of the universe. The ordinary distinctions between mind and matter, human and other life forms, nature and human beings, and even our species and the divinity were not considered valid ways of understanding experience. Life was a complex matrix of entities, emotions, revelations, and cooperative enterprises and any abstraction was considered stupid and dangerous, destructive of spirit and reductionist in the very aspects that made life important. A great many non-Indians have intuited this "togetherness" from observing Indians and reading of the "Indian way," but have failed to understand the remarkable system of relationships which undergirds a seemingly innocent and simple life.

Relatedness is a much better description of the Indian way of looking at the world. Here we are not describing a comparative knowledge in which no absolute value exists. Indeed, all values are absolute because they are experiences and because they deal with specific relationships between specific individuals. A good example of this specificity is the manner in which the Osage Indians fed themselves. In the early spring they would plant their corn along the bottomlands of the Missouri River about the place where St. Louis is today. After they had sown their crop they would depart for the far Rocky Mountains in Colorado and Wyoming to do their summer hunting. The Osage would spend most of the summer in the high mountains hunting deer, buffalo, antelope and other large game animals, and they would dry their meat in the sun, making it suitable for preservation.

In the middle of July they would begin to examine one of the mountain flowers and when this flower began to turn to seed they would know that it was time to begin their journey back to their winter homes. They would pack up their summer's hunting surplus and return to Missouri where their corn would now be ready for the harvest. Such behavior may seem the utmost of simplicity except that to accomplish such a task required that the Osage know the relationships of plants, animals, and lands over a distance of some 1,000 miles and know these complex relationships so well that they could transfer an abstract sense of time, time in the sense of organic growth, from plant to plant over that distance and use the growth of a mountain plant as a gauge or calendar for their corn.

Here we have no general knowledge, no principles valid in all cases, no knowledge that can be tested in the laboratory. We have a knowledge totally unlike western scientific knowledge and yet an understanding of great profundity. Within this scope of knowledge we have an intuitive understanding of the spiritual nature of life which enables people to act in a purposive and predictive sense. Classifications, in this system of thinking, defy western categorization; they are not deductive and cannot be reached through any complicated logical path. Yet they exist and serve amazingly well in determining how a specific people will relate to an environment. Thus if we can learn anything from this example the first lesson must be that classifications, as we have been used to them in the western schemata of knowledge, are useless when we approach a more intimate relationship with the universe.

The hallmark of relatedness or synthesis is experience rather than interpretation. In the synthetic process we first experience the unity of existence and then, upon reflection and further experience, we begin to separate elements of that experience into useful categories of knowledge in which similarities and intimacies are the most important criteria. For that reason most Indian classifications of birds, animals, reptiles, and other life forms begin with the activities of these creatures and seek to identify similar purposive behaviors. Simple morphology, as western peoples have conceived the organic world, have little part in the Indian format; when they do, the morphological features that are chosen are understood as indicating similarity of temperament, not evolutionary origins. Thus our species, birds, and bears are considered to be the "two-leggeds," and we behave in many respects as if we were a single species. A good Indian medicine man can conduct a sophisticated tour of human and animal personality by describing the traits that convinced Indians long ago that the "two-leggeds" were a specific group.

The shift from isolating things to relating them involves the recognition of a different form of preserving knowledge. When we isolate and then interpret phenomena, our basic intent is to derive principles from which we can predict future behavior, illustrate mechanical operations, or analyse into further component parts. Our interpretation and rearrangement of data is most important. In the tradition which relates everything in specific terms the immediate experience is most critical and everything is oriented toward a preservation of the exact conditions under which something happened. Little effort is devoted to rearranging the elements of the incident or experience, for it was the uniqueness of that particular experience that first attracted us and made it seem important. Thus the tradition seeks to preserve as accurately as possible everything that took place.

When we look at the traditions of the North American peoples we discover that they have carried down over the generations many accounts of phenomena we would consider amazing today. The Ojibway of western Ontario, for example, relate stories of the water monster who lived in the lakes and rivers and tipped over the canoes of the unwary and unlucky. Pictures of this creature are liberally scattered over much of Ontario and eastern Canada. The Sioux also relate the story of water monsters and their description correlates to an astounding degree with the Ojibway tale. Further west the Indians of the Pacific Northwest have traditions that the lakes of the region were formerly much larger and contained monsters who stirred the waves unmercifully whenever humans ventured out on the water. A correlation of all accounts, of petroglyphs and pictographs of the various tribes, and an acknowledgment that this particular set of stories is always intimately tied to specific lakes should be sufficient to inform us that at one time within the memory of these tribes, a different and perhaps more spectacular form of life inhabited this continent. If we use our imaginations we can see in this tradition the presence of the group that we have always called "dinosaurs."

Now to suggest that human beings have been living in North America since the Mesozoic is radical only when we restrict our interpretation of human knowledge to that already accumulated by western peoples through the process of isolating elements of experience. The suggestion seems less radical when we remember that the oral traditions do not seek to interpret as much as they attempt to recall and remember precisely the unusual events of the past. The possibility that these stories contain the elements of past experiences is heightened considerably when we view contemporary research on the dinosaurs and discover that the latest and most precise interpretation of this group conceives them as warmblooded, bearing their young live, and traveling in herds, all characteristics of mammals and not reptiles, and possessing behavior patterns not unlike those which the Indian water monster tales relate.

What are we to do when a tradition which has always been seen by western peoples as primitive and superstitious now threatens to become an important source in a new and important revolution in paleontology? Are there other important areas of experience that have been preserved by oral traditions that have been neglected or discarded by the scientific mind because of the all-consuming goal of achieving truth by the isolation of elements of experience? Here we have a dilemma of major proportions which strikes the western mind at precisely the most vulnerable point. Isolation has not produced truth as much as it has produced specialists who studiously avoid synthesis in favor of a continuing subdivision of information into increasingly separated disciplines. We finally arrive at the fundamental question underlying the scope of human knowledge: is truth divisible into categories or is it synthetic, incorporating all aspects of experience and understanding?

The present situation calls for a sense of maturity between cultures that no other period of human history has required. We must now begin to transcend all other parochial considerations in our understanding and move forward into a new period of synthesis in which all information is brought into a coherent whole. Alfred North Whitehead remarked rather casually in *Science and the Modern World* that "it takes a very unusual mind to undertake the analysis of the obvious." Now the obvious always refers to those things that are so commonly accepted as to be considered beyond serious consideration by scholars. So the task of moving human knowledge forward has generally fallen to the amateur, to those who simply wish to know, and to the humble souls who refuse to surrender an idea to the guardians of human knowledge, the academics; those souls who understand knowledge as the possession of the whole human species and not the plaything of the specialist.

North American peoples have an important role to play in the determination of knowledge in the future. They represent thousands of years of experience in living on this continent and their customs and traditions, the particular and sometimes peculiar ways they have of approaching problems, of living, and of protecting the lands, are not simply the clumsy adjustments of primitives but the seasoned responses of people who synthesized and summarized the best manner of adapting themselves to the world in which they lived. Insofar as their insights can be translated into principles which can reorient western thinking, scientific and social, and insofar as North American peoples can understand their own traditions and abide by them, to that degree we can produce a more sophisticated, humane, and sensible society on this continent.

So the provinciality of which Whitehead speaks is really the provincial manner in which we today look at the experiences and memories of our ancestors and define the history of our species and planet. World history, Arnold Toynbee once remarked, is a parochial affair comparable to a map of the Mediterranean area being considered a true and accurate map of the world. Human knowledge cannot be provincial, but must enclose the planet and render an accurate account of its nature and growth. We are today on the threshhold of a new era in which this task will be accomplished— and it is perhaps the most exciting time of any that our species has experienced. Let us have the emotional and intellectual maturity to bring it to pass.

❦ ❦ ❦

from KISS OF THE SPIDER WOMAN

fiction by MANUEL PUIG

from FICTION

nominated by Bobbie Bristol, Michael Gross, Barbara Grossman and Max Zimmer

—"Let me reach out to you once more, my love . . . The night is still and begs for me to talk to you . . . And now I'm wondering if you're recalling too . . . The sad, sad dreams of our strange love. . . ."
　—What is that, Molina?
　—A bolero called *My Letter*.
　—Only you'd come up with something like that.
　—Like what? What's wrong with it?
　—You're crazy. It's a lot of romantic nonsense.

—I happen to like boleros, and that one's really very pretty. I'm sorry if it wasn't very tactful, though.

—What do you mean?

—Well, you got that letter and now you're really down.

—And what's that got to do with it?

—Well, next thing you know I start humming songs about sad letters. But I didn't do it on purpose . . . really I didn't, O.K.?

—No, I know.

—Why so sad?

—It was some bad news. You could tell?

—How should I know. . . . Well, yes, you look pretty depressed.

—It was some really bad news. You can read the letter if you want.

—No, better not . . .

—Don't start all over again like last night. You've got nothing to do with my problems, nobody's going to ask you anything. Anyway they already opened it and read it before they let me have it. You're really on the ball. . . .

—Hey, that's right.

—If you want to read it you can read it here.

—The writing looks like chicken scratching to me. Why don't you read it to me if you feel like it?

—It's from a girl without much education, poor kid.

—I can't believe what a stupid woman I am, it never dawned on me, that they open letters here if they want to. So, sure, it doesn't matter if you read it to me.

—"Dearest: I haven't written to you for a real long time because I didn't have the courage to tell you everything about what happened and you can understand why, can't you? Because you're the intelligent one, not me, that's for sure. I also didn't write to tell you the news about poor Uncle Pedro. Because they told me his wife already sent you a letter. I know how much you don't like to dwell on this type of thing. Because life has to go on somehow, and, well, we all need strength to continue the struggle to make our way through life and its trials. But as far as I'm concerned that's the worst part about growing old." It's all in code. Could you tell?

—Well, it's not very clear, that much I could tell.

—When she says "growing old," that means becoming part of the movement. And when she says "life and its trials," that's fighting for the cause. And Uncle Pedro, unfortunately, . . . he's a fellow who

was only twenty-five years old, one of our comrades in the movement. I didn't know anything about his getting killed. The other
letter never reached me. They must have torn it or something when
they opened it up here.

—Ah . . .

—Which is why this letter was such a shock to me. I had no idea.

—I'm very sorry.

—Well, what can you do . . .

— . . .

— . . .

—Tell me the rest of the letter.

—Let's see . . . ". . . growing old. Still, at least you've got lots of
strength. I wish I was that way. So you're probably taking it O.K. For
me, the worst of it's how much I miss Uncle Pedro. Because he kind
of left the family in my hands, and that's some responsibility. Listen,
baldy, I heard they really gave you a good shaving. What a shame I
can't get a load of you that way for a change. Too bad about those
goldilocks of yours. But I always keep in mind the stuff we used to
talk about. Above all about not letting ourselves get down in the
dumps over personal stuff. So I try sticking to your advice by making
the best of things, whatever way they fall." When she says that he
left the family in her hands that means that she's in charge of our
group now.

—Ah . . .

—So . . . "I kept missing you more and more and that's why,
especially after the death of Uncle Pedro, I finally had to take the
responsibility on myself. Of letting my niece Mari start in having
relations with a nice boy you never met. Who comes over to the
house and seems decent enough about his plans to hold down a
steady job. But I warned my niece not to get too serious. Because
that just makes for more headaches. And not to try for anything more
than a little nice companionship. Which after all, everybody needs,
to have the strength to get by with life and its trials." The niece
named Mari is herself, and by saying some fellow is decent about
holding down a steady job she means he's devoted to the cause, you
get it? To the struggle.

—Mmm hmm, but I don't understand the business about having
relations.

—That means she's been missing me too much, and we, well, we
commit ourselves, as comrades, to avoiding intense relationships of

that kind because they can only be a hindrance when it comes time
to act.

—Act how?

—Act decisively. Risk one's life.

—Ah . . .

—We can't get caught up in subjective feelings for one another,
because naturally either person would want the other to stay alive.
Then you both tend to be afraid of death. Well, not exactly afraid, but
. . . it's painful if anyone suffers because you choose to risk your life.
So to avoid that she's begun to have relations with another comrade.
. . . I'll go on. "I kept wondering whether I had better tell you or
not. But I know you enough to realize you'd rather have me tell you
all of it. Fortunately things are going well now. And we all feel
optimistic that someday soon our house will turn out to prosper after
all. It's night and I'm thinking maybe you're thinking about me too.
Here's a big hug for you, Ines." When she says house, it means
country.

—But I don't understand what you said last night then, about how
your girlfriend isn't really like you described her.

—Damn! I'm dizzy again, just from reading a letter. . . .

—You must be really weak. . . .

—I feel slightly nauseous.

—Lie back and close your eyes.

—Damn! I swear, I was feeling so much better.

—Rest quietly, it's just from focusing your eyes too much. Keep
them closed awhile.

—Mmm, it feels as if it's subsiding now. . . .

—You shouldn't have eaten, Valentin. I told you not to.

—I was hungry, that's all.

—You were doing so well yesterday until you ate, and that
screwed up your whole system. Now today you do it again, and this
time the whole plate! Promise me you won't touch a bite tomorrow.

—Don't even talk about food, it makes me . . .

—I'm sorry.

—Know something? There I was laughing at your bolero, but the
letter I got today says just what the bolero says.

—You think so?

—Mmm, I do . . . It seems to me I don't have any right to be
laughing at your bolero.

—You were probably just laughing because it struck too close to the bone, and you laughed . . . so as not to cry. Like in another bolero I know. Or tango.

—How does it go? That one you were singing before?

—Which part of it?

—The whole thing.

—"Let me reach out to you once more, my love . . . The night is silent and begs for me to talk to you . . . And now I'm wondering if you're recalling too . . . The sad, sad dreams of our strange love . . . Although life may never let us meet again, sweetheart . . . And we—because of fate—must always live apart . . . I swear, this heart of mine will always be all yours . . . My thoughts, my whole life, all yours too . . . Just as this pain . . . Belongs to you. . . ." "Pain" or "hurt," I don't remember which. It's one or the other.

—That's not bad, really.

—To me it's divine.

—What's the name of it?

—*My Letter*, by Mario Clavel. He's from Argentina.

—Really? I would have thought he was Mexican, or Cuban.

—I also know lots by Agustin Lara, almost all of them.

—I don't feel quite as dizzy now, but the cramps are starting up again.

—Try to relax.

—It's my fault for having eaten.

—Don't think about the pain if you can help it, and try to relax. It's when you get all tense . . . Just talk to me a little. About anything. . . .

—What I was trying to explain last night was that the girl I talked about, the very liberated one, from the bourgeois family. She's really not my girl, not the one who wrote to me.

—So who's the one who wrote to you?

—No, see, the one I always talk about entered the movement at the same time that I did. But then later on she decided to quit, and she insisted I do the same.

—Why?

—She became too attached to life, too happy with me. Our relationship alone sufficed for her. And that's when all the trouble began. You see, she would get upset whenever I disappeared for a few days, and each time I came back there she was crying again. And that was nothing. She stopped telling me about phone calls from my comrades, and toward the end even intercepted letters. Well, that was the last straw.

—Has it been a long time since you've seen her?

—Almost two years. But I still think about her. If only she hadn't started acting that way . . . like some castrating mother. . . . Anyway, I don't know . . . it seems like we were destined to be separated.

—Because you loved each other too much?

—That sounds like another bolero, Molina.

—Listen, big man, don't you know by now, boleros contain tremendous truths, which is why I like them.

The healthy thing about her, though, was the way she stood up to me. We had a genuine relationship going for us. She never just . . . how can I explain it? She never let herself be manipulated, like the typical female. . . .

—What do you mean?

—Aghhh, Molina, my friend . . . it feels like I'm getting sick all over again.

—Where does it hurt?

—Down in my gut . . .

—Don't tense up, Valentin, that'll make it worse, try to stay calm.

—Yes.

—Lie back.

—I just feel so sad I can't tell you.

—What's the matter?

—That poor kid, if you only knew. What a wonderful person he was, poor guy. . . .

—Who?

—The one they killed.

—Well, he won his place in heaven, that's for sure. . . .

—If only I could believe in that, it would be such a consolation sometimes, to believe that decent people ultimately find their reward. But I just can't buy it. Ugh . . . Molina, I'm going to have to pester you again—quick, call the guard to open up.

—Hold it just a second . . . I'm just . . .

—Aghhh . . . aghhh . . . no, don't call. . . .

—Don't be upset, I'll get you something to wipe yourself right away.

—Aghh . . . aghh . . . the pains are so strong, as if my guts were about to burst. . . .

—Loosen up your body, just let it come out and afterward I'll wash your sheet.

—Please, bundle up the sheet under me. Because it's coming out all liquid.

—Yes . . . sure, like this, there, you keep yourself calm now. Let it come out. Later on I'll just take the sheet in to the showers with me. It's Tuesday, remember?

—But that's your sheet. . . .

—It doesn't matter, I'll be washing yours anyway, and luckily we still have plenty of soap.

—Thanks Molina. . . . I think I'm starting to feel a little better now. . . .

—You just relax, and don't worry. You're usually such a pisser anyway. Tell me when you're finished and I'll help you clean yourself up.

— . . .

—All finished?

—I think so, but now I'm freezing.

—Let me give you my blanket. That way you'll stay warm.

—Thank you.

—But first roll over so I can clean you up. If you think you're all done.

—Better wait a little longer. . . . Molina, I'm sorry for laughing that way before, at what you were saying about boleros.

—What a time you pick to talk about boleros.

—Listen, I think I'm finished now, but I'm the one to clean myself . . . if I don't start to faint again when I lift my head.

—Try slowly . . .

—No use, I'm still too weak, there's no other way . . .

—I can clean you up, don't worry about it. You just relax.

—Thank you. . . .

—O.K. . . . that's it, and a little over here . . . turn slowly . . . that's right. Nothing went through to the mattress after all, so it's not so bad. And fortunately there's plenty of water. I can just wet a clean tip of the sheet to wipe you off, that's easy enough.

—I don't know what to say.

—Don't be silly. Let's see now . . . lift up a little over here. That's right . . . very good.

—Honestly, I can't thank you enough, because I don't have the strength to make it to the showers.

—Of course not, and that's all you need is some icy water on your body.

—Uh . . . uh . . . the wet sheet's cold too.

—Spread your legs a little more. . . . That's it.

—But it doesn't disgust you?

—Be quiet. Now I'll wet some more of the sheet . . . like this . . . — . . .

—Well, you're getting to look all tidied up now . . . just a little drying with the other end. . . . What a shame I've got no talcum left.

—Doesn't matter. It's so great just being dry.

—Good, and there's one more corner of the sheet to pat you off. . . . Like that. Now you're good and dry.

—I feel so much better, really. Thank you, my friend.

—Wait now . . . here we go . . . let me wrap you up tight in the blankets, just like a papoose. There we go . . . lift up a little on this side.

—O.K.?

—That's right. . . . Wait, . . . and now the other side, so you won't catch a chill. Are you comfortable now?

—Mmm hmm, fine. . . . Thank you so much.

—And don't you dare move, not until the dizziness goes away completely.

—We'll see, it'll probably go away soon.

—But whatever you want, I'm the one who gets it for you. You don't budge.

—And I promise not to laugh at your boleros any more. I like the lyrics from that one you were singing before . . they're O.K.

—I especially love the part that goes, ". . . And you, maybe you're also remembering . . . Our dreams, sad dreams of a love that seemed strange. . . ." Divine, isn't it?

—You know what? . . . I actually changed diapers on that poor comrade's baby boy, the guy they killed, I mean. We were all hiding out together in the same apartment, he and his wife, and their little son. . . . Who knows what's to become of him now? He can't be more than three years old. What a cute little tyke. . . . And the worst of it is I can't write to anyone about it, because the slightest move on my part would compromise them . . . or even worse, identify them.

—Can't you just write to your girl?

—That would be the worst choice of all. She's the head of the group now. No, not to her, not to anyone. And it's just as it says in your bolero, "because this life will never bring you back," because I'll never be able to write to that poor fellow either, or talk to him or anything.

—Actually what it says is, "*Although* life *may never* let us meet again, sweetheart . . ."

—Never! What an awful word. Until now I had no idea . . . how awful . . . that word . . . could . . . I'm sorry. . . .

—It's O.K., Valentin, get it off your chest, cry as much as you want, let yourself go until you're all cried out.

—It's just that it all feels so rotten. . . . And not being able to do anything, locked up here, unable to even . . . take care of his wife, his li . . . little . . . kid. . . . Oh, my friend, it's . . . so sad. . . .

—But what can we do?

—Molina, help me to . . . to lift my arm out . . . from under the blanket . . .

—What for?

—Give me . . . give me your hand, tight.

—Sure, grip it as hard as you can.

—I just want to stop shaking so damn much, that's all.

—But who cares whether or not you're shaking, if it gives you some relief.

—But there's something else, and it bothers me so much. Something really terrible, something despicable . . .

—Tell me, get it off your chest.

—It's that the one I'd. . . . I'd really like to write me . . . the one I'd like to be with most of all, and to hold . . . isn't my girl . . . isn't my real girl. It's the other one . . . it's the one I talk to you about that I want to see.

—But that's simply how you feel. . . .

—Yeah . . . because I talk a lot but . . . but deep down inside, what I . . . what I really like is . . . is the other kind of woman. Inside I'm just the same as all the other reactionary bastards who helped to murder that poor guy . . . I'm just like them, exactly.

—That's not true.

—Oh yes it is, let's not kid ourselves.

—If you were like them you wouldn't be in here.

—" . . . sad dreams of a love that seemed strange . . ." And you know why I became so annoyed when you started in with your

bolero? Because it reminded me of Marta, not my girlfriend. That's
why. And I even think that, with Marta, I don't feel attracted to her
for any good reasons, but because . . . because she has *class* . . .
that's right, class, just like all the class-conscious pigs would say . . .
in their son-of-a-bitching world.

—Don't torture yourself. . . . Close your eyes and try to rest.

—But whenever I do, I start to feel dizzy again.

—I'll heat up some water for some camomile tea. Yes, it turns out
that we still have some. We just forgot about it.

—I don't believe you. . . . Really?

—I swear. It was under all my magazines, so we lost track of it.

—But it's yours, and you like having tea in the morning.

—Listen, it'll help you relax. Just stay quiet for a while. You'll see
what a difference a good rest makes. . . .

$$* \quad * \quad *$$

*—a fellow with a plan on his mind, a fellow who accepts his
mother's invitation to visit her in the city, a fellow who lies to his
mother assuring her of his opposition to the guerilla movement, a
fellow who dines by candlelight alone with his mother, a fellow who
promises his mother to accompany her on a trip to all the fashionable
winter resorts like when he was a child just after the war, a mother
who goes on about all the eligible young beauties of the European
aristocracy, a mother who goes on about all the wealth that he will
eventually inherit, a mother who proposes to already place a substantial fortune in her son's name, a mother who hides the real reason
why she can't accompany him to Europe just yet, a fellow who
inquires into the whereabouts of the ex-manager, a fellow who finds
out that the same man is actually the brains behind the Ministry of
Internal Security, a fellow who finds out that the ex-manager is
actually the head of secret service in the office of counterinsurgency
operations, a fellow who wants to convince his mother to go off with
him to Europe, a fellow who wants to take title to his fortune and
repeat his childhood European voyage in order to ski with his lovely
mother, a fellow who decides to leave everything behind and fly off
with his mother, a fellow whose mother rejects his proposal, a mother
who confesses to already having other plans, a mother who has plans
to rebuild her own emotional life, a mother who goes to see him off at
the airport and there confides to him the news of her imminent*

marriage to the ex-manager, a fellow who pretends to be enthusiastic over the projected marriage, a fellow who gets off the plane at the first stopover and takes a return flight home, a fellow who joins up with the guerillas in the mountains, a fellow determined to rehabilitate the good name of his father, a fellow who meets up with that same peasant girl who once led him through the sierra when he first met the guerillas, a fellow who can see that she's pregnant, a fellow who doesn't want to have an Indian for a child, a fellow who doesn't want to mix his blood with the blood of an Indian, a fellow who feels ashamed about all his feelings, a fellow who feels revolted to caress the future mother of his own child, a fellow who doesn't know how to make up for his faults, a fellow who leads a guerilla assault against the plantation where his mother and the ex-manager happen to be, a fellow who surrounds the mansion, a fellow who opens fire on his own home, a fellow who opens fire on his own flesh and blood, a fellow who orders the occupants of the house to surrender, a fellow who watches the ex-manager come out of the house hiding like a coward behind the mother as his hostage, a fellow who orders his men to fire, a fellow who listens to the heartrending screams of his mother as she begs for mercy, a fellow who delays the execution, a fellow who demands a full confession relating to the complete facts of his father's death, a mother who breaks loose from the arms imprisoning her and confesses to the whole truth, a mother who explains how her lover dreamed up a plan designed to make the father seem a murderer of his own faithful overseer, a mother who confesses how her husband was actually innocent, a fellow who orders his men to execute his own mother after giving the order to execute the ex-manager, a fellow who completely loses his mind and seeing his mother agonizing on the ground picks up a submachine gun to execute the very soldiers who've just riddled her with bullets, a fellow who in turn is immediately executed, a fellow who feels guerilla bullets burn into his stomach, a fellow who manages to glimpse the accusing eyes of the peasant girl among the faces of the firing squad, a fellow who before dying wants to beg for forgiveness but can no longer emit any sound, a fellow who sees in the eyes of the peasant girl an eternal condemnation

MINISTRY OF THE INTERIOR OF THE ARGENTINE RE-PUBLIC

Penitentiary of the City of Buenos Aires
Report to the Warden, prepared by Staff Assistants

Prisoner 3018, Luis Alberto Molina

Sentenced July 20, 1974, by the Honorable Judge Justo José Dalpierre, Criminal Court of the City of Buenos Aires. Condemned to eight years imprisonment for corruption of minors. Lodged in Pavillion B, cell 34, as of July 28, 1974, with sexual offenders Benito Jaramillo, Mario Carlos Bianchi, and David Margulies. Transferred on April 4, 1975, to Pavillion D, cell 7, housing political prisoner Valentin Arregui Paz. Conduct good.

Detainee 16115, Valentin Arregui Paz

Arrested October 16, 1972, along Route 5, outside Barrancas, National Guard troops having surrounded group of activists involved in promoting disturbances with strikers at two automotive assembly plants. Both plants situated along said highway. Held under Executive Power of the Federal Government and awaiting judgment. Lodged in Pavillion A, cell 10, with political prisoner Bernardo Giacinti as of November 4, 1974. Took part in hunger strike protesting death of political prisoner Juan Vicente Aparicio while undergoing police interrogation. Moved to solitary confinement for ten days as of March 25, 1975. Transferred on April 4, 1975, to Pavillion D, cell 7, with sexual offender Luis Alberto Molina. Conduct reprehensible, rebellious, reputed instigator of above hunger strike as well as other incidents supposedly protesting lack of hygienic conditions in Pavillion and violation of personal correspondence.

GUARD: Remove your cap in front of the Warden.
PRISONER: Yes sir.
WARDEN: No need to be trembling like that, young man, nothing bad is going to happen here to you.
GUARD: Prisoner has been thoroughly searched and has nothing dangerous on his person, sir.
WARDEN: Thank you, sergeant. Be good enough to leave me alone with the prisoner now.

GUARD: Shall I remain stationed in the hallway, sir? With your permission, sir.

WARDEN: That will do fine, sergeant, you may go out now. . . . You look thin, Molina, what's the matter?

PRISONER: Nothing, sir, I was sick to my stomach, but I'm feeling much better now.

WARDEN: Then stop your trembling. . . . There's nothing to be afraid of. We made it look like you had a visitor today. Arregui couldn't possibly suspect anything.

PRISONER: No, he doesn't suspect anything, sir.

WARDEN: Last night I had dinner at home with your sponsor, Molina, and he brought me some good news for you. Which is why I had you summoned to my office today. Oh, I know it's rather soon . . . or have you learned something already?

PRISONER: No, sir, nothing yet. I feel I need to proceed very cautiously in this kind of situation. . . . But what did Mr. Parisi have to say?

WARDEN: Very good news, Molina. It seems your mother is feeling a lot better, since he spoke to her about the possibility of a pardon. . . . She's practically a new person.

PRISONER: Really? . . .

WARDEN: Of course, Molina, what would you expect? . . . But stop your crying, what's this? You should be pleased . . .

PRISONER: It's from happiness, sir . . .

WARDEN: But come on now. . . . Don't you have a handkerchief?

PRISONER: No, sir, but I can just use my sleeve, it's no problem.

WARDEN: Take my handkerchief at least. . . .

PRISONER: No, I'm really O. K. Please excuse me.

WARDEN: You know, Parisi is like a brother to me, and it was his interest in you that led us to come up with the present option, but Molina . . . we're expecting you to know how to manage things. Do you seem to be making any headway, or what?

PRISONER: I think I'm getting somewhere . . .

WARDEN: Was it helpful to have him weakened physically, or no?

PRISONER: Actually I had to eat the prepared food the first time.

WARDEN: Why? That was certainly a mistake. . . .

PRISONER: No, it wasn't, because he doesn't like rice, and since one plate had more than the other . . . he insisted I have the bigger portion, and it would have been suspicious had I refused. I know you warned me that the prepared one would come in a new tin plate, but they loaded it up so much I had to eat it myself.

WARDEN: Well, good work, Molina. I commend you, and I'm sorry about the mix-up.

PRISONER: That's why I look so thin. I was sick for two days.

WARDEN: And Arregui, how's his morale? Have we managed to soften him up a little? What's your opinion?

PRISONER: Yes, but it's probably a good idea to let him begin to recover now.

WARDEN: Well, that I don't know, Molina. I think the matter had best be left to our discretion. We have here appropriate techniques at our disposal.

PRISONER: But if he gets any worse there's no way he can remain in his cell, and once he's taken to the infirmary, there's no chance left for me.

WARDEN: Molina, you underestimate the proficiency of our personnel here. They know exactly how to proceed in these matters. Weigh your words, my friend.

PRISONER: Excuse me, sir, I only want to cooperate. Nothing else . . .

WARDEN: Of course. Now another thing, don't give out the slightest hint about a pardon. Hide any sign of euphoria when you go back into your cell. How are you going to explain this visit?

PRISONER: I don't know. Perhaps you can suggest something, sir.

WARDEN: Tell him your mother came, how does that sound?

PRISONER: No, sir, impossible, not that.

WARDEN: Why not?

PRISONER: Because my mother always brings some bags of food for me.

WARDEN: We have to come up with something to justify your euphoria, Molina. That's definite. I know now, we can requisition some groceries for you, and pack them up the same way, how does that strike you?

PRISONER: Fine, sir.

WARDEN: This way we can also repay you for your sacrifice, over that plate of rice. Poor Molina!

PRISONER: Well, my mother buys everything in the supermarket a few blocks from the prison, so as not to have to carry everything on the bus.

WARDEN: But it's easier for us to requisition everything from supplies. We can make the package up right here.

PRISONER: No, it would look suspicious. Please don't. Get them to go to that market, it's just down the street.

WARDEN: Wait just a minute. . . . Hello, hello. . . . Gutierrez, come into my office a moment, will you please.

PRISONER: My mother always brings me the stuff packed in two brown shopping bags, one for each hand. They pack it for her at the store, so she can manage everything.

WARDEN: All right. . . . Yes, over here. Look, Gutierrez, you'll have to go buy a list of groceries which I'm going to give you, and wrap them up in a certain way. The prisoner will give you instructions, and it all has to be done in . . . let's say half an hour, take out a voucher and have the sergeant go make the purchases with you according to the prisoner's instructions. Molina, you dictate whatever you think your mother would be likely to bring you. . . .

PRISONER: To you, sir?

WARDEN: Yes, to me! And quickly, I have other things to attend to.

PRISONER: . . . Guava paste, in a large package. . . . Make it two packages. Canned peaches, two roast chickens, still warm, obviously. A large bag of sugar. Two boxes of tea, one regular and the other camomile. Powdered milk, condensed milk, detergent . . . a small box, no, a large box, of Blanco, and four cakes of toilet soap, Suavísimo . . . and what else? . . . Yes, a big jar of pickled herring, and let me think a little, my mind's a complete blank . . .

*   *   *

—Look what I've got!

—No! . . . your mother came? . . .

—Yes!!!

—But how great. . . . Then she's feeling better.

—Mmm hmm, a little better. . . . And look at what she brought me. I mean, for *us*.

—Thanks, but all of that's for you, no kidding.

—You be quiet, you're convalescing, remember? Starting today a new life begins . . . the sheet's almost dry, feel . . . and all this food to eat. Look, two roast chickens, *two*, how about that? And chicken is perfect, it won't upset your stomach at all. Watch how fast you get better now.

—No, I won't let you do that.

—Please take them. I don't care for chicken anyway. I'll just be

glad to do without any more stink from you and your barnyard. . . .
No, seriously, you have to stop eating that damn stuff they feed us
here. Then you'll start feeling better in no time. At least try it for a
couple of days.

—You think so? . . .

—Absolutely. And once you're better then . . . close your eyes,
Valentin. See if you can guess . . . come on, try . . .

—How do I know? I don't know . . .

—No peeking. Wait, I'll let you handle it to see whether you can
guess.

—Here . . . feel.

—Two of them . . . packages . . . and heavy ones. But I give up.

—Open your eyes.

—Guava paste!

—But you have to wait for that, until you feel O.K., and you can
be sure you only get half of that. . . . I also took a chance and left the
sheets alone to dry . . . and nobody walked away with them, how
about that? They're just about dry. So tonight we both have clean
sheets.

—Nice going.

—Just give me a minute while I put this stuff away . . . and then
I'll make some camomile tea because my nerves are killing me, and
you, you have a leg of this chicken. Or no, it's only five o'clock . . .
better you just have some tea with me, and some crackers here,
they're easier to digest. Dilicadas, see? The ones I had as a kid
whenever I was sick . . . before they came out with Criollitas.

—How about one right now, Molina?

—O.K., just one, with a dab of jam, but orange for the digestion.
It's lucky, almost everything she brought is easy to digest, so you can
have lots of it. Except for the guava paste . . . for the time being. Let
me light the burner and presto, in a few minutes you'll be licking
your fingers.

—But the leg of chicken, may I have it now?

—Come on, a little self-control. . . . Let's save it for later, so when
they bring us dinner you won't be tempted, because, lousy as it is,
you gorge yourself every time.

—But you don't realize, my stomach feels so empty when the
pains stop that it's like all of a sudden I'm starving.

—One minute, let's get this straight. I expect you to eat the
chicken, no, chickens, *both* of them. On condition, though, that you

don't touch the prison chow, which is making you so sick. Is it a deal?

—O.K. . . . But what about you? I won't let you just sit around and drool.

—I won't, cold food doesn't tempt me, really.

—Oh, it definitely agreed with me. And what a good idea to have camomile tea first.

—Calmed your nerves, didn't it? Same with me.

—And the chicken was delicious, Molina. To think we have enough for two more days still.

—Well, it's true. Now you sleep a little, and that will complete your cure.

—I'm not really sleepy. You go ahead and sleep. I'll be fine, don't worry.

—But don't you start dwelling again on some nonsense like before, or it'll interfere with your digestion.

—What about you? Are you sleepy?

—More or less.

—Because there is one thing that's still lacking to complete the usual program.

—Christ, and I'm the one who's supposed to be degenerate here.

—No, no kidding. We should have a film now, that's what's missing.

—Ah, I see . . .

—Do you remember any others like the panther woman? That's the one I liked best.

—Well sure, I know lots of supernatural ones.

—So let's hear, tell me, like what?

—Oh, . . . *Dracula* . . . *The Wolf Man* . . .

—What else?

—And there's one about a zombie woman . . .

—That's it! That sounds terrific.

—Hmm . . . how does it start . . .

—Is it American?

—Yeah, but I saw it eons ago.

—So? Do it anyway.

—Well, let me concentrate a minute.

—And the guava paste, when do I get to taste it?

—Tomorrow at the earliest, not before.

—Just one spoonful? For now?

—No. And better I start the film. . . . Let me see, how does it go?
. . . Oh, that's it. Now I remember. It begins with some girl from
New York taking a steamer to an island in the Caribbean where her
fiancé is waiting to marry her. She seems like a very sweet kid, and
full of big dreams, telling everything about herself to this ship's
captain, really a handsome guy, and he's just staring down at the
black waters of the ocean, because it's night, and next thing he looks
at her as if to say "this poor kid has no idea what she's getting herself
into," but he doesn't say anything until they've already reached the
island, and you hear some native drums and she's like transported,
and then the captain says don't let yourself be taken in by the sound
of those drums, because they can often as not be the portents of
death. *cardiac arrest, sick old woman, a heart fills up with black
seawater and drowns*

—*police patrol, hideout, tear gas, door opens, submachine gun
muzzles, black blood of asphyxiation gushing up in the mouth* Go on,
why did you stop?

—So this girl is met by her husband, whom she's married by
proxy, after only knowing each other a few days in New York. He's a
widower, also from New York. Anyway, the arrival on the island,
when the boat's docking, is divine, because her fiancé is right there
waiting for her with a whole parade of donkey carts, decorated with
flowers, and in a couple of carts there's a bunch of musicians, playing
nice soft tunes on those instruments which look like some kind of
table made up out of little planks, that they whack with sticks and,
well, I don't know why, but that kind of music really gets to me,
because the notes sound so sweet on that instrument, like little soap
bubbles that go popping one after another. And the drums have
stopped, fortunately, because they'd sounded like a bad omen. And
the two of them arrive at the house, it's pretty far from town, off in
the countryside, under the palm trees, and it's such a gorgeous
island with just some low hills, and you're way out in the middle of
these banana groves. And the fiancé is so very pleasant, but you can
tell there's a real drama going on inside him, he smiles too much, like
someone with a weak character. And then you get this clue, that
something's wrong with him, because the first thing the fiancé does
is introduce the girl to his majordomo, who's around fifty or so, a
Frenchman, and this majordomo asks him right then and there to
sign a couple of papers, about shipping out a load of bananas on the

same boat that the girl arrived on, and the fiancé asks him to do it later, but the majordomo, he's like insistent about it, and the fiancé looks at him with eyes full of hatred and while he's busy signing the papers you notice how he can hardly keep his hand steady to write, it's trembling so much. Anyhow, it's still daylight, and the whole welcome party, which rode back there in those little flowery carts, is out back in the garden waiting to toast the new couple, and they're all holding glasses full of fruit juice, and at this point you notice the arrival of a couple of black peons, sort of delegates from the sugar-cane plantations, with a keg of rum to honor the master, but the majordomo sees them too and looks furiously at them, and grabs an ax that happens to be lying around, and he chops away at the keg of rum until it all pours out on the ground.

—Please, no more talk about food or drinks.

—And don't you be so impressionable then . . . crybaby. Anyhow, the girl turns to the fiancé as if to ask him why all the hysterics, but just then he's busy nodding to the majordomo how that's exactly what he should do, and so, without wasting any more time, the fiancé raises his glass of fruit juice and toasts the islanders there before him, because the next morning the two of them will be married, as soon as they go sign the papers at some government office there on the island. But that night the girl has to stay by herself, in the house, because he has to go to the farthest banana plantation on the whole island in order to show his gratitude to the peons, and by the way, to avoid any gossip and thus protect the girl's good name. The moon is marvelous that night, and the garden surrounding the house, just stunning, with all those fabulous tropical plants which seem more fantastic than ever, and the girl has on a white satin chemise, under just this loose peignoir, it's white too but transparent, and she's tempted to take a look around the house, and she walks through the living room, and then into the dining room, and twice she comes across those folding type of frames with a picture of the fiancé on one side but with the other side blank, because the photo is gone, which must have been the first wife, the dead one. Then she wanders around the rest of the house, and goes into some bedroom which you can tell was once for a woman, because of the lace doilies on the night table and on top of the dresser, and the girl starts rummaging through all the drawers to see if some photograph might still be around but doesn't find anything, except hanging in the closet is all the clothes from the first wife, all of them incredibly fine imports. But at this point the girl hears something move, she spots a shadow passing by the window. It scares the daylights out of her and she goes out into the garden, all lit up with moonlight, and sees a cute little frog jumping into the pond, and she thinks that was the noise she heard, and that the shadow was probably just the swaying of the palm trees in the breeze. And she walks still farther into the garden, because it feels so stuffy back in the house, and just then she hears something else, but like footsteps, and she spins around to see, but right at that moment some clouds blot out the moon, and the garden gets all black. And at the same time, off in the distance . . . drums. And you also hear more steps, this time clearly, and they're coming toward her, but very slowly. The girl is suddenly quaking with fear, and sees a shadow entering the house, through the same exact door that she'd left open. So the poor thing can't even make up her mind which is scarier at this point, to stay out there in that incredibly dark garden, or to go back into the house. Well, she decides to get closer to the house, where she peeks in through one of the windows but she doesn't see a thing, and then she hurries to another window, which turns out to look in on the dead wife's bedroom. And since it's so dark she can't make out much more than like a shadow gliding across the room, a tall silhouette, moving with outstretched hands, and fingering all the knicknacks lying around inside there, and right next to the window is the dresser with the doily and, on top of that, a really beautiful brush with the handle all worked in silver, and a mirror with the same kind of handle, and since the girl is right up against the window she can make out a very thin deathly pale hand, fingering all the bric-a-brac, and the girl feels frozen on the spot, too terrified to even budge, *the walking corpse, the treacherous somnambula, she talks in her sleep and confesses everything, the quarantined patient overhears her, he's loath to touch her, her skin is deathly white* but now she sees the shadow gliding out of the room and toward who knows what part of the house, until after a tiny bit she hears footsteps out there on the patio once more, and the girl shrinks back trying to hide in all those vines clinging to the walls of the house when a cloud finally passes by so that the moon comes back out again and the patio's lit up once again and there in front of the girl is this very tall figure wearing a long black duster, who scares her half to death, the pale face of a dead woman, with a head of blond hair all matted up and hanging down to her waist. The girl wants to scream for help but there's no more voice

left in her, and she starts backing away slowly, because her legs don't
work any more, they're just rubber. The woman is staring straight at
her, but all the same it's like she doesn't see her, with this lost look, a
madwoman, but her arms stretch out to touch the girl, and she keeps
moving ahead very slowly, and the girl is backing away, but without
realizing that right behind her there's a row of dense hedges, and
when she turns around and finally realizes how she's cornered she
lets out a terrible scream, but the other one keeps right on coming,
with her arms outstretched. Until the girl faints dead away from
terror. At that point someone grabs hold of the weirdo lady. It's that
the kindly old black woman has arrived. Did I forget to mention her?
*a black nurse, old and kindly, a day nurse, at night she leaves the
critically ill patient alone with a white nurse, a new one, exposing her
to contagion*
    —Yes.
    —Well, this kindly old black woman amounts to more or less a
housekeeper. Big and fat, her hair's already turned completely gray,
and always giving the girl these sweet looks ever since she arrived on
the island. And by the time the girl regains consciousness the old
housekeeper's already carried her inside to bed, and she makes the
girl believe that what happened was just a nightmare. And the girl
doesn't know whether to believe her or not, but when she sees how
nice the housekeeper treats her she calms down, and the housekeeper brings her tea to help her sleep, it's camomile tea, or something like that, I can't remember exactly. Then the following day the
marriage ceremony is to take place, so they have to go see the mayor,
and pay their respects to him and sign some papers, and the girl is
busy getting dressed for the occasion, in a very simple tailored dress,
but with a beautiful hairdo which the housekeeper fusses over, to put
it up in a kind of braid, how can I explain it, well, back then the
upsweep was a must on certain occasions, to look really chic.
    —I don't feel well. . . . I'm all dizzy again.
    —You sure?
    —Yes, it's not really bad yet, but I feel the same way I did when it
started the other times.
    —But that meal couldn't have done you any harm.
    —Don't be ridiculous. What makes you think I'm blaming it on
your food?
    —You seem so irritated . . .

—But it's got nothing to do with your food. It's a matter of my system, that something's still wrong with it.

—Then try not to think about it. That only makes it worse.

—I just couldn't concentrate any longer on what you were saying.

—But honestly, it must be something else, because that food was totally healthy for you. You know how sometimes after an illness you're still suggestible for a while?

—Why not tell a little more of the film, and just see if it goes away. Maybe it's because I'm feeling so weak. I probably ate too fast or something. . . . Who the hell knows why. . . .

—But that must be it, you're just very weak, and I noticed how fast you were eating, like a kid, without even chewing your food.

—Ever since I woke up this morning I've been thinking about only one thing, and it must be getting to me. I can't get it off my mind.

—What is it?

—The fact that I can't write to my girl . . . but to Marta, yes. And you know, it would probably do me some good to write her, but I can't think of what to say. Because it's wrong for me to write her. Why should I?

—I'll go on with the film then?

—Yes, do that.

—O. K., where were we?

—It was just when they were getting the girl ready.

—Ah, that's right, and she was having her hair done up in . . .

—Yeah, it's up I know already, and what do I care if it is? Don't get so bogged down in details that have so little importance. *crudely painted effigy, a sharp blow, the effigy is made of glass, it splinters to bits, the fist doesn't hurt, the fist of a man*

—*the treacherous somnambula and the white nurse, the contagious patient stares at them in the darkness* What do you mean don't! You just keep still because I know what I'm saying. Starting with the fact that wearing the hair up is—pay attention—important, because women only wear it up, it so happens, or they used to back then, when they wanted to really give the impression it was an important occasion, an important date. Because the upsweep, which bared the nape of the neck because they pushed all the hair up on top of the head, it gave a woman's face a certain dignity. And with that whole mass of hair pushed up like that the old housekeeper is making her a

braid, and decorating her hair with sprigs of local flowers, and when
she finally drives off in the little chaise, even though it's modern-day
times they go off in this little carriage pulled by two tiny donkeys, the
whole town smiles at her, and she sees herself en route to paradise.
. . . Is the dizzy spell going away?

—Seems like it is. But continue the story, O.K.?

—So they go along, her and the housekeeper, and on the steps of
that kind of Town Hall-type place they have there, in a Colonial
style, her fiancé is waiting for her. And then you see them later on,
they're out in the dark night air, her lying in a hammock, with a good
close-up of the two faces, because he bends down to kiss her, and it's
all lit up by the full moon kind of filtering through the palm trees.
Oh, but I forgot something important. You see, the expression on
their faces is like two lovers, and so contented looking. But what I
forgot is that while the black housekeeper's still brushing her hair up
for her, the girl . . .

—Not that hairdo again?

—But you're so irritable! If you don't make any effort yourself
you'll never calm down.

—I'm sorry, go on.

—So the girl asks the housekeeper some questions. Like, for
instance, where did he go to spend the night. The housekeeper tries
to conceal her alarm and says he went to say hello to some people out
in the banana groves, including the ones that lived on the farthest
plantation of all, and out there most of the peons believe in . . .
voodoo. The girl knows it's some kind of black religion and she says
how she'd very much like to see some of that, some ceremony,
perhaps, because it must be quite lovely, with lots of local color and
music, but the housekeeper gives her a frightened look, and tells her
no, she better just stay away from all that stuff, because it's a religion
that can get very bloody at times, and by no means should she ever
go near it. Because . . . but at this point the housekeeper stops
talking. And the other one asks her what's the matter, and the
housekeeper tells her how there's a legend, which probably isn't
even true but just the same it scares her, and it's about the zombies.
Zombies? what are they? the girl asks her, and the housekeeper
motions her not to say it so loud, only in a very low voice. And she
explains that they're the dead people that witchdoctors manage to
revive before the corpses get cold, because the witchdoctors themselves are the ones who kill them, with a special poison they pre-

pare, and the living dead no longer possess any will of their own, and they obey only the orders of the witchdoctors, and that the witch-doctors use them to do whatever they want them to, and they make them work at anything, and the poor living dead, the zombies, they don't have any will at all beyond the witchdoctor's. And the house-keeper tells her how many years ago some of the poor peons from a few of the plantations decided to rebel against the owners because they paid them almost nothing, but the owners managed to get together with the chief witch doctor on the island to have him kill all the peons and turn them into zombies, and so it came to pass that after they were dead they were made to work at harvesting bananas, but at night, so as not to have the other peons find out, and all the zombies work and work, without any talk, because zombies don't say a word, or think, even though they suffer so much, because in the middle of working, when the moon shines down on them you can see the tears running down their faces, but they never complain, be-cause zombies can't talk, they haven't any will left and the only thing they get to do is obey and suffer. Well, all of a sudden the girl, because then she remembers the dream that she still thinks she had the other night, the girls asks her whether there's such a thing as a zombie woman. But the housekeeper manages to get off on a tangent somehow and tells her no, because women are never strong enough for such hard work in the fields and so that's why no she doesn't think there's any such thing as a zombie woman. And the girl asks her if the young fiancé isn't afraid of all that business, and the housekeeper answers no, but naturally he has to put up with a certain amount of superstition in order to stay on friendly terms with the peons, so he just went out there to receive the blessing from the witchdoctors themselves. And then the conversation ends, and like I told you, later on you see them together on their wedding night, and happy looking, because for the first time, you see the kid, the husband, has a look of peace on his face, and all you hear is the *bzz-bzz* of tiny bugs outside and water running in the fountains. And then later you see the two of them lying asleep in their bed, until something wakes them up and gradually they hear, louder and louder, off in the distance, the beating of the drums. She shivers, a chill runs up and down her back. . . . Are you feeling any better? *night rounds for the nurses, temperature and pulse normal, white cap, white stockings, good night to the patient*

—A little . . but I can barely follow what you're saying, *the*

endless night, the cold night, endless thoughts, cold thoughts, sharp
slivers of broken glass

—But I ought to stop then. *the strict nurse, the very tall cap stiff*
with starch, the slight smile not without cunning

—No, honestly, when you distract me a little I feel better, please,
go on. *the endless night, the icy night, the walls green with mildew,*
the walls stricken with gangrene, the injured fist

—O. K., so . . . how did it go next? They hear drums way off in the
distance, and the husband's expression changes, all that peace is
gone, he can't sleep now, so he gets up. The girl doesn't say anything, discretion itself, she doesn't move a muscle, making like she's
fast asleep, but she really pricks up her ears and hears this noise of a
cupboard door being opened and squeaking, and then nothing
more. She doesn't dare get up and actually investigate, but then it
gets later and later and still no sign of him. She decides to look, and
finds him lying across an easy chair, completely drunk. And she
quickly eyes all the furniture and discovers a little open cabinet,
hardly big enough for one bottle, the empty bottle of cognac, but the
husband also seems to have another bottle, next to him, and that one
is just half empty. So the girl wonders where it came from, because
there's no liquor kept in the house at all, and then she notices how,
just underneath the bottle in the cabinet, certain things have been
tucked away, and it's a bunch of letters and photographs. And it's a
job for her to drag him back into the bedroom, where she just lies
down beside him, trying to cheer him up because she loves him and
promises him he's not going to be alone any more, and he looks
gratefully at her and falls back asleep. She tries to get some sleep too,
but now she can't, although before she was so contented, but seeing
him drunk like that makes her incredibly upset. And she realizes
how right the marjordomo was to smash that rum keg. She puts on
her negligee and goes back to the cabinet to look at the photos,
because what intrigues her incredibly is the possibility of finding a
picture of the first wife. But when she gets there she finds the
cabinet closed, and locked too. But who could've locked it? She
looks around but everything is swallowed up in complete darkness
and absolute silence, except for those drums, which you can still
hear. Then she goes over to shut the window so as not to have to
listen to them, but right at that very moment they stop, as if they'd
spotted her from miles and miles away. Anyhow, the next morning
he looks as if he doesn't remember anything, and he wakes her with

their breakfast all ready, and smiley as can be, and informs her that he's going to take her on a ride by the sea. She becomes totally infected with his excitement, and off they go into the tropics, in a great convertible with the top down, and there's a peppy musical background, calypso type, and they drive past a couple of divine beaches, and here it's a very sexy scene because she feels the urge to go for a swim, because by then they've already seen the lovely coconut groves, and rocky cliffs looking out to sea, and here and there some natural gardens with gigantic flowers, and the sun is scorching hot but she's forgotten to bring along a bathing suit, so he says why not swim in the raw, and they stop the car, she undresses behind some rocks and then you see her off in the distance running to the ocean in the nude. And later on you catch them lying on the beach together, under the palms, her with a sarong out of his shirt, and him with just his pants on, nothing else, and barefoot, and you have no idea where it comes from, but you know the way it happens in movies, you suddenly just hear the words of this song, saying how when it comes to love it's a question of earning it, and at the end of some dark trail, strewn with all kinds of hardships, love awaits those who struggle to the last in order to earn that love. And you can see the girl and he are completely enchanted with each other once again and they decide to let bygones be bygones. And then it begins to get dark, and when they drive up a little ridge of road, you just manage to catch in the background, not too far from there, all glinty from the sun which is like this fiery red ball, a very old colonial house, but pretty, and very mysterious, because it's completely overrun by vegetation, which covers it up almost totally. And the girl says how some other day she'd like to go for a ride to that house, and she asks why it's been abandoned. But at this point he seems to get very nervous and tells her like very rudely, never, never go near that house, but he doesn't offer the slightest explanation, just saying that he'll tell her why some other time. *the night nurse is inexperienced, the night nurse sleepwalks, is she asleep or awake? the night shift is long, she's all by herself and doesn't know where to turn for help* You're so quiet, you're not even cracking any comments . . .

—Somehow I'm not feeling very good, just go on with the film, it's good to take my mind off things for awhile.

—Wait, now I lost the thread.

—I don't understand how you manage to keep so many details in

your head anyway. *the hollow head, the glass skull, filled with mass cards of saints and whores, someone throws the glass head against the putrid wall, the head smashes, all mass cards fall onto the floor*
—In spite of the great time they were having that whole day, the girl gets upset all over again now, because she saw how nervous he became the minute she asked about that house, the one that looked abandoned. Well, when they arrive back at the mansion, he takes a shower, and that's when she can't resist looking through his pockets for the keys in order to search through that cabinet of the night before. And she goes and searches through his pants, and finds a key ring, and runs to the cabinet: on the key ring there's only one tiny key, she tries and it fits. She opens the cabinet. There's a full bottle of cognac inside, but who put it there? Because she hasn't left her husband's side for a second since the night before, so he didn't do it, she would have seen him. And underneath the bottle there's some letters, love letters, signed by him and others signed by the first wife, and underneath the letters some photographs, of him and some other woman, was that the first wife? The girl seems to recognize her, it's as if she's seen her somewhere before, surely she's come upon that face before, but where? An interesting type, very very tall, long blond hair. The girl goes on looking through each and every photograph, and then she discovers one in particular that's like a portrait, just of the face, the eyes very pale, that slightly lost look . . . and the girl remembers! It's the woman who chased her in the nightmare, with the face of a madwoman, dressed all in black down to her toes. . . . But at that point she notices the water isn't running in the shower, and her husband could easily catch her going through his things! So she tries frantically to put away all that stuff, setting the bottle back on top of the letters and photographs, closing the cabinet, and then going back into the bedroom, where she finds him right there! all wrapped up in this huge bath towel, but smiling away. She doesn't know what to do, so she offers to dry his back, she has no idea how to keep him busy, how to distract him, *the poor nurse, so unlucky, they assign her to a patient on the critical list and she doesn't know how to keep him from dying or killing her, the danger of contagion is stronger than ever* because he's already about to start getting dressed, but she's terrified that she has the key right in her hand, and he might notice that fact any minute now. But she goes on drying his shoulders with one hand, looking over at his pants draped on the chair, and doesn't know what to do to get the keys back

into his pocket. Until she gets an idea, and says she'd like to comb his hair. And he answers, wonderful, the comb is in the bathroom if you want to get it, and she says, that's no way for a gentleman to act, saying that, so then he goes to look for it himself and meantime she takes the chance to slip the keys back into his pocket just in the nick of time, and when he comes back she starts combing his hair and massaging his bare shoulders. And the poor little newlywed she just breathes a sigh of relief. Then a few days go by, and the girl realizes how the husband always gets up around midnight because he can't sleep, and she pretends to be sound asleep, because she's afraid of bringing up the subject face to face with him, but in the early morning she gets up to help him back into bed, because he always ends up bombed out of his mind and collapsed in the armchair. And she always checks the bottle, and it's a different one each time, and it's full, so who's putting it there in that cabinet? The girl doesn't dare ask him a thing, because when he comes back every evening from the plantations he's so happy to see her waiting there for him, embroidering something, but at midnight you always begin to hear those drums again, and he gets all obsessed about something, and can't sleep any more, unless he gets himself into a drunken stupor. So obviously, the girl gets more and more uptight about the whole thing, and at one point when her husband is outside somewhere she tries to have a word with the majordomo, to discover some possible secret from him maybe, about why the husband seems so nervous at times, but the majordomo tells her with a big sigh how they're having lots of problems with the peons, etcetera etcetera, and in the end he really doesn't say too much about anything. Well, the thing is, the girl, one time when the husband tells her he's going off for that whole day with the majordomo, to that plantation that's the farthest away of all, and won't be back until the following day, she decides to go off by herself on foot to that same abandoned house, because she's sure she'll find out something there. And so just after tea, around five o'clock, when the sun isn't so strong any more, the husband and the majordomo set out on their trip, and the girl eventually goes off too. And she's looking for the road to that abandoned house, but she gets lost, and soon it's getting late, and already almost nightfall, when she manages to find that ridge in the road from where you got to see the house, and she doesn't know whether to turn back or not, but her curiosity gets the best of her, and she goes on to the house. And she sees how suddenly, inside there, a light goes on, which

encourages her a little more. But once she reaches the house, which
is, no exaggeration, almost buried by wild plants, she doesn't hear
anything, and through the windows you can see how on the table
there's a candle burning, and the girl gets up enough courage to
open the door and even take a look inside, and she sees over in the
corner a voodoo altar, with more candles burning, and she goes
farther inside to see what's on top of the altar, and she walks right up
to it, and on top of the altar she finds a doll with black hair with a pin
stuck right through the middle of the chest, and the doll is dressed in
an outfit made to look exactly like what she was wearing herself on
her own wedding day! And at this point she almost faints with fright
but spins around to run away through the same door that she came in
by . . . and what's in the doorway? . . . this incredibly huge black
guy, with bulging eyeballs, wearing only a ragged pair of old pants,
and with the look of somebody who's totally out of his mind, staring
at her and blocking any escape. And the poor thing, all she has left to
do is let out a desperate scream, but the guy, who's actually what
they call a zombie, one of the living dead, he keeps coming closer
and closer, with his arms reaching out, just like the woman from the
other night in the garden. And the girl lets out another scream, and
runs into the next room and locks the door behind her, the room's
almost dark, with the window almost covered with jungle growth so
only a tiny bit of light comes through, a little twilight, and the room
has a bed in it, which little by little the girl begins to make out, as she
becomes more accustomed to the darkness. And every inch of her
shudders, nearly suffocated by her own cries and her terror, as she
sees there on the bed . . . something moving . . . and it's . . . that
woman! Incredibly pale, all disheveled, the hair hanging down to
her waist, and with the same black duster on, she slowly rises and
begins to move toward the girl! In that room without escape, all
locked up. . . . The girl would like to drop dead she's so frightened,
and now she can't even scream, but suddenly . . . from the window
you hear a voice ordering the zombie woman to stop and go back to
her bed . . . it's the kindly black housekeeper. And she tells the girl
not to be scared, that she's going to come right in and protect her.
The girl opens the door, the black woman hugs her and calms her
down; and behind her, in the front doorway, is that black giant, but
he's totally obedient now to the housekeeper, who tells him he must
look after the girl, and not attack her. The giant black zombie obeys,

and the zombie woman too, all disheveled, because the house-keeper orders her back to her bed, and the woman completely obeys. Then the housekeeper takes the girl affectionately by her shoulders and tells her she's going to get her back safely to the main house, in a little donkey cart, and along the way she tells her the whole story, because by now the girl's realized that the zombie woman with the blond hair down to her waist . . . is her husband's first wife. And the housekeeper begins to tell how it all happened. *the nurse trembles, the patient looks up at her, asking for morphine? asking to be caressed? or does he just want the contagion to be instantaneous and deadly?*

—*the skull is glass, the body is glass too, easy to break a toy made out of glass, slivers of sharp cold glass in the cold night, the humid night, gangrene spreading through the hand shredded by the punch* Do you mind if I say something?

—*at night the patient gets up and walks barefoot, he catches cold, his condition deteriorates* What? Go ahead.

—*the glass skull full of mass cards of saints and whores, old yellowed mass cards, dead faces outlined in cracked paper, inside my chest the dead mass cards, glass mass cards, sharp, shredding, spreading the gangrene into the lungs, the chest, the heart* I'm very depressed. I can hardly follow what you say. I think it'd be much better to save the rest for tomorrow, don't you? And this way we can talk a little.

—Fine, what do you want to talk about?

—I feel so awful . . . you have no idea. And so confused . . . anyhow, I . . . I see it a little more clearly now, it's the business I was talking about that had to do with my girl, how afraid I am for her, because she's in danger . . . but that the one I long to hear from, the one I'm longing to see isn't my girl. And longing to touch, it's not her I'm dying for, to hold in my arms, because I'm just aching for Marta, my whole body aches for her . . . to feel her close to me, because I think Marta is really the only one who could save me at all, because I feel like I'm dead, I swear I do. And I have this notion that nothing except her could ever revive me again.

—Keep talking, I'm listening.

—You're going to laugh at what I want to ask of you.

—No I won't, why should I?

—If it's not a bother, would you mind lighting the candle? . . .

What I'd like is to dictate a letter to you for her, I mean for the one I always talk about, for Marta. Because I get dizzy if I use my eyes for anything.

—But, what could be wrong with you? Couldn't it be something else? Besides the stomach problem, I mean.

—No, I'm just terribly weak, that's all, and I want to unburden myself a little somehow. Molina, my friend, because I can't stand it any more. This afternoon I tried myself to write a letter, but the page kept swimming.

—Sure then, wait till I find the matches.

—You've been really good to me.

—There we are. Shall we do a rough draft on scratch paper first, or what would you like to do?

—Yeah, on scratch paper, because I've no idea of what to say. Use my ball-point.

—Wait, I'll just sharpen this pencil.

—No, take my ball-point, I'm telling you.

—Fine, but don't start foaming at the mouth again.

—I'm sorry, I just see everything black right now.

—O.K., start dictating.

—Dear . . . Marta: It must be strange for you . . . to get this letter. I feel . . . lonely, I need you so, I want to talk with you, I want . . . to be close, I want you to . . . give me . . . some word of comfort. I'm here in my cell, who knows where you are right now. . . and how you're feeling, or what you're thinking, or what you might be needing right this minute. . . . But I just have to write you a letter, even if I don't send it, who knows what'll happen actually . . . but let me talk to you anyway . . . because I'm afraid . . . afraid that something is about to break inside of me . . . if I don't open up to you a little. If only we could actually talk together, you'd understand what I mean . . .

—". . . you'd understand what I mean." . . .

—I'm sorry, Molina, how did I tell her that I'm not going to send her the letter? Read it to me, would you?

—"But I just have to write you a letter, even if I don't send it."

—Would you add, "But I will send it."

—"But I will send it." Go ahead. We were at "If only we could actually talk together you'd understand what I mean."

—. . . because at this moment I could never go to my comrades and talk with them, I'd be ashamed to be this weak. . . . Marta, I feel as if I have a right to live a little longer, and that someone should pour a little . . . honey . . . on my wounds . . .

—Yes . . . go on.

—. . . inside, I'm all raw, and only someone like you could really comprehend . . . because you were raised in a clean and comfortable house like me and taught to enjoy life, and I'm the same way, I can't adjust to being a martyr, it infuriates me, I don't want to be a martyr, and right now I wonder if the whole thing hasn't been one terrible mistake on my part. . . . They tortured me, but still I didn't confess anything . . . I didn't even know the real names of my comrades, so I only confessed combat names, and the police can't get anywhere with that, but inside myself there seems to seem to be another kind of torturer . . . and for days he hasn't let up . . . And it's because I seem to be asking for some kind of justice. Look how absurd what I'm about to say is: I'm asking for some kind of justice, for some providence to intervene . . . because I don't deserve to just rot forever in this cell or, I get it . . . I get it . . . now I see it clearly, Marta. . . . It's that I'm afraid because I've just been sick . . . and I have this fear in me . . . this terrible fear of dying . . . and of it all ending like this, with a life reduced to just this rotten bit of time, but I don't think I deserve that, I've always acted with generosity, I've never exploited anyone . . . and I fought, from the moment I possessed a little understanding of things . . . fought against the exploitation of my fellow man. . . . And I've always cursed all religions, because they simply confuse people and prevent them from fighting for any kind of equality . . . but now I find myself thirsting for some kind of justice . . . divine justice. I'm asking that there be a God . . . write it with a capital G, Molina, please . . .

—Yes, go on.

—"What did I say?

—"I'm asking that there be a God."

—. . . a God who sees me, and helps me, because I want to be able, someday, to walk down streets again, and I want that day to come soon, and I don't want to die. But at times it runs through my mind that I'm never, never going to touch a woman again, and I can't stand it . . . and whenever I think about women . . . I see no one but you in my mind, and it would be such a comfort to somehow believe that at this moment, from here on, until I finish this letter to you, you're really thinking about me too . . . while you run your hand over your body which I remember so well . . .

—Wait, don't go so fast.

—. . . your body which I remember so well, and that you're pretending it's my hand . . . and what a deep consolation that could be for me . . . my love, if that were happening . . . because it would be just like my touching you, because a part of me is still with you, right? Just the way the scent of your body is still inside my nostrils . . . and beneath the tips of my fingers I too have the sensation of feeling your skin . . . as if I'd somehow memorized it, do you understand me? Even though it has nothing to do with understanding . . . because it's a question of believing, and at times I'm convinced that I've kept something of yours with me too . . . and that I've never lost it . . . but then sometimes, no. I feel like there's nothing here in this cell except me . . . all alone.

—Yes . . . "Me . . . all alone . . ." go ahead.

—. . . and that nothing leaves a trace of itself, and that the luck of having been so happy together, of having spent those nights with you, and afternoons, and mornings of pure enjoyment, is absolutely worthless to me now, and actually works against me . . . because I miss you like crazy, and the only thing I feel is the torture of loneliness, and in my nostrils there's nothing but the disgusting smell of this cell, and of myself . . . but I can't wash myself because I'm so sick, so totally debilitated, and the cold water would probably give me pneumonia, and beneath the tips of my fingers what I really feel is the chill fear of dying, and in my very marrow I feel it . . . that same chill. . . . It's so terrible to lose hope, and that's what's happening with me . . . the torturer that I have inside of me tells me everything is finished, and that this agony is my last experience on earth . . . and I say this like a true Christian, as if afterward another life were waiting . . . but there's nothing waiting, is there?

—Can I interrupt? . . .

—What's wrong?

—When you finish, remind me to tell you something.

—What?

—Well, that there is something we could do, actually . . .

—What? Say it.

—Because if you wash yourself in that freezing shower it certainly will kill you, as sick as you are right now.

—But what is to be done? For the last time, tell me, goddamn it!

—Well, I could help you clean yourself. Look, we can heat some water up in the pot, we already have two towels, so one we soap up and you wash the front of yourself, I can do the back for you, and with the other towel slightly wet we sponge off the soap.

—And then my body wouldn't itch so much?

—That's right, we can do it bit by bit, so you don't catch any chill, first your neck and ears, then your underarms, then your arms, your chest, your back, and so on.

—And you'd really help me?

—Obviously.

—But when?

—Right now if you like, I'll heat up some water.

—And then I can sleep, without the itching? . . .

—Peaceful as can be, without any itching. The water will be warm enough in just a few minutes.

—But that kerosene is yours, you'll waste it.

—It doesn't matter, in the meantime we'll finish your letter.

—Give it to me.

—What for?

—Just give it to me, Molina.

—Here . . .

—. . .

—What are you going to do?

—This.

—But why are you tearing up your letter?

—Let's not discuss it any further.

—Whatever you say.

—It's just no good getting carried away like that, out of desperation. . . .

—But it's good to get something off your chest sometimes, you said so yourself.

—Well, it doesn't work for me. I have to just put up with it. . . .

—. . .

—Listen, you've been very kind to me, honestly, I mean that with all my heart. And some day I expect to be able to show my appreciation, I swear I will. . . . so much water?

—Mmm hmm, we'll need at least that much. . . . And don't be silly, there's nothing to thank.

—That much water . . .

—. . .

—Molina . . .

—Mmm?

—Look at the shadows that the stove's casting on the wall.

—Mmm, I always watch them, you never saw them before?

—No, I never noticed.

—Mmm, it helps me pass the time, watching the shadows when the stove's lit.

Translated from the Spanish
by Thomas Colchie

RUNNING AWAY FROM HOME

by CAROLYN KIZER

from KAYAK

nominated by KAYAK

Most people from Idaho are crazed rednecks
Grown stunted in ugly shadows of brick spires,
Corrupted by fat priests in puberty,
High from the dry altitudes of Catholic towns.

Spooked by paster madonnas, switched by sadistic nuns,
Given sex instruction by dirty old men in skirts,
Recoiling from flesh-colored calendars, bloody gods,
Still we run off at the mouth, we keep on running.

Like those rattling roadsters with vomit-stained back seats.
Used condoms tucked beneath floor-mats.
That careened down hairpin turns through the blinding rain
Just in time to hit early mass in Coeur d'Alene!

Dear Phil, Dear Jack, Dear Tom, Dear Jim.
Whose car had a detachable steering-wheel:
He'd hand it to his scared, protesting girl
Saying, "Okay, *you* drive"—steering with his knees;

Jim drove Daddy's Buick over the railroad tracks,
Piss-drunk, just ahead of the Great Northern freight
Barrelling its way thru the dawn, straight for Spokane.
O the great times in Wallace & Kellogg, the good clean fun!

Dear Sally, Dear Beth, Dear Patsy, Dear Eileen,
Pale, faceless girls, my best friends at thirteen,
Knelt on cold stone, with chilblained knees, to pray.
"Dear God, Dear Christ! Don't let him go All the Way."

O the black Cadillacs skidding around corners
With their freight of drunken Jesuit businessmen!
Beautiful daughters of lumber-kings avoided the giant
Nuptial Mass at St. Joseph's, and fled into nunneries.

The rest live at home: bad girls who survived abortions,
Used Protestant diaphragms, or refused the sacred obligation
Of the marriage bed, scolded by beat-off priests,
After five in five years, by Bill, or Dick, or Ted.

I know your secrets: you turn up drunk by 10 a.m.
At the Beauty Shoppe, kids sent breakfastless to school.
You knew that you were doomed by seventeen.
Why should your innocent daughters fare better than you?

Young, you live on in me: even the blessed dead:
Tom, slammed into a fire hydrant on his Indian Chief
And died castrated; Jim, fool, fell 4 stories from the roof
Of his jock fraternity at Ag. & Tech.;

And the pure losers, cracked up in training planes
In Utah; or shot by a nervous rookie at Fort Lewis;
At least they cheated the white-coiffed ambulance chasers
And death-bed bedevillers, and died in war in peace.

Some people from Oregon are mad orphans
who claim to hail from Stratford-upon-Sodom.
They speak fake B.B.C.; they are Unitarian fairies,
In the Yang group or the Yin group, no Middle Way.

Some stay Catholic junkies, incense sniffers who
Scrawl JESUS SAVES on urinal walls, between engagements;
Or white disciples of Black Muslims; balding blonds
Who shave their pubic hair, or heads, for Buddha.

I find you in second-hand bookstores or dirty movies,
Bent halos like fedoras, pulled well down,
Bogarts of buggery. We can't resist the furtive questions:
Are you a writer too? How did you get out?

We still carry those Rosary scars, more like a *herpes*
Simplex than a stigmata: give us a nice long fit
Of depression; give us a good bout of self-hate;
Give us enough Pope, we pun, and we'll hang.

Hung, well hung, or hungover, in the world's most durable
Morning after, we'd sooner keep the mote and lose the eye.
Move over Tonio Kroger; you never attended
Our Lady of Sorrows, or Northwestern High!

Some people from Washington State are great poetasters,
Inbibers of anything, so long as it makes us sick
Enough to forget our sickness, and carry on
From the Carry Out: Hostess Winkies and Wild Duck.

We "relate", as they say, to Indians, bravest of cowards
Furtively cadging drinks with a shit-faced grin:
Outcasts who carry our past like a 90 lb. calcified foetus
We park in the bus-station locker, and run like sin.

Boozers and bounders, cracked-up crackerbarrel jockeys,
We frequent greasy bistros: Piraeus and Marseilles,
As we wait for our rip-off pimps, we scribble on napkins
Deathful verse we trust our executors to descry.

Wills. We are willess. As we have breath, we are wilful
And wishful, trusting that Great Archangel who Still Cares,
Who presides at the table set up for celestial Bingo.
We try to focus our eyes, and fill in the squares.

Some people from Spokane are insane salesmen
Peddling encyclopedias from door to door,
Trying to earn enough to flee to the happy farm
Before they jump from the Bridge, or murder Mom;

Or cut up their children with sanctified bread-knives
Screaming, "You are Isaac, and I am Abraham!"
But it's too late. They are the salutary failures
Who keep God from getting a swelled head.

Some shoot themselves in hotel rooms, after gazing
At chromos of the Scenic Route through the Cascades
Via Northern Pacific, or the old Milwaukee & St. Paul:
Those trains that won't stop rattling in our skulls!

First they construct crude crosses out of Band-Aids
And stick them to the mirror; then rip pages
From the Gideon Bible, roll that giant final joint,
A roach from *Revelations*, as they lie dying.

Bang! It's all over, Race through Purgatory
At last unencumbered by desperate manuscripts
In the salesman's sample-case, along with the dirty shirts.
After Spokane, what horrors lurk in Hell?

I think continually of those who are truly crazy:
Some people from Montana are put away;
They shake their manacles in a broken dance
With eyes blue-rimmed as a Picasso clown's.

Still chaste, but nude, hands shield their organs
Like the original Mom & Dad, after the Fall;
Or they dabble brown frescoes on the walls
Of solitary: their Ajanta and Lascaux.

While the ones that got away display giant kidneys
At the spiral skating-rink of Frank Lloyd Wright,
Or framed vermin in the flammable Museum
Of Modern Mart. But they're still Missoula

In their craft and sullen ebbing, Great Falls & Butte.
Meanwhile, Mondrian O'Leary squints at the light
Staining the white radiance of his well-barred cell,
Till ferocious blurs bump each other in Dodgem cars.

O that broken-down fun-house in Natatorium Park
Held the only fun the boy Mondrian ever knew!
Now seven-humped, mutated radioactive Chinook salmon
Taint the white radiance of O'Leary's brain.

O mad Medical Lake, I hear you have reformed:
No longer, Sunday afternoon, the tripper's joy.
Watch the nuts weep! or endlessly nibble fingers.
Funny, huh? The white ruin of muscular men.

Twisting bars like Gargantua; lewd Carusos,
Maimed Chanticleers, running off at the scars.
They hoot their arias through the rhythmic clashing
Of garbage-can lids that serve as dinner trays;

Inmates are slopped, while fascinated on-
Lookers watch Mrs. Hurley, somebody's grandma,
Eating gravy with her bare hands. Just animals, Rosetta.
She's not *your* mother. Don't let it get you.

Suddenly, Mr. Vincente, who with his eleven brothers
Built roads through the Spokane Valley
Where Italians moved like dreams of Martha Graham
As they laid asphalt over subterranean rivers,

Spots a distant cousin, Leonard, an architect
Until seventh grade, who seems to know him:
Leonard displays, by way of greeting.
His only piece of personal adornment:

How the tourists squeal! Watch them fumble at coat, and fly!
Girdled and ginghamed relatives disperse
Back to the touring car, the picnic basket
With its home-made grappa in giraffe-necked bottles.

As sun-scarred men urge olive children on,
Grandma Hurley, who thought the treat was for her,
Shyly waves her gravy-dappled fingers,
Couple-colored as her old brindled cat.

Enough of this madness! It's already in the past.
Now they are stabbed full of sopers, numbed & lobotomised
Is the privacy of their own heads. It's easier for the chaplain:
They're nodding. If you consent to be saved, just nod for God.

It's never over, old church of our claustrophobia!
Church of the barren towns, the vast unbearable sky,
Church of the Western plains, our first glimpse of brilliance.
Church of our innocent incense, there is no goodbye.

Church of the coloring-book, crude crayon of childhood,
Thank God at last you seem to be splitting apart.
But you live for at least as long as our maimed generation
Lives to curse your blessed plaster bleeding heart.

♦ ♦ ♦

THE BIOGRAPHY MAN

fiction by GARY REILLY

from THE IOWA REVIEW

nominated by THE IOWA REVIEW

"YOUR AUTOBIOGRAPHY!" he said to them, standing gilded in the morning sun like a sparkling tournament trophy. "We will write your very own story! Take it from me. My company. . . ." His company, a back-Eastern somewhere wholesale publisher making books inexpensive like fine wines in the cellar. "The more who buy, the cheaper they come!" hailing them from the wagon all circus curlicue red yellow and golden with a steed stamping and whinnying on the dusty streets. The children first saw him arrive, an edge of town voyager in the dawn with leather straps, champing horse, all silver buckles, spokes and copper rims, pulling into the townsquare at daybreak and throwing the side open for everyone to gaze upon leather and

441

goldtrim books. "Your own biography, your own life story!" printed
on quality paper, inexpensive labor of speciality house ". . . can
afford it because . . ." because of pot-boilers which allow the philanthropist owner (everyone knows how crazy philanthropist mil-
lionaires are) to take huge trash-novel profits and send wagonmen
through green little midwest towns to offer books, books, " . . .
everyone loves books!" books about your very own life. Bound and
goldtrimmed, don't forget that, printed and sent to you and see
these here on display now, from Bainbridge over in Ohio, and Star
City back in Indiana. Anyone have relatives in Star City? The crowd
pushing closer to the wagon now like leaves blown against autumn
trees, staring up at the traveling salesman, possible snake-oil man
for the suspicious sheriff to run out of town. Up closer now, necks
like marionettes, twisting to see the books. "Step up! Browse!
Thumb through the life stories of your cousins!" Children dashing
under the quiet nibbling horse's legs, chasing with gunsticks, and
parents hollering to be quiet. The leading citizens, the mayor and
city councilmen, all pinstripe and tophat and smile-vote formality,
standing to one side on the way to the office for coffee and business.
"Only ten dollars!" he shouts, "to leave a legacy for your children,
your grandchildren, your great-grandchildren!" This last striking
that golden note in the hearts of all men who sire children, as every
man wants to be immortal, every man has his pride. Now perking
up, husbands turning and smiling and nodding at wives, a twinkle in
their eyes, this sounds nice doesn't it now, a life story to give to the
heirs of a hundred years from now? Wives squint-eyed, doubting
with a slow nodding of the head, arms akimbo, listening to the wagon
man, counting egg-money hidden from the small-town husband who
drinks a little too much, but, oh well, it sorta would be nice now,
wouldn't it, to have a book like this here to pass on down through the
generations, of course, after all, what is there to say about our lives
here in the flatlands? "Remember that day you had your first
smoke?" he hollers from the wagon. "Remember that first drink?
Hey, remember that first kiss?" and a crowd of milling people now
grin foolishly down at the ground and, "Then again, maybe you'd
rather not say anything about that around the spouse!" and guffaws
from the crowd and everyone shy together on the townsquare.
"Remember that hunting trip? How about that fishing trip where
you almost caught that giant bass, pike, trout, pneumonia? The day
your first wagon made tracks on your front lawn?" And everyone

toe-digging the street, with far-off looks in men's eyes and the stories they told around whiskey campfires, and the women at their sewing circles, and well, it didn't seem all that important then, but now that you mention it, there was a thing or two in my life that. . . . "How many of you were kids?" he laughs, little kidhands clapping and dogs barking. "Any you people ever had parents who got you up and sent you off to a schoolhouse? Or whipped you when you got up to no good? Or sat with you on cold October evenings in front of the fireplace?" And the crowd now in mystic memory of childhood and "The smells! Do the smells of childhood come back to you? Fresh paint, smoke, pinewood and clover? The things you wish you could tell your descendants, what it was like in this midwest valley? Ten dollars!" Only ten dollars and everyone now early-morning shuffling as the crowd grows to hear the biography man. Ten dollars and a nice leatherbound and gold wholestory book.

Now the mayor passes through the crowd, everyone separating because he's a friend of the people (including the ones who didn't vote for him) and also the law in town whose job it is with the sheriff to determine just who among traveling salesmen are out to cheat the people, climbing up onto the wagon in front of the polished wood display with two hundred books at least, velvet drapes and glass, very home-in-the parlor America, now standing there introducing himself to the wagon man as the mayor with a solid judge-a-man handshake. The mayor picks up a book to determine the quality of the literature, being a literary man himself who has been known to dabble in Dickens late at night. He looks at a book about a man in Idaho, farmer, wife, children, so much like these people here, the words coming together and a scene of farming on a day when the sun is just coming up over the morning fields. The mayor reads along and nods his head. Everyone in the crowd nods along with the mayor and now a clerk from the grocery shyly steps up to the wagonstage and lifts a book and fingers the delicate pages and stops to read a passage, nodding with the mayor in the sales morning in the square.

"Now, folks! Folks, only ten dollars to have your lifestory printed up in leather and kept next to the family Bible. Poembooks they are, the narrative-lyric of your life." The mayor nods, ascertaining the fine prose value of the books, putting one aside, picking up another about a dock worker out of New Orleans, reading until he grows embarrassed dwelling overlong on a particularly bawdy description of a New Orleans cathouse while the salesman shouts to the people

"Only ten dollars!" putting the book down and picking up another about a young woman in eastern Kansas who lived in a prairie sod-house, with Indians coming at one time to steal corn and horses. "Very nice, very nice," says the mayor, nodding to the wagon man and stepping down to the street so that no one really knows what to think as the mayor smiles, shaking vote-hands and standing back in the crowd to watch while others cautiously ascend the steps to examine the library until soon the whole town is caught up in the circus atmosphere of the strangest salesman yet to come in to town with novel novelties with next-to-Bible-over-the-fire-place pos- sibilities to hand down through descendants to attain immortality.

The biography man raises the remaining sides on struts and a breeze flows through the lacquered shiny wagon as more people ascend to see the books, to browse, and to stand and study in thoughtful never-make-a-quick-deal wisdom of old Yankee trader stock. "Remember, this offer is made possible. . . . " Possible. "Possible thorough the generous personal contributions. . . ." of a terribly rich quick-buck bestseller publisher and eastern philan- thropist who knows the lifestory of everyman is a story in itself which should not be lost. "You do not have to be rich! You do not have to be famous! You *do* have to have ten dollars!" and laughter from the crowd of suspender-snapping and bonnet-adjusting smalltown folks of the prairie day.

Stores unopened on the ten o'clock street, all the customers now crowded around the bright carnival wagon, men stamping dust off their boots and spitting discreetly. Soda-fountain and dry-goods doorlocks untouched, hours late now as the town gathers around. No one worried—though banker-types with inbred duty rush to open businesses, only to stand in doorways alone while the wagon man draws bigger crowds, the money lying in tellercage drawers, the tweed and wool suits itchy in the already hot summer sun. Dogs barking and children chasing each other through the holiday-from- school streets, ducking down wooden alleys, tipping over rain- barrels in fun, the electricity catching like a disease, everyone wondering and hemming-and-hawing, and a few I-don't-knows in the crowd who set their heads at an angle and figure out the advan- tages of having their own biography on the shelf over the mantle- piece, next to the family Bible.

The display books well-looked-at now, people stepping back down off the wagon, lifting skirts and glancing back thoughtfully. Men pulling watches from burgundy vests and gazing at timepieces, already late this morning.

"Ten dollars! We make all the arrangements, place the orders and begin the publication process and you will receive one hardbound book guaranteed to last past a lifetime!" to be handed down, and will look so fine on the shelf and it will cause a chuckle or a tear to reopen the book on fall evenings to read once more about that time the boys all got together and raided the orchard, and laugh, slapping knees, because those fellows wrote it down just exactly the way it was, got it down to a T, and lissen here, that night we drove to the dance out at the armory, remember that? Oh yeah, yeah, and riding back home in the buggy past Miller's lake where the moon was oh so, yeah, they wrote it up just exactly like it was, and ain't it nice to have it up there, even if it is sorta, you know. . . . And then the people begin to look at one another out of the corners of their eyes, and everyone is beginning to think the same thing. The sin of Pride, and how would it look to go around having a book about yourself. Shameful? Is it not rather, well, but still. . . . "Abraham Lincoln was one of your kin! There are literally hundreds of biographies about our sixteenth president! And he was the humblest among men!" and they look up at him and nod, well, yes, ol' Honest Abe was a humble and great man and we study him in school, but, it seems, I don't know, we are not a famous poeple and have nothing to crow about, but still, there were nice times which would be pleasant to read about in our old age and to show the grandchildren. "But it's a shame," old ladies in the crowd whispering Christian Duty and sinful Pride-dreaming until people begin to stroll away, trying to think now, ol' Abe, yes, but still, and there is that Pride to watch out for, but famous people got to be that way, and, well, better think it over, although it certainly does sound nice, and so cheap, only ten dollars, which we certainly can afford in these times which are not so bad. "Everyman has a story to tell!" People wondering, not quite sure now, turning and heading for banks, dry-goods stores, blacksmiths, time for business and thinking it over, though I'm not gonna be the first to climb those steps and plunk down ten dollars in front of the whole town to have them think I'm some kind of looking-glass fiend, we'll just wait to see if anyone else does it first.

Hot windy dusty day of dry wood and heat rising from hardbaked street-dirt. The biography man sitting sunshaded on a wooden folding chair with pillow, now gazing out with a sad smile on his lips as townsfolk drift by on wooden storefront sidewalks in gingham dresses and bluejeans workpants, children racing past the lone wagon on dares while kids shoot like Indians at the covered-wagon in their territory. Sipping on a cherry phosphate from the soda fountain, resting next to the golden leather books standing on the polished brownwood display case, leaning back for more shade, head nodding at the folks who look up and maybe smile or nod with approval and howdy while stepping on down the street to go to the hardware store or even to the saloon for an afternoon beer before getting back to work. The salesman slyly peeking out from under the brim of his hat and mind-nodding to himself without moving. There goes the mayor, and the salesman nods to himself at the mayor who imagines himself a great orator whose legend befits a man of his stature, sitting up late into the night, drinking tumblers of scotch, staring at his cluttered desktop, he will look down over the town from the third-story pinnacle room of City Hall and spy on the biography man in the street, thinking maybe he'll just slip out in the dark and pay that salesman a visit and just keep the book locked up in a safe until old age, handing his lifestory to his son when he reaches his majority, still wondering about Pride, but thinking no one shall see him in the dark, the biography man promising to stay all night until moving-on time in the morning.

The salesman now glancing at the young farmhand looking out through the grimy hardware store window, and the salesman nods to himself again at this young buck who fancies himself a pirate-casanova with a tale or two to tell, getting back to work later that afternoon and recollecting those nights when he slipped over into the next county to drink moonshine with the Willamet boys, and that horse race he won out at the lake last summer impressing not-yet girlfriends, and all the man-adventures he'd had in the valley since he was a boy which would impress a girl or two the next time he was dressed up and out for a dance at the armory, raking hay and sweating in the workafternoon sunshine, thinking maybe he'd just grab a ten-spot out of his ol'sock buried under the floorboards of his bedroom in the shed out back of the barn and maybe just hop on over there after dark when no one can see him to poke fun or laugh about his Pride.

The salesman sips his phosphate, leaning back and shuffling his shoulders against the wall of the wagon, brushing buzzing summerheat flies away from his face, crossing his legs, rubbing his nose, tipping his hat and nodding at the young girl shyly looking away behind her mother as they come from the millinery and dry-goods with bolts of calico for dresses, curtains, bedspreads, walking prim down the sidewalk, and the salesman nodding at the girl who sits up late at night with gothic novels from the five-and-ten, secreted away from Ma and Pa, to be read in candle-lit darkness, alone in the bedroom where every night dashing young heroes lie on her bed to gather her up in their arms and caress her hair and press lips against hers while she wide-eyed and breathless reads page after page of a novel that, really now, is quite a bit like her own life. After all, did she not kiss that Roberts boy at the dance in Waynesville that time she went to visit her relatives in Illinois that year after high school graduation? Certainly her life would be as exciting to read as anything written by famous female gothic novelists. Those days of lake-wading, love-discovering, classroom beaus, friendship rings, all culminating in a passionate novel. Why, if her biography were ever put on paper, it might become an eastern bestseller, leading perhaps to starring roles with Broadway New York Nightingales and opening-night parties, and after-dinner drinks in blood-red candle-lit apartments with handsome leading actors and famous novelists as she herself might someday be. Her heart pounding at the thought of maybe taking just a little, only ten dollars, from the graduation money her parents surprised her with for hopechest dowry with a possible trip to visit her aunt in Philadelphia someday. Just to take a walk in the evening streets past the townsquare and when no one was around, step out into the street and maybe get nerve to talk to the good-looking stranger, always did like older men really, that Roberts boy was *such* a child, and after all, only ten dollars, Ma and Pa never to know about it, hiding the biography in back of her closet where Pa never looks and Ma doesn't bother with. Really, it would seem a wise, if not sensible, investment. Only ten dollars. And that salesman, well, she knew about salesmen. She would giggle about this, following her mother down the street into the notions shop.

Handing the empty glass to a short-haircut boy who turns to dash back to the drugstore to show the wagon man that he is the fastest runner of any kid in town, he leans back, his head not moving, but always watching, waiting, in the hot summer afternoon of clouds and a cool breeze now and then, no customers yet, but knowing, always knowing what is in the hearts of the people who will come in the night.

A farmer now, rigging by with horses and wagon, tipping his straw hat very politely, wife beside him, happy-gone kids sitting on flour sacks in back, squatting up and down, grinning at the carnival wagon as they start back to the farmhouse now just a mile or so out of town. The salesman looks into the farmer face and nods with a hat-tip and smile as the wagon rumbles clink past with dust rolling from under wheels and the leather smack of reins on horses' backs. He nods. And the farmer will drive on now, past and out of town, thinking with a grin of dadburn good ol' days of swimming and helping birth foals, and barnfires, and that time in Texas when he rode the bull in the rodeo and now wouldn't that make a whopper of a story to go sticking in a book! Not the cathouse stuff now, wife would kill him with an ax, but still all the good times when he belonged to the militia long ago in Oklahoma and all those oil-rich Indians causing trouble, and him staying out two whole weeks during the riots and almost getting to fire his rifle. Exciting days. That mule trip back into Wyoming not ten years ago for hunting and maybe goldfinding before he finally came home and settled down and got hitched and, oh yeah, there were a couple things that might make good reading just for fun and all, and I don't care, I think it'd be damn nice to have a book about myself to read when I'm old and to give to the kids and I don't give a goddam but that I think I just might ride back into town towards nightfall and maybe drop in on that salesman and chew the fat and see what it's all about here now. I don't care what anybody'd think. I think it'd be damn nice.

So flies buzz in the heat shimmering off the street as the sun goes down and cool shadows start to sprout all over town with evening pulling in, and the salesman gets up and stretches his legs and goes into the tiny bed-back-shack part of the wagon to get out forms and pens and ink and wait now for the customers who'll be coming in the night to whisper secret dreams, coming in the dark so that no one might see them and think them just a little too Proud and avoid them maybe on the streets later, now that they want one of the books.

And they came in the night. Quietly tapping on wagon wheels, the salesman leaning out into the dark and inviting each customer into the yellow light of the office-bedroom to discuss details and explain publishing. The street lit silver by a crescent moon making barely-discernible silhouettes flitting in and out of the darkness whenever the street seems deserted and no one seems to be there to see what anyone might be up to around the biography wagon at this time of night.

Silent, still, crickets in the weeds.

Dawn in the town, people crowded around now, staring at the wagon tracks coming into town but not leaving. Great silent horse hoofmarks still embedded in the dirt, wagon tracks coming into town to vanish in thin air, like spook-waif, gone in the morning sun. The sheriff examining the tracks, not knowing what to make of the strange mysterious disappearance of the wagon, suspecting foul play, wondering if it was possible those crazy Willamet kids from the next county mighta come in the night and spirited away the whole set-up in a practical joke, like the wagon in the courthouse foyer last Halloween, but no, no tracks, just a few footprints, no clues. Then, a panic-stricken mother running up to the sheriff, daughter gone, salesman gone, get a rope, catch him, hang him for fooling a young girl and whisking her off to the east, New York! A tear-streaked face crying up at him, the perplexed sheriff not knowing what to tell her or where the salesman could even be. And then a councilman stopping by and asking where the mayor is, had a meeting at eight o'clock and hasn't shown. Then a wagon from out of town with a farmwife frantic to know if her husband got drunk and is in jail sobering up, and the sheriff having no answer for her nor the cowering children on the buckboard. The street crowds with people in the town-square, stepping all over the wagon tracks which come into town but do not leave. Roll right up and stop across the street from the dry-goods store, then vanish like morning fog, and every-one scratching their heads and looking around at each other and wondering, and wives, husbands, fathers, clamoring, pulling on the sheriff's vest, "Where are they? Where are our husbands? Our wives? Our daughters? Our sons? Where have they gone?" And the sheriff shouting, trying to calm down the people and looking worried over his shoulder, wishing the mayor would come strolling down the street to help solve the mysterious disappearances. Crying in the street, wailing, embarrassed folk shyly looking away, not used to emotion and tears of shocked mothers and distressed pale husbands and bawling children. The sheriff finally telling the ones with lost relatives to come to the office one at a time and he will fill out a form and, well, I'll just take down the information and we'll send it up to the state capitol and maybe they'll send someone down here that knows about these kinds o' things. Now y'all just calm down and everyone else go home and the rest of you come over to my office and we'll just try to get things straightened out here now.

Months, seasons, rainfall, silent mourning nights pass slowly, quiet wagons moving down the streets now, the crying and wailing ceasing long ago, reports to the capitol going back-and-forth until red-eyed mothers and white-faced husbands have melted into silent giving-up. Streets a little sadder now, no word from outlying districts.

An afternoon by the dry-goods store, teamsters pull up with deliveries, unloading crates onto the street, receipts, back-breaking heaving of boxes and storeroom shelving, the clerk frowning as wagons drive off to the next county with more deliveries as he counts the number of crates and rechecks the stockroom until he finds the mistake which is a crate that he opens, and there, goldtrimmed leather books which the clerk stares at for only a moment until he is running across the street and dragging the sheriff over to his store to look before word gets around town. But the frantic running to the sheriff's office has the town interested, now that the loss of relatives in the mysterious sad summer has been all but forgotten. They begin to follow, to drift into the store, and back into the stockroom where the sheriff silently pulls out book after book, and looks at titles. Biographies. All familiar names of souls lost, dozens, every name on the report to the capitol. People crowding around for a better look until a scream shocks everybody and a woman is grabbing at a book with tears falling, clutching the book to her breast, her daughter, the book, held with knuckle-white fingers. The sheriff wide-eyed as the crowd turns slowly, like water coming to a boil, until arms are grabbing and pulling and knocking stock to the floor with the clerk shouting frantically to stop, please now, hold on, until the sheriff, not knowing what, begins to shout orders and people back up and the scurry on the floor of men and women settles.

Books now being pulled out one-by-one and handed back into the crowd as silent onlookers gaze in fear at the names printed in gold on each of the book covers. The store silent, lone figures leaving, stepping out into the street, books dwindling until a few lie untaken by relatives who had packed up and moved on. These he will send to the state capitol.

THE NERVES OF A MIDWIFE: CONTEMPORARY AMERICAN WOMEN'S POETRY

by ALICIA OSTRIKER

from PARNASSUS: POETRY IN REVIEW

nominated by PARNASSUS: POETRY IN REVIEW

> I am obnoxious to each carping tongue
> Who says my hand a needle better fits.

Thus briskly wrote the pilgrim mother Anne Bradstreet in a "Prologue" to her book of poems, first published in 1650, and thus meekly two stanzas later the first woman poet in America apologized:

> Men have precedency and still excel.
> Men can do best and women know it well.
> Preeminence in each and all is yours;
> Yet grant some small acknowledgment of ours.

A fraction over three centuries later, Erica Jong observed in "Bitter Pills for the Dark Ladies" (1968) just how small the acknowledgment could be:

451

If they let you out it's Supermansaint
& the ultimate praise is always a question of nots:
    viz. not like a woman
    viz. "certainly not another poetess"

meanin'
    she got a cunt but she don't talk funny
    & he's a nigger but he don't smell funny
& the only good poetess is a dead.

The "certainly not another poetess" remark was Robert Lowell's at
the advent of Sylvia Plath's *Ariel*, and Plath, who certainly did not
want to be another poetess, might well have been pleased by it. But
Plath and Jong have in fact both contributed to an extraordinary tide
of poetry by American women poets since the late 1950's* which
shows no sign of abating.

An increasing proportion of this work is explicitly female in the sense
that the writer has consciously chosen not to "write like a man" but to
explore experiences central to her sex, to find the style necessary to
express such experiences, and therefore, at least at first, often to
invite the scorn of conventional literary critics, editors, and male
poets.

    In the 1970s, dozens of little magazines and presses have sprung
up which print only women's poetry. Universities across the country
run series of women's poetry readings, as do, on a more modest
level, coffee-houses; conferences of women poets occur and recur.
The audience upon which these activities depend takes its poetry
avidly and personally. One young woman poet I know calls the work
of other women "survival tools." Another writes me:

> About women poets. I like them and read them because I think
> they're writing more exciting poetry than most men. Their poetry is
> about discovery and breaking new ground and it feels more like life to
> me . . . like work that comes to grips with what I feel is essential in all

---

* Among the breakthrough volumes initiating this period are Adrienne Rich, *Snapshots of
a Daughter-in-Law: Poems 1954–62* (published 1963), Muriel Rukeyser, *The Speed of
Darkness* (1960), Anne Sexton, *To Bedlam and Part Way Back* (1960) and *All My Pretty
Ones* (1962), Denise Levertov, *The Jacob's Ladder* (1961) and *O Taste and See* (1963),
Diane Wakoski, *Inside the Blood Factory* (1962), Carolyn Kizer, *Pro Femina* (1963), Sylvia
Plath, *Ariel* (1963).

arts—what are we doing in our lives? Why do we do it? How do we see each other? How can we change what we have into what we want?

Among commercial and university presses, good women poets are widely published and recognized for their individual voices. Their books on the whole receive thoughtful reviews, written with clearer understanding and less condescension every year. True, instead of "certainly not another poetess," the highest praise in some circles is "certainly not another feminist," but even this is changing.*

What has not changed is that most critics and professors of literature, including modern literature, deny that "women's poetry," as distinct from poetry by individual women, exists. Many women writers agree. Some will not permit their work to appear in women's anthologies.

The superficial plausibility of this position rests on the undeniable fact that women writers are a diverse lot, adhering to no single set of beliefs, doctrines, styles, or subjects. Yet would anyone deny the usefulness of the term "American poetry" (or "French poetry" or "Brazilian poetry") on the grounds that American (or "French, or Brazilian) poets are diverse? Should we call Whitman, Frost, Pound, and Stevens "poets" but not "American poets?" Did T.S. Eliot's rejection of America make him any less quintessentially an American poet? In all these cases, the poet's nationality is central to his work; we might even argue that the more deeply an artist represents a nation, the more likely that artist is to represent humanity. Shakespeare was thoroughly English, Dante thoroughly Italian, and so on.

---

* Anthologies of women's poetry fare differently from books of poems by individual women. I read *Parnassus* for enlightened, stimulating criticism of poetry and poetics, and am seldom disappointed. But in the Spring/Summer 1975 *Parnassus* I find a review which spends six lines on Segnitz and Rainey's *Psyche: An Anthology of Modern American Women Poets* and calls it "petite" (it is 256 pages, or about the same size as Donald Hall's *Contemporary American Poetry*, which for years was a standard volume). "The twenty poets are good," says the reviewer, but does not name one, or quote one line; and then proceeds to six encomiastic pages on Rothenberg and Quasha's *America A Prophecy*, finding it "a big anthology." That is rather extreme old-school. Yet the Fall/Winter issue of the same year contains a review of two other women's anthologies, in which the reviewer, though far more conscientious and detailed in analysis—he distinguishes intelligently between the two volumes, argues soundly against the editorial polemic of one of them while allowing the justice of its essential points, and appreciates excellence in the poems of both—nevertheless confesses discomfort with the existence of such anthologies. He praises Levertov for "triumphing on tiptoe over biology and destiny," Rich for "the emotional distance that enables her to perfect aesthetic form," and gives his opinion that many of the poets "would prefer to be read as women second, as poets first." What causes him, I wonder, to think so? Must we prefer one of those terms to the other?

Because of the critical assumption that poetry has no gender, we have not learned to see women poets generically, or to discuss the ideas, apart from the temporary ideologies, that the flowering of their poetry generates. In what follows, I make the assumption that "women's poetry" exists in much the same sense that "American poetry" exists, and that from it we should discover not only more of what it means to be a woman but also more of what it means to be human. Athough we may not be able to guess just which poems or poets from the present lively moment will in the long run endure, we can reasonably expect that whatever is shallow will evaporate by itself, and that whatever is profound and strong will ultimately enrich the mainstream of letters. Here I would like to touch, speculatively, on four elements in women's poetry which seem to me original, important, and organically connected with one another. These are the quest for autonomous self-definition, the intimate treatment of the body; the release of anger; and what I call, for want of a better name, the contact imperative. Each of these themes appears in the work of many more writers than I will be able to quote, and some of those I quote will be familiar names while some will not, precisely because the ideas, the feelings, are not merely the property of individuals. I will also say a few hesitating words about stylistic and formal considerations in women's poetry, and how they may correlate with certain emotional requirements.

First of all, then, it appears that to define oneself as authentically as possible from within has become the major female enterprise in poetry. "No more masks!" is a line from Muriel Rukeyser and the title of an anthology. Not what our fathers and mothers told us, not what our teachers expected, not what our lovers suppose, nor necessarily what literature and mythology, however beautiful and compelling, tells us: what are we then? As soon as the question is asked, certain typical rifts appear. Denise Levertov in the poem "In Mind" discovers two incompatible selves: one a woman

> of innocence, unadorned but
> fair-featured, and smelling of
> apples or grass. She wears
> a utopian smock . . .
>   And there's a
> turbulent moon-ridden girl
> or old woman, or both,

> dressed in opals and rags, feathers
> and torn taffeta . . .

The first "is kind" but lacks imagination. The second "knows strange songs" but is not kind. A self approved by others, modest, decorous, and humanistically valuable (it has written, I think, Levertov's poems of social and political compassion), stands against a darker, more mysterious and dangerous self. Both are natural—it is not a question of one being real, one hypocritical—although the latter might perhaps better be called preternatural. Levertov, perhaps the sweetest and most life-celebratory of poets writing today, nevertheless writes of a "coldness to life," an inner-directedness which seems "unwomanly" because insufficiently nurturing of others. Or she writes of cherishing a "madness . . . blue poison, green pain in the mind's veins" though she has always been the sanest of her friends, the one they came to for comfort. The split is a central one in Levertov, and many young women warm to her work because it expresses both clearly and gently a dilemma they find in themselves. More flamboyantly, Diane Wakoski in "Beauty" parades a self something like Levertov's moon-ridden girl, asking:

> and if I cut off my long hair,
> if I stopped speaking,
> if I stopped dreaming for other people about parts of the car,
> stopped handing them tall creamy flowered silks,
> and loosing the magnificent hawks to fly in their direction . . .
> if I stopped crying for the salvation of the tea ceremony,
> stopped rushing in excitedly with a spikey bird-of-Paradise,
> and never let them see how accurate my pistol-shooting is,
> who would I be?

The dilemma in Wakoski, and again it is a common one, is a sense of overpowering pride, vitality, and imaginative energy crossed by a selfdestructive dependence on others for its confirmation. "Where is the real me I want them all to love," she asks self-mockingly, as she swings from one father-lover figure to another—George Washington whom she excoriates at one end of her pendulum, Beethoven to whom she clings at the other, and the easy riders whom she invites to make her life hard in between.

Not only roles and temperaments may come into question, but sexual identity itself, as it does in Adrienne Rich:

> *I do not know*
> *if sex is an illusion*
>
> *I do not know*
> *who I was when I did those things*
> *or who I said I was*
> *or whether I willed to feel*
> *what I had read about*
> *or who in fact was there with me*
> *or whether I knew, even then*
> *that there was doubt about these things*
> ("Dialogue")

> If I am flesh sunning on rock
> if I am brain burning in fluorescent
> light
>
> if I am dream like a wire with fire
> throbbing along it
>
> if I am death to man
> I have to know it
> ("August")

I have to know it. That is the unspoken theme behind the self-regard which dominates many women's work, whether the work is a delicate blend of feeling, sensation, and thought like Levertov's, passionately exhibitionistic like Wakoski's, or essentially intellectual like Rich's. The fact that the question of identity is a real one, for which the thinking woman may have as yet no satisfactory answer, may turn her resolutely inward. It may also make her poetry urgent and emotional, insofar as feelings initially inhibited, whether from within or without, have permission to erupt into the poem—and she will not know who she is until she lets them. In such work, academic distinctions between art and life, or between the self and what we in the classroom call the speaker or the persona of a poem (persona, recall, means "mask"), move to vanishing point.

A good deal of the confusion felt by some readers confronted with women's poetry may be a simple matter of fashion. Our present critical milieu expects and rewards the maintenance of low profiles in poetry: "reticence," for example, is the term Richard Howard employs to recommend Ammons' *Sphere*, and Ashbery's *Self-Portrait in a Convex Mirror* enjoys a *success d'estime* for implying that a distorting lens tells us all we know and all we need to know about the self. "Control" and "distance" make good buzzwords on any book-jacket, while the phrase "confessional poetry" has become equivalent to wrinkling up one's nose as at a nasty odor, something vulgar. But when a woman poet says "I" she is likely to mean the actual "I" as intensely as her verbal skills permit, much as Wordsworth or Keats did—or Blake, or Milton, or John Donne of the *Holy Sonnets*, before Eliot's "extinction of personality" became the mandatory twentieth-century initiation ritual for young American poets.

Another problem is that the woman poet who seeks herself puts trivial material, that is, the material of her own daily life and feelings, into poems. "Some women marry houses," begins Anne Sexton's terse and deadpan "Housewife:"

> It's another kind of skin; it has a heart,
> a mouth, a liver and bowel movements.
> The walls are permanent and pink.
> See how she sits on her knees all day,
> faithfully washing herself down.
> Men enter by force, drawn back like Jonah
> into their fleshy mothers.
> A woman *is* her mother.
> That's the main thing.

Or, again, "They say women are too personal. We are not personal enough," begins Penelope Schott, in a poem which speaks of insufficient empathy with other women, who push baby carriages she has grown free of. She remembers how it felt to push the baby carriages, laden with groceries, down curbstones. She remembers that her mother lied to her about growing pubic hair, and about the pain of childbirth, and that "I have already lied to my daughter." To tell the truth to our daughters requires that we acknowledge it ourselves. The poem becomes the tribunal where a persona will not suffice; it is oneself who will be found innocent or guilty.

As the two poems just quoted already indicate, one subject that all women have in common to tell the truth about is anatomy; not, perhaps, as destiny but as priority, especially since in a world where perhaps not much is to be trusted, "the body does not lie." *Tota mulier in utero*, says the Latin, although until recently anatomy was not a subject for women's pens. While Lawrence, Joyce and Henry Miller wrote and let censorship be damned, Virginia Woolf in a lecture on "Professions for Women" recalled her impulse, when young, to describe "something about the body . . . which it was unfitting for her as a woman to say. Men, her reason told her, would be shocked . . . For though men sensibly allow themselves great freedom in these respects, I doubt that they realize or control the extreme severity with which they condemn such freedom in women." In the 1970's, descriptions of bodily experiences have become the most common sign of female identification in poetry. Tactility and orality abound—Sexton and Jong are particularly oral, for example, their poems filled with images of food, eating, sucking, licking. Sex receives graphic treatment hot and cold—Lynn Lifshin is probably the silkiest siren among the Wife of Bath's daughters, Elizabeth Sargent and Alta the lustiest. Looking at and touching oneself, dressing and adorning oneself, menstruation, pregnancy and birth, abortion, rape, the surgeon's knife, the process of aging, the handling of children—because women have been traditionally been defined by and confined to the secret gardens of their physical selves, while being forbidden to talk in mixed company about them, they now have much to say. The abundance and variety of body images in women's poetry presently outweighs that of men's, as does the non-air-brushed intimacy of focus.

The range of attitudes women take toward the body is also startling. At one extreme, which would be medieval were it not so modern, Sylvia Plath perceives the flesh as infinitely and fascinatingly vulnerable. "I am red meat," she realizes in "Death & Co.," and her poems form a *totentanz* of the body's subjection to laceration, mutilation, disease, paralysis, rendered in chillingly vivid images of passivity and pain:

> They have propped my head between the pillow and the sheet-
> cuff
> Like an eye between two white lids that will not shut.
> Stupid pupil, it has to take everything in . . .

My husband and child smiling out of the family photo;
Their smiles catch onto my skin, little smiling hooks.

The world of Plath's imagination is bounded by the brutal destruction of flesh in the Nazi holocaust and the everyday brutality of "The butcher's guillotine that whispers 'How's this, how's this?' " More recently, the young poet Ai depicts a rural Southwest in which men and women alike exist at a level of ruthless bodily hungers. When a man beats a runaway woman:

> The corner of your mouth bleeds
> and your tongue slips out, slips in.
> You don't fight me, you never do.

When a midwife does her job:

> A scraggy, red child comes out of her into my hands
> like warehouse ice sliding down the chute.

The bondage of a female body takes another form in poems which deal with the ambivalence of beauty. To cosmetize or not to cosmetize? This is a sub-genre in itself, opening a rich vein of comic possibilities. Carolyn Kizer in "Pro Femina" remarks on "Our masks, always in peril of smearing or cracking," attention to which keeps a woman from serious work, neglect of which keeps her without a love life, catching up on her reading. Honor Moore's "My Mother's Mustache" gives the pros and cons of depilatories. Karen Swenson worries about a bosom less ample than Monroe's. "It's a sex object if you're pretty/love and no sex if you're fat," observes Nikki Giovanni. Jong writes a hilarious poem on "Aging," with a surprise happy ending. These poems are as undignified as they are funny—we are off the pedestal—and of course, like all good clowning, work of this sort spins from a painful core. Raised up to be narcissists, which is a game every woman ultimately loses, we must laugh that we may not weep.

Also among the poems just beginning to be written are some which treat the female body as a power rather than a liability. In Sharon Barba's "A Cycle of Women," the poet evokes.

> that dream world Anaïs speaks of
> that dark watery place
> where everything is female,

and imagines a new Venus emerging from it, "a woman big-hipped, beautiful and fierce." Sexton writes "In Celebration of my Uterus," comparing "the central creature and its delight" to a singing schoolgirl, a spirit, a cup, "soil of the fields . . . roots," and hyperbolically declares:

> Each cell has a life.
> There is enogh here to feed a nation . . .
> Any person, any commonwealth would say of it,
> "It is good this year that we may plant again
> and think forward to a harvest."

Robin Morgan's long "Network of the Imaginary Mother" recounts the poet's conversion from loathing to loving her own body, precipitated by the baptismal experience of nursing her dying mother, and defines her biological capacities in terms of goddess-figures representing a triumphant will to love and nurture, opposed to the killing abstractions of technology. Muriel Rukeyser has developed a language similarly rooted in gender and ramifying into politics, which envisions radical social change impelled by principles of maternity. The power of the maternal drive to transform even the most intimate grief and guilt into strength appears in Lucille Clifton's "The Lost Baby Poem:"

> the time i dropped your almost body down
> to meet the waters under the city
> and run one with the sewage to the sea
> what did i know about waters rushing back
> what did i know about drowning
> or being drowned . . .
>
> if i am ever less than a mountain
> for your definite brothers and sisters
> let the rivers pour over my head
> let the sea take me for a spiller
> of seas let black men call me stranger
> always for your never named sake

And for Adrienne Rich, in the difficult yet triumphant close to "The Mirror in Which Two Are Seen as One," it is ourselves to whom we must heroically give birth:

> your mother dead and you unborn
> your two hands grasping your head
> drawing it down against the blade of life
> your nerves the nerves of a midwife
> learning her trade.

It will be interesting to see whether such female metaphors will come to take their place alongside more conventional metaphors for heroism. Meanwhile, whether engaged or not in ideology, it would be difficult to find a woman poet writing today who does not treat the facts of her and our physical experience as essential material for poetry.

If we turn to sexual politics in the sense coined by Kate Millett, we find less pleasure, more anger, and a striking development of poems about violence, although (or because) neither violence nor anger has been a traditionally acceptable mode of expression for women. When women perceive themselves as victims, suppressed, confined, their strengths denied and their weaknesses encouraged under the collective and personal system feminists have come to call patriarchy, they write self-pity poems, mad-housewife poems, off-our-back poems, all of which are interesting at least symptomatically. The most interesting of them are those which generalize, or make generalization possible, by plunging to the principles which animate persons.

One recalls Plath's archetypally authoritarian male figure in "Lady Lazarus," the composite Doctor-Nazi-sideshow manager, "Herr God, Herr Lucifer." In the eyes of this figure the poet is, she knows, an object to be manipulated, a freak, "your jewel . . . your valuable." In Mona Van Duyn's complex and witty "Death by Aesthetics," the same unpleasant figure appears as a physican-lover, probably also psychoanalyst, an icy Doctor Feelgood:

> His fluoroscope hugs her. Soft the intemperate girl
> disordered. Willing she lies while he unfolds
> her disease, but a stem of glass protects his fingers
> from her heat, nor will he catch her cold . . .

He hands her a paper. "Goodbye. Live quietly,
make some new friends. I've seen these stubborn cases
cured with time. My bill will arrive. Dear lady,
it's been a most enjoyable diagnosis."

In vain the patient begs:

meet me, feel the way my body feels,
and in my bounty of dews, fluxes and seasons,
orifices, in my wastes and smells
see self.

He has already gone, saying "Dont't touch me," and his
prescription reads "Separateness."

The experimental playwright and poet Rochelle Owens,
in the ironically titled "The Power of Love: He Wants Shih,"
has composed a sadistic fantasy for a practicioner of martial
arts. The hero explains that a woman's love for him is his
weapon, that as her feeling increases, his disappears:

> It's heaven's will, shau hsi!
> In my mind I smear the mucus
> from my nose on her breasts . . .
> & drop ants into her two mouths . . .
> I fill up all her orifices—
> I'm very generous . . .
> & she calls me the divinity
> of mountains & streams &
> I think of how it would be
> to piss on her!

May Swenson's "Bleeding" takes the form of a dialogue between a
cut and a knife, the former apologetic, the latter angry about being
made "messy with this blood." Similarly grim is the dialogue in
Marge Piercy's "The Friend," in which a man across the table tells a
woman to cut off her hands because they poke and might touch him,
to burn her body because it is "not clean and smells like sex." She
agrees and says she loves him. He says he likes to be loved and asks
her if she has cut off her hands yet.

Such poems, it seems to me, probe deeply into the sources of male-female misery, directing one's horror almost equally against the hypocrite male's inaccessibility to emotion, and the female's compliance in her victimization. Men, in poems about male domination, are always authority figures associated with technology, abstract and analytical thinking instead of feeling, a will to exercise control, and a gluttonous demand for admiration. But the women are helpless petitioners: all they need is love, they make no demands, they will do anything and permit anything to be done to them, they are all too ready to obey. Nor is it an accident that the scenes of these poems are all intimately physical. The presumably male idea of the uncleanness of flesh, and of women's flesh in particular, which we inherit with the rest of our Judeo-Christian dreamlife baggage (e.g. Tertullian, "Woman is a temple over a sewer") is one that perhaps few women themselves evade. Self-disgust is a strong drink, and to the passive woman an intoxicant: "Every woman adores a fascist/The boot in the face."

One need not believe that individual men necessarily fill the role which so many women's poems have men play, that of aggressive or impassive villain; or that women themselves are universally innocent of such vices. Some men mop the floor. Some women are bitches. One of the excellences of a poem like Swenson's is that it assigns no explicit gender to the cut and the knife—the masochistic cut in fact sounds very much like Shakespeare's Shylock. Such games can be played by persons of any sex, in any combination; compare Ginsberg's "Master" in *The Fall of America*. But this does not invalidate the individual suffering in the poems, or the generic applications implied by them. We know the bleeding cut feels feminine, we know the knife which wants to be hard and shiny feels masculine.

What follows, then, at any rate in a significant number of poems, is the fantasy of vengeance. Plath imagines a ritual slaying of the father she loves and hates in "Daddy," and a return from the grave to devour men in "Lady Lazarus." Rich in "The Phenomenology of Anger" dreams of becoming an acetylene torch, to burn away the lie of her enemy, the killer of babies at My Lai, the defoliator of fields. She desires, she says, to leave him a new man, yet one cannot escape the sense of her compulsion to punish. In her more down-to-earth manner, Diane Wakoski dedicates *The Motorcycle Betrayal Poems* "to all those men who betrayed me at one time or another, in hopes they will fall off their motorcycles and break their necks." In one of the poems of that volume, Wakoski imagines shooting a lover in the back with a Thompson Contender, and watching him topple over once for every man—from her father to the President—who has neglected her. In "They Eat Out," Margaret Atwood punctures, with a fork, a self-important gentleman friend. Grisliest of the lot, perhaps, is Cynthia Macdonald's "Objets d'Art." Having been told by a stranger in a railway station that she was "a real ball-cutter," she thinks it over, goes into the business, finds that freezing is the best method of preservation—and is interested, of course, only in volunteers:

It is an art like hypnosis
Which cannot be imposed on the unwilling victim.

which brings us full circle on the fine line between fear and need in human motivation.

But if the release of anger is a major element in women's poetry, so, to an even greater degree, is the release of a contrary passion, which in part explains the vehemence of women's rage. The superiority of male over female (or the mind over the body, or the impersonal over the personal) appears to be the more intolerable to many women poets because of intense cravings for unity, for a sense of relationship which escapes the vertical grid of dominance and submission altogether. Mutuality, continuity, connection, identification, touch: this theme in women's work is one which we might call the contact imperative, and it strongly affects the way women write about love, time, history, politics, and themselves.

In love poetry, the contact imperative means goodbye to the strong silent type. "I like my men/talky and/tender," says Carol Bergé, and in poem after poem describing gratified desire, those lovers and husbands are praised who are most gentle and warm; i.e., who release rather than suppress their "feminine" qualities. Conversely, the poets seem best satisfied with themselves when they quit passivity and take some form of initiative, like Nikki Giovanni in "The Seduction," forthrightly undressing her man while he lectures on about the revolution. Domestically, women tend to envision love as something natural, normal, and shared, as in Lisel Mueller's "Love Like Salt." To explain ecstasy, women consistently seem to employ the idea of interpenetration between two lovers, the dissolving of boundaries between individual selves, and at especially blissful moments, the elimination of distinctions between human and nonhuman existence. A couple makes love in a bedroom, and then there is

> the hot joy spilling
> puddles on the bed, the rug,
> the back yard, the earth
> happy with us, needing our joy.

"Anybody could write this poem," insists Alta in her title. "All you have to say is Yes." Again, in Maxine Kumin's "We Are," the lovingly-developed metaphor for a pair of lovers is that of a pond, complete with frogs whose legs open like very small children's, skimmed by waterbugs, surrounded by blackberry bushes: "We teem, we overgrow." Still again, in Daniela Gioseffi's quasi-surrealistic, quasi-pornographic "Paradise Is Not a Place," the lovers sail the seas on their mattress, and ultimately fuse into a giant Mount Androgynous which becomes a permanent tourist attraction in the mid-Pacific. One would think of Donne's "The Canonization," except that for Gioseffi, as for women love poets in general, love does not signify transcendence of carnality or mortality, nor does it involve trials, tests, obstacles. The images are of relaxation and immanence rather than strenuousness. The motion of love is down, not up: down toward the earth, down into the flesh, easily.

The need for connection can also express itself in terms of exploring continuities between generations. Daughters write of parents or grandparents, mothers write of children. Women write of continuities from one writer to another (not, *pace* Harold Bloom, on the Oedipal model of killing and superceding, but on the Demeter-Kore model of returning and reviving), or the love-and-support relationships (sexual or not) generated and reinforced by the feminist movement.

Among politically radical writers such as Rich, Piercy, and Morgan, desire for personal affection assumes the status of a non-negotiable demand. Intimacies between friends and lovers become a model for the conduct of political life. What resists the self-surrender of love in the microcosm of private relationships is also what resists it in Vietnam, Biafra, Harlem, and these poets want to break that resistance, tear off the armor, and liberate the willing lover at the core of the unwilling enemy. Thus an embrace is a "guerrilla tactic" in Piercy's "Agitprop," and the woman who inflicts it on an unresponding man is sending his deeper self "promises . . . of interim relief/and ultimate victory."

These women are also the writers who make poems for and from the lives of lost women, the insulted and injured of present and past history, and an occasional heroine. Working-class girls appear in several of Piercy's poems, and Piercy has done a fine lament for Janis Joplin. The lives of frontierwomen are celebrated and mourned in Rich's "From an Old House in America"; Rich has also written about Marie Curie and Caroline Herschel. Morgan's "Network of the Imaginary Mother" includes a recital of the names of witches executed, or tortured and executed, up until the eighteenth century. Susan Griffin writes equally of welfare mothers, her own middle-class alcoholic one, and Harriet Tubman. Judy Grahn writes a sequence of poems entitled "The Common Woman," concluding with Marilyn Monroe. One of the most powerful statements about the personal and social dimensions of women's love for women is Grahn's *A Woman Is Talking to Death*. To extract quotations from this work is to mutilate it, but Grahn should be better known. The following passage is from a mock interrogation:

What about kissing? Have you kissed any women?

I have kissed many women.

When was the first woman you kissed with serious feeling?

The first woman ever I kissed was Josie, who I had
loved at such a distance for months. Josie was not only
beautiful, she was tough and handsome too. Josie had
black hair and white teeth and strong brown muscles.
Then she dropped out of school unexplained. When
she came back she came back for one day only, to
finish the term, and there was a child in her. She was
all shame, pain and defiance. Her eyes were dark as
the water under a bridge and no one would talk to
her, they laughed and threw things at her. In the
afternoon I walked across the front of the class and
looked deep into Josie's eyes and I picked up her chin
with my hand, because I loved her, because nothing

like her trouble would ever happen to me, because I
hated it that she was pregnant and unhappy, and an
outcast. We were thirteen.

You didn't kiss her?

How does it feel to be thirteen and having a baby?

You didn't actually kiss her? . . . .

In a later section of the poem, Grahn is knocked down in a diner by a
Spanish-speaking youth who calls her "queer." Counterman and
police prove indifferent. Weeks later it occurs to her that this might
be Josie's son. In a still later section, she and her "pervert" friends
encounter a 55-year old Chinese woman who has been raped by a
cabdriver and left bleeding in the snow. They kiss and try to reassure
her, knowing it is not enough. Grahn burns with desire to rule the
city with this woman, but she lets her go in the ambulance with the
bored policemen, guiltily unable to enact her defiance, to "get the
real loving done."

Within the symposium of the self, a number of women poets
evidently wish to reverse Yeats's dictum that from the quarrel with
ourselves we make poetry. They struggle rather to make poetry
about coming to peace with ourselves by reconciling internal anti-
monies. Coleridge, Rimbaud, and Woolf are invoked for the idea of
the androgynous being who combines both intellect and emotion,
strength and gentleness. Rukeyser, in a poem on Kathe Kollwitz,
quotes Kollwitz' testimony that her own work required a masculine
element. Rich, in "Diving into the Wreck," discovers as she descends to the depths of personal and communal history, "I am he . . .
I am she." Although Rich has since repudiated the ideal of an-
drogyny, it remains attractive to others, and perhaps is responsible
for the tough-but-tender style of a writer like Grahn.*

I believe that it is the contact imperative which finally accounts for
the confessional or diarist mode in women's writing, because of the

---

* An exception that seems to me to prove the rule of women's concern for unifying relationships is Margaret Atwood. Atwood is an important poet, most of whose work seems to express
a steely and mistrustful avoidance of, rather than desire for, human closeness. On the other
hand, the "Circe-Mud Poems" which conclude her recent *You Are Happy* appear to move
toward the possibility, at least in imagination, of transcending isolation and hoping for
harmony of male and female in the natural world, as is also the case with the heroine of her
novel, *Surfacing*.

intimacy this mode imposes on the audience. One cannot read, for example, a Wakoski or a Sexton poem without feeling that the ordinary objectivity of readership comes under severe attack, and the same is true, if to a less breathtaking degree, with many other women poets. "No more masks" means something for reader as well as writer. As the poet refuses to distance herself from her emotions, so she prevents us from distancing ourselves. We are obliged to witness, to experience the hot breath of the poem upon us. Or perhaps we want to wrestle loose. The poem is impolite, crude, it imposes too much. In either case, we have been obliged to some degree to relinquish our roles as readers, and to respond personally. That, evidently, has been the aim of the poet. In a sense beyond what Plath intended, these are disquieting muses.

Having said this much, I do not suppose I have exhausted the themes and modes of contemporary women's poetry, any more than I have mentioned all the "good" women writers. I suspect, for example, that the need to define pre-social strata in female nature is producing a revival of mythology in poetry, much as the compulsion to explore non-rational human passions led Coleridge to the supernatural, Keats and Shelley to classical Greek myth, Blake to a self-invented mythology, Yeats to occultism, Eliot to *The Golden Bough*. I would not be surprised to find that certain traditional images and symbols reveal new facets for women artists. Water, in women's poetry, seems to function as an image not of chaos and danger, but of security and a potential for rebirth. Another instance is the symbol of the flower, which in women's poetry today repeatedly signifies vitality, power, sensuousness to an almost predatory degree, much as in the visual imagery of Georgia O'Keeffe or Judy Chicago. Still another is blood, which becomes in many poems an image for creativity.

Nor do I suppose that the issues I have been outlining are the exclusive property of women writers. Poets like Ginsberg, Duncan, and Bly work intensively on some of the same problems that beset women, and in fact each of these men has identified his concerns as symbolically female. Theodore Roethke's profound sensuousness and discomfort with abstractions had a feminine cast (although through most of his career his explicit self-identifications were emphatically with plants and animals, and his treatment of women thoroughly conventional). Paul Goodman's poetry shares many anti-authoritarian ideas with that of the radical feminist poets, including the idea of congruence between the body and the body politic. Galway Kinnell dives faithfully into his own wreck, and his essay on "Poetry, Personality and Death" eloquently discusses the limitations of impersonality in poetry, pointing out that while a *persona* may enable a writer to dramatize otherwise hidden aspects of his own personality, it may also release him from the painfulness of a full examination. The poet, Kinnell remarks, "knows himself to be of a more feminine disposition than the banker." To a greater or lesser extent, such writers defy the dominant "modern" mode of weary irony which has characterized English and American poetry for fifty years, deviations from which have usually been anti-academic, grassroots movements of one sort or another. Yet at the present moment, the flying wedge of dissent and quest is composed mainly of women, who collectively are contributing an extraordinary intellectual, emotional, and moral exhilaration to American poetry, and who may be expected to have an impact on its future course.

FORGIVE US. . .

by GEORGE VENN

from POETRY NORTHWEST and OFF THE MAIN ROAD (Prescott Street Press)

nominated by Prescott Street Press

Fifty years of your butchering art
are here, Grandfather. I hear the crash
of your falling ax into alder, the whisk
of your keen knife on the blue steel
while lambs and wethers bleat in the barn.

They knew your one quick stroke across
their throats would make their ends
the best you could create. I still don't
like the blood, Grandfather, but I know
now the need for meat.

"Nothing should suffer," you said,
and sought out old dying queens in hives
and pinched their heads. Mensik's calf—
you told us not to watch; bad dreams
would come, you said, so we walked out

and watched you anyway through a crack
in the wall—one deadly swing, no more—
from the spiking maul buckled the calf
instantly to its knees on the hay.
We knew your power then, and ran away.

And now this God, Grandfather, this God
whose songs you sang, whose church

your worship built, whose book you read,
whose name you never said in vain—
He's got you here in His shepherd's barn.

Oh, he's a shoddy butcher, Grandfather.
He's making you suffer his rusty dull
deathknife for years, crippling your legs,
then cutting off your speech to tremble,
then tying you up in a manured bed.

He won't bring you down with any grace
or skill or swift humane strike of steel.
Day after day, you sit in His hallway
in your wheelchair and nurses walk by
like angels and shout half your name.

Ah, this God of yours, Grandfather, this
God has not learned even the most simple
lesson from the country of your hands.
You should have taught him how to hone
His Knife, that the slaughtering of rams
is the work of those brave enough to love
a fast deft end.

🔥 🔥 🔥

THE HAT IN THE SWAMP

by PAUL METCALF

from MILK QUARTERLY

nominated by Raymond Federman and Ron Sukenick

(editor's note—The following tale is from a wonderfully wacky special edition of Milk
Quarterly *devoted entirely to the subject of hats and titled "The Hat Issue".)*

> *(this bit of frontier humor emanates
> from the early days of southern Ill-
> inois, when much of the land was
> covered with cypress swamp)*

"A weary wayfarer was floundering through the mire . . . sometimes wading to the saddle girth in water; sometimes clambering
over logs; and occasionally plunged in quagmire. While carefully
picking his way by a spot more miry than the rest he espied a man's
hat, lying with the crown upwards in the mud, and as he approached
was not a little startled to see it move. This happened in a dismal
swamp where the cypress waved its melancholy branches over the
dark soil, and our traveler's flesh began to creep . . . the solitary
rider checked his nag and, extending his long whip, fairly upset a
man's head, a living, laughing head . . . [the traveler] promptly
apologized for the indecorum of which he had been guilty, and
tendered his services to the gentleman in the mud puddle. 'I will
alight,' said he, ' and endeavor to draw you forth.' 'Oh, never mind,'
said the other, 'I'm in rather a bad fix it is true, but I have an excellent
horse under me who has carried me through many a worse place
than this—we shall get along.'"

THESE WOMEN

fiction by CHRISTINE SCHUTT

from GALLIMAUFRY

nominated by GALLIMAUFRY *and Anne Tyler*

W HEN I CONTRADICT MY GRANDMOTHER, her mouth will work as if she were pulling on a knotted straw, and she will say to me, "You're just like your mother." Who else would know better than my grandmother? "I wish you wouldn't stay out past twelve, Eugenie. You know I never could persuade your mother to come in." Behind each word disaster dangles like some dangerous fruit, for it's a fearful thing to resemble a woman no one likes. I try to contradict my grandmother less and less. She means to get the best out of me, and will take credit for nothing else. When I have failed in math or morals, I am like my mother. When my half-sister, Katie, argues, stays out late, swears or sulks, she is like her unpopular father. We worry over these comparisons.

Katie is six years old and I am thirteen. It is October; everything is orange. The caretaker is driving us into the country to my grandmother's house where the land's been pocketed with glaciers. There are many lakes here, deep, tealcolored, cold. We are sitting on either side of my grandmother in the backseat of her green car. My grandmother says, "Sumac," and Katie looks out the window in alarm. My grandmother is a squat woman with a center part and black hair crimped to the chin. She is freckled and gap-toothed. She runs her tongue over the space between her two front teeth and gazed absentmindedly at us. In her even voice she says, "I'm glad you girls have decided to live with me." She folds her small, perfectly manicured hands in her lap.

Her hands are beautiful, pearly, magnetic. Sometimes I watch her, after dinner, at the study chair, dip her fingertips into the small, gray bowl of hot, sudsy water. She holds her hand, paw-like, until the pads of her fingers shrivel. Then she spreads her fingers on the towel, where the bright instruments are laid out, and she presses down on the softened cuticle with the tip of the scored metal file. "My hands," she often says, "are my best feature."

With her small hands she has lifted large stones, planted annuals, pulled up shaggy weeds in the great effort to complete her rock gardens. I have watched her in her overalls and sensible brown shoes help the gardeners fit in the slabs of lannon stone that make up the paths and beds and benches of the gardens. I am told that at age five I helped her plant. One morning, the story goes, I follow her from bed to bed as she twists the root-colored tulip bulbs into the earth. She knows what blooms—red, yellow, white—will come out of each bulb. Some distance from her I am pulling out the bulbs. When she has almost finished, I come up behind her. "Look," I say, pointing to my basket, "I've picked up all of these for you." My grandmother is aghast. That year the color of the garden comes as a complete surprise to her. "Oh dear," she exclaims whenever she tells this story to prove it doesn't pay to lose your temper, "Now," she asks, "what good would it have done?" I shrug my shoulders. "You remembering doing that, don't you, Eugenie?" And though, in fact, I really don't remember, I say, "Yes, I think I do." She smiles then and contentedly asks, "When have you ever seen your grandmother mad?" "Never," I say, "never."

My grandmother arranges flowers, types letters, sews. She is capable: her touch is sure. She pats Katie's dimpled knee and half whispers, "I want you to think of this as home." My sister looks at me to see what this means. I've told Katie she'll see her babysitter's farm again. "We'll visit Ernie," I said to her as we watched Frank load the suitcases into the trunk of the green car. "When mother's well, we'll come back to ride the ponies." Here, at my grandmother's, there are no horses. The gardens are formal; the trees are various, gnarled, large. Frank opens the car doors and I step out to look at this new house of ours, a place I've visited many times during my mother's divorce, but which is somehow different today, grand, alert. Over the windows the maroon and white awnings have been rolled back and tied for winter. Some bushes are under burlap. The red brick structure with its graph-work of speckled ivy grows imposing and one-dimensional in the October dusk. Everything happens very fast. The maid moves through the house turning on lamps. The fan light goes on: the black hedges spring back, green, fragrant, alive. I want to spend my life here.

"Is Mama going to visit us?" Katie asks my grandmother, who answers, cautiously, "When she's able." Katie picks at the treble clef embroidered on her dress. One morning, when I put it to her differently and asked if she might like to live with me, she said coyly, "Only if I can swim in the lake when I want to." I said, "You can do almost anything at grandma's." Now she's here and she's crying. "Damnit, Katie!" I say, "why don't you get some decent kneesocks. Nobody wears those queer nylon things." My grandmother shakes her head at me in a gentle reprimand. "Oh, no," she says and puts her arm around my sister, "we'll have Katie looking like all the rest of the little girls soon enough. And when we visit Mommy, she'll say, 'Now who can that pretty girl be?'". For a moment my sister stops crying. "Now," my grandmother asks, "it's not going to be so bad here, is it?"

In my new school—clannish, private—the girls I most admire have small feet, cinched waists. For two years, until I realize it's too late to reshape what I've inherited, I wear a girdle to bed and every morning put on loafers two sizes too small. In the class above mine, there is a handsome girl who has learned to speak, like her mother, with an aristocratic accent, which is quite musical and coy. Sometimes I imitate her accent. What it amounts to is slowly sliding down every syllable. Even a sentence like, "Maahgrit is veery unhahhpy," comes out as good news. You talk through clenched teeth as if to talk was against your will, and so that anyone who does get you to speak is led on not just by the sound you make but by the fact that you make it at all. It's giving whomever it is you talk to a sense of mastery. Friends say I imitate this girl's speech very well.

I collect, too, stories about families of girls I envy. Like a string of useless worry beads, I go over these stories again and again. In a local family of famously beautiful girls—all with distinctive slanted eyes, long noses, golden hair—I once overheard the oldest daughter say that she tanned so easily because of the Italian blood on her father's side. This dark man's sister is said to have given birth to her equally attractive daughter—same eyes, golden hair, smaller nose—on a sled on the way to the hospital in the middle of the big snowstorm of 1947. Moreover, the woman whose son married the dark man's oldest daughter is said to have met her husband at a Marshall Field's luncheon where she was modelling satin lingerie. With this last lady my mother once gave a successful reading of the *Madwomen of Chaillot*. My mother likes to tell the story of how this woman upstaged her by swatting at imaginary tsetse flies. This reading took place two summers before my mother's divorce, when she wasn't drinking and they were still friends.

I am in the dim, cramped locker room and taking off my hockey shins, my tunic. The smell in here is rich and heady, like burning rubber. I am happy to be here with these pretty, Nordic girls. It works this way: my mother has never fit in. The mothers of many of these girls know my mother. They know of the divorce, the sanitarium. In the afternoons, when they are parked and waiting for their sons and daughters, I sometimes catch them looking at me. I smile back with just a hint of sadness in my face. Yesterday, a classmate of mine walked me to Frank's car and said, "My mother wanted me to tell you that if you should ever want to live at our house, we'd like to have you." I thanked her but said I thought I'd be living with my grandmother.

Another afternoon, this time with a different classmate, a small, muscular girl with red-blonde hair and a skim milk complexion. We are inners, stragglers, slowly trudging up the worn, rocky path from the hockey field to the school. I've run so hard today it hurts to breathe. I lick my lips and taste the sour crust of lipstick. A boy trots past us and says hello to me. My companion says, "You're going to turn out just like your mother." I could say a dozen things to hurt this girl, but I don't. Instead, I quietly announce, "I will never turn out like my mother. We're not at all alike." She continues, "You always tease the boys. You swing your hips. You wear lipstick." "I don't mean to," I say and run ahead. I don't want to provoke her; women friends are important. Without them a silence spreads in the ear like fungus. There's no shaking it out, no relief. They will chatter in locker rooms and when you walk in, they will all stop talking. It is called the freeze out. It can happen at any age.

"Damnit, Katie," I shout when I get home and find my sister has left her doll clothes floating in my tub. "Wash your filthy rags somewhere else. Will you?" I fling the small wet dresses against the bedroom door. Then I lock myself in and run a hot tub until the windows steam and water beads on the mirror. In here the air is sweet and thick; I soak.

The boys in the grade school car pool call Katie "bucket". Every day she squeezes into the cramped backseats of the various station wagons that take her to and from the small school and she hopes—it's in her face, puckered, worried—that nothing will be said. She is very quiet in the car, pressing her nose against the cool window. She keeps a steady eye on the dark landscape; she is last out. She concentrates on small objects, stones, twigs, shoelaces, with a high-stake intensity that pounds in her head. Sudden noises, scuffles, pluck new notes of terror. Let me be small, be sick, be home, be dead. "Bucket," someone hollers, and the word ricochets off the squat, square buildings.

I sometimes tell Katie, "Kids used to do that to me. Don't pay any attention to them."

Each night after dinner Katie goes up to her room with a small can of diet supplement. "What do you drink that for?" I ask her. She looks at me fiercely. "To lose weight, dummy," she says. She sits cross-legged on the bed underneath the fishnet canopy and daintily sips her drink. She looks at nothing in particular or at me on the floor in the middle of my sit-ups. One Saturday I find her stretched across the bed and sobbing. Staticky music of a melancholy sort is playing on the radio. When I ask her what's the matter she says, "It's just been such a lonely fall. I'm so sad." I put my hand on her shoulder. "Things will get better," I say, suppressing a smile.

"What do you know?" she snaps, turning on her side, scowling at me.

"I've gone through the same things. You've just got to buck up."

Then I smile at her. "That music's so corny." She listens and begins to laugh a little. "Really, Katie," I say, sitting on the edge of the bed, stroking her dark head of matted curls. "It's a matter of waiting things out until you know you've got the upper hand, until you're prettier than they are." She makes a long face and shakes her head in disbelief. "These years are like swimming under water. If you're going to get through them at all, you've got to hold your breath. The people who used to tease me now want to be my friends." She rests her cheek against the pillow. "Scratch me, will you?" she asks. I pull a strand of hair behind her hot wet ear. We stay like this for a while, me rubbing her back and she not saying anything.

In late November, when the lake turns a dull metal, the cold churns up a spine of foam which runs from the south to the north shores. The lake is a cell in the process of division. Every day that sudsy roadway widens, until one morning I pull back the damask curtains and am stunned by the bald landscape and the thin skin of ice, blue-black, smooth, with its one white seam running dead center down the lake. As the ice thickens the surface grows knobby, pale; the seam buckles. But all winter long the lake yawns. The noises it makes are deep and far-reaching, a thrum, ping, ping, ping, ping. My grandmother says to Katie, "The dead Indians are gathering."

Katie thinks the Indians will come to the house to take back the arrowheads we've found along the lake paths. She runs around the house, dodging into different rooms as her mood changes from excitement to fear and back again. "You're a wild Indian!" the maid hollers at her as she races in and out of the kitchen. Sometimes her hysteria grows on me, and we both run in and out of rooms, screaming. "Indians!" Katie turns the lights on and off, on and off. "it's lightning!" she shrieks, then flees the dark room. I run up behind the maid, "Got ya!" I shout, and Tessie turns around, still spooked, uncertain. "Get out of here!" she snaps. Sometimes, if I am on the phone or entertaining friends, I take Tessie's side and protest against the racket myself. "God, Katie," I whine at her, "relax."

With great care and an eye on the time when the demonstration will be over, I am practicing scales on the piano. Katie seats herself on the opposite stool and begins to play chopsticks. "Katie," I shout, "Quit it!" Some distance behind us my grandmother is sitting on the tufted yellow loveseat. She murmurs, "Katie." My sister glowers at me. She jumps off her seat and pounds the keys. "I want to play, damn you," she screams, and she picks up the antique stool on which she's been seated. She lifts it over her head and is about to hit me with it when my grandmother catches hold of her shoulders and swings her toward he empty room where Katie throws the chair. The little stool with its prickly seat snaps like a wishbone. "You could have killed me!" I say in an astounded voice. My grandmother stoops to pick up a curved leg with a pretty carved knee. "My dear!" she says to Katie. "Do you know what you've done?" Katie runs from the room. "I hate you," she screams, "I want to go home".

We endure; we adjust. Next year this is history.

It is my grandmother's kitchen that my husband, Ted, first makes up the game, "Who Am I?" Katie and I have followed him from the library into the kitchen where the rich aroma of turkey, like the thick smell of burnt fat, still drifts in the air. Ted is hungry and begins opening cupboards in search for the pies. Given Tessie's cranky ways, they could be anywhere. I know, but I won't tell. Ted's grown florid and beefy. Twenty pounds since our wedding, and it worries me, living with the superstition that all fat people are unhappy. This noon, after dinner, he unbuttoned his bright vest and loosened his tie. "Going to take a snooze, old man?" Katie asked.

"Don't eat anything," I say now, "Please. You don't need it." He frowns at me. Katie teases. "Ted," she says, "I thought you were on a diet." She stretches out on the speckled tiles and to a count of five raises first her right leg, then her left. "You ate more this afternoon than anyone else, Katie," Ted says in his high-pitched, merry voice. "Your Uncle Pete kept nudging me in the ribs every time you passed your plate for another helping." Ted's standing over her with his cheeks puffed out.

"Ted!" she says, drawing out his name. He presses his foot lightly on her stomach. She squeals and tries to fend him off, but her arms go weak with all the tickling. Finally, she protects herself and rolls just out of reach. I sit on the damp drain board under the harsh tube of light. "Ted's getting angry," I holler. He opens the top corner cupboard and finds the pecan and pumpkin pies under clear wrap. "You're going to be as fat as your Dad!" I shout at him. "And I won't be responsible. You learned this someplace else." Suddenly he turns around and begins to work his mouth in and out, in and out. He stares at me. "Who am I?" he asks. His mouth puckers, then flattens in a faint smile. "Who am I?" he asks again, in a fierce, husky voice. I make a disgusted face. Katie boos him. "That's so easy," I answer, "Gram." It's suddenly quiet in the kitchen.

My grandmother is resting in her small porch bedroom on the second floor. She's wrapped herself in the hot electric blanket and cranked up the foot of her mechanical bed to ease the pressure on her legs. To me she's said, "Don't let me sleep too long. I don't want to be up all night." I'll give her another hour. Katie props herself up against the bank of glass cupboards where the dishes are kept. I close the doors to the kitchen and the butler's pantry. "Do Gram again," Katie says to Ted, but he shakes his head. "No," he says, grinning, "I've got a better idea," and he walks over to the kitchen table with its Ball jars of scumming cuttings. His head falls forward. "I must compose myself," he says. Our eyes are fixed on him.

He throws his head back and runs his fingers through his long, brown hair in a gesture of exhaustion. "I've fought this family all my life." His brow furrows; his temper takes another track. "All my life," he says in an angry voice and pounds the table with his fist. Then, in a quicksilver change, in the lightest, highest voice, "I don't have to anymore." He smiles—a moist, luminous smile—and enuciates with care, "It's that simple."

"Wow!" Katie says. "No good," I say, "no good," though I doubt even my mother, with her wilful blind eye, her fearful temper, would deny she had just been well imitated. At this moment, nothing about Ted's family stands out. I think fast. I fix on Pete's wife, Marjorie. I push myself off the drain board and shake my head in astonishment and in my smallest voice say, "That's so cute. Yes. So cute. Don't you think so, Petes?" The sound I want is almost birdlike, like Marjorie herself, silly and frail. Katie says—very seriously, for she is completely taken with this game—"Aunt Marjorie always does this," and she crosses her arms over her waist as if she were struck by some bright pain.

I see Ted looking at me to see what might happen next. But like my grandmother, I smile back—a closed-mouth, colorless smile, the most enigmatic look I know—and he can't tell what I'm thinking.

I recently saw an old friend of mine, a freckled, pretty girl, with a son, almost two. When I asked her who she thought her little boy looked like, she answered, "He looks like himself." And I thought if she means this, if it's true for her that he looks quite himself, well, then that's very good. My mother-in-law says people in the same family begin to look like one another. She will not admit that any one of her children looks more like her husband than herself. I've grown up to isolate features and identify origin. Whenever I meet someone, I find myself studying the face and wondering, "whose eyes? whose height?" Katie has my stepfather's ears, heavy-lobed and large. My mother's smile, with the skinny upper lip and perfect melon shape has been pointed out to me in pictures of myself. There is nothing wrong, I think, in looking for resemblances.

One afternoon, before a Christmas dinner, my sister and I are dressing together in her bedroom. I am perched on the edge of the sink before the triptych mirror with its bands of light and in that light applying, very carefully, a dark brown mascara. Katie is in the old walk-in shower with its raggy white curtain and wooden bench. I can see her sitting on that bench and shaving her legs, very carefully. Our family dinners are contests; everyone is keen to come looking better than ever. One aunt of mine still persists in hugging me and my two cousins to see which of the three girls, born the same year, is now heaviest. She clasps a waist like a caliper. "What a skinny thing you are," she'll say or, "A little money in the bank never hurt anyone." On this afternoon, though, Katie surprises me, and not just as she emerges from the shower—very suddenly, dark, wet, hardy—but early on, when she's still shaving and says, "I recently got a B+ on a paper I wrote for my Milton seminar. The professor said it was a very well-researched paper, but the writing was over-cautious. So the grade. Another girl in my class got an A for the same assignment. Her mother's a professor at Columbia. This girl's a natural. She's got flair. Maybe I write cautiously because so much depends upon my succeeding." Her eyes meet mine, and I see her inner eye shift rapidly. She's blushing. "Do you ever wish," she asks, giggling, pointing upward, "*He'd* dealt you another mother?"

In the year my mother spent at the sanitarium, Katie and I saw her twice. The first visit dates late winter with a white sky and black-pocked mounds of snow. I keep my mouth on the cold window pane and inhale. The sound this makes is of a storm. My grandmother says calmly, "Your mother cut her hair, girls. It is very short now." Frank drives slowly; nothing else is said. We drive down a narrow street with identical shingled houses set close on a hump of lawn. The home is at the end of this street up a long asphalt drive. Or maybe it's not on this street, but just beyond the city limits. I am sure of the asphalt drive and of a hill and a large brick building. When I open the car door the air is coastal.

We are led down a streaky, flesh-colored hallway to a room of the same color where my mother sits in a straight-back chair facing the far wall. Her haircut is patchy; in places the scalp comes through, bony, white, vulnerable. Later, she will pick up an inch of hair and say to my grandmother. "Like it? I did this with a nail scissors."

"Mama?" Katie asks, and my mother turns to see us. "Babies!" she screams and she comes at us like a harpie. "Mama!" Katie cries and she is immediately enfolded in the wings of my mother's blue-black velvet dress, the same dress she wore for her reading of Joan in *The Lark*. My mother is on her knees on the hard tile floor. "Baby, baby, baby," she moans. She kisses Katie's face, her hands, her hair. They embrace for a long time. When my mother stands up Katie holds onto the hem of the velvet dress. My mother cocks her head at me and, in a voice full of drama, stutters, "Don't, Don't look at me like that!" She embraces me suddenly. Around her neck she is wearing a very large amethyst cross. It presses against my breast bone so that the pain is real, localized and focused. "Honey girl," she croons in a steadier voice. I say nothing. I concentrate on the cross; the smell of soap; her soft, soft cheek. She pulls away. "I am your mother," she announces in her grand, noisy way, and with that, hatred rushes to my head like blood. This is all I remember about the first visit—the hot bursts of anger like the pop of flashbulbs when my sight fails and everything is colorless and starred.

It is midsummer when we see her again. Driving towards the cool portico with its row of empty rockers, we see her walking around the edge of the driveway, which, like the bulding, seems to have changed and is now gravel. My mother is wearing a dress I remember from the summer before, a striped, purple shirtwaist with an amazingly full skirt. The dress does not fit her well anymore. It is too small and puckers in the back. She holds her arms out from the skirt in a dreamy way. She is like a child, playing dress-up. Only these are her clothes. When she sees us, she waves her right arm in broad, sleepy arcs, as if she is at a great distance from us. Katie hollers from the window, "Mom!" There are no tears when we meet; it is too sunny for that.

My mother's hair has grown out in bangs and she has wound around the crown of her head a brown fall. The bobbie pins are visible everywhere. When she hugs me, I notice a line of tawny make-up, which ends at the jaw bone. Her neck is very pale and the two scars at the throat, from where she once ran the razor blade, very lightly, but to good effect, are pink and rucked, like the borders of states on landscaled maps.

At lunch my mother talks about how well she feels. "I've made some wonderful friends here," she says and nods to me. "Look at him," she whispers and points to a boy, not more than fifteen. He stands at the edge of the burnt out garden with his hands thrust deep into the pockets of his jeans. She frowns at the skinny figure. "Psychotic," she snaps, then lowers her voice, grows ruminative, "but I've reached him. All it takes is a little love, just a little," and her voice trails off as she gazes beyond us to where the boy is standing. She is close to tears when she abruptly sits up. "I want you to meet him, Eugenie. It'll do you good." I'm about to answer her, but she's turned to address my grandmother.

"You know, I've met some wonderful, wonderful people here, Mama." She speaks in a confidential tone as if she has not said this to anyone before. "I want you to meet Dr. Johnny. He's been very, very good to me." My grandmother answers in a colorless voice. "Yes, Nancy" she says, "I'm sure he's been nice to you." It's hard—it has always been hard—to know what my grandmother thinks. But we do meet Dr. Johnny.

Just as we are about to leave the sanitarium, he emerges from some other part of the garden. Maybe he's been watching us throughout our lunch. All of a sudden, there he is: a large, grey man with a criminal haircut. He doesn't talk or smile much. He has a long, fleshy mouth and a nose like a fighter's, broad, flat, crooked. At the car door he says to my grandmother, "Your Nancy's quite a gal," and my mother begins to cry.

When I get home, I put on my bathing suit and walk down a hill through the spikey grass to where a small wobbly pier has been set up in the shallows. The lake at this hour is hot and mysterious. The water in the low sun glints like coins. I walk into the water, which becomes water again, cooler, greener than I expected. It takes me by surprise before I dip under and begin swimming out.

Much later, when my sister has left home, gone to college, grown bitter, we meet for a brief vacation with my mother at her new house in California. The rooms in the small house are pastel and pretty with views of the valley and other houses. This is a village of condominiums. My mother likes it here and dresses as a native in

nautical clothes, bold prints. Mexican cottons. Her antiques look
different, less formal, blonder. The white carpet has a spring to it.
But some things remain the same. On the tables are still the feathery
plants, Battersea boxes, china eggs and rabbits and owls, "little
doodads" my mother calls these things. Formal pictures of her
girls—in debutante gowns, on horses—are everywhere. In the
clean, blue kitchen there are two cherry spoon racks with the tin
wells filled with philodendron. We are eating tacos at the kitchen
table. My mother has pushed her sunglasses on top of her head. She
has started the game, "What do you want of mine?" with the unspoken, parenthetical (when I die?)

"Nothing," Katie says in a low, angry voice.

"Okay with me," my mother answers.

"Well," I say, looking from my sister to my mother, "I wouldn't
mind a thing or two, maybe the Pembroke table in the hall?"

My mother smiles slyly. "So you like the Pembroke table, do you?
That's a very lovely table." Between her thumb and middle finger
she balls a shred of lettuce. "I won't be giving it up for a while."

"I'd like something now. How about the tortoise-shell tea caddy?"

"We'll see," my mother says.

"Oh, mother," Katie whines, "cut it out."

"So," my mother says, "what's the matter with you? No one's
talking to you."

Katie thumps her elbows on the table and sighs loudly into her
cupped hands.

I say, "Think about the caddy, Mom," and leave the table to
shower. Eat, bathe, sleep: I take care of myself in California.

I use up lots of the hot water. The shower nozzle is tight and the
water comes out hard and fast. It bites; it feels good. Then the glass
door slides open and the rush of cold air almost knocks me out. My
mother's face has collapsed, like a fist, when it's opened, and the
knuckles disappear.

"Your sister's mad at me. I don't know why, but she won't talk to
me. She just looks at me with those big cow eyes." She shudders.
"I'm so tired, Eugenie. All I've ever wanted was to make you girls
happy."

"Mom?" I ask, and cross my arms over my chest and clack my
teeth in a noisy shiver.

The features of her face pull back into place, like railroad cars reversing and colliding on the track. "I can stand you," she says, "your eyes are just like mine, small and cold. It's your baby sister's look—" and she slams the glass partition shut.

When I get out of the shower, I am hot and rosy. My mother, emerging from an equally hot shower in the guest bathroom, says her idea of luxury is to dry off under the cool covers of her bed. Not me. I wrap up in a large bath towel, sit on the edge of the sink, my feet in the bowl, and examine my face under the harsh light, at close range.

JOHNNY APPLESEED

fiction by SUSAN SCHAEFER NEVILLE

from APALACHEE QUARTERLY

nominated by APALACHEE QUARTERLY

HE TOLD ME THAT HIS ANCESTOR had left his hard black seeds in neat rows where scrub pine or thistle, cockle or thorns would have grown and that when people stopped just long enough to eat the apples he had planted, they felt their feet become like iron and their heads become drugged and when they tried to move, found that they, like the trees, couldn't. And in turn, he said, the people planted squash and corn and ate the apples freely, spreading more black seeds whose roots joined under the earth in dark rivers which spread under the houses which also grew from the seeds, wrapping around children's knees, strangling pipes until they had to dig more and more wells.

And he told me I was still under the spell of those trees of his ancestor and I said I didn't believe that until he said would I leave in the morning with him for Zanzibar and I said no. And he pointed to the trees behind my house, black as obsidian against the darkening sky, and he said the black branches were the rivers from the apple trees, spreading out like sap at this time of night and that to him they were a cut-out in the sky. If I looked closely, I could see stars where the bark should be. I looked closely and didn't see stars, but there were stars outlined with gunmetal on the hat he wore and I liked it when he stroked his beard a certain way and I didn't care about the trees or the bark or his illusions. He said he was a direct decendent of Johnny Appleseed, that he had the same name, and that once he had even seen him in a bar in Kansas City, the original Johnny toting glossy catalogues, posing as an undergarment salesman so he could say 'negligee' and 'brassiere' to the women who came in. He said that he himself was an itinerant magician, specializing in appearing and disappearing, that I'd already seen one half of his act. He put his arms on my shoulders and asked was I anxious to see the other half and I said no, I wasn't. Then he asked again if I would leave for Zanzibar and I said no, but I'd put him up in the garage for the night. He said that was a trick question: since I'd said no I was in need of help and he would stay around until I said yes. I told him he sounded crazy, I thought he was just a tramp, but he pulled his beard and bent his knee slowly so that rings of cloth crawled up his leg and I thought, what could be the harm. Stay, but only for one night. By that time the cut-out trees had bled into the rest of the sky; there were stars around his head as well as on it.

I pulled a mattress into the garage while he sat crouched on a high shelf watching, hanging by rakes, shovels, hoes. His eyes the same silver gray as the gunmetal, they glinted in the dark unevenly, like crumpled tinfoil. He mumbled while I worked, eyes always on me while he mumbled. I covered the mattress with fresh sheets, sprayed lavender between, set a Chinese enamelled lamp on a short table, asked him if he needed a blanket. I tried to ignore his incantations. They started low.

Johnny Johnny Johnny Johnny whoops Johnny whoops Johnny Johnny Johnny Johnny

I placed a piece of chocolate

> whoops Johnny whoops Johnny
Johnny Johnny Johnny Johnny
> > on his pillow
> Johnny whoops Johnny whoops Johnny
Johnny Johnny

Sweet cream in a pitcher beside the bed.

I left him in the garage. I locked the door. The bed had looked nice, like a movie set looks—complete where the light reached, but framed by dark and oil and hard metal beaks of machinery. I tried to imagine him sleeping in it.

I went into the house, opened doors and windows for air, locked screens. Stopped by a window and touched the screen with my tongue. It was bitter and the taste lasted. I thought about the song I would probably go upstairs to write about a woman whose only sense was taste. About all the things she could touch with her tongue before she died a tragic death from rare infectious germs. The last thing she tasted before she died would be the hair on her lover's chest, slightly salty, slightly sour.

But when I opened the door to my room, Johnny Appleseed was there waiting, the hat with the gunmetal stars slid halfway under the bed. I asked him how he'd found his way past me. He told me that I hadn't really locked anything, that I'd allowed him to come in. I picked up the hat and put it on the dresser. He flipped open a pocket knife and took out a block of wood from between the sheets. Soon he had wood shavings all over the bed. He said the block of wood had once been a whole tree, that he made tiny smooth rings from the wood, that I would find them useful. I said if you're really Johnny Appleseed, shouldn't you have a bag of seeds. He motioned to the empty side of the bed with the blade of his knife.

I said, if you're really a magician Johnny Appleseed, show me some tricks. He sat on a moon-lit tree limb in the cemetery, carving faces in the bark, chips falling on a stone by my feet. Leaping to the ground, he moved the pocket knife toward my eyes, brandished it in the air. See the lights on the blade, he said. I'm carving chips from the moon. Catch one. I touched a reflection of the moon, buried in the hair on his chest. **Now watch the blade, Johnny Johnny Johnny. See the blade bend, Johnny, stroke it, stroke the blade**. I stroked it. The blade didn't bend. **Stroke it, Johnny Johnny**, he said. He moved my hand along the metal, **stroke the blade, watch it bend**.

It's flat, I told him. His face moved closer to mine, the hard edge of his hat brushed my ear, he winked. Isn't it amazing that the blade is bending, he said. Bending to match the contour of the earth, he said. The earth is flat here, I said. It looks flat, he said, but it's really bending; it has to, you know, it has to bend everywhere. Not around here, I said. A circle bends everywhere, he said; it appears flat like the earth, but it's really bending. It's flat, I said. Very very flat.

He tossed the knife at the tree. It folded in half and fell to the ground. He turned his wrist and a wooden ring appeared in his hand, rough-hewn. I'm sure I saw it slide down your sleeve, I said. The satin shirt had rippled, I'd seen it ripple. Sit, he said. I sat on the stone amid the shavings. He slipped the ring over my foot, around my left ankle. Another turn of the wrist and another ring appeared, this one smooth sanded, varnished. He slid it over my right hand. A larger one appeared, he slid it up my right leg, around my thigh. That's enough of that, Johnny Appleseed, I said. I feel very unbalanced. He slid one up my left thigh and asked me to stand. I clacked when I tried to walk toward him. Now where's the trick, Johnny Appleseed, I said. Try to take them off, he said. I tried and they wouldn't come off, they were stuck, and I said they must have shrunk from my sitting on the ground. I said at least-clack clack-help-clack-me remove-clack clack clack-one from one thigh-clack. One of the rings slid from my legs as if it were greased. I'll figure out how to do it, I said. I know it's an illusion.

He took my hand and led me to a flat grave stone, pallid white and cold. He chanted **Johnny Johnny** and I lay down on the stone. The letters were indented deep in the rock; I could feel someone's name and dates digging into my back. He lay down on top of me, his hair falling into my face, brown curls brushing my lips. I was moist and he entered hard, the wooden ring burning on my thigh from the pressure. I could feel him up high; he was urgent and quick. Then he rolled over onto the grass and said that some people say that's what death feels like. If so then it's not too bad, I said, and I brushed the wet hair back from his eyes. He said Johnny Appleseed had planted the apples because he had been afraid to leave the land to the dead things. That his own destiny was to face the dead things, that he was building a power, that there was no security for him. He gripped my hand and stared at the sky; it was filled with clouds and moving violently. I could sense that the emptiness frightened him. The cemetery was quiet. Then he threw his legs into the air in an arc, did a kip to his feet and pulled me up with him. I fingered the ring clutching my wrist. Mirrors, I said. You must do it with trick mirrors.

He came once to watch me where I worked, coming in late after I'd finished most of my set, wearing the hat with the gunmetal stars and jeans and a muslin shirt and a floor-length apron with stenciled colored moons and seaweed on the bib. He asked for a table up front and the waitress gave it to him. He ordered a pitcher of sweet cream and ten ounces of bourbon. His table was in the light from the stage; he sat in the shadow. All I could see were his disembodied hands pouring the cream and bourbon into a glass, lifting the glass into the air and setting it down. The place I worked was decorated like a speak-easy—dim lights, waitresses in flapper costumes, pictures of gangsters on the wall. I was dressed like a moll in a red satin dress, greasy red lipstick. I carried a plastic carbine. I sang old jazz, mostly Billie Holliday and Bessie Smith, sometimes some of my own songs that I wrote to sound like that same style jazz. I was glad he'd come because it seemed to be my chance to mesmerize him. The satin dress molded my body with stripes of moving lights, clung tightly to my hips. There was a slit up the side to my waist and I wore a black leotard and black hose, though it was difficult getting the hose through the wooden ring on my thigh. My voice wasn't great, I knew, but was throaty and rich and my movements were good. Men were always coming up to me after the show, wanting to give me a ride home. I had always said no. I sat on a round table and did a turn, easy with the satin dress. I lay back on the table, legs crossed, carbine on my knee. I caressed the microphone with my finger as I sang, looking over to the table where Johnny was sitting.

> "If I should get a notion
> To jump right in the ocean
> Aint nobody's business if I do."

I slid off the table and walked over to Johnny. I stroked his hair with the point of the carbine. It tangled in one place and I pulled it out gently. I still couldn't see his whole face, just half of it with a reddish glow from the floor lights. He was half smiling, elfin. The stars on his hat glowed red, more like planets. I walked away and did a few grinds as I sang, something I don't usually do. I walked over to the upright piano and played with the band during the riffs. I looked at Johnny's table, the glass still rising and falling as if by levitation. Suddenly his fingers began to move fast, at the same rate as mine

moved on the piano keys. I looked and gold coins began to slide out
from between his fingers and clatter on the table. More and more
coins appeared in the air. He dropped handfuls; they formed a
mound in front of him. I played more intricate riffs; we began to
improvise, the band and I. Playing wilder. More coins appeared.
Soon the stage manager focused an amber light on Johnny's table.
The crowd thought he was part of the show and they applauded. I
noticed the band was beginning to play background to him, slowing
when his hands slowed, at times becoming frenetic when his hands
began to blur. Birds appeared in the air, flapped around the table,
tiny globes of blue lights like moons circled among the birds, cards
materialized and vanished and still coins were pouring onto the table
and off, clattering to the floor. Waitresses stopped bringing drinks.
There were no more conversations. Just the sound of the band and
the birds and Johnny's silent seductions. He picked up the pitcher of
sweet cream and turned it over on the table. No liquid ran out and
when he picked it up again, there was a mound of apples which
rolled lopsided and thudded off the table. He squashed one beneath
his heel. He reached into the air and held each bird, each coin, each
moon with his hand and when he opened his hand they were gone.
Then both of the hands moved suddenly, pushing the gold coins off
the table. Some of them rolled toward me, landing at my feet. **Oh
Johnny Johnny**, I whispered. **Oh Johnny**.

I finished my set and he was waiting by the door when I left. He
winked and said, you know where I can find any bootleg whiskey,
baby. All of that stops at this door, I told him. The illusion stops here,
doesn't it? I stepped into the night air. This is real isn't it? He turned
me to face him. The apron was slung over his shoulder. His shirt was
unbuttoned, the hair on his chest thick and matted. His hand slid
down my satin dress, fingered the ring on my thigh. You make a good
moll, he said. I put my hand in his shirt, ran up and down his side.
I'm looking for cards, I said. Trick cards. You won't find them, he told
me. You definitely won't find them. I felt something cold graze my
ear lobe. He produced a fifty cent piece. Come on, he said. I'll buy
you a cup of coffee. I reached for the coin and it disappeared. **Oh
Johnny Johnny**, I whispered again. **Oh Johnny Johnny.**

Wooden rings holding back the kitchen curtains, hanging from the
ceiling like mobiles. Five wooden rings on each arm which clattered
when I moved. One ring hugging my neck, rings hidden beneath

tables and chairs, between the sheets on my bed, thin ones between the leaves of books, filling pans and skillets, sandwiched between slices of bread. I sealed a drawer in the kitchen shut, the drawer that contained the knives. I sealed the drawer with paraffin because the knives had begun to bend toward me when I neared them. Without stroking, they were all bending toward me. Knives bending, rings appearing. I stood looking out the window with Johnny Appleseed. I said I see it Johnny. The trees are bleeding, the sap is flowing. He took out his knife. Stroke the blade, he said. Stroke the blade. It bent upward toward the sky. I see it bending, I said. I see it bending, they're all bending. More rings on my arm, a flat one around my waist. Two more flat ones which circled my breasts. A brass tea kettle rocking on the stove like a blind singer. Johnny Appleseed went up to bed. I went to sleep in the garage.

I found a box in the garage, filled with toys, my artifacts. I lay on the mattress, surrounded by stuffed bears with music boxes, brass key wings plunged deep in their backs, rotating like hummingbirds. I caught a wing in my teeth, felt the metal cold and bitter on my tongue, let the notes out slowly. I held a bear to my chest, felt the humming of the song in the bear like a heartbeat. The bears stopped one by one, I continued holding onto them. I saw the door open; I'd known he would come. **Johnny Johnny Johnny Johnny whoops Johnny whoops Johnny**. He sat down cross-legged by the enamelled lamp, the light modeling his face. Give me those, he said, it's the only way you'll live. I handed him the bears. He put them back in the box, pushed the box away, outside of where the light reached. He lay his hat over the lamp; it dimmed the light. He slipped off the apron. The shirt beneath was made without buttons and was open at the collar. He pulled it off over his head, the thick hair on his chest, the hair. He turned off the light then; the garage blackened. My blouse unbuttoning, jeans sliding off, catching on rings. Hands moving up my belly to my breasts, nipples rising as if by magic. Plant some, Johnny plant. There is no garage Johnny, I said. There is no house. No trees. No earth. Just this mattress, cool sheets, your voice in my ear. I can be in Zanzibar Johnny, I said. I'm already there, I said. And I love it Johnny, it's nothing Johnny, it feels good Johnny Johnny, empty Johnny, it's real Johnny Johnny, it's real Johnny, it's real.

SOME CARRY AROUND THIS

by SUSAN STRAYER DEAL

from FIRELANDS ARTS REVIEW

nominated by FIRELANDS ARTS REVIEW

Some carry around this
coal of sorrow.
As children they were
given the black gift
because they saw a
dog or sparrow die and
stopped childhood to wonder.
Later some gathered
it on the beaches
of war when a
country was blackened
to death. Some
pulled it out of
the sky when no one
would answer.
It is used to warm
the cold soul when
deserted to meaning,
or to darken the
pages of life with
a scribble.
If you have one
you know what I'm
talking about.

If you have one you know
you can not let
the coal die out.

THE STONECUTTER'S HORSES

by ROBERT BRINGHURST

from THE MALAHAT REVIEW

nominated by Mary Kinzie and George Payerle

April 4, 1370

Ego Franciscus Petrarca scripsi qui
testamentum aliud fecissem
si essem dives ut vulgus insanem putat.

Io, Francesco   io   io
I, Francesco, this April day,
death stirs like a bud in the sunlight, and Urban
has got off his French duff and re-entered Rome
and for three years running has invited me to Rome,
over the bright hills and down the Flaminia,
into Arezzo one more time,
my age sixty-five and my birthday approaching,
the muggers on the streets in broad daylight in Rome,
the hawks and the buzzards . . .
                                        Take this down.

No one has thought too deeply of death.
So few have left anything toward or against it.
Peculiar, since thinking of death can never be
wasted thinking, nor can it be come to
too quickly. A man carries his death with him
everywhere, waiting, but seldom thinking
of waiting. Death is uncommonly like the soul.

495

Beyond that, what I own ought to fall
of its own weight and settle. But beggars and tycoons
and I are concerned with our possessions.
And a man with a reputation for truth
must have one also for precision.
                                        I leave
my soul to my saviour, my corpse to the earth.

And let it be done without any parades.
I don't care very much where I'm buried,
so it please God and whoever is digging.
Still, you will ask. You will badger me.
If I am dead you will badger each other.
But don't lug my bones through the public streets
in a box to be gabbled at and gawked at and followed.
Let it be done without any parades.

If I die here in Padova, bury me here
near the friend who is dead who invited me here.
If I die on my farm, you can use the chapel
I mean to build there, if I ever build it.
If not, try the village down the road.

In Venezia, near the doorway.
If in Milano, next to the wall.
In Pavia, anywhere. Or if in Rome . . .
if in Rome, in the centre, of course, if there's room.
These are the places I think I might die in
in Italy.
            Or if I happen to be in Parma,
there is a cathedral of which, for some reason,
I am the archdeacon. But I will avoid
going to Parma. It would scarcely be possible,
I suppose, in Parma, not to have a parade.

At any rate, put what flesh I have left
in a church. A Franciscan
church if there is one.
I don't want it feeding a tree from which
rich people's children swipe apples.

Two hundred ducats go to the church in which
I am buried, with another hundred to be given
out in that parish to the poor, in small doses.
The money to the church, let it buy a piece of land
and the land be rented and the rental from the land
pay for an annual mass in my name.

I will be fitter company in that sanctuary
then, present in spirit and name only,
than this way, muttering to the blessed virgin
through my hemorrhoids and bad teeth. I should be glad
to be rid of this sagging carcass.
                                        Don't write that.

I have cleared no fields of their stones. I have built
no barns and no castles. I have built a name
out of other men's voices by banging my own
like a kitchen pan. My name to the church
with the money it takes to have it embalmed.

Very few other things. My Giotto to the Duke.
Most men cannot fathom its beauty. Those
who know painting are stunned by it. The Duke
does not need another Giotto, but the Duke knows painting.

To Dondi, money for a plain ring to remind him
to read me.
          To Donato—what? I forgive him
the loan of whatever he owes me. And I
myself am in debt to della Seta. Let it
be paid if I haven't paid it. And give him
my silver cup. Della Seta drinks water.
Damned metal ruins the wine.

To Boccaccio I am unworthy to leave
anything and have nothing worthy to leave.
Money, then, for a coat to keep himself warm
when he works after dark, as he frequently does,
while the river wind stutters and bleats at his window
and his hand-me-down cordwood fizzles and steams.

My lute to Tommaso. I hope he will play it
for God and himself and not to gain fame
for his playing.
                    These are such trivial legacies.

Money to Pancaldo, but not for the card-table.
Money to Zilio—at least his back salary.
Money to the other servants. Money to the cook.
Money to their heirs if they die before I do.

Give my bible back to the church.
                              And my horses. . . .
My horses.
      Let two of my friends, who may wish to,
draw lots for my horses. Horses
are horses. They cannot be given away.

The rest to my heir and executor, Brossano,
who knows he is to split it and how he is to split it
and the names I prefer not to put into this
instrument. Names of no other importance.
Care for them. Care for them here in this house
if you can. And don't sell off the land to get money in any case.
Selling the earth without cause
from the soul is simony, Brossano. Real-estate
hucksters are worse than funeral parades.
I have lived long enough in quite enough
cities, notwithstanding the gifts
of free lodging in some of them, long enough, Brossano,
to know the breath moves underfoot in the clay.

Though we ride to Rome and back aboard animals,
nothing ever takes root on the move.
The heart splits like a chinquapin pod,
spilling its angular seed on the ground.

I have seen houses and fields bartered
like cargo on shipboard. But nothing takes root
without light in the eye and earth in the hand.

Phaleas knew it and the Duke knows it
and Urban knows it and I know it.
And I must ask Boccaccio, what was it
Plato knew that made him say
the men the city needed most,
laborers and leaders, should be landless?
The land is our solitude and our silence.
A man should hoard what little silence
he is given and what little solitude he can get.

Just the one piece over the mountains
ought, I think, to be given away. Everything
I have ever done that has lasted began there.
And I think my heir will have no need to go there.

If Brossano die before I do,
look to della Seta, and for his part let him
look into that cup. He will know my mind.

A man who can write as I can ought not
to talk of such things at such length. Keep this
back if you can. Let the gifts speak
for themselves if you can, small though they are.
But I don't like the thought of what little there is
spilling into the hands of lawyers through lawsuits.
The law is no ritual meant to be practised
in private by scavengers. Law is the celebration
of duty and the ceremony of vengeance.
The law has nothing to do with my death
or with horses.
    Done.
    Ask the notaries to come over
not later than noon. I will rewrite it
and have it to sign by the time they arrive.

GRANDMOTHER
(1895–1928)

by CLEOPATRA MATHIS

from AMERICAN POETRY REVIEW

nominated by Tess Gallagher

When her father said she was a fool
to go with the white man, she only smiled,
thinking how his eyes waked blue in the foxglove
and looked away to hide her face.

She wasn't frightened: the journey down the ouachita
at flood stage, the spring swelling.
She showed him the golden raintree raining
gold buds, how to pound filo,
strip cane. She gathered aniseed, split alevara

for the time of the child
who stretched inside, but never told,
practiced in a squat. At night they lay belly to back,
the baby thrust its weight against him.

For twelve seasons of the river rising
babies cried in the black wood cabin.
She made them shifts of calico and darning string;
he brought her flowers from the milkwort,
long reeds. He loaded river mud and carp,
planted collards on the banking slope.
They lived the choctaw way,
apart from others like flint arrows.

The fourteenth year, she tended their needs
the same. Winter shoved into april,
they kept the windows stuffed with paper.
At the time of birth, she sent them out.
For years he spoke of how he left, his betrayal
to the blood he joined. And when he died
he saw her by the bed, the infant
in her arms, her hair soaked red.

𝑏 𝑏 𝑏

RICH

fiction by ELLEN GILCHRIST

from INTRO

nominated by Mary Peterson and Raymond Carver

T OM AND LETTY WILSON were rich in everything. They were rich in friends because Tom was a vice-president of the Whitney Bank of New Orleans and liked doing business with his friends, and because Letty was vice-president of the Junior League of New Orleans and had her picture in *Town and Country* every year at the Symphony Ball.

The Wilsons were rich in knowing exactly who they were because every year from Epiphany to Fat Tuesday they flew the beautiful green and gold and purple flag outside their house that meant that Letty had been queen of the Mardi Gras the year she was a debutante. Not that Letty was foolish enough to take the flag seriously.

Sometimes she was even embarrassed to call the yard man and ask him to come over and bring his high ladder.

"Preacher, can you come around on Tuesday and put up my flag?" she would ask.

"You know I can," the giant black man would answer. "I been saving time to put up your flag. I won't forget what a beautiful queen you made that year."

"Oh, hush, Preacher. I was a skinny little scared girl. It's a wonder I didn't fall off the balcony I was so scared. I'll see you on Monday." And Letty would think to herself what a big phony Preacher was and wonder when he was going to try to borrow some more money from them.

Tom Wilson considered himself a natural as a banker because he loved to gamble and wheel and deal. From the time he was a boy in a small Baptist town in Tennessee he had loved to play cards and match nickels and lay bets.

In high school he read *The Nashville Banner* avidly and kept an eye out for useful situations such as the lingering and suspenseful illnesses of Pope Pius.

"Let's get up a pool on the day the Pope will die," he would say to the football team, "I'll hold the bank." And because the Pope took a very long time to die with many close calls there were times when Tom was the richest left tackle in Franklin, Tennessee.

Tom had a favorite saying about money. He had read it in the *Reader's Digest* and attributed it to Andrew Carnegie. "Money," Tom would say, "is what you keep score with. Andrew Carnegie."

Another way Tom made money in high school was performing as an amateur magician at local birthday parties and civil events. He could pull a silver dollar or a Lucky Strike cigarette from an astonished six year old's ear or from his own left palm extract a seemingly endless stream of multicolored silk chiffon or cause an ordinary piece of clothesline to behave like an Indian cobra.

He got interested in magic during a convalescence from German measles in the sixth grade. He se t off for books of magic tricks and practiced for hours before his bedroom mirror, his quick clever smile flashing and his long fingers curling and uncurling from the sleeves of a black dinner jacket his mother had bought at a church bazaar and remade to fit him.

Tom's personality was too flamboyant for the conservative Whitney Bank, but he was cheerful and cooperative and when he made a mistake had the ability to turn it into an anecdote.

"Hey, Fred," he would call to one of his bosses. "Come have lunch on me and I'll tell you a good one."

They would walk down St. Charles Avenue to where it crosses Canal and turns into Royal Street as it enters the French Quarter. They would walk into the crowded, humid excitement of the quarter, admiring the girls and watching the Yankee tourists sweat in their absurd spunglass leisure suits, and turn into the side door of Antoine's or breeze past the maître d' at Galatoire's or Brennan's.

When a red-faced waiter in funeral black had seated them at a choice table, Tom would loosen his Brooks Brothers' tie, turn his handsome brown eyes on his guest, and begin.

"That bunch of promoters from Dallas talked me into backing an idea to videotape all the historic sights in the quarter and rent the tapes to hotels to show on closed-circuit television. Goddamit, Fred, I could just see those fucking tourists sitting around their hotel rooms on rainy days ordering from room service and taking in the Cabildo and the Presbytere on T.V." Tom laughed delightedly and waved his glass of vermouth at an elegantly dressed couple walking by the table.

"Well, they're barely breaking even on that one, and now they want to buy up a lot of soft porn movies and sell them to motels in Jefferson Parish. What do you think? Can we stay with them for a few more months?"

Then the waiter would bring them cold oysters on the half shell and steaming pompano *en papillote* and a wine steward would serve them a fine Meursault or a Piesporter, and Tom would listen to whatever advice he was given as though it were the most intelligent thing he had ever heard in his life.

Of course he would be thinking. "You stupid, impotent son of a bitch. You scrawny little frog bastard, I'll buy and sell you before it's over. I've got more brains in my balls than the whole snotty bunch of you."

"Tom, you always throw me off my diet," his friend would say, "Damned if you don't."

"I told Letty the other day," Tom replied, "that she could just go right ahead and spend her life worrying about being buried in her wedding dress, but I didn't hustle my way to New Orleans all the way from north Tennessee to eat salads and melba toast. Pass me the french bread."

Letty fell in love with Tom the first time she laid eyes on him. He came to Tulane on a football scholarship and charmed his way into a fraternity of wealthy New Orleans boys famed for its drunkenness and its wild practical jokes. It was the same old story. Even the second, third, and fourth generation bluebloods of New Orleans need an infusion of new genes now and then.

The afternoon after Tom was initiated he arrived at the fraternity house with two Negro painters and sat in the lowhanging branches of a live oak tree overlooking Henry Clay Avenue directing them in painting an official-looking yellow and white striped pattern on the street in front of the property. "D-R-U-N-K," he yelled to his painters, holding on to the enormous limb with one hand and pushing his black hair out of his eyes with the other. "Paint it to say D-R-U-N-K-Z-O-N-E."

Letty stood near the tree with a group of friends watching him. He was wearing a blue shirt with the sleeves rolled up above his elbows and a freshman beanie several sizes too small was perched on his head like a tipsy sparrow.

"I'm wearing this goddamn beanie forever," Tom yelled. I'm wearing this beanie until someone brings me a beer," and Letty took the one she was holding and walked over to the tree and handed it to him.

One day a few weeks later, he commandeered a Bunny Bread truck while it was parked outside the fraternity house making a delivery. He picked up two friends and drove the truck madly around the Irish Channel, throwing fresh loaves of white and whole wheat and rye bread to the astonished housewives.

"Steal from the rich, give to the poor," Tom yelled, and his companions gave up trying to reason with him and helped him yell.

"Free bread, free cake," they yelled, handing out powdered donuts and sweetrolls to a gang of kids playing baseball on a weed-covered vacant lot.

They stopped off at Narby's, an Irish bar where Tom made bets on races and football games, and took on some beer and left off some cinnamon rolls.

"Tom, you better go turn that truck in before they catch you," Narby advised, and Tom's friends agreed, so they drove the truck to the second precinct police headquarters and turned themselves in.

Tom used up half a year's allowance paying the damages, but it made his reputation.

In Tom's last year at Tulane a freshman drowned during a hazing accident at the Southern Yacht Club, and the event frightened Tom. He had never liked the boy and had suspected him of being involved with the queers and nigger lovers who hung around the philosophy department and the school newspaper. The boy had gone to prep school in the East and brought weird-looking girls to rush parties. Tom had resisted the temptation to blackball him as he was well connected in uptown society.

After the accident, Tom spent less time at the fraternity house and more time with Letty, whose plain sweet looks and expensive clothes excited him.

"I can't go in the house without thinking about it," he said to Letty. "All we were doing was making them swim from pier to pier carrying martinis. I did it fifteen times the year I pledged."

"He should have told someone he couldn't swim very well," Letty answered. "It was an accident. Everyone knows it was an accident. It wasn't your fault." And Letty cuddled up close to him on the couch, breathing as softly as a cat.

Tom had long serious talks with Letty's mild alcoholic father, who held a seat on the New York Stock Exchange, and in the spring of the year Tom and Letty were married in the Cathedral of Saint Paul with twelve bridesmaids, four flower girls, and seven hundred guests. It was pronounced a marriage made in heaven, and Letty's mother ordered masses said in Rome for their happiness.

They flew to New York on the way to Bermuda and spent their wedding night at the Sherry Netherland Hotel on Fifth Avenue. At least half a dozen of Letty's friends had lost their virginity at the same address, but the trip didn't seem prosaic to Letty.

She stayed in the bathroom a long time gazing at her plain face in the oval mirror and tugging at the white lace nightgown from the Lylian Shop, arranging it now to cover, now to reveal her small breasts. She crossed herself in the mirror, suddenly giggled, then walked out into the blue and gold bedroom as though she had been going to bed with men every night of her life. She had been up until three the night before reading a book on sexual intercourse. She offered her small unpainted mouth to Tom. Her pale hair smelled of Shalimar and carnations and candles. Now she was safe. Now life would begin.

"Oh, I love you, I love, I love, I love you," she whispered over and over. Tom's hands touching her seemed a strange and exciting passage that would carry her simple dreamy existence to a reality she had never encountered. She had never dreamed anyone so interesting would marry her.

Letty's enthusiasm and her frail body excited him, and he made love to her several times before he asked her to remove her gown.

The next day they breakfasted late and walked for awhile along the avenue. In the afternoon Tom explained to his wife what her clitoris was and showed her some of the interesting things it was capable of generating, and before the day was out Letty became the first girl in her crowd to break the laws of God and the Napoleonic Code by indulging in oral intercourse.

Fourteen years went by and the Wilsons' luck held. Fourteen years is a long time to stay lucky even for rich people who don't cause trouble for anyone.

Of course, even among the rich there are endless challenges, unyielding limits, rivalry, envy, quirks of fortune. Letty's father grew increasingly incompetent and sold his seat on the exchange, and Letty's irresponsible brothers went to work throwing away the money in Las Vegas and L.A. and Zurich and Johannesburg and Paris and anywhere they could think of to fly to with their interminable strings of mistresses.

Tom envied them their careless, thoughtless lives and he was annoyed that they controlled their own money while Letty's was tied up in some mysterious trust, but he kept his thoughts to himself as he did his obsessive irritation over his growing obesity.

"Looks like you're putting on a little weight there," a friend would observe.

"Good, good," Tom would say, "makes me look like a man. I got a wife to look at if I want to see someone who's skinny."

He stayed busy gambling and hunting and fishing and being the life of the party at the endless round of dinners and cocktail parties and benefits and Mardi Gras functions that consume the lives of the Roman Catholic hierarchy which dominates the life of the city that care forgot.

Letty was preoccupied with the details of their domestic life and her work in the community. She took her committees seriously and actually believed that the work she did made a difference in the lives of other people.

The Wilsons grew rich in houses. They lived in a large Victorian house in the Garden District, and across Lake Pontchartrain they had another Victorian house to stay in on the weekends, with a private beach surrounded by old moss-hung oak trees. Tom bought a duck camp in Plaquermines Parish and kept an apartment in the French Quarter in case one of his business friends fell in love with his secretary and needed someplace to be alone with her. Tom almost never used the apartment himself. He was rich in being satisfied to sleep with his own wife.

The Wilsons were rich in common sense. When five years of a good Catholic marriage went by and Letty inexplicably never became pregnant, they threw away their thermometers and ovulation charts and litmus paper and went down to the Catholic adoption agency and adopted a baby girl with curly black hair and hazel eyes. Everyone declared she looked exactly like Tom. The Wilsons named the little girl Helen and, as the months went by, everyone swore she even walked and talked like Tom.

At about the same time Helen came to be the Wilsons' little girl, Tom grew interested in raising Labrador retrievers. He had large wire runs with concrete floors built in the side yard for the dogs to stay in when he wasn't training them on the levee or at the park lagoon. He used all the latest methods for training Labs, including an electric cattle prod given to him by Chalin Perez himself and live ducks supplied by a friend on the Audubon Park Zoo Association Committee.

"Watch this, Helen," he would call to the little girl in the stroller, "watch this." And he would throw a duck into the lagoon and its secondary feathers neatly clipped on the left side and its feet tied loosely together, and one of the Labs would swim out into the water and carry it safely back and lay it at his feet.

As so often happens when childless couples are rich in common sense, before long Letty gave birth to a little boy, and then to twin boys, and finally to another little Wilson girl. The Wilsons became so rich in children the neighbors all lost count.

"Tom," Letty said, curling up close to him in the big walnut bed, "Tom, I want to talk to you about something important." The new baby girl was three months old. "Tom I want to talk to Father Delahoussaye and ask him if we can use some birth control. I think we have all the children we need for now."

Tom put his arms around her and squeezed her until he wrinkled her new green linen B. H. Wragge, and she screamed for mercy.

"Stop it," she said, "be serious. Do you think it's all right to do that?"

Then Tom agreed with her that they had all the luck with children they needed for the present, and Letty made up her mind to call the cathedral and make an appointment. All her friends were getting dispensations so they would have time to do their work at the Symphony League and the Thrift Shop and the New Orleans Museum Association and the P.T.A.s of the private schools.

All the Wilson children were in good health except Helen. The pediatricians and psychiatrists weren't certain what was wrong with Helen. Helen couldn't concentrate on anything. She didn't like to share and she went through stages of biting other children at the Academy of the Sacred Heart of Jesus.

The doctors decided it was a combination of prenatal brain damage and dyslexia, a complicated learning disability which is a fashionable problem with children in New Orleans.

Letty felt like she spent half her life sitting in offices talking to people about Helen. The office she sat in most often belonged to Dr. Zander. She sat there twisting her rings and avoiding looking at the box of Kleenex on Dr. Zander's desk. It made her feel like she was sleeping in a dirty bed even to think of plucking a Kleenex from Dr. Zander's container and crying in a place where strangers cried. She imagined his chair was filled all day with women weeping over terrible and sordid things like their husbands running off with their secretaries or their children not getting into the right clubs and colleges.

"I don't know what we're going to do with her next," Letty said. "If we let them hold her back a grade it's just going to make her more self-conscious than ever."

"I wish we knew about her genetic background. You people have pull with the sisters. Can't you find out?"

"Tom doesn't want to find out. He says we'll just be opening a can of worms. He gets embarrassed even talking about Helen's problem."

"Well," said Dr. Zander, crossing his short legs and settling his steel-rimmed glasses on his nose like a tiny bicycle stuck on a hill, "let's start her on dexadrine."

So Letty and Dr. Zander and Dr. Rothschild and Dr. Farber and Dr. Smith decided to give Helen five milligrams of dexadrine every day for twenty days each month, taking her off the drug for ten days in between.

Children with dyslexia react to drugs exactly the opposite to normal children. If you give them tranquilizers it peps them up, but if you give them ritalin or dexadrine it calms them down and makes them able to think straight.

"You may have to keep her home and have her tutored on the days she is off the drug," Dr. Zander reminded Letty, "but the rest of the time she should be easier to live with." And he reached over and patted Letty on the leg and for a moment she thought it might all turn out all right after all.

Helen stood by herself on the playground of the beautiful old pink brick convent with its drooping wrought-iron balconies covered with ficus. She was watching the girl she liked talking with some other girls who were playing jacks. All the little girls wore blue and red plaid skirts and navy blazers or sweaters. They looked like a disorderly marching band. Helen was waiting for the girl, whose name was Lisa, to decide if she wanted to go home with her after school and spend the afternoon. Lisa's mother was divorced and worked downtown in a department store, so Lisa rode the streetcar back and forth from school and could go anywhere she liked until 5:30 in the afternoon. Sometimes she went home with Helen so she wouldn't have to ride the streetcar. Then Helen would be so excited the hours until school let out would seem to last forever.

Sometimes Lisa liked her and wanted to go home with her and other times she didn't, but she was always nice to Helen and let her stand next to her in lines.

Helen watched Lisa walking toward her. Lisa's skirt was two inches shorter than those of any of the other girls and she wore high white socks that made her look like a skater. She wore a silver identification bracelet and Revlon nail polish.

"I'll go home with you if you get your mother to take us to get an Icee," Lisa said. "I was going last night but my mother's boyfriend didn't show up until after the place closed so I was going to walk to Manny's after school. Is that O.K.?"

"I think she will," Helen said, her eyes shining. "I'll go call her up and see."

"Naw, let's just go swing. We can ask her when she comes." Then Helen walked with her friend over to the swings and tried to be patient waiting for her turn.

The dexadrine helped Helen concentrate and it helped her get along better with other people, but it had an unpleasant side effect. Helen was already chubby and, after she began to take the drug, she grew even fatter. The Wilsons were afraid to force her to stop eating for fear they would make her nervous so they tried to reason with her.

"Why can't I have any ice cream?" she would say. "Daddy is fat and he eats all the ice cream he wants." She was leaning up against Letty, stroking her arm and petting the baby with her other hand. They were in an upstairs sitting room with the afternoon sun streaming in through the French windows. Everything in the room was decorated with different shades of blue, and the curtains were white with old-fashioned blue and white checked ruffles.

"You can have ice cream this evening after dinner," Letty said, "I just want you to wait a few hours before you have it. Won't you do that for me?"

"Can I hold the baby for awhile?" Helen asked, and Letty allowed her to sit in the rocker and hold the baby and rock it furiously back and forth crooning to it.

"Is Jennifer beautiful, mother?" Helen asked.

"She's O.K., but she doesn't have curly black hair like you. She just has plain brown hair. Don't you see, Helen, that's why we want you to stop eating between meals, because you're so pretty and we don't want you to get too fat. Why don't you go outside and play with Tim and not try to think about ice cream so much?"

"I don't care," Helen said, "I'm only nine years old and I'm hungry. I want you to tell the maids to give me some ice cream now," and she handed the baby to her mother and ran out of the room.

The Wilsons were rich in maids, and that was a good thing because there were all those children to be taken care of and cooked for and cleaned up after. The maids didn't mind taking care of the Wilson children all day. The Wilsons' house was much more comfortable than the ones they lived in, and no one cared whether they worked very hard or not as long as they showed up on time so Letty could get to her meetings. The maids left their own children with relatives or at home watching television, and when they went home at night they liked them much better than if they had spent the whole day with them.

The Wilson house had a wide white porch across the front and down both sides. It was shaded by enormous oak trees and furnished with swings and wicker rockers. In the afternoons the maids would sit on the porch and other maids from around the neighborhood would come up pushing prams and strollers and the children would all play together on the porch and in the yard. Sometimes the maids fixed lemonade and the children would sell it to passersby from a little stand.

The maids hated Helen. They didn't care whether she had dyslexia or not. All they knew was that she was a lot of trouble to take care of. One minute she would be as sweet as pie and cuddle up to them and say she loved them and the next minute she wouldn't do anything they told her to.

"You're a nigger, nigger, nigger, and my mother said I could cross St. Charles Avenue if I wanted to," Helen would say, and the maids would hold their lips together and look into each other's eyes.

One afternoon the Wilson children and their maids were sitting out on the porch after school with some of the neighbors' children and maids. The baby was on the porch in a bassinet on wheels and a new maid was looking out for her. Helen was in the biggest swing and was swinging as high as she could go so that none of the other children could get in the swing with her.

"Helen," the new maid said, "it's Tim's turn in the swing. You been swinging for fifteen minutes while Tim's been waiting. You be a good girl now and let Tim have a turn. You too big to act like that."

"You're just a high yeller nigger," Helen called, "and you can't make me do anything." And she swung up higher and higher.

This maid had never had Helen call her names before and she had a quick temper and didn't put up with children calling her a nigger. She walked over to the swing and grabbed the chain and stopped it from moving.

"You say you're sorry for that, little fat honky white girl," she said, and made as if to grab Helen by the arms, but Helen got away and started running, calling over her shoulder, "nigger, can't make me do anything."

She was running and looking over her shoulder and she hit the bassinet and it went rolling down the brick stairs so fast none of the maids or children could stop it. It rolled down the stairs and threw the baby onto the sidewalk and the blood from the baby's head began to move all over the concrete like a little ruby lake.

The Wilsons' house was on Philip Street, a street so rich it even had its own drugstore. Not some tacky chain drugstore with everything on special all the time, but a cute drugstore made out of a frame bungalow with gingerbread trim. Everything inside cost twice as much as it did in a regular drugstore, and the grown people could order any kind of drugs they needed and a green Mazda pickup would bring them right over. The children had to get their drugs from a fourteen-year-old pusher in Audubon Park named Leroi, but they could get all the ice cream and candy and chewing gum they wanted from the drugstore and charge it to their parents.

No white adults were at home in the houses where the maids worked so they sent the children running to the drugstore to bring the druggist to help with the baby. They called the hospital and ordered an ambulance and they called several doctors and they called Tom's bank. All the children who were old enough ran to the drugstore except Helen. Helen sat on the porch steps staring down at the baby with the maids hovering over it like swans, and she was crying and screaming and beating her hands against her head. She was in one of the periods when she couldn't have dexadrine. She screamed and screamed, but none of the maids had time to help her. They were too busy with the baby.

"Shut up, Helen," one of the maids called. "Shut up that goddamn screaming. This baby is about to die."

A police car and the local patrol service drove up. An ambulance arrived and the yard filled with people. The druggist and one of the maids rode off in the ambulance with the baby. The crowd in the yard swarmed and milled and swam before Helen's eyes like a parade.

Finally they stopped looking like people and just looked like spots of color on the yard. Helen ran up the stairs and climbed under her cherry fourposter bed and pulled her pillows and her eiderdown comforter under it with her. There were cereal boxes and an empty ice cream carton and half a tin of English cookies under the headboard. Helen was soaked with sweat and her little Lily playsuit was tight under the arms and cut into her flesh. Helen rolled up in the comforter and began to dream the dream of the heavy clouds. She dreamed she was praying, but the beads of the rosary slipped through her fingers so quickly she couldn't catch them and it was cold in the church and beautiful and fragrant, then dark, then light, and Helen was rolling in the heavy clouds that rolled her like biscuit dough. Just as she was about to suffocate they rolled her face up to the blue air above the clouds. Then Helen was a pink kite floating above the houses at evening. In the yards children were playing and fathers were driving up and baseball games were beginning and the sky turned gray and closed upon the city like a lid.

And now the baby is alone with Helen in her room and the door is locked and Helen ties the baby to the table so it won't fall off.

"Hold still, Baby, this will just be a little shot. This won't hurt much. This won't take a minute." And the baby is still and Helen begins to work on it.

Letty knelt down beside the bed. "Helen, please come out from under there. No one is mad at you. Please come out and help me, Helen. I need you to help me."

Helen held on tighter to the slats of the bed and squeezed her eyes shut and refused to look at Letty.

Letty climbed under the bed to touch the child. Letty was crying and her heart had an anchor in it that kept digging in and sinking deeper and deeper.

Dr. Zander came into the bedroom and knelt beside the bed and began to talk to Helen. Finally he gave up being reasonable and wiggled his small gray-suited body under the bed and Helen was lost in the area of arms that tried to hold her.

Tom was sitting in the bank president's office trying not to let Mr. Saunders know how much he despised him or how much it hurt and mattered to him to be listening to a lecture. Tom thought he was too old to have to listen to lectures. He was tired and he wanted a drink and he wanted to punch the bastard in the face.

"I know, I know," he answered, "I can take care of it. Just give me a month or two. You're right. I'll take care of it."

And he smoothed the pants of his cord suit and waited for the rest of the lecture.

A man came into the room without knocking. Tom's secretary was behind him.

"Tom, I think your baby has had an accident. I don't know any details. Look, I've called for a car. Let me go with you."

Tom ran up the steps of his house and into the hallway full of neighbors and relatives. A girl in a tennis dress touched him on the arm, someone handed him a drink. He ran up the winding stairs to Helen's room. He stood in the doorway. He could see Letty's shoes sticking out from under the bed. He could hear Dr. Zander talking. He couldn't go near them.

"Letty," he called. "Letty come here. My god, come out from there."

No one came to the funeral but the family. Letty wore a plain dress she would wear any day and the children all wore their school clothes.

The funeral was terrible for the Wilsons, but afterward they went home and all the people from the Garden District and from all over town started coming over to cheer them up. It looked like the biggest cocktail party ever held in New Orleans. It took four rented butlers just to serve the drinks. Everyone wanted to get in on the Wilsons' tragedy.

In the months that followed the funeral Tom began to have sinus headaches for the first time in years. He was drinking a lot and smoking again. He was allergic to whisky and when he woke up in the morning his nose and head were so full of phlegm he had to vomit before he could think straight.

He began to have trouble with his vision.

One November day the high yellow windows of the Shell Oil Building all turned their eyes upon him as he stopped at the corner of Poydras and Carondelet to wait for a street light, and he had to pull the car over to a curb and talk to himself for several minutes before he could drive on.

He got back all the keys to his apartment so he could go there and be alone and think. One afternoon he left work at two o'clock and drove around Jefferson Parish all afternoon drinking Scotch and eating potato chips.

Not as many people at the bank wanted to go out to lunch with him anymore. They were sick and tired of pretending his expensive mistakes were jokes.

One night Tom was gambling at the Pickwick Club with a poker group and a man jokingly accused him of cheating. Tom jumped up from the table and grabbed the man and began hitting him with his fists. He hit the man in the mouth and knocked out his new gold inlays.

"You dirty little goddamn bondpeddlar, you son of a bitch! I'll kill you for that," he yelled, and it took four waiters to hold him while the terrified man made his escape. The next morning Tom resigned from the club.

He started riding the streetcar downtown to work so he wouldn't have to worry about driving his car home if he got drunk. He was worrying about money and he was worrying about his gambling debts, but most of the time he was thinking about Helen. She looked so much like him that he believed people would think she was his illegitimate child. The more he tried to talk himself into believing the baby's death was an accident, the more obstinate his mind became.

The Wilson children were forbidden to take the Labs out of the kennels without permission. One afternoon Tom came home earlier than usual and found Helen sitting in the open door of one of the kennels playing with a half-grown litter of puppies. She was holding one of the puppies and the others were climbing all around her and spilling out onto the grass. She held the puppy by its forelegs, making it dance in the air, then letting it drop. Then she would gather it in her arms and hold it tight and sing to it.

Tom walked over to the kennel and grabbed her by an arm and began to paddle her as hard as he could.

"Goddamn you, what are you trying to do? You know you aren't supposed to touch those dogs. What in the hell do you think you're doing?"

Helen was too terrified to scream. The Wilsons never spanked their children for anything.

"I didn't do anything to it. I was playing with it," she sobbed.

Letty and the twins came running out of the house and when Tom saw Letty he stopped hitting Helen and walked in through the kitchen door and up the stairs to the bedroom. Letty gave the children to the cook and followed him.

Tom stood by the bedroom window trying to think of something to say to Letty. He kept his back turned to her and he was making a nickel disappear with his left hand. He thought of himself at Tommie Keenen's birthday party wearing his black coat and hat and doing his famous rope trick. Mr. Keenen had given him fifteen dollars. He remembered sticking the money in his billfold.

"My god, Letty, I'm sorry. I don't know what the shit's going on. I thought she was hurting the dog. I know I shouldn't have hit her and there's something I need to tell you about the bank. Kennington is getting sacked. I may be part of the housecleaning."

"Why didn't you tell me before? Can't Daddy do anything?"

"I don't want him to do anything. Even if it happens it doesn't have anything to do with me. It's just bank politics. We'll say I quit. I want to get out of there anyway. That fucking place is driving me crazy."

Tom put the nickel in his pocket and closed the bedroom door. He could hear the maid down the hall comforting Helen. He didn't give a fuck if she cried all night. He walked over to Letty and put his arms around her. He smelled like he'd been drinking for a week. He reached under her dress and pulled down her pantyhose and her underpants and began kissing her face and hair while she stood awkwardly with the pants and hose around her feet like a spancel. She was trying to cooperate.

She forgot that Tom smelled like sweat and whisky. She was thinking about the night they were married. Every time they made love Letty pretended it was that night. She had spent thousands of nights in a bridal suite at the Sherry Netherland Hotel in New York City.

Letty lay on the walnut bed leaning into a pile of satin pillows and twisting a gold bracelet around her wrist. She could hear the children playing outside. She had a headache and her stomach was queasy, but she was afraid to take a valium or an aspirin. She was waiting for the doctor to call her back and tell her if she was pregnant. She already knew what he was going to say.

Tom came into the room and sat by her on the bed.

"What's wrong?"

"Nothing's wrong. Please don't do that. I'm tired."

"Something's wrong."

"Nothing's wrong. Tom, please leave me alone."

Tom walked out through the French windows and onto a little balcony that overlooked the play yard and the dog runs. Sunshine flooded Philip Street, covering the houses and trees and dogs and children with a million volts a minute. It flowed down to hide in the roots of trees, glistening on the cars, baking the street, and lighting Helen's rumpled hair where she stooped over the puppy. She was singing a little song. She had made up the song she was singing.

"The baby's dead. The baby's dead. The baby's gone to heaven."

"Jesus God," Tom muttered. All up and down Philip Street fathers were returning home from work. A jeep filled with teenagers came tearing past and threw a beer can against the curb.

Six or seven pieces of Tom's mind sailed out across the street and stationed themselves along the power line that zig-zagged back and forth along Philip Street between the live oak trees.

The pieces of his mind sat upon the power line like a row of black starlings. They looked him over.

Helen took the dog out of the buggy and dragged it over to the kennel.

"Jesus Christ," Tom said, and the pieces of his mind flew back to him as swiftly as they had flown away and entered his eyes and ears and nostrils and arranged themselves in their proper places like parts of a phrenological head.

Tom looked at his watch. It said 6:15. He stepped back into the bedroom and closed the french windows. A vase of huge roses from the garden hid Letty's reflection in the mirror.

"I'm going to the camp for the night. I need to get away. Besides, the season's almost over."

"All right, " Letty answered. "Who are you going with?"

"I think I'll take Helen with me. I haven't paid any attention to her for weeks."

"That's good," Letty said, "I really think I'm getting a cold. I'll have a tray up for supper and try to get some sleep."

Tom moved around the room, opening drawers and closets and throwing some gear into a canvas duffel bag. He changed into his hunting clothes.

He removed the guns he needed from a shelf in the upstairs den and cleaned them neatly and thoroughly and zipped them into their carriers.

"Helen," he called from the downstairs porch. "Bring the dog in the house and come get on some play clothes. I'm going to take you to the duck camp with me. You can take the dog."

"Can we stop and get donuts?" Helen called back, coming running at the invitation.

"Sure we can, honey. Whatever you like. Go get packed. We'll leave as soon as dinner is over."

It was past 9:00 at night. They crossed the Mississippi River from the New Orleans side on the last ferry going to Algier's Point. There was an offshore breeze and a light rain fell on the old brown river. The Mississippi River smelled like the inside of a nigger cabin, powerful and fecund. The smell came in Tom's mouth until he felt he could chew it.

He leaned over the railing and vomited. He felt better and walked back to the red Chevrolet pickup he had given himself for a birthday present. He thought it was chic for a banker to own a pickup.

Helen was playing with the dog, pushing him off the seat and laughing when he climbed back on her lap. She had a paper bag of beignets from the French Market and was eating them and licking the powdered sugar from her fingers and knocking the dog off the seat.

She wasn't the least bit sleepy.

"I'm glad Tim didn't get to go. Tim was bad at school, that's why he had to stay home, isn't it? The sisters called Momma. I don't like Tim. I'm glad I got to go by myself." She stuck her fat arms out of the window and rubbed Tom's canvas hunting jacket. "This coat feels hard. It's all dirty. Can we go up in the cabin and talk to the pilot?"

"Sit still, Helen."

"Put the dog in the back, he's bothering me." She bounced up and down on the seat. "We're going to the duck camp. We're going to the duck camp."

The ferry docked. Tom drove the pickup onto the blacktop road past the city dump and on into Plaquemines Parish.

They drove into the brackish marshes that fringe the Gulf of Mexico where it extends in ragged fingers along the coast below and to the east of New Orleans. As they drove closer to the sea the hardwoods turned to palmetto and water oak and willow.

The marshes were silent. Tom could smell the glasswort and black mangrove, the oyster and shrimpboats.

He wondered if it were true that children and dogs could penetrate a man's concealment, could know him utterly.

Helen leaned against his coat and prattled on.

In the Wilson house on Philip Street Tim and the twins were cuddled up by Letty, hearing one last story before they went to bed.

A blue wicker tray held the remains of the children's hot chocolate. The china cups were a confirmation present sent to Letty from Limoges, France.

Now she was finishing reading a wonderful story by Ludwig Bemelmans about a little convent girl in Paris named Madeline who reforms the son of the Spanish ambassador, putting an end to his terrible habit of beheading chickens on a miniature guillotine.

Letty was feeling better. She had decided God was just trying to make up to her for Jennifer.

The camp was a three-room wooden shack built on pilings out

over Bayou Lafouche, which runs through the middle of the parish.

The inside of the camp was casually furnished with old leather office furniture, hand-me-down tables and lamps, and a walnut poker table from Neiman-Marcus. Photographs of hunts and parties were tacked around the walls. Over the poker table were pictures of race horses and their owners and an assortment of ribbons won in races.

Tom laid the guns down on the bar and opened a cabinet over the sink in the part of the room which served as a kitchen. The nigger hadn't come to clean up after the last party and the sink was piled with half-washed dishes. He found a clean glass and a bottle of Tanqueray gin and sat down behind the bar.

Helen was across the room on the floor finishing the beignets and trying to coax the dog to come closer. He was considering it. No one had remembered to feed him.

Tom pulled a new deck of cards out of a drawer, broke the seal, and began to shuffle them.

Helen came and stood by the bar. "Show me a trick, Daddy. Make the queen disappear. Show me how to do it."

"Do you promise not to tell anyone the secret? A magician never tells his secrets."

"I won't tell. Daddy, please show me, show me now."

Tom spread out the cards. He began to explain the trick.

"All right, you go here and here, then here. Then pick up these in just the right order, but look at the people while you do it, not at the cards."

"I'm going to do it for Lisa."

"She's going to beg you to tell the secret. What will you do then?"

"I'll tell her a magician never tells his secrets."

Tom drank the gin and poured some more.

"Now let me do it to you, Daddy."

"Not yet, Helen. Go sit over there with the dog and practice it where I can't see what you're doing. I'll pretend I'm Lisa and don't know what's going on."

Tom picked up the Kliengunther 7mm. magnum rifle and shot the dog first, splattering its brains all over the door and walls. Without pausing, without giving her time to raise her eyes from the red and gray and black rainbow of dog, he shot the little girl.

The bullet entered her head from the back. Her thick body rolled across the hardwood floor and lodged against a hatrack from Jody

Mellon's old office in the Hibernia Bank Building. One of her arms landed on a pile of old *Penthouse* magazines and her disordered brain flung its roses north and east and south and west and rejoined the order from which it casually arose.

Tom put down the rifle, took a drink of the thick gin, and, carrying the pistol, walked out onto the pier through the kitchen door. Without removing his glasses or his hunting cap he stuck the .38 Smith and Wesson revolver against his palate and splattered his own head all over the new pier and the canvas covering of the Boston Whaler. His body struck the boat going down and landed in eight feet of water beside a broken crab trap left over from the summer.

A pair of deputies from the Plaquemines Parish sheriff's office found the bodies.

Everyone believed it was some terrible inexplicable mistake or accident.

No one believed that much bad luck could happen to a nice lady like Letty Dufrechou Wilson, who never hurt a flea or gave anyone a minute's trouble in her life.

No one believed that much bad luck could get together between the fifteenth week after Pentecost and the third week in Advent.

No one believed a man would kill his own little illegitimate dyslexic daughter just because she was crazy.

And no one, not even the district attorney of New Orleans, wanted to believe a man would shoot a $3,000 Labrador retriever sired by Super Chief out of Prestidigitation.

PIG 311

by MARGARET RYAN

from CEDAR ROCK

nominated by CEDAR ROCK

"In an experimental atomic explosion off the island
of Bikini. . . . among the animals exposed to
radiation was one pig, bearing the number 311. He
was placed in an old warship and was thrown into
the sea by the blast. He swam to an atoll, lived
for a long time and procreated in a perfectly
normal manner."

> —One Hundred Thousand Years of Man's
> Unknown History, by Robert Charroux

I was pickled in brine for a while,
all of me, not just the delicate feet;
the bristling body, the ugly snout,
even the much-maligned ears were blown
into the sea by a blast I knew nothing about.

The sleek-bodied goats, the intelligent monkeys,
even the obese sheep in their expensive coats
disappeared into the unseen slaughter.
A great wind delivered me into the water.
I set my short legs churning the salt into foam.

I don't know who set this circle of coral
like a ring in the water, who gave me palmtrees,
coconuts, paradise—this other hard-nosed pig,
my bride. We have had daughters and sons
in a perfectly normal manner.

Our children cover the island now, a chosen,
cloven-footed race. They breed, repeople the land.
The children read about me, their father, how
I survived the great blast. Already the hooves
of the poets engrave my name in the sand.

🔥 🔥 🔥

AMERICAN POETRY: LOOKING FOR A CENTER

by ISHMAEL REED

from BLACK AMERICAN LITERATURE FORUM

nominated by BLACK AMERICAN LITERATURE FORUM

IN *Our Time*, a book edited by Allan Katzman, and published in February of 1972 by Dial Press, there appeared an interview of Buddhist monk Kina Murti Bhikku, described by interviewer Jakkov Kohn as "a gentleman whose deep clear eyes tend to pierce the vacuum around him." Bhikku was appealing to an audience of liberal intellectuals and artists on behalf of the Buddhist monks who were being murdered in "the tens of thousands" by the invading Chinese communists. Bhikku accused the communists of "annihilating Tibetan culture." The Chinese communists, according to Bhikku, had destroyed most of the monasteries and used the remainder for "camps, barracks, and horse stables."

In order to "corrupt" the monks, the Chinese communists—who entered Tibet in 1959—accosted them with homosexuals and prostitutes. Some, like Chogyam Trungpa, Rinpoche, made it across the Himalayas to safety. Rinpoche landed in India, and from there he went to England. According to one report, Rinpoche's unorthodox approach to Buddhism dismayed some of his English followers and so he came to America. The immigrant Buddhists appealed to the American left-wing cultural establishment because they were both oppressed and had a psychedelic angle.

May 14, 1977

There was some conflict between Robery Bly and Allen Ginsberg backstage at the KPFA radio benefit poetry reading held at the Greek Theatre in Berkeley. Whispers were trickling out of Boulder, Colorado, America's Tibet, where Rinpoche was now enthroned, surrounded, according to the secret All-Colorado Hamadryas News Agency, by "young foolish money" or, as Richard Dillon said, "weaker personalities who bounce off stronger ones."

Agitated, Bly said to me that he considered Boulder Buddhism a "con job," and that "some of those people up there are no more Buddhist than my grandmother." William Burroughs, mentioned with photo in the Naropa catalog, "represented the Death Principle," Bly had said in the *Co-Evolution Quarterly*. Bly was for the Great Mother principle.

Organizer Alan Soldofsky hustled about backstage like a white-suited chicken. The poets were drinking wine and eating deli sandwiches. It was a U.C. football Saturday and 4,000 people turned out for the reading. Backstage, black slavemasters were selling books I put my guts and sweat into and which these squatters had no part in making. They didn't want to pay me and so I had taken my black slavemasters to court just as Dred Scott had done his.

The audience heard Ginsberg, Bly, McClure, Dorn, Bobbie Louise Hawkins, Alta, Joanne Kyger, Lewis MacAdams, Jana Harris, Jessica Hagedorn, Simon Ortiz, David Henderson, and Victor Cruz.

When it came my time to read I was told to limit it to 10 minutes because "Allen wanted to come back and chant some more." Soldofsky told me afterwards, a cigar wiggling in his lips, hands clasped in his suspenders, "Kid, you were great. You were only supposed to take ten, but I'm glad you took twenty." Another day in the poetry business. It's an industry, with conglomerates, companies, and mom-and-pop stores. If the kind of crowd Soldofsky was able to raise continues to attend them, poetry readings might even become big business. It shouldn't have any difficulty fitting in since it includes many of the other attitudes characterized by a "modern urban civilization": competition, greed, sexism, and racism. Some kind of caucus was now criticizing the *American Poetry Review* for featuring the works of white males, in the eyes of the major book reviews the only people among us gifted with writing talent, and demanding it be put on a rotating editorship. Being the intimidated liberals that they are they hurriedly put Ethridge Knight on the cover and gave Sonia Sanchez a column. Al Young, co-publisher of *Y'Bird* magazine, wrote our position. He said that we had no more right to tell the *American Poetry Review* what to do than we had telling the Ku Klux Klan. The comparison is not strained. The Ku Klux Klan originated not in the backwoods, but on the American campus. The *American Poetry Review* printed mostly imitative academic poetry.

When I said in the *Berkeley Barb*, December 12, 1975, that the New York School, and the Bolinas clique, composed an A. T. &T. of American poetry I came into conflict with a local San Francisco Buddhist who heads the Poetry-In-The-Schools program. I was supposed to read with Fictionist Richard Grossinger but didn't show up because the Buddhist, complimenting his friends in their bios, said in mine that I "lived and raved in Berkeley." Though he told Herb Caen that he meant it as a "compliment," the *Berkeley Barb* quote was the first thing he brought up when he came over to Floyd Salas' (*Tatoo the Wicked Cross*) house to "apologize." My non-attendance at his poetry program was introduced into the discussion concerning my tenure at the University of California by a critic whose work on the Beats omits Bob Kaufman. Somewhat like doing the Lord's Supper and not painting in the central figure. What did me not attending a poetry reading at San Francisco State, because I felt I'd been slighted, have anything to do with getting tenure at Berkeley? I didn't get tenure. A Local Buddhist, and a Professor who'd done a book on the Beats. The Buddhist had studied at Jack Kerouac's School of Disembodied Poetics, which was Naropa's poetry program. I began to put two and two together.

Black Mountain and Beat Studies dominate the Naropa catalog.

Everything else is French. French Studies in Colorado. I wonder what the early miner and pioneer women writers would think about that.

The self-assured East underestimates the cultural explosion now taking place west of the Rockies. I was editing an anthology of California Poetry—*Calafia*—from 1845 to the present and can only describe the range as astonishing. 19th-century Latinos writing about trips to Chinatown; a black voodoo poet of the same period named Buelah Mae, a list of mine names which in terms of images are richer than those of many contemporary poets.

After what seemed to me to be reprisals for the remark made in the *Barb*, mostly said from humor and to stir up mischief, I began to think it might have some basis in fact. I felt like the cartoonist who'd issued an unflattering portrait of Rasputin and the Czarina and, as a consequence, was being hunted all over Moscow. I figured I'd do the hunting. I found out later that Bolinas was a mere watering hole of a constellation of international artists, intellectuals, and people who grew up in households of five maids. Actually, there were some good writers there. It would be foolish to ignore the accomplishments of Di Prima, Kyger, MacAdams, Hawkins, and Rollins. There were much bigger fish around than Bolinas.

Some of the luminaries in this constellation were gay. Though I understand that there are some rather ardent, and extremely passionate, heterosexual relationships going on at Boulder, some of the people on the faculty are identified with Homosexual Studies. Bly's remarks about Burroughs representing the Death Principle. Bly the exorcizer romping about the Greek theatre with a Nixon mask on muttering, "I am the soul of America," or something. (So many avant-garde novelists and poets are doing Nixon that I expect any day that Nixon will submit an experimental novel to the Fiction Collective, with them as characters, using their real names. I wonder how Nixon would do Bly, Coover, Roth, Baraka, me?)

Anne Waldman was quoted in *Time* magazine, February 14, 1977, as saying that "Naropa was fast becoming the center of American poetics." I knew different and so did Anne. What did they know that I didn't know? Was *Time* serious? Or was this merely a manifestation of the old well-known Luce "Orientalism"? *Time* sounding like an underground newspaper circa 1967—ex-undergrounders were designing the editorial pages of *The New York Times*—said of Chogyam Trungpa, Rinpoche, that "when he appeared, according to one legend, pails of water turned to milk and a rainbow spread across the sky."

When the 1960s East Village crowd returned from Millbrook where Timothy Leary was "guru" they'd talk about the children of famous people who were turning on. Had one of them grown up to influence *Time* magazine?

April 22, 1977

Twenty-two is a key number for me. It either sets me back or means a breakthrough. Today is a good twenty-two day. I arrive on the Boulder campus to hear Ron Sukenick (98.6) arguing with a spinster cartoon of the teacher, beak nose and everything. The argument is loud and can be heard through the halls. Ron comes back to us and tells me he's resigning from something. Appropriately, the students are celebrating the birthday of a Colorado Cannibal.

After my reading, we have dinner at the Gold Hill restaurant in the mountains above Boulder on a little strip that looks like Dog Patch. We share a table with a lady from *Time* magazine who's dressed in a frilled blouse and one of those coats Lord Byron used to wear. A man at the end of the table with Dali eyes is introduced to me as a photographer from *People*. The fiction reading I've given earlier at the University has excited my appetite and so I have a trout, and some red wine. The restaurant was added to the bar, so the story goes, because the owner felt so guilty about the people who drove off cliffs when they only served liquor. We go to a party given me by Steve, and David Winn. The party jumps and some of the people from Naropa attend. I spend some time with a librarian who fills me in on some details about one of my heroes of antiquity, Julian the Apostate, who fought the good fight against official religion.

The next morning I've scheduled an interview with Dick Gallup and Michael Brownstein, Naropa teachers and poets, to take place at the Hotel Boulderado. At the party I meet a Naropa dissident and invite him along. Turns out he's a reporter for *Soldier of Fortune* magazine and one of Idi Amin's employees—Idi Amin, the present hero of Afro-American intellectuals of the "freedom struggle."

The tape recorder is on the breakfast table. Not only will it pick up the voices of the speakers but the rock music in the background. Carol Berge described the rock singers as sounding like Pinocchio.

Pinocchio supported by space-age electronics. A few months before. E. Power Biggs had died. The last holdout against the electric organ.

Brownstein tells me that Naropa grew out of a "high energy grab-bag-everything arts festival held in the summer of 1974."

I remembered the 1960s love generation Be-Ins and Love-Ins which took place in Golden Gate and Tompkins Square Parks. This must have been something like those since it included the same personnel. The love generation didn't realize that it's his demons which make man's life interesting as much as his love. Naropa began in 1976.

What is a clique? Brownstein argued convincingly that different "lineages" were represented at Naropa. Ginsberg was descended from the Beats while "Anne [Waldman] and me are more into a New York thing." I would hear more about New York in the hour-and-a-half interview than about Boulder.

When I asked Al Young, poet and novelist, whether he thought Boulder was "fast becoming the center of American poetics," he said, "None of those people are from Boulder, they're from the East." I found it curious that Colorado's cultural traditions weren't mentioned during the interview. Colorado is the Spanish for "red" but not once did I hear a reference to Hispanic poetry though Hispanic poets were present in Boulder: Corky Gonzalez, Kris Guiterrez, Jesus Luna, and Arturo Rodriguez. Were these people refugees from a dying planet unable to explore the New World? Sukenick said that the University at Boulder and Naropa were into a kind of cultural exchange: they shared teachers and poets. The relationship between Naropa and the University at Boulder didn't end there.

The Tibetan Buddhist Ceremony of the Vajra Crown was held on the University campus. Normally, according to the *Colorado Daily*, anybody raising revenue using the University must account for the money immediately and deposit it somewhere. The Buddhists claimed that, under Tibetan tradition, the money was "blessed," and if the money is put into an account and later withdrawn it loses its blessedness. Bert Lance should have had a Buddhist lawyer.

Brownstein, who sometimes looks like a guy who wore a prep school cap and shorts at one time, says he thought "the hottest scene in the country was taking place in Boulder," which he called an "energy center." Between sips of coffee, I sat there taking it all in while in the background that music which always seems to include a loud drummer, pounded and crashed.

Gallup didn't say much. Silence is Buddhist, which right there prevents it from gaining any mass following in a rowdy country raised on noise. The land of the Hallelujah and the Yahoo. The country of Bang-a-Lang-a-Ding-Dong.

The publicity about Boulder was all wrong, said Brownstein, a poet from Tennessee, "We're not rich, the classroom equipment is inadequate and we're not paid very well. There's not enough for the programs." A teacher in the Poetics program receives 200 dollars per week, I was told.

That information didn't square with what the All-Colorado Hamadryas News Agency was feeding me and what I was hearing from other sources. The suite Rinpoche rented in Chicago during an appearance. The real estate holdings.

Judith Hurley, a former disciple, complained in the *Colorado Daily* about the Boulder Buddhists' opulent living. In a piece called "Buddhism Schmoodism" she described what happened during the Gyalwa Karmapa's recent visit: "His Holiness," it seems, lived it up! She reported there were walls covered with satin, and sewn cushions, table cloths in satin and brocade; Tickets to a Vajra Crown Ceremony went for 8 dollars; In the ballroom hung "floor to ceiling satin;" Present to protect Trungpa Rinpoche were the Vajra Guards, a para-military organization said by some to be a bully squad. "He's very charismatic," explained Buddhist Michael Brownstein.

Of the Crown Ceremony's audience Hamadryas said, "The men were dressed in starched white suits and formal neckties, and women in their Sunday best." Like a Kiwanis convention.

Hurley concluded her article, "So let me remind you that Tibet, where these people come from, was a theocracy. You know what that means? That means they're used to being treated like kings." Kings? That rings a bell. Camelot! The overwhelming image in the "liberal arts" books white boys are required to read. Toadying up to the court isn't anything new for the artist, the world over. Early art is sometimes described as "court art." They had some in Europe, in China, and in Africa. The musician had to write a concerto for his patron. Benin sculpture emerges from this tradition.

The descendents of Holy Roman Empire monarchies became feeble-minded in the 20th century and after World War I had been done in by the democracies; some were kept on to entertain the tourists, like the one they have in England. A lot of this "Lost Generation" whining is merely western writers mooning over the fact that they didn't have some earl or somebody to pick up the bills.

They complained, and still do, about the stupidity of the bourgeoisie because to them the bourgeoisie doesn't have any smarts and won't bow down to their "genius." It was inevitable that they'd find a substitute, and so they adopted Shang-Ra-Lai.

Brownstein disassociated himself from Trungpa and the Boulder Buddhists and their "blessed" bank accounts and real estate holdings; Brownstein said that Rinpoche wasn't his guru but "Allen's." He and Anne had a guru who was in India.

Although they file taxes together, and Rinpoche is all over the catalog, Brownstein insisted that the Poetics program was separate from the Buddhists and that the Poetics faculty had "carte blanche" to do what they wanted to do. What was going on here?

Would the Buddhists unite behind a Presidential candidate and extend Naropa to the White House? Would the Vajra Squad become that candidate's Palace Guard? Somebody at the party said, "Be careful of the Vajra Squad," when they heard I was writing an article. I told them that I wasn't a guest in this country. I had read about the silent deportation of the Moonies. When the upper-middle-class parents who run the nation find out what some of these kids are into—don't you think they're going to put pressure on the government to do something about Naropa? After they deport the Boulder Buddhists and the man *Time* called "The Precious Master of the Mountains"—just as they have a white King of Swing, a white King of Rock (secret niggers say Jagger sold his soul to the devil for that spot and Altamont was the payoff), a white King of Rock and Roll, there will emerge a white "Precious Master of the Mountains." They already got one in the bull-pen according to *Head* magazine. Watch.

Dillon and Brownstein got into a big hassle about whether Buddhism was a religion. Brownstein claimed that Buddhism didn't have any gods, though the art associated with Buddhism, shown in Tibetan monasteries, depicts gods and goddesses, some of them of Indian origin, and some black. "It's all in here," Brownstein said, pointing inward. "Sort of like a psychological diagram," Dillon added. "What about a situation in which people are treated as gods?" Dillon said, obviously referring to Rinpoche, whose name, according to a text called *A Cultural History of Tibet*, by David Snellgrove and Hugh Richardson, was the one given "the most sacred of Tibetan images," the "Jopbo Rinpoche," "the Precious Lord," brought to Tibet by the Chinese wife of Srong-brtsan-sgam-po, the first of the great Buddhist kings who died in 650 A.D. Unlike Boulder's Rinpoche, Srong-brtsan-sgam-po valued words and fixed a new script for the Tibetan language.

I had been an admirer of William Burroughs. As a joke I used to read his "Astronaut's Return" to largely black audiences and then ask them to identify the author. They'd usually say Elijah Muhammad or Malcom X. Here was a white intellectual who was aware of the horrors visited upon the world by technology. Some of his ideas of history were quite comfortable with those of pioneer, and outlaw, black historians like Hansbery, Rogers, and Van Sertima. For some of us Burroughs towered over the Mailers and the Bellows with their bent for Nixonian literary racist flummery. Mailer had to know better than some of the racist things carried in his books. He was a popular "Intellectual" who often faked knowledge like a slide trombonist faking riffs.

Where did Burroughs stand on Naropa? James Grauerholz, who signed a letter to me "Assistant to William Burroughs," wrote on August 21st that he had heard that I planned to discuss Boulder Buddhism in an article entitled the "Poetry Business." He wanted to be sure that Burroughs' viewpoint was accurately presented.

In the article "Obeying Chogyam Trungpa," Burroughs and Rinpoche disagree on some matters, the most important of which appears related to psychic phenomena. Burroughs feeling that astral projection and telepathy exist, while Trungpa dismisses them as distractions. Much "evidence" would support Burroughs. Their essential disagreement can be summed up in what Burroughs wrote: he said that Rinpoche didn't give the matter of words as much importance as he did. Claiming that when Huxley got Buddhism, he stopped writing novels and wrote Buddhist tracts, Burroughs challenged, "Show me a good Buddhist novelist."

More and more investigation is being given to the matter of coincidence. Koestler argued in his *The Roots of Coincidence* that coincidence was not such a mysterious thing after all but something which happens in everyday life to such an extent that it can be measured. I was beginning to believe this and had begun to record coincidences and found that they happened frequently. Victor Cruz

(*Tropicalization*) didn't know that I was writing an article and called up on September 18 to tell me about a book called *The Job* written by William Burroughs. His criticisms sounded like those of Robert Bly. I turned on the tape recorder next to the phone.

In *The Job*, according to Cruz, Burroughs argued that there were cells inside a man's body which could produce a fetus. Vic thought that to be cold-blooded and accused Burroughs of advocating the elimination of women. It sounded cold-blooded to me too. I finally understood why Mrs. Frankenstein cried her entire honeymoon night. "He's produced by heterosexuals and so his stance is contradictory," Cruz said. He felt that it was also anti-"Third World," a term both of us were uncomfortable with; it was created by politicians who hate culture and so permit words to become their traps. We produced a multi-cultural magazine called *Y'Bird*. The literary wholesalers, those publications which forecast magazines and tell the book sellers what to buy, continually refer to the magazine as third world, and black, when in the last issue we included 26 white contributors.

Cruz accused homosexuals of desiring to become women without paying the price. Without suffering labor pains, which I'm glad I don't have to suffer. "They just want the theatrics, and the gestures." He compared this attitude with that of Disco music where you can learn a latin dance for 25 dollars and an afternoon of your time. "Some of those dances, which originated in Africa, involve an hour's exercise of toe movement."

"Intricate lip-motions and eye-movement go with the Salsa, but you don't see these Disco dancers doing it. It's the difference between the Tower of Power and Tito Puente," Cruz said. Cruz has written songs for Ray Barretto.

Boulder was where they wrote Disco poetry, Cruz said. It's like the design art he associated with Andy Warhol in which one relies upon plastic formulas. "How can it be the center of American poetry when American poetry is more than one language." The new multi-cultural writing contained images, symbols, diction, and the textures of different traditions. The Beats, and Black Mountain, operate from basically a European tradition. Pick up the standard "American anthology" and you'll find included works from people who share similar values. The writers I interviewed at Boulder, Naropa critic and defender, like French poetry and what happened among white exiles of the 1920s. Non-white poets knew that and more. If you were a victim of American super-race "education" you couldn't miss Shakespeare & Co. The non-white poets also seemed to be influenced by more than writing. Houston poet Lorenzo Thomas, who said some good things about Boulder, but didn't think it was the center, named among his influences "living down South in the country." New York, the traditional center of Afro-American writing, was not that any longer. A revolt had occurred in the early '70s which had sent Afro-American poetry into the West and the South. The first issue of *Callaloo*, a New Orleans magazine edited by former Umbra poet Tom Dent, Charles Rowell, and Jerry Ward, carried Dent's editorial which read:

> So many of our friends are tired and disgusted with the New York scene. . . . So one of the things we are about is redressing the balance between the so-called advanced progressive N.Y. & the backwards countrified South.

Cyn Zarco, a Filipino-American, one of four poets included in the internationally acclaimed anthology *Jambalya*, said she could sympathize with the 1920s expatriate movement, being an expatriate herself, "but I'm not fascinated by it," she said.

I said in the same *Berkeley Barb* interview that the '70s would bring about a multi-cultural poetry and that both the 1960s Black Aesthetic, and that of the counter-culture, were racist and limited. When Amiri Baraka, the literary Black Power guru, became LeRoi Jones, the communist revolutionary, after a bold public reconsideration of his views, he left his groupies in intellectual disarray. Addison Gayle, Jr., the Chief Black Aesthetic proponent, sneaked away from his position via hardcover in a book where he admits that he quoted Keats when contemplating suicide. So much for the Black Aesthetic, which critic Larry Neal characterized as the spiritual sister of the Black Power movement in an important anthology, *Black Fire*, he co-authored with Jones.

Now, for the first time, a truly national poetry, made up of the many writing cultures, was on the scene. It cut across gender, race and region. Music, painting, and dance had already been there for about fifty years. A Japanese-American student said that what he enjoyed most about dancer Twyla Tharp's *Dance-In-America* show was the footage of black dancer Bill Robinson. Tharp, in that sense, was a multi-cultural artist and synchronizer, sometimes using the work of Fats Waller. Choreographer Carla Blank had scored a number called "Eccentric Chorus Line," accompanied by Scott Joplin's music and performed in Tokyo, long before the Joplin craze.

Besides knowing about "Modern Literature," the multi-cultural poets I interviewed mentioned dance, music, and other influences on their work.

They were influenced by Salsa, Be-bop, the Japanese avant-garde, the poetry of Latin America, Africa, and of the Harlem Renaissance, probably a movement more important than the 1920s expatriate one, in terms of international influence.

On September 3, 1977, I invited Simon Ortiz (*Going for the Rain*), David Meltzer (*The Two-Way Mirror*), and Bob Callahan, publisher of Turtle Island Press and editor of *The New World Journal*, whose latest book is *Winter Poles*, to come to my home and discuss the Boulder situation. Shawn Wong, head of the Combined Asian Resources Project, flew down from Seattle, Washington. He is the author of a novel and the editor of *Yardbird Reader*, Vol. 3, which, according to Shawn, was the first publication to recognize an Asian-American tradition which wasn't limited to exotica or mimicry.

Callahan didn't feel that Boulder had enough variety to be the center of American poetics. He said that it was merely the Saint Mark's project gone west. The Saint Mark's project grew out of the readings which were held at Saint Mark's Church-in-the-Bowery on the Lower East Side in the middle '60s. The first reading happened because William Burroughs was persuaded to read there instead of at the Metro cafe where a racist incident had occurred. Joel Oppenheimer was the first head of the poetry program; I headed the fiction program. Anne Waldman came on later and edited a magazine from there called *World* and St. Mark's, through her energies and talent, became famous. Recently, it was the scene of a reading including Allen Ginsberg and the late Robert Lowell, which, in terms of literary politics, was equivalent to Begin sitting down for lunch with Arafat and reminiscing about mutual relatives. Robert Lowell, to some, represented the Academy the Beats sought to overthrow. He said that he and Ginsberg merely came from opposite ends of William Carlos Williams. At about the same time, *The New York Times Book Review*, in a daily review, divided the American Poetry world between The Beats and The Academy. Women, "Third World," etc., according to the *Times* article, were on the outs.

A glance at the Naropa catalog reveals that its idea about "art" revolves about a constellation of 1950s' personalities. People whose "experiments" had been picked up by everything from big-time television to Schrafft's Ice Cream. Sukenick talked about Naropa being the last stand of a major American cultural movement.

David Meltzer said that the idea of Naropa being the center to him sounded like someone's overblown enthusiasm. Kind of like baseball scorecards—baseball being a cult subject for the literary avant-garde—as in the expression "My team can beat your team."

Naropa, to Callahan, was part of a 200-year-old American tradition, "the dude ranch." Rinpoche's Dude Ranch!

Meltzer and Callahan were poets who worked in factories when they were 15. They don't look like young foolish money, to me. Meltzer is a Caballa scholar, and Callahan is Irish-American. Both Meltzer and Callahan knew the riches of their backgrounds. So did the rest of those who met that day, at my house, over cookies and coffee. We knew our heritages, and weren't having identity problems. We communicated because we were Americans, which meant that we knew about comic books, movies, World War II, Milton Berle, Red Foxx, Yiddish Theatre, John F. Kennedy, Muhammad Ali, Toscanini, John Coltrane, Black Power, KKK, Ice Cream, Mickey Mouse, etc. We were also bookish and our reading didn't stop when were were "educated." Meltzer and Callahan were rare white poets who knew the works of other cultures. They didn't sneer at American culture as it was fashionable to do back east. After Jerzy Kosinski, The New York Intellectuals' token dissident, made an ignorant tirade against American culture before a delighted French audience, I got up and asked him as a truck driver would ask him, "If you don't like the United States then why don't you go back to Poland and take Polanski with you." Muriel Rukeyser, that grand lady, criticized a letter I wrote saying that I couldn't relate to P.E.N., the American Writer's Organization, because it was headed by a foreigner—Kosinski—who couldn't possibly know the problems of an American writer. Now I feel justified in writing that letter kind Muriel called "lousy."

Meltzer charged Naropa with adopting the slick merchandising techniques of the modern corporation. When Bob Callahan once asked Rinpoche why he was charging 50 dollars for tickets, Rinpoche told him that they had to operate Buddhism like an American business. Callahan, once Rinpoche's San Francisco host, found this enough reason to disassociate himself from Rinpoche, though he respects him and believes that he's good at TM. But charging 50 dollars a ticket was foreign to Callahan's "communalistic principles."

When Robert Creeley was invited to a Rinpoche lecture, according to Richard Dillon, he refused; Ashbery begged out claiming that "I'm Episcopalian." Why were Jewish intellectuals associated with Naropa? "Because they don't find enough reinforcement in their own backgrounds,"Meltzer said.

"Literature belongs to the people," claimed Simon Ortiz, who often includes Acoma chants in his readings. "I would guide any Native-American away from the idea that one place is the center of American poetry today." Ortiz wondered whether the C.I.A. had anything to do with Naropa. Carl Bernstein had written in the *Rolling Stone* that Luce's publications had something to do with the C.I.A. It was *Time* in which the "Precious King" article appeared.

"There's always some story about a wealthy European going to Tibet only to return and start Nazism or something," Meltzer said.

What worried Shawn Wong about Naropa was its "official language."

Meltzer thought it ironic that those who had waged "holy war" against a former establishment, dedicated to white notions of literature, had themselves become victims of their own revolution and in danger of being overthrown. "Maybe they're calling themselves the center because they're a hole in the clouds." Meltzer said.

The last publicized center of American writing was Manhattan. They became known as The New York Intellectuals. With important connections with publishing, and universities, with access to the major book reviews, they were able to pose as the vanguard of American culture when they were so obsessed with the two Joes—McCarthy and Stalin—that they were only to produce two artists, Saul Bellow and Philip Roth, who left town. That's why everybody in the Berkeley theatre laughed at the "Dysentery" joke in the Woody Allen movie *Annie Hall*. There was that sad issue of the *Partisan Review*, 44, No. 2 (1977), called "New York and National Culture: An Exchange," in which a panel of New York Intellectuals claimed to represent National Culture when in reality they sounded like village people whispering about haunted houses. Forms they claimed to have invented were classical ingredients of American art, but they wouldn't know that because they hate "liberal Democracy," and popular cultures, and are still reading those books in the rusty trunks brought over from Europe. To them an intellectual is someone who uses big words, lives in the suburbs, and has read *Crime and Punishment* 88 times. Egoists that they are, to them, the rest of us are stupid, and "simple-minded." California, to those culturally medievel map-makers, is a place where "gurus" live.

When Charles Pruett asked from the audience why no blacks, women, or Puerto Ricans were on the panel claiming to represent national culture, he was wisecracked down by a demogogic Irving Howe, using a tactic the New Left he abused so much made famous.

Just as the Boulder minds are still in New York, the N.Y.I. mind was in France, or Russia, anywhere but this—to them—disgusting place. Putting on airs, and claiming the rest of the country to be "envious" of them. Another thing the panel agreed on. The New York Intellectual was dead.

Defying the N.Y.I. machine they embarassed, the Beats originated in the Be-bop subculture, perhaps the most important modern "artistic" movement. Native-Americans have been doing "Abstract Expressionism" for thousands of years, even before somebody invented a critical term for it. "I don't know what they mean by Cubism," Picasso said, "My art is African art."

The Beats adopted the values of Be-boppers—the language, as well as the interest in "Eastern Religion." Long ago, Lynn Hope, a Newark saxophonist, had quit the country for Egypt. Pre-Be-bopper Cab Calloway was singing "psychedelic" songs in the twenties. Bob Kaufman, the most admired Beat poet among the young multicultural poets, provided the bridge between the Beats and Be-bop. Armed with my tape recorder I ran into Kaufman on Broadway in San Francisco and asked him for an interview; he refused. He is still the enigma of the Beat movement and future multi-cultural critics would probably consider him the most important poet of the movement. For now, local criticism was in the hands of the Beat critical bureaucracy. They were white males. One had written up the KPFA reading as if the non-white poets didn't even appear.

Though he didn't originate it, Amiri Baraka, due to his strong publicity connections with Beats, and also because of the notoriety of his play *Dutchman*, was made the founder of the New Black Poetry. He was the first to admit "there were others before me," but

Richard Ellman didn't read that and so, since Baraka had been influenced by Olson and Williams, wrote, in *The Norton Anthology*, how the New Black Poetry was dependent upon white forebears, thus recalling the quaint racist American notion that heathens can do nothing on their own.

Baraka's abstract Zen words were replaced by the abstract works of Kawaida, only to be succeeded by the abstract words of Marxist Leninism. Everything other than the jargon showed a brilliant, tight, original, witty, coruscating, even humorous work, which excelled as Be-bop did, and like African art, not on the basis of facts, but the resemblances to facts. Somebody called it elliptical; Baraka was Miles Davis.

While Ginsberg took guruism into the counter-culture, Baraka, who once described himself as Sammy Davis, Jr., to Ginsberg's Frank Sinatra, introduced it into "Black Arts." He built a cult around his personality. His public denial of the white Beats proved an effective strategy; for about eight years counter-culture people kept asking me when Baraka was going to talk to them.

Now, he was back home on the cover of *The Village Voice*, renouncing his racist period. Ginsberg and Baraka, both from Newark, shared influences, and, shortly after *Dutchman* was on, Baraka said on New Jersey television that he had read Pound before Marx.

Perhaps Pound led both Baraka and Ginsberg to the East. In David Meltzer's *The San Francisco Poet*, Kenneth Rexroth mentions the upside-down ideograms in Pound's *Cantos*. He told the publisher of New Directions about it who in turn passed it on to T. S. Eliot who, amused, said, "But, you know, no one pays any attention at all to that stuff. You know, that Chinese thing. Nobody reads Chinese anyway." Baraka was so good at the self-deprecating interior monologue that it was no surprise that he'd abandon guruism for "the people." He was just too much the New Yorker to take himself that seriously. His father was probably a Democrat like mine.

As for Ginsberg. He said of Rinpoche in the June issue of the short-lived *National Screw* magazine, that "he [Rinpoche] seems to have carried forward a practical, visible, programmatic practice of egolessness, and provided a path for other people to walk on." While Brownstein strove to separate the Poetics program from the Buddhist program, Ginsberg described the Kerouac School of Disembodied Poetics as "a branch" of Naropa. To the outside, all of this was confusing.

October 4, 1977
Whittmore House, Washington University, St. Louis

Howard Nemerov bought me lunch. I have a Crab Louis. They say that Nemerov doesn't talk much, but I spring an interview on him anyway. He turns out to be one of the wittiest people I've talked to. He said that he was too involved in his own work to give much thought to a center of American poetry. Anne Waldman was his student at Bennington, but "She showed no signs of doing what she's doing now."

"Anne's ambitious," Nemerov said, "I think she wanted to be an actress." I thought of the Rita-Hayworth-circa-1940s poster that went up for her reading of "Fast Speaking Woman."

What were his opinions of contemporary American poetry? "I was a judge in last year's National Book Awards, and after reading one hundred books I doubted not only my judgment but my sanity." He characterizes much of today's poetry as "Kleenex poetry. You look at it and throw it away."

"Young people like to think of themselves as poets. If there are two million poets today, I'm partly responsible," Nemerov said. "I taught them and then they went out and taught others. Like a chain letter."

He said that Allen Tate had once told him that you had to be homosexual to get over in the poetry world. Fifteen years later you had to be asylum material. And by the 1970s you had to be dead, preferably by your own hand.

He said that literary Chinoiserie dated back to at least Pope's time in the 18th century and that he had studied Buddhism at Harvard long before it became fashionable.

"For someone who has survived 5 poetry movements and 2 wars, the idea of a Disembodied School of Poetics strikes me as funny."

His picture is in this week's *New York Times Book Review* in connection with the publication of *The Collected Poems of Howard Nemerov*.

The interview is over. They have a picture of Vincent Price in this faculty club. I've been told that the Price home is on this very street.

Later, Charles Wartts, Jr., wanted to show me a short story and so we adjourned to Washington U's Rathskeller, which is celebrating its anniversary. There's a guy dressed up as an animal running around giving people free beer. In another room students are watching soap operas on the biggest TV screen I ever saw.

Wartts said that he was in Boulder in the early '70s when the Buddhists were sending a red van around to recruit people in Pizza Parlors and Beer Halls. He said that a sweet looking blonde took him to a meeting where people were told that if they chanted long enough they'd get what they desired. Then people started testifying like in the Baptist Church about what Buddhism had done for them. He said that people talked about giving up all of their material possessions. The little blonde said that she was starving and that after she chanted somebody brought her a big pizza. Then they wanted to go to Denver to recruit people, he said, but he left.

When I told Wartts, a director of Journalism at Webster College, about the lavish display accompanying the Vajra Crown Ceremony, he couldn't believe that this was the same ragged band of holy rollers he'd met in the early '70s.

Quincy Troupe, co-author of the multi-cultural anthology *Giant Talk*, published by Random House, said that the guruism of Baraka and Ginsberg could be attributed to their "huge egos."

The New Black Poetry, Troupe claimed, had come a long way from the "burn down America" poems of the 1960s. He saw black poets returning to jazz, blues, folklore, and liberating themselves from "weighty diction."

"Poets fall into a guru complex," Troupe said, because their traditional role in some cultures has been that of "mediator between heaven and earth."

He did not see Boulder as the center; he found the poetry of blacks, Latinos, and some Asians to be much more interesting.

Thomas and Troupe were both members of the "New Black Poetry," which, like the Beats, broke away from the Academy. With the exception of Langston Hughes, Sterling Brown, and others, much of the poetry by blacks before that was indistinguishable from that found in an old *Oxford Book of Verse*.

19th-century black poetry, like 19th-century black painting, was very much imitative of European forms. The Harlem Renaissance was a dramatic departure from that tradition.

Other American groups had found their "national voices" and the revolt begun by the Beats and picked up by the blacks was spreading. P. R. Felipe Luciano referred to black poets born between 1928 and 1938 as "Older Brothers."

The Beats influenced us. I read *On The Road* in my late teens and shortly afterwards took off for San Francisco. I thought that North

Beach was where you went swimming. We discussed "Howl" in poetry classes at the University of Buffalo. I must have read Don Allen's *The New American Poetry* so many times that when I arrived in New York at 22 my copy was falling apart; my favorite was Helen Adams. The first apartment I lived in, on Spring Street, in 1962, had been abandoned a month before by Jack Kerouac who told the other roommates that he was going to Las Vegas to get drunk.

Shawn Wong said that in 1971 Asian-American kids couldn't name a single Asian-American writer and now some of them were writers themselves. "Asian-American art isn't about business," Shawn said, "It's about educating artists."

Since Buddhism came out of Asia I was interested in what some of the Asian-Americans thought about American Buddhism.

Shawn said that Asian-American writers were more interested in the Cantonese folk gods, the Chinese loas which had been suppressed by Christian missionaries. Kwan Kung was one. This folk god had become the loa of Asian-American artists in San Francisco. He was the symbol of plunder, revenge, drama, and literature. Playwright Frank Chin invited me to purchase a statue of the fierce-looking god on display in a New York Chinatown shop window. It would have cost me 300 dollars. Chin, the leading spirit behind the Asian-American Renaissance taking place in Seattle, San Francisco, Los Angeles, and New York, regarded the Buddhists as just another Christian sect.

Filipino-American poet Cyn Zarco said that she was into a revolutionary Buddhism, which was gaining popularity among the Asian-American avant-garde in San Francisco. It was called Nichiren Shoshu, and involved chanting twice a day. It was a religion in which one fulfilled one's goals and desires in the real world. She said that the idea of Boulder being the center of American poetics was "Bull!"

Some of the same crowd who were after Buddhahood were also into "shamanism," formerly an area for anthropologists and tourist poets; the Native-Americans were now claiming their traditions for themselves.

Cherokee-American writer, Gerald Hobson, in his "The Rise of the White Shaman as a New Version of Cultural Imperialism," wrote: ". . . knowledge of Indian cultures has, unfortunately, been formed too often by the romantic [and now the neo-romantic] writers/artists/ethnologists who have avidly and imperiously staked out their claims as unequivocal experts on our Indian cultures."

The Hispanic-American poets have been coming on so strong that soon Spanish will be a required language for those citizens living west of the Rockies. Their magazines are named *Tin Tan*, *Maize*, *Rejidos*, *Puerto Del Sol* and *De Colores*.

I asked Ron Sukenick why someone at the Paris conference—where Kosinski dropped his load on American culture—said that Americans had no tradition when the Native-Americans were writing out of traditions which extended back to 30,000 years. Sukenick said that there was a tendency in America to ignore traditions which weren't derived from Europe.

They've made me and Ron into Bureaucrats and businessmen because it's better that we have an influence on getting authors published and magazines started than some people I know. His remark that Naropa was the last stand of an important movement stuck with me. There's no center of American poetry. People in centers see themselves as the center because they can't see the whole scene with an eye for detail. If the poetry scene were the landscape at night and you were looking down at it you'd see flickering patches of light distributed over great distance. Knowing Anne, she was probably misquoted. Some of the women out here asked, "Why did you publish that bitch?" when I had "Fast Speaking Woman" in an anthology called *Yardbird Reader* I used to edit. She's an important part of a significant culture. She's openminded to show an interest in a variety of cultures and art forms, as displayed in "Fast Speaking Woman." I once wrote her a letter warning her, in green ink, not to be Guinevere in somebody's Fairy Kingdom. I'm convinced that Gallup and Brownstein are earnest, and based upon the works I've read I believe Boulder to be an important center. Sympathetic critics ask them only to examine their relationship to an official religion with its Abbots and its Hierarchy. Bob Callahan talked about how the old Druids handled the situation. ". . . whenever the Monkish drift ran too closely towards one Godism and one Kingism—historically, the two run hand-in-hand—some old Druid would appear magically and cast an oath or give a charm, and the Monks would all scatter back inside their castles again." A lot of American poets can't sit in one position that long because they're itching from spirits and can't keep still. Demons pour out of their mouths and issue from their fingertips. Others may have their Fourth Estate but poets have their Estate of the Second Sight Seers.

In that 1972 book, Bhikku questioned whether Tibetan Buddhism could exist outside of Tibet. There was that famous encounter when Rinpoche and an old Zen Master who died the following year met on Page Street. They talked about what shape an American Buddhism would take. They opened a Mental hospital in upstate New York. Millions of Americans are "depressed," that unmysterious word they created to describe what the old folks used to describe as a "haunt ridin' you" or "death on your back" or "bad loas in your head." TM may be one way of dealing with the increasing madness occurring in highly technological societies. It was almost as if the devil had become immune to the dominant psychiatric techniques of the last century.

I understand that Rinpoche wants to get rid of the beards and long hair so that he might recruit some of the power elite: generals, industrialists, and politicians. Disco Buddhism, kind of like Shang-Ra-Lai entering Holiday Inn.

His abandoning them might be the best thing to happen to the Boulder poets, which the publicity called the "center of American poetics."

When I asked Okinawan-American poet Geraldine Kudaka, who reads with a band called Mugicha, featuring a musician named Snakepit Eddy, where she felt the center of American poetry was, she replied, "In every poet's heart."

I SHOW THE DAFFODILS TO THE RETARDED KIDS

by CONSTANCE SHARP

from SOUTHERN POETRY REVIEW

nominated by SOUTHERN POETRY REVIEW

I don't make them name it
like I did with the wooden pig and horse
and the rest in the "animal unit."
I don't even name it myself, or if I do
I don't say it distinctly
with the message, remember!
I take them by the hand and say
I want to show you
something.
When we get to the school steps,
I arrange them around the beds.
Stacy laughs
and opens her palms in a little dance.
I bend down and show them
how to smell: I half close my eyes,
draw my breath in deep,
and look dreamy and delighted. Latasha
pulls a pistil out. David
scolds a whole bed of them with his finger.
Robby bends down with me
and caresses a petal. He gives it a kiss
and one more pat
then he puts the yellow horn to his ear
and listens.

DREAM

by JOHN WILLSON

from BOXSPRING

nominated by BOXSPRING

Sometimes through binoculars
I scan the neighborhood for flaws.
Today there is nothing—only
a loose thread in someone's
curtain

but I reach two fingers
down the lenses
tug this thread gently
and the fabric
tears into a living room.
A man is reading in a chair.
He is reading the journal
of an anteater

in a zoo: "Today
there is nothing—
only a new crack in the cement.
But along this crack my tongue
feels a delicious black thread—
I tug this gently."

LIVING WITH ANIMALS

by MARGARET KENT

from GREENSBORO REVIEW

nominated by GREENSBORO REVIEW

It has been said that dogs drink at the River
Nile while running along that they might not be
seized by crocodiles.

These mornings I lie awake listening for signs
of life in the house: the scurrying of mice
in the eaves, the tick of birds in the gutters,
the sure-footed step of love outside my door.
Grumbling, I rise. The darkness has washed me
clean of shadows. I am a groundhog emerging
on the last day of the year, squinting down
light tumbling in pieces behind me, shapes of
where I've been, no idea of what's to come.

Of a concrete nature, it's Sunday: ribs and
God and rest, the long slow grinding down of
afternoon, the inevitable ride toward darkness,
animals fading in the fields, at the sides of
roads. We cross the bridge to Arkansas, our
hands in our laps, the radio playing hymns,
"this blinding light that comes with love"
is nothing now, a failure, the sad overloading
of the heart's circuits, this dark house
condemned by love, condemned by love.

It is another light that divides us now, clear
shapes again in the fields, in the mirror, at
the edge of roads: yellow dogs, for instance,

their fur muddied and bedraggled, casualties
of the river, perhaps, or of morning: how when
I see white teeth bared sideways to the sun,
the pale conversion of tongue to dust, the
befuddled cowlick along the spine, I think of you,
how we outran the danger but surrendered to time.

It is growing dark. At the edge of the fields
the levee rises like a brown serpent feeding on
fireflies. Our separate lives, I suppose, have
never stood much of a chance. But think of
the animals we have known and feared and
nurtured in this black of night and know
fear leaves us all head down at last, running
blindly along some river and always alone.

At home in my room I listen: the pear tree
outside my window is a blasphemy of evening birds.
They chatter as if daylight had never before abandoned
them. I think it is so. Sometime later, I make tea
and write you these words: in a forest of peccaries,
a wart-hog is the sole dissenter. In a forest of
wart-hogs, a peccary is a welcome sound. In a forest
of both, bread crumbs make not a hair's breadth of difference.

THE TRIAL OF ROZHDESTVOV

by the Russian SAMIZDAT underground

from A CHRONICLE OF CURRENT EVENTS, 47 published by Amnesty International

nominated by Amnesty International

(editor's note—The poet and reformer Vladimir Rozhdestvov, has endured years of jailing, harassment and compulsory treatment in psychiatric hospitals "of a special type." The following account of his torment was originally circulated in illegal typewritten samizdat, the Russian version of small press publishing.)

PREFACE
by Amnesty International

A Chronicle of Current Events *was initially produced in 1968 as a bimonthly journal. In the spring of that year members of the Soviet Civil Rights Movement created the journal with the stated intention of publicizing issues and events related to Soviet citizens' efforts to exercise fundamental human liberties. On the title page of every issue there appears the text of Article 19 of the Universal Declaration of Human Rights, which calls for universal freedom of opinion and expression. The authors are guided by the principle that such universal guarantees of human rights also similar guarantees in their domestic law) should be firmly adhered to in their own country and elsewhere. They feel that 'it is essential that truthful information about violations of basic human rights in the Soviet Union should be available to all who are interested in it'. The* Chronicles *consist mostly of accounts of such violations. . . .*

In February 1971, starting with number 16, Amnesty International began publishing English translations of the Chronicles *as they appeared.*

This latest volume, containing Chronicle 47, *is, like previous ones, a translation of a copy of the original typewritten text.*

THE TRIAL OF ROZHDESTVOV

On 23 November the Kaluga Regional Court ruled that Vladimir Rozhdestvov, charged under article 190-1 of the R S F S R Criminal Code, was not responsible, and sent him for compulsory treatment to a psychiatric hospital of special type.

Vladimir Pavlovich Rozhdestvov (b. 1937) graduated from the Tomsk building institute.

On 6 November 1970, when he was travelling to Moscow to circulate leaflets he had written calling for the democratization of the Soviet system, he was removed from the train at Kalinin and forcibly hospitalized in a psychiatric hospital, where he was diagnosed as a schizophrenic. Rozhdestvov was treated with insulin therapy. He left the hospital in May 1971.

In October 1971, when the K G B found out about the group of seven people organized by Rozhdestvov which was propagating dissenting views, they hospitalized him once again. He was treated with neuroleptic drugs and sulphazin. He was released in March 1972. Since then Rozhdestvov, as recorded in the history of his illness, 'has been on a special K G B list as a socially dangerous sick person'.

On the night of 9-10 September Rozhdestvov was forcibly placed in Kaluga regional psychiatric hospital No. 1. There was subjected to treatment with neuroleptic drugs.

On 7 October Alexander Podrabinek wrote to the chief psycho-neurologist of the U S S R Ministry of Health, Churkin:

We ask you to investigate this case and make every effort to release Rozhdestvov.

We consider it necessary to inform you that if Rozhdestvov is not released by 12 October we shall be compelled to appeal to the special committee for investigating complaints about the use of psychiatry for political ends, set up recently by the World Psychiatric Association.

On 11 October Rozhdestvov was transferred to the Kaluga investigation prison.

On 4 November procurator Amarov of the regional procuracy told Rozhdestvov's mother that a criminal case under article 190-1 of the R S F S R Criminal Code had been brought against her son and that compulsory treatment in a special psychiatric hospital awaited him.

The trial took place on 23 November. Deputy president of the Kaluga regional court Kuznetsov presided, procurator Dmitriyev was the prosecutor, barrister N. Ya. Nimirinskaya spoke for the defense, and doctor L. P. Tronina of the Kaluga regional psychiatric hospital was the psychiatric expert.

The trial was open, and everyone who wanted was allowed into the hall. N. P. Gaidukova and Voronin had been summoned to the trial as witnesses. Gaidukova did not appear: she presented a sickness certificate. The court determined to hear the case in her absence after reading out the evidence given by her at the pre-trial investigation. The court also determined to hear the case in the absence of the accused, 'in connection with his sick condition'.

The mother of the accused, Olga Efimovna Rozhdestvova, petitioned for the admission of Alexander Podrabinek as legal representative for her son. Barrister Nimirinskaya—in 1974 she defended V. Khaustov (*Chronicle* 32) and V. Nekipelov (*Chronicle* 32), and in 1976, V. Igrunov (*Chronicle* 40)—upheld her petition. Procurator Dmitriyev objected. The Court ruled against the petition of Rozhdestvova.

The 'Resolution on sending the case to court to resolve the question of the application of compulsory measures of a medical character to V. P. Rozhdestvov' said:

> Since 1970 Rozhdestvov has systematically spread deliberately false fabrications slandering the Soviet political and social system. This is confirmed by the evidence of witnesses . . .
>
> Witnesses Krivorotov, Gutovsky, Reingardt, Nekrasov, Nadyshev and Naumenko have testified that in the period 1970-1977 Rozhdestvov listened to anti-Soviet broadcasts of Western radio-stations, commented on their content in an anti-Soviet vein, voiced complaints against the alleged incorrectness of policies conducted in the USSR, and tried to exercise a negative influence on them politically. He was interested in people who expressed political dissatisfaction with living conditions in our country, and praised life in capitalist countries . . .
>
> In February-March 1977 he handed over a manuscript to Gaidukova which contained slanderous fabrications against the mate-

rial conditions of the Soviet people, its economic and political rights, and also against the internal policies of the U S S R. He suggested to Gaidukova that she listen to broadcasts of foreign radio-stations . . .

On 6-7 September 1977 he tried to foist anti-Soviet fabrications on Voronin. He tried to convince him of the necessity of struggling for the reconstruction of Soviet society on the model of the West, of circulating these fabrications amongst the population, and of joining an anti-Soviet organization allegedly in existence in the USSR. He suggested that he listen to broadcasts of anti-Soviet radio-stations and copy out the text of an ideologically harmful poem composed by him . . .

According to the conclusion of a forensic psychiatric examination, he expresses delusional ideas of reformism and of struggle with the socio-political system existing in the Soviet Union . . .

Because of his psychic condition Rozhdestvov needs compulsory treatment in a psychiatric hospital of special type . . .

From the interrogation of witness Voronin:

Judge: Where and under what circumstances did you become acquainted with Rozhdestvov?

Voronin: We lived together for two days in a hotel.

Judge: Tell us everything you know about the case.

Voronin: On 6 September I arrived in Maloyaroslavets for military training. I stayed in a hotel, in a room for two, room No. 4. On the evening of 7 September, when I was writing synopses, a conversation struck up between us—Rozhdestvov and myself. Rozhdestvov asked me why I was not working in my speciality (by profession I am a builder). I replied that I was forced to leave my job because of a conflict with the director. Then he said that not only small bosses are bad, but the bosses at the top as well. In the evening he listened to the Deutsche Welle radio-station and said that Italian communists were not allowed in to the USSR and that it was time to put an end to that. I asked: 'Aren't you afraid of trying to convert me?' He replied: 'First I size a person up, then I draw conclusions'. After this the conversation turned to labour-camps. In the evening I went to see a film on a patriotic military theme. Rozhdestvov did not go to see the film and said that he did not watch such films because everything in them was lies. I did not sleep all night and thought: how should I act? In the morning I went to the KGB and told them everything. They ordered me to write a statement. They instructed me how to conduct the conversation and on what topics. In the evening I introduced a conversation about struggle. Rozhdestvov told me about an underground organization and suggested that I participate in it. I asked how I could help. He said that it was necessary to try to convert good people, to conduct propaganda amongst pupils of senior classes. He said that it was possible to circulate 1000 leaflets in three months, then to take a break for about three months. He said that branches of the organization exist in 130 towns, a journal comes out—some *Chronicle*. He suggested I form a circle in Kaluga and move there with that aim. He suggested I have a talk about all this with my brother. He showed me his poem, suggested I copy it out for clandestine circulation amongst the masses. The following morning we parted after exchanging addresses. He did not mention his surname in order to preserve security.

Judge: What further conversation was there?

Voronin: I asked what the aim of the organization was. He said that it was necessary to change the system by peaceful means, to disband the army, to divide up the land into approximately 50 hectares per person, to introduce private property for factories and so on, like in the West.

Judge: What is the aim of the organization?

Voronin: To change the system.

Judge: Over how long?

Voronin: In a maximum of ten years.

Judge: What did he urge you to do personally?

Voronin: He urged me to join the struggle.

Judge: In what way?

Voronin: To campaign, to circulate leaflets, to move to a town where I could be closer to the masses.

Judge: What exactly did he say about the leaflets: what should they contain, who will prepare them, how will you receive them?

Voronin: He said that he would provide the leaflets, and that if a journal exists, leaflets are a trifle. He described how they scatter leaflets in Moscow.

Judge: Does the underground organization already exist?

Voronin: I don't know. Rozhdestvov said it was necessary to form a circle.

Judge: Is the journal he was talking about the *Chronicle of Current Events?*

Voronin: Yes.

Judge: By whom is it published, by what organization, where?
Voronin: I don't know.
Judge: What radio-stations did Rozhdestvov listen to? When?
Voronin: The first evening he listened to Deutsche Welle.
Judge: What was the content of the broadcast?
Voronin: About Italian communists who were not allowed into the Soviet Union.
Judge: What stations did Rozhdestvov suggest you listen to? What are they called?
Voronin: Voice of America, Radio Liberty, BBC. I said that everything these radio-stations broadcast was slander. Rozhdestvov said they speak the truth, as strong nations would not slander weak ones.
Judge: Did not doubts arise in you as to the psychic health of Rozhdestvov?
Voronin: No. He produced many quotations, including from Lenin, and gave the impresssion of being an intelligent person.
People's assessor: Was he drinking?
Voronin: No, he didn't even drink beer.
People's assessor: So in your opinion he is not a sick man but an enemy of the people?
Voronin: Yes.
Prosecutor: What is the content of the poem?
Voronin: The poem called for struggle and in general its content was prohibited.
Prosecutor: Does he slander in it or not?
Voronin: Yes, he slanders.
Prosecutor: What other slanderous things did he say?
Voronin: That worker's pay is low, there is no meat or milk in the shops, that there are no rights like in the West, that some exhibition in Moscow was torn down, that the system of elections is undemocratic.
Prosecutor: In other words, he denigrated and slandered the Soviet way of life?
Voronin: Yes.
Counsel for the defence: What days were you in the hotel?
Voronin: The 7th and 8th. On the 9th I left after work. There was no work on the 10th.
Defence: What slander did Rozhdestvov communicate to you on 7 September, what facts?

Voronin: About the party and the government, that there are the same bad people at the top as down below. He spoke of an underground organization.

Defence: I am asking you not about an organization but about what you regard as slanderous.

Voronin: For example, about the money system—he said that wages are low.

Defence: Did you talk about the money system that day—on 7 September?

Voronin: Yes.

Defence: You wrote the statement to the KGB the following day?

Voronin: Yes.

Defence: Why is it dated 9 September?

Voronin: I wrote it on the 8th but finished it on the 9th.

Defence: Who started the conversations on the second day of your acquaintance?

Voronin: Rozhdestvov was writing down the poem. I asked him about the poem.

Defence: What facts of a slanderous nature were contained in the poem?

Voronin: He wrote that the people drink because they have nothing to do, and he called for struggle.

Defence: You copied out the poem. Did you know that it was not allowed?

Voronin: No, I didn't.

The psychiatric examination had diagnosed Rozhdestvov as a 'paranoid schizophrenic with delusions of reformism'. The psychiatric expert L. P. Tronina stated at the trial that Rozhdestvov 'considered it possible to change the Soviet political system by peaceful means'.

The judge rejected the petition of the defence counsel to arrange another psychiatric examination and to call the other witnesses. The judge several times rudely interrupted the barrister's speech. He forbade those present to take notes.

On 25 November the Working Commission to Investigate the Use of Psychiatry for Political Purposes published a 'Report on the Trial of Rozhdestvov'.

The same day a member of the commission, Alexander Podrabinek, addressed an open letter to the World Psychiatric Association. The letter concludes thus:

> And before it is too late, before the appeal hearing begins, I call on the World Psychiatric Association to intervene in this case. May the resolutions adopted in Honolulu not remain on paper. May Soviet psychiatrists feel the firmness of their foreign colleagues in upholding the humane principles of medicine.

CONTRIBUTORS NOTES

AI is the author of *Cruelty* (1973) and *Killing Floor* (1979). She won the Lamont Poetry award, a Guggenheim Arts Foundation fellowship and a Radcliffe Fellowship.

KRISTINE BATEY's work has appeared in *Nexus* and *Snakeroots*. She is married, lives in Chicago and earns money typing hospital pathology reports.

ROBERT BRINGHURST's books include Bergschrund (Sono Nis, 1975) and *Jacob Singing* (Kanchenjunga, 1977).

LORNA DEE CERVANTES lives in San Jose, California where she is the editor and printer of a Chicano literary magazine, *Mango*.

THADIOUS M. DAVIS lives in Boston and teaches at The University of Massachusetts.

R. C. DAY lives in Arcata, California and has published in *Kenyon Review*, *Massachusetts Review* and elsewhere.

SUSAN STRAYER DEAL teaches in North Platte, Nebraska. She has published work in *Cape Rock*, *Attention Please*, *Fault* and elsewhere.

VINE DELORIA, JR. holds degrees in theology and law and is a practising attorney in Golden, Colorado.

M. R. DOTY's forthcoming books are *An Introduction To The Geography of Iowa* (Great Raven Press), *An Alphabet* (Alembic Press), *Climbing the Wet Islands* (Moondance Press) and *Shabby Love* (Thunder City Press).

TESS GALLAGHER's books are *Instructions to the Double* and *Under Stars* both published by Graywolf Press.

ELLEN GILCHRIST has published poetry and fiction in various literary magazines and lives in New Orleans.

GERALD GRAFF is Chairman of the English Department at Northwestern University and author, most recently, of *Literature Against Itself.*

JAMES B. HALL teaches at the University of California, Santa Cruz.

MICHAEL HARPER directs the graduate writing program at Brown University. His new and selected collection of poems, *Images of Kin*, was published in 1977.

FELISBERTO HERNÁNDEZ (1902–1964) was born and died in Uruguay. A professional pianist, he remained almost unknown as a writer during his lifetime. Much of his work was collected after his death by his longtime friend, José Pedro Diaz, from personal papers and lost editions. His translator, LUIS HARSS, teaches at West Virginia University.

BRENDA HILLMAN lives in Kensington, California and works in a bookstore. Penumbra Press recently issued a collection of her poems.

JUDITH HOOVER is a recent graduate of Bennington College. "Proteus" is her first published story.

SHIRLEY KAUFMAN lives and works in Israel and is the author of *Gold Country* and *Carbon*.

MARGARET KENT lives in Greensboro, North Carolina and has been published in several literary magazines including *Poetry* and *Paris Review*.

CAROLYN KIZER has long been active with small presses. She now lives in Berkeley, California.

STANLEY KUNITZ teaches at Columbia University. His selected poems will soon be published by Atlantic Monthly Press.

JAMES LAUGHLIN founded New Directions publishing house in 1936. He is married, has four children and lives in Norfolk, Connecticut.

LARRY LEVIS is the author of *The Afterlife*. He won the Lamont Poetry award in 1976 and teaches at the University of Missouri and helps edit *The Missouri Review*.

JOHN LOVE is a poet, teacher and journalist. His first book of poetry, *The Touch Code*, was published by Release Press in 1977.

BARBARA LOVELL lives in North Carolina and teaches at the University of North Carolina, Charlotte.

CLEOPATRA MATHIS lives in Trenton, New Jersey and has appeared in many small press publications.

PAUL METCALF, the great-grandson of Herman Melville, is the author of several novels, including *The Middle Passage*, *Genoa* and *Patagoni*.

CHARLES MOLESWORTH is the author of a book of poems, *Common Elegies* (New Rivers, 1977) and of the forthcoming study of contemporary American poetry, *The Fierce Embrace* (University of Missouri Press).

BARBARA MYERHOFF is Chairperson of the Anthropology Department at The University of Southern California and the author of numerous books and articles. Her documentary film, *Number Our Days*, won an Academy Award in 1976.

SUSAN SCHAEFER NEVILLE lives in New Castle, Indiana and received a NEA Fellowship in 1978.

MARY OLIVER's most recent collection of poetry is *Twelve Moons* (Little Brown). She lives in Provincetown, Massachusetts.

ALICIA OSTRIKER is professor of English at Rutgers University and the author of three books of poetry. Penguin published her fully-annotated edition of Blake's *Complete Poems* last year.

LON OTTO teaches at the College of St. Thomas in St. Paul Minnesota and is the winner of the Sixth Annual Iowa School of Letters Award for Short Fiction.

JAYNE ANNE PHILLIPS is a co-winner of the 1979 St. Lawrence award for fiction. Her *Sweethearts*, originally published by Truck Press, has just been reissued. Delacorte/Seymour Lawrence will publish her book of stories, *Black Tickets*.

ROBERT PHILLIPS' collection *The Pregnant Man*, was recently published by Doubleday.

STANLEY PLUMLY's *Out of the Body Travel* (Ecco Press) was nominated for the 1977 National Book Critics Circle Award in poetry.

JOE ASHBY PORTER's novel, *Eelgrass* was issued in 1977 by New Directions.

MANUEL PUIG's most recent novel was published by Knopf. He lives in New York City.

ISHMAEL REED's most recent book is *Shrovetide in Old New Orleans*. He lives in El Cerrito, California and heads The Before Columbus Foundation.

GARY REILLY is a Vietnam veteran and presently attends the University of Colorado in Denver.

WILLIAM RUECKERT teaches at the Geneseo branch of The State University of New York and is a fellow at The National Humanities Institute at The University of Chicago.

MARGARET RYAN lives in New York and is a free lance writer.

MAX SCHOTT's collection of stories, *Up Where I Used to Live*, was published recently by The University of Illinois Press and a novel is forthcomimg from Harper and Row.

CHRISTINE SCHUTT lives in New York City with her husband and son. "These Women" is her first published story.

CONSTANCE SHARP has taught children with learning problems for several years. She studied with Philip Levine and Louise Glück. "I Show The Daffodils to the Retarded Kids" is her first published work.

RON SILLIMAN's latest volume is *The Age of Huts* (Pod Books). He lives in San Francisco.

JANE SMILEY's first novel will be published by Harper and Row. She lives in Iowa and is looking for a job.

DAVE SMITH, the author of *Cumberland Station*, teaches at the University of Utah.

GJERTRUD SCHNACKENBERG SMYTH has published in *The Carolina Quarterly, The Mississippi Review, Beloit Poetry Journal* and elsewhere. She was appointed a Fellow In Poetry at Radcliffe, earlier this year.

WILLIAM STAFFORD teaches at Lewis and Clark College in Portland, Oregon. His two most recent books are *Stories That Could Be True* and *Writing The Australian Crawl.*

DAVID ST. JOHN is the author of *Hush* (Houghton Mifflin). He teaches at Johns Hopkins University.

SHIRLEY ANN TAGGART lives in Lexington, Massachusetts. "Ghosts Like Them" is her first published story.

JOHN UPDIKE, born in Pennsylvania in 1932, is a professional writer who lives in Massachusetts. His most recent novel was *The Coup;* a collection of short stories, *Problems*, will soon be published.

CÉSAR VALLEJO was a widely published poet and his translator, ALVARO CARDONA-HINE, is the author of *Words on Paper* and co-author of *Two Elegies*, both books published by Red Hill Press.

MONA VAN DUYN has published five books of poetry and was awarded both The National Book Award and The Bolligen Prize.

GEORGE VENN teaches at Eastern Oregon State College in La Grande, Oregon.

JEFF WEINSTEIN co-edits *Only Prose* in New York. He is also restaurant reviewer for the *Soho Weekly News.*

DALLAS WIEBE grew up in Newton, Kansas and now lives in Cincinnati. Many of the names and places and some of the materials for "Night Flight to Stockholm" were taken from K. M. Briggs' book *The Anatomy of Puck* (1959). He writes "for materials taken from Briggs' extraordinary book the readers should see pages 63, 179, 198 and 207."

JOHN WILLSON writes in Portland, Oregon where he is employed as a landscaper.

🔥 🔥 🔥

OUTSTANDING WRITERS

(The editors also wish to mention the following important works published by small presses in 1978. Listing is alphabetical by author's last name.)

NON-FICTION

What Was Modernism?—Robert Martin Adams (Hudson Review)

Mimesis and the Motive for Fiction—Robert Alter (TriQuarterly)

Dialogue of Poets: Mens Animi and the Renewal of Words—Helen Bacon (Massachusetts Review)

Interview with Larry Eigner—Peter Bates (Stony Hills)

Neruda's Memoirs: A Reading from Homer—Ben Belitt (Bennington Review)

Memories of Uncle Neddy—Elizabeth Bishop (Southern Review)

Moral Fiction?—Robert Boyers (Bennington Review)

How To Read The New Contemporary Poem—Paul Breslin (American Scholar)

De Improvisations—Gerald Burns (Iowa Review)

Concert: Notes from A Mideast Journal—Florence Cohen (Story Quarterly)

Witness—Mary Doyle Curran (Massachusetts Review)

On the Formal Function of Plot—Jane de Lynn (la-bas)

Super-, Sur-, Meta-, Para-, or Anti?: Reflections on Post-Modern American Fiction—Louis Gallo (X. A Journal of the Arts)

The Dilemma of Literature in An Age of Science—David J. Gordon (The Sewanee Review)

Robespierre and Santa Claus: Men of Virtue in Drama—Robert Heilman (The Southern Review)

Home—William Heyen (Manassas Review)

Towards An Allusive Referential—Dick Higgins (Printed Editions)

Our Contributors—William Harmon (Kayak)

The Gay Frank O'Hara—Randy Kikel (Gay Sunshine)

Poetry in the Novel—Jerome Klinkowitz (Precisely:One)

Recovering Reality—Christopher Lasch (Salmagundi)

Captive Audience—Barbara Lefcowitz (New Letters)

How Do You Tell A Story?—Jack Matthews (Sun & Moon)

Big Charles: A Gesture Towards Reconstituiton—Paul Metcalf
(United Artists)

An Essay on Murder—Leonard Michaels (Portland Review)

Khlebnikov and Makhno—David Miller (Interstate)

The Golden Age of the American Novel—Roger Sale (Ploughshares)

Being Fair About Lyof Nikolayevich—W. M. Spackman (Canto)

Criticism, Starting from Scratch—M. L. Rosenthal (The Missouri
Review)

Interview with Keorapetse Kgositsile—Charlies Rowell (Callaloo)

A $500,000 Grant May Be Yours—William Ryan (Newsart)

Lunching with Hoon—Theodore Weiss (American Poetry Review)

A Bibliography on Edward Dorn for America—Donald Wesling
(Parnassus)

The Black People, Excerpts From A Work in Progress—John A.
Williams (Y'Bird)

Portrait of A Forgotten Poet; Bob Kaufman—A. D. Winans
(dramatika)

Interview With John Oliver Killens—Revish Windham (Black
Forum)

FICTION

Eyes—Tamas Aczel (Massachusetts Review)

A Way Out—Jonis Agee (Gallimaufry)

Story in A Mirror—Ilse Aichinger (Fiction)

Modern Medicine—Alexander Austin (beyond baroque)

The Caul—Russell Banks (Mississippi Review)

The Beast Grows Silent—Isaac Babel (Ardis)

Indisposed—Russell Banks (Matrix)

Wedding—John Bennett (Story Quarterly)

Stepping Westward—Doris Betts (Mississippi Review)

Duck Hunting—T. Alan Broughton (Ploughshares)

How Mrs. Fox Married Again—Rosellen Brown (Penmaen Press)

Picaroon—Virgil Burnett (TriQuarterly)

Company—Frederick Busch (Ploughshares)

Writing Through Finnegans Wake—John Cage (James Joyce Quarterly)

Marriage—Helen Chasin (Paris Review)

Forecast of the Balloon Man—Carol Conroy (Gallimaufry)

from Let The River Answer—Melvin Dixon (Callaloo)

The Bottom Line—Stanley Elkin (Antaeus)

A Voice In The Closet—Raymond Federman (Fiction Collective, Coda)

·The Rememberers—Eugene Garber (Four Quarters)

A Record As Long As Your Arm—George Garrett (Ploughshares)

Susu, I Approach You In My Dreams—William Gass (TriQuarterly)

Marquitos Drasinover's Baptism—Isaac Goldemberg (Persea)

The Storm Doll—William Goyen (Ontario Review)

Mr. Evolution—Phillip Graham (Release Press)

Contagious—Güneli Gray (Gallimaufry)

The Last Survivor of Sierra Flat—Robert Greenwood (Southwest Review)

One Night In the Life Of A Cocktail Waitress—Camden Griffin (The Smith)

Sawdust—Gregory Hayes (Kansas Quarterly)

Life—Bessie Head (The Spirit That Moves Us)

A Running Conversation—Roberta Israeloff (North American Review)

On the Island—Josephine Jacobsen (Jackpine Press)

A Metamorphosis—Greg Johnson (Ontario Review)

A Bus, A Bridge, A Beacon—Neil Jordan (Longship Press)

The Stolen Stories—Steve Katz (Cornell Review)

Phantom Silver—William Kittredge (Iowa Review)

Dead Weight—Timothy Koskinen (Lynx)

Everything Uncertain—Michael Lally (Salt Lick Press)

What Is Left—Gordon Lish (Ploughshares)

Monday All the Time—Ullalume Gonzales de Leon (Fiction)

Bolgako—André Malraux (Antaeus)

The Execution—Jack Matthews (Ohio Review)

Forty In The Shade—John McCluskey (Obsidian)

The Sound—Joseph McElroy (Fiction)

An Otherwise Happy Life—Joanne Meschery (Fiction)

Holland—Mary Morris (Paris Review)

Characters—Alice Munro (Ploughshares)
The Translation—Joyce Carol Oates (TriQuarterly)
The Hobbyist: A Scientific Examination—Bette Pesetsky (Ontario Review)
The Leprosarium—Natalie L. M. Petesch (New Letters)
from Kiss of the Spider Woman—Manuel Puig (TriQuarterly)
Black Dreams—David Reich (The Smith)
Three Points—Henry H. Roth (Croton Review)
Summer—Teo Savory (Unicorn)
Excerpt from A Novel-In-Progress—Mary Lee Settle (Blue Ridge Review)
The Tribes of Night—Anna Sidak (beyond baroque)
Magic—Dinita Smith (Hudson Review)
The Mockingbird Room—Elizabeth Ann Tallent (Pikestaff Forum)
"I Tell You This. . ."—June Todd (Chicago Review)
A Confederacy of Dunces—John K. Toole (New Orleans Review)
Per Ominy Ah—Eoghan O Tuairisc (Longship Press)
Crabs—Lowell Uda (Petronium Press)
Miss Buick of 1942—Sara Vogan (Quarry West)
Stoke Sobel In Polk—Diane Vreuls (Massachusetts Review)
from "The Magi"—Millie Mae Wicklund (Mudborn Press)
A Nocturne: Childhood—Edmund White (Shenandoah)
"Child Posed As Doll"—Gayle Whittier (Carolina Quarterly)

POETRY

The Fair Young Wife—Helen Adam (River Styx)
After Love—Vicente Aleixandre (Iowa Review)
Traveling Shows—A. R. Ammons (Poetry Miscellany)
Five Poems for Grandmothers—Margaret Atwood (Open Places)
Erhart—John Balaban (Pivot)
Barriers 6—Gerald W. Barrax (Nimrod)
To Know The Dark—Wendell Berry (Poets In The South)
Firewood—Chana Bloch (Southern Poetry Review)
An Evening When the Full Moon Rose as the Sun Set—Robert Bly (Georgia Review)
Jonah Remembers The Great Fish—Martha Bosworth (Blue Unicorn)
The Sideways Suicide—Michael Burkard (American Poetry Review)

Rogue River Jet Boat Trip, Gold Beach, Oregon, July 4, 1977—
    Raymond Carver (Antioch Review)
The Time of the Doormouse—Bartolo Cattafi (Small Moon)
Apology—Richard Cecil (American Poetry Review)
A. B. B. C. Documentary—Tony Connor (Red Fox Review)
Three Riddles from the Anglo-Saxon—Wesli Court (Poetry News-
    letter)
Later—Robert Creeley (Toothpaste Press)
Early Morning—Mary Louise Curtis (Placebo Press)
Royal Visit: Orlando, 1977—Mary Louise Curtis (Placebo Press)
Proud Riders—H. L. Davis (Ahsahta Press)
Alligators and Paris And North America—William Dickey (Massa-
    chusetts Review)
Prologue to A Longer Story—Wayne Dodd (Georgia Review)
Apple—M. R. Doty (Alembic)
A Winter Elegy to the Sioux—Norman Dubie (American Poetry
    Review)
The Optical Prodigal—Russell Edson (Oink!)
The Power of the Doe—Ron Ellis (Pikestaff Press)
Untitled—Theodore Enslin (Pentagram)
Yes—Charles Entrekin (Berkeley Poets Cooperative)
from School—Leon Felipe (Blue Moon News)
papyri—Ellen Gilchrist (Kayak)
Elegy for Ann Green—Lorrie Goldensohn (Seneca Review)
The Way Things Work—Jorie Graham (Poetry Northwest)
The Faithful Wife—Barbara L. Greenberg (Poetry Northwest)
The Stories—Jonathan Greene (Truck)
Myopia—Deborar Greger (Antioch Review)
One More—Linda Gregerson (Ironwood)
The Beginning of Summer—Robert Haas (Antaeus)
Wisdom From The Whelping Ground—Karla Hammond (absinthe)
You Won't Love Me and I Learn Death—Eloise Klein Healy (rara
    avis)
Field Work—Seamus Heaney (New England Review)
Two Friends—Robert Herz (L'Epervier Press)
Sun Dream/Daughter Dream—William Heyen (Rook Press)
Father, Son, Ghost—Mark Jarman (Antaeus)
Probably the Farmer—Laura Jensen (Antaeus)
Do Not Forget—Lamuel Johnson (Ardis)
Delight—Lawrence Kearney (Poetry)

End Song—Ruth Krauss (Burning Deck)

The Choice—Philip Levine (Missouri Review)

Adah—Larry Levis (Iowa Review)

Garcia Lorca: A Photograph of the Granada Cemetery, 1966—Larry Levis (Antaeus)

Story—Larry Levis (Skywriting)

The Viscous Sleep—Janet Little (Calliope)

Solo Native—Tom Lux (Antaeus)

To The Savage Child—John Mahnke (Ploughshares)

Los Americanos—Cleopatra Mathis (American Poetry Review)

Ballad—Anne Maxwell (American Poetry Review)

Eve of Easter—Bernadette Mayer (United Artists)

What's Meant For Pleasure—Bernadette Mayer (Sun&Moon)

Love—Gary McEachern (Gargoyle)

Mask of the North North East—Gail McKay (Prism)

Repechages On the Last Morning—Jay Meek (Yale Review)

Twilight—Samuel Menashe (Proteus)

Sculpture—Jane Miller (Antaeus)

Portrait In Available Light—Sara Miles (Ordinary Women Books)

Ars Poetica—Czeslaw Milosz (Antaeus)

A Man In Space—Paul Monette (Shenandoah)

An American Book—Todd Moore (road/house)

Piecing—Robin Morgan (Feminist Studies)

Salisbury—Hilda Morely (Endymion)

Catfishing In Natchez Trace—G. E. Murray (Ascent)

Ransom—Carol Muske (New England Review)

I Explain A Few Things—Pablo Neruda (Choice)

Messages—Mary Oliver (Yale Review)

Applause—Charles Olson (Olson #8)

Rottenrock Mountain—Elder Olson (South Carolina Review)

A Letter From A Saint—Steve Orlen (Antaeus)

A Poem—Grace Paley (Persea)

Sonnet On Lessons, Wasted—Leslie Palmer (Laurel Review)

Letting Up—John Peck (Godine)

Approaching Absolute Zero—Joyce Peseroff (Small Moon)

Poems of Alberto Caeiro—Fernando Pessoa (Bleb)

from *Counting*—Jayne Anne Phillips (Gallimaufry)

The Twenty-Fifth Anniversary—Kenneth Pitchford (KP Newsletter)

In Memorium, Jim Murray—Alan Planz (Choice)

Flowers Die In Hiroshima—Lefteris Poulious and Kimon Friar (Footprints)

Called Sleeping—Carol Ann Russell (Cutbank)

Chameleos —Dennis Saleh (New Rivers)

Draft Dodger—Peter Schjeldahl (Sun)

Swimming—Lloyd Schwartz (Poetry Now)

St. Joan In California—Lauren Shakely (Pequod)

Poem In Praise of Divorce—Judith Johnson Sherwin (Countryman Press)

Note Slipped Under A Door—Charles Simic (Manassas Review)

School For Dark Thoughts—Charles Simic (Manassas Review)

Snowstorm In The Country—John Skoyles (Shankpainter)

Pig Poem—Edward Smallfield (Choice)

Laura's Bread—Lorna Smedman (Pulp)

Black Widow—Dave Smith (Aura)

In Snow, A Possible Life—Dave Smith (Western Humanities Review)

Assurance—William Stafford (Handbook)

Saying A Big Word—William Stafford (Jeopardy)

Alcestis—Maura Stanton (Columbia)

The Bee—Ricardo Sternberg (American Poetry Review)

The Pears—Pamela Stewart (Antaeus)

The Story—Mark Strand (Antaeus)

The Pilgrimage Revealed: A Newly Discovered Manuscript Shedding Light on Modern Man—Laurie Stroblas (Pulp)

The Way Corn Works—Dick Sweeney (Alternative Press)

The Rats Remain—Anna Swinszczynska (Mr. Cognito)

Renoir—Carolyn Tipton (Blue Unicorn)

For. M. W.—Jean Toomer (Indigene)

Foundations—Leonard Trawick (Cornfield Review)

The Star Apple Kingdom—Derek Walcott (American Poetry Review)

Salad—Michael Waters (Missouri Review)

The First Word—Bruce Weigl (New Honolulu Review)

The Polar Bear At Crandon Park Zoo, Miami—Barbara Winder (New South)

Willie's Women—Donna Wintergreen (Groundwater)

for The Girl Drowned Off The Provincetown Breakwater, March 1975—Ellen Wittlinger (Aspect)

Self-Portrait—Charles Wright (New England Review)
Virginia Reel—Charles Wright (Antaeus)
(Poem)—Suzanne Zavrian (Y'Bird)
Hiding In Public—Christine Zawadiwsky (Bieler Press)

⚙ ⚙ ⚙

OUTSTANDING SMALL PRESSES

(These presses made or received nominations for the 1979–80 edition of *The Pushcart Prize*. See the *International Directory of Little Magazines and Small Presses*, Dustbooks, Box 1056, Paradise, CA 95969, for subscription rates, manuscript requirements and a complete international listing of small presses.)

Abraxas Press, 2322 Rugby Rd., Madison, WI 53705

Absinthe, % Indian Tree Press, Barryville, NY 12719

Accent Press, Inc., Open Places, Box 2085, Stephens College, Columbia, MO 65201

Aegean Books, 615 Frenchmen St., New Orleans, LA 70116

Aegis, Student Press, University of New Hampshire, Durham, NH 03824

Aesopus Press, Woodstock Poetry Review, 27 Oriole Dr., Woodstock, NY 12498

Agni Review, P. O. Box 349, Cambridge, MA 02138

Ahashta Press, Dept. of English, Boise State U, Boise, ID 83725

Ailanthus Press, 200 W. 83rd St., New York, NY 10024

Akwesasne Notes, Mohawk Nation via Rooseveltown, NY 13683

The Alchemist, Box 123, La Salle, Québec, Canada

Aldebaran, Roger Williams College, Bristol, RI 02809

Alice James Books, 138 Mt. Auburn St., Cambridge, MA 02138

Allegany Mountain Press, 111 North 10th St., Olean, NY 14760

Allegra Press, 526 Forest, E. Lansing, MI 48823

Alta Napa Press, Box 407, Calistoga, CA 94515

Alternative Press, 3090 Copeland Rd., Grindstone City, MI 48467

American Rag, 1 E. 104th St., New York, NY 10029

American Poetry Review, 1616 Walnut St., Philadelphia, PA 19103

American Scholar, 1811 Q St. NW, Washington, D.C. 20009

American Visual Communications Bank, 196 West Simpson, Tuscon AZ 85701

Anemone, 550 Alta Vista Way, Laguna Beach, CA 92651

Angst World Library, 2307-22nd Ave. E., Scattle, WA 98112

Anima Publications, 1053 Wilson Ave., Chambersburg, PA 17201

Antares Foundation, Box 14051, San Francisco, CA 94114

Antaeus, 1 W. 30th St., New York, NY 10001

Anthelion Press, 5643 Paradise Dr., Corte Madera, CA 94925

Antietam Press, Box 62, Boonsboro, MD 21713

Antioch Review, Box 148, Yellow Springs, OH 45387

Apalachee Quarterly, Box 20106, Tallahasee, FL 32304

Applezaba Press, 333 Orizaba, Long Beach, CA 90814

Aquila, Box 174 B, Petersburg, PA 16665

Artaud's Elbow, Box 1139, Berkeley, CA 94701

Ararat, 628 2nd Ave., New York, NY 10016

Ardis Publishers, 2901 Heatherway, Ann Arbor, MI 48104

Ariadne Press, 4400 P St., NW., Washington, D.C. 20007

Arizona Quarterly, Univ. of Arizona, Tuscon, AZ 85721

Ark River Review, Box 14- WSU, Wichita, KS 67208

Art Form Magazine, 1112 Montana Ave., El Paso, TX 79902

As Is, 6302 Owen Place, Bethesda, MD 20034

Ascent, English Dept., University of Illinois, Urbana, IL 61801

Aspect, 66 Rogers Ave., Somerville, MA 02144

Association of National Non-Profit Artists Centres, 970 Rachel St. E., Montreal, Quebec, Canada

Asylum's Press, 464 Amsterdam Ave., New York, NY 10024

Aura 8, Box 11126, Birmingham, AL 35202

Aurable Press, 4834 California St., San Francisco, CA 94118

Back Roads, Box 543, Cotati, CA 94928

Backroads, Box 370, Wilson, WY 83014

Barataria, Box 15060, New Orleans, LA 70175

Barkfeather Publishing, 115 Fair Oaks St., San Francisco, CA 94110

Bellevue Press, 60 Schubert St., Binghamton, NY 13905

Beloit Poetry Journal, Box 2, Beloit, WI 53511

Bennington Writers Workshop, Bennington, VT 05201

Berkeley Poets Cooperative, Box 459, Berkeley, CA 94701

Bertrand Russell Today, Box 431, Jerome Ave. Station, Bronx, NY 10468

Beyond Baroque Foundation, 1639 W. Washington Blvd., Venice, CA 90291

Bieler Press, 4603 Shore Acres Rd., Madison, WI 53716

Big Moon, Box 4731, Modesto, CA 95352

Big River Association, 7420 Cornell Ave., St. Louis, MO 63130

Bilingual Review, % Dept. Foreign Languages, York College of the City University of New York, Jamaica, NY 11451

Bits Press, Dept. of English, CWR University, Cleveland, OH 44106

Black American Literature Forum, Parson Hall 237, Indiana State University, Terre Haute, IN 47809

Black Forum Magazine, Box 1090, Bronx, NY 10451

Black Scholar, Box 908, Sausalito, CA 94965

Black Sparrow Press, Box 3993, Santa Barbara, CA 93105

Blacksmith, 5 Walnut Ave., Cambridge, MA 02140

Blackswell Press, Watsonville, CA 95076

BLEB, Box 322, Times Square Station, New York, NY 10036

Bloodroot, Box 891, Grand Forks, ND 58201

Blue Leaf Editions, Box 857, New London, CT 06320

Blue Moon Press, UA English Dept., Tuscon, AZ 85721

Blue Mountain Press, 511 Campbell St., Kalamazoo, MI 49007

Blue Oak Press, 2555 New Castle Rd., Newcastle, CA 95658

Blue Ridge Review, Box 7484, Charlottesville, VA 22901

Blue Unicorn, 22 Avon Rd., Kensington, CA 94707

Blue Wind Press, 820 Miramar, Berkeley, CA 94707

Boggle Publications, 425 E. 6th St., New York, NY 10009

Book Forum, 38 E. 76th St., New York, NY 10021

Boston University Journal, 704 Commonwealth Ave., Boston, MA 02215

Boundry 2, Univ. of New York at Binghampton, Binghampton, NY 13901

Bottomfish Magazine, 21250 Stevens Crk., Cupertino, CA 95014

Boxspring, Hampshire College, Amherst, MA 01002

Branching Out, Box 4098, Edmonton, Alberta, T6E 4T1, Canada

Brilliant Corners, 1372 W. Estes #2N, Chicago, IL 60626

Broken Whisker Studio, 4225 Seeley, Box 54, Downers Grove, IL 60515

Buckle, English Dept., State Univ. College, 1300 Elmwood Ave., Buffalo, NY 14222

Calamus Books, 323 N. Geneva St., Ithaca, NY 14850

California Quarterly, 100 Sproul Hall, Univ. of Calif., Davis, CA 95616

The Call/El Clarin, Box 5597, Chicago, IL 60680

Callaloo, English Dept., Univ. of Kentucky, Lexington, KY 40506

Calliope, Roger Williams College, Bristol, RI 02809

Calyx, Rt. 2, Box 118, Corvallis, OR 97330

Cambric Press, 912 Stowbridge, Huron, OH 44839

Canadian Fiction Magazine, Box 46422, Station G, Vancouver, B.C. V6R 4G7, Canada

Canto, 11 Bartlet St., Andover, MA 01810

The Cape Rock, Southeast Missouri State, Cape Girardeau, MO 63701

Capra Press, 631 State St., Santa Barbara, CA 93101

Carolina Quarterly, Box 1117, Chapel Hill, NC 27514

Cedar Rock, 1121 Madeline, New Braufels, TX 78130

Center, Box 7494, Albuquerque, NM 87194

Center for Southern Folklore, 1216 Peabody Ave., Box 4081, Memphis, TN 38104

Center for Writers, English Dept. USM, Box 37, Hattiesburg, MISS 39401

Challenger Press, 46 College St., Brockport, NY 14420

Chariton Review, NE Missouri State U., Kirksville, MO 63501

Chicago Review, Univ. of Chicago, Chicago, IL 60637

Choice, % Logan, 1396 Amherst St., Buffalo, NY 14216

Chomo-Uri, Box 1057, Amherst, MA 01002

Chowder Review, 2858 Kingston Dr., Madison, WI 53713

Chronicle Books, 870 Market St., Suite 915, San Francisco, CA 94102

Chrysalis, 1727 N. Spring St., Los Angeles, CA 90012

Chthon Press, 77 Mark Vincent Dr., Westford, MA 01886

Circinatum Press, Box 99309, Tacoma, WA 98499

City Lights Books, 261 Columbus Ave., San Francisco, CA 94133

City Miner, Box 176, Berkeley, CA 94701

Cleveland State University, Poetry Center, Cleveland, OH 44115

Cliff Catton Press, Box 61, West New York, NJ 07093

Coffee Break Magazine, Box 103, Burley, WA 98322

Colorado North Review, Univ. Center, Univ. of Northern Colorado, Greeley, CO 80631

Colorado Quarterly, Univ. of Colorado, Boulder, CO 80302

CS Review, 360 Liberal Arts, Colorado State Univ., Ft. Collins, CO 80523

Columbia, School of the Arts, 404 Dodge, Columbia Univ., New York, NY 10027

Conch Magazine Ltd., 102 Normal Ave., Buffalo, NY 14213

Conditions, Box 56, Van Brent Station, Brooklyn, NY 11215

Confrontation, English Dept., Long Island University, Brooklyn, NY 11201

Connecticut Fireside, Box 5293, Hamden, CT 06518

Constructive Action For Good Health, 710 Lodi St., Syracuse, NY 13203

Consummated Productions, Austin, TX

Consumptive Poets League, Koff, 27 First Ave. #9, New York, NY 10003

Contact/11 Publications, 11 Broadway, New York, NY 10004

Contemporary Quarterly, Box 41110, Los Angeles, CA 90041

Contraband Press, Box 4073, Sta A., Portland, ME 04101

Copper Beach Press, Box 1852, Brown Univ., Providence, RI 02912

Copper Canyon Press, Box 271, Port Townsend, WA 98368

Cornell Review, 108 N. Plain St., Ithaca, NY 14850

Cornfield Review, Ohio State Univ., 1465 Mt. Vernon Ave., Marion, OH 43302

Coteau Books, Thunder Creek Co-op, 1188 Duffield Cr., Moose Jaw, Saskatchewan S6H5M4, Canada

Cottege Industries, Box 244, Cobalt, CT 06414

Country Man Press, Taftsville, VT 05073

Cowell Press, Dept. of English, San Diego State Univ., San Diego, CA 92182

Crawl Out Your Window, % Warren Writing Q-022, UCSD, La Jolla, CA 92923

Crazy Paper, 160 6th Ave., New York, NY 10013

The Creative With Words Club, Box 46173, W. Hollywood, CA 90046

Croissant & Company, Route 1, Box 51, Athens, OH 45101

Cross-Cultural Communications, 239 Wynsum Ave., Merrick, NY 11566

Crosscut Saw, 1806 Bonita, Berkeley, CA 94709

Croton Review, Box 277, Croton-On Hudson, NY 10520
Curbstone Press, 321 Jackson St., Willimantic, CT 06226
Cutbank, Univ. of Montana, Missoula, MT 59812
CWWC Publications, Box 46179, West Hollywood, CA 90048

Dacotah Territory, Box 775, Moorhead, MN 56560
David Godine Publisher, 306 Dartmouth St., Boston, MA 02116
Decatur House Press Ltd., 2122 Decatur Place NW, Washington, DC 20008
December Press, 4343 N. Clarendon, Chicago, IL 60613
Deck, 71 Elmgrove Ave., Providence, RI 02906
Dekalb Literary Arts Journal, Dekalb College, 555 N. Indian Creek Dr., Clarkston, GA 30021
Denver Quarterly, Univ. of Denver, University Park, Denver, CO 80208
Diana's Bimonthly Press, 71 Elmgrove Ave., Providence RI 02906
Doodly-Squat Press, Box 40124, Albuquerque, NM 87106
Downtown Poets Co-op, G.P.O. Box 1720, Brooklyn, NY 11202
Dragon's Teeth Press, El Dorado National Forest, Georgetown, CA 95634
Dramatika, 429 Hope St., Tarpon Springs, FL 33589
deBois Zone Press, 516 11th Ave., Grafton, WI 53024
Dustbooks, Box 100, Paradise, CA 95969

Earth's Daughters, Box 41, Station H, Buffalo, NY 14214
Ecco Press, 1 W. 30th St., New York, NY 10001
El Fuego de Aztlar, 3408 Dwinelle Hall, U.C., Berkeley, CA 94720
El Passant/Poetry, 1906 Brant Rd., Wilmington, DL 19810
Ellen's Old Alchemical Press, Box 161915, Sacramento, CA 95816
Ellipsis, 2157 Bartola Dr., Meraux, LA 70075
Embers Publications, 2150 Portola Dr., Santa Cruz, CA 95062
Emerald City Press, Box 40814, Tucson, AZ 85717
Endeavors In Humanity Press Inc., 1112 Montana Ave., El Paso, TX 79902
Endymion, 562 West End Ave. #6A, New York, NY 10024
Epoch, 245 Goldwin Smith Hall, Cornell Univ., Ithaca, NY 14853
Erin Hills Publishers, 1390 Fairway Dr., San Luis Obispo, CA 93401
Exile, Box 546, Downsview, Ontario, Canada
Evener, Putney, VT 05346

Event, Douglas College, Box 2503, New Westminister, B.C. V3L 582, Canada

Eyes & Ears Foundation, 6515 Sunset Blvd., Suite 200-B, Los Angeles, CA 90028

The Falcon, Mansfield State College,Mansfield, PA 16933

Feminist Studies, University of Maryland, College Park, MD 20742

Fiction, Dept. of English, City College of NY, Convent Ave. & 138th St., New York, NY 10031

Fiction Collective, % George Braziller, Inc., 1 Park Ave., New York, NY 10016

Fiction International, St. Lawrence University, Canton, NY 113617

Fiction Texas, 8001 Palmer Highway, Texas City, TX 77590

Fiddlehead, The Observatory, Univ. of New Brunswick, Box 4400, Fredericton, NB E3B 5A3, Canada

Field, Rice Hall, Oberlin College, Oberlin, OH 44074

Figment, 34 Andrew St., Newton, MA 02161

Film Library Quarterly, Box 348, Radio City Station, New York, NY 10019

Floating Island Publications, Box 516, Point Reyes Station, CA 94956

Flying Buttress Publications, Box 83, University Station, Syracuse, NY 13210

Folio, 2207 Shattuck Ave., Berkeley, CA 94704

Foothill Quarterly, 12345 El Monte Rd., Los Altos Hills, CA 94022

Footprint Magazine, 150 W. Summit St., Somerville, NJ 08876

Four Quarters, La Salle College, Philadelphia, PA 19141

Free Passage, 24 N. 4th, Grand Forks, ND 58201

The Front Press, Box 1355, Kingston, ON K7L5C6, Canada

Frontiers, Hillside Court 104, Univ. of Colorado, Boulder, CO 80309

Gallimaufry, 3208 N. 19th Rd., Arlington, VA 22201

Gargoyle, 160 Boylston St. #3, Jamaica Plain, MA 02130

Gay Community News, 22 Broomfield St., Boston, MA 02108

Gay Sunshine, Box 40397, San Francisco, CA 94140

Gemini Press, 625 Pennsylvania Ave., Oakmont, PA 15139

Georgia Review, Univ. of Georgia, Athens, GA 30602

Georgia State University Review, Georgia State Univ., Dept. of English, University Plaza, Atlanta, GA 30303

Ghost Dance Press, 526 Forest, E. Lansing, MI 48823

Gibbons Press, 610 35th Ave., San Francisco, CA 94121

Glassworks, Box 163, Rosebank Station, Staten Island, NY 10305

Glitch, 515 Lamar Apt. 271, Arlington, TX 76011

Gluxlit Press, Box 11165, Dallas, TX 75223

Grand River Publications, Box A, Fairwater, WI 53931

Graywolf Press, Box 142, Port Townsend, WA 98368

Great Society Press, 451 Heckman St. #368, Phillipsburg, NJ 08865

Green Mountain Review, J. S. C., Johnson, VT 05656

Green River Press Inc., SVSC Box 56, University Center, MI 48710

Greenfield Review, Box 80, Greenfield Center, NY 12833

Green House, 53 Beacon St., Dedham, MA 02026

Greenhouse Review Press, 126 Escalona Dr., Santa Cruz, CA 95060

Greensboro Review, Dept. of English, Univ. of N. Carolina, Greensboro, NC 27412

Grilled Flowers Press, Box 809, Iowa City, IA 52240

Groundwater, 237 E. 88th St. #5B, New York, NY 10028

Grove, English Dept., Pitzer College, Claemont, WI 91711

Growing Without Schooling, 308 Boylston St., Boston, MA 02116

Gnomon Press, Box 106, Frankfort, KY 40601

Gusto, 2960 Philip Ave., Bronx, NY 10465

Haiku Society of America Inc., Japan House, 333 E. 47th St., New York, NY 10017

Hampshire Typothetae, 30 Market St., Northampton, MA 01060

Hampden-Sydney Poetry Review, Box 126, Hampden Sydney, Virginia, 23943

Handbook, 184 West North Broadway, Columbus, OH 43214

Hanging Loose Press, 231 Wyckoff St., Brooklyn, NY 11217

Happiness Holding Tank, 170 Grand River, Okemos, MI 48864

Harbour Publishing, Box 119, Maderia Park, BC von 2H0 Canada

Harian Creative Enterprise, 47 Hyde Blvd, Ballston Spa, NY 12020

Harris-Storm Press, 261 Cypress St., Providence, RI 02906

Heidleberg Graphics, Box 3404, Chico, CA 95927

Helen Review, Tiresias Press, 162 Clinston St., Brooklyn, NY 1120

Helix House Publishers, Box 1595, La Mesa, CA 92041

Heyday Books, Box 9145, Berkeley, CA 94709

Hills, 1220 Folsom, San Francisco, CA 94103
Hob Nob, 715 Dorsea Rd., Lancaster, PA 17601
Hoka Hey Press, Box 756, Springville, CA 93265
Holy Cow!, Box 618, Minneapolis, MN 55440
Hounslow Press, 124 Parkview Ave., Toronto M2N345, Canada
House of Anansi Press Lt., 471 Jarvis St., Toronto, 284, Canada
Hudson Review, 65 E. 55th St., New York, NY 10022
Hudson River Press, Rhinecliff, NY 12574
Hurricane Company, Box 426, Jacksonville, NC 28540

Icarus Press, Box 8, Riderwood, MD 21239
Images, English Dept., Wright State University, Dayton OH 45431
Imaginary Press, Box 193, Cambridge, MA 02139
Impetus, Columbia University, New York, NY
Indian Village Press, 79 Donald St. #51, Weymouth, MA 02188
Indiana Writes, 110 Morgan Hall, Indiana Univ., Bloomington, IN
    47401
Indigené, Box 15057, Philadelphia, PA 19130
International Poetry Review, Box 2047, Greensboro, NC 27402
International University Press, 501 E. Armour Blvd., Kansas City,
    MO 64109
Interstate, Box 7068, Austin, TX 78712
Intro 9, 4951 Top Line Drive, Dallas, TX 75247
Iowa Review, 308 EPB, Univ. of Iowa, Iowa City, IA 52242
I. Reed Books, 285 E. 3rd St., New York, NY 10009
Irish Writers' Co-operative, 27 Herbert Place, Dublin 2, Ireland
Iron Mountain Press, Box 28, Emory, VA 24327
Ironwood Press, Box 40907, Tuscon, AZ 85717
Isadora Press, 2754 SE 27th, Portland, OR 97202
Ithaca House, 108 N. Plain St., Ithaca, NY 14850

Jackpine Press, 3381 Timberlake Lane, Winston-Salem, NC 27106
Jam To-day, Box 249, Northfield, VT 05663
James Joyce Quarterly, Univ. of Tulsa, 600 S. College Ave., Tulsa,
    OK 74104
Jawbone Press, 17023 Fifth Ave. NE, Seattle, WA 98155
Jeopardy, Western Washington University, Bellingham, WA 98225
Jewel Publications, 2417 Hazelwood Ave., Ft. Wayne, IN 46805
John Kirchoff, Box 272, Wixom, MI 48096
Journal Books, 704 Baylor St., Austin, TX 78703

The Kanchenjunga Press, 22 Rio Vista Lane, Red Bluff, CA 96080

Kansas Quarterly, Dept. of English, Denison Hall, Kansas State Univ., Manhattan, KS 66502

Karl Bern Publishers, 9939 Riviera Dr., Sun City, AZ 85351

Kayac, 325 Ocean View, Santa Cruz, CA 95062

The Kenyon Review, Kenyon College, Gambier, OH 43022

King Publications, Box 19332, Washington, D.C. 20036

Konglomerati Press, Box 5001, Gulfport, FL 33737

Kosmos, 2580 Polk, San Francisco, CA 94109

Là-bas, Box 431, College Park, MD 20740

Lame Johnny Press, Box 66, Hermosa, SD 57744

Language, 464 Amsterdam Ave., New York, NY 10024

Lapis Lazuli, 712 NW 4th St., Corvallis, OR 97330

Laurel Review, W. Virginia Wesleyan College, Buckhannon, WVA 26201

L'Epervier Press, 1219 E. Laurel, Ft. Collins, CO 80521

Light: A Poetry Review, Box 1105 Stuyvesant P. O., New York, NY 10009

Lion Enterprises, 2024 E. Epler, Indianapolis, IN 46227

The Literary Review, Fairleigh Dickinson Univ., 285 Madison Ave., Madison, NJ 07940

Little Free Press, 715 E. 14th St., Minneapolis, MI 55404

The Little River Press, R. Edwards, 10 Lowell Ave., Westfield, MA 01085

Little Wing Publishing, 865 Embarcadero Del Mar E, Goleta, CA 93017

Long Pond Review, Dept. of English, Suffolk Comm. College, Selden, NY 11784

Longship Press, Crooked Lane, Nantucket, MA 02554

Lost Glove, 161 W. 86th St. Apt. 6A, New York, NY 10024

Louisville Review, Dept. of English, University of Louisville, Louisville, KY 40208

LSM Press, Box 2077, Oakland, CA 94604

Luna Bisonte Prods., 137 Leland Ave., Columbus, OH 43214

Lynx Magazine, Box 800, Amherst, MA 01002

Maggot Brain, 105 Arden St. #5-A, New York, NY 10040

Makara Magazine, 1011 Commercial Dr., Vancouver, BC, Canada

Malahat Review, University of Victoria, Box 1700, Victoria, BC, Canada

Malki Museum Press, 11-795 Fields Road, Banning, CA 92220

Manassas Review, N. Virginia Comm. College, Manassas, VA 22110

Mango Publications, 329-A S. Willard, San Jose, CA 95126

Massachusetts Review, Memorial Hall, Univ. of Mass., Amherst, MA 01003

Mati, Salome: A Literary Dance Magazine, 5548 N. Sawyer Ave., Chicago, IL 60625

Matrix, Ida Noyes Hall, Univ. of Chicago, Chicago, IL 60637

Maxy's Journal, Box 1203 Station B, Nashville, TN 37235

Merging Media, 59 Saudra Circle A-3, Westfield, NJ 07090

Metis Press, 815 W. Wrightwood, Chicago, IL 60614

Merlin Papers, Box 5602, San Jose, CA 95150

Miam, Box 14083, San Francisco, CA 94114

Micah Publications, 255 Humphrey St., Marblehead, MA 01945

Michael Joseph Phillip's Editions, 5840 Washington Blvd., Indianapolis, IN 46220

Michigan Quarterly Review, University of Michigan, Ann Arbor, MI 48109

MidAtlantic Review, Box 398, Baldwin Place, NY 10505

Mid-Summer Press, Box 370, Madison, WI 53701

Mississippi Review, Univ. of Miss., Southern Station, Box 5144, Hattiesburg, MS

Missouri Review, 231 Arts & Science, Univ. of Missouri-Columbia, Columbia, MO 65211

Modus Operandi, Box 136, Brookeville, MD 20729

Molly Yes Press, R. D. 3 Box 70B, New Berlin, NY 13411

Momentum Press, 512 Hill St. #4, Santa Monica, CA 90405

Momo's Press, Box 14061, San Francisco, CA 94114

Montemora Foundation Inc., Box 336 Cooper Station, New York, NY 10003

Moonfire Press, 1817 E. Windsor Place, Milwaukee, WI 53202

Moonshine Review, Route 2, Box 488, Flowery Branch, GA 30542

Moretus Press Inc., 350 Fifth Ave., Suite 1104, New York, NY 10001

Mr. Cogito Press, Box 627, Pacific University, Forest Grove, OR 97116

Mu Publications, Box 612, Dahlgren, VA 22448

Mudborn Press, 209 W. De la Guerra, Santa Barbara, CA 93101

NRG Magazine, 228 SE 26th, Portland, OR 97214

Negative Press, 848 E. 28th St., Brooklyn, NY 11210

Neuter Press, 37 Callodine, Buffalo, NY 14226

New America, Dept. of American Studies, Univ. of New Mexico, Albuquerque, NM 87131

New England Review, Box 170 Hanover, NH 03755

New Letters, Univ. of Missouri–Kansas City, 5100 Rockhill Road, Kansas City, MO 64110

New Mexico Humanities Review, Box A, New Mexico Tech., Socorro, NM 87801

New Orleans Review, Loyola University, Box 195, New Orleans, LA 70118

New Renaissance, 9 Heath Road, Arlington, MA 02174

New River Press, 1602 Sellsy Ave., St. Paul MN 55104

The New South Company, 4480 Park Newport, Newport Beach, CA 92660

New Wilderness Foundation, 365 West End Ave., N.Y., N.Y. 10024

New York Arts Journal, 560 Riverside Dr., New York, NY 10027

Newscribes, 1223 Newkirk Ave., Brooklyn, NY 11230

Nimrod, University of Tulsa, Tulsa, OK

Nit and Wit, 1908 W. Oakdale, Chicago, IL. 60657

No Deadlines Publisher, 241 Bonita, Portola Valley, CA 94025

Nobodaddy Press, 100 College Hill Rd., Clinton, NY 13323

Nonmenon Press, Box 7068, University Station, Austin, TX 78712

North American Review, University of Iowa, Cedar Falls, IA 50613

North Country Star, Box 550, Boonville, CA 95415

Northwoods Press Inc., RD1, Meadows of Dan., VA 24120

Obsidian, English Dept., State University College, Fredonia, NY 14063

Oconee Review, Box 6232, Athens, GA 30604

Ohio Review, 346 Ellis Hall, Ohio University, Athens, OH 45701

Oink! Press, 7021 Sheridan Rd., Chicago, IL 60626

Oleander Press, 17 Stansgate Ave., Cambridge CB2 2QZ England

Omango d'Press, Box 255, Wethersfield, CT 06109

Ontario Review, 6000 Riverside Dr. East, Windsor, Ontario N8S 1B6, Canada

Oolichan Books, Box 10, Lantzville, BC V0R2H0 Canada

Open Places, Box 2085, Stephens College Columbia, MO 65201

Ordinary Women Books, Box 664 Old Chelsea Station, New York, NY 10011

Origins, Box 5072, Station E, Hamilton, Ontario L8S4K9 Canada

Origins Press, 87 Dartmouth St., Boston, MA 02116
Osiris, Box 297, Deerfield, MA 01342
Out of the Ashes Press, Box 42384, Portland, OR 97242
Out of Step, Box 103, Hudson, NY 12534
Oyez, Box 5134, Berkeley, CA 94705

Pacific Perceptions, 1906 Parnell Ave., Los Angeles, CA 90025
Pacific Poetry & Fiction Review, San Diego State U., San Diego, CA 92182
Pacifica Publishing Co., 26313 Purissima Rd., Los Altos Hills, CA 94022
Padan Aram, 52 Dunster St., Cambridge, MA 02138
The Painted Bride, 527 South St., Philadelphia, PA 19147
Pajarito Publications, 2633 Granite NW, Albuquerque, NM 87104
Palaemon Press Ltd., Box 7527, Reynolds Station, Winston-Salem, NC 27109
Panhandler, English Dept., Univ. of West Florida, Pensacola, FL 32504
Panjandrum Books, 99 Sanchez St., San Francisco, CA 94114
Parnassus, 205 W. 89th St., New York, NY 10024
Paris Review, 541 E. 72nd St., New York, NY 10021
Partisan Review, Boston University, 128 Bay State Rd., Boston, MA 02215
Pawn Review, Box 4255, Overland Park, KS 66204
Peace & Pieces Foundation, Box 99394, San Francisco, CA 94109
Permanent Press, Box 43, Sagaponack, NY 11962
Pembroke Magazine, Box 756, Pembroke, NC 28372
Penca Books, San Antonio, TX
Pendas Productions, 14 Fourth St., Toronto M5J 2B1, Canada
Penmaen Press, Old Sudbury Rd., Lincoln, MA 01773
Pentagram Press, Box 11609, Milwaukee, WI 53211
Pequód, Box 491, Forest Knolls, CA 94933
Perishable Press, Mt. Horeb, WI 53572
Perivale Press, 13830 Erwin St., Van Nuys, CA 91401
Persea Books, Box 804, Madison Square Station, New York, NY 10010
Persona Press, Box 14022, San Francisco, CA 94114
Peterson, 77 Lakewood Place, Highland Park, IL 60035
Petronium Press, 1255 Nuuanu Ave, #1813, Honolulu, HI 96817
Phoebe, 4400 University Drive, Fairfax, VA 22030

Phone-A-Poem, Box 193, Cambridge, MA 02139

Pig Iron Press, Box 237, Youngstown, OH 44501

Pikestaff Press, Box 127, Normal, IL 61761

Pivot, 221 S. Barnard St., State College, PA 16801

Placebo Press, 6880 W. Fairfield #53, Pensacola, FL

Pleasure Dome Press, Long Island Poetry Collective Inc., Box 773, Huntington, NY 11743

Plainswoman, Box 8027, Grand Forks, ND 58202

Ploughshares, Box 529, Cambridge, MA 02139

Plucked Chicken Press, Box 160, Morgantown, WV 26505

Pocket Poetry Press, Box 70, Key West, FL 33040

Poésie-USA, Box 811, Melville, NY 11746

Poetry, Box 4348, Chicago, IL 60680

Poetry, Box 842, Iowa City, IA 52240

Poetry Miscellany, Box 165, Signal Mt., TN 37377

Poets In The South, University of South Florida, Tampa, FL 33620

Poets Monthly, 1 Union Square West #512, New York, NY 10003

Poetry Newsletter, Dept. of English, Temple Univ., Philadelphia, PA 19122

Poetry Northwest, Univ. of Washington, 4045 Brooklyn Ave., Seattle, WA 98105

Poetry Now, 3118 K Street, Eureka, CA 95501

Poets On:, Box 255, Chaplin, CT 06235

Poetry Symposium, Fort Worden State Park, Port Townsend, WA

Pomegranate Press, Box 181, North Cambridge, MA 02140

Porch, Dept. of English, Arizona State Univ., Tempe, AZ 85281

Portland Review, Box 751, Portland, OR 97207

Prairie Schooner, 201 Andrews Hall, Univ. of Nebraska, Lincoln, NB 68588

Precisely, Box 73, Canal St. Station, New York, NY 10013

Prescott Street Press, 407 Postal Building, Portland, OR 97204

Primavera, Univ. of Chicago, 1212 E. 59th St., Chicago, IL 60637

Printed Editions, Box 842, Canal St. Station, New York, NY 10013

Prism International, Dept. of Creative Writing, Univ. of B.C., Vancouver, BC, Canada

Programmed Studies, Box 113, Stowe, MA 01775

Proletariat, Box 3774, Merchandise Mart, Chicago, IL 60654

Proteus Press, 1004 N. Jefferson St., Arlington, VA 22205

Puckerbrush Press, 76 Main St., Orono, ME 04473

Pulp, 720 Greenwich St., Apt 4-H, New York, NY 10014

Pulp Press, Box 48806, Stn. Bental, Vancouver, BC, Canada

Quarry West, College V, USC, Santa Cruz, CA 95064

Quarterly Review of Literature, 26 Haslet Ave., Princeton, NJ 08540

Quarterly West Press, 312 Oloin Union, Univ. of Utah, Salt Lake City, UT 84112

Raccoon, 561 Ellsworth St., Memphis, TN 38111

Ragnarok Press, 59 Sandra Circle, Westfield, NJ 07090

Raincrow Press, 3332 E. Flower, Tucson, AZ 85716

rara avis, 1400 Macbeth St., Los Angeles, CA 90026

Red Cedar Review, English Dept., Michigan State Univ., E. Lansing, MI 48824

Red Clay Publications, 6366 Sharon Hills Rd., Charlotte, NC 28210

Red Dust, Inc., Box 630, Gracie Station, New York, NY 10028

Red Earth Press, Box 26641, Albuquerque, NM 87125

Red Fox Review, Mohegan Community College, Norwich, CT 06360

Red Herring Press, 629 E. Green St., Champaign, IL 61820

Red Hill Press, 6 Sam Gabriel Dr. Fairfax, CA 94930

Release Press, 411 Clinton St., Brooklyn, NY 11231

Revista Chicano-Riquena, Indiana Univ. Northwest, 3400 Broadway, Gary, IN 46408

Rhiannon Press, 608 Putnam Drive, Eau Claire, WI 54701

Rhino, 77 Lakewood Place, Highland Park, IL 60035

Richard Thrift, 108 Clarke Court, Charlottesville, VA 22903

Richmond Literature and History Quarterly, Box 12263, Richmond, VA 23241

Right Press, Box 2366, Park City, UT 84060

Riversedge Press, Box 1547, Edinburg, TX 78539

Road/House, 900 W. 9th St., Belvidere, IL 61008

Room, Box 40610, San Francisco, CA 94140

The Rook Press, Box 144, Ruffsdale, PA 15679

Round River, 215 N. Paterson St., Madison, WI 53703

Rubicon Press, Dusty Garage Books, Box 2141, Salem, OR 97308

Ruhtra, Box 12, Boyes Hot Springs, CA 95416

Rumba Train Press, 6023 Village Road, Lakewood, CA 90713

S.H.Y., % Poste Restante, Hydra, Greece

St. Andrews Review, St. Andrews Presbyterian College, Laurinburg, NC 28352

St. Croix Review, Box 244, Stillwater, MN 55082

Salmagundi, Skidmore College, Saratoga Springs, NY 12866

Salt Lick Press, Box 1064, Quincy, IL 62301

Sam Houston Literary Review, Sam Houston State Univ. Press, Huntsville, TX 77340

Samisdat, Box 10 Brigham, Quebec, Canada

San Jose Studies, San Jose State Univ., 174 Administration Bldg., San Jose, CA 95192

San Marcos Review, Box 4368, Albuquerque, NM 87106

Santana Publishing Society, 3100 White Sulphur Springs Rd., St. Helena, CA 94574

Sandscript, Cape Code Writers, Inc., Box 333, Cummaquid, MA 02637

Seal Press, 533 11th East, Seattle, WA 98102

The Seattle Review, Univ. of Washington, Padelford Hall, GN-30, Seattle, WA 98195

Second Coming Press, Box 31249, San Francisco, CA 94131

Seems, Dept. of English, Univ. of Northern Iowa, Cedar Falls, IA 50613

Shadow Press, Box 207, Gananoque, Ontario, K7G2T7, Canada

Shadow Press, Box 8803, Minneapolis, MN 55408

Shankpainter, Fine Arts Work Center, Box 565, Provincetown, MA 02657

Shenandoah, Box 722, Lexington, VA 24450

Shore, 1405 Madison Ave. #4B, New York, NY 10021

Sibyl-Child, Box 1773, Hyattsville, MD 20788

Sing Heavenly Muse, Box 14027, Minneapolis, MN 55414

Sing Out, 595 Broadway, New York, NY 10012

Sitnalta Press, 1881 Sutter St. #103, San Francisco, CA 94115

Small Moon, 52½ Dimick St., Somerville, MA 02143

The Smith, 5 Beekman St., New York, NY 10038

The Smudge, Box 19276, Detroit, MI 48219

Sheep Meadow Press, 145 Central Park West, New York, NY 10023

A Shout in The Steet, English Dept., Queens College, Flushing, NY 11367

Slow Loris Press, 6359 Morrowfield Ave., Pittsburgh, PA 15217

So & So, 1730 Carleton, Berkeley, CA 94703

Soft Press, 1525 McRae Ave., Victoria, BC V8P 1G4, Canada

Solo Press, 1209 Drake Circle, San Luis Obispo, CA 93401
Some, 309 W. 104th St., Apt 9D, New York, NY 10025
Sou'wester, Southern Illinois University, Edwardsville, IL 62025
South Carolina Review, Dept. of English-Strode Tower, Clemson University, Clemson, SC 29631
Southern Exposure, Box 230, Chapel Hill, NC 27514
Southern Libertarian Messenger, Box 1245, Florence, SC 29501
Southern Poetry Review, Dept. of English, Univ. of North Carolina, Charlotte, NC 28223
Southern Review, Drawer D, University Station, Baton Rouge, LA 70893
Southport Press, Dept. of English, Carthage College, Kenosha, WI 53141
Southwest Review, Southern Methodist Univ., Dallas, TX 75275
Spanner, 85 Ramilles Close, London SWZ, 5 DQ England
Sparrow Press, 103 Waldron St., W. Lafayette, IN 47908
Spindrift Press, Box 3252, Cantonsville, MD 21228
The Spirit That Moves US Press, Box 1585, Iowa City, IA 52240
Spiritual Community, Box 1080, San Rafael, CA 94902
Spoon River Quarterly, Dept. of English, Bradley Univ., Peoria, IL 61625
Standard Editions, Box 1297, Peter Stuyvesant Station, New York, NY 10009
Stony Hills, Box 715, Newburyport, MA 01950
Story Press, 7370 S. Shore Drive, Chicago, IL 60649
Story Quarterly, 820 Ridge Rd., Highland Park, IL 60035
Strawberry Press, 11 Broadway, New York, NY 10004
Street, Box 555, Port Jefferson, NY 11777
Stroker Magazine, 129 2nd Ave. #11, New York, NY 10003
Sulphur River, Box 155, Bogota, TX 75417
Sun, 456 Riverside Drive #5B, New York, NY 10027
Sun & Moon, 4330 Hartwick Road #418, College Park, MD 20740
sun rise fall down artpress, 447 St. Louis, Lewisburg, PA 17833
Sunbury, Box 274, Jerome Ave. Station, Bronx, NY 10468
Sunken Forum Press, Dewittville, Quebec, JOS1CO, Canada
Swallow Press, 811 W. Junior Terrace, Chicago, IL 60613
Swamp Press, 4 Bugbee Rd., Oneonta, NY 13820
Syncline, 2630 N. Hampden Ct., Chicago, IL 60614

Tamarack, Box 455, Potsdam, NY 13676

Tamarisk, 188 Forest Ave., Ramsey, NY 07446

Templar Press, Box 98, F.D.R. Station, New York, NY 10022

10 Point 5, Arts Magazine, Box 124, Eugene, OR 97440

Tendril, Box 512, Green Harbor, MA 02041

Thelphini Press, % Eleni Fourtouni, 1218 Forest Rd., New Haven, CT 06515

Third Eye, 250 Mill St., Williamsville, NY 14221

13th Moon, Inc., Box 3, Inwood Station, New York, NY 10034

Thunder City Press, Box 11126, Birmingham, AL 35202

Tide Publications, 8706 Cadillac Ave., Los Angeles, CA 90034

Tideline Press, Box 786, Tannersville, NY 12485

Tightrope, Swamp Press, 4 Bugbee Rd., Oneonta, NY 13820

Tinderbox, 334 Molasses Lane, Mt. Pleasant, SC 29464

Tomatoe Publications, Ltd., 70 Barrow St., New York, NY 10014

Toothpaste Press, 626 E. Main St., West Branch, IA 52358

Tottel's 17, % Bernstein, 464 Amsterdam Ave., New York, NY 10024

Touchstone, Drawer 42331, Houston, TX 77042

Trailings, Box 32, Hancock, MI 49930

Trask House Books, 2754 S. E. 27th, Portland, OR 97202

TriQuarterly, Northwestern Univ., University Hall 101, Evanston, IL 60201

Truck, 2163 Ford Parkway, St. Paul, MN 55116

True Seed Exchange, Rural Route 1, Princeton, MO 64673

Turt Press, 25 E. 4th St., New York, NY 10003

Tuumba Press, 2639 Russell St., Berkeley, CA 94705

Umbral, Box 2042, Ft. Collins, CO 80522

Unicorn Press, Box 3307, Greensboro NC 27402

University of Connecticut Library, Special Collections Dept., Storrs, CT 06268

University of Illinois Press, Urbana, IL 61801

University of Missouri Press, 107 Swallow Hall, Columbia, MO 65211

University of Pittsburgh Press, Pittsburgh, PA 15260

University Press Books, 2431 B Durant Ave., Berkeley, CA 94704

Unrealist Press, Box 53, Prince, WV 25907

United Artists, Box 718, Lenox, MA 01240

The Unspeakable Visions of the Individual, Box 439, California, PA 15419

Urthkin, Box 67485, Los Angeles, CA 90067

US-1 Worksheets, 21 Lake Dr., Roosevelt, NJ 08555
Uzzano, Shimer College, Mount Carmel, IL 61053

Vagabond, 1610 N. Water, Ellensburg, WA 98926
Van Dyk Publications, 10216 Takilma Rd., Cave Junction, OR 97523
Vegetable Box, English Dept., Univ. of Washington, Seattle, WA 98195
Vehicle Editions, 100 Clark St., Montreal, Quebec, H22159, Canada
Ventura Press, Box 1076, Guerneville, CA 95446
Vermont Crossroads Press, Box 30, Waitsfield, VT 05673
Vesta Publications, Box 1641, Cornwall, Ont., Canada
Virginia Quarterly Review, Univ. of Virginia, Charlottesville, VA 22903

Washington Review, Box 50132, Washington, D.C. 20004
Washington Writers Publishing House, 1346 Connecticut Ave., N.W., Room 1013, Washington, D.C. 20036
Washoe Press, Box 91922, Los Angeles, CA 90009
Water Mark Press, 175 E. Shore Rd., Huntington Bay, NY 11143
Wayside, Box 475, Cottonwood, AZ 86326
West Salem Books, Box 10481, Winston-Salem, NC 27108
West Branch, Dept. of English, Bucknell Univ., Lewisburg, PA 17837
Westerly Review, 229 Post Rd., Westerly, RI 02891
Western Humanities Review, Univ. of Utah, Salt Lake City, UT 84112
Westigan Review, English Dept., Western Michigan Univ., Kalamazoo, MI 49008
Wolf Run Books, Box 10671, Eugene, OR 97440
Word Works, Box 4054, Washington, D.C. 20015
Whetstone, Box 226, Bisbee, AZ 85603
Whimsy Press, 1822 Northview, Arnold, MO 63010
White Ewe Press, Box 996, Adelphi, MD 20783
White Mule, 2710 E. 98th Ave., Tampa, FL 33612
White Pot Press, 1718 P. St. N.W., Apt 620, Washington, D.C. 20036
White Walls, Box 8204, Chicago, IL 60680
Wind Literary Journal, RFD Rt. 1, Box 809K, Pikeville, KY 41501
Windless Orchard, Purdue English Dept., Ft. Wayne, IN 46805

Window Press, 7005 Westmoreland Ave., Takoma Park, MD 20012
Wingbow Press, % Bookpeople, 2940 Seventh St., Berkeley, CA 94710
Winter, Autumn, Box 125, Salem, MA 01970
Wolfsong, Box 252, Iola, WI 54945
Women Talking, Women Listening, Box 2414, Dublin, CA 94566
Woolmer/Brotherson Ltd., Andes, NY 13731
World Poetry Society International, 208 W. Latimer Ave., Campbell, CA 95008
Wormwood Review, Box 8840, Stockton, CA 95204
Writers Forum, Univ. of Colorado, Colorado Springs, CO 80907
WPA, Palo Alto Cultural Center, 1313 Newell Rd. Palo Alto, CA 94303

X, A Journal of the Arts, Box 2648, Harrisburg, PA 17105

Yale Review, 1920A Yale Station, New Haven, CT 06520
Yanagi, Box 466, Bolinas, CA 94924
Y'Bird, 2140 Shattuck Ave., Room 311, Berkeley, CA 94704
Yellow Press, 2394 Blue Island Ave., Chicago, IL 60608

Zahir, Box 715, Newburyport, MA 01950
Zonepress, Box 194 Bay Station, Brooklyn, NY 11235

CALEDONIA, the type in which this book was set is one of those referred to by printers, as a "modern face". It was designed around 1939 by W.A. Dwiggins (1880–1956) and it has been called "the most popular all-purpose typeface in U.S. history".

It is an original design, but, as from the beginning, fresh and exciting designs have often evolved from variations on the old, done by competent and disciplined hands. Caledonia shows marks of the long admired Scotch roman type-letters cut by Alexander Wilson in Glasgow in the 19th century. It also shows a trace from the types that W. Bulmer & Company used, cut in London, around 1790 by William Martin.

That Dwiggins was aware of the particular needs of our time is soundly attested to in the enduring good reception his "hard working, feet-on-the-ground" type has received from countless printers, authors and readers alike.

This book was designed and produced for the publisher, by RAY FREIMAN & COMPANY, Stamford, Connecticut.